HISTORICAL INTRODUCTIONS
TO
THE ROLLS SERIES

HISTORICAL INTRODUC-TIONS TO THE ROLLS

SERIES. By WILLIAM STUBBS, D.D., FORMERLY BISHOP OF OXFORD AND REGIUS PROFESSOR OF MODERN HISTORY IN THE UNIVERSITY

COLLECTED AND EDITED BY

ARTHUR HASSALL, M.A.

STUDENT, TUTOR, AND SOMETIME CENSOR
OF CHRIST CHURCH

AMS PRESS
NEW YORK

Reprinted from the edition of 1902, New York

First AMS EDITION published 1971

Manufactured in the United States of America

International Standard Book Number: 0-404-06302-0

Library of Congress Catalog Number: 77-158211

AMS PRESS INC.
NEW YORK, N.Y. 10003

PREFACE

THE publication of the historical portions of the late Bishop Stubbs' Introductions to certain volumes of the Rolls Series is due to the courtesy of the Controller of His Majesty's Stationery Office, who has given me permission to collect in one volume those investigations of Bishop Stubbs which are at present scattered among the numerous volumes of the Rolls Series.

Historical students have for many years appreciated the subtle delineations of character and the invaluable suggestions and conclusions which are to be found in the Bishop's Introductions. The immense learning and the critical acumen which appear on every page of his work are too well known to need further mention.

Everyone, indeed, who is interested in English History in the Middle Ages has recognised that in these Introductions may be found the clue to much that is difficult to comprehend; no sounder guide to the times of Henry II., Richard I., John, Edward I. and Edward II. has ever been written; but, unfortunately, the volumes of the Rolls Series can as a rule only be consulted in some of our better equipped libraries.

I imagine that no better tribute to the memory of the late Bishop can be paid, and no greater boon conferred on historical students, than to bring within their reach the only possible means for a right understanding of the Angevin period. Written in vigorous language, which is always lucid and frequently eloquent, these Introductions reveal to us a depth of learning, a knowledge of men and affairs, and a fund of charity—so characteristic of Bishop Stubbs.

No better judge of the value of Henry II.'s work ever lived; no historian has ever given us a truer and more forcible picture of King John. It is to be hoped that the perusal of these pages will induce many students to consult the Chronicles, Memorials, and Historical Collections themselves, to explain which these Introductions were written. These historical works are published *in extenso* in the Rolls Series, and many of the references in the Introductions are to the volumes in that series. Students ought to regard these Introductions as merely steps to a further and more detailed investigation of the Angevin period.

Probably no historian has ever lived who did more for the study of English History than Bishop Stubbs. The perusal of these Introductions will do much to enable historical students in all parts of the world to appreciate the debt which they owe to him, and to realise the true value of accurate historical scholarship.

ARTHUR HASSALL.

CHRIST CHURCH, OXFORD:
October 1902.

CONTENTS

MEMORIALS OF SAINT DUNSTAN,

ARCHBISHOP OF CANTERBURY

[In the first seventy-two pages of the Introduction to the 'Memorials of Saint Dunstan' Bishop Stubbs draws attention to the importance of Dunstan as a historical personage, and then discusses the value of the various biographies of the Archbishop. The Priest B., Adelard, Osbern, Eadmer, and William of Malmesbury wrote lives of Dunstan, and their works are here subjected to a careful criticism. The relation of these biographies to the Chronicles—' the more weighty and direct evidences of our national history '—is then touched upon. 'The determination of the chronology and the identification of the places and persons that come into Dunstan's history' is not, according to Bishop Stubbs, a very easy task, as the authorities are vague on each point.]

* * * * * *

DUNSTAN is said to have 'sprung to light' in the reign of Athelstan. We may question whether the word 'oritur'[1] refers to his birth or to his coming before the eye of history, in what year of Athelstan's reign the event took place, and in what year Athelstan began to reign. All our authorities agree in referring the word to Dunstan's birth. The Anglo-Saxon Chronicles, which Osbern follows, fix the first year of Athelstan as the date, and for that first year we have to choose between 924 and 925, the former date being given in four MSS. of the Chronicle and by Florence of Worcester, the latter by two MSS. of the Chronicle. Unfortunately the exact date of the death of Edward the Elder is unknown, but, as Athelstan in his charters speaks of 929[2] as his sixth year, his first must at all

Date of Dunstan's birth

---

[1] See B. p. 6; Flor. Wig. A.D. 924; Chr. S. A.D. 924, 925.

[2] Alford had seen a charter in which 925 is called the first year of Athelstan, Annales, iii. 242 :—A.D. 929 is the sixth year in Kemble, Cod. Dipl., Nos. 347, 348. A.D. 931, Nov. 12, is in the seventh year, ibid. 353 ; A.D. 934, May 28, is in the tenth year, ibid. 364; A.D. 931, Mar. 23, is in the seventh year, ibid. 1102; and July 31 also, ibid. 1103 ; A.D. 932, Aug. 28, is in

the eighth year, ibid. 1007. If these dates are calculated on one principle, his reign must have begun after Nov. 12, 924; but I should not venture to take this for granted. The reign of Athelstan lasted, according to the MS. Tiberius A. 3, fourteen years and seven weeks and three days, which, calculated back from Oct. 27, 940, the day of his death, would fix his coronation about the first week in September, 926. The Chronicle gives him a

B

events have begun in 924. Alford places Dunstan's birth in the spring of 925, arguing that if his mother were pregnant in February, as must be supposed to have been the case if Adelard's miracle of the candles has any semblance of truth, and if Athelstan's accession took place about the middle of the year 924, the child must have been born in 925.[1] And this computation is borne out by an entry in an ancient Anglo-Saxon Paschal Table, preserved in the Cotton MS., Caligula A. 15, under the year 925, ' on thison geare wæs sce Dunstan geboren.' The matter is not in itself of great importance, but it is complicated with questions touching the date of archbishop Athelm, and the age at which Dunstan took holy orders.

His parents

Dunstan's parents were, as the Saxon priest tells us, Heorstan and Kynedritha; his near kinsmen were among the ' palatini' or

His connexion with the royal house

members of the court and household of Athelstan; Elfege the Bald, bishop of Winchester, and bishop Kinesige of Lichfield, were also near relations. Dunstan had a brother named Wulfric. The great lady Ethelfleda was also connected with him by the ties of relationship, and she was of royal descent, being Athelstan's niece. These circumstances certainly give some foundation for the statement of Dunstan's nobility, made by the later biographers, who, however, have a strong tendency to define what the earlier writer has left

His other relations

indefinite. Adelard goes further, making archbishop Athelm his uncle. Osbern and Eadmer make his parents noble, and turn the lady Ethelfleda into Elfgifu or Æthelgifu. They also ignore the existence of Wulfric, making Dunstan an only son.

Kynedritha

The probability is in favour of Dunstan's noble birth. Of Heorstan nothing more is known, but Kynedritha is very probably the same as Keondrud, a lady whose name is found among those members of Athelstan's court who were made partakers of the prayers of the monks of S. Gall, when in the year 929 they were

Wulfric

visited by bishop Kynewald of Worcester.[2] Wulfric, who is described

reign of fourteen years and ten weeks, which may have been calculated from his father's death, and would fix that event about August 10 :—if for fourteen we read sixteen, Edward's death would be determined on or about August 20, 924; if not, Athelstan

must have been crowned two years after his reign began, which is improbable. Perhaps the day may yet turn up in some monastic kalendar. It is, however, very curious that all the ancient regnal lists give him a reign of only fourteen years.

[1] Annales, iii. 242.

[2] The form is printed by Goldastus in the Scriptores Rerum Alamannicarum, vol. ii. part II. p. 153, and also in the Appendix to the Report on the Fœdera. It is so closely connected with Dunstan's period that it is worth while to give it entire:—

' Anno ab Incarnatione Domini 928, indictione ii. (lege 929) Keonwald venerabilis episcopus profectus ab Anglis, omnibus monasteriis per totam Germaniam, cum oblatione de argento non modica, et in id ipsum rege Anglorum eadem sibi tradita, visitatis, in idibus Octobris venit ad monasterium Sancti Galli; quique gratissime a fratribus susceptus et ejusdem patroni nostri

as managing the secular affairs of Glastonbury under the title of præpositus or reeve, may also with some probability be identified with Wulfric, the 'comes' or 'gesith' of the kings Edmund and Edred, to whom many grants of land were made which ultimately became the property of Glastonbury. The estates thus bestowed were situated at Idemestone, Nellington, Grutelington, Langleath, and other places not far from Glastonbury, and the gifts may possibly have been made with the intention of their being appropriated to the monastery; they begin as early as 940, when Dunstan could scarcely have become abbot, and Wulfric the recipient must have been an elder brother, if he were brother at all. Another glimpse of him may be caught in a curious MS. of the Irish collection of canons, now among the Hatton MSS. in the Bodleian, entitled 'Liber Sancti Dunstani,' which belongs to the date, possibly to the school or hand of Dunstan. The scribe has drawn in one place the head of a boy, in rubric, with the name 'Wulfric Cild.'

The lady Ethelfleda bears a name too common among the Anglo-Saxons to furnish any basis for identification, and the fact that she is called Athelstan's niece scarcely helps the inquiry. A certain lady, Ælfleda, has, like Wulfric, grants of land from Athelstan and Edmund,[1] which came to the same monastery. This lady is not to be identified with Ethelfleda of Mercia, Athelstan's aunt,

Ethelfleda

festivitatem cum illis celebrando, quatuor ibidem dies demoratus est. Secundo autem, postquam monasterium ingressus est, hoc est in ipso depositionis S. Galli die, basilicam intravit et pecuniam secum copiosam attulit, de qua partem altario imposuit, partem etiam utilitati fratrum donavit. Posthæc eo in conventum nostrum inducto, omnis congregatio concessit ei annonam unius fratris, et tandem orationem quam pro quolibet de nostris, sive vivente, sive vita decedente, facere solemus pro illo facturam perpetualiter promisit. Hæc sunt autem nomina quæ conscribi jussit vel rogavit: rex Anglorum Adalstean, Kenowald episcopus, Wigharth, Kenwor, Conrat, Keonolaf, Wundych, Keondrud.' A longer list appears in the general catalogue of the Fratres Conscripti (Goldast. p. 156):—

'Hic regis Angliæ et comitum suorum nomina denotata sunt;

Adalsten, Rex.	Wolfhelmus, archiepisc.		Elwinus, episc.	Eotkarus, episc.
Winsige, episc.	Sigihelm, episcopus.		Oda, episcopus.	Fridosten, episc.
Kenod, abba.	Albrich, abba.		Cudret.	Erdulf.
Fridolef.	Wulfun.	Ortgar.	Osfred.	Elfsie.
Adalwerd.	Elwin.	Adalwin.	Berectwin.	Wulfilt.
Wighart.	Conrat.	Kenwin.	Wundrud.	Kenowald, episc.
Kenolaf.	Keondrud.'			

cum ceteris.

The bishops are Wulfhelm of Canterbury; Elfwin of Lichfield; Edgar of Hereford; Winsige of Dorchester; Sigelm of Sherborne; Odo of Ramsbury; Frithstan of Winchester; and Kynewold of Worcester. Of the abbots, Kenod belongs to Evesham or Abingdon, and Cudret to Glastonbury. Elfric, abbot (Albrich); Osferth, ealdorman; Wulfhun, bishop; Wihtgar, minister; and others may be identified with the witnesses of Athelstan's charters.

[1] MS. Wood, I. folios 223, 240; Kemble, C. D. No. 389, where she is called 'religiosa fœmina.'

who died in 922 at the latest, nor with Ethelfleda of Damerham, the second wife of king Edmund ; nor with Eadfleda, Athelstan's sister. Ethelfleda of Romsey, abbess, virgin, and patron saint, cannot, if her recorded history be true, have been the widowed friend of Dunstan. The main part, however, of the history of the abbess of Romsey is apocryphal, and the dates assigned to her are inconsistent with one another. It is therefore possible that she was the person whom we are seeking. She is said to have been the daughter of an ealdorman Ethelwold and his wife Brihtwina.[1] If this ealdorman be identical with Elfweard, Athelstan's brother, who died in 924, his daughter would be the king's niece ; but this is barely probable.

Called also Ethelgifu The fact that Osbern and Eadmer give her the name of Ethelgifu or Elfgifu would show that in their time no such identity was recognised, nor can the latter name with any probability be regarded as the true one, although the practice assigned to her, of ministering of her goods to the kings and the seed royal, does curiously coincide with the office which has been with great probability ascribed to that more famous Ethelgifu [2] who exercised so baneful an influence on the career of king Edwy. We know Ethelfleda only on the testimony of the Saxon priest, who, however, distinctly asserts her relationship with both Dunstan and Athelstan.

Relation between Athelm and Dunstan Our earliest authority does not determine the degree of relationship between Elfege, Kinesige, and Dunstan, but Adelard makes Athelm, archbishop of Canterbury, the brother of Heorstan. In this by itself there is nothing improbable ; Athelm had been bishop of Wells, and was very likely to have been connected with the royal family, as one at least of his successors was ; his name occurs also in the list of bishops given by William of Malmesbury as having been monks of Glastonbury.[3] Adelard, however, is so manifestly mistaken in making him the patron as well as uncle of Dunstan, that no weight can be attached to his evidence. Athelm died either when Question as to Wulfhelm Dunstan was a baby, or before he was born.[4] Wulfhelm, who succeeded him, had likewise been bishop of Wells, and among the Dunstan letters there is found a copy of verses addressed to him, which may point to some connexion between the two, but he is nowhere

---

[1] Her life is in Capgrave, abridged from the MS. Lansd. 436. See Hardy, Catalogue, &c. i. 568.

[2] Robertson, Historical Essays, pp. 200 sq.

[3] Ant. Glast. ap. Gale, p. 324.

[4] There are no genuine charters to which the name of Athelm is attached. The name of Wulfhelm, his successor, appears in 923 and onwards. The statement of Florence (A.D. 924) that Athelm crowned Athelstan is derived from Adelard, p. 55. If the evidence of charters as to Wulfhelm in 923 be rejected, still it is certain that Athelm was dead long before Dunstan could have gone to court. See Chr. S. A.D. 924, 925, from which it would seem that Athelm and Edward the Elder died the same year.

said to have been connected with Glastonbury, or to have been a patron of Dunstan.

Glastonbury, or its immediate neighbourhood, was the place of the saint's birth and early teaching; he was a pupil of the Irish pilgrims who had taken up their abode at the resting-place of the younger Patrick.[1] Whilst quite a boy he lived also in the palace of Athelstan, at no great distance from Glastonbury, it would seem, as he had already received the tonsure, and was serving in the church of S. Mary, in which he had been baptized. After his expulsion from Athelstan's court, he stayed a long time at Winchester with Elfege, who prevailed on him to become a monk. After this we again find him at Glastonbury in attendance on the lady Ethelfleda, who had built herself a house there, and who left her estates to be disposed of by him. He next appears in attendance on king Edmund at Cheddar, and, after a short disgrace, is made by him abbot of Glastonbury, in which office he continues until he is made bishop.

Dunstan born at or near Glastonbury

Dunstan's early life

For this part of Dunstan's life we have very few dates. Athelstan died in the year 940, when Dunstan would be about sixteen, no doubt a clever, somewhat precocious boy, whose dreams and prayers might very likely expose him to the rough treatment of his playfellows. His appointment to Glastonbury is placed by the Canterbury copy of the Chronicle in the year 943, and by Florence of Worcester, whose authority, if independent of that copy, is preferable, under the date 942, but only as one of the remarkable acts of king Edmund. The direct evidence being so slight, we may rest on the authority of the charters, in which Dunstan as abbot appears among the witnesses only in 946, the year of Edmund's death. The only charter of earlier date in which he is mentioned is one of the year 940, which is apparently admitted by Kemble as genuine, and which is a grant, made to him as abbot, of land at Christian Malford.[2] But although this document has no overt evidence of fabrication, it is found only in a copy, like the other Glastonbury charters, and either the name of Dunstan or the title of abbot may have been an insertion of the copyist. Dunstan, as one of the sons of the nobles, might have had a grant of folkland at sixteen, the age at which the young warrior received his arms; but it is very improbable that if he had

Date of Dunstan's appointment to Glastonbury

---

[1] The Arras MS. says the younger Patrick, the other two MSS. the elder Patrick. This is a trace of the growth of the legend that connects Patrick with Glastonbury, and may be the germ of the tradition. Whether the later MSS. altered *junior* into *senior* in the idea of enhancing the greatness of Glastonbury, or whether the writers knew of the existence of Sæn-Patric, Patricius senior, who is said to have been bishop second in succession after the great Patrick, and who might safely be called either senior or junior, I cannot take on myself to decide. By William of Malmesbury's time Glastonbury claimed not only the great Patrick but his successor Benignus.

[2] Kemble, C. D. No. 384.

then become abbot, and that in a church so near the royal court, his name should not appear in the charters for six years longer.[1] I think, however, that the date cannot be thrown later than 946, and I see in the chronology no difficulties that need hinder the belief in the story of Edmund's hunt in Cheddar as substantially true.

Condition of Glastonbury

A more important point, perhaps, and certainly a more interesting one, is the condition of Glastonbury at this time; and although it cannot be touched on here except in the most cursory manner, it cannot be dismissed with a word. The Saxon priest represents it as an ancient sanctuary, a retired spot possessing a church to which a more than human origin was ascribed, a holy place to which Athelstan resorted for the purpose of prayer, a place of pilgrimage colonised by Irishmen, who had gathered at the tomb of Patrick.

Antiquity claimed for Glastonbury in later times

As the place of Dunstan's birth, education, and promotion, Glastonbury had a later history, much of which is coloured by its connexion with the Canterbury saint; it became a rich abbey, and laid claim to an early history and remote antiquity; not content with claiming the senior as well as the junior Patrick, it adopted Joseph of Arimathea as its first founder, and produced evidence of its existence and sanctity under kings and in times long anterior to the West Saxon rule; not only Edmund the Magnificent ruler of Britain, and Edgar the Peaceful, and Edmund Ironside, but king Arthur himself slept there. Such claims doubtless provoked criticism, and criticism forced on the monks the need of a forged history to assert,

Fabricated evidence

and of forged monuments to support them. And the fabrication of such evidences must have gone on at Glastonbury on a scale proportioned to these claims. Westminster claimed the apostle Peter as its founder, but that by a miracle. S. Alban's rejoiced in the protomartyr of Britain, but contented itself with Offa as the restorer rather than the founder of its greatness. But Glastonbury would have a history without a miracle, and a continuous existence which needed no restoration. William of Malmesbury, it would almost seem, undertook to erect the story out of materials which he distrusted, but this did not content his employers, and they interpolated his work to a degree which makes it impossible to rely with confidence upon any part of it.

True evidence on the point

The later developments, however, of Glastonbury history need not make us shut our eyes to such early evidence as is afforded by the Saxon priest. Further, we have in a MS. of the same date, or even

---

[1] Dunstan attests only one charter of Edmund: No. 406, marked by Kemble as suspicious, a grant to Ethelnoth, in the Glastonbury Cartulary: ' ego Dunstan abbas nolens sed regalibus obediens verbis hanc cartulam scribere jussi.' Mr. Robertson regards as his first historical appearance his attestation to a charter of Edred in 946, Kemble, C. D. 411.

a few years later, a list of the abbots of Glastonbury, which runs up
to the age of Ina.[1] Ethelwerd mentions the cœnobium of Glaston- Early
notices of
Glastonbury
bury as the burial-place of the ealdorman Eanulf;[2] its early history
is indeed unnoticed by Bede, or by the authors of the chronicle, but
its existence as a monasterium is proved by an incontrovertible
authority, the letters of S. Boniface, and the life of the same great
West Saxon saint written by his countryman and disciple S. Willibald.[3] And this mention by S. Boniface carries us back to the days
of Ina, who according to William of Malmesbury, writing apart
from Glastonbury influences, was the founder, and to the early
abbots of the ancient list just mentioned. And the certainty of this

[1] It is very useful, in order to get an idea of the Glastonbury workmanship,
to compare the list of abbots given in the Tiberius MS. with that given by
William of Malmesbury, and the few dates ascertainable from early historians
and charters with the elaborate array of years which he produces, possibly in
some degree from the same materials.

Tiberius B. 5.		W. Malmesb. Ant. Glaston.	
1. Hæmgils.	Bp. Hereford in 731	After five British	
2. Wealhstod	(Bede).	abbots, Patrick,	
		Benignus, Wor-	
3. Coengils.	Contemporary with	gret, Lademund,	
4. Beorhtwald .	S. Boniface, epist.	and Bregored:—	
		1. Beorthwald .	670–680 ; abp.
5. Cealdhun.	At the Council of		Canterbury.
6. Muca . .	Clovesho in 805.	2. Hemgisel .	680–705.
		3. Beorwald .	705–712.
7. Wiccea.		4. Aldbeorth .	712–719.
8. Bosa.		5. Atfrith . .	719–729.
9. Stitheard.		6. Kemgisel .	729–743.
10. Herefyrth.		7. Guba . .	743–744.
11. Hunbeorht.		8. Ticca .	744–752.
12. Andhun.		9. Cuma . .	752–754.
13. Guthlac.		10. Walthun .	754–786.
14. Cuthred .	Confr. S. Gall. above,	11. Tumberth .	786–795.
	p. 3.	12. Beadulf . .	795–802.
15. Ecgwulf.		13. Muca . .	802–824.
16. Dunstan .	A.D. 940 or 946–958.	14. Gutlac . .	824–850.
17. Elfric.		15. Ealmund .	850–866.
18. Sigegar . .	Bp. of Wells in 975.	16. Herefyrth .	866–880.
19. Ælfweard .	975 onwards.	17. Stiwerd . .	880–905.
		18. Ealdhun .	905–927.
		19. Elfric . .	927.
		20. Dunstan .	940.
		31. Elfward . .	962.
		22. Sigar . .	972.

The order and dates of Malmesbury's list seem to be quite at random; yet
there is enough likeness between the two lists to show that he had older
materials to work upon.

[2] Mon. Hist. Brit. p. 513.

[3] There is a letter of Brihtwald,
archbishop of Canterbury, to Forthere,
bishop of Sherborne, referring to abbot
Beorwald (Mon. Moguntina, ed. Jaffé,
p. 48); this Beorwald is called by
Willibald abbot of Glastonbury ' cœnobium . . quod antiquorum nuncupatu
vocabulo Glestingaburg' (ibid. 439);
and there is a letter from the priest
Wiehtberht to 'patribus et fratribus
in monasterio Glestingaburg con-
stitutis' (ibid. 246), written during
the life of Boniface.

Possible
genuineness
of the early
charters
much of the early history gives probability to many of the charters, the place of which in the Glastonbury Cartulary would afford by itself very little presumption of their credibility.

Condition
of the
monastery
On such evidence we may assume that there was an ancient ecclesiastical settlement at Glastonbury, dating from the seventh century at the latest, which had shared the changes and experienced the fate that had befallen most of the establishments of the centuries of the conversion ; the churches and other buildings standing, the libraries perhaps in a few cases continuing entire,[1] but the monastic life extinct, the name preserved only as giving a title to the ownership of the lands, and the abbots and monks, if there were any that

The Irish
pilgrims
called themselves so, being really secular priests and clerks.[2] The Irish pilgrims who instructed Dunstan may or may not have been members or officers of this establishment, but the right of patronage

Low state of
monachism
at the time
was clearly in the hands of the king, and the state of monastic rule, discipline, and pretension was so attenuated that the contemporaries of Dunstan regarded him as a founder rather than a reformer. Monachism there was in England, although it was not after the rule of S. Benedict, and a monk Dunstan had already become ; but that Dunstan's monachism had little or nothing in common with the state of things existing at Glastonbury at the time appears from the words which the biographer puts in the mouth of Edmund : 'Be thou of this seat the lord and potent occupant, and whatsoever from thine own means shall be lacking for the increase of divine service, or for the completeness of the sacred rule, that I will supply devoutly by my royal bounty.'[3] It is clear that the abbacy must

---

[1] Asser's account of the state of the monastic institute in Alfred's time was true of the next half-century : 'per multa retroacta annorum curricula monasticæ vitæ desiderium ab illa tota gente, necnon et a multis aliis gentibus funditus desierat, quamvis perplurima adhuc monasteria in illa regione constructa permaneant, nullo tamen regulam illius vitæ ordinabiliter tenente, nescio quare, aut pro alienigenarum infestationibus . . . aut etiam pro nimia illius gentis in omni genere divitiarum abundantia,' &c. Mon. Hist. Brit. 493. According to Alfred himself the books remained, but there was no one who could use them. Pref. to S. Gregory's Pastoral Care.

[2] Elfric the biographer of Ethelwold, the earliest describer of this state of things, draws a sad picture of the old Minster at Winchester, and although it may be exaggerated it is the testimony of an eye-witness :

'malemorigerati clerici, elatione et insolentia ac luxuria præventi, adeo ut nonnulli eorum dedignarentur missas suo ordine celebrare, repudiantes uxores, quas illicite duxerant, et alias accipientes, gulæ et ebrietati jugiter dediti.' Hist. Abend. ii. 260. The biographer of Oswald, after telling us that Oswald bought himself 'monasterium quod est in Wintonia positum . . . donando digno pretio,' proceeds, 'in diebus illis non monastici viri nec ipsius sanctæ institutionis regulæ erant in regione Anglorum, sed erant religiosi et dignissimi clerici, qui tamen thesauros suos quos avidis adquirebant cordibus non ad ecclesiæ honorem sed suis dare solebant uxoribus,' folio 4.

[3] Osbern's own expansion of the speech is also worth noting. For it is impossible to suspect either the Saxon priest or Osbern of a desire to undervalue the antiquity of Glaston-

have been vacant and the lands of the monastery in the king's hands, Condition of Abingdon much as was the case at Abingdon at the same time. The words of the biographer of S. Ethelwold might be applied to the one as well as to the other; it 'was a place in which a little monastery had been kept up from ancient days, but it was then desolate and neglected, consisting of mean buildings and possessing only a few (in the case of Abingdon, forty) hides; the rest of the land of the place the king possessed by his royal right.' [1] That is, there was still a monastic establishment, but it had become ruinous and impoverished. It was in name an abbey, but really served by clerks, or altogether neglected. The renewal of discipline was really a foundation rather than a revival.

The name of the abbot who had vacated the seat taken by Dun- Dunstan's predecessor stan, as given by William of Malmesbury, is Elfric, the successor of Aldhun, under whom he says Dunstan had been educated. In the ancient list, however, Dunstan's immediate predecessor is named Ecgwulf; and the next in order, counting backwards, is Cuthred, whom I am inclined to identify with that 'Cudret' who appears among the courtiers of Athelstan in the compact with the monks of S. Gall.

It might be difficult to define the monastic character that Dun- Dunstan's early monachism stan had assumed; but it differed as much from the system which it superseded as it did from the more perfect form into which it ultimately grew. No doubt the name and dress of the monk were resumed. Wulfred, Dunstan's early friend, is called a deacon, but the companions of his retirement whilst he is abbot are called monks. He himself in the famous drawing, which with very much probability is ascribed to his own hand, appears in the dress of a monk. Yet the establishment at Glastonbury under him is much more of a school than a convent: the words 'scholasticus' and 'discipulus' come more naturally than 'monachus.' In this again there is nothing peculiar to Glastonbury; exactly the same processes are traceable at Abingdon. I conclude that there had taken place, probably under the influence of Elfege the Bald, a strong tendency towards pure Benedictinism: that tendency was represented by Dunstan and Ethelwold in their early efforts, but it was not crowned with success, or brought into perfect accord with the Benedictine discipline, until Dunstan had seen the old rule in working at Blandinium, and Oswald and Ethelwold had brought instructors from Fleury. The difference between the laxer rule of Dunstan and the stricter discipline of the other two may be partly attributed to the difference of their foreign relations, partly also to the fact that

bury as compared with Canterbury.   [1] Elfric's Life of Ethelwold, Hist. Comp. Robertson, Hist. Essays, p. 190.   Abend. ii. 257.

Dunstan's
discipline
milder than
that of
Oswald and
Ethelwold

Dunstan, being a statesman, and, after the accession of Edgar, in a position of supreme importance, was obliged, whatever his own wishes may have been, to avoid a policy of persecution. In the biographies of Ethelwold and Oswald, Dunstan plays a part quite secondary to theirs in the expulsion of the clerks from the monasteries ; and in his own churches, Canterbury, London, and Worcester, he attempted no such measure : it is possible that he acted as a check rather than a spur on the zeal of Edgar. At the same time it cannot be supposed that the clerks were expelled without his permission ; and although the stories of his active participation, detailed by Osbern and Eadmer, were borrowed and adapted from the career of Ethelwold, there is evidence enough in the first life to show that he sympathised with the movement, and that his own life and personal influence were guided by an ascetic spirit.

Edmund reigned but a short time after Dunstan's appointment as abbot, dying on May 26, 946.[1] Edred, who succeeded him, reigned until November 23, 955.[2] The former king was eighteen when he began to reign, twenty-four when he died. Edred must have been within a year of the same age as Dunstan. These dates help to reconcile us to the fact that Dunstan became abbot at twenty-two. They serve to account for his close intimacy with Edred ; they had been playfellows probably at the court of Athelstan. Edred was a sickly young man ; the Saxon priest has drawn a picture of his ill-health too graphic to be an invention of his own. His mother Eadgifu was his chief adviser, and next to her Dunstan, who acted as treasurer of the royal estates, and perhaps in an official position somewhat like that of the later chancellors. His time was divided between his abbey at Glastonbury, where he was teaching and

building, and his attendance on the king, who seemed to have kept court, not in the western shires like Athelstan and Edmund, but chiefly at Winchester. His reign was on the whole a successful one ; for, whether by his own energy, by Dunstan's policy, or by the divisions of his enemies, he acquired finally the allegiance of Northumbria. It was, no doubt, during a visit paid with Edred to the north that Dunstan saw the remains of S. Cuthbert.

It is to these years, no doubt, that Dunstan's period of active teaching is to be referred. It was Edred who by his mother's advice placed Ethelwold as abbot at Abingdon ; and this is the time of Oswald's mission to Fleury.[3] The part taken by archbishop Odo in the government of the country has been obscured by the glory of the younger men, and by the fact that his life was not written until a

---

[1] Chr. Sax. A.D. 946.
[2] Ibid. A.D. 955.
[3] Elfric's Life of Ethelwold, Chron.

Abend. ii. 257 ; Hist. Ramsey, Gale, p. 391.

century and a half after his death. It is, however, certain that he did nothing to thwart the policy of Dunstan, and enough of his ecclesiastical legislation remains to show that, in a determination to enforce the observance of both monastic vows and the laws of marriage, he came in no degree behind his more famous successor.[1]

In 953, the death of Ethelgar, bishop of Crediton, gave Edred and Eadgifu an opportunity of promoting Dunstan to the episcopate. It may or may not be true that, as Adelard relates, a like offer was made to him on the death of Elfege the Bald in 951. He was not yet of canonical age for consecration, and he refused the bishopric, alleging as the reason, if we are to credit the later writers, his unwillingness to leave the court as long as Edred lived. There can, I think, be no doubt about this part of the story, or about the dream which followed his refusal. Elfwold was appointed at his recommendation to Crediton, and as bishop of Crediton Elfwold attests the charters of Edred from 953 onwards.

Proposal to make Dunstan a bishop

Edred's death must have been sudden; he was at Frome;[2] Dunstan, who was at Glastonbury, was summoned to attend him, but the king died before he arrived, and the crown fell to Edwy, the elder of the two sons of Edmund by his first wife Elfgifu.[3] Edred's reign is said in the table of the kings to have lasted nine years and six weeks:[4] a computation which agrees but imperfectly with the dates given by Florence of Worcester for his coronation and death, the former event being placed on the 16th of August 946, and the latter on the feast of S. Clement, November 23, 955. The rougher computation of the Chronicle, nine years and a half, dating from the death of Edmund, is nearer the mark.

Date of Edred's death

As Edwy reigned three years, thirty-five weeks, and five days,[5] and died on the 1st of October 959, his coronation must have taken place on the first or second Sunday after Epiphany, 956. He could scarcely at this time have been more than fifteen years old. Dunstan was still at court, and on him and his kinsman Kinesige[6] was thrown the disagreeable task of bringing back the careless and obstinate boy,

Date of Edwy's coronation

---

[1] See his Constitutions, published in the reign of Edmund, in Wilkins, Concilia, i. 212 sq.

[2] Chron. Sax. A.D. 955.

[3] Chron. Sax. A.D. 955; Mon. Hist. Brit. p. 662.

[4] MS. Tiberius, A. 3; Chr. S. ed. Thorpe, i. 233.

[5] 'Four years less seven weeks,' MS. Tiberius, B. 5; Rel. Ant. ii. 171; 'quadriennio' Ethelwerd, p. 520; 'three years, thirty-six weeks, less two days, MS. Tiberius, A. 3; Thorpe, Chr. S. p. 233.

[6] Kinesige appears first in a charter of Athelstan to Abingdon, Kemble, C. D. 1129, as bishop of Berkshire. Berkshire was properly in the diocese of Ramsbury, of which Odo was bishop at the time. In the lists of bishops (M. H. B. 624) he is bishop of Lichfield; he may have been administering Berkshire for Odo at the date of the earlier charter. He attests charters from 931 to 934, and from 949–963; but possibly enough there were two persons of the name.

Story of the coronation feast

from the chamber of Ethelgifu and her daughter, to the solemn banquet. On this event much has been written, and an amount of criticism spent, altogether out of proportion to the materials for its history.[1] The narration of the Saxon priest is the primary authority; written forty years after the event, and not by an eye-witness, it bears marks of having been coloured by popular tradition. The distinction which I have already drawn, as to the narrative of our author, where it concerns Dunstan's private history and where it touches on public events, may be applied here. The monstrous lust of such a mere child as Edwy was could not have been a main feature of a story told by Dunstan himself, who knew the truth, and who, although he had been persecuted by Ethelgifu, had no temptation to pervert facts. The offence given to Dunstan may easily be accounted for by the relationship of Edwy and Ethelgifu, and the bulk of our historians have so construed it.

Dunstan in exile

Edgar still at court

Edgar becomes king of Mercia

Dunstan's flight to Flanders must have followed early in the year 956; the charters of Edwy which are attested by him [2] may some of them be referred possibly to the day of the coronation. Edgar continued much longer at his brother's side, at least until the summer of 957.[3] The rebellion of the Northumbrians and Mercians cannot be thrown later than the spring of 958. In that year Edgar begins to issue charters as king.[4] The revolt is placed by Florence of Worcester in 957, and as bishop Kynewald of Worcester, whose death made room for Dunstan as bishop, disappears in that year from the charters, the recall of Dunstan probably followed immediately on the revolt. Edgar is reckoned to have reigned two years at the time of his brother's death.

Dunstan made a bishop

Dunstan's return was followed by his promotion to the episcopate. Glastonbury was in the hands of Edwy, and for the time it appeared that he had no chance of recovering it. It was accordingly determined, in a council of the witan attached to Edgar, that Dunstan

[1] On this subject may be read with advantage Mr. Allen's Essay, appended to his work on the Prerogative, p. 220, and Hallam's note in the History of the Middle Ages. The former is very speculative. Hallam's conclusion is in defiance of his argument.

[2] These are, a grant to Wilton, dated 955, Kemble, 436; one to Abingdon, dated 956, Kemble, 441; one dated 956 at Cirencester, in favour of Worcester, Kemble, 451; one to Ælric, in the Abingdon Cartulary, dated 956, Kemble, 1186, 1187.

[3] Edgar attests charters of his brother as late as May 9, 957, Kemble, 465. A charter to bishop Oskytel, which is attested by him, dated 958 (Kemble, 472), is shown by the indiction to belong to 956.

[4] These of course are not numerous: one from the Peterborough Cartulary, dated 958, in which Edgar calls himself 'rex Anglorum,' is signed by Oskytel of Dorchester, Dunstan of Worcester, Kinsige of Lichfield, Athulf of Hereford, and Leofwine of Lindsey, Kemble, 471; another, dated 959, from the same Cartulary, has the signature of Dunstan as bishop of London, and Oskytel as archbishop of York (Kemble, 480), Edgar calling himself king of the Mercians.

should be made a bishop. This council was held at a place called in the various MSS. of the first life Bradanford or Brandanford.[1] If the latter reading be right, and it is the reading which Mabillon recognised in the Arras MSS., and is clearly that of the Cottonian, the place was probably Brentford, the earlier form of which, Bregentnaford, was probably lost. If the other reading be the true one, Bradford in Wiltshire would seem to be the place meant; but if so, then Edwy's kingdom must have been much more circumscribed than we have any other reasons for supposing it to have been. The Wiltshire Bradford must, I think, have been in Edwy's hands, and the balance of probability is in favour of Brentford.

Council of Brandanford

The story further reads as if the resolution of the witan merely was that Dunstan should be promoted. No see is mentioned, perhaps no see was vacant. We are not told that Dunstan was consecrated upon this recommendation, and Adelard probably records the truth when he describes him as consecrated by Odo to the see of Worcester. Yet it is quite possible that he was consecrated as an unattached bishop, as the Saxon priest describes, to attend personally on Edgar and give him the benefit of his counsel. Such an appointment would not have been entirely out of keeping with the system of diocesan episcopacy that had prevailed in Wessex, where from the time of Ethelwulf there had been occasionally shirebishops with no fixed see. On this hypothesis might be explained the tradition preserved by Adelard that Odo consecrated Dunstan, 'titulo ecclesiæ cui episcopus datus est conticito'; the idea that he did so by divine instruction, that he might succeed him at Canterbury, being an after-thought.

The question as to Dunstan's consecration

The tradition

Whether or no this was the case, the death of Kynewald, bishop of Worcester, gave the new bishop a see. Kynewald's name appears for the last time in a charter of 957; and, in the few charters of 958 which were issued by Edgar during his brother's lifetime, Dunstan appears as bishop. If the festival kept on the 21st of October at Canterbury, as the ordination of S. Dunstan,[2] commemorates his episcopal consecration, it must, I think, be referred to the year 957. In 959 he received the see of London, and held it together with Worcester until the settlement that followed Edwy's death. This arrangement may not improbably have been made either because Odo was dead, or because Canterbury, where a new bishop would have had to seek consecration, was in the hands of Edwy.

He is bishop of Worcester

and of London

Reason for the plurality

---

[1] The account of this council given by Wilkins, Concilia, i. 224, is an extract from archbishop Parker's *Antiquitates*.

[2] From the Obituary or Martyrology of Canterbury, Wharton, Angl.

Sacr. i. 54: 'xii. Cal. Novembris, Cantuariæ, ordinatio B. Dunstani archiepiscopi, cujus vita quam fuerit pontificatu digna etiam divina revelatione innotuit.'

Date of
Edwy's
marriage

Edwy's marriage must have taken place in 956, or early in 957; the charter of Abingdon, attested by Elfgifu the king's wife, and Ethelgifu the king's wife's mother, bearing also the attestation of bishop Kynewald.[1] It is not attested by Odo, who had no doubt been offended with the marriage. Edwy's charters in which Odo'e name appears in 957 may have been granted most probably before that event: those of 958, after the forced reconciliation, following the separation of Edwy and Elfgifu, which is placed by the Anglo-Saxon Chronicle of Worcester [2] in that year.

The next point to be considered is one of the most complex in our early annals, but it is also one on which our Saxon priest is

Question as
to the date
of Odo's
death

a primary authority: the circumstances that followed the death of Odo, and the appointment of Dunstan as his successor. Our author, who gives no dates, tells us that, on Odo's death, Elfsin or Elfsige, bishop of Winchester, succeeded him; that Elfsige on his way to Rome crossed the Alps in deep snow, and caught the cold which killed him. His companions returned. Byrhthelm,

Succession
of Elfsige
and Byrht-
helm

the bishop of Dorset, was chosen in his place, and having shown himself incompetent to enforce discipline was sent back to his see by the king, who then with the advice of his witan appointed Dunstan.[3] We are not told who was king when Elfsige and Byrhthelm were appointed; the king who nominated Dunstan was of course Edgar. There is thus nothing in the original story that

Who
promoted
them?

is fatal to the belief that Elfsige and Byrhthelm were the nominees of Edwy, and the humiliation of the latter prelate a result of the

---

[1] Hist. Abend. i. 218; Kemble, C. D. No. 1201. The charter is not quite simple. Edwy bestows Kennington on the priest Brihthelm, with the date 956, and the attestation of Odo, Edgar, Elfsige, Oswulf, Wulfsige, Kynewold, and Daniel; that is clearly before the revolt of the north, and probably before the marriage. After this Brihthelm, now a bishop, exchanges the Kennington estate for one at Crydanbridge with abbot Ethelwold of Abingdon; this exchange being without date, and attested by 'Ælfgifu thæs cininges wif, and Æthelgifu thæs cyninges wifes modur,' Elfsige, Oswulf, and Coenwald, bishops. This exchange is undated, but it must have taken place some time after the grant. Brihthelm had in the meanwhile become a bishop, Odo and Edgar were away from the court, and Elfgifu and her mother supreme for the time. All then that it proves is the fact of the marriage, and that it took place

during the life of Kynewald, Dunstan's predecessor.

[2] Tiberius, B. 4, 'Her on thissum geare Oda arcebiscop totwæmde Eadwi cyning and Ælfgyfe, forthæm the hi wæron to gesybbe.' It is to be remembered that this is all the evidence we have on the subject except the tradition prevalent a hundred and fifty years after. The Saxon priest says nothing about the completion of the marriage, and the biographer of Oswald gives a different story, making Edwy an adulterer: 'sub uxore propria alteram adamavit quam et rapuit . . . Antistes autem (Odo) . . . equum ascendit et ad villam qua mulier mansitabat pervenit, eamque rapuit et de regno perduxit.' (Nero, E. 1. fo. 1.)

[3] The life of Oswald (Nero, E. 1), which is the original authority for the insult offered by Elfsige to Dunstan, is also silent as to the king who appointed Elfsige.

changes that followed Edwy's death. The Anglo-Saxon Chronicle, except in its latest and most questionable edition, does not mention either the death of Odo or the names of Elfsige and Byrhthelm; and Adelard also is silent on the whole transaction.

When, however, we come to the time of Osbern and Florence, we find an immediate difficulty. Osbern attributes the appointment of Elfsige and Byrhthelm to Edgar: Florence of Worcester, perhaps wavering in his own mind, places the election of Elfsige before, and that of Byrhthelm after, the accession of Edgar to the whole kingdom.[1] William of Malmesbury follows Osbern in ascribing the appointment of Elfsige to Edgar, and although in the Life of Dunstan he adopts the same statements about Byrhthelm, does not mention him among the archbishops in the Gesta Pontificum. Eadmer, who might have been expected to be accurate, follows Osbern. Such an array of writers, who possessed, in the records of their churches, authorities which have not come down to us, might be supposed to afford a conclusive comment on the original statement, strong enough certainly to refute an argument founded on the first reading of that statement.

Later statements at variance

The later writers refer the promotion of Elfsige to Edgar

Such, however, is the scantiness of all information added by these writers to the original stock preserved in the Chronicle, that we can scarcely give them credit for possessing or for using materials that have not come down to us. We have recourse, therefore, to the information which we may find in charters and kalendars, and in a more precise examination of the chronology.

Real scantiness of evidence

Edwy died on the 1st or 2nd of October 959.[2] Odo died on the 2nd of June;[3] but in what year? His name is found attached to an Abingdon charter dated May 17, 959, which has no decisive mark of forgery.[4] If he died in June 959, there is still time before the 1st of October for Elfsige to go as far as the Alps, thirty-three days' journey, for his companions to return home, and Byrhthelm to be elected. And the existence of a charter of Edwy, dated 959, and attested by Byrhthelm as 'Dorobernensis ecclesiæ episcopus,' may be regarded as conclusively proving that he was appointed by that king.[5] On the other hand, such a succession of events is so rapid as to be almost unprecedented. Elfsige would hardly have found the

What time elapsed between the death of Odo and that of Edwy?

---

[1] Flor. Wig. A.D. 958, 959.

[2] Four MSS. of the Chronicle give the year 959; two 958; one Oct. 1, 958. Florence gives 959; the Kalendar printed by Hampson gives the day Oct. 2; the charters afford ample proof that Edwy was alive in 959.

[3] Obituary of Canterbury, Angl. Sacr. i. 54.

[4] Kemble, Cod. Dipl. No. 1224, an Abingdon charter, attested not only by Odo but by Eadgiva the king's grandmother, Hist. Abend. i. 169-172. It is worth observing that of the two copies of this charter one (Claudius, c. 9) omits the name of Odo.

[5] This charter, which is not in Kemble, is in the Book of Hyde (ed. Edwards), p. 177.

Odo died
probably
in 958
Alps so blocked with snow in June that he should be really frozen
to death ; and Florence of Worcester distinctly places Odo's death
in the year in which he separated Edwy and Elfgifu, that is in 958.
It is important, too, to observe that one copy of the Abingdon
charter omits the name of Odo. On the whole we may safely conclude that sufficient ground is found for setting aside the statements
of Osbern as to the nomination of his two successors, and for inter-
preting the Saxon priest accordingly.

What was
Byrhthelm's
see ?

A minor question is this: Byrhthelm is called by our first
author the bishop of Dorset, that is, of Sherborne ; but the lists of
the bishops of Sherborne contain no such name, that see having
been occupied successively by Wulfsige, who, as we know from
charters, disappears in 958, and Elfwold, who signs first in 961. It
is true that between these years there is room for Byrhthelm, but
the lists, which are nearly contemporary, do not admit him. On
the other hand, we find prelates of this name at this period, in the
sees of Wells, Winchester, and London. It is not by any means
impossible that the bishop who was elected to Canterbury was the
bishop of Wells, who is called *electus* in 956,[1] and who may either
have held Sherborne after Wulfsige's death in 958, as well as Wells,

Wells or
Sherborne,
or both

just as Dunstan held London, or have been called bishop of Dorset
in mistake for Somerset. We find his name, however, so often in
the Abingdon charters that it seems more natural to adopt the

More than
one of the
name

former supposition. The fact that we find two bishops of the name
constantly attesting together [2] hinders us from identifying this
Byrhthelm with the occupants of the sees of London and Winchester ; but it is obvious that if Canterbury were practically vacant,
as we have supposed, from June 958 to October 959, any bishops
appointed in the meantime must have either sought consecration
elsewhere or have held sees in plurality. I think that on the whole
it is most likely that Byrhthelm, who is called the king's kinsman,[3]
was a competitor with Dunstan in more ways than one ; he was
probably Edwy's prime minister, as Dunstan was Edgar's, and
Edgar's triumph was the decisive cause for his final defeat.

Dunstan
becomes
archbishop

Dunstan then became archbishop of Canterbury in 959 ; the
entries in the Chronicle which place this event in 961 [4] being

---

[1] Kemble, C. D. No. 349 : from a
Bath Cartulary. Byrhthelm of Wells
succeeded a bishop named Wulfhelm
in 956 : Wulfsige of Sherborne disappears from the charters in 958; and
his successor Elfwold first appears in
961. I am strengthened in this conjecture by finding that Mr. Robertson,
Hist. Essays, p. 194, note, also supposes Byrhthelm to have succeeded

Wulfsige in 958.
[2] E.g., Kemble, C. D. No. 1225.
[3] Kemble, C. D. 469.
[4] See Thorpe's edition, pp. 218,
219, where it will be seen that the
passage is an interpolation in one MS.,
is altogether omitted in four, and at
home only in the Canterbury MS.
Dom. A. 8, which is the least valuable
as an authority.

late insertions, and at variance with the evidence of charters. The commemoration of his ordination on October 21,[1] before mentioned, may possibly refer to his installation at Canterbury; and if this be the case, no time could have been lost after Edwy's death in removing Byrhthelm, a fact which is moreover proved by two charters of 959[2] which Dunstan witnesses. After the settlement of the kingdom he went to Rome for the pall. This he received from Pope John XII. probably in 960, in which year very few charters contain his name. In 961 he consecrated Elfstan and Oswald his successors in the sees of London and Worcester, probably also the new bishop of Sherborne. In 963 he consecrated Ethelwold, his old fellow-pupil or disciple, to the see of Winchester,[3] and from that date begins the struggle of the monks and clerks which furnishes most of the historians of the reign with their chief subject of discussion. We must, however, dismiss this famous question with a very few remarks in addition to those already made.

Goes to Rome

Struggle between the monks and clerks

All evidence seems to show that, whilst the monastic movement had taken its rise at Winchester, it had been received with the most fervour in Mercia. Dunstan received his impressions in its favour from Elfege the Bald. Ethelwold was a native of Winchester, and Oswald had been trained and held preferment in the same city. The revival of Glastonbury and Abingdon, under the patronage of Edred, was the limit of success in Wessex for a long time, and the four years of Edwy's rule were unfavourable to its extension. The statements of Osbern and Eadmer, that Edwy confiscated all monastic property, are not borne out by the authority of the earlier writers, but Glastonbury had certainly been seized, and the condition of Winchester under Ethelwold seems to show that such monachism as had existed under Elfege was extinguished under his successor. We may safely infer that the monastic party shared in the disgrace of Dunstan, and was made to bear the effects of the quarrel between Edwy and Odo. Accordingly, when the revolt of the Mercians and Northumbrians placed Edgar in the position of a rival, and a too powerful rival, to his brother, it was natural that he should find support in the monastic party; it is also quite possible that that revolt was prompted by the leaders of the religious reform, who were provoked by Edwy's foolish and unlawful marriage. The story that Edgar in his early youth had been moved by the sight of the ruined monasteries to make a vow of restitution[4]

Rise of the new monachism

Connexion of the monastic party with Mercia

[1] Ang. Sac. i. 54.
[2] Kemble, C. D. Nos. 1221, 1225.
    Chr. S. A.D. 963.
[4] Regularis Concordia: preface.

' Clericos perosos habuit, nostri habitus viros sicut diximus honoravit,' says the monk of Ramsey. (V. Oswaldi, Nero E. 1. f. 8.)

Edgar's monastic zeal

may very well be true ; he owed his crown to men who were sincere in their desire to bring about the same end. Unquestionably there were many other points at issue. Wessex and Mercia were held together by a very slight thread, as both earlier and later history show ; but there can, I think, be no doubt either that religious questions entered into the struggle, or that the results bound Edgar, even more firmly than they bound Dunstan, to the monastic interest. The very scanty notices of the Chronicle during Edgar's reign illustrate this, and what little truth can be sifted from the exaggerations of the later monastic writers seems to confirm the conclusion.

Monachism in Mercia

Oswald, under the protection of the East Anglian ealdorman Ethelwin, was working at Ramsey. Ethelwold was nursing a scheme of extension which was to revive the churches which had perished in the Danelaw. Archbishop Oskytel of York, the near kinsman of Oswald and Odo, and of the half mythic Thurkytel, abbot of Bedford, whom Crowland afterwards claimed as founder, must have been one leader of the 'populus brumalis,' when they renounced Edwy. Edgar's success placed these men in possession of all the power they could desire. With Dunstan at Canterbury, Ethelwold at Winchester, and Oswald at Worcester, their course was clear. Ethelwold was the moving spirit, Oswald tempered zeal with discretion, Dunstan's hand may be credited with such little moderation and practical wisdom as can be traced.

Importance of the revival

The movement, with all its drawbacks, was justifiable, perhaps absolutely necessary. The cleansing of Winchester from the ' spurcitiæ clericorum' may not have been indispensable to the welfare of Ramsey, Ely, Peterborough, and Thorney ; but we cannot doubt that a monastic mission system was necessary for the recovery of middle England from the desolation and darkness which had been brought upon it by the Danes, or that the monastic revival was in those regions both successful and useful.

Process of recovering monastic estates

In his first year, 964, Ethelwold, with Edgar's assistance, expelled the seculars from the two great monasteries of Winchester, from Chertsey, and from Milton,[1] and, after doing so, carried out his scheme in middle England. He recovered Ely, Peterborough, and Thorney from the hands into which they had fallen, and established a body of monks in each, under abbots of his own training. Oswald acted with less energy ; instead of driving the clerks out of his cathedral at Worcester, he removed his episcopal chair to the neighbouring monastery ; but he carried on his educational and missionary work at Ramsey with not less zeal than was shown by Ethelwold. It is accordingly on this part of England that the storm falls when the old causes of quarrel revive after the death of Edgar.

[1] Chr. S. A.D. 964.

The only other question of interest in the career of Dunstan during the reign of Edgar is that which concerns the king's coronation at Bath, and, in connexion with it, the story of the nun of Wilton and the septennial penance. According to Osbern, Edgar violated a nun at Wilton, who became mother of Edward, his successor, and Dunstan imposed as a penance, besides other observances, the disuse of the crown for seven years and the foundation of a nunnery at Shaftesbury. Eadmer denies that the young woman in question was a nun, or that she was the mother of Edward, but admits the fact of the crime and the penance, with the exception of the foundation of Shaftesbury, which was known to have been a work of King Alfred. Gotselin, the biographer of S. Edith, and a contemporary of Osbern, gives to the lady of Wilton the name of Wulftrudis, and asserts that Edgar would have married her had she not retired to take the veil at Wilton.[1] Nicolas of Worcester, Eadmer's friend, denied the connexion between the disuse of the crown and the sin of Edgar, and gave the name of S. Edward's mother as Æthelfleda, daughter of Ordmær, ealdorman of the East Angles.[2] William of Malmesbury, in the Gesta Regum, whilst he related three legendary stories of Edgar's vices, attempted to harmonise the several accounts which he had read, and gave the full account of the murder of Ethelwold and marriage of Edgar and Elfthritha, adding that the nunnery of Werewell was founded as an expiation for the crime.[3]

So far as direct evidence goes, the story of the nun of Wilton rests on the testimony of Osbern, which is in itself suspicious, and is told with circumstances that supply a partial refutation. As on this the truth of the septennial penance depends, it may fairly be argued that the whole story stands or falls together. The life of S. Edith, however, which represents a quite independent tradition, clearly shows that there was an ancient scandal about a veiled lady at Wilton; William of Malmesbury's legend of the murder of Ethelwold proves a tradition as to the foundation of an expiatory monastery. The words of the Anglo-Saxon poet, imbedded in the Chronicle, are a telling proof of Edgar's vices.[4] The coronation taking place in 973, just seven years after the marriage of Edgar

---

[1] Mabillon, AA. SS. O. S. B. sæc. v. p. 623.

[2] The biographer of Oswald (Nero E. 1) says that Elfthritha was the daughter of Ordmer, ealdorman of the 'Occidentales Angli;' but he also makes her mother of both Edward and Ethelred; so that he must have confounded two of Edgar's wives. The Chronicle says that

Elfthritha was daughter of Ordgar.

[3] Gesta Regum, lib. I. (ed. Hardy, p. 254).

[4] A.D. 958. Canute thought Edgar 'vitiis deditus, maximeque libidinis servus in subjectos propior tyranno fuisset.' W. Malm. G. P. (ed. Hamilton), p. 190: from Gotselin's Life of S. Edith; Mabillon, sæc. v. p. 626.

Impossible of any certain inference

and Elfthritha, affords a presumption as to some connexion between the story of the seven years' penance and that ill-omened marriage. But the very circumstances which seem to us to afford a practical clue to the explanation may have themselves suggested the legend. It may be quite as wise to reject the whole of the legendary matter, and deny, with Nicolas of Worcester, the connexion of the coronation with the penance.[1] If this be done, we cannot do better than accept the theory which has been recently worked out with great research and ingenuity by one of our most eminent historical scholars,[2] that Edgar's coronation at Bath was a solemn typical enunciation of the consummation of English unity, an inauguration of the king of all the nations of England, celebrated by the two archbishops, possibly with special instructions or recognition from Rome, possibly in imitation of the imperial consecration of Edgar's kinsmen, the first and second Otto, possibly as a declaration of the imperial character of the English crown itself.

Scantiness of details from 965 to 973

The Anglo-Saxon Chronicle supplies only three facts during the seven years that intervene between the marriage and the coronation: the war in Westmoreland, the ravaging of Thanet by the king, of which no explanation is given, and the appointment of Oswald to the see of York. Florence of Worcester throws into these vacant years the several stages of monastic progress: the year 967 is marked by the foundation of Romsey; in 968 Edgar placed monks at Exeter; in 969 the clerks were banished from the monasteries of Mercia; in 970[3] the relics of S. Swithun at Winchester were translated; and in 972 the new minster was dedicated. The great coronation at Bath took place at Whitsuntide 973, and the homage of the eight kings shortly after at Chester. Two years after, on July 8, 975,

Death of Edgar

Edgar died, and was buried by Dunstan by his father's side at Glastonbury.

No authentic history of Dunstan's later years

Dunstan survived his friend for thirteen years, during which the biographers do not supply a single item of independent information. The Saxon priest tells us little of the reign of Edgar, and does not

---

[1] The Life of Oswald, which gives a full detail of this coronation, has not a word about the penance, and represents as ' de more solito.' However, as it gives at length the Promissio Regis, as taken on the occasion, it is clear that it was not a mere crown-wearing festival.

[2] Robertson, Hist. Essays, pp. 203–215, a most learned and instructive essay.

[3] This translation must be distinguished from the more famous dedication of the church celebrated by

Wulfstan in the poem published by Mabillon, sæc. v. pp. 614 sq., at which Dunstan was present, and the bishops Elfstan, Ethelgar, Elfstan, Escwig, Elfege, Æthelsige, and Athulf :—

' Quorum summus erat vultu maturus et actu
Canitie niveus Dunstan et angelicus.'

The names of the bishops fix the date, I think, to the year 980, in which Ethelgar was consecrated; Elfstan of Ramsbury died in 981.

even mention his successors. Adelard records that the saint crowned and anointed both Edward and Ethelred, and that he possessed sufficient influence with the latter to induce him to appoint Elfege to Winchester. The Chronicle does little more than record the reversal of Edgar's monastic policy under his youthful successor by the agency of Elfhere, ealdorman of Mercia. Florence adds that the influence of Elfhere was counteracted by the three East Anglian and East Saxon nobles, Ethelwin, Elfwold, and Brihtnoth, and gives an account of the election of Edward which bears a somewhat suspicious likeness to the language of Osbern. It is to the Chronicle that we owe our knowledge of the council of Kirtlington in 977, and that of Calne in 978, the history of which was interwoven by Osbern into his account of the monastic quarrel. The murder of the young king is there recorded without the mention of the names of the guilty. It is in Osbern that we first find it laid to the charge of Elfthritha. But the Chronicler, who records under the year 980 the translation of Edward's body from Wareham to Shaftesbury, by Elfhere and Dunstan, the former the leader of the secular, the latter the patron of the monastic party, shuts out the probability that Edward was sacrificed to political rather than personal aims. The inference drawn from the silence of the contemporary chronicles is unfavourable to Elfthritha; the statement that Edward's kinsmen would not avenge him [1] does not warrant us in supposing that he was the victim of a conspiracy. Dunstan crowned his successor at Kingston, and then attempted to impress upon him the binding character of his royal obligations in a document, the 'Promissio Regis,' with its commentary, which is still preserved. We may ask, but we cannot answer, who guided the state during the childhood of Ethelred. The political history of Dunstan ends with his accession.

It is, however, to this period of his life that the letter of Abbo belongs, and the picture of his daily occupations drawn by the Saxon priest. His chief employment was on the divine service, prayer and psalmody, and holy vigils ; now and then he resumed the employments of his youth, exercising his old skill in handicraft in the making of musical instruments like the organs which were kept at Malmesbury, or the bells that were known at Canterbury as his own work ; the early hours of the morning he gave to the very needful task of correcting the faulty manuscripts of the library. Even after he had retired from political life, leaving Ethelred to mismanage his kingdom as he chose, the great domains of his church afforded him abundance of public work ; it was his delight to make peace between man and man, to receive and assist the

Side notes:
How supplied by later authorities

Elfthritha probably contrived the murder of Edward

Idea of Dunstan's life in his old age

[1] Chron. Sax. A.D. 975.

widows and fatherless, pilgrims and strangers of all sorts; as an
ecclesiastical judge he never stayed his hand against unlawful
marriages, or in the maintenance of ecclesiastical order. He was
an admirable steward of the church's wealth, a founder and endower
of new churches, and indefatigable in the work of instruction,
Picture of Dunstan's old age gathering young and old, men and women, clerk, monk, and lay, to
listen to his teaching. 'And thus all this English land was filled
with his holy doctrine, shining before God and men like the sun and
moon. When he was minded to pay to Christ the Lord the due
hours of service, and the celebrations of the mass, with such entire-
ness of devotion he laboured in singing that he seemed to be speaking
face to face with the Lord, even if just before he had been vexed
with the quarrels of the people; like S. Martin, he constantly kept
eye and hand intent on heaven, never letting his spirit rest from
prayer.'

Probable truth of the sketch The idea of the sketch is that of a good and faithful servant;
there is nothing grotesque about the man as he appears in the pages
of the eye-witness; nothing of the tyrannical ascetic. It is the
crowning of a laborious life, of a man who has had great power and
has used it for his country, and who, now that other rulers have
arisen who do not know or love him, falls back on the studies of his
youth, and spends his last years in the promotion of pious and
learned works. The end, if we set aside, as I think we may safely
do, the strange story of the miracle, is quiet and peaceful. He was
only sixty-four when he died, but his public life had begun early and
lasted long, and his fame lived both at home and abroad, in the
praises of the strangers whom he had befriended, the churches that
he had planted, the scholars whom he had taught, but chiefly in the
longing remembrance of the peace and glory which Edgar under his
teaching had maintained: the peace and glory which were written
in the hearts of the English, although they left vacant pages in the
chronicles, and which were the last glimpses of national prosperity.
Yet Dunstan's memory was worshipped not only from a feeling of
regret; as I have remarked more than once, his beatification in
His early beatification popular regard scarcely waited for his death; and it is no small
proof of the estimation in which his memory was held that when, in
1017, Canute set the laws civil and ecclesiastical upon the ancient
and national footing, together with the feast on the anniversary of
S. Edward, a perpetual protest against the line of Ethelred, he
ordered the solemn and universal observance of S. Dunstan's mass
day.[1]

Dunstan's share in Edgar's legislation The true mark of Dunstan's mind must be looked for in Edgar's
legislation, and in the few canons passed at the ecclesiastical

[1] Leges Canuti (Schmid, p. 265), I. 17.

assemblies of the reign. These will all be found among the ancient laws and institutes of the Anglo-Saxons, published by Wilkins, Thorpe, and Schmid.[1] That Dunstan had a chief part in the enactment of these is a necessary inference from the fact that throughout the reign he was the king's closest friend and adviser, the chief of his witan, the ecclesiastical head of the nation. The laws that bear Edgar's name must bear the impress of Dunstan's mind. We cannot follow the writers who argue that because Edgar's canons do not forbid the marriage of the clergy they must be referred to the period of his reign when Dunstan was not yet archbishop, and argue, therefore, that they were the work of a king of fifteen years old who was under the guidance of a party far more monastically inclined than Dunstan himself.[2]

Of the secular laws of Edgar, the institution of the Hundred seems to be a reconstruction and development of the old German Hundred system, for special purposes of police, from which no inference can be drawn as to the policy of its author. The secular ordinances and the 'Supplementum' are in this respect more important ; and the preamble to the first of these asserts a noble principle : 'I will that every man be worthy of folkright, as well poor as rich, and that righteous dooms be judged to him.' The enactments that follow are few but definite, and touch on the remedial jurisdiction of the king, the regular holding of the popular courts, the general system of 'borh' or security for appearance in the gemots, and the uniformity of coins and measures. In the Supplementum the hand of Dunstan is distinctly traceable ; it is an enactment in the time of pestilence, that the wrath of God may be turned from the people. 'I and the archbishop command,' says the king, 'that ye anger not God' by robbing him or his church. The practices of religion are enjoined, the rights of the king and his thegns, the legal freedom of the Danes, and their possession of their own laws, are secured ; the points included in the earlier laws are repeated, and the observance of the peace enforced by threats and promises. Although these few ordinances bear but a slight proportion to the laws of Ethelred and Canute, they are distinctly constructive : the administration of justice, the equal rights of poor and rich, Dane and English, and the careful maintenance of the 'frith' by the hundred system, are

---

[1] Thorpe (folio ed.) pp. 109–118. Schmid, pp. 182–199.

[2] Johnson's Canons, ed. Baron, i. 408, 'Though these laws and the first set of canons following next after them are ascribed to king Edgar, yet they have nothing of the spirit of Dunstan in them : I mean they inflict no punishments or hard censures on the married clergy, as they certainly would if Dunstan had been at the making of them.' Also, p. 412, 'these canons, which I place before Dunstan's accession to the see of Canterbury, as containing no censure against the married clergy.'

progressive measures of reform. If Dunstan's work is here, we have some justification of the praises of his biographers.

Ecclesiasti-
cal laws of
the period

The ecclesiastical laws of the period are of the same constructive and progressive stamp. Those few enactments which are included among Edgar's laws touch chiefly on payments to the churches, church scot, tithe, and Rome penny, and on the observance of

Canons of
the reign
of Edgar

festivals and fasts. The canons which touch on spiritual matters have a wider interest;[1] but, like most canonical legislation, they incorporate very much of earlier law. They fall into two classes; the first are called the sixty-seven canons of Edgar, many of which are taken from the Karolingian capitularies, and which touch on synods, the exercise of spiritual discipline, the abolition of the relics of heathenism, the observance of Sundays, festivals, and fasts, the decent and solemn celebration of the sacraments, and the guidance of the lives of the clergy. One or two are characteristic, we may

Dunstan's
hand in
them

think, of Dunstan: 'That no priest receive a scholar without the leave of the other by whom he was formerly retained;' 'that every priest do teach manual arts with diligence;' 'that no learned priest reproach him that is less learned, but mend him if he know how;' 'that no noble born priest despise one of less noble birth; if

Penitential
canons

it be rightly considered, all men are of one origin.' The penitential canons which are found in connexion with these are a compilation of the period from the earlier penitential books of the church, and contain nothing original. Nor do they contain anything that connects them with the reign of Edgar or the pontificate of Dunstan. It is in these only that any mention is found of clerical marriages : 'If a mass priest or a monk or deacon had a lawful wife before he was ordained, and dismisses her and takes orders, and then receives her again by lying with her, let every one of them fast as for murder and vehemently lament it;'—a very necessary safeguard in an age in which it was so common to play fast and loose with sacred obligations. But this canon, on which apparently depends the charge of persecuting the married clergy made so commonly against Dunstan, is an extract from penitentials of much earlier date, and cannot with any certainty be assigned to him as its re-enactor.[2]

Tradition
preserved by
William of
Malmesbury
touching the
drinking
custom

William of Malmesbury has preserved a tradition which serves to present Dunstan in a light that can hardly offend popular reformers of this day. He introduced the custom of inserting pegs in the

---

[1] Thorpe, pp. 395 sq. Johnson, i. pp. 412 sq.

[2] It is taken from the fourth book of the Pseudo-Egbertine Penitential, which again is from the Pseudo-Theodore, which takes it from the Pœnitentiale Romanum, published by Halitgar of Cambray; here it is taken from the Penitential of Columbanus, and the earlier writers. See Wasserschleben, Bussordnungen der Abendländische Kirche, p. 365. Thorpe pp. 408, 378, 283.

drinking cups, that no man might run into excess without knowing it.[1] Human nature, which is so apt to mistake a limit for a law, a maximum for a minimum, soon put the pegs to the opposite use, and required legislation that forbade the custom 'of drinking to pegs,' or, as we should say, 'allowing no heeltaps.'

The early and more trustworthy writers connect the memory of Dunstan with no cruel or barbarous asceticism. The evidence of the laws does, I think, confirm the testimony of the Lives. Dunstan is a constructor, not a destroyer; a consolidator, not a pedantic theorist; a reformer, not an innovator; a politician, not a bigot; a statesman, not a zealot. His merits as a scholar, an artist, a musician, a cunning craftsman, are a part of the contemporary picture which ought not to be disregarded. His zeal for education is a far more authentic trait than his zeal for celibacy. His vindication of the law of marriage can never be regarded as a blot by those who know anything of the state of society, especially in the royal houses of his day; or consider the strange way in which religion and courtly adulation could be combined when the uncorrupted body of a king like Edgar was believed to work miracles. Yet this has scarcely been fairly recognised. Dunstan's zeal for the purity of marriage is acknowledged as a matter of merit when it was exercised against the corrupt papacy; yet because by the command of the witan of the kingdom he draws a wanton boy of fifteen from the dangerous society of a girl whom it was unlawful for him to marry, we are told that 'a young king was persecuted and dethroned by the insolence of monkery exciting a superstitious people against him.'[2] There must be a sacredness, it would seem, about the very sins of kings.

Dunstan an educator rather than an ascetic

His zeal for the law of marriage

Strange misrepresentation

It is strange that of a life so important and diversified as that of Dunstan not a single literary monument survives; not a single letter that can with any possibility be attributed to him, although several addressed to him are extant, and will be found in the Rolls Series. Diligent in his ecclesiastical work, diligent in his political work, diligent as a student and as a teacher, he has left, beyond a few lines of writing, the endorsement of a charter, and the prayer put into the mouth of a kneeling figure in an illumination, no writings whatever.[3]

No literary remains of Dunstan

It is true that during the middle ages, when the study of alchemy was rife, a tract bearing the name of Dunstan was circulated among the initiated; but it was no doubt assigned to him as to a celebrated

The tract on Alchemy

---

[1] Ed. Hardy, p. 237.
[2] Hallam, Middle Ages, ii. 267.
[3] The statement that one of the MSS. of the Chronicle is supposed to be in Dunstan's handwriting (Allen, Prerogative, 223) is based on the merest conjecture.

saint and philosopher, whose name might gain for it a circulation that it could not demand upon its merits. This work, the 'Tractatus maximi Domini Dunstani archiepiscopi Cantuariensis vere philosophi de lapide philosophorum,' was printed at Cassel in 1649, in the ' Clavis portæ aureæ' of George Ripley.[1] It is also found in a fifteenth century MS. in the Library of Corpus Christi College, Oxford.[2]

The Regularis Concordia

Another book which has been attributed to Dunstan is the ' Regularis Concordia,' a body of rules for monks, which has been at least twice printed : first by Reyner in the ' Apostolatus Benedictinorum,' and again in the preliminary matter of the ' New Monasticon.' It is an interesting and valuable work, written very shortly after the monastic revival, and so early received as authoritative that it was translated into Anglo-Saxon before the Norman conquest. It cannot, however, be ascribed to Dunstan, who is mentioned in it as ' egregius hujus patriæ archiepiscopus, præsago afflatus spiritu,' although it is easy to see that it might, by a very natural mistake, be regarded as his work. It has a considerable historical value, giving an account of the way in which Edgar was induced to promote the monastic revival, the missions from Fleury and Ghent, and the council of Winchester, of which so much is said in the lives of Dunstan by Osbern and Eadmer. It may conjecturally be referred to the abbot Elfric.

The Concordia is not Dunstan's

There is in the Royal Library, in the British Museum,[3] a large commentary on the Benedictine rule, written in the twelfth or thirteenth century, and illustrated with a very fine full-page picture of a bishop. This has been attributed with some confidence to Dunstan, but the MS. contains nothing to justify such a statement ; neither the Latin style nor the general arrangement of the book is at first sight consistent with the assumption ; and if there be among the minuter points of the work anything that suggests it, I have been unable in a careful examination to discover it.

Commentary on the Benedictine Rule, not Dunstan's

Of the other books with which the name of Dunstan, not as author but as traditionary owner, is connected, the most important is the well-known Bodleian MS. marked Auctarium F. iv. 32.[4] This volume consists of a bundle of very ancient remains, the chief of which are, a large part of the *Liber Euticis Grammatici de*

Books that have belonged to Dunstan

[1] Clavis portæ aureæ, p. 240. See Wright's Biographia Literaria, i. 462.

[2] No. 128. Coxe's Catalogue of MSS., C.C.C. p. 47. It is a fifteenth century MS., once the property of Brian Twyne.

[3] MS. Reg. 10 A. 13. See Wright, Biogr. Lit. i. 461.

[4] Described in Macray's Annals of the Bodleian, p. 20 ; Hickes, Thesaurus, i. p. 144, where the first page is engraved ; and iii. p. 63 ; Villemarqué's Notices des principaux MSS. des Anciens Bretons, Paris, 1856.

discernendis Conjugationibus, a quantity of extracts from the Scriptures in Greek and Latin, Tables for calculating the Full Moon, a Paschal table reaching from A.D. 817 to 832, the first book of Ovid's Art of Love, a homily in Anglo-Saxon on the Invention of the Cross, and several minor fragments or notes on measures and numbers. Several of these pieces contain British glosses and furnish some of the earliest written specimens of Welsh. On the first leaf of the volume is a large drawing of our Saviour, holding in his right hand a long rod or sceptre, and in his left a book, with a monk kneeling at his feet. On the sceptre is inscribed the text, ' Et virga recta est virga regni Tui ' ; on the book, ' Venite filii, audite me, timorem Domini docebo vos ' : from the mouth of the monk proceeds a scroll, and over his head is the couplet— *[The Bodleian MS. with a drawing of Dunstan]*

> " Dunstanum memet clemens rogo, Christe, tuere
> " Tenarias me non sinas sorbsisse procellas."

A later inscription at the top of the page tells us that this is Dunstan's work : ' Pictura et scriptura hujus paginæ subtus visa est de propria manu sancti Dunstani.' This drawing was engraved in Hickes's Thesaurus, vol. i. p. 144, and in other later works. The manuscript itself is described in a very early catalogue of the Library of Glastonbury, now in the Library of Trinity College, Cambridge, and is also mentioned by Leland as seen by him there, with the note that the book had been Dunstan's.[1] It is one of the most curious volumes in existence, and would go further to prove the antiquity of Glastonbury and its connexion with early British as well as Anglo-Saxon history than all the forged charters even if they were genuine.

Another Glastonbury book in the Bodleian is among the Hatton MSS., No. 30 ; a copy of S. Augustine on the Apocalypse, at the end of which in large capitals is the inscription, ' Dunstan abbas hunc libellum scribere jussit,' a note evidently made before Dunstan had reached the rank of either archbishop or saint.[2] *[The Hatton MS., No. 30]*

The Hatton collection contains another book (No. 42) inscribed on the back ' Liber Sancti Dunstani,' which has been already mentioned as the volume in which the head of ' Wulfric Cild ' is drawn. This is a collection of canons ; the first portion written about the time of Dunstan, the latter about a century earlier. The more ancient part consists of the Apostolic canons, and decrees of councils which form part of the early collections of decretals. The rest of the volume comprises a copy of the great Irish collection of canons in sixty-seven chapters, which is found in the much damaged Cotton MS. Otho E, 13, in the S. Gall MS. 243, and in the Paris MSS. 3182 *[The Liber Sancti Dunstani]*

---

[1] Leland, Collectanea, iii. 154.
[2] Also mentioned by Macray, Annals, p. 20.

and 12021, which was prepared for the press by the late Mr. Arthur Haddan as a part of the second volume of the councils, and has just been printed in Germany from a collation of various MSS. by Dr. Wasserschleben of Giessen. The Hatton MS. furnishes a somewhat enlarged edition, such as Dunstan might be supposed likely to make. Besides this it contains the canons of Adamnan, a selection of passages from the Roman and Frank law books, and a quantity of regulations about degrees of kindred. The fact that it contains the Irish canons adds a presumption that it was written at Glastonbury, an inference we should be inclined at first sight to draw from the company in which it is found. If it was really Dunstan's book, we may see in it reflected the nature of his studies : the Irish canons he might get from his teachers at Glastonbury ; the Frank and Roman law during his exile at Ghent; the regulations touching marriages and the degrees of kindred would illustrate those peculiar points which come out most strongly in the traditions of his discipline.

The Sherborne Pontifical at Paris

The National Library at Paris possesses what is called the Pontifical of Dunstan, a magnificent folio of the tenth century, which once belonged to the church of Sherborne in Dorsetshire, and may not improbably have been given by Dunstan or one of his early successors. Its number in the catalogue of Latin MSS. is 943. It contains besides the Pontifical, on vacant leaves, a number of interesting pieces touching English church history. Amongst these is a list of the bishops of Sherborne, ending with Ethelric, who became bishop in the year 1001 ; [1] the letter of Pope John XII. to Dunstan ; the letter of an archbishop, whose name is not given, to bishop Wulfsige, printed in the Rolls Series, and a list of the books ' quos custodit Dodo ' ; perhaps the Sherborne Library. This list, which may possibly have been printed, mentions amongst other books, ' Liber Legis Salicæ,' ' Liber Bernelini in Abaco,' and ' Liber Helprici artis calculatoriæ.' Other articles in the volume are an Anglo-Saxon sermon ' de dedicatione ecclesiæ ' ; the order for the benediction of an abbot, ' tempus inter hominis mortem et ultimam resurrectionem ' ; and ' this is thæra gerædnessa sum the bisceopas geræd habbath.' Besides these there are some Sherborne charters which have been printed by Kemble.

Dunstan's penmanship

Of Dunstan's penmanship, besides the picture in the Bodleian MS., there are possibly two or three specimens existing in charters. The cathedral church of Christ at Canterbury possesses one, a grant

---

[1] I give the list from this MS. :—
1. Aldhelm. 2. Forthere. 3. Herewald. 4. Æthelmod. 5. Denefrith. 6. Wigberht. 7. Ealhstan. 8. Ealhmund. 9. Æthelheah. 10. Wulfsige. 11. Asser. 12. Æthelwerd. 13. Waerstan. 14. Æthelbald. 15. Sigelm. 16. Ælfred. 17. Wulfsige. 18. Alfwold. 19. Æthelsige. 20. Wulfsige. 21. Æthelric. It agrees exactly with MS. Tiberius B. 5. See Registrum Sacr. Angl. p. 165.

by king Edred dated in the year 949, in which he gives the monastery of Reculver to the mother church. A duplicate of this exists among the Cotton charters, and has been photographed by order of the trustees of the British Museum. Dunstan professes himself to be the writer : 'Ego Dunstan indignus abbas rege Eadredo imperante hanc domino meo hereditariam kartulam dictitando conposui et propriis digitorum articulis perscripsi.'[1] Another is said by Mr. Wright to have been in the possession of the church of Winchester.[2]

Of Dunstan's musical ability it is possible that we have a trace in the trope or cantus ' Kyrie rex splendens,' which according to the Salisbury use is appointed to be sung on his festival, after the *officium*. The text of this composition will be found in the Rolls' volume, p. 357, taken from the Gradual,[3] collated with the printed editions of the Missal. All, however, that can be said of it is that it may be Dunstan's. The history of it is this. Eadmer relates a story of Dunstan falling asleep one Sunday at mass, whilst waiting for Edgar, who had gone out hunting. In his sleep he heard a solemn service in heaven, and when he awoke dictated to his servants a ' Kyrie Eleyson,' which he had learned there, which, according to the biographer, was in his days sung in many places among the solemn ceremonies of the mass.[4] It would seem a natural conclusion that the ' Kyrie rex splendens ' which was sung only on the feasts of Dunstan and S. Michael should be identified with this ; and although William of Malmesbury does not notice it except in a very cursory way, it must have been believed soon after his day. Higden is, however, the first writer who distinctly states that the ' Kyrie ' which Dunstan learned contained the ' modulos harmoniæ ' which were contained in the trope so famous among the English, ' Kyrie rex splendens.' The statement is copied by Capgrave, and appears also in Bromton, and possibly in other writers of the fifteenth century.[5] If, however, we venture to assume thus much, it may reasonably be questioned whether the words or the music only should be attributed to Dunstan. Higden's language seems to refer to the music, that of Eadmer to the words. It has indeed been thought that as the peculiar tropes or variations on the ' Kyrie ' are not found until the thirteenth century in the common missals, the music only of this one could even by tradition be Dunstan's. But this is a mistake, for we possess a tropary dating nearly if not quite from

The Kyrie rex splendens

Development of its history

---

[1] Kemble, C. D. No. cccxxxv.
[2] Wright, Biog. Lit. i. 459.
[3] In the Bodleian, among the ' Gough Missals.'
[4] The Kyrie Eleyson story, however, occurs much earlier in the life of Oswald, Nero E. 1, fo. 16 : ' Hoc non

conticescendum puto quod et Kyrie Eleyson eximium e superis auditum agminibus, quod nostrates satis dulciter personare consuescunt.'
[5] Higden, ap. Gale, p. 270 ; Bromton, ap. Twysden, c. 879.

Dunstan's days, which contains a large number of ' Kyries,' both words and music. In this we do not find ' Kyrie rex splendens,' but several forms of expression more or less coinciding with it.[1] If we suppose that Dunstan wrote the trope, it would not of course appear at once in the service books, but there is nothing in it inconsistent with this antiquity. It may have been many times remodelled like the other ' Kyries ' and rearranged afterwards.

Question of the translation of Dunstan's bones

In the later pages of the Rolls' volume much will be found about the claim of the monks of Glastonbury, first asserted in the twelfth century and stoutly maintained down to the age of the Reformation, that they possessed the bones of Dunstan. They had been removed, according to the story, in the reign of Edmund Ironside, and proved

No reason to believe the story of Dunstan's translation

their genuineness by working miracles. Into the details of this story we need not enter : there is no reason whatever for believing that such a translation ever took place, or that Glastonbury ever possessed a single bone of Dunstan. The tale, like so many other marvels of hagiology, has its parallels elsewhere : no doubt relics were stolen on a large scale as well as given and purchased. King Edmund was believed to have removed from the north to Glastonbury the bones of Aidan, Ceolfrith, and Hilda ;[2] and these saints had special commemorations at Glastonbury so early that the invention of the story cannot fairly be ascribed to William of Malmesbury.[3] Edred and Odo again were believed to have carried off the body of S.

Parallel traditions

Wilfrid from Ripon to Canterbury. These were cases in which the bodies of the saints were removed to save them from the profane hands of the Norsemen. A still closer parallel may be found in the history of Ely. Ecgfrid, the abbot of S. Alban's, according to the Ely historians, flying at the command of Stigand from the Normans, carried with him to Ely the shrine containing the bones of the proto-martyr, and, in order to obtain admission into the brotherhood, deposited them or allowed them to be deposited with the bones of S. Etheldreda.[4] The S. Alban's historians denied the truth of this. The flight of the abbot—Fretheric they call him—is admitted, and his death and burial at Ely ; 'whence,' says Matthew Paris, 'they of Ely, lying against their own heads, assert that he brought thither with him the bones of S. Alban, not fearing to allege against the holy man the crime of sacrilege.' The reverence paid to S. Alban was therefore diminished, as was the case also with other saints of the kingdom,

[1] MS. Bodl. 775.
[2] W. Malmesb. Gesta Pontiff. p. 198.
[3] See especially the Kalendar in MS. Cotton, Nero A. 2 ; and that in the Missal of Leofric in the Bodleian Library.
[4] Liber Eliensis (ed. Stewart), p. 227.

and miracles in their churches became less frequent.[1]   Before 1129 Story at
S. Alban's
another competitor, 'quoddam collegium in Dacia,' falsely asserted the
possession of the relics, and in that year the coffin at S. Alban's was
opened and the bones counted.   Still the men of Ely contended
that miracles constantly proved them in the right.   At last, under
papal pressure, early in the reign of Henry II. they confessed that
they had been deceived by a pious fraud.[2]   Not so the monks of
Glastonbury, who carried on the battle until the eve of the Reformation.   There is no probability that Dunstan's remains ever left Canterbury; they rested in the shrine which so many ages of pious
affection had provided and adorned until the Reformation, when, if
they escaped the blind profanity of Henry VIII., it was because the
glories of S. Dunstan had been eclipsed by a more famous ecclesiastical hero.[3]

Of the cultus of Dunstan the illustrations given in the eighth
section of this volume in the Rolls Series will probably prove sufficient
to content the reader.

I shall not attempt to draw a minute character of Dunstan, for Dunstan's
character
the materials before us afford too small data to make it possible
to do so with any definiteness.   But I think we may, from the
language of the first biographer, the letters of Abbo and the other
writers included in this volume, get a glimpse of the man, truer if
fainter than the fancy portraits drawn by later writers who have
seen no mean between indiscriminate adulation on the one hand and
the most hateful detraction on the other.   Dunstan has been repre- Misrepre-
sentation of
Dunstan
sented by a very learned recent writer as a man whose whole life was
'a crusade, cruel, unrelenting, yet but partially successful, against
the married clergy, which in truth comprehended the whole secular
clergy of the Anglo-Saxon kingdom.'   'Dunstan was, as it were, in
a narrower sphere, a prophetic type and harbinger of Hildebrand.
Like Hildebrand, or rather like Damiani doing the work of Hildebrand,
in the spirit not of a rival sovereign but of an iron-hearted monk, he
trampled the royal power under his feet.   The scene at the coronation
of king Edwy, excepting the horrible cruelties to which it was the
prelude, and which belong to a more barbarous race, might seem to
prepare mankind for the humiliation of the emperor Henry at Canosa.'[4]
For this invective there is not in the writings of contemporaries, or
in any authentic remains of Dunstan's legislation, the shadow of a

---

[1] Gesta Abbatum (ed. Riley), i. 51.
[2] Ibid. p. 176.
[3] In the twelfth and thirteenth
centuries the great bells which he had
made for Abingdon were preserved;
and at Glastonbury, crosses, chasubles,
censers, and vestments of his making.
Wright, Biogr. Lit. i. 435, 459.
[4] Milman, Latin Christianity, vol.
iv. p. 25 (ed. 1867).

foundation.   What Dunstan did at Edwy's coronation he did by the
order of the assembled witan of the kingdom.   The cruelties which are
said to have followed are asserted on the authority of Osbern and
Eadmer, the earlier of whom wrote nearly a century and a half after
the death of Edwy, and depend on no other testimony.   If they ever
took place at all, they took place during Dunstan's exile, during the
war that preceded the election of Edgar.   Such at least is the statement of Osbern, who is the sole witness ; Eadmer's additions in his
life of Odo resting on no evidence at all.[1]   The charge of persecuting
the married clergy is as baseless.   We have no means of judging
what proportion of the secular clergy was married : the secular clerks
who held monastic property were married, and the same evidence
which proves their marriages proves also how lightly the marriage

No evidence
as to Dun-
stan's harsh-
ness towards
the married
clergytie sat upon them.   But against these it was not Dunstan chiefly,
but Oswald and Ethelwold who took the measures of reform which
are represented as persecution, and which were no doubt severe and
undiscriminating.   In this Dunstan, as I have already remarked,
takes only a secondary part : he does not remove the clerks from his
own cathedral churches ; his sympathy with the monastic movement
is only to be gathered by inference from the fact that he did not
oppose it.   As to the married clergy in general there is absolutely
no evidence whatever ; and here is the most astounding amount of
assumption.   It is scarcely to be believed that our canonists, in
discussing the date of the little ecclesiastical legislation that belongs
to Edgar's reign, have determined that it does not belong to Dunstan's
pontificate because it contains no enactments against the married
clergy.   Yet Dunstan became archbishop as soon as Edwy was dead,
and beyond a doubt inspired whatever ecclesiastical law was made

Silence of
his genuine
legislation
on this pointin that reign.   In fact the only laws which can with any probability
be ascribed to Dunstan are altogether silent on the point.   We know
that when he was a young man in minor orders he intended to marry,
and it was the taking of monastic vows that showed his renunciation
of the design.   It is the enforcement of monastic discipline, not the
compulsory celibacy of the clergy, that is the object of the clerical
reforms ; and in this Dunstan only partly sympathised.   As for the
charge of trampling on the royal authority, it may be dismissed in a
word.   Men's views of what constitutes vice may differ, but any rule
that condemns Dunstan condemns John the Baptist also ; and if any
error on the side of severity is pardonable, it is when the rebuke is

I will content myself with a
general reference to Mr. Robertson's
invaluable essay on Dunstan's policy,
Hist. Essays, pp 189 sq. : and to Dr.
Hook's Life of Dunstan.   I think little can be added to the exhaustive
summary of the former writer.   Both
works stand, as might be expected, in
strong contrast with Milman, Hallam,
and Lingard.

addressed to the vices of princes : why is Dunstan to be blamed for that which is the glory of Ambrose and Anselm?

But in truth the career of Dunstan was no anticipation of that of Hildebrand : it was the very counterpart of that of Gerbert, the student, the practical workman, the wise instructor of a royal pupil, the statesman, the reformer, and the patriot. Osbern and Eadmer drew the character of their saint in the spirit with which they were themselves inspired, imputing to him qualities which in their imagination were virtues, as in the eyes of more modern writers they have seemed to be vices, but which the world may be almost said to have learned from the life of Gregory VII. They drew the picture of the saint in lines and colours that seemed to them indispensable to sanctity, and read the history of Dunstan through the history of Henry IV.

No likeness between Dunstan and Hildebrand

Another point has been already referred to, which receives some important illustration from the early lives and letters here printed : the connexion of England with Flanders, especially in the point of monastic reform. It must not be forgotten, that while monasticism had become under Alfred practically extinct in England, on the continent it had merely languished. The monasticism of Flanders was active and energetic compared with that of England, just as the monasticism of Fleury was definite and severe as compared with that of Flanders. Count Baldwin had married the daughter of Alfred ; she took a part in the monastic revival in her adopted country, such as Alfred had attempted at home, and which was carried out by two men of very different character in the two countries, Edred and Arnulf, both grandsons of Alfred. In the year 918 the monks of Blandinium had received from Etheldritha, or Elstrudis as they called her, a grant of lands in Kent which were in their hands when the Domesday Survey was made.[1] Whilst Edred was reviving Glastonbury and Abingdon, Arnulf was rebuilding and refilling S. Bertin, S. Vedast, and Blandinium. Eighteen great monasteries were restored by him. All this was well known to the West Saxon princes. Elstrudis was buried at Blandinium. Edwin, the brother of Athelstan, who perished at sea by his brother's cruelty, it was said, found his resting-place at S. Bertin.[2] The so-called monks who were expelled in the process of reform and would not accept the revived Benedictine rule, found refuge with Athelstan in England.[3]

Connexion of England with Flanders

Revival of monachism

[1] Meyer, Annales Rerum Belgicarum, p. 20. 'A.D. 929. Obiit Elstrudis magni principis mater 7mo kalendas Junias, jacetque sepulta prope maritum Blandinii in ædicula parentis virginis. Hæc Blandiniensibus cœnobitis amplas donavit possessiones in Anglia in finibus Cantii, unde tabulas habent anno 918.' A charter confirming the grant of Etheldritha, made by Edward the Confessor, is printed in Kemble, C. D. No. dcclxxi.

[2] Meyer, p. 20.

[3] Ibid. p. 21.

D

It is thus easy to account for the hospitable treatment which Dunstan found in the territories of Arnulf, and for the letters addressed to Edgar, to Dunstan and his successors, by the Flemish and North French monasteries, asking or returning thanks for help.

Continental relations of the West Saxon Kings

This serves to open a comparatively untrodden field of ecclesiastical history, for the illustration of which it is probable that more remains are extant than is generally suspected. It is extremely desirable that the history of the foreign relations of England, political, ecclesiastical and literary, in the tenth and eleventh centuries, should be more carefully explored. There is no reason to suppose that the invasion of the Danes, when they destroyed so much else, really interrupted the intercourse of England with Germany. The marriages of the daughters of Alfred and Edward do not stand alone. The political negotiations of Odo placed Lewis d'Outremer on the throne of the West Franks; the wanderings of Kynewald brought Athelstan and his court into close ecclesiastical affinity with the monasteries of Germany. It is true that there is some uniformity in the result: English gold is as ingenuously asked for, and as freely bestowed, as it continues to be for ages after. English manuscripts are borrowed, of which there is no notice of

Intercourse of England with the continent

return. Few and far between are the notices of Englishmen in continental authors, but nevertheless there are traces of a continuous and lively intercourse, which might be multiplied by close examination, and might yield an unexpected harvest to patient labour.

Greek words in the Latin of the time

The number of Greek words that occur in the early lives and letters will necessarily attract the notice of scholars. This is no peculiarity of English writers; it is a common feature of the period; and it is one the examination of which has never been thoroughly carried out. The superficial use of glossaries, without any knowledge of grammar, will account for some part of the vocabulary which so curiously diversifies the Latin of the Saxon priest. The use of Greek hymns or Greek versicles in the services of the church may account for a phrase here and there. The occasional visit of a Greek pilgrim or exile awoke from time to time the desire of knowing a few Greek words, or the forms of the Greek letters. But the exact amount of knowledge of Greek literature is not easy to calculate; the few references that occur seem to be stock quotations, drawn probably, if not certainly, through the medium of the Latin Fathers. Phenomena like John Scotus Erigena were rare indeed; yet the age of Dunstan almost reaches the age of John Scotus, and what was possible for one scholar was not quite impossible for others. The struggles of the Saxon emperors in Southern Italy probably did something to bring spoken Greek to the ears of western ecclesiastics.

     *   *   *   *   *   *

THE HISTORICAL WORKS OF MASTER RALPH DE DICETO, DEAN OF LONDON

[IN two volumes of the Rolls Series are contained 'the whole of the historical matter which claims him as author or collector.' Ralph de Diceto not only wrote many treatises, he also made compilations from his own larger works. In the latter part of the Preface, which is not printed in this volume, Bishop Stubbs gives an account of the several MSS. which he used in editing Ralph's writings. In another place he examines Ralph's value as a historian. The following account of Ralph's life throws an interesting light upon the duties of an Archdeacon and Dean in the twelfth century, upon the Becket dispute, and upon the ecclesiastical greatness of London in the reigns of Henry II. and Richard I.]

IN the roll of English Historians of the twelfth century no name stands higher than that of Ralph de Diceto. He has been more fortunate than either Roger of Hoveden or the author of the ' Gesta Regis Henrici '; for the great ecclesiastical position which he occupied for more than fifty years made him, modest and retiring as he seems to have been, a definitely public man. As a public man, he left traces of his presence in the record of public affairs, and these traces furnish us with some important points of his personal biography I propose, in the following pages, to attempt a sketch of the career of the author, and to give an account of the external history of the book now before us, reserving for the introduction to the second volume what has to be said about the intrinsic value of his labours, the sources of his information, and the relations of the *Imagines Historiarum* to the other contemporary annals of the same age.

Prominence of Ralph de Diceto, as a public man

The most obscure point, perhaps, in our author's personal history is his name. It is peculiar to himself. History and record alike give him the name of 'Radulfus de Diceto,' and the surname he shares with no other. He almost invariably uses it in full, whenever he writes about himself; he prefixes it at length to his literary works; he inserts it in the salutation of his letters; he heads the acts in which he and his chapter join with his full name ' Ralph de

Obscurity of his name

Diceto the dean of the church of S. Paul at London, and the chapter of the said church, to all to whom these presents shall come, greeting'; and he dates his survey of the estates of his church by this among other notes : 'per Radulfum de Diceto decanum Lundoniensem, anno primo sui decanatus.' It may be thought that in the latter documents he used this form merely for the purpose of distinguishing his own acts as dean from those of his predecessor Ralph of Langford ; but the same peculiarity is found whilst he is acting as archdeacon before he became dean ; and it is carefully observed by his contemporaries : Gilbert Foliot, John of Salisbury, William FitzStephen, Arnulf of Lisieux, distinguish him as 'Radulfus Dicetensis' or 'Radulfus de Diceto.' It would almost seem that he prided himself for some reason on the surname which he had assumed, or else that he held so humble an opinion of his own importance that he though it requisite on every occasion to distinguish himself from the more conspicuous persons who bore the same Christian name. Illustrations of this practice will abound as we proceed. Any conclusion, however, to which we may come upon the point, must be regarded as showing that, at a period at which surnames, whether patronymic, local or official, were becoming much more common than they had been, Ralph de Diceto was one of the very first to use such a name distinctively and invariably. It is this peculiarity which enables us to detect his presence on occasions and in documents in which, if he had been content to follow the common practice, it would have been unnoticed.

Significance of the author's name

Not a family name

The fact that no other person has been discovered who bore the name of 'Diceto' is a very strong argument against the hypothesis that it is a patronymic or family name like Biset or Belet, Basset, Foliot, or Lycett.[1] If it be interpreted as denoting the birth-place of the bearer, or some benefice which he held in early life, there seems to be an insuperable difficulty in the identification. The word might be a Latinised form of an English local name such as Dicet or Disset ; but no place of such name is known to exist. Possibly it may lurk still in some remote Shropshire or Essex manor, but it has yet to be discovered. Ditcheat in Somersetshire might tempt us, in its present form, to identify it with Dicetum, but in the days of Ralph it was still Dichesyeat. It might also be a Latinised form of a French Dicy, Dizy, or Dissai, and of such places there is no lack, but there is nothing in Ralph's personal history to connect him with them. Under such circumstances any lengthened speculation would be simply a waste of ingenuity. As, however, the name is a part of the history of the man, it demands some brief consideration.

Is it a local name ?

[1] Bishop Bancroft calls Ralph de Diceto Ralph Dycett; Statutes of S. Paul's (ed. Simpson), p. 279.

The first and indeed the only positive claimant of the honour of giving name to our author is the town of Diss, in Norfolk. In this case neither the antiquity of the claim nor the grounds upon which it is based entitle it to more than the character of a guess. Diss appears in Domesday Book in several places and invariably in the form of ' Dice.' [1] Now, supposing the final 'e' of Dice to have been sounded, the Latin form Dicetum might be a probable translation of Dicé ; but no such form is known to occur. Diss is never, so far as records have thrown light upon the point, Latinised as Dicetum. It appears as 'Dize' in the Pipe Rolls of Henry II. [2]; as 'Disze' in the Pipe Rolls of Richard I. [3] ; as 'Disce' in the Patent Rolls of John. [4] It is 'Dysse' in the Taxation of Pope Nicholas in 1291. [5] The records of the abbey of Bury S. Edmund's show that among the inmates or officers of that house there were, contemporary with our author, three at least who took their names from Diss. Jocelin of Brakelond mentions Master William of Dice, who was master of the schools : his son Walter, who was a candidate for the living of Chevington ; and a monk named John : they are John, Walter, and William 'de Dice' and 'de Dicia.' [6] The list of the sacrists of S. Edmund's, printed in the Monasticon, contains the name of 'Willel-'mus de Disce,' who filled the office for four days in Abbot Sampson's time. [7] The Royal Library, now in the British Museum, contains a volume with the inscription 'Hunc librum scribi fecit Willelmus de Dice, servus et monachus S. Edmundi, ad honorem S. Edmundi.' [8] In a document appended to Jocelin's Chronicle, William of Diss is called 'Willelmus de Dicia.' Dyssa is the form used by Alexander III. These facts seem to show that without further evidence the claim of Diss should not be allowed, and there are circumstances which tend to show that Dicetum should be sought elsewhere.

In the first place, the common practice of calling a beneficed clergyman by the name of his parish may suggest that Ralph was the rector of Dicetum. But he was not rector of Diss. Uncertain as are the number and situation of his several preferments, we know

[1] Domesday, vol. ii. ff. 114, 129, 149, 154, 176, 210, 215, 228, 263, 269, 272, 276, 278.
[2] Rot. Pip., Hen. II., ed. Hunter.
[3] Rot. Pip., 1 Rich., ed. Hunter, p. 39.
[4] Rot. Pat., ed. Hardy, i. 190.
[5] Taxatio P. Nicol., p. 84 b.
[6] 'Walterus filius magistri Wil-lelmi de Dice ; ' 'Johannes de Dice ; ' 'Willelmus dictus de Dicia.' Joc. Brakelond (Camd. Soc.). pp. 32, 83, 84, 102.

[7] 'Waltero de Banham successit Willelmus de Disce, qui cum modo electus fuisset ad illud officium, et in illo a die Sancti Thomæ martyris usque ad Circumcisionem Domini, per quatuor videlicet dies stetisset, interim sompnum oculi sui capere non potue-runt ; qui videns se ibidem proficere non posse, suam ab abbate Sampsone (A.D. 1182–1211) petiit cessionem.' Mon. Angl. iii. 163.
[8] Casley's Catalogue, p. 127.

that the church of Diss was held during his life by two persons with whom he seems to have had no connexion. This is proved by a document which so greatly struck the fancy of Bishop Bale that he twice mentions it in different works, once in the 'Scriptores'[1] and once in the 'Votaryes,' as showing that two persons, father and son, were at this period successively parsons of Diss. He had seen a decretal epistle of Pope Alexander III., addressed to John of Oxford when bishop of Norwich, and written, therefore, between 1175, when John of Oxford was consecrated, and 1181, when Alexander III. died. In this letter the Pope 'commaundeth that Wyllyam the new person of Dysse, for clayminge the benefyce by inheritaunce, after the decease of his father person Wulkerell which begate him in his presthode, should be dispossessed, no appellacyon admitted.'[2] The letter itself has not been found, and is not among the collected epistles of Alexander III., but Bale's authority on such a point is not to be questioned. By the name Wulkerell we may take it for granted that the common East Anglian Wulfketell is meant, and in the story we have one of many instances of the tenure of ecclesiastical benefices in hereditary succession, a practice which the popes found it extremely difficult to suppress, and which is the subject of many extant letters of Alexander himself, preserved among Foliot's epistles and in the appendix to the Acts of the Lateran Council of 1179. Wulfketell and William would leave no room for Ralph, unless we suppose him very early in life to have held the benefice and afterwards to have resigned it. Such a supposition, however, is scarcely reconcilable with the fact that he clung so tenaciously to the name.

Hereditary parsons of Diss.

In the second place, if Ralph had been, either by birth or preferment, connected with Diss, we might fairly expect that we should be able to trace the connexion in his books ; we might expect to find some minute particulars or some special words of respect or disrespect, touching the Lords of Diss, to whose patronage he might be indebted, or whose acquaintance he must have made. The Lord of Diss during great part of Ralph's life was Richard de Lucy, the chief minister of Stephen and the great justiciar of Henry II. Richard died the year before Ralph was promoted to the deanery of S. Paul's, and was succeeded in his lordship by his son-in-law,

Was Ralph a native of Diss ?

Ralph shows no special connexion with Diss or its lords

---

[1] Bale, Scriptores (second edition), p. 217 : 'in Nordovolgia Wulkerellus presbyter Guilhelmo filio, ut legitimo heredi, sacerdotium de Dyssa reliquit.' We have no further knowledge of the dispute. The patronage of the church must, however, have been claimed by the lords of Diss ; for in 1216 Robert de Goldingham has letters of presentation from the king to the church of 'Disce,' owing to the fact that the lands of Robert FitzWalter were then in the king's hands. Rot. Pat. (ed. Hardy), i. 190.

[2] Bale, Votaryes (ed. 1551), fo. 98 b. See Blomfield, Hist. Norfolk, i. 11, which first called my attention to this fact.

Walter FitzRobert.[1] Although the great position and high character of Richard de Lucy would give the historian an ample opportunity of dilating on the virtues of a fellow-townsman, he nowhere mentions him with such special remark. The Bigods and the Mandevilles, on the contrary, the patrons of the priories of Thetford and Walden, under whom Ralph held the livings of Finchingfield and Aynho, receive especial mention : the former with additional particulars of personal history, and the latter in terms of exceptional compliment.[2]

In the third place, it is to be considered that, with one possible exception, no historical writer before the seventeenth century seems to have thought of identifying Dicetum with Diss. The one apparent exception is that of the author of the 'Livere des Reis de Britanie,' who wrote in the time of Edward I.[3] This writer, translating directly or mediately from the Imagines, describes the pious founder of the cemetery of S. Thomas of Canterbury at Acre as William the chaplain of 'Rauf de Disze, le haut den de Londres.' In this case it is probable that Disze (or Diszé) is simply a retranslation of Diceto, but at first sight it looks like an intentional identification with Diss. Setting aside, however, this instance, we find such a number of curious misreadings of the name as proves that the early writers had no idea of connecting it with a well-known English town. Gilbert Foliot, when he first made acquaintance with Ralph, called him Diotecensis, a sufficient proof that he did not recognise the place from which the name was derived. Some still stranger forms are mentioned by Selden in the Prolegomena to Twysden's 'Decem Scriptores.' Thomas of Walsingham, the learned and industrious compiler at St. Alban's, calls our author Radulfus de Luzeto ;[4] the manuscripts of Higden's Polychronicon have Radulfus de Byzeto, which Trevisa translated 'Raulf le Bruys,' and which appears in Caxton as 'Raph de Bruys ;'[5] Bale in the first edition of the Scriptores called him 'Radulphus de Rizeto' ;[6] John Ross of

The claim of Diss is not ancient

Early writers do not identify Diceto with Diss

Various misreadings of the name

---

[1] Blomfield, Hist. Norf. i. 2.

[2] William of Mandeville is specially spoken of in connexion with his expedition to the east, when he presented several churches with cloths brought from Constantinople (Rolls Series ed. vol. i. p. 428) ; his marriage, which took place at Pleshey, within Ralph's archidiaconal jurisdiction (vol. ii. p. 3) ; his victories in Flanders ii. 32) ; and his death (vol. ii. p. 73). For particulars about Hugh Bigod see vol. i. pp. 248, 377, 378, 385. Richard de Lucy is mentioned as excommunicated by Becket in 1166 (vol i. p. 318), and in connexion with the foundation of Lesnes Abbey in 1178 (ib. p. 425) ; but in the account of the rebellion of 1173 not even his name occurs.

[3] 'Le livere de reis de Angleterre,' p. 256. See also Mr. Glover's note in the Introduction, p. xii, where Decize is suggested as the true Dicetum. Diss does not seem to have occurred to Mr. Glover.

[4] Walsingham, ed. Camden, p. 55 ; ed. Riley, vol. i. p. 34.

[5] Higden, lib. vii. cap. 39, ed. 1538.

[6] Scriptores (ed. 1549), fo. 97. It is corrected in the second edition.

Warwick had read it 'Ralph de Duceto'; and John Pyke, who largely used the books before us, referred to the writer more than once as 'Ralph de Doiceto.'[1] In the collections made by Edward I. on the question of the over-lordship of Scotland, the name appears in the printed copies as 'Dizeto.'[2] The early bibliographers were content to call him by the name by which he called himself, but were in some doubt as to his nationality. Leland confessed himself unable to determine whether he was an Englishman,[3] and did not include him in the list of the writers of Britain. Bale called him an Englishman, but he contented himself with the usual generalities that show how little he knew about him beyond the existence of his works. Pits followed Bale and Leland. The identification with Diss appeared first, I believe, in the second edition of Dugdale's History of S. Paul's, published in 1716, with the author's own corrections, by Dr. Maynard.[4] We are not told whether in this particular case the addition had Dugdale's authority, and the loose, inaccurate way in which it is given would seem to suggest that it had not. In the list of the deans Ralph de Diceto is said, in a parenthesis, to be of 'Disca in com. Suffolk.' Dugdale himself must have known that Diss was in Norfolk. However this may be, Henry Wharton either was ignorant of the conjecture, which was published several years after his death, or refused to accept it;[5] and Gale, who mentions that he had seen the form 'Dissetum' in the chronicles of Walden Abbey, does not proceed to argue from the fact.[6] Tanner does not notice it in his Bibliotheca. Yet it commended itself to the authors of the Histoire Littéraire de France, who, finding somewhere the name of 'Thomas de Disce, a priest of the province of York,' withdrew somewhat hastily a claim which they had prepared to make on behalf of France as the native country of Ralph de Diceto.[7] There were several places in France which might be understood by Dicetum, but there was a Diss in England, which furnished to them a satisfactory solution of the question. It

The origin of the claim of Diss

Accepted in recent times

[1] Selden, Proleg. to Twysden's 'Decem Scriptores,' p. xxix.

[2] Fœd. i. 769.

[3] 'Fuit doctor Theologiæ, at non satis mihi constat num etiam Anglus fuerit;' Dugdale, S. Paul's (ed. 1658), p. 283. Bale and Wharton call him English, and their judgment would be valuable if we were certain that the contrary view had ever been presented to them. See Wharton's Appendix to Cave's Historia Litteraria, and Bale as quoted above.

[4] It does not appear in the edition of 1658, pp. 9, 48; it is in Maynard's edition, pp. 10, 51; and repeated in Ellis's, p. 7.

[5] Wharton, 'de decanis Londoniensibus,' p. 203. Cf. Ang. Sac. ii. p. xxvii.

[6] In the preface to the 'Quindecim Scriptores,' A.D. 1691. The MS. which Gale saw, and which is now MS. Arundel 29, is a seventeenth century transcript. The name is spelled Diceto in the text of this MS., but the form Disseto may occur in the margin. See below, p. 63.

[7] Hist. Litt. vol. xvi. p. 499.

is on their authority, we may presume, that recent writers have called our author ' Ralph of Diss.'

Spelling of the name

The proper form of the name is ' Diceto,' as it is given in all the manuscripts and records which proceeded directly from the author's hand ; but very soon after his death, in the records of his cathedral it is found written ' Disceto ' ;[1] the modern copy of the Chronicle of Walden has the same form, and it is found also in a document which will be adduced farther on, issued by Bishop Hugh of Lincoln before the death of Ralph. There seems to be no ancient authority for the form Disseto ; and Dizeto rests on a document issued a hundred years after his time.

Apparent etymology of the name

The form ' Dicetum ' itself, according to the analogies of mediæval Latin and French, would naturally represent the French Dissai, as Alnetum represents Aulnay, Fraxinetum Fresnay, Salicetum Saussai, or as Virenetum represents the English Verney. But the parallel halts in one important point, for there is no tree ' dicus,' ' dica,' or ' dix,' which is required to make it complete ; nor does the word occur in French geography any more than in English. It seems lawful to infer from this that it is an artificial name, adopted by its bearer as the Latin name of a place with which he was associated, but which had no proper Latin name of its own. So explained it may belong to some English place, Diss, Dicton, Ditton, or other, or to a French Dissai, Dizy, or Dissé ; but with this differ-ence, that whilst it has no proper relation with the English names, it stands in a true etymological relation to the French. There are in the province of Maine three places of the name required :[2] Dissai-sous-de-Lude, known in Latin documents as Diceium ; Dissé-sous-Ballon, and Dissai-sous-Courcillon, near Château du Loir, Latinised as Disiacus. In other parts of France are found Dizy, in the de-partment of the Marne in Champagne, and Dizy in that of the Aisne in Picardy ; while there is Dicy in that of the Yonne in Burgundy. The neighbourhood of Le Mans has perhaps the first claim, if we consult the internal evidence of our author's writings. The great care bestowed on the history of the counts of Anjou is sufficient to call attention to it. Either Dissai-sous-Courcillon, which was be-stowed by Bishop Siegfrid[3] on Fulk the good count of Anjou, might allege in its favour the prominence given to that count in the *Abbreviationes* ; or Dissé-sous-de-Lude, one half of which was given by Bishop Ulger of Angers to his cathedral, might adduce the verses

Places in France which might be called Dicetum

---

[1] See Statutes of S. Paul's (ed. Simpson), pp. 33, 109, 125, 174, where it is written Disceto ; at p. 63 Dean Baldock (A.D. 1294-1303) writes Dyceto ; and at p. 153 Bishop Bray-brooke (A.D. 1382-1405) writes Disseto.

[2] Cauvin, Géographie ancienne du diocèse du Mans ; Institut des Pro-vinces de France, vol. i. s. vv.

[3] Gallia Christiana, ii. 135.

about Ulger which Ralph has written in the margin of his book
under the years 1139–1142. At the utmost, however, we can only
say that etymologically the balance inclines in favour of one of these
towns, and would give Ralph a French nationality which there is little
in his books to refute and some slight circumstances to countenance.

Obscurity of
nationality
Internal evidence on a point like this may be read almost any
way. Our author's writings nowhere contain any statement that he
was an Englishman; if they did, such a statement at the period at
which he wrote might mean no more than that he was born of
French descent in England. Neither do they contain any assertion
that he was a Frenchman; if they did, it might mean no more than
that he was sprung from the Normans of the Conquest. As to the
indirect evidence which may be sought in the tone and spirit of his
narrative, little can be said. The early portions of the *Abbreviationes*,
in which, if he were English, some signs of English sympathy might
be expected, are merely extracts from previous writers. No definite
Some points
suggest a
French
nationality
inferences can be drawn from the plan of selection, from the modifications, the omissions, or additions of the compiler. The descriptions
of Angers and Aquitaine which are the purple patches of the first
pages of the *Imagines*, and which may be thought to prove that Ralph,
when he began that work, contemplated something more ambitious
in tone, and more comprehensive in character, than a mere book of
annals, are in this respect worthy of special attention. The picture of
Angers is drawn by one who was fairly well acquainted with the site;
no such picture of an English city occurs in the book. We are not
indeed assured that the description is not extracted from the work of
some other author; in common with the other Angevin memoranda
it is claimed for another hand; and, although I hope to be able to
show that the grounds upon which that particular claim is based are
untenable, the disproof of the claim of one competitor does not prove
the claim of the other. Another indication, stronger perhaps than
this, may be found in the fact that towards the close of the *Abbreviationes*, at that point, that is, of the work at which the author is
passing from his extracts from earlier writers to the record of his
own personal reminiscences, the greater part of the matter which
cannot be referred to older authority concerns either the church of
S. Paul in London, which was his final home, or contemporary events
in France. As the memoranda touching S. Paul's may be easily accounted for by his connexion, lifelong as it would seem to have been,
with that cathedral, the references to French history, to the visit of
Eugenius III. to Paris, the election of the archbishop of Bourges
and consequent interdict, the crusade and the taxation which was
caused by it, may be due to the fact that in his youth, in a native
home in France, he had been struck with these events. But it is

quite as probable that he remembered them because at the time they Nothing determined by these occurred he was a student in the University of Paris. The question of nationality is really involved in the same obscurity as the meaning of the name; but that Ralph was an Englishman of the period of amalgamation, an Englishman in his sympathy with the sound legislation of Henry II., and with the national aspirations of the reconstituted England, there can be no doubt.

Equally uncertain are the point of our author's parentage and Probable date of our author's birth the date of his birth. Although we can follow him through fifty years of a somewhat distinguished career, we find no traces of great age at the close, no signs of youthful action or premature promotion at the beginning. If he had been more than eighty when he died, some one of the many annalists of the time would almost certainly have recorded the date and circumstances of his death. Yet, unless we suppose him to have been exceptionally young when, in the year 1152, he was made archdeacon, he could not have been much under eighty when he died. As, however, it is necessary to have some hypothetical string on which to arrange the known events of his life, we may suppose him to have been born between 1120 and 1130. His notices of events touching the history of S. Paul's begin in 1136, and certainly have the appearance of personal recollections.

There are some points, which now meet us, that suggest a not Was he connected with the family of Belmeis? impossible theory of the parentage of Ralph de Diceto. He was appointed to his archdeaconry by Bishop Richard II. of Belmeis; the office of archdeacon was very frequently reserved by the bishops for their nearest kinsmen; the family of Belmeis for more than half a century was all-powerful in the chapter of S. Paul's; and Ralph more than once betrays a tenderness as to clerical marriage and the propriety of a son succeeding to his father's benefice. Some illustration of the scenes in which his early years were passed may result from a short examination of these points.

In 1108 Richard I. of Belmeis was made bishop of London. Family of Belmeis His family derived their name from the Norman village of Beaumais on the Dive, Bellus Mansus. He had himself risen to importance in the service of the house of Montgomery, had been sheriff of Shropshire under the earls of that house, Roger, Hugh, and Robert of Belesme,[1] and had probably recommended himself to the king by his fidelity and loyalty at the time of the rebellion of the last-mentioned earl. In his own person and by his kinsmen he founded an important Shropshire family, before he became a bishop. As bishop he

---

[1] Orderic. Vital. lib. xi. cap. 31; Ann. Winton. Ang. Sac. i. 297; Eadmer, Hist. Nov. pp. 96, 97. The best account of the family will be found in Eyton's History of Shropshire, vol. ii. pp. 193 sq.; a pedigree, partly conjectural, is there given, which cannot be entirely accepted.

Bishop
Richard I.

showed himself a great prelate of the true Norman type, a magnificent
builder, a great state official, and a most liberal benefactor to his
church. He is said to have devoted the whole of his episcopal
revenue to the restoration of his cathedral ; he founded the cathedral
schools ; he obtained great privileges for the chapter from the king ;
and, by purchasing and enclosing land and houses round S. Paul's,
he formed the churchyard and neighbouring streets into a sort of
cathedral close.[1] As was the common practice, he provided out of

How
Richard of
Belmeis
promoted
his kinsfolk

the patronage of the see for several of his kinsmen. One nephew,
William, son of his sister Adelina, was dean of S. Paul's from 1111
to 1138 ; Ralph of Langford and Richard of Belmeis, sons of Walter
the bishop's brother, were made canons ;[2] a still nearer kinsman,
Walter the bishop's son, was prebendary of Newington, and appears
in the Great Roll of the Pipe for the 31st year of Henry I. as 'filius
episcopi Londoniensis,' paying ten marks for a right judgment
touching the church of Illing.[3] Another of the family, William, was
archdeacon of either London or Colchester.[4] The position thus
created for the family was defended by them as a part of their inheritance, and not without the quarrels incidental to family parties

Richard II.
of Belmeis

of the kind. Shortly before his death in 1127, the bishop appointed
his nephew Richard, who was still a child,[5] archdeacon of Middlesex.
Gilbert the Universal, who succeeded to the see in 1128, held it for
only six years, and his death in 1134 was followed by a disputed

Quarrel in
the chapter
of S. Paul's

election and a vacancy which lasted until 1141. It is possible that
the dean William wished to be elected, or to force his nominee upon

---

[1] Wharton, Episc. Lond., pp. 46–50.
[2] Eyton regards Ralph of Langford
as sister's son to the bishop, and
supposes that his mother had married
a man of the name ; but the words of
our author (R. S. ed. vol. i. p. 250) seem
clearly to prove that he was brother of
the second bishop Richard, and in that
case his name of Langford would be
derived from one of the many Lang-
fords or Longfords where he may have
had preferment.
[3] Rot. Pip. 31 Hen. I. ; Newcourt,
Repertorium, i. 186.
[4] See below, p. 45. This enumeration probably does not exhaust the
list of the bishop's kinsmen in the
chapter. Richard of Belmeis was
buried in the priory of S. Osyth, which
he founded, with the epitaph, ' Hic
jacet Ricardus Beaumeis cognomento
Rufus Londoniensis episcopus, vir
probus et grandævus per totam vitam
laboriosus, fundator noster religiosus,
qui multa bona nobis et ministris

ecclesiæ suæ S. Pauli contulit ; obiit
xvi. kal. Jan. 1127 ; cujus animæ
propitietur Deus.' Weever, Sep. Mon.
p. 607 ; Mon. Angl. vi. 308 ; Newcourt, ii. 455 ; Eyton, ii. 200. I do
not know the date of the inscription,
but it is curious that a Richard Ruffus
was archdeacon of Essex for several
years during the century, and that
another Richard Ruffus was prebendary of Twyford in 1181 and holding certain lands of the church which
had been let to his predecessor of the
same name. Moreover, Ailwardus
Ruffus was archdeacon of Colchester
from 1150–1162 or thereabouts ; and
Guido Ruffus was the last dean of
Waltham. Archdeacon Hale, however, doubts whether the archdeacon
Richard is rightly called Ruffus ;
Domesday of S. Paul's, p. lxxxvii.
[5] ' Nondum plene pubes ' ; it was a
common practice to nominate very
young men as archdeacons and send
them to Paris or Bologna to be educated.

the chapter, but he was opposed by his kinsmen; a large party of the canons joined, however, in electing Abbot Anselm of S. Edmund's. The dean appealed, but his relations took part against him, carried their treasures to Rome, where they found the church in a state of schism, and obtained for a time at least possession of the estates of the see for Anselm. The dean was supported by Ralph of Langford and Richard of Belmeis, who in 1138 obtained from the Pope a definitive sentence which sent Anselm back to his abbey. The custody of the bishopric was, however, intrusted to Bishop Henry of Winchester, and the death of the dean, which occurred the same year, left the see unclaimed until, in 1141, the empress gave it to Robert de Sigillo.

The hold of the family on the church was not shaken by this. Ralph of Langford was elected as successor of his cousin in the deanery, and Richard of Belmeis, whose archdeaconry had been held in trust for him by a chaplain of the bishop named Hugh, obtained from Rome a commission of judges, who compelled Hugh against his will to resign in his favour. The reign of Stephen was altogether a stormy time for S. Paul's. When the empress lost her hold upon London, her Bishop Robert went into exile. William the archdeacon, 'cum gente eorum qui a Bello Manso traxere cognomen,' [1] so far from showing proper filial obedience, did their utmost to reduce their bishop to destitution; and again in 1148, when the English bishops were suspended by the Pope for not attending the council of Rheims, the archdeacon and his party set an example of contumacy by appealing against the sentence. In the obscure intrigues of this period of Stephen's reign it is impossible to speak with confidence on such a point; but if we may depend on the *Historia Pontificalis*, which records the fact, and which is now believed to be the work of John of Salisbury, the archdeacon and his party were now playing into the hands of the king. We cannot, however, trace more consistency in the ecclesiastical than in the baronial intrigues of this complicated time.

Margin note: Continued hold of the family on S. Paul's

Margin note: Independence of the family in chapter

---

[1] *Historia* Pontificalis, Pertz, Mon. Hist. Germ. vol. xx. p. 532 : ' Verum primi omnium crimen inobedientiæ incurrerunt Lundonienses, confugientes ad appellationem (sc. in 1148), cum tamen in litteris apostolicis esset inhibita appellatio. Fecerant hoc jam alia vice, quando episcopus eorum, bonæ memoriæ Robertus, expulsus est; cui hanc exhibuere devotionem, ut omni diligentia procurarent ne patri exul anti in aliquo prodessent. Horum signifer et in hac et in illa causa fuit Guillelmus archidiaconus cum gente eorum qui a Bello Manso traxere cognomen.' Who this archdeacon was is not quite clear. There was a William archdeacon of Colchester in 1162, S. T. C. iv. 37 ; and in 1150 the four archdeacons were Richard Belmeis of Middlesex, Richard [Ruffus] of Essex, and William and Ailward of London and Colchester. This William is called archdeacon of London in 1152 (S. T. C. v. 184), but the expression may be used loosely ; and I cannot be quite sure whether there were one or two archdeacons of the name, or which archdeaconry Ailward really held. But see p. 57 below.

Question of
episcopal
election

In 1151 the see of London was again vacant : Robert de Sigillo
was dead, and there was an evil report of poison. Eugenius III., acting
doubtless at the instigation of the empress's party, directed the canons
to elect within three months a fit candidate, 'virum honestum et
litteratum et religionis habitu decoratum.' The demand that the
bishop of London should be a monk, or regular canon, struck the
chapter with dismay ; the majority of the canons applied to Rome
and obtained an explanation of the last words as including the
order of secular canons.[1] But the king also interposed difficulties : [2]
unable to force a nominee of his own upon the chapter, he determined to make at least a pecuniary profit out of the election ; and

Election of
Richard II.
of Belmeis

although he had by charter at the beginning of his reign confirmed
the right of free election to the cathedral churches, he exacted a sum
of five hundred pounds from S. Paul's for leave to act upon the
canonical right. At last enabled to proceed to election, the chapter
fixed on Richard of Belmeis, the archdeacon of Middlesex, on whom
of course devolved the duty of making good the fine which Stephen
had demanded. The debt thus incurred hampered him all his life.
The election was not acceptable to the magnates, and the family
interest had to be employed at Rome before it was recognised.
Eugenius III. had to use his direct influence in securing the appointment,[3] and Gilbert Foliot, the energetic counsellor of the Angevin
party, had an important share in the negotiation.[4] The bishop elect
was already in possession of considerable preferment, and he had
held the deanery of S. Alkmund's at Shrewsbury, one of the ancient
collegiate foundations that had survived the reforming zeal of the
Norman lords. Like his uncle and predecessor, he favoured the
religious orders ; the earlier Richard had founded the priory of
S. Osyth in Essex for Austin canons ; his nephew transferred his
collegiate endowment to found an Arroasian priory at Lilleshull.[5]

---

[1] Historia Pontificalis, Pertz, xx. 545.

[2] 'Rex vero eis eligendi libertatem
concedere noluit antequam quingentas
libras exemplo monachorum Sancti
Augustini ei appenderint. Quo facto
electus est Ricardus, ejusdem ecclesiæ
archidiaconus, qui præfatam pecuniam
non sine nota symoniæ dinoscitur
exsolvisse. Ea namque tempestate
sub optentu libertatis redimendæ
pravitatem symoniacam plurimi pal-
liabant.' Hist. Pont., Pertz, xx. 545.

[3] Gilbert Foliot writes to the Pope :
'Londoniensis nimirum episcopus
adeo manuum vestrarum opus est et
creatio, ut ei recte in faciem possit
objici, tu quid habes nisi quod a
domino papa accepisti ? ' S. T. C. v. 120.

[4] Foliot speaks of the bishop as a
kinsman, S. T. C. v. 40 ; he assisted
in obtaining his election to the see,
ibid. 122.

[5] There is a charter of Henry I., in
which he gives to Richard of Belmeis,
nephew of the bishop of London, all
that the bishop had held of the king,
which formerly was Godebald's and
Robert's ; the same Richard is called
archdeacon in a charter of Stephen,
so there seems to be no doubt of his
identity. The Arroasian house at
Lilleshull was founded on the land of
Richard's prebend. Mon. Angl. vi.
262, 263. See too Eyton's Shropshire,
vol. viii. p. 218.

But he was neither monk nor priest. He had been ordained deacon in 1138. On the 20th of September 1152 at Otford he was ordained priest by Archbishop Theobald, and on the 28th of the same month he received episcopal consecration at Canterbury, the archbishop and his brother Walter bishop of Rochester, Hilary of Chichester, and Gilbert Foliot himself, officiating.[1] Nearly all the bishops of England were present on the occasion. The bishop of Winchester, who was absent, signified his consent to the consecration in a letter to the archbishop, which our author has preserved, perhaps as being the first document that came into his hands as the bishop's official servant ; for Richard's first act as bishop was to appoint Master Ralph de Diceto as his successor in the archdeaconry of Middlesex.

Consecration of Richard II. of Belmeis

He makes Ralph archdeacon

Considering the great pains with which the ruling family had tried to concentrate and strengthen their interest in the chapter, it is improbable that the new bishop should bestow his first piece of preferment on a stranger. That interest was not exhausted, and afterwards, when Ralph was dean, we find William of Belmeis, a nephew of the second Richard, bestowing on the canons his church of S. Pancras for the health of the soul of his uncle, and of his father Robert of Belmeis.[2] The hereditary instinct which worked in the chapter was extremely likely to affect the appointment to the archdeaconry. It was very common for the bishops to appoint their nearest kinsmen to this confidential office. Numberless examples may be given at this very period. Archbishop Ralph had given the archdeaconry of Canterbury to his brother John ; Archbishop Theobald, who succeeded him, gave it to his brother Walter ; Bishop Nigel, of Ely, had made his son Richard his archdeacon ; at Hereford, Gilbert Foliot had given or procured the appointment for his kinsman Ralph ; Robert Peche, bishop of Lichfield, had given the archdeaconry of Coventry to his son Richard, who, after two intervening appointments, succeeded him in his see ; Walkelin, archdeacon of Suffolk, was nephew of Bishop Everard of Montgomery ; [3]

Cases of bishops who appointed their near kinsmen archdeacons

---

[1] Gervase, c. 1370 ; Rolls Series, vol. i. pp. 295, 296.

[2] Newcourt, Repertorium, i. 190. MS. Harleian 6956, fo. 84. This MS., which I shall have again to refer to, contains Dr. Matthew Hutton's excerpts from the records of the dean and chapter of S. Paul's. Most of the books that Hutton saw, if not all, are still in the muniment room of the cathedral, and I have to thank the dean, Dr. Church, and the librarian, Dr. Sparrow Simpson, for a liberal permission to use them. I refer, however, to the Hutton MS. as easier

for verification. The early registers of S. Paul's are of immense value for the illustration of the ecclesiastical and civic history of London, and it is to be hoped that some of them may soon be printed.

[3] Walkelin was one of the class of archdeacons whose lives led to the conclusion that ' no archdeacon could be saved.' He gave great trouble to Archbishop Theobald and John of Salisbury, and defied the Pope as his uncle Robert of Belesme had defied the king. He had a ' focaria ' who on one occasion of his return from

at Salisbury, Bishop Roger appointed his nephew Alexander, and
Jocelin, who succeeded him, appointed his son Reginald; at York,
Geoffrey the archdeacon was nephew of Roger the archbishop. If
then we should incline to the conjecture that Ralph de Diceto was a
near relation of Richard of Belmeis, we should not wrong the
bishop by imputing to him exceptional nepotism. Nor, as I have
remarked, are there wanting in our author's own works some indications that the question of clerical marriage and legitimacy had a
special interest for him. Dean Milman, in his short sketch of
Ralph's career, in the annals of S. Paul's, has noticed particularly
the words which occur in the *Abbreviationes* under the year 1074
on the measures taken by Gregory VII. against the married clergy.
The dean adduces the passage as showing that Ralph was not
thoroughly imbued with Hildebrandine principles, at all events upon
this point. It is true that the words are not really our author's,
but part of an extract from Sigebert of Gemblours, who nearly a
century before had written against the allegations made by laymen
against married priests ; but the fact that Ralph had incorporated
them without reservation in his own compilation may reasonably be
regarded as showing that he did not disapprove of the sentiment
they contained. His special references, again, to the Panormia of
Ivo of Chartres for precedents in which sons had succeeded their fathers
in high clerical preferment look the same way : ' The apostolic see
has permitted the sons of priests, whose conversation has been
approved in monasteries or religious churches, to be promoted to the
priesthood and even to the highest grade of the ministry ; in some
instances we have heard of the sons of bishops being promoted, after
some intermediate appointment, in the very churches in which their
fathers had ministered.' This was in fact one of the three canonical
points on which Ralph was specially interested, the other two being
the restoration of a deposed prelate and the lawfulness of translation,
the latter of which was brought prominently to his notice when he
had to transact the business of Foliot's removal from Hereford to
London. One famous passage which has often been quoted from
the *Abbreviationes* seems to militate against this view. In 1137, he
tells us, the ' focariæ of certain canons who are called secular were
carried off and dragged to the Tower, not without dire disgrace, and
kept there bound for many days ; they returned to their own, but
not without personal mockery, loss of reputation, and cost of money.'
It is not probable that Ralph, if he wrote these words at all, meant
them to apply to his own church. They appear in only one of the

Tenderness
of Ralph on
the question
of clerical
marriage

Rome, presented him with a child,   the Pope. See John of Salisbury,
whom for the sake of the jest he   Epist. 27.
christened Adrian, or Adriana, after

manuscripts drawn up under his own eye, and in that not without suspicious marks of erasure. If they are genuine, however, they seem, from the very reticence with which they are introduced, to indicate some feeling in the writer that he was not upon safe ground. It is not then, I think, improbable that Ralph de Diceto was son or nephew to Ralph of Langford, whom, with one person intervening, he succeeded in the deanery of S. Paul's. The supposition would not indeed explain the meaning of his name, but a clerical pedigree might account for the fact of his bearing a name not elsewhere recognised.

Bishop Richard was not able to secure the promotion of his nominee without a considerable effort, such as again he would have scarcely made in behalf of any but a near friend. It is in a letter upon this point that we get our first documentary illustration of our author's career. Gilbert Foliot, now bishop of Hereford, writes to Pope Eugenius III. on behalf of Bishop Richard. Both Foliot and the Pope were strong partisans of the empress and her son, and from the way in which the former speaks of the bishop as having been indebted for his promotion to the Pope's direct action, in opposition to the wishes and in spite of the conspiracies of the magnates, we may conclude that Richard was likewise, as Ralph de Diceto certainly was, a supporter of the house of Anjou. The Pope seems, not perhaps without cause, to have thought himself entitled to some share in the fruits of victory, and he had bestowed the archdeaconry vacated by the bishop's consecration on John of Canterbury, a young clerk who, with Thomas Becket and Roger of Pont l'Evêque, was running the race for preferment in Church and State, and who afterwards, as John 'aux blanches mains,' was bishop of Poictiers and archbishop of Lyons. Richard had, however, before the papal appointment was made, or certainly before it was announced, conferred the post on Ralph de Diceto. Foliot, in the letter referred to, brings this fact in a very determined way to the Pope's notice. The newly made bishop was so completely the creation of the Pope that he could scarcely be supposed to claim anything as his own; but as a matter of fact he had bestowed the archdeaconry before he knew the Pope's pleasure concerning it; he was persuaded that it was in ignorance of Ralph's appointment that the Pope had ordered it to be given to John of Canterbury,[1] and if evidence was necessary the bishop of Lincoln, Robert de Chesnei, a faithful friend of both bishop and archdeacon, and a man whose

Marginal notes: Opposition to Ralph's appointment as archdeacon — Foliot's letter to the Pope on Ralph's promotion

---

[1] 'Archidiaconatum enim quem liberalitate laudabili domino Johanni Cantuariensi donandum mandastis, ante concessum alteri fuisse vestram credimus latere prudentiam.' S. T. C. v. 121.

E

word could not be disputed, was ready to swear to the fact.[1] The Pope must not put the newly made bishop to shame by overruling the appointment. Nor was the new archdeacon a man to be set aside ; he was a man of established character for both probity and learning. The request seems to have been granted, and Ralph retained the archdeaconry. The disappointed competitor found a rich compensation in the treasurership of York, to which he succeeded in 1153 or 1154 ; and it is interesting to note the way in which our author sets down the several steps of his late preferment,[2] and the friendly way in which he consults him on points of history.

Ralph's residence in the University of Paris

This letter throws some light on Ralph's age. He is already 'magister,' probably not much under the age for ordination as priest. The same word indicates that he had already studied in a university, which could be no other than that of Paris, where we know him to have passed two periods of work.[3] If this were so, we may fairly infer that he himself witnessed the reception of Eugenius III. at S. Geneviève's, in 1146, on the occasion when the Pope's servants were wounded ; he may have been in France during the interdict imposed on account of the quarrel at Bourges, and have seen the starting of the second crusade. If we suppose him to be now thirty, he may have been at Paris as early as the year 1140 and have heard with his own ears the teaching of Hugh of S. Victor, which directly or indirectly impressed him so deeply that he not only incorporated one long passage of his writing in the 'Abbreviationes,' but introduced an

His friendship with Arnulf of Lisieux

extract from it into the statute book of his cathedral.[4] Whatever may have been the precise limits of his first residence at Paris, it was during that residence that he made the acquaintance of Arnulf of Lisieux, the ambitious, clever prelate whose letters preserve so many interesting notices of the time. In one of these letters Arnulf writes to Ralph as a friend and contemporary, not as we should

[1] 'Ipse quidem Lincolniensis testatur et jurare paratus est, dominum Londoniensem, antequam voluntatem vestram aut scripto aut aliquo referente cognoverit, prædictum archidiaconatum magistro Radulfo Diotecensi [so the MS.], cui et ad doctrinam scientia et ad honestatem mores exuberant, concessisse.' S. T. C. v. 121. In another letter to the bishop of London (S. T. C. v. 169, 170), Foliot refers to this or a similar case occurring in 1152 or 1153: 'quod ante susceptas domini papæ litteras in personam omnium testimonio idoneam procuratoris beneficium contulisti, ratum manere desideras.'

[2] His consecration is recorded in 1163, R. S. ed. vol. i. p. 311 ; his promotion to Lyons and resignation of that see, vol. ii. p. 120 ; and his pilgrimage to Canterbury in 1194. The letter on the subject of the precedence of the see of Lyons and John's answer are entered on the first page of the Abbreviationes; see vol. i. pp. 5, 6. Ralph introduces him as putting down a rebellion in Poictou in 1176.
[3] See next page, note. Bulæus, Hist. Univ. Paris, ii. 769.
[4] Abbreviationes, R. S. ed. vol. i. p. 31. Registrum Statutorum, ed. Simpson, p. 9.

expect a patron to write to a protégé.[1] The two had been intimate friends, and had had a common friend, Ralph de Flur, whose early death was a grief to both of them. Arnulf became bishop in 1141 ; if the friendship were formed whilst Arnulf was a student, we might bring Ralph to Paris long before the death of Hugh of S. Victor, which is said to have occurred in 1141. When Arnulf in 1182 retired from his see, after an episcopate of forty years, he took refuge in a house which he had built within the precincts of the abbey of S. Victor. Likely enough it was there that he and Ralph with him had studied in his youth, after he had learned all that he could learn in his brother's schools at Séez. That Ralph's first residence at Paris cannot have been much earlier than this may be inferred from his silence as to the history of Abelard and the other great men who

Arnulf of Lisieux

Ralph was junior to John of Salisbury

[1] Arnulf. Lexov. Ep. 16. The interest of the extract, for the whole letter cannot be here given, may excuse its great length:— 'Audivi te causa studiorum Parisios advenisse, audivi et lætatus sum; lætatus equidem ut ejus quem diligebam præsens me lætificaret aspectus et jucunda collocutionis alternæ collatio delectaret. Optabam quoque ut aliqua exhibendi tibi officii refulgeret occasio, cujus me dudum merita prævenerunt. Licet enim solum veritas amicitiæ requirat affectum, liberale tamen obsequium non excludit, sed eo potius illustratur, quoniam ut ait sanctus ille, "probatio dilectionis exhibitio est operis." Movet autem quod cum secundo jam veneris, noluisti ad amicum nec ad momentum etiam declinare, neque saltem per cursorem debitæ salutationis alloquium paucis consignatum apicibus destinare. Hæsi diutius, quotiesque ab illis partibus aliquis apparebat, divinabam quod ille mihi jucundum Radulfi mei nuntiaret adventum. Frustratus toties ex hoc nunc nihil audeo divinare, sed caritatem tuam duxi litteris præsentibus, si forte obdormierit, excitandam, aut si quem forte concepit falsa suspicione languorem de perseverantiæ meæ nuntio convalescat; noveris enim nihil tibi apud me de pristina caritate perisse, sed quasi duplicatus amor est, cum eum tibi mea mens cogatur exsolvere, quem aliquando duobus impendebat affectum. Sublatus siquidem est e medio communis amicus noster Radulfus de Flur, qui dimidium animæ meæ videtur moriens abstulisse. Ipsius mihi semper est colenda memoria, ipsius amor semper quibuscunque modis id fieri potuerit instaurandus. Duobus autem modis defuncto vicem amicitiæ judico rependendam, ut primo scilicet piis apud Deum intercessionibus adjuvetur, secundo hi quos ipse dilexerat dilectione vicaria diligantur. Inde est quod amor noster ab illo in te quasi quodam hæreditariæ successionis jure transfusus est, ut jam te non simplici sed duplicato complectar affectu. Tibi enim præ ceteris hæc est deferenda successio, quem ille præ ceteris diligebat, tibique eam quasi quodam testamento specialis amicitiæ prærogativa consignat. Gere igitur suum amicitiæ morem, certisque clarescat indiciis ipsam novas vires de nova duplicatione traxisse. Scribe autem interim aliquid ut in alterius utriusque videar suscepisse sermonem. Injunge quod vis ut in altero utrique videar obsequium præstitisse; visita nos ut possim utriusque personam in altero contemplari. Scribe, inquam, quia si scripseris, hoc ipsum tibi studii poterit augere materiam, nec propositi operis provectum impediet aut proventum. Injunge aliquid, ut aliqua amicitiæ perseverantis argumenta procedant, quia eam efficacius comprobat petendi fiducia quam liberalitas offerendi. Visita nos quia te cum desiderium nostrum, tum loci propinquitas, tum etiam solemnitas invitat. Dominus quoque Willelmus de Ver ex promissione tenetur ut veniat, vobisque invicem solatiari poteritis et nobis sanctæ solemnitatis gaudia duplicare. Valete. Ad Radulfum de Diceto archidiaconum Londoniensem.'

were teaching at Paris during the few preceding years. He must have been a few years junior to John of Salisbury,[1] who in the Metalogicus furnishes us with an exact list of the masters under whom he himself studied, and who were then in the zenith of their fame. It is true that Ralph wrote so long after that he may not have thought it worth while recording mere scattered reminiscences ; but it is perhaps more likely that he was too young at the time of Abelard's death to take much heed of the closing scenes of an eventful history.

Possible traces of Ralph in attendance on his bishop

For the ten years that followed Ralph's promotion to the archdeaconry, we know nothing distinctly of his movements. His notices of the acts of his bishop are, perhaps, a ground for supposing him to have occasionally attended him as a chaplain. In that capacity he may have been present at the consecration of archbishop Roger of York,[2] at the coronation of Henry II., and at the baptism of the younger Henry, which was performed by the bishop of London, in 1155. All these events are noted in the ' Imagines,' and are not derived, as the early entries in that work largely are, from the Chronicle of Robert de Monte. After the year 1155, the mention of several events that happened at Paris and in the neighbourhood possibly indicates that this was the period of Ralph's second residence in the great university. The letter of Arnulf of Lisieux, which has been already quoted, is addressed to him as archdeacon, and it was very common for newly appointed archdeacons to return to the schools to complete their legal education. Thus Gilbert Foliot had two of his archdeacons at the same time studying law at Bologna.[3] It is not, however, probable that this second visit of Ralph to Paris would be deferred beyond the tenth year of his appointment.

Ralph's second residence in Paris

Ralph rector of Aynho

One other event of our author's life may be placed here. Ralph had acquired the rectory of Aynho, in Northamptonshire, either by the direct gift of one of the Mandevilles, probably Earl Geoffrey II., of Essex, or from the mónastery of Walden, which the Mandevilles had founded, and on which they bestowed the patronage of Aynho.[4] Some time before the year 1164, during the priorate of Prior William, who died in that year,[5] Ralph de Diceto, as parson of Aynho, appointed, as his perpetual vicar or curate, Turbert the son of Turbert. No doubt Robert de Chesnei, the bishop of Lincoln, the intimate friend of Richard of Belmeis, helped

---

[1] John of Salisbury is said to have been seventy at the time of his death in 1180.

[2] Gervase, c. 1376.

[3] Richard Foliot, archdeacon of Colchester, and Robert Banastre, archdeacon of Essex ; S. T. C. v. 335, 336 ; probably about 1170. Cf. Spici-

legium Liberianum, pp. 610, 618.

[4] Aynho was given to Walden by the founder, Mon. Angl. iv. 141, 149. Earl Geoffrey II. held the earldom from 1144 to 1167.

[5] Hist. Walden, Mon. Angl. iv. 134.

in making the arrangement, and certainly instituted Turbert to the vicarage.[1] Evidence of this institution was adduced long after in a trial held to determine who the rightful patron of Aynho was. Besides Aynho, Ralph held also the living of Finchingfield, in Essex, which he had received either from the Bigods or from the priory of Thetford, of which they were the benefactors. From this also he drew a pension, and served the church by a vicar. But at what date he received Finchingfield there is nothing to show.[2]

Rector of Finching-field

The office of archdeacon was no sinecure. Although a spiritual office, conferred by investiture of ring and book,[3] it was concerned chiefly with matters of legal and secular interest, the judicial and pecuniary disputes which in the English Church never abounded more than at the period before us. It was this constant entanglement in temporal business which made the archdeacon, of all clerical officers, the most unpopular with the laity, and which among the more religious of the clergy suggested an important doubt, which John of Salisbury amusingly states in a letter to a newly made archdeacon. Nicolas de Sigillo, a canon of S. Paul's, had been promoted, no doubt by the influence of the Bishop Robert de Sigillo, and had perhaps been disappointed at not being made archdeacon earlier. He had denied that it was possible for an archdeacon to be saved. Yet in 1155, when the archdeaconry of Huntingdon was offered him, he accepted it, and John of Salisbury wrote to congratulate him in a bantering letter, expressing his pleasure that the bishop of Lincoln had convinced him that salvation was possible for him.[4] Ralph's archdeaconry comprised within its jurisdiction about fifty parishes in Middlesex, three deaneries in Essex, and one deanery in Hertfordshire. That it was the archdeaconry of Middlesex is certain ; it was the same archdeaconry that Richard of Belmeis had held, and is specially named by our author himself. Dr. Matthew Hutton, an eminent antiquary of the seventeenth century, who himself held Ralph's living of Aynho,[5] worked out the proof of this at considerable length and with much learning.

Ralph de Diceto as archdeacon of Middle-sex

---

[1] See the document given in the Appendix to the Preface of vol. ll. No. II. R. S. ed.

[2] Hubert Walter, when archbishop of Canterbury, confirmed a pension of forty shillings per annum, granted by the prior of Thetford out of the church of Finchingfield to the abbot and monks of Reading, after the death of the then incumbent, Ralph de Diceto. (*E reg. vet. Eliens. inter archiv. ep. Eliens.*) Blomefield, Hist. Norfolk, i. 448. On these pensions see Hale, Domesday of S. Paul's, pp. xlv, xlvi.

[3] So the archdeacon of Derby was invested, G. T. C. vi. 60.

[4] Joh. Salisb., Ep. 166. It is to be feared that Nicolas made his archdeaconry a stepping-stone to still more secular promotion ; he acted as a clerk of the Exchequer and a tallager in 1174, Madox, Hist. Exch. p. 485. He farmed the manor of Ardley under the chapter of S. Paul's in 1181. Domesday of S. Paul's, pp. 112, 113.

[5] His argument is given by Newcourt in the Repertorium, vol. i. 34.

But it is beyond doubt, and wherever Ralph is called archdeacon of London it is only loosely, in reference to the fact that he was one of the four archdeacons of the diocese. The archdeaconry of Middlesex was the third in dignity of the four, coming after those of London and Essex.[1] In the choir of S. Paul's the stall of the archdeacon of Middlesex was the last on the left side.[2] It was not by itself richly endowed ; like the archdeaconry of London, which Peter of Blois described as a 'draco,' that had to live on air, a sort of chameleon, it had very little in the way of revenue to maintain the dignity of the post.[3] A century after Ralph de Diceto held it, it appears as endowed with procurations and synodals,[4] but it is by no means certain that it possessed these resources in his time. The revenue from his livings, or from his prebend, if he held one, must have been his chief provision. Richard of Belmeis was not able to do much for him.

Troubles of Richard of Belmeis

The poor bishop never overcame the difficulties which he had to encounter immediately on his promotion. Although he ruled the diocese of London for ten years, he never got out of debt.[5] His judicial sentences were constantly appealed against, his rights of patronage infringed, and his supremacy in the chapter disputed. One great quarrel was with Master Henry of London, the librarian and master of the schools of S. Paul's, who claimed the archdeaconry of Colchester.[6] Archdeacon Nicolas of London was somehow ousted from his archdeaconry, and although his conduct in office had been just and moderate, and his competitor had no real claim to it, the

His legal decisions disputed

bishop failed to set matters straight, and he had recourse, through Foliot, to the Pope for redress.[7] Some dozen letters of John of Salisbury preserve the memory of appeals from the bishop's tribunal to Archbishop Theobald, or to the Pope.[8] The same writer, who acted as secretary to Archbishop Theobald, tells the Pope on one occasion that he has had to invest a certain clerk, named Hugh, contrary to the will of the bishop, with a prebendal stall at S. Paul's :[9] possibly that Hugh de Marinis, or Hugh de Marney, who succeeded

---

[1] Statutes of S. Paul's, p. 20.

[2] Ibid. p. 25.

[3] Cf. Statutes, &c., p. 21.

[4] ' Ultimo est archidiaconus Middelsexiæ, cujus victus in procuratione consistit.' Statutes, p. 25.

[5] Joh. Salisb., Ep. 7; S. T. C. v. 58.

[6] On this obscure matter, the date of which is difficult to determine, see Joh. Salisb., Ep. 35.

[7] It is not clear whether the letter in question (S. T. C. v. 151) is addressed to Adrian IV. or to Alexander

III. Foliot, however, writes in favour of the archdeacon Nicolas, who ' absens et innoxius archidiaconatu quem et juste possidebat et ministrabat sobrie, nulla juris aut ordinis observatione spoliatus est.' Nicolas had applied to his bishop for redress, but failed to obtain it : but he was in full possession before the bishop's death.

[8] See especially letters 10, 11, 13, 18, 22, 39, 58, 87, 117, 118, 132.

[9] Joh. Salisb., Ep. 36.

Ralph of Langford as dean. To complete his misfortunes, the The bishop is paralysed bishop became a paralytic,[1] and when, about the year 1160, his brother Ralph of Langford died, he was no longer considered fit to manage his own affairs, and the state of his affairs was so bad that he had great difficulty in finding agents to manage them.[2] Robert de Chesnei, bishop of Lincoln, and Gilbert Foliot, of Hereford, his relation, who, perhaps, had an eye to the succession, did their best for him; they compelled the new dean, Hugh, and Nicolas, the archdeacon, to undertake the administration of his property, and they, after his death, had to maintain tedious proceedings at law against his creditors. In all this we hear nothing of Ralph de Diceto. No judgments of our archdeacon are impugned in the archiepiscopal court; he is not mentioned as one of the stewards of the poor bishop's property. He seems, as we shall see, even to have lost or missed his chance of obtaining a prebendal stall in the cathedral, and when we find him next it is in Paris. We may, I think, infer that Ralph at Paris he had spent a considerable part of these years in study there.

Richard of Belmeis died on May 4, 1162, three weeks before the election of Thomas Becket to the primacy. It was not then he, but Gilbert Foliot, his successor, whom the biographers of S. Thomas represent by anticipation as bishop of London, that singly opposed the election of Becket, if any such opposition were offered.[3] Ralph had perhaps returned to England to attend the deathbed of his patron, or was summoned to the chapter that elected his successor. Anyhow, he was employed as the agent of the canons in procuring Employed in negotiating the translation of Foliot the confirmation of their choice. It was not a simple matter. Since the conquest no bishop in England proper had been translated from the see of his consecration except to one of the two metropolitan sees. Before the conquest there were one or two questionable instances, and since the conquest Bishop Hervey of Bangor had been transferred from a Welsh see to an English one; but the 'postulation' of Foliot, involving his translation from Hereford to London, was regarded as exceptional, and as requiring special confirmation by the Pope. Fortunately, Alexander III. was at Paris. Ralph de Diceto knew Parisian ways. Furnished with letters from the king, from Becket, and from his fellow canons, he laid the matter before the Pope,[4] and was listened to. London, it was pleaded, was an

---

[1] Imagines, R. S. ed. vol. i. p. 304.
[2] S. T. C. v. 158, 180.
[3] Grim, S. T. C. i. 15; Rog. Pontigny, S. T. C. i. 107. 'Mentiuntur plane qui dicunt Londoniensem electioni Thomæ archiepiscopi restitisse, quia sedes illa Londoniæ scilicet illis diebus vacavit et postea usque ad Nativitatem Domini.' Gervase, c. 1383.

[4] 'Ex relatione dilecti filii nostri Radulfi ecclesiæ vestræ archidiaconi accepimus quod idem rex desiderat plurimum, &c.' Imagines, vol. i. p. 309; S. T. C. v. 193, 194.

exceptionally important place ; Gilbert Foliot—and this was equally true—was an exceptionally able man. The king required his services ;

Translation of Foliot

even Becket pleaded for him, an act which caused him bitter remorse afterwards, when he saw that he had helped to raise the man who was to overthrow him. Ralph very briefly notes the dates of the transaction ; it is from the papal letter of confirmation that we learn that he had himself negotiated. The postulation was made, it would seem, on March 6 ; on the 19th the Pope wrote to Foliot that he approved of the translation, and on April 28, all the preliminaries being completed, the new bishop, ' in accordance with the desire of the whole chapter, was solemnly introduced into his see.'

Ralph favoured by Foliot

The fortunes of Ralph de Diceto had suffered from the embarrassments and incapacity of his patron. He seems to have run a risk of losing his prebend. But he had an old friend in the new bishop, who no doubt felt under some obligation towards him for the way in which he had helped on the translation. An early letter of Gilbert Foliot, written to the king soon after he became bishop of

His introduction to the king

London, shows that our archdeacon required powerful aid.[1] He is introduced, curiously enough, to Henry II., in nearly the same formula as that in which ten years before Foliot had recommended him to the Pope ; ' eo securius commendamus quod ei et scientiam ad doctrinam et ad honestatem mores exuberare jamdiu experientia rerum certa cognovimus.' But to this general recommendation the writer adds one which was perhaps more potent, his entire love and full devotion of affection towards the royal person. The special prayer of the letter is that the king would help Ralph in his great necessity ; that the portion of his prebend, granted to him and confirmed by apostolic and royal authority, may be restored to him in its integrity. What this prebend was we are not told, and the records of S. Paul's do not, so far as I can discover, tell what stall

[1] ' Domino regi dominus Londoniensis salutem et devotum debitæ fidelitatis obsequium. Vestra, domine, dignos speramus gratia quos in ecclesia Dei et litteratura commendat et vita. Inde est quod apud excellentiam vestram clericum nostrum beati Pauli archidiaconum, Radulfum de Diceto, eo securius commendamus, quod ei et scientiam ad doctrinam et ad honestatem mores exuberare jamdiu experientia rerum certa cognovimus. Accedit ad hoc amor integer et affectionis erga vos plena devotio, ut vos ulnis caritatis corde complectens honori vestro gloriæque congratulans felices vobis in Domino successus semper exoptet, et sibi commissos, ut a summo rege vobis id impetrent cum se præstat opportunitas, indesinenter admoneat. Quem in oborta sibi necessitate recurrentem ad vos, nilque nisi quod juri debetur et æquitati postulantem, cordis intimo supplicamus affectu quatenus ob Dei reverentiam nostræque petitionis et honestatis ejus, et exhibitæ vobis et semper exhibendæ fidelitatis, intuitu, clementer exaudiatis, et ut præbendæ suæ portio, quam sibi et apostolica et regia vestra concedit et confirmat auctoritas, ipsi in integrum restituatur, juxta datam vobis a Domino sapientiam, tam juste quam misericorditer efficiatis.' S. T. C. vi. p. 1.

Ralph de Diceto held before he became dean, when he likewise became prebendary of Tottenhale. It is possible that the person He is in danger of losing his prebend instituted by Archbishop Theobald, as John of Salisbury has recorded, ousted Ralph from his prebendal stall ; or he may by non-residence during his stay at Paris have disqualified himself for retaining it. We are not told that he recovered it. Another letter of Foliot, the address of which is lost, probably refers to a similar disappointment ; in it the bishop prays the person to whom he writes to give up ' to our archdeacon R., who has been so long our clerk and friend, the church of S. John which we have heard was granted to him by Lambert.' [1] The letter of introduction to the king had, however it may have answered its immediate purpose, the effect of making Ralph personally known to Henry. From this point of time he is found occasionally about the court or taking part in public affairs, although he never, so far as we know, became a chaplain or official clerk of the king. We get two or three glimpses of him during the Becket struggle.

His position during that stormy period must have been very Ralph during the Becket struggle trying. His bishop, from whom he had received distinct marks of confidence and regard, was the chief enemy of Becket in the episcopal body—the ' archisynagogus ' whose skill and learning were made to conduct the king's defence in the memorable dispute. Ralph's devotion to the king, which is attested not only by Foliot's

---

[1] ' Inde est quod dilectionem vestram . . . rogamus quatenus R. archidiacono, jamdudum clerico et amico nostro, ecclesiam Sancti Johannis, quam sibi a Lamberto cessam esse accepimus, concedatis.' S. T. C. vi. 36, 37. The following table of the archdeacons of the church of London will show that for a great part of Ralph's tenure of office he was the only person who could be described as ' R. archidiaconus ' ; but it may be added that the title of Essex or Colchester is generally given to the holders of those two archdeaconries, so that really the only two between which confusion was likely to arise were London and Middlesex :

Archdeacons of London.—William, 1148 (Hist. Pont. Pertz, xx. 532) ; subscr. 1150 ; archdeacon at the time of the election in 1152, S. T. C. v. 184. Nicolas, in office before the death of Richard of Belmeis, S.T.C. v. 158 ; as early as 1160, when he attests a grant to Walter Durdent, bishop of Coventry ; in 1181 (Domesd. of S. Paul's). Peter

of Blois, appointed before 1192.
Archdeacons of Middlesex. —Roger, ob. cir. 1127. Hugh, as administrator for Richard of Belmeis, 1127–1138. Richard of Belmeis, 1138–1152. Ralph de Diceto, 1152–1180. Gilbert archdeacon in 1192.
Archdeacons of Essex.— Richard [Ruffus], 1142, 1150, 1162. Robert Banastre, 1168, 1192, 1194 ; educated at Bologna, S. T. C. v. 336.
Archdeacons of Colchester.—Ailward, 1150. Henry of London claimant between 1152 and 1162. William archdeacon in 1162, S. T. C. iv. 37. Richard Foliot archdeacon about 1168 and 1170 : at Bologna, S. T. C. v. 308, 309 ; nephew of Gilbert Foliot, ib. 319, 353. Ralph de Alta Ripa, archdeacon, 1186, 1189 ; a crusader at Acre.
I have remarked above that I cannot be certain whether Ailward or William in 1150 was archdeacon of London. Archdeacon Hale, however, agreed with this arrangement, Statutes of S. Paul's, p. 173.

assertion but by the general tone of his writings, drew him the same way. But Becket had been a canon of his own cathedral,[1] and no doubt had attached to himself the partisans of the now reigning house by his faithful service before he was made arch-

Ralph's caution in the Becket dispute

bishop; and Ralph had too much learning and too much ecclesiastical feeling not to apprehend great mischief from the threatened downfall of the primate. That he was very cautious we may be sure; for there is an almost total silence in his writings as to the politico-ecclesiastical side of the contest. Yet his memorials were not drawn up until long after the martyrdom and canonisation had tuned all voices to the praises of S. Thomas of Canterbury. If, like the rest of the religious people of England at the time, he sympathised more or less with the archbishop, he loved the king and respected Foliot. We are not, however, to suppose that such devotion as he showed to the martyr was of a posthumous sort only.

His appearance at the Council of Northampton

William FitzStephen, the biographer of Becket, telling the story of the Council of Northampton in October 1164, the great council in which Becket was tried and from which he fled, sets Ralph de Diceto for once before us as a distinct personality. It was on the sixth day of the council, when Becket had resolved to carry his cross into the king's presence, at once proclaiming his distrust of his own safety and declaring himself a candidate for martyrdom. Resisting the arguments of the bishops, he persisted in his resolution and called forth from Foliot the bitter sneer, 'A fool he was ever, and a fool he will ever be.'[2] Herbert of Bosham suggested that Becket should be ready to pronounce the sentence of excommunication in case anyone laid hands on him. The biographer himself interposed; 'Be it far from him; not so did the holy apostles and martyrs of God when they were taken and carried away to death; rather, if this befall him, let him pray and pardon, and in patience possess his soul.' He proceeded further to urge patience, and moved two of the company to tears. John Planeta, hearing these words, laboured to restrain his rising tears; likewise Ralph de Diceto, the archdeacon, afterwards dean of London, wept there very much on that day.[3] William FitzStephen was no doubt a friend of Ralph's; they seem to have been in full sympathy on the occasion, and afterwards we find them telling the story of the martyrdom in words so similar that it is clear that they must have compared notes

---

[1] According to Newcourt's list he held the prebend of Reculverland: that he was a canon of S. Paul's is probably implied in our author's words.

[2] W. FitzStephen, S. T. C. i. 225.

[3] 'Johannes Planeta hæc audiens lacrymas erumpentes laborabat retinere. Similiter et Radulfus de Diceto archidiaconus Londoniensis postea decanus, plurimum ea die ibi lacrymatus est.' S. T. C. i. 227. This was written, then, after the year 1180.

upon it. Patience was the safest and soundest course; the tears were both sincere and politic. If Ralph as a patriotic churchman had much cause for weeping, as archdeacon of Middlesex he had much occasion for anxious silence. It could have required no great penetration to see that the breach between Becket and Foliot, if not that between Becket and the king, was now become irreparable, and that henceforth, both in public and in private, a wise man must be cautious and reticent. Such, however he was actuated, was the course that he maintained, and by it he seems to have gained reputation as a discreet and temperate man.

So high at this time stood his character for learning and prudence that in 1166, after Becket, in the might of his newly acquired legation, fulminated his sentence of excommunication against the king's friends, Ralph was consulted by the astute and experienced minister Richard of Ilchester, as to the way in which the sentence was to be respected. He has preserved his own answer, shrouding himself in the 'Imagines' under the term 'Amicus,' but in the 'Series Causæ' acknowledging it as his work. It is a very cautious production; the minister is warned that Becket's voluntary exile has not deprived him of his spiritual authority, and that Richard's position as archdeacon of Poictiers did not exempt him from the obedience which, as a native of the diocese of Bath,[1] he owed to the primate of the English Church. Nothing could be gained by contemning the sentence, nothing could be lost by respecting it. Such a curse could be valid only against the guilty: Christian humility and public policy alike dictated obedience. It is probable that Richard submitted to the sentence in accordance with this advice, as Gilbert Foliot himself did under like circumstances in 1169. The calm and conciliatory tone of the letter perhaps suggested the employment of Ralph de Diceto as a mediator, or at least as a messenger, between the bishops who adhered to the king and the angry archbishop.

Becket became legate on the 24th of April 1166; his excommunication of the ministers was proclaimed at Vézelay, according to Ralph de Diceto, writing long afterwards, on Ascension Day; according to the better authority of John of Salisbury, who wrote at the time, on Whit Sunday, the 12th of June.[2] The English bishops

Marginal notes:
Ralph is consulted by Richard of Ilchester on the validity of Becket's sentence

His letter to Richard of Ilchester

Ralph goes as messenger to Becket

---

[1] The right of the church of Canterbury to sanction or forbid the promotion of Englishmen in foreign churches appears in the negotiation for the promotion of John of Salisbury to the bishopric of Chartres.

[2] Joh. Salisb., Ep. 145. I follow Canon Robertson's arrangement of these details. There is a graphic letter in S. T. C. iv. 225-227, describing the presentation of the letters of legation by Berengar to the priest officiating at high mass at S. Paul's on Ascension Day. The archdeacon Nicolas was present; but as nothing is said about Ralph we may presume that he was not.

who had, from the moment they heard of the issue of the legatine commission, been in dread of having the same sentence issued against themselves, met at London on Midsummer Day, and appealed to the Pope against the threatened excommunication. They also drew up a long letter in which they announced to Becket the fact of their appeal and the date assigned for it, Ascension Day in the following year.[1] The letter was entrusted to Ralph, who was, besides his personal qualifications, archdeacon to Foliot, who drew up the letter. The king had been abroad since the preceding March, and Ralph was no doubt instructed to maintain a direct communication with the court. The letter was one of spirited and urgent but still temperate remonstrance : the suffragans prayed their chief to exhibit the prudence, humility, and pastoral carefulness which are the greatest virtues of a prelate. The king, he was told, was ready to do justice, and, in all points of dispute between himself and the archbishop, to abide by the judgment of the Church of England. The archdeacon delivered the letter, but whether at Pontigny, where Becket seems to have resided for some weeks after the excommunications, or at S. Colombe at Sens, whither he removed after the king in September had urged the Cistercian chapter to force him away from Pontigny, we cannot determine. The archbishop returned an answer which is at once scornful, argumentative, and sanctimonious.[2] The reference which it contains to the bearer of the letter of the suffragans is slight enough ; but Ralph seems to be treated to a full share of the contempt that Becket so liberally bestowed on his opponents : 'from your letters which I have received through your archdeacon I have gathered thus much, for I could not expect to gather grapes of thorns or figs of thistles.'[3] The archdeacon does not seem to have prided himself on the reception he met with, for in his abridgment of the primate's answer he omits all reference to himself as conducting the negotiation. John of Salisbury, in a letter to Bishop Bartholomew of Exeter, mentions him as bearing an epistle from the king to Foliot, in which Henry committed himself, his whole kingdom and his cause, to the bishop of London as his most faithful friend, and ordered his officials to obey him in all things.[4] This letter seems to

He carries a letter from the bishops

Becket's mention of Ralph

He carries a message from the king to Foliot

---

[1] The letter is given more fully in Hoveden, i. 262 ; S. T. C. vi. 185. It is identified as the letter described by John of Salisbury in his epistle 184, by the extracts which he gives.

[2] Hoveden, i. 256 ; S. T. C. iii. 283.

[3] 'Sed de litteris tuis, quas per archidiaconum tuum destinatas accepi, talia collegi ; neque enim de spinis uvas aut ficus de tribulis colligere

potui.' S. T. C. iii. 283.

[4] 'Scripsit ei nuper dominus rex per Radulfum Dicetensem archidiaconum suum, quod se, totum regnum suum, et causam quæ inter eum et ecclesiam vertitur, ipsius, tanquam patris et fidelissimi amici, committit arbitrio, et præcepit ut sui officiales ei in omnibus usquequaque obediant.' Joh. Salisb., Ep. 184.

prove, if it were necessary, that Ralph de Diceto was the archdeacon who carried the letter to Becket, and that he had returned by the way of the royal court. He does not appear again in these negotiations, but his relations with Foliot gave him the opportunity of learning all that took place; he watched them with care, and although his 'Imagines' were probably not put in their present form until several years after the events, and thus his descriptions have none of the exactness and vividness that might have been expected if they had been written whilst the recollection was fresh, they are, coming from the hand of a careful and by no means partial eye-witness, an invaluable addition to the letters and lives of Saint Thomas of Canterbury.

One or two notes of Bishop Foliot's movements during the remaining years of the controversy occur in the 'Imagines,' and show that Ralph, if not in his company, received exact information from him. In the spring of 1169 Foliot was in anticipation of an immediate sentence of anathema to be directed against himself by name. The king had received a letter from Alexander III., dated in the preceding June,[1] and telling him that the archbishop was no longer forbidden to excommunicate; there was no doubt that the bishop of London would be the first object of attack, and accordingly on the 18th of March he called together the clergy and people of London at S. Paul's and solemnly appealed to the Pope.[2] The appeal did not stay the sentence, which Becket pronounced on Palm Sunday at Clairvaux. At Michaelmas Foliot started for Rome to prosecute his appeal. In dread of treachery he chose the longer route, and instead of proceeding through Burgundy, the ordinary road followed as of old by English travellers, he went through Guienne and Provence and across the Alps to Milan.[3] He reached Milan in the spring of 1170, and there he received letters dated February 14th, in which the Pope told him that he had directed the archbishop of Rouen and the bishop of Exeter to absolve him.[4] Cheered by the news he returned at full speed to the north, and reached Rouen in time to be absolved on Palm Sunday, March 29. Most of these dates are recorded in the 'Imagines,' and this might lead us to suppose that the author went with the bishop; but we find from the letters of Master David, a canon of S. Paul's, whose literary remains were a few years ago published in the Spicilegium Liberianum,[5] that Foliot had employed other officers in his negotiation

Marginal notes: Business of Foliot's absolution — His solemn appeal — His journey to Italy — His return and absolution

[1] S. T. C. iv. 130.
[2] S. T. C. vi. 218; R. Diceto, i. 333.
[3] Joh. Salisb., Ep. 293; Spicilegium Liberianum, p. 642.
[4] Vol. i. p. 337 R. S. ed. S.T.C. iv. 93.
[5] 'Quiete et prospere ad Sanctum Ambrosium devenientes,' Spicileg. Liberian. p. 644. Compare the words of Ralph, vol. i. p. 337 R. S. ed.: 'veniens ad Sanctum Ambrosium.'

Master
David

with the Pope. David had himself been one of the messengers. In a letter addressed to him, bidding him wait at Rouen, the bishop announces his arrival at Milan in nearly the same words as those used in the ' Imagines,' and states that the king had communicated with him through Nicolas, the archdeacon of London.[1] This being the case, it seems more probable that Ralph was left at home to manage the diocese, and that his precise details of the bishop's movements were derived from similar letters addressed to himself.

Coronation
of the
younger
king, and
murder of
Becket

The security obtained for Foliot by the absolution was destined to be short lived. In the following June the coronation of the younger Henry involved him in new difficulties. One of Becket's first acts on his return was to declare the bishop of London excommunicate under papal letters; and his refusal to withdraw the sentence except on terms of abject submission was one of the points of his altercation with his murderers. The murder of Becket left the hostile bishops in greater danger than they had ever been before,

Foliot
absolved
from his
guilt in the
coronation

but the Pope was not implacable. The sentence of anathema issued on account of his participation in the coronation was withdrawn, and the bishop, on undertaking to abide by the Pope's judgment, was absolved from that part of his guilt by the bishops of Nevers and Beauvais, at Chaumont, near Gisors, in August 1171.[2] But he was not yet restored to the exercise of his episcopal functions; before that could be done he had to purge himself of all complicity in the death of Becket. He was not disposed to take another journey to Rome, and, alleging ill-health as a cause, sent one of his archdeacons and two clerks, named Richard and Hugh, to perform the ceremony

Restored to
his episcopal
functions

as his representatives.[3] That done, the Pope wrote on the 27th of February 1172 to the archbishop of Rouen, giving him leave to receive the bishop's personal purgation and to rehabilitate him; and this was done on the 1st of May at Aumale.[4] In this negotiation we are again tempted to trace the hand of Ralph. The archdeacon who was employed is denoted by the initial ' R.'; but as it is probable that both Richard Foliot, archdeacon of Colchester, and Robert Banastre, archdeacon of Essex, were studying at the time at Bologna,

---

[1] Spicileg. Liberian. p. 644.

[2] The papal letters were directed to the archbishop of Bourges and the bishop of Nevers, April 24, S. T. C. vi. 59; Bened. i. 23. The bishops of Nevers and Beauvais and the abbot of Pontigny performed the absolution.

[3] The Pope writes from Tusculum, Feb. 27, 1172: ' Sane cum nulli apparuissent qui vellent eos impetere, et prædictus Londoniensis, obstante sibi debilitate corporis, ad tantum

laborem suscipiendum non esset sufficiens, et in via plurima discrimina et pericula imminerent, dilectos filios nostros R. archidiaconum suum et magistrum Ricardum et magistrum Hugonem clericos ejus ad presentiam nostram transmisit, ut pro se coram nobis purgationem præstarent.' S. T. C. iv. 68.

[4] The archbishop of Rouen and the bishop of Amiens officiated.

one of these was more probably the bishop's agent on the occasion. Master David also was again employed. With the restitution at Aumale Foliot's troubles ceased, and the remaining years of his episcopate were peaceful.

Archidiaconal acts of Ralph de Diceto

For several years we have no data that would enable us to trace our author's occupation, except one or two matters of archidiaconal business in which a glimpse of him may be caught. In the Chronicle of Walden Abbey we find him authorising the exemption of the chapel which the Earl of Essex had built at Pleshey from the jurisdiction of the archdeacon and his officials.[1] On another occasion he appears more jealous of his official rights; a letter of Foliot's exhibits him struggling for his rightful jurisdiction over the church of S. Margaret, Westminster, in opposition to Abbot Laurence.[2] The church of Bulmer, in Essex, was the subject of another dispute between Walter of Bulmer, a clerk, and Ralph de Hauterive, a canon of S. Paul's, master of the schools, and afterwards archdeacon. In this Ralph had an interest, and joined in an agreement referring it to the bishop for arbitration on the 4th of December 1178.[3] If we attempt to trace him in public affairs during the same

[1] MS. Arundel 29, fo. 6; Fundatio Walden. lib. ii. c. 3: 'Præter hæc concessimus ut capella cum cimiterio apud Plessetum, quam ipse ædificaverat, dedicaretur, quia longe erat ecclesia matrix de Estra, difficilis vero et longa, maxime tempore hyemali corpora mortuorum ad sepeliendum ferentibus, via. Remansit autem ad servitium ejusdem capellæ tota decimatio cum obventionibus habitantium in Plesseto cum decima insuper duarum virgatarum de Berewik Granciæ videlicet Plesseto propinquioris, quæ ad ecclesiam de Estra usque ad illum tempus pertinebat. In dedicatione autem illa, multis coram astantibus, episcopo insuper Gileberto ordinante, Radulfo etiam de Disceto archidiacono Middlesexiæ assensum præbente, statutum est ut capella jam dicta omnino sit libera, neque archidiacono, neque ejus officialibus teneatur respondere: crisma autem ad baptismum et oleum infirmorum de matrice ecclesia, Estra scilicet, accipere ei concessum est.' See also Newcourt, Rep. Lond. i. 34.

[2] 'Ecclesiam quippe Sanctæ Margaretæ, super qua recens hæc est orta dissensio, a primis suis fundamentis usque ad dies hos episcopis Londoniensibus et eorum archidiaconis sine contradictione et reclamatione fuisse subjectam, consonum totius undique viciniæ testimonium clamet; et hanc meo quoque tempore R. archidiacono debitum et consuetum cathedraticum exsolvisse in illis fere partibus nullus ignorat.' S. T. C. v. 368. Laurence was abbot 1160–1176.

[3] 'Composition or award made by Gilbert bishop of London in the presence of Robert bishop of Hereford, in 1178, for settlement of the controversy between the churches of Bulemere and Brundon, moved against Ralph de Hauterive by Walter de Bulemere, clerk, and his accomplices, and referred to the said bishop by common consent of all claiming rights in the said church of Bulemere, viz. Ralph de Disceto, archdeacon of London; Gilbert Geldham, dean; and the aforesaid Walter; and also John Le Manant, knight, patron of the church of Brundone, and the said Ralph de Hauterive, the parson of the said church. At S. Paul's, London, 4 non. Dec. Witnesses, Robert, bishop of Hereford; Hugh, dean of S. Paul's; Richard, archdeacon of Colchester; Henry of Northampton, Richard Stortford, Gilbert Foliot, canons of S. Paul's; Ralph Foliot, canon of Hereford; Roger FitzMaurice, and

period, it is only by following the proceedings of Foliot or observing the occasions on which, like any other archdeacon, he would be summoned to ecclesiastical assemblies. Possibly he witnessed the election and consecration of the bishops when he records the dates and circumstances of the ceremony. He was no doubt present when Archbishop Richard visited S. Paul's on the 24th of October 1174 ; probably he attended the court in 1177, when many deans and arch-deacons were summoned to hear the award between the kings of Castile and Navarre, of which he preserves an imperfect record.[1]

His silence about him-self
But he tells us nothing about himself ; his omission to notice the great disturbances which took place in London in 1177 [2] indicates either that he was absent or that he wrote after the importance of the matter was forgotten. In this obscurity the career of Master David affords a ray of light, and shows us that nearly thirty years after his first appointment at S. Paul's his position was not so secure as might have been expected.

Account of Master David
Master David, whom we have seen employed as Foliot's envoy[3] on two occasions in Italy, was an ambitious and a needy man. He called himself David of London, and was perhaps prebendary of Brownswood.[4] He had studied with profit at Clermont, at Paris, and at Bologna. On one occasion we find him applying to Dean Hugh and the Chapter for leave of non-residence.[5] Foliot, who seems to have been his first patron, had a high opinion of his character and attainments,[6] and he was on very friendly terms with Robert Foliot, the bishop of Hereford, a kinsman of Gilbert, and with Roger, the bishop of Worcester, the king's cousin. He was resident at Bologna when the two archdeacons were reading there,[7]
and acted in the business of his patron's absolution both in 1169 and
David at Bologna
in 1171. At Bologna apparently he got into debt, and, in trying to extricate himself, showed himself ungrateful and greedy. After a long series of self-commendatory begging letters, he went to seek

others.' Charters of the duchy of Lancaster, 35, Report of the Deputy Keeper, App. p. 29. Bulmere is in Essex, but in the old archdeaconry of Middlesex. Newcourt, ii. 99, 103.

[1] R. de Dic. i. 418 ; Benedict, i. 145 : ' Venerunt etiam illuc tot abbates, tot decani, tot archidiaconi quot sub numero non cadebant.'

[2] Benedict, i. 155. Another reason for omitting to mention these trans-actions may have been that the Bucquints, who were implicated in them, were tenants of the chapter of S. Paul's. Humfrey Buccuinte was farmer of Kensworth. (MS. Hutton, 6956, p. 158.)

[3] Above, pp. 61, 63. Compare S. T. C. iv. 62, 94.

[4] If he was either, Newcourt has confounded him with another person called Brand, or his name was David Brand. See Newcourt's list of the prebendaries of Brownswood. Archdeacon Hale (Domesday, &c., p. cxviii) seems to doubt whether he was a canon : anyhow he had a demesne at Willesdon ; ib. p. 152.

[5] Spicileg. Liberian. pp. 603–606.

[6] S. T. C. vi. 34.

[7] Spicil. Lib. p. 610, ' Adventanti-bus Boloniam dominis meis archidia-cono et nepotibus domini mei lætus factus sum.' Cf. S. T C. iv. 68.

his fortune at Rome. Foliot had done for him what he could, and had perhaps held out the hopes of succession to an archdeaconry when one should be vacant. He had certainly assigned him a pension of ten pounds on the archdeaconry of Middlesex, and for more than two years Ralph de Diceto, as archdeacon, had continued to pay it. Then he quarrelled with his friends. The dean Hugh was an old man, and a vacancy might be expected any day in the chief dignity of the church.[1] For that dignity there can be little He aims at the deanery question that Ralph de Diceto had long been marked out; it was an elective office, and he had been for nearly thirty years a member of the chapter; he was the depository of all the traditions of the church, and no doubt had much personal influence, if not also, as might be suspected, a family influence in the cathedral body. The news that Master David, fortified with letters from the bishops of Hereford and Worcester,[2] was on his way to Rome to secure the Opposition of Ralph and the bishop papal nomination to the deanery, may well have disgusted both bishop and archdeacon. Ralph stopped Master David's pension, and the bishop wrote letters to oppose him. This proceeding seems

[1] Foliot writes to the bishop of Worcester : 'Arma sumit adversum nos familiaris vir et quondam domesticus noster, magister ille David, et quem laudum titulis extulimus, quem beneficiis honoravimus, quem sperabamus amicissimum, non solum experimur ingratum sed etiam infestissimum. Hic cupidæ mentis injecit oculos in præcipuam ecclesiæ nostræ dignitatem, et ut eam nobis invitis obtineat ad dominum papam iter parat, ut ejus auctoritate nos lædat et ipsum circumveniendo, quod nostri juris est non violenter solum sed impudenter extorqueat.' He had applied for letters to the bishops of Worcester and Hereford. Spicil. Liber. p. 641.

[2] The bishop of Worcester writes thus to the Pope : Master David of London is a devout, faithful, and learned man ; the bishop of London, 'considerata mediocritate immo parvitate redditus sui, et viri honestate et litteratura, ei decem libras argenti in archidiaconatu Middelsexiæ annuatim percipiendas assignavit, donec eidem in pari vel ampliori beneficio ecclesiastico provideatur ; quod et carta sua quam inspeximus confirmavit, et litteris a sigillo dependentibus, ut memorato magistro David solveret præfatas libras decem, R. archidiacono Middelsexiensi præcepit. Qui de mandato ei per biennium continuum et infra terminis statutis persolvit. Ortis autem quibusdam controversiis inter jam dictos, episcopum et archidiaconum et magistrum David, episcopus et archidiaconus arbitrium commutaverunt, ut quod archidiaconus in magistro David solvere consuevit deinde episcopo persolveret.' The archdeacon had accordingly stopped payment. Now, however, the bishop had restored David to his favour, but as his pecuniary position was precarious, the bishop of Worcester prays the Pope to order Foliot to assign him ten pounds a year from the first vacant benefice : 'interim vero, donec vacaverit beneficium in quo sufficienter decem libræ ei recompensentur, districte præcipiatis prædicto archidiacono, ut illas de archidiaconatu in quo ei constat fuisse assignatas, absque vexationis molestia persolvat. In hujus ergo interventus pro viro digno exhibiti exauditione, experiatur nostræ parvitatis devotio, pater reverende, consuetæ benignitatis affectum ; et ne tanti viri labores alicujus tergiversatione deludantur, in severitate et districtione mandati præcipiatis prænominato archidiacono, ut decem libras quas magistro David solvere consuevit, occasione et appellatione cessante integre persolvat.' Spicil. Liber. pp. 757, 758.

F

to have nipped Master David's ambition in the bud. The last we hear of him is in a letter from the bishop of Worcester to the Pope, praying that, now that Bishop Foliot has admitted him again to favour, the archdeacon may be ordered to resume payment of the pension until David could be provided with a benefice of the same value. This correspondence must have taken place before 1179, in which year Bishop Roger died. In 1180 the deanery was vacated and Ralph de Diceto was elected to fill it.

Ralph becomes dean of S. Paul's

Although as a rule promotion was slow except for servants of the Court, Ralph de Diceto must have seen himself outstripped in the race for preferment by many who had started with him. Thomas Becket, his junior probably in the capitular body, had long ago reached the honours not only of the primacy but of martyrdom and canonisation. John of Canterbury, his competitor for the archdeaconry, had been for nearly twenty years a bishop, and was shortly to be chosen to fill the half-independent see of Lyons. Richard of Ilchester, his friend, had become in 1174 bishop of Winchester, and Robert Foliot, archdeacon of Oxford, with whom he had been long associated under Bishop Gilbert, had become the same year bishop of Hereford. Of his Parisian acquaintance, Robert of Melun had been made a bishop in 1163; and Adam, the canon of Notre Dame, who had been associated also with John of Salisbury, had been, in 1175, promoted to the see of S. Asaph. A new generation and school was springing up around him in his own cathedral, but there were still with him William de Vere, the early friend and fellow-student; William of Northall, the archdeacon of Gloucester and residentiary of S. Paul's; Paris, the archdeacon of Rochester, nephew of the great Robert Pullus, and himself closely associated with the Sicilian clergy; some remnants of the Belmeis family party, and more than one Foliot. It is not impossible that Ralph during some portion of his career acted as Master of the Schools of S. Paul's, in that office which later bore the name of chancellor. Between Master Henry, who in the time of Richard of Belmeis had contended for the archdeaconry of Colchester, and Ralph de Hauterive, the military archdeacon who led the English reserve at the siege of Acre, there is abundant room for another 'magister.' But whether or no Ralph filled the office, he must have exercised over the resident body of younger canons an enlightened and beneficial influence. The election to the deanery was a free election.[1] No congé d'élire from the bishop was requisite, and although the episcopal confirmation after the election was necessary, there could be no question about the ratification of the election in the case of

Ralph's early friends promoted before him

Remaining friends in the chapter

---

[1] Statutes of S. Paul's (ed. Simpson), p. 14.

so old and tried a servant. Ralph does not note either the Date of his promotion
death of his predecessor or his own appointment. The exact date,
then, is not ascertained, but as we find him at work on the
survey of the chapter property as early as January 8th, 1181, it is
clear that he must have been settled in his office before the end
of 1180.

It is not easy under the altered circumstances of the modern Importance of his new position
cathedral system to realise the importance of such a position as that
to which Ralph was now called. The High Dean of S. Paul's [1] was
not only the head of a great body of rich and active clergy, but the
chief administrator of a very large estate in land, one of the chief
citizens of the capital city of England, and the foremost secular
priest in the southern province. He was the dean of London,
'decanus Lundoniensis,' for he did not, except in official documents,
call himself dean of S. Paul's, or admit the dean of S. Martin's, his
near neighbour, to any superficial parity of dignity. Ralph brought
long experience and a strong love of his church to his new office, and
he left on the administrative history of his cathedral a deep and
lasting mark. His historical labours were by no means the whole
of his work; his reputation as a theologian was considerable, and
the scriptorium of S. Paul's produced postills, as well as chronicles
and compilations, of which he was the author; but his hand is as
distinctly traceable in the register, the survey, and in the statute
book; the same strikingly beautiful penmanship, the Pauline hand,
as I shall venture to call it, which under his superintendence recorded
the great events of history, may be recognised among the extant
muniments of his cathedral.

We are prone, in examining into the municipal and mercantile Ecclesiastical greatness of London
history of London, to forget that it was a very great ecclesiastical
centre. The fact that the cathedral of Canterbury was in the hands
of a monastic chapter left S. Paul's at the head of the secular clergy
of southern England; it was an educational centre too, where young
statesmen spent their leisure in something like self-culture. London
with its 40,000 inhabitants had a hundred and twenty churches, all
looking to the cathedral as their mother.[2] The resident canons had
to exercise a magnificent hospitality carefully prescribed in ancient
statutes; twice a year each of them had to entertain the whole staff
of the cathedral, and to invite the bishop, the mayor, the sheriffs,
aldermen, justices and great men of the court.[3] Rich as the church
was, no canon was allowed to become residentiary who could not

---

[1] 'Rauf de Disze le haut den de
Lundres,' 'Livere des reis,' p. 256.
The dean of Rouen cathedral also
bore the title of 'haut doyen.' 1st

Report of Cathedral Comm., App. p. 2.
[2] Pet. Bles. epistt. (ed. Giles), ii. 85.
[3] Statutes, pp. 125, 126.

afford to spend seven or eight hundred marks the first year : at York the qualification was not less than a thousand marks.[1] If this were the case with the canons, the obligation lay more heavily and continuously on the dean. Ralph's first thought seems to have been how to become a good husband to his church.

The survey of the estates of the chapter

The first act which he undertook as dean was the great survey of the lands and churches belonging to the chapter of his cathedral.[2] It was an exact account, drawn up in a most orderly manner, like the Domesday survey of the Conqueror, or the great Durham survey of ' Boldon Buke.' A precious fragment of the original is preserved in the Bodleian Library (MS. Rawlinson, B. 872), and has been edited with notes and large illustrative apparatus by the late Archdeacon Hale among the publications of the Camden Society. The

Extant fragment of the survey

penmanship of the fragment exactly resembles that of the original manuscripts of the dean's historical works, and would afford a proof, if such proof were wanted, that might suffice for their identification. Although his survey is comparatively well known to antiquaries through Dugdale and Newcourt, as well as through Archdeacon Hale's ' Domesday of S. Paul's,' it forms too important a part of our author's history to be left with a scanty notice here.

The title and date of the document, which are important as fixing the time of Ralph's appointment to the deanery, run as follows :

Title of the survey

' Annus ab Incarnatione Domini millesimus centesimus octogesimus primus. Annus pontificatus Alexandri papæ tertii vicesimus primus. Annus regni regis Anglorum Henrici secundi vicesimus septimus. Annus regni regis Anglorum Henrici filii regis undecimus. Annus translationis episcopi Herefordensis Gilberti Folioth in Lundoniensem episcopum octavus decimus tunc temporis effluebat, quando facta fuit inquisitio maneriorum[3] beati Pauli per Radulfum de Diceto decanum Lundoniensem ; anno primo sui decanatus, assistentibus ei tam magistro Henrico de Norhamtona quam domino Roberto de Cliforde.'[4] The regnal years are not exact, for the 21st year of Alexander III. ended in September 1180, whilst the 27th year of Henry II. began on the 19th of the following December. As,

[1] First Report of the Cathedral Commissioners, Appendix i. p. 17. Bishop Braybrook in 1399 fixed the more reasonable sum of 300 marks, Statutes of S. Paul's, p. 152.

[2] It does not contain a survey of the prebendal estates, only of the chapter lands, the ' communa,' and churches.

[3] ' The manors forming the communa of the chapter were Caddington,

Kensworth, Sandon, Luffenhale, Ardleigh, in Hertfordshire ; Beauchamp, Wickham, Thorpe and Kirkby, and Walton, Tidwolditun, Tillingham, Barling, Runwell, Norton, Navestock, and Chingford, in Essex ; Sutton and Drayton in Middlesex ; and Barnes in Surrey.' Simpson, Statutes, pref. p. xxvii.

[4] Hale, Domesday of S. Paul's, pp. 112, *sq.* ; Dugdale, S. Paul's, p. 306.

however, Alexander died on August 30, 1181, the survey must have been thrown into its present form in the January of that year. The Inquest on which the survey is based lasted twenty-two days, beginning at Caddington, in Hertfordshire, on January 8, and ending at Sutton, in Middlesex, on the 30th. The articles of inquiry are stated in the distinct and cautious order that marks the rest of Ralph's work : ' ut facilius veritas erueretur, pro maneriorum capacitate, pro numero colonorum modo plures modo pauciores eligendos decrevimus artatos præstita jurisjurandi religione, quod ad interrogata nec verum supprimerent nec assererent falsum scienter, sed juxta conscientiam suam in commune proferrent pro quot hydis unaquæque villa se defenderet tempore regis Henrici, tempore Willelmi decani, versus regem, quid tunc fiscalibus commodis appenderetur per annum vicecomiti scilicet vel hundredi præposito, quidve modo ; quid modo solvatur collegio canonicorum, quot hydæ in dominio, quot assisæ, quot liberæ, quot geldabiles, quot in dominio sint arabiles acræ, quot in prato, quot in nemore sive vestito sive non vestito ; quid instauramenti possit apponi vel in marisco vel in alia pastura ; qui colonorum libertate gauderent quive gravarentur operibus, qui censuales, quive cottarii ; quid meliorationis accreverit in unoquoque manerio, quidve manerium senserit detrimentum vel in deterioratione domorum vel in vastatione nemorum ; quis terminos moverit vel præterierit. Quia vero pravorum intentio semper est prior ad detrahendum, si lector de reprehensione sollicitus circa maneriorum inquisitionem aliquid omissum notaverit, non id inquirentium negligentiæ deputet sed juratorum vel errori vel fraudi.'

Journal of the Inquest on which the survey was based

Apart from the social and economical value of the survey, matters which cannot be touched on now, it has considerable interest in pointing out to us the sort of men with whom Ralph de Diceto was associated in the management of the estates and business of his church. Of the farmers of the seventeen manors visited by the dean and his assessors, five were canons of the cathedral or high dignitaries elsewhere. The first, who farmed Caddington and Kensworth, was Herbert, archdeacon of Canterbury, the son of Richard of Ilchester, bishop of Winchester, and himself afterwards bishop of Salisbury.[1] Ardleigh was farmed by Nicolas de Sigillo, archdeacon of Huntingdon and clerk of the Exchequer, probably a son or brother of Bishop Robert de Sigillo, who had one son at least in the chapter.[2] Richard Ruffus, the prebendary of Twyford, farmed Sandon, Eadulfsnase, Barling, and Runwell and Belchamp : the lease of

Farmers of the capitular estates

[1] Domesd. of S. Paul's, p. 110.
[2] Domesd. of S. Paul's, p. 111 Madox, Hist. Exch. p. 485. Henry,

son of Bishop Robert, was prebendary of Mora. (Newcourt.)

some of which had been granted to a predecessor of the same name who was archdeacon of Essex; Richard was a great man in his way, and possessed a house of his own within the cathedral precincts. William of Northall, who farmed Drayton, was archdeacon of Gloucester and afterwards bishop of Worcester; and Nicolas, the archdeacon of London, held Sutton. John de Marigni or Marney farmed Navestock, probably by favour of Dean Hugh de Marigni; Robert of Fulham held Wickham, Gilbertus Manens held Titwolditon, William and Theodoric, two brothers, held Tillingham,. and Odo of Dammartin held Norton; Walter and John held Barnes. Of these seven we have only the names.[1]

Survey of the churches belonging to the chapter The survey of the manors [2] was followed by a visitation of the churches, a complete abstract or transcript of which, as well as of the survey, is preserved among the cathedral registers.[3] The report of the visitation is introduced by an instructive and characteristic preface, addressed by the dean, perhaps, to his successors :—

' Patrimonium beati Pauli doctoris gentium in ecclesia Londoniensi liberalitate regum, oblatione fidelium, canonicis ibidem Deo servientibus collatum antiquitus, ordine quo supra descriptum est cum de maneriis ageretur. Si volueris diligentius perscrutari per ordinem vires locorum occultatas hucusque, non poteris amodo causari tibi prorsus incognitas. Ad communem igitur utilitatem respiciens, si primam vocem habueris in capitulo, si vel fueris ascriptus in matricula canonicorum, nulla ratione sustineas ut si firmariorum potestas, qui modo possident, exspiraverit, quoquo casu, quod aliquis vel canonicus vel extraneus simul ad firmam possideat. et manerium et ecclesiam ; sed ne promiscuis actibus rerum turbentur officia, sit semper in eadem villa distinctio personarum ; sit alter qui temporalibus præsit, sit alter qui spiritualia subministret : sit alius qui decimas solvat, sit alius qui recipiat. Ordinetur autem vicarius in ecclesiis juxta dispositionem capituli, qui, si facultates ecclesiæ patiantur, dum servit altari sit contentus altario ; si non patiantur, victus capellano suppleatur ex decimis ad arbitrium tale quod semper honestati sit conscium. Reliqui vero fructus, quos in ecclesia propriis sumptibus excoluerit, majores quoque decimæ reserventur canonicis vel ad annuum censum capellanis vel aliis clericis tradantur ad firmam. De regulari jure faciendum est quod supradiximus, nisi necessitas urgens interdum aliud aliquid fieri pro ratione temporis et utilitate magna capituli flagitaverit. Ordinetur autem vicarius in ecclesiis juxta dispositionem tam decani quam capituli. Quæ sit ergo dos ecclesiarum, quid solvatur capitulo, quid per clericos, quidve per firmarium ecclesiæ nomine ; quid in aliquibus

---

[1] Domesday of S. Paul's, p. 111.   [2] Ibid. p. 140.
[3] Ibid. pp. 146–152.

locis ecclesiæ matrici jure parochiali solvatur, a qua noster firmarius, a qua nostri coloni recipiant spiritualia ; quid solvatur pro sinodalibus, quis colligat beati Petri denarium ; quid solvatur archidiaconis Huntedoniæ vel Bedefordiæ, quis ecclesiarum ornatus, diligenter annexum invenies in sequentibus. Explicit prologus.' [1]

Of the character of the visitation, the report on Navestock may serve as a specimen :—' Ecclesia de Nastocha est in dominio canonicorum et reddit eis lx. solidos per manum firmarii ; et solvit nomine sinodalium xii. d. ; de denario beati Petri iii. solidos quos colligit sacerdos et solvit. Et habet in dominio de terra arabili xlvii. acras, in bosco xl. acras, et defendit eas versus regem pro quater viginti acris. Habet etiam decimas plenas totius villæ et de dominio tertiam garbam.' The case of Navestock might be a good illustration of the wisdom of the dean's suggestion that the farm of the manor and the rectory should not be in the same hands. S. Paul's held the two together until the Reformation, when the two were finally divided ; but long before that, probably, the eighty acres of glebe and wood which belonged to the church had been lost among the lands of the manor ; the vicar holds now about twenty acres, and the rectors possess no land in the parish. The whole record of survey and visitation throws light on the temporal and spiritual administration of church property which is very valuable ; the use of the inquest by sworn recognitors for the valuation of the land ; the confusion of lay and clerical duties in the hands of the great men of the chapter ; the institution of vicarages often very scantily endowed on the rich manors, intended to exonerate the great clerks from the duty of serving their churches, are all significant points. The period was one at which the appropriation of tithes was very largely extended, and at which the claims of the ministering priest of the parish were universally set aside in favour of those of the beneficed parson, who might on those terms hold any number of livings and be scarcely, even in name, a clerk. Ralph, who held Aynho and Finchingfield in this loose way, did not scruple to throw the cure of the parishes on the newly instituted vicarages ; it is to his credit that he tried to obtain for them a sufficient endowment.

Report on Navestock

Ralph's first act as dean of S. Paul's was the beginning of a long and careful administration of the property of his church. In 1447 [2] the chapter still possessed three registers bearing the name of Ralph de Diceto ; time, however, has not spared us one that answers to the character of a decanal register. But the general registers of the cathedral and the muniment room of the chapter still contain, either in original charters or in early copies, a large number of documents

Documents issued by Ralph de Diceto as dean

[1] Domesday of S. Paul's, pp. 146, 147. [2] Domesday of S. Paul's, p. xvi.

drawn up and sealed by him. Many of these have been used by Newcourt, who employed them with pious zeal in the composition of his Repertorium Ecclesiasticum Parochiale Londinense ; and the antiquarian industry of Dr. Matthew Hutton prompted him to extract from the mass some of the most important of the Pauline records, the abstract of which is preserved among the Harleian Manuscripts. But many more still lie unnoted on the registers and in the charter drawers, full of interest for the history of London and the church, but far too numerous and various to be even cited in this place. Many of these are in the form of leases granted to the farmers of the chapter lands, and form a valuable continuation to the series of earlier leases printed by Archdeacon Hale from a still earlier register, in the Domesday of S. Paul's. Thus there is a lease of Norton to John of Dammartin, granted no doubt on the death or termination of the tenure of Odo of Dammartin,[1] a lease of Sandon to Thomas and Alan of Bassingburn,[2] and a lease of Belchamp,

Chapter acts executed by Ralph de Diceto as dean dated in 1185, to Richard Ruffus.[3] Others record the presentation to churches : Ralph de Diceto and the chapter grant the church of Ardleigh to John of Winchester, and again to Hamo of Winchester ; [4] they receive Master Gilbert of Cranford as clerk to the chapel of East Twyford on the presentation of Payn FitzHenry ; [5] the church of Barnes is granted to Richard, a kinsman of Henry of Northampton, at a rent of half a mark ; but this is probably a lease of tithes to be supplemented by the institution of a vicar.[6] Some of the grants are of the nature of monastic endowments, bestowed perhaps with a view of increasing the influence of the chapter. It was probably under the influence of the Justiciar Ranulf Glanvill that the church of S. Olave, Jewry, and two-thirds of S. Stephen's, Coleman Street,

[1] MS. Hutton, p. 27. 'Sciant præsentes et futuri quod ego Radulfus de Diceto decanus ecclesiæ Sancti Pauli Lundoniæ et ejusdem capitulum concessimus Johanni de Dammartin Nortonam cum omnibus pertinentiis suis tenendam de nobis ad firmam . . . reddentes inde nobis annuatim centum solidos. Testibus Radulfo de Diceto decano, Nicholao archidiacono, Henrico thesaurario, Ricardo de Storteforde magistro scholarum, magistro Henrico, Roberto de Clifforde, Hugone de Raculfe, Henrico filio episcopi, magistro Hugone, Ricardo Juveni, Rad. de Chiltona, Gileberto Banastre.' See Newcourt, ii. 439.

[2] Hutton MS., p. 122.
[3] Hutton MS., part 2, p. 117.
[4] Hutton MS., pp. 68, 87.
[5] Newcourt, i. 759; Hutton MS., p. 53.

[6] Hutton MS., p. 48. 'Sciant omnes quod ego R. de Diceto, decanus ecclesiæ Sancti Pauli Lundoniæ, et ejusdem ecclesiæ capitulum concessimus Ricardo cognato magistri Henrici de Norhamtune ecclesiam de Berne cum terris et decimis et obventionibus et omnibus rectitudinibus ad eandem pertinentibus ; reddet autem inde nobis annuatim dimidiam marcam. Hanc vero concessionem ipsi facimus salvo jure universo quod dominus archiepiscopus Cantuariensis habet in ecclesia illa. Testibus Rad. decano, Nic. archid. Lundon., magistro Ricardo, magistro Radulfo, Hugone de Raculf, Roberto de Clifforde, magistro Henrico, magistro Hugone, Ricardo juniore, magistro Ricardo fratre Nicholai et Ricardi.'

were granted or secured to the monastery of Butley, of which he was
the founder. In this case the prior and convent were to act as
vicars of S. Olave's and supply the pastoral care : a clumsy arrangement which was afterwards superseded by a formal appropriation
and the ordination of a vicarage.[1] There is also a grant of land at
Ludeburn to the prior and convent of Merton in Surrey.[2] A more
interesting series of documents are the grants of land, houses, and
other property, with which the resources of the church were enlarged
during the same period. And amongst these Ralph himself deserves   Ralph's
the first place, both as a benefactor and as a promoter of good works   benefactions
in others. He built himself a deanery-house and chapel within the   church
precincts of S. Paul's, which when completed he bestowed with the
land on which they stood, and the ornaments and books with which
he had furnished them, on the deans his successors for ever. For
the securing of this benefaction he obtained letters of confirmation
from Gilbert Foliot and Richard FitzNeal, successively bishops of
London, from Richard archbishop of Canterbury, and Pope Lucius III.
This must have been done soon after he became dean, as Archbishop
Richard died in 1184 and Lucius III. in 1185. The papal confirmation, dated at the Lateran in March, limits it to the years 1182 or
1183. In consideration of this gift every succeeding dean had to
pay ten shillings for a pittance on the anniversary of the death of
the donor, and to give security for the payment at his institution to
the deanery.[3] Ralph settled, moreover, on the chapter the tithe of
the demesne of his prebendal estate of Tottenhall,[4] with a view
towards the endowment of a new hospital founded by Master Henry
of Northampton, prebendary of Kentish Town, within the cathedral
liberties. Henry of Northampton, who was one of the canons of   Other
Archbishop Baldwin's projected college at Lambeth, and whom he   benefactors
nominated to the church of Monkton in Thanet, was likewise a   of the
benefactor ; he left certain houses to the chapter for the sustentation   period
of the almonry ;[5] probably it was by way of compensating his

[1] Newcourt, i. 512; MS Hutton,
p. 111.

[2] MS. Hutton, pt. 2, p. 134.

[3] Newcourt, i. 34; MS. Hutton,
part 2, p. 146. The original charters
may be still in S. Paul's ; the confirmation by Bishop Richard III. will be
found, extracted from the register, in
the Appendix to the Preface to vol. ii.
(Roll Series).

[4] Newcourt, i. 212. 'Radulfus de
Diceto decanus ecclesiæ Sancti Pauli
Londoniæ universis, &c. Noverit
caritas vestra me . . . concessisse
capitulo canonicorum Sancti Pauli

integram totam decimam de dominio
præbendæ meæ de Tothale in blado et
in omnibus fructibus de terra pro-
venientibus, &c. Testibus Nicholao
archidiacono Lond., &c.' MS. Hutton,
p. 112.

[5] Newcourt, i. 169 ; MS. Hutton, p.
52. 'R. de Diceto ecclesiæ S. Pauli
Lundoniensis decanus et ejusdem
ecclesiæ capitulum omnibus, &c.
salutem. Noverit universitas vestra
quod nos concessimus magistro Ricardo de Lulinge domos quæ fuerunt
magistri Henrici de Norhamptun con-
canonici nostri, quas idem Henricus

relations that we find Richard his kinsman made lessee of the church of Barnes. Another valuable gift was that of William of Belmeis, the nephew of the second Bishop Richard, and the last of the name whom we find connected with S. Paul's. He, for the health of the souls of his father Robert of Belmeis and his uncle Richard, gave to the canons his church of S. Pancras, which was consequently appropriated to the chapter and a vicarage ordained ; the tithe of S. Pancras, however, went towards the maintenance of Henry of Northampton's hospital.[1] Richard of Stortford, the 'magister scholarum,' imitated the example of the dean, and settled the stone house, which he had built within the close, on his successor in his own prebend, subject to an annual rent of a mark of silver to maintain an obit.[2] Among minor charters is one in which Bishop Richard the third grants to Ralph de Diceto and the chapter Ralph Blund 'our man and native,' of Hadham, free and quit of all bond of servitude.[3]

Ralph's work in the statute book of his church

Not less distinctly than in the domestic economy of the cathedral[4] is the work of Ralph to be traced in the statute book. The customs and statutes of the cathedral were reduced to their existing form and probably first codified by Dean Ralph Baldock, afterwards bishop of London and chancellor to Edward I., a man who seems to have succeeded to some portion of Ralph de Diceto's love of order. In the process of arrangement he has not preserved the exact wording of such statutes as had been previously enacted, and there is perhaps far more than at first meets the eye, in which a critical examination could determine the authorship of the several parts.[5] In more than one place the customs approved in the time of

nobis ad sustentationem elemosinæ beati Pauli dedit . . . tenendas de nobis . . . pro iii. solidis annuatim in anniversario die obitus magistri Henrici. Testibus, &c.' Henry can scarcely be the same Henry of Northampton who is noticed by Mr. Foss among the judges. Cf. Epp. Cant., p. 342.

[1] Newcourt, i. 190; MS. Hutton, p. 84.
[2] Newcourt, i. 151.
[3] 'Omnibus Christi fidelibus, etc. Ricardus divina miseratione Lundoniensis ecclesiæ minister salutem in Domino. Ad communem omnium notitiam pervenire volumus nos concessisse et dedisse Radulfo de Diceto decano et capitulo beati Pauli Radulfum Blundum hominem et nativum nostrum de Haddam, liberum et quietum ab omni nexu servitutis ; et ut hæc nostra, &c. Testibus, &c.' Regist. S. Pauli. One R. Blondus was a

scholar at Oxford ; mentioned by Peter of Blois, Epp. (ed. Giles), i. 184 ; but the name was very common.

[4] Dr. Simpson, Statutes, p. 132, mentions a seal used by Ralph de Diceto, described in MS. Ashmole, 833, fol. 401 ; bearing the inscription, 'Sigillum capituli Sancti Pauli Londonie. S. Paule standing upon a little building like a church, holding up his right hand, and in his left a booke, open as if he were preaching, on each hand several people, some of which hold up their hands.'

[5] Such a critical examination has been given to the Statutes in the edition of Dr. Sparrow Simpson, not only in reference to the original forms of the several enactments, but with illustrations from the usages of other cathedrals, and indeed with every appliance that is required for the elucidation of the subject.

Ralph de Diceto are referred to as a sort of primary authority, or as defining a period of limitation beyond which it was needless to seek for the origin of the particular rule. In some few instances a constitution of Ralph may be given entire; such a statute is that ' de servientibus,'[1] which orders that all the servants of the church shall be in the church in winter at the first stroke of the compline bell, and in summer at the first stroke of the curfew; that they are to guard against the admission of suspicious strangers, and to be answerable for all furniture carried outside the vestibule; several other directions are added, especially one which establishes a graduated table of fees for gravedigging.[2] If a statute like this shows the dean's attention to the minute regulation of the lowest of the church's inmates, another set of constitutions touch the most important of the cathedral institutions, the law of residence. The great statute of residence which was accepted by the chapter in 1192 is not given by Baldock in its proper form, but only by means of extracts; and, curiously enough, another set of regulations prescribing the duties of the residentiaries appears in a later part of the book under the title of ' constitutions, statutes, and declarations of ancient and approved customs published in the time of Master Ralph de Disceto, dean of S. Paul's.' The text of the statute of residence, which seems to be our author's own work, will be found in an appendix to the preface of vol. ii. (Roll Series). It prescribes with great exactness the amount of absence which disqualifies a canon from receiving a share in the distribution of the common fund; it defines the sense in which a canon can be said to have well served the church, and orders that equitable consideration shall be given to necessary causes of absence. In particular two cases are provided for, which Ralph knew from his own experience were likely to recur; a canon who was absent at a university was allowed forty shillings annually from the common fund; and one who was obliged to carry on a trial in defence of his right was allowed to count the days of necessary absence as days of residence. The approved customs are a much more striking series of articles;[3] they lay down the duties of hospitality to be performed by the canons, the number of feasts which they are to make, the duty of entertaining the mayor, sheriffs, aldermen, justices, and the great men of the court who may stand in good stead to the church in difficult times. The new residentiary

The statute of residence drawn up in 1192

The approved customs of residence

Duties of a residentiary canon

---

[1] Statutes, pp. 109, 124: ' Ordinatum fuit tempore Radulfi de Diceto decani, quod,' &c. See also Dugdale, S. Paul's (ed. 1658) p. 270.

[2] ' Item quod pro fovea mortui facienda non accipiat ultra iii^d., et hoc a divite; a mediocri ii^d. vel i^d.; a puero nisi tantum i^d.' Statutes, pp. 110, 124.

[3] Statutes, pp. 125 sq.: ' Constitutiones et statuta et declarationes consuetudinum antiquarum et approbatarum editæ tempore magistri Radulfi de Disceto, decani Sancti Pauli.'

is forbidden to dwell in the house of the Earl of Hereford, or in the house of Diana or Rosamond ; he is not to be bled at all in the first quarter of his residence, and in the other quarters once a month ; he is bound to take part in the expenses and festivities of Childermas and the boy bishop.[1] These customs are many of them extravagant and burdensome, and the whole were cancelled by Bishop Braybrook in 1399 as a pretended statute of Ralph de Diceto.[2] It is quite possible, however, that they were a genuine record of customs which prevailed when the canons were all great and rich men, and when the duty of hospitality was recognised as second only to that of divine service.

Ralph's institution of a fraternity A more interesting act, which bears the name of Ralph de Diceto and the date 1197, is the institution of a fratery or fraternity for the celebration of the office for the dead members, and the mass of the Holy Ghost for living ones, and for the relief of the sick and poor, at four annual meetings.[3] The society, which does not in its main features differ from the ordinary type of the religious guild, is memorable only as a proof of the dean's anxiety that his church should not be lacking in the more popular forms of charity and devotion.

Besides the enactments which bear his name, the extract from Hugh of S. Victor which has been more than once mentioned as inserted by way of preamble to the statutes, and possibly the extracts from the rule of Chrodegang, which are rather of antiquarian value than of practical validity, may have been drawn out of the Character of the cathedral establishment scholarlike memory of Ralph de Diceto. The impression produced by a careful examination of those parts of the volume which reflect the conditions of the twelfth century is that the cathedral establishment was organised on a plan not altogether unlike a college of the present day ; residence was very much determined by the will of the individual canon ; certain funds were divisible among the residents only, each canon drew his bread and beer, and bread and

[1] Statutes, p. 129: 'Debet etiam novus residentiarius post cenam die Sanctorum Innocentium ducere puerum suum cum daunsa et chorea et torchiis ad elemosinariam, et ibi cum torticiis potum et species singulis ministrare, et liberatam vini, cervisiæ et specierum et candellarum facere,' &c.

[2] Statutes, p. 153: 'Statuta vero prætensa ac consuetudines ejusdem ecclesiæ canonicos in primo anno residentiæ ad majores expensas . . . sive ad sumptuosa et excessiva convivia et pastus voluptuosos, et alias excessivas expensas, quam ut præ æfertur necnon choreas et complenas per vicos et plateas . . . necnon statutum prætensum editum tempore Radulfi de Disseto quondam decani dictæ ecclesiæ . . . cassamus, irritamus et annullamus.'

[3] Statutes, pp. 63, 64 : 'de Frateria beneficiorum ecclesiæ Sancti Pauli London., anno ab Incarnatione Domini MCXCVII. in crastino Annunciationis Beatæ Mariæ, auctoritate Radulfi de Dyceto, ecclesiæ Sancti Pauli London. decani, &c.'

beer for his dependents ; of the non-residents, some were farmers of
the manors of the corporation, some held the livings either bestowed
by the chapter or belonging to their several prebends ; some of the
canons were very young and waiting for prebends, some accumulated
duties in church and state, some were resident as exhibitioners in
foreign universities. Devotion, hospitality, education, were the chief
occupation of the residents. Great men, English and foreign, were
entertained at great cost ; kings and foreign prelates were received
with solemn processions, in which from time to time the city joined
the church, and great holy days were kept 'coronata civitate,' the
streets being hung with garlands. The great establishments of the
friars were not yet instituted. S. Paul's stood at the head of the
religious life of London, and by its side, at some considerable interval
however, S. Martin's le Grand, S. Bartholomew's, Smithfield, and
the great and ancient foundation of Trinity, Aldgate, which had
sprung out of the more ancient foundation of the English cnihten-
gild. Ralph de Diceto was, for zeal, learning, and local faithfulness,
a very fair representative man under a system which was soon to be
greatly modified.

The value set upon the relics of the saints at this time was very Ralph's
collection
of relics
great, and the reputation of the system had not been so seriously
damaged as it was later on by detected imposture. Ralph de Diceto
was a collector of relics, and he bestowed no small store of them on
his church. A list of these gifts is preserved in the register, and
has been several times printed.[1] They included a portion of the
knife of our Lord, of S. Mary Magdalene's hair, fragments of the bones
or dress of S. Stephen the Pope, S. Laurence, S. Martin, S. Oswald,
and many others. The vestry too in 1295 contained at least one
chasuble of Ralph de Diceto, made of red samite with vineated dorsal
of pure orfreys, a small contribution, perhaps, compared with the
more numerous and more costly vestments bestowed or bequeathed
by his contemporaries.[2] The choir, however, and the library preserved more precious memorials of him ; there was his psalter, with

[1] Dugdale, S. Paul's, ed. 1658, p.
234 ; ed. Ellis, p. 337 : ' Hæ sunt
'reliquiæ quas Radulfus de Diceto
decanus contulit S. Paulo. [MS. Cod.
B. penes D. and C. fol. 1 b.] De cul-
tello Domini ; de capillis S. Mariæ
Magdalenæ ; de S. Stephano papa et
martyre ; de osse beati Laurentii
martyris ; de pallio aliisque reliquiis
S. Martini Turonensis episcopi ; de
S. Marco et Marcellina martyribus ; de
S. Victore martyre ; de testa S. Ypo-
liti martyris ; de baculo S. Martini
Turonensis episcopi ; de S. Oswaldo

rege et martyre ; de stola et pallio
S. Maximini ; de baculo S. Maximini
Treverensis episcopi ; de capite S.
Eugenii martyris ; ossa cujusdam
martyris de sociis S. Mauritii ; de
sandaliis et sudario et casula S. Re-
macli confessoris ; de osse et vesti-
mento S. Walburgæ Virginis et de
margaritis armillæ ipsius ; de osse
Alexandri papæ et martyris, de pulvere
reliquiarum.'

[2] These articles are mentioned in
the surveys of the treasures of the
church taken in 1295 by Ralph Baldock

a list at the beginning of the ornaments which he gave to the church ; a homily book ' de peroptima litera,' in the finest Pauline hand, we may be sure ; another book of homilies and martyrology bearing his own name ; another martyrology containing copies of the cathedral charters ; a great and fair and well noted gradual, a capitularium and collectarium, good and new and of good penmanship, which belonged to him ; last but not least, the volume of chronicles printed in these volumes, the very MS. from which our text is taken. Besides these there were in the library postills on the books of Ecclesiasticus and Wisdom,[1]—the dean's own sermons or lectures delivered in church or school.

House, land, furniture, chapel, tithes, relics, vestments and books, all testified to a long and deep attachment of the venerable dean to his grand world-famed cathedral.

In this scanty sketch of Ralph's work as dean, and of the relics which long remained to preserve his memory, we have far outstripped the strict lines of our chronology, and must return to the date of

the dean ; Dugdale, ed. 1658, p. 212 ; ed. Ellis, p. 320 :—

Item, casula Radulfi de Diceto de rubeo sameto, cum dorsali puri aurifrigii vineata,' pp. 215, 322.

' Item, psalterium in quo præmittuntur ornamenta quæ Radulfus de Diceto contulit ecclesiæ Londoniensi,' pp. 217, 324.

' Item, Omelium magnum de peroptima litera, quod fuit Radulfi de Diceto decani, incipiens in prima rubrica " quid in festo primæ dignitatis ; " initio primæ legendæ " primo tempore," alleviata cum litera auri in qua depingitur puerperium beatæ Virginis, et finit in rubrica in Octabis Sancti Erkenwaldi, lectio S. Evangelii,' &c., pp. 218, 324.

' Item, aliud omelium ejusdem de grossiori litera male ligatum, incipiens præter ea quæ scribuntur in custodiis dominica prima Adventus in illo Evangelio, " cum appropinquasset Jesus Jerusalem ; " et finit in Evangelio dominica prima ante Adventum " cum sublevasset oculos Jesus," præter ea quæ scribuntur in custodia.'

' Item, Omelium Sanctorum, male ligatum, magnum de grossa, intitulatum in grossiori litera, " respice libro Radulfi de Diceto decani ; " incipiens in Nativitate Domini in Evangelio " exiit edictum," et finit in legenda Jeremiæ de Virginibus.'

' Item, liber Radulfi de Diceto decani nomine suo intitulato in tertio folio a principio scilicet " Omelia et martylogium," et finit in epistola " Nolite peregrinari," ' pp. 218, 325.

' Item, aliud martylogium ejusdem quod incipit " ego Theodricus,' et postea intitulatur nomine ejusdem in sexto folio a dextra noviori litera ; et post incipit " in nomine Domini nostri " in cartis concessis terrarum et in capella decani,' pp. 219, 325.

' Gradale magnum et pulchrum et bene notatum quod fuit Radulfi de Diceto, nullo præmisso. Incipit " ad te levavi animam meam," ' pp. 219, 326.

' Item capitularium et collectarium bonum et novum et de bona litera, cum canone missæ, quod fuit Radulfi de Diceto decani, incipiens in magna rubrica " sicut in festo primæ dignitatis," et finit " in secreto unius virginis," ' pp. 221, 327.

' Cronica composita a Radulfo de Diceto ; et incipit liber a rubrica " In opusculo sequenti trium temporum," et finit in penultimo folio in rubrica " comites Flandrenses," ' pp. 222, 328.

[1] ' Item, postilla R. de Diceto super Ecclesiasticum et super librum Sapientiæ, 2ndo folio, " vel unumquodque translatum." ' Dugdale, pp. 277, 393.

his appointment to trace the thin thread of his more public appearance.

For several years after his appointment to the deanery we know nothing, from other sources, of our author's history, and his own works illustrate it only by the occasional record of the promotion of a friend or fellow canon. Thus, in 1182, he mentions the resignation of the see of Lincoln by Geoffrey the king's son, and the election of Walter of Coutances, who was afterwards his most faithful correspondent. The consecration and enthronisation of the latter prelate are noted, as well as his speedy translation to Rouen. Walter is described by Peter of Blois as a member of a family, doubtless of Norman extraction, settled in Devonshire or Cornwall,[1] and his friendship with Ralph may have begun either at the university or at court, where he had been for some years vice-chancellor or keeper of the seal to Henry II. We know him best as justiciar in the reign of Richard. In 1186 William de Vere, canon of S. Paul's, the friend of Ralph at Paris, was consecrated to the see of Hereford, and William of Northall, another canon and archdeacon of Gloucester, to that of Worcester. Early in 1187 Ralph lost his old friend and patron, Bishop Foliot, and the see of London was not filled up for nearly three years. Within a few weeks after Foliot's death he had to receive the archbishop of Canterbury, Baldwin, who visited the church on Mid-Lent Sunday, and he took advantage of the opportunity to obtain from him an injunction forbidding the persons who were in charge of the temporalities of the see to interfere with the spiritual officers in the discharge of their duties. They had infringed the rights of the archdeacon of Middlesex in the church of Hormead, in Hertfordshire. The guardians of the temporalities were Ralph de Hauterive, archdeacon of Colchester, and Richard Brito, archdeacon of Coventry, the latter acting as a clerk of the Exchequer.[2] Probably the dean, by himself or in conjunction with some of the other members of the chapter, was acting as guardian of the spiritualities, for the dispute on this point between the chapter and the archbishop does not seem to have begun as yet.[3] Baldwin, in the letter referred to, makes no mention of any such officials, but it must have been in this capacity that the dean officiated at the coronation of Richard I., when, because ' the church of London was vacant at the time, Ralph de Diceto, the dean of the church of London, ministered to the archbishop in the holy oil and chrism.'

Henry II. had, shortly before his death, determined to fill up the

Marginal notes:
- Notes of occurrences which he may have witnessed
- The see of London during a vacancy
- Ralph officiates at the coronation

---

[1] P. Blesens. Epistt. (ed. Giles), i. p. 252.

[2] Pipe Roll of Richard I., pp. 11, 12.

[3] See the final agreement on this point in the Statutes of S. Paul's, p. 382 ; and the Appendix to Wharton's Historia de Episcopis.

A new
election,

vacant see, and he and Archbishop Baldwin had summoned the dean with eight of the canons to attend the royal court, wherever it might be, on the Sunday 'Isti sunt dies' March 26, 1189.[1] Ralph and

and journey
to France

his companions obeyed the citation and were abroad for fourteen weeks, during which time it would seem that Henry, harassed to death as he was by misfortune and illness, found no leisure to attend them. Forty pounds, as the Pipe Roll records, and as Ralph has himself noted, were paid to them for their expenses, out of the revenues of the see which were now in the king's hands.

The new
bishop
Richard
Fitz Neal

Henry died on the 6th of July. On the 15th September, at Pipewell, the see of London was filled up by the election of one of the canons, who was likewise dean of Lincoln, Richard, the son of the late bishop of Ely, Nigel, treasurer to the king, and well known to us as the author of the Dialogus de Scaccario. No doubt the canonical ceremony of election was gone through, but it was well understood that Richard, like the other prelates appointed at the time, was the king's nominee. He had been freely chosen bishop of Lincoln under Henry II., but that king had refused to allow his promotion, alleging that he was rich enough already, and that thenceforth he would make bishops only such men as the Lord should choose.[2] His son had no such scruples, and the chapter were probably glad to elect a member of their own body, instead of such a man as the Chancellor Longchamp.

Friendship
of Ralph
and bishop
Longchamp

Richard of London and William of Ely were consecrated together on the 31st of December at Lambeth. It would be the duty of Ralph to present the elect of London to the archbishop and to assist at his enthronisation, which took place the same day. We may presume that he improved the opportunity of cultivating the acquaintance of Longchamp, for whose great abilities he seems to have entertained a profound admiration. To a man of Ralph's age and understanding it would be wrong to impute the character of a flatterer or even of a courtier ; but the letter which he addressed to Longchamp on his elevation to the offices of legate and justiciar, and which he prefixed, as a sort of dedication, to the royal tables and other *opuscula* contained in the volume now preserved at Ripley Castle, shows that he was dazzled by the rapid and brilliant promotion of the chancellor. Great as was the fall of Longchamp and grievous as were the faults of his administration, Ralph writes of him throughout with moderation, and, when he wishes to point the moral, borrows from Sidonius Apollinaris the description of the character and career of Arvandus.

The important positions held by these two bishops during Richard's absence on the Crusade enabled them to furnish our

[1] The statement of the Pipe Roll, p. 12, is: ' Et canonicis Sancti Pauli de Londoniis qui transfretaverunt ad   eligendum episcopum, pro expensis suis xl. libras per breve regis.'
[2] Ben. Pet. i. 345, 346.

author, who was now known to be writing the annals of the time, with direct and most valuable information. He was indeed singularly well placed for knowing all that was passing both in the council of government and among those who were discontented with the administration of Longchamp. At the same moment he was the trusted friend of William Longchamp, Walter of Coutances, and Richard FitzNeal. Probably his sympathies were chiefly with the last, who was throughout the period faithful to the cause which he saw to be most beneficial to the king, and who was free from the influence of those motives, whether of arbitrary self-will or of ambitious self-seeking, which derogate from the equally proved fidelity of the other two. But the dean does not employ, in any part of his description of the contest, language that implies any strong feeling on his part. Even in speaking of the great session of the barons in the chapterhouse of S. Paul's, he makes little further remark than that the bishop of London was the only person present who in his oath to the king made any reservation of the rights of his order ; a point which looks as if his mind was more employed with the controversies of 1163 than those with 1191.

Ralph now known to be writing a history

In 1194, on Richard's return from captivity, he was received with a solemn procession at S. Paul's on the 23rd of March, and on the 19th of May the Archbishop of Rouen visited the cathedral with similar pomp, and preached to the people, being entertained, after mass, with a feast in the bishop's palace. On both occasions no doubt the dean was present. In 1196 he seems to have been an eye-witness of the riot caused by William FitzOsbert. Even here he does not go out of his way to make strong remarks. It seems that he looked on the popular grievance as a real grievance, but that he knew the demagogue to be a bad man, and regarded the severities of the Government as justified, and the precautionary measures of the justiciar as wise and politic. In 1197 he records the death of William Longchamp and the promotion of his brother Robert to be abbot of S. Mary's at York. One of Longchamp's last communications had been the letter in which he transmitted the epistle of the Old Man of the Mountain, exonerating the king from the charge of procuring the murder of Conrad of Montferrat. In 1198 he has to record for the third time the death of his bishop. Richard Fitz-Neal died on the 10th September : how much Ralph owed to him in the preparation of his history it is easier to conjecture than to prove. Richard had himself in his 'Tricolumnis' written the early annals of the reign of Henry II., and living as he did, first as canon and afterwards as bishop, in close neighbourhood with Ralph de Diceto, may very probably have imparted to him his own views on the great crisis of that reign. But if it were so, it is impossible,

Richard at S. Paul's

Riot of William FitzOsbert

Other memoranda of personal interest

without better knowledge than we possess of the contents of the 'Tricolumnis,' to show that our author had the privilege of using it. The vacancy of the see again involved a journey to France for the chapter. On the 9th of November the king summoned a committee of seven canons to meet him on the 7th of December. The dean was not required to attend, probably in consideration of his age, and it was ordered that the precentor Walter, who was with the archbishop in Normandy at the time, should be one of the committee as a substitute, perhaps, for his superior. Ralph, however, did not let himself be overlooked. Whether he took the journey or not we are not informed, but he specially records that it was at his postulation, or on his presentation, that the bishop elect was consecrated. The ceremony was performed on the 23rd of May, 1199, in S. Katharine's Chapel at Westminster, four days before the coronation of John. William of S. Mere l'Eglise, the new bishop, was, like his predecessor, a canon of S. Paul's, whose advancement Ralph had watched for several years. As early as 1178 a contemporary hand recorded in the margin of the 'Imagines,' that it was in that year William of S. Mere l'Eglise had come to the king's court, and in 1189 he had become dean of S. Martin's.

The 'Imagines' contain after this only one or two incidental notices of personal observation. The demolition of Archbishop Baldwin's church at Lambeth provokes from the dean the severest remark that occurs in the whole book :—' to Peter was given the power of building up, of multiplying and transferring sees, but by what law or canon was bestowed on him licence to lay waste a holy place may be left to the judgment of Him who gave the power to build up.' Under the year 1200 we find a complaint of the burdensome exaction from the religious houses of London, which resulted from the entertaining of Philip, the Pope's notary; and another severe remark on the natural and innate greediness of the Romans. In December 1200, the dean seems to have witnessed the benediction of Ralph Arundel, a Londoner, as Abbot of Westminster, the ceremony being performed in S. Paul's ; and in September 1201, to have attended the reception of the legate John of Salerno in his cathedral church. The last entry but one in the 'Imagines' notes the summoning of the bishop of London and others to Normandy, whither the archbishop sailed on the 14th of December.

The letters of Walter of Coutances which, from 1196 onwards, occupy the largest part of the pages of the 'Imagines,' contain little that is of historical interest, and less still that illustrates the personal history of our author. One letter of Ralph's, anonymous, and containing, besides the usual generalities of comfort and

---

Marginal notes:

Another episcopal election

Ralph at the consecration of William of S. Mere l'Eglise

Ralph on the demolition of the college church at Lambeth

Other personal reminiscences

Correspondence with Walter of Coutances

sympathy, a couple of verses apparently of his own composition, is in this aspect the most valuable part of the correspondence.

Two or three of the later notices of local events and matters of personal interest must close our survey of the life of Ralph de Diceto. The record of the visits of prelates and princes to the church of the ' doctor of the nations ' is a marked feature throughout the ' Imagines.' Thus, in 1183, we find Archbishop Richard celebrating mass in S. Paul's a few days before his death; in 1184 Philip of Heinsberg, archbishop of Cologne, was solemnly received, and for the first time in our dean's experience, the city was ' crowned,' and there was joy, honour, and dancing in the streets in honour of the prelate and his companion, the Count of Flanders; in 1187 Archbishop Baldwin was solemnly received, and, the see being vacant, consecrated the chrism on the Thursday in holy week, and celebrated mass on Easter Day. In 1194 Richard, as we have seen, found time to visit S. Paul's ' coronata civitate,' and the Archbishop of Rouen followed in a few weeks. The reception of John of Salerno is nearly the last event recorded. We may imagine how attentively the old annalist would listen to the discourse of his great guests for something to embody in his book. Visits of princes and prelates to S. Paul's

The statute of residence drawn up in 1192 contains the names of several of the canons who stood round the dean in these last days, and enable us to trace the changes which must have affected the tone of society in the chapter. The Archdeacon Nicolas, whose experiences must have run parallel with Ralph's for forty years, is gone, and in his place is Peter of Blois, the learned rhetorician and theologian, who is so well known to us by his collected epistles. It is somewhat significant that Ralph de Diceto never mentions him; doubtless the dean saw through the pretentious, ambitious, self-seeking adventurer. Another name, also calculated to increase the literary tone of the chapter, is that of Walter Map, the archdeacon of Oxford, whose appointment to the precentorship of Lincoln is specially recorded in the ' Imagines.' Walter's poems and his book ' De Nugis Curialium,' the latter of which contains some marvellous tales not at all unlikely to have come out of Ralph's store, would no doubt recommend him to the dean. The schools of the cathedral were now under Master Richard of Stortford. Master Alard, who succeeded Ralph in the deanery, appears as a deacon; Robert Clifford and Henry of Northampton are still alive; the families of the late bishops are well represented; there is still Henry, the son of Bishop Robert de Sigillo; and Richard Ruffus, a relic perhaps of the house of Belmeis; there are Gilbert archdeacon of Middlesex, Ralph archdeacon of Hereford, and Robert Foliot, all kinsmen and nominees of the great Gilbert. Other names recall the court and

Names of the canons who were Ralph's latest companions

Peter of Blois

Walter Map

Richard of Stortford

Other canons

council of Henry II. ; Osbert de Camera, Richard of Windsor, Brand the king's clerk, and William of Ely, who was, after the death of Bishop Richard, the king's treasurer. He, perhaps, was a kinsman of Richard FitzNeal, and a descendant of the organiser of the Exchequer. One name occurs very suggestive of a new principle of papal policy afterwards to be dangerously developed, Laurence, the nephew of Pope Celestine III. Ralph de Hauterive, the brave archdeacon of Colchester, must have been dead ; his successor Richard appears among the confirming canons ; Archdeacon Paris, too, and many others whose names may be found in the ancient lists of the canons, and whose contributions towards our author's narrative may here and there be detected. We are not, however, obliged to regard the old age of the dean as desolate or dull ; there are old friends still about him, and he keeps up his interest in the public history and the promotion of his fellow canons to the very last. He cannot have lived long after the last event noted in the 'Imagines.'

Society at S. Paul's

The date of the death of Ralph de Diceto has never been exactly ascertained. Bale, who in his first edition had fixed the period of his 'flourishing' (claruisse fertur) in the year 1200, in his second edition substituted for it the year 1210.[1] This statement, which may have been a mere error of the press, was accepted as probable, or at least as proving that the dean was alive as late as 1210. The date was accepted, however, as a conjecture, only for lack of a better. Wharton and Le Neve both expressly stated Bale to be their authority, and the latter was unable to reconcile the statement with the fact pointed out by Newcourt,[2] that Alard of Burnham, the successor of Ralph, was dean in 1204. So high, however, was Bale's authority—that, rather than suppose him to have been mistaken, it was suggested that Ralph probably resigned the deanery before his death. As there can be no doubt that Bale's date was a mere conjecture, the question must be further argued.

Difficulty in ascertaining the date of Ralph's death

Bale's date

The last place in which Ralph in his own book mentions himself is in 1199, when he tells that he presented William of S. Mere l'Eglise to the archbishop to be consecrated to the see of London on the 23rd of May. The 'Imagines' are continued for nearly three years longer, and if the latter pages were drawn up under his eye, he must have been alive as late as March 25, 1202. The authority for the latter pages of this work is not beyond dispute, and as the original MS. closes at the coronation of John, we cannot certainly prolong the author's actual superintendence of the work longer than June 1199. It is, however, probable that the statement made under

Evidence of the 'Imagines'

He was probably alive as late as March 25, 1202

---

[1] 'Claruit anno Servatoris nostri 1210, quo Chronica finiebat sub Johanne Anglorum rege.' Possibly 1210 is a misprint for 1201.

[2] Repertorium, i. 34.

the year 1201, that the Cardinal John of Salerno was solemnly received at S. Paul's on the 31st of August, was made by the Pauline scribe, and proves the continuation to have been written at S. Paul's. If this is the case, we can scarcely suppose the dean to have died in the interval, for that event would almost of necessity have been noted in its place. It may then, I think, be allowed that on the evidence of the MSS. of the 'Imagines,' Ralph de Diceto was certainly alive in June 1199, and most probably as late as March 1202.

We have next to look for the further limit, the date at which his successor appears in office. This is supplied by Newcourt: the first recorded act of Dean Alard was ' the confirmation of the church of Shoreditch to the office of precentor of S. Paul's,'[1] and if that confirmation was made soon after the grant of that church by King John, which was dated on the 25th of March in the fifth year of his reign, 1204, as in all likelihood it was, Alard must have been dean early in 1204. The obit of Ralph de Diceto was kept on the 22nd of November.[2] If these two limits be accepted he must have died on the 22nd of November either in 1202 or in 1203. The following consideration may lead to the conclusion that the former is the true date.

His successor was in office in March 1204

Giraldus Cambrensis was at this moment carrying on one of his long struggles with adverse destiny in the shape of an appeal to Rome and a trial before apostolic judges delegate in England. It is not worth our while to discuss the exact nature of the contest, or the reasons which may have led Innocent III. to appoint Ralph de Diceto one of the judges, still less to speculate on the course which the dean may be supposed to have taken. It is enough to remark that early in the year 1201[3] Innocent III. had nominated as judges Eustace bishop of Ely, the dean of London, and the archdeacon of Buckingham. Letters from the Pope to these judges preserved by Giraldus, dated July 27, 1201,[4] and July 29, 1201;[5] and a letter of Giraldus himself, addressed to the same, and dated before October, 19, 1202, is likewise extant.[6] The judges had in fact held, or proposed to hold, five sessions upon his cause. On the 26th of January 1202 he had appeared at Worcester. The judges had

Ralph employed as a judge on the appeal of Giraldus Cambrensis

Various sessions of the judges

---

[1] Newcourt, Repertorium, i. 35, 97; Rot. Chart. (ed. Hardy), p. 124. It is to this foundation of the precentorship that the letter of Peter of Blois to Innocent III. refers; Ep. 217; Opp., ed. Giles, ii. 170.

[2] Dugdale, S. Paul's; Milman, Annals of S. Paul's, p. 513.

[3] Gir. Camb. Opp. iii. 68, 69. The chronological relation of the following references will be found explained in the Councils and Ecclesiastical documents (Haddan and Stubbs), vol. i. pp. 419–429.

[4] Gir. Camb. Opp. iii. 68, 69.

[5] Ibid. iii. 70.

[6] Ibid. iii. 237.

appointed deputies, the archdeacon of Gloucester was to represent
Bishop Eustace; the prior of S. Mary's was to act as substitute for
the dean and archdeacon; and he only appeared to represent the
three.[1] Again, Giraldus appeared at Newport on the 4th of May;
the bishop did not attend, and the dean again sent a substitute.[2]
On the 18th of June at Brackley the bishop was present; the dean
and archdeacon sent substitutes.[3] At Bedford, on the 1st of August,
another session was held;[4] and at last, on the 9th or 16th of
September, all the three judges met at S. Alban's in person.[5] On
the 16th of October the judges intended to make their report before
the archbishop and his suffragans, but, the week before that,
Giraldus, finding his safety endangered, fled from England and

Ralph's name not included in the commission of 1203 betook himself to Rome.[6] The next papal document issued in the
case is an order for a new election to the see of S. David's dated
May 25 or 26, 1203.[7] This is addressed to Bishop Eustace, the
archdeacon of Buckingham, and the bishop of Worcester. It seems
most probable that, if the dean of London were yet alive, the delegation would have been continued to him, for in the many long
records of suits carrried on at Rome at this period it is difficult to
find instances in which a change in the body of judges delegate is
made without strong cause. It is true we are not quite certain that
in this case the dean of London was Ralph de Diceto,[8] but it is
extremely probable that he was the person so designated, and that
he was not superseded by the nomination of a new judge,[9] but vacated

Probable date of his death, Nov. 22, 1202 his place by death. If this be true he died on the 22nd of November,
1202. If on further investigation it should appear that he was
superseded, then, if the dean were indeed Ralph de Diceto, his death
must be fixed on the 22nd of November 1203; if he were not Ralph,
but his successor Alard, the date must be thrown back to the year
1201. But there can be little doubt that the venerable scholar was
himself employed as papal judge, and that we may thus approximate
to, if we cannot actually determine, the date of his death.[10]

---

[1] Gir. Camb. Opp. iii. 203.
[2] Ibid. iii. 215.
[3] Ibid. iii. 218.
[4] Ibid. iii. 221.
[5] Ibid. iii. 223, 228.
[6] Ibid. iii. 237.
[7] Ibid. iii. 281: cf. pp. 71 sq.
[8] It is just possible, but most improbable, that the dean of London might be the dean of S. Martin's le Grand. See Rot. Chart., ed. Hardy, p. 64.
[9] It is also possible that the Pope might regard the commission issued

in 1203 as the beginning of a new business; certainly the bishop of Worcester had been taking part with Giraldus before the older commission had concluded its work; and his name may have been now inserted at Giraldus's application; but it is less probable than that the dean was dead,

[10] Ten shillings were paid to the major canons annually on this day: 'Istam solutionem decanus in institutione sua cavebit facere, et hæc et alia pro domibus suis in atrio S. Pauli ordinata fideliter observare.' List of Obits in

Archbishop Parker has preserved, in an extract from an ancient fragment, a story of the death of a dean of S. Paul's which must be noticed here, not for its importance or probability, but to guard against the possibility of its being referred to Ralph de Diceto. In the time of Archbishop Hubert Walter, he says, a dean of the church of S. Paul at London was keeper of the king's treasury, or, as it is called, the treasurer. In that office he collected a great treasure. On his deathbed he was advised by the bishops and magnates to receive the Holy Eucharist, but, from fear and dread, he constantly deferred doing so. Wondering at this, the friendly lords requested the king to visit him and compel him to receive the sacrament. The dean promised to do so the next day, and then proceeded to dictate his will to a single scribe. Having turned the rest of his attendants out of the room, he kept the notary waiting for some time. 'In the name of the Father and of the Son and of the Holy Ghost,' the formula began. When the dean found that this was being written, he angrily ordered the writer to erase it and to write these words only : ' I leave all my goods to my lord the king, my body to the grave, and my soul to the devil.' Then he died, and the king gratefully ordered his body to be carried in a cart and thrown into a river.[1] That the archbishop somewhere found the story we need not doubt, but it is not likely ever to have been anything but a fable, and there is no dean of S. Paul's to whom it could be made to apply. The only dean who died during Hubert's pontificate was Ralph de Diceto, and he was not the king's treasurer. The only treasurer who died during the same period was Bishop Richard, who died in England when the king was absent in France. William of Ely, his successor, was a canon of S. Paul's, but not dean, and he long outlived both Hubert and his master, retaining his office until

Marginal notes: Legend of the death of a dean of S. Paul's

Marginal note: Not applicable to Ralph de Diceto

S. Paul's, by Archdeacon Hale, at the end of Milman's Annals of S. Paul's, p. 513.

[1] Antiquitates (ed. Drake), p. 228. ' Nam et eodem tempore ecclesiæ Paulinæ Londonensis decanus ærarii regii custos fuit, sive ut vocant thesaurarius ; is, eo fungens officio, ingentem clam thesaurum coacervavit ; tandem in lethalem morbum incidit ; cumque jam valetudinis nulla spes esset, ab episcopis et magnatibus admonetur de sumendo corpore Christi. Quo audito cohorruit remque consulto distulit. Quod illi mirati regem rogant ut ad sacramenti perceptionem eum compelleret. Accedens rex eum rogavit, monuit atque jussit. Is se id facturum crastino promisit. Interea ad testamentum condendum monitus est ; ad quod paratus exire præter unum scriptorem ceteros voluit. Is testamentum scripturus exspectans quid decanus dictaret, ex more testamentorum sic orsus est : " In nomine Patris et Filii," etc. Quod cum decanus comperisset, iratus jussit id deleri et hæc verba tantum scribi : " Lego omnia bona mea domino regi, corpus sepulturæ, et animam diabolo.' Quo dicto expiravit ; rex cadaver illius jussit curru exportari atque in amnem projici et demergi.' [Ex fragmento quodam veteri.]

the year 1223.   I have not tried to explore the origin of the story ;
it is sufficient to prove that it cannot be true here.   Ralph de Diceto
left behind him no such tradition of wickedness and despair ; the
canons of his church observed his anniversary as the day of the
death of 'Ralph de Diceto, the good dean.'

*   *   *   *   *   *

THE CHRONICLE OF THE REIGNS OF HENRY II. AND RICHARD I. (A.D. 1169–1192)

KNOWN COMMONLY UNDER THE NAME OF BENEDICT OF PETERBOROUGH

[THE following is one of the most celebrated of the Prefaces written by Bishop Stubbs. It contains a very interesting description of the character and aims of Henry II., an explanation of the many difficult problems which he was called upon to solve, and an account of the measures adopted to 'eliminate feudalism from government.' Henry's judicial, fiscal, religious, and military systems are fully dealt with, and a valuable criticism on the results of the King's life work concludes a very remarkable piece of English history.]

HAVING devoted the Preface to the first volume to the discussion of the literary history of this book, I will now proceed to sketch the character and position of the great prince whose reign forms the subject of far the largest portion of its contents.

It is almost a matter of necessity for the student of history to work out for himself some definite idea of the characters of the great men of the period he is employed upon. History cannot be well read as a chess problem, and the man who tries to read it so is not worthy to read it at all. Its scenes cannot be realised, its lessons cannot be learned, if the actors are looked on merely as puppets. A living interest must invest those who played a part in making the world what it is : those whose very existence has left indelible traces on its history must have had characteristics worthy of the most careful investigation. *Some realisation of character necessary for the student of history*

Such a judgment as may be formed in the nineteenth century, of a king of the twelfth may well seem unsatisfactory. With the utmost pains it is hard to persuade ourselves that a true view is obtained, or is even obtainable. We know too little of his personal actions to be able in many cases to distinguish between them and those of his advisers ; or to say whether he was a man of weak will or of strong ; whether his good deeds proceeded from fear or from virtue, or from the love of praise ; whether his bad ones were the *Such realisation only approximate at best* workings of hasty impulse, or the breaking out of concealed habit, or the result of a long struggle between good motives and evil passions.

Opinions of contemporary writers as to character are not to be depended upon

Neither can we accept the delineations of contemporary writers without carefully testing them at every step. They are almost always superficial, but if that were the only fault we might be content to accept them as the verdict of ordinary judges, and it is always satisfactory to know what a a man's contemporaries thought of him, even if they were neither close observers nor judicious critics. But their descriptions are seldom to be trusted even in this respect, for they betray almost universally a bias for or against the hero. The one in a thousand who is so far removed from personal feeling as to wish to take a philosophical or consistent view, is probably too far removed from acquaintance to be able to distinguish the truth from falsehood. The contemporary historian cannot view the career of his leading character as a whole ; he sees it too closely, or else he sees it through a distorting medium. Hence the unsearchableness of the king's heart is so often given by mediæval writers as the reason for measures the bent of which they do not see, and as to which, for the want of acquaintance with other acts of the same kind, they cannot generalise.

Kings must be judged by their acts, and that judgment tested by their reputation in their own days

The heart of kings is unsearchable ; but on the other hand their freedom of action is, or rather was in the middle ages, uncontrolled by external restraints. In them, as in no other men, can the outward conduct be safely assumed to be the unrestrained expression of the inward character. It is from observing the general current of the life, from the examination of the recorded acts of it, that the only reasonable view of the character can be obtained. Standing too far off in time and mode of thought to be in much danger of imputing modern principles and motives, we can generalise somewhat as to the inward life of a man if we know what his outward life was ; and then we can compare our conclusion with the judgment of contemporaries, and see whether such men as they were would be likely to think as they have done of such a man as we have described to ourselves.

Such judgment possible in the case of a long reign

If we know enough of the facts of a man's life we can draw such a picture. Character that is not shown in act is not strong enough to be worthy of the name. The man whose character is worth study must be one whose acts bear the marks of character. In the view of a long life, some generalisations can almost always be drawn, from the repetition of acts, from the uniformity or uncertainty of policy. A king who lets his advisers act for him in one case will show the like weakness in others ; will act in different ways under different personal influences. But one who all his life chooses his counsellors on one principle, and follows with them a uniform line A uniform policy a key to character of policy, chooses them because he approves their policy, or rather because they will carry out his own. And that policy, if such be traceable, is the expression of the strongest principles of his own character ; it may be confused or perplexed by his minor traits, but it cannot be suppressed by them, and if it exists it will be seen in operation.

A careful reading of the history of the three centuries of Angevin Curse on the race of Plantagenet kings might almost tempt one to think that the legend of their diabolical orgin and hereditary curse was not a mere fairy tale, but the mythical expression of some political foresight or of a strong historical instinct. But, in truth, no such theory is needed ; the vices of kings, like those of other men, carry with them their present punishment ; whilst with them, even more signally than with other men, the accumulation of subsequent misery is distinctly conspicuous, and is seen to fall with a weight more overwhelming the longer their strength or their position has kept it poised.

It was not that their wickedness was of a monstrous kind ; such Their sins not tragic wickedness indeed was not a prominent feature in the character of the mediæval devil ; nor was it mere capricious cruelty or wanton mischief. Neither were their misfortunes of the appalling sort wrought out by the Furies of Attic tragedy. Of such misery there were not wanting instances, but not enough to give more than an occasional luridness to the picture. Nor was it, as in the case of the Stewarts, that the momentum of inherited misfortune and misery had become a conscious influence under which no knightly or kingly qualities could maintain hope, and a meaner nature sought a refuge in recklessness. All the Plantagenet kings were high-hearted men, rather rebellious against circumstances than subservient to them. But the long pageant shows us uniformly, under so great a variety Common characteristics of the race of individual character, such signs of great gifts and opportunities thrown away, such unscrupulousness in action, such uncontrolled passion, such vast energy and strength wasted on unworthy aims, such constant failure and final disappointment, in spite of constant successes and brilliant achievements, as remind us of the conduct and luck of those unhappy spirits who, throughout the middle ages, were continually spending superhuman strength in building in a night inaccessible bridges and uninhabitable castles, or purchasing with untold treasures souls that might have been had for nothing, and invariably cheated of their reward.

Only two in the whole list strike us as free from the hereditary Exceptions in the cases of Edward I. and Henry VI. sins : Edward I. and Henry VI., the noblest and the unhappiest of the race ; and of these the former owes his real greatness in history, not to the success of his personal ambition, but to the brilliant qualities brought out by the exigencies of his affairs ; whilst on the latter, both as a man and as a king, fell the heaviest crash of accumulated misery. None of the others seem to have had a wish to carry out the true grand conception of kingship. And thus it is with the extinction of the male line of Plantagenet that the social happiness of the English people begins. Even Henry VII., though, perhaps, as selfish a man as any of his predecessors, and certainly less cared for or beloved, seems to open an era during which the vices of the monarchs have been less disastrous to their subjects than before, and the prosperity of the state has increased in no proportion to the ability of the kings.

Varieties of individual character among the Plantagenets

And yet no two of these princes were alike in the constituent proportions of their temperament. The leading feature of one was falsehood, of another cruelty, of another licentiousness, of another unscrupulous ambition : one was the slave of women, another of unworthy favourites ; one a raiser of taxes, another a shedder of the blood of his people. Yet there was not one thoroughly contemptible person in the list. Many had redeeming qualities, some had great ones ; all had a certain lion-like nobility, some had a portion of the real elements of greatness. Some were wise ; all were brave ; some were pure in life, some gentle as well as strong ; but is it too hard to say that all were thoroughly selfish, all were in the main unfortunate ?

Henry II. combined most of these

In the character of Henry II. are found all the characteristics of this race. Not the greatest, nor the wisest, nor the worst, nor the most unfortunate, he still unites all these in their greatest relative proportions. Not so impetuous as Richard, or Edward III., or Henry V. ; not so wise as Edward I. ; not so luxurious [1] as John or Edward IV. ; not so false as Henry III., nor so greedy as Henry IV., nor so cruel as the princes of the house of York ; he was still eminently wise and brave, eminently cruel, lascivious, greedy, and false, and eminently unfortunate also, if the ruin of all the selfish aims of his sagacious plans, the disappointment of his affections, and the sense of having lost his soul for nothing, can be called misfortune.

Apparent anomalies in the character of Henry II.

It would be a great mistake to view the personal and political character of Henry as one of unmingled vice. It was a strange compound of inconsistent qualities rather than a balance of opposing ones, yet the inconsistencies were so compounded as to make him restless rather than purposeless, and the opposing qualities were balanced sufficiently to suffer him to carry out a consistent policy. His fortunes, therefore, bear the impress of the man. He was

---

[1] William of Newburgh compares him with his grandfather to the disadvantage of the latter : 'In libidinem pronior, conjugalem modum excessit, formam quidem in hoc tenens avitam, sed tamen avo hujus intemperantiæ palmam reliquit.' Hist. Angl. iii. 26.

a brave and consummate warrior, yet he never carried on war on a large scale, or hesitated to accept the first overtures of peace.[1] He was impetuous and unscrupulous, yet he never tempted fortune. He was violent in hatred, yet moderate in revenge ;[2] a lover of good men, a corrupter of innocent women ; at once religious and profane, lawless and scrupulous of right ; a maker of good laws, and a seller of justice ;[3] the most patient and provoking of husbands ; the most indulgent and exacting of fathers ; playing with the children, whose ingratitude was breaking his heart, the great game of statecraft as if they had been pawns. He was tyrannical in mood without being a tyrant either in principle or in the exigencies of policy. In power and character, by position and alliances, the arbiter of Western Europe in both war and peace,[4] he never waged a great war or enjoyed a sound peace ; he never until his last year made an unsatisfactory peace or fought an unsuccessful battle. The most able and successful politician of his time, and thoroughly unscrupulous about using his power for his own ends, he yet died in a position less personally important than any that he had occupied during the thirty-five years of his reign, and, on the whole, less powerful than he began. Yet if we could distinguish between the man and the king, between personal selfishness and official or political statesmanship, between the ruin of his personal aims and the real success of his administrative conceptions, we might conclude by saying that altogether he was great and wise and successful.

Contrast between his personal and administrative successes

In so mixed a character it would be strange if partial judges could not find much to praise and much to blame. In the eyes of a friend the abilities of Henry excuse his vices, and the veriest experiments of political sagacity wear the aspect of inventions of profound philanthropic devotion. To the enemy the same measures are the transparent disguise of a crafty and greedy spirit anxious only for selfish aggrandisement. The constitutional historian cannot help looking with reverence on one under whose hand the foundations of liberty and national independence were so clearly marked and so deeply laid that in the course of one generation the fabric was safe for ever from tyrants or conquerors. The partisan of ecclesiastical immunities or monastic discipline can see in him only the apostate and the persecutor. The pure moralist inclines to scrutinise personal vices and to give too little credit to political merit. It is by such that the character of Henry has for the most part been written.

Variety of judgments upon the character of Henry II. by the constitutionalist,

the ecclesiastic,

and the moralist

---

[1] 'Pacis publicæ studiosissimus.' W Newb. iii. 26.
[2] 'Inter ipsos triumphales eventus ummam clementiam . . . conservavit.' Gir. Camb. De. Inst. Pr. ii. 3.
[3] 'Justitiæ venditor et dilator.'

Giraldus, De Inst. Pr. ii. 3. Yet it was justice that he sold.
[4] It was no mere flattery when the author of the Dialogus de Scaccario called him ' Rex illustris mundanorum principum maxime,' p. 2 (ed. 1711).

Whilst we accept the particulars in which they agree, we may, without pretending to be free from prejudice, attempt to draw from our own survey of his acts a more probable theory of the man and of his work on the age and nation.

His character as interpreted by history

Interpreted by the history of his acts, the main purpose of Henry's life is clear. That was the consolidation of the kingly power in his own hands. Putting aside the disproportioned estimate of his ambition formed by contemporary writers, and encouraged perhaps by some careless or ostentatious words of his own,[1] we see in that purpose no very towering idea of conquest, or shortsighted appetite for tyranny. If ambition were ever really his ruling passion, it was one which he concealed so well that its definite object cannot be guessed, which at an early period of his reign he must have dismissed as impracticable, and which never led him to forego by precipitate ardour one of the advantages that might be secured by delay and moderation. He may have had such an aim, he may have thought of the empire,[2] or that the deliverance of Spain or Palestine was reserved for his arms ; but that he really did so we have not the most shadowy evidence. We know that he was a powerful, unscrupulous man, a man of vast energy and industry, of great determination, the last man in the world to be charged with infirmity of purpose ; but we also know that he knew mankind and had read history, and we see that as the actual results of his plans were of no immoderate dimensions, so also the details of his designs were carried out with a care and minuteness only credible on the supposition that they were ends in themselves. We need not suppose gratuitously that he intended to base on the foundation of consolidated power a fabric of conquest that would demand half a dozen lives to complete.

Ambition not his ruling passion ; but rather the desire of consolidating his power

This great purpose not liable to be thwarted by his passions

Such a theory as I have stated at once gives him a fitting aim for a moderate sensible ambition, and explains the relation between the influences of passion and policy by which he was actually

---

[1] 'Solet quippe, quoniam ex abundantia cordis os loquitur, animosum pariter et ambitiosum coram privatis suis nonnunquam verbum emittere "totum videlicet mundum uni probo potentique viro parum esse."' Gir. Camb. De Inst. Prin. ii. 1.

[2] 'Verum ad Romanorum imperium, occasione werræ diutinæ et inexorabilis discordiæ inter imperatorem Fredericum et suos obortæ, tam ab Italia tota quam urbe Romulea sæpius invitatus, comparata quidem sibi ad hoc Morianæ vallis et Alpium via, sed non efficaciter obtenta, animositate sua ambitum extendit.' Gir. Camb. De Inst. Pr. ii. 1. This is a curious passage taken in connexion with the statement of Peter of Blois, Ep. 113. 'Vidimus et præsentes fuimus, ubi regnum Palæstinæ, *regnum etiam Italiæ*, patri vestro aut uni filiorum suorum, quem ad hoc eligeret, ab utriusque regni magnatibus et populis est oblatum.' A design of seizing Aix-la-Chapelle and the empire itself had been at one time ascribed to the Conqueror, in 1074. Lambert Hersf., ed. Pistorius, p. 377.

swayed. His moral character, his self-will and self-indulgence, his licentious habits, his paroxysms of rage, his covetousness, faithlessness, and cruelty, did not come into any violent collision with his political schemes, or if they threatened to do so were kept (except perhaps in the single exception of the forest laws) in abeyance until the pressing necessity of policy was satisfied. That they were so restrained proves that this leading purpose is not to be regarded as imaginary. That they did sway him on almost every recorded occasion of his life in which they did not clash with his purpose is so certain as to prevent us from listening for a moment to any theory which would represent him as a beneficent, unselfish ruler. His ambition may not have been the one which his moral character and circumstances might lead us to expect; but to say this is merely to repeat that that character was rather a compound of inconsistent qualities than a balance of opposing forces. *Where this purpose did not interfere he was ruled very much by passion*

Take for example his relations with France, the conquest of which is the only conceivable and was the most feasible object of the ambition with which he may be credited. In such a purpose his passions and his unscrupulous policy would have run in the utmost harmony—pride, passion, revenge, the lust of dominion, the love of power. He hated Lewis the Seventh, he had every right to hate him, both as injurer and as injured. He was more or less at variance with him as long as he lived; he knew him to be weak and contemptible, and yet to be the source of all his own deepest unhappiness. At many periods of his reign Lewis and France lay at his mercy. The net of alliances was spread all around him. Italy, Spain, Flanders, were in close alliance with Henry. From 1168 to 1180 the position of Henry the Lion in Germany was such as must have prevented Lewis from looking for any help from the house of Hohenstaufen, even if he and the emperor had not been the champions of rival popes. If the king of England and ruler of half of France abstained from taking what a man of vulgar ambition would have taken, what Edward III. and Henry V. nearly succeeded in taking, we are not indeed to ignore other possible reasons for his forbearance, but the most probable reason is that he did not want it. *He cannot have wished to conquer France* *His ambition more moderate than that of Edward III. or Henry V.*

Such possible reasons may be suggested, but for the most part they are much too weak to stand before a resolute passionate ambition, and the certainty that they must have occurred to so clear-headed a man as Henry tells that the ambition they served to restrain could not have been of such a nature, if it existed at all; but it is needless to speculate upon them. Unscrupulous as men were, the idea of unrighteous conquest from a Christian prince did not enter into the ordinary morality of the age. They fought for *Possible reasons for restraining such ambition in the case of France* the settlement of quarrels, or for the decision of doubtful claims, or for rivalry, or for the love of war, but not for illegal conquest. In Henry's own wars this fact is clear, he never waged a war but on the ground of a legal claim. Further than this, his own feudal superstition, if it is not worthy of a higher name, with regard to the person of Lewis, was so strong as to exercise a visible restraint on his actual hatred. His political common sense might well have told him that the force which was enough to crush Lewis was not strong enough to hold France. The difficulties he experienced in ruling the dominions which he already possessed, and the variety of nationalities already crowded under one sceptre, were considerations that could not have escaped him, and they were just the considerations which, powerless before the lust of dominion, would commend themselves most forcibly to his characteristic caution.

Henry's external aims

The consolidation of his continental dominions

The real object of Henry's external ambition was the consolidation of his dominions. To effect this but a moderate extension was necessary. These dominions on the continent were a long territory of varying breadth, the cohesion of which was of course weakest at its narrowest part. The reduction of Brittany from the condition of nominal to that of real dependence, and the extinction of any formidable power in Angoumois, La Marche, Saintonge, and Limousin, were necessary for the maintenance of the desired unity of estates. Second in importance was the enforcement of feudal claims over Toulouse and Auvergne, which might be more useful as independent allies than as unwilling vassals. The recovery of the Vexin and the establishment of Eleanor's rights over Berry gave a strength to the frontier and an apparent compactness to the mass ; but these, like Brittany, Henry chose to secure by marriages rather than by arms ; and in the same way the only considerable acquisition which he contemplated was attempted in the abortive proposal for the marriage of John with the heiress of Savoy and Maurienne.

His procedure rather politic than openly aggressive

In the pursuit of his object Henry went to work very much in the way in which a rich man in the eighteenth century created an estate and founded a family.[1] He was anxious to increase the mass of his inheritance and his local influence by advantageous marriages and judicious purchases. He was scarcely less anxious to extinguish copyholds and buy up small interloping freeholders. In the choice of his acquisitions, that stood first in his consideration which could be brought within a ring fence. If Henry II. occasionally had recourse to chicanery [2] and oppression, he has not wanted followers

---

[1] For instance, his purchase of the county of La Marche in 1177. R. de Monte ad ann., and R. S. ed vol. i. p. 197. R. de Diceto, 600.

[2] 'Omne jus poli jure fori demutavit. Scripta authentica omnium enervavit.' 'Hæreditates retinuit aut vendidit.' R. Niger, 169.

on both a large and a small scale whom his moderation even in these points might put to shame.

The character of his insular acquisitions was determined on a similar principle. Wales, Ireland, and Scotland were all desirable conquests, but no great cost should be spent on them. If internal divisions could be turned to profit, or if the scheme of aggression could be made available for the diversion of uneasy spirits from home, Henry was ready to take advantage of the circumstances, but would not waste much treasure or many men. In each of these cases he had a legal claim ; to Ireland by the gift of Pope Adrian IV. ; to Scotland and Wales by his inheritance of the ancient supremacy of the Anglo-Saxon kings, and the simple application of feudal principles to that inheritance. The case with regard to Ireland was even stronger, if we consider him as succeeding to the like ancient claim to supremacy, and as at once the nominee of the sovereign of all islands [1] and the invited arbiter of domestic quarrels. Yet, according to Robert de Monte, the original design upon Ireland was formed for the purpose of finding a kingdom for William Longespee of Anjou, and the final conquest was carried out in order to provide a suitable settlement for John.[2] William the Lion and David of North Wales were reconciled by a royal or quasi-royal marriage.[3] Galloway was not attacked until a like bond had proved too slight or too frail to hold it.

Henry's division of his dominions among his sons was a measure which, as his own age did not understand it, later ones may be excused for mistaking ; but the object of it was, as may be inferred from his own recorded words, to strengthen and equalise the pressure of the ruling hand in different provinces of various laws and nationalities.[4] The sons were to be the substitutes, not the successors of their father ; the eldest as the accepted or elected sharcr

His policy in the islands

The legal pretexts for aggression

His distribution of his dominions, how to be explained

---

[1] See the Bull ' Laudabiliter,' Gir. Camb. De Inst. Pr. ii. 19. ' Sane Hiberniam et omnes insulas quibus sol justitiœ Christus illuxit, . . . ad jus beati Petri et sacrosanctæ Romanæ ecclesiæ . . . non est dubium pertinere.' By a misinterpretation of the forged donation of Constantine.

[2] Ad ann. 1155. ' Circa festum Sancti Michaelis Henricus rex Anglorum, habito concilio apud Wincestrum de conquirendo regno Hiberniæ et Guillemo fratri suo dando, cum optimatibus suis tractavit. Quod quia matri ejus imperatrici non placuit intermissa est ad tempus illa expeditio.' Cf. Cont. Anslem of

Gemblours ad 1156 : ' Exercitum . . . quem proposuerat ducere in Hiberniam ut eam suo dominio subjugaret et fratremque suum concilio episcoporum et religiosorum virorum illi insulæ regem constitueret.' See also Alberic of Trois Fontaines, ad 1156, ed. Leibnitz, p. 329.

[3] Emma, the bastard daughter of Geoffrey Plantagenet, was married to David, prince of North Wales, in 1174. R. de Diceto, 585.

[4] ' Addens etiam in illo mandato quod quando ipse solus erat in regimine regni nihil de jure amittebat, et modo dedecus esset cum sint plures in regenda terra aliquid inde perdere.'

of the royal name, as feudal superior to his brothers, and first in the
royal councils, stood in the same relation to his father as the king
of the Romans to the emperor; he might rule with a full delegated
power, or perhaps with inchoate independence, but the father's hand
was to guide the helm of state. Unhappily the young brood of the
eagle of the broken covenant were the worst possible instruments
for the working of a large and complex policy; the last creatures in
the world to be made useful in carrying on a form of government
which the experience of all ages has tried and found wanting.

His grand
position in
Europe

Yet how grand a scheme of western confederation might be
deduced from the consideration of the position of Henry's children,
how great a dream of conquest may after all have been broken by
the machinations of Lewis and Eleanor! What might not a
crusade have effected headed by Henry II., with his valiant sons,
the first warriors of the age, with his sons-in-law Henry the Lion,
William of Sicily, and Alfonso of Castile; with Philip of France,
the brother-in-law of his sons, Frederick Barbarossa, his distant
kinsman and close ally, the princes of Champagne and Flanders, his
cousins? In it the grand majestic chivalry of the emperor, the
wealth of Sicily, the hardy valour and practical skill of Spain, the
hereditary crusading ardour of the land of Godfrey of Bouillon and
Stephen of Blois, the statesmanlike vigour and simple piety of the

What a
crusade he
might have
led

great Saxon hero, under the guidance of the craft and sagacity, the
mingled impetuosity and caution of Henry II., might have presented
Europe to Asia in a guise which she has never yet assumed. Yet
all the splendour of the family confederation, all the close-woven
widespread web that fortune and sagacity had joined to weave, end
in the cruel desertion, the baffled rage, the futile curses of the chained
leopard in the last scene at Chinon. The lawful sons, the offspring,
the victims, and the avengers of a heartless policy,[1] the loveless
children of a loveless mother, have left the last duties of an affection
they did not feel to the hands of a bastard, the child of an early,
obscure, misplaced, degrading, but not a mercenary love.

His home
policy deter-
mined by
the same
ruling
principle

The same idea of consolidating the kingly power is apparent in the
legal and social measures of Henry II. His position was in these
respects, indeed, more fortunate than in his foreign relations. He
had not here to originate a policy which was to unite heterogeneous
provinces, but inherited the experience of a century, the able
ministers of his grandfather, and the plans which had been initiated
in the reigns of William the Conqueror and William Rufus. But
it certainly is not in the power of an ordinary administrator to adapt
and develop the ideas of others, and embody them in a policy of his

[1] See Giraldus Camb. De Inst. Pr. ii. 3; and William of Newburgh, iii. 26.

·own. What credit Henry loses for originality he more than recovers when we consider the energy, skill, and industry with which he pursued his main object.

The bent of his internal policy may be described as the substitution of the king's government for the state of things which had prevailed more or less ever since the Conquest, which was partly coeval with the existence of the Norman race, partly owing to the incrustation of feudal institutions; against which the Conqueror had had to struggle, which William Rufus had to repress by the strong hand, which Henry I. by dint of time and skill had but in a degree weakened, and which had regained in the anarchy of Stephen's reign all the power that it had lost under his predecessor. The exact aim of this policy The creation of a strong central government

The idea of a kingly government administered by the king's servants, in which the action of the feudal nobility where it existed was simply ministerial, and was not, so far as the executive was concerned, even necessary to the maintenance of the plan, was the true remedy for the evils of anarchy inherent in the Norman state. Such a system could not be devised by a weak or ambitious head, or worked by feeble or indolent hands. Nor could it be brought to maturity or to easy action in one man's lifetime. The elements of discord were not extinguished in Henry's reign; they broke out whenever any other trouble distracted the king's energy or divided his power. Still he was in the main successful, and left to his successors the germ of a uniform administration of justice and system of revenue. His ministers, who at the beginning of his reign were little more than officers of his household, at the end of it were the administrators of the country.[1] The position of England in the affairs of Europe was, from this time, owing, not to the foreign possessions of the sovereign, but to the compactness of her organisation, and the facility with which the national strength and resources could be handled. The government to be by the king and his ministers, eliminating the feudal element

It does not matter much whether we consider the several measures of Henry's administrative reforms as parts of a matured definite scheme, or as the expedients and experiments of an adroit manager. The more carefully we study the remaining monuments of the earlier reigns, or the character of Henry's ministers, the more we may be Character of the details of Henry's system of government: philosophical or experimental?

---

[1] This great extension of the power and importance of the king's ministers during the reign has frequently been remarked in the case of the chancellor. Yet the difference of the position of Henry I.'s chancellors as compared with that of Becket and Longchamp is trifling compared with the position of the marshal at the beginning and ending of Henry II.'s reign With regard to the lay official, the contrast is more significant, because the aggrandisement is personal rather than official. The constable, on the other hand, seems to have retained some of the prestige of the position of the Stallere from earlier times.

convinced that his genius was rather adaptive and digestive than originative. When on the other hand we examine the actual results of his reforms as exemplified in the succeeding reigns, the more certainly we see the difference between the earlier fragmentary attempts at legislation and the definite system which Henry left behind him ; but on any view the industry, energy, and readiness of his working were qualities of the man himself.

Two opposite views of his character drawn from the examination of his system. (1) Was he a tyrant ?
It is obvious that Henry's great design as well as the subordinate parts of it may, taken apart from the general tenour of his character, be read in two ways, or rather that two opposing views of his character may be drawn from the bare consideration of his objects and measures. It may seem that he wished to create a tyranny, to overthrow every vestige of independence among the clergy and nobles, and to provide himself from the proceeds of taxation with means of carrying out personal selfish designs. He might be a man who could endure no opposition, and to whom it was enough to make a thing intolerable that it should be originated by any other than himself. Such a reading would explain much of his avarice, cruelty, and greediness in acquiring territory.

(2) Was he a benefactor ?
Or it might be argued that as so many of his schemes did actually result in the amelioration of the condition of his subjects, as his judicial reforms were the basis on which the next generation was enabled to raise the earlier stages of civil liberty ; and as his ecclesiastical measures have in nearly every particular been sanctioned and adopted by the practice of later ages, he is therefore entitled to the praise of a well-intentioned, benevolent ruler, as well as to the credit of a far-sighted statesman.

or (3) a far-sighted statesman ?
None of these views tenable
Both of these views have been advocated, the first by some of his contemporaries, and those who in later times have approached the history from their point of prejudice ; the latter by those who, both anciently and recently, have been inclined to look with too professional an eye on the character of his reforms. I have stated already that I think neither of them tenable ; and as it is at present Henry's personal character that is before me, I will give the reasons.

(1) Neither in policy nor in character was he a despot
As to the first theory, which, in the mouths of his contemporaries, seems so condemnatory, it must be said that gratuitous baseness was no part of Henry's character, if we may judge by his actions. He was thoroughly unscrupulous and unprincipled, but he was not a tyrant ; he was not wantonly cruel or oppressive. His crimes against public law and order, such as they were, were not purposeless, nor is it in any way necessary to suppose that he had that intolerance of all opposition which pursues tyranny for its own sake. He had definite aims, and followed them unrelentingly ; whatever could be

made to minister to their furtherance was forced to its use. As his
passions gave way to his policy, so the minor measures of his policy
were sometimes compelled to give way to the occasional exigencies
of his great design. But where there was no definite object he was
not a tyrant.

The theory that he was a benevolent governor or a far-sighted
statesman is not supported, either by the apparent purpose of his
reforms, or by their actual result. It requires no particular
benevolence to teach a king that his subjects are more contented
when justice is fairly administered than when violence reigns
unrepressed; and that where they are contented they are more
likely to be industrious, and more able to pay taxes; that where
they have more at stake they are more ready to make sacrifices to
purchase security; but this is no lesson of far-sighted statesmanship,
for it is the simplest principle of the art of government. If there
were any sign of benevolence, any glimpse of the love of his people
apparent in his actions, he ought by all means to have the credit of
it; if there were any such general tone in his private life it might
be allowed to give the key of interpretation of his public life, and a
harmony to his whole character. But his life was violent and
lawless; his personal design, wherever it clashed with his established
measures, set them at once aside.

Again, such parts of his system as have been approved by the voice
of late posterity, such as, especially, the restrictions on papal power
and on ecclesiastical immunities, are capable of very simple discussion.
There is no need to enter into a question of the personal merit of
S. Thomas of Canterbury, or of the exact point for which he held
out, and for which, in fact, he perished. We may respect the stout-
heartedness of the prelate without approving his cause, or we may
approve his cause without shutting our eyes to the violent and
worldly spirit in which he conducted it; but when we find that in
this cause all the piety and wisdom of three centuries saw the
championship of Divine truth and justice against secular usurpation,
we are not surely wrong in supposing that the Constitutions of
Clarendon were dated three centuries too soon. Was Henry really
three centuries before his age? If the answer is affirmative, we
deny his character as a statesman, and reduce him to a theorist.
In truth, it was as ancient customs [1] that he wished to restore them,
not to force them as innovations. His mistake was not that he
anticipated the age of the Reformation, but that he neglected to
consider that such was the rapid progress of papal assumption, and

Margin notes:
(2) He was too entirely selfish to be called a benefactor

Uniform selfishness of Henry II.

He was a statesman, not a theorist; and cannot claim credit for far-sightedness

---

[1] 'Avitas consuetudines.' Gerv.
1385. 'Leges avi mei Henrici regis
recordatæ et conscriptæ publice coram
omnibus recitentur ne novum aliquid
tradidisse quisquam nobis præsumat
imponere.' Grim. S. T. C. i. 31.

its acceptance, both in England and on the continent, since the age of Hildebrand, that his 'ancestral rights' were really left high and dry behind the advancing flood which he vainly thought to stem. The policy to which feudal antiquity had been forced to yield was really powerless against the increasing tide of ecclesiastical authority. The point which eluded the sagacity of Henry was identical with that which the Conqueror himself had overlooked when he established ecclesiastical courts to take cognisance of the secular offences of the clergy. Both saw the impossibility of reconciling royal supremacy with the claims of feudal antiquity; but in ecclesiastical matters William yielded to, or perhaps helped on, the first trickling of the stream which Henry had to withstand in its full force. It was as necessary to William to strengthen as it was to Henry to weaken the power of the clergy. Henry should not have expected to find in Becket one who would at once fill the seat and reverse the measures of Lanfranc.

In his secular and ecclesiastical reforms alike, he had an object to gain which demanded unusual measures; and he, without scruple and without remorse, tried to enforce them by all means, fair and foul. If he was not a mere tyrant, he was a man who was never deterred by any considerations but those of expediency from trying to win his game.

It seems, then, that there is a third and a truer reading of this eventful life, one which makes no demand on our credulity like the second, and which requires no harsh construction of simple actions like the first. Henry wished to create, at home and abroad, a strong government. In this itself there was nothing deserving the name of tyrannical; at the worst it was less of a tyranny than that which had been in use in the three Norman reigns, and had been exercised on both sides in the contests of that of Stephen. As governments were in those days, any might be accounted good which was conducted on the principle of law, not on caprice. The notions of constitutional sovereignty and liberty were still locked up in the libraries, or in embryo in the brains of the clergy.

Such a theory makes Henry neither an angel nor a devil. He was a man of strong nature; strong will, strong affections, and strong passions. His ambition was not a wanton one. He began his reign without any temptation to be oppressive; but from the beginning we can read his purpose of being master in his own house. The humbling of the barons was no hard task; the initiation of law and order was an easy consequence; but the attempt to apply the principles of law and order to the clergy, in a way that was not sanctioned by the public opinion of his day, and which made his ablest counsellor his most inveterate foe, brought

Margin notes:

The difference of his success against feudal and against ecclesiastical usurpation respectively

Though not a tyrant, he would have been if it had been necessary

The desire to create a strong government no proof of tyrannical designs, or of a despotic spirit

Constitutional government still in embryo

His bad points brought out by opposition

up an opposition which called into play all the violence of his nature. It was not that his character changed, but that circumstances brought out what was in him in a stronger light. After Becket's death, the circumstances became even stronger still, and brought out in a still stronger light the same characteristics.

By that most disastrous event all the elements of opposition were restored to life. Lewis had now a cause which, to his weak and wicked conscience, justified all the meanness and falsehood that he could use against his rival. The clergy dared not side with the king in such a quarrel. The barons took immediate advantage of the general disaffection. The king's sons lighted the flames of war. Not, I think, that there is any evidence to show that the death of S. Thomas was actually or nominally the pretext for revolt; but it was a breaking up of the restraints which had so far been effectual; and all who had grievances were ready and able to take advantage of the shock. *Actual results of Becket's murder*

Under the circumstances, Henry did not show himself a hero, but he behaved as a moderate and politic conqueror. It was not revenge, but the restoration of the strength of his government that he desired. He did not break off his plans of reform : year after year saw some wise change introduced into the legal or military administration ; and practically he managed the church without any glaring scandal. He ruled for himself, not for his people; but he did not rule cruelly or despotically. His character contained much that was tyrannical, but his policy was not such as to curse him with the name of tyrant.[1] *Henry's policy weighed more with him than his desire of revenge*

Is Henry, then, to have no credit for his sagacious measures ? Yes; the credit due to a man who, having come to his crown with a power limited by circumstances rather than by law, and having overcome those circumstances, has chosen to sacrifice somewhat of the licence of despotism for the safety of order ; has chosen to place his power on the basis of public security and common justice.[2] Such merit was his, although, doubtless, the love of power was stronger in him than the love of order. His wisdom was not less wisdom because it was the wisdom of a selfish man. *What credit is due to him?*

In the elaborate descriptions of Henry II. which are given by Peter of Blois, Giraldus Cambrensis, and Ralph Niger, we cannot doubt that we have the accurate delineation of the man as he *Can the portraits drawn of him by his contemporaries be harmonised?*

---

[1] R. de Dic. 578.

[2] 'Illustris Anglorum rex Henricus hoc nomine participantium regum secundus dictus est, sed nulli modernorum fuisse creditur in rebus componendis animi sua virtute secundus : ab ipso enim suæ dominationis exordio totum in hoc direxit animum ut paci rebellantes et dyscolos multiplici subversione conteret, et pacis ac fidei bonum in cordibus hominum modis omnibus consignaret.' Dial. de Scacc. p. 38.

appeared through the different mediums of liking and dislike. The main lines of the portraits are the same, though they are seen as it were through variously-coloured glass. They are well-marked and defined, as we might expect in the most superficial view of such a man. But although well-marked and strongly defined, they do not combine, even under the hand of a professed panegyrist, into the outlines of a hero.

He does not look like a hero

We see a hard-headed, industrious, cautious,[1] subtle,[2] restless man ; fixed in purpose, versatile in expedients ; wonderfully rapid in execution ; great in organising, without being himself methodical ; one who will always try to bind others, whilst leaving himself free ; [3] who never prefers good faith to policy or appearances to realities ; who trusts rather to time and circumstances than to the goodwill of others ; by inclination parsimonious and retiring, but on occasion lavish and magnificent ; liberal in almsgiving,[4] splendid in building,[5] but not giving alms without an ulterior object, nor spending money on buildings, except where he can get his money's worth. As with treasure, so with men, he was neither extravagant nor sparing ; rather economical than humane ; pitiful after the slaughter of battle, but not chary of human life where it could be spent with effect.[6]

Abstract of the characters given by contemporaries

He had the one weakness of great minds, without which no man ever reached greatness : never to be satisfied without doing or taking part himself in everything that was to be done ; [7] and he had not what

---

[1] 'Omnia prius quam arma pertentans.' Gir. Camb. ' Martios congressus quoad potuit semper evitans.' Ib. iii. 24.

[2] His dissimulation is a great point with Becket. S. T. C. iii. 63, 140, 225. No one who ever had anything to do with him escaped his mousetraps (muscipulas). Epp. Cant. 260. Tendiculas, S. T. C. iii. 302. He was a complete Proteus. S. T. C. iii. 302.

[3] 'Naturali quadam inconstantia, verbi plerumque spontaneus transgressor ; nam quoties res in arctum devenerat, de dicto malens quam de facto poenitere, verbumque facilius quam factum irritum habere.' Gir. Camb.

[4] 'Incomparabilis eleemosynarum largitor et praecipuus terrae Palestinae sustentator.' Gir. Camb. Cf. Dial. de Scacc. p. 2. See his will in Giraldus, De Inst. Pr. ii. 17 ; also Ralph de Diceto, 613 ; Gervase, 1459.
The orders of Grammont and Fontevraud were his favourites, as the Cluniac was of Henry I. and the Cis-

tercian of Richard I. The monks of Fontevraud registered him in their obituary as 'secundus probitate Alexander, alter Salomon scientia,' Note on Ralph of Coggeshall in Bouquet.

[5] 'Ad pacem populi spectat immensitas illa pecuniarum quam donat, quam recipit, quam congregat, quam dispergit. In muris, in propugnaculis, in munitionibus, in fossatis, in clausuris ferarum et piscium, et in palatiorum aedificiis, nullus subtilior, nullus magnificentior invenitur.' P. Bles. See especially the list of his buildings in R. de Monte, 897, ad ann. 1161.

[6] 'Amissos in acie plus principe plangens et humanior exstructo militi quam superstiti, longeque majori dolore mortuos lugens quam vivos amore demulcens.' Gir. Camb.

[7] Even Richard I., like Napoleon Bonaparte, complained that he could not be everywhere. ' Nemo potest esse ubique.' Itin. R. R. p. 267. R. de Diceto, 560. ' Per provincias currens

may be called the strength of little minds, inability to see good in what he did not himself devise.

He was eloquent, affable, polite, jocose ;[1] so persuasive in address that few could resist the charm of his manner. He had the royal prerogative of never forgetting names and faces ;[2] he loved to encourage the retiring and to repel the presuming.[3] He was a most excellent and bountiful master.[4] He was very faithful, both in friendships and enmities, where they did not interfere with his policy.[5]

He was not without elegant tastes ;[6] he loved the reading of history, delighted in the conversation of acute and learned men like his uncles the kings of Jerusalem, and his sons-in-law William of Sicily and Henry of Saxony. He had a wonderful memory,[7] well stored with the lessons of past times, and with the experiences of constant journeys, on which he was careful to see everything that was to be seen. *His taste for history*

He had little regard for more than the merest forms of religion ;[8] like Napoleon Bonaparte, he heard mass daily, but without paying decent attention to the ceremony. During the most solemn part of the service he was whispering to his courtiers, or scribbling, or looking at pictures.[9] His vows to God he seems to have thought might be *His religiousness*

explorat facta omnium, illos potissimum judicans quos constituit judices aliorum.' Pet. Bles.

[1] '.Nemo est argutior in consiliis, in eloquio torrentior.' 'Nullus rege nostro honestior est in loquendo, in comedendo urbanior, moderatior in bibendo.' P. Bles. 'Princeps eloquentissimus. . . . Vir affabilis, vir flexibilis et facetus.'

[2] 'Quemcunque vel semel in facie attentius inspexerat, quanquam in tanta quotidie multitudine constitutus, nunquam amplius ignotum habebat.' Gir. Camb.

[3] 'Nullus mansuetior est afflictis, nullus affabilior pauperibus; nullus importabilior est superbis . . . studuit opprimere fastuosos, oppressos erigere.' Pet. Bles.

[4] 'In augendis dignitatibus sibi militantium semper aspirat.' Dialogus de Scaccario, p. 30.

[5] 'Quem semel dilexit vix dediligit; quem vero semel exosum habuit vix in gratiam familiaritatis admittit.' Bles. 'Quem semel exosum habuerat, vix in amorem, quem semel amaverat vix in odium revocabat.' Gir. Camb.

[6] 'Quoties enim potest a curis et sollicitudinibus respirare, secreta se occupat lectione, aut in cuneo clericorum aliquem nodum quæstionis laborat evolvere: nam cum rex vester bene [*i.e.* William of Sicily] litteras noverit, rex noster longe litteratior est . . . Verum tamen apud regem Anglorum quotidiana ejus schola est, litteratissimorum conversatio jugis, et discussio quæstionum.' P. Bles. 'Quod his temporibus conspicuum est, litteris eruditus . . . Historiarum omnium fere promptam notitiam et cunctarum rerum experientiam propemodum ad manum habebat.'

[7] 'Quicquid aliquando memoria dignum audierat nunquam a mente decidere poterat.' Gir. Camb.

[8] He was occasionally, like John, violently blasphemous. See Gir. Camb. de Inst. Pr. iii. 11. He neglected confession, ib. iii. 13.

[9] This may be a libel of Ralph Niger, but it is graphic enough to be true: 'Oratorium ingressus, picturæ aut susurro vacabat,' p. 169. Giraldus says the same, 'Sacræ vix horam hostiæ mittendæ divinis accommodans, et id ipsum temporis, ob regni forte negotia tanta reique publicæ causa, plus consiliis et sermone quam devotione consumens.'

evaded as easily as his covenants with men; his undertaking to go on crusade was commuted for money payments, and his promised religious foundations were carried out at the expense of others.[1] *His morals* His regard to personal morality was of much the same value and extent. He was at no period of his life a faithful husband; and when he had finally quarrelled with Eleanor he sank into sad depths of licentiousness.[2]

He was an able, plausible, astute, cautious, unprincipled man of *His temper* business. His temper was violent, and he was probably subject to the outrageous paroxysms of passion which are attributed to his Norman ancestors, and which, if they have not been exaggerated by the historians, must have been fearful proofs of a profane and cruel disposition, on which discipline had imposed no restraints.[3]

Abstract of the contemporary accounts of his appearance His personal appearance did not approach the heroic. He was slightly above the middle height,[4] square and substantial, with a decided tendency to corpulence.[5] His head was round, and well proportioned;[6] his hair approaching to red, sprinkled in his later years with white, but always kept very short as a precaution against *His face and figure* baldness.[7] His face is described by one authority as fiery,[8] by another as lion-like. His eyes were grey, and full of expression, but rather prominent, and occasionally bloodshot.[9] His nose was

---

[1] 'Ralph Niger's account of this is very characteristic: ' Juratus se tria monasteria constructurum, duos ordines transvertit, personas de loco ad locum transferens, meretrices alias aliis, Cenomannicas Anglicis substituens.' This of course refers to the Amesbury transaction. The Waltham one was of much the same kind. Giraldus also is severe on this very shabby business, and is unable to say what the third monastery was by the construction of which his vow was fulfilled, unless it were the Charterhouse at Witham. De Inst. Pr. ii. 7.

[2] Ralph Niger says that he imprisoned Eleanor that she might not interfere with his amours (p. 168). He says also of him, ' Corruptor pudicitiæ et avum sequens in flagitiis, primo in sponsas, post in filias procerum illecebras exercens.' Giraldus says that after Eleanor's imprisonment, 'qui adulter antea fuerat occultus, effectus postea manifestus, non mundi quidem rosa, juxta falsam et frivolam nominis impositionem, sed immundi verius rosa vocata, palam et impudentius abutendo'; a statement which settles two traditionary statements about Rosamond, namely, that she was

the mother of Geoffrey, who was born about 1158, and that she was put out of the way by Eleanor. Walter de Mapes says that Geoffrey's mother was a low woman named Ykenay.

[3] Cf. S. T. C. iv. 260.

[4] ' Statura ejus mediocris est, ut et inter parvos magnus appareat, nec inter majores minimus videatur.' Pet. Bles. ep. 66. Henry and Richard were taller than their father, John and Geoffrey shorter. Gir. Camb. ii. 29.

[5] ' Corpore carnoso . . . ventre peramplo.' Giraldus Camb.

[6] 'Amplo capite et rotundo.' Gir. Camb. ' Caput ejus sphæricum,' ' ut collo et toti corpori proportionali moderatione respondeat.' Pet. Bles.

[7] 'Subrufus.' Gir. Camb. ' Subrufum . . . nisi quia colorem hunc venerabilis senectus et superveniens canities aliquantulum alteravit.' Pet. Bles. ' Cæsaries ejus damna calvitiei non veretur, superveniente tamen artificii capillorum tonsura.' Ibid.

[8] 'Facie ignea.' Gir. Camb. 'Leonina facies quasi in quadrangulum se dilatat.' Pet. Bles.

[9] ' Oculis glaucis, ad iram torvis et rubore suffusis.' Gir. Camb. ' Oculi ejus orbiculati sunt; dum pacati est

well formed, and denoted no more pride or fastidiousness than was becoming to a king.[1]

He had a short bull neck,[2] a broad square chest,[3] the arms of a boxer,[4] and the legs of a horseman [5] (the author does not say whether of a groom or a cavalier). His feet were highly arched,[6] but his hands were clumsy and coarse.[7]

He paid very little attention to dress,[8] and never wore gloves but when he went hawking. He took a great deal of exercise, being both restless by habit and anxious to keep down his tendency to fat. He was a great hunter and hawker ; [9] he never sat except at meals or on horseback.[10] He transacted all business standing, greatly to the detriment of his legs. He was very moderate in both meat and drink,[11] cared very little for appearances, loved order in others without observing it himself ; he was a good and kind master, who chose his servants well, but neither trusted them too much, nor ever forgave their neglect of his interests. *His personal habits*

The picture is not a pleasant one ; in spite of his refined taste and his polite address he must have looked generally like a rough, passionate, uneasy man. But his frame, though not elegant, was very serviceable, qualified him for great exertion, and was proof against privation or fatigue. He was an adroit and formidable man at arms, but there was little at first sight to denote either the courteous knight or the skilful general, or the self-possessed intriguer, or the ingenious organiser, or the versatile administrator, or the profound politician. *General impression derived from these*

---

animi columbini et simplices, sed in ira et turbatione cordis quasi scintillantes ignem et in impetu fulminantes.' Pet. Bles.

[1] Pet. Bles.

[2] ' Collo ab humeris aliquantulum demisso.'' Gir. Camb.

[3] ' Pectore quadrato.' Gir. Camb. ' Thorax extensior.' Pet. Bles.

[4] ' Brachiis validis.' Gir. Camb. ' Lacerti pugiles.' Pet. Bles.

[5] ' Equestres tibiæ.' Pet. Bles.

[6] ' Arcuati pedes.' Pet. Bles.

[7] ' Manus ejus quadam grossitie sua hominis incuriam protestantur ; earum enim cultum prorsus negligit, nec unquam nisi aves deferat utitur chirothecis.' Pet. Bles.

[8] ' Ocreis sine plica, pileis sine fastu, et vestibus utitur expeditis.' Pet. Bles.

[9] ' Semper in manibus ejus sunt arcus, enses, venabula, sagittæ.' Pet. Bles.

[10] ' Semper a mane usque ad vesperam stat in pedes, et licet tibias habeat frequenti percussione calcitrantium equorum enormiter vulneratas et lividas, nisi tamen equitet vel comedat, nunquam sedet.' Pet. Bles. So also Gir. Camb. ' Cum tibiarum pedumque tumore frequenti . . . cæteras id ipsum corporis incommoditates accelerabat.'

[11] ' Caro siquidem ejus se mole pinguedinis enormiter onerasset, nisi quia ventris insolentiam jejuniis et exercitio domat.' Pet. Bles. · Erat enim cibo potuque modestus ac sobrius. . . . Pacis quoque tempore sibi nec pacem ullam nec requiem indulgebat ; venationi enim trans modestiam deditus, summo diluculo equo cursore transvectus, nunc saltus lustrans, nunc montium juga transcendens dies ducebat inquietos ; vespere vero domum receptum, vel ante cœnam vel post, rarissime sedentem conspexeris.'

Importance
of his
position in
English
history
But if the character of Henry contained none of the elements of
real greatness, if the leading principle of it was one which is actually
incompatible with the highest degree of excellence in a ruler, the
position of the nation he governed was such, and the influence
exercised upon it by his character and the events of his reign was so
salutary, as to make him one of the most conspicuous actors in the
drama of English history.   He was a link in the chain of great men
by whom, through good and evil, the English nation was drawn on
to constitutional government.   He was the man the time required.
It was a critical time, and his actions and policy determined the
crisis in a favourable way.   He stands with Alfred, Canute, William
the Conqueror, and Edward I., one of the conscious creators of
English greatness.

Period of
amalgama-
tion
His reign was the period of amalgamation,[1] the union of the
different elements existing in the country, which, whether it be
looked on as chemical or mechanical, produced the national character
and the national institutions.

Possible
speculation
on national
character
If there is really such a thing as national character, we may
speculate thus.   The Anglo-Saxon temperament had run to seed
in the age preceding the Conquest.   The efforts of Canute, directed
to the thorough union of the Danish with the Anglo-Saxon
population, had ended as such efforts general do, in the assimilation
of the smaller to the larger constituent in the union of the kindred
races.   The Danish provinces had become before the Conquest
scarcely distinguishable from the Anglo-Saxon, as far as concerned
national feeling, and the more important questions of law and
manners.   What differences yet remained served to intensify the
weakness which was inherent in the character of the mass.

Self-reli-
ance, the
character
produced by
Anglo-Saxon
institutions
The tendency of all the Anglo-Saxon institutions was to produce
a spirit of self-dependence ; that was the strength of the system.
Its weakness was the want of cohesion, which is a necessary condition of particles incapable of self-restraint in the absence of any
external force to compress them.   The power of combination was
not indeed wanting, but it was exercised only in very small aggrega-
tions, for very small purposes, and those private rather than national.
The allodial system left the owner of land dependent on no earthly
lord.   The principle of combination in gilds and tithings, which to a
certain extent was voluntary, on the one hand, and the system of
commendation, which was entirely so, on the other, supplied a very

---

[1] ' Jam cohabitantibus Anglicis et
Normannis et alterutrum uxores
ducentibus vel nubentibus, sic per-
mixtæ sunt nationes ut vix discerni
possit hodie, de liberis loquor, quis
Anglicus, quis Normannus sit genere ;
exceptis duntaxat ascriptitiis qu
villani dicuntur, quibus non est
liberum obstantibus dominis suis a
sui status conditione discedere.' Dialogus, &c., p. 26.

indifferent means of national union.   The unity of the tithing was far closer than that of the hundred ; that of the hundred than that of the county ; that of the county, or of the district governed by the same law, was far stronger than that of the kingdom.   Self-reliance in great and small alike, without self-restraint, without the power of combination, with a national pride and yet no national spirit, laid England an easy though unwilling prey at the feet of the Conqueror. Hating to submit, it was yet unable to unite except in the same small clusters in which throughout its early history the nation had exhausted its power of cohesion ; hence the special character of the struggles which occupied the early years of William's reign. *Self-reliance carried to an extreme, ends in the loss of the power of cohesion*

For such a condition the feudal system was undoubtedly the fitting cure.   There is much truth, though only half the truth, in Mr. Carlyle's observation that the pot-bellied equanimity of the Anglo-Saxon needed the drilling and discipline of a century of Norman tyranny.   The grinding process by which the machinery of feudalism forced into a common mass all the different interests, desires, and habits of the disunited race was, however, only one part of its operation.   The feudal system was very far from being altogether bad.   Like the Holy Alliance, it would have been a very excellent device if it could háve been administered by angels ; and all Norman nobles were by no means such men as William Rufus or Robert of Bellesme.   The essence of the system was mutual fidelity, and its proper consequence the creation of a corporate unity, and the recognition of it by every member, from the king to the villein. The bond was not a voluntary one, to be taken up and put aside at pleasure ; the principle of cohesion was uniform throughout the mass.   If then on the one hand the maladministration of the system forced the different constituents of the nation into a physical union of interests, the essential character, which no maladministration could neutralise, supplied the very elements which were wanting for moral strength.   Self-reliance was proved not to be incompatible with order, mutual faith, and regard to law ; and these are indispensable for national strength and national spirit. *The feudal system helped to restore this power (1) by its bad administration, and (2) by its inherent soundness of principle*

It was not, however, necessary that the pressure of this discipline should be perpetual ; it was enough that the lesson should be learned, and the rod might be cast aside ; but very much must depend on the treatment applied at the moment.   Had the crucible been taken from the furnace too soon the elements would never have combined ; if it had been kept there too long the fusion would have ended in an explosion, or in the formation of an insensate, unductile mass.   The reign of Henry II. was the time of the crisis, and the hands by which the happy moment was seized were his own and those of his ministers.   If Henry had been a better man his work would have *The pressure of feudal discipline was temporary only*

Henry's
reign a
critical one
been second to that of no character in history; had he been a
weaker one than he was, England might have had to undergo for
six hundred years the fate of France.

National
character
in relation
to national
institutions
Such a speculation may be a mere flight of fancy, but it accords
in its main features with the facts of history, and if there be such a
thing as national character it must be closely connected with national
institutions. In one state of society they grow out of it ; in another
it is fashioned by them until it seems to grow out of them : they
develop together in a free state, in a subject one they affect one
another by assimilation or opposition according to the nature and
duration of the pressure.

Fusion of
Anglo-Saxon
and Norman
elements
What is merely a probable speculation at the best, in regard of
character, is, however, a true story applied to institutions. The
Anglo-Saxon and the Norman institutions had been actually in a
state of fusion since the Conquest, and the reign of Henry gave to
the united systems the character which has developed into the
English constitution. It destroyed the undue preponderance of one
Henry's
reign in
regard to
the amalga-
mation
power in the State over the others; it secured the firm position of
the central force, and it opened the way for the growth of wealth in
social security ; it prevented England from falling under a military
monarchy, or into a feudal anarchy ; it so balanced the forces
existing in the State as to give to each its opportunity of legitimate
development. Magna Carta could never have been won by lawless
barons for a crushed and spiritless nation, nor would the people
when they learned their strength have satisfied themselves with the
moderate aims that contented the heroes of the thirteenth century,
had they been left too early without restraint, or been kept under
prolonged oppression. The Angevin kings, the Norman nobles, the
English churls, the Roman clergy, become in one century the
English people.

He extin-
guishes the
remains of
feudalism
in the
government
The reign of Henry II. saw the end of feudalism, so far as it had
ever prevailed in England, as a system of government ; the executive
power was taken altogether out of its hands ; the military strength
of it was subordinated to the general aims of government ; the
legislative capacities of the system were held in formal existence,
but in practical abeyance, for better times and better administrators.
Feudalism continued to exist legally as the machinery of land
tenure, and morally in its more wholesome results as a principle of
national cohesion and the discipline of loyalty.

Three
influences in
opposition
from 1066
to 1154
During the ninety years that followed the conquest in England,
three distinct interests were either in active conflict or in passive
opposition : that of the royal power, that of the Norman feudatories,
and that of the people.

The fourth interest, that of the clergy, does not in this view assume the prominence which it exhibited later on. It is doubtless true that the privileges of the church in the Norman era should be considered as the franchises of the people ;[1] it was through the clergy only that the voice of the people could be heard. From the unity of the national church the unity of the kingdom had itself sprung, and the liberties of the church were almost the only liberties that were left under the change of dynasty. Nor can we forget that in the English constitution, that system which it was the Conqueror's object to retain and administer by his own vassals, far the most important place was given to the clergy, the prelates being by virtue of their spiritual character the chief members of the royal council, and the archbishop of Canterbury occupying a position co-ordinate with royalty itself. The king was not a king until he was crowned, and before he was crowned he must bind himself to maintain the liberties of the church and to act by the counsel of the primate.

For these reasons the Church of England even more than the churches of the continent was in a position to enforce her claims as ' the pillar and ground of the truth,' as the upholder of righteousness in a degraded and most licentious court, and as the sole monument and bulwark of liberty in an oppressed people. And this consideration gives to the position of Anselm, and even of Thomas Becket, a dignity and a constitutional importance which the particular points for which they contended did not involve. But their position as yet was morally rather than politically definite. It would be to shut our eyes to the plain truth of facts if we were to view the action of Anselm or Thomas as the action of either church or people. The bishops and higher clergy were for the most part on the king's side, appointed to their places as the rewards of services done to him, or as safe instruments of his policy. The king's court and chapel, full of ecclesiastics, represented the actual status of the clergy at the time more truly than Anselm or Thomas, even with the national spirit of the monasteries at their back. The freedom of the church only on occasions and emergencies appeared as a real thing. The counsel of the primate might be given, but it depended on the will of the king and the influence of his court whether or no it should be taken. Lanfranc and Theobald could influence even William Rufus and Henry II. ; Anselm and Thomas, men probably of more force of character, though not more righteous and earnest, took a different course and signally failed.

The constitutional action of the church had yet to be revived and developed, and it owed much more to Hubert Walter and Stephen Langton than to the two saints of the twelfth century. The personal

Marginal notes:

What was the position of the church?

Earlier and present importance of the position of the clergy

The actual and theoretical standing points of the clergy during this period were not the same : Anselm and Becket occupied one, the majority of the clergy another

The constitutional action of the church is really

---

[1] Palgrave, *Normandy and England*, iv. 169.

of more
importance
at a later
period
quarrel of William Rufus and Anselm, and the contest on investitures under Henry I., had not a direct bearing on the national life, and tended, especially the latter, which had its origin in circumstances external to England, to place matters on a false issue. Throughout the period the higher clergy ruled with the king, and the lower suffered with the people. The baronial importance of the bishops, and the distinct recognition of the interest of the clerical estate, apart from the king and nobles, date from the later years of Henry I. and the reign of Stephen. Roger of Salisbury and Henry of Blois may be regarded as the founders of the secular as S. Anselm was of the ecclesiastical independence of the clergy. They were in different ways the precursors of Thomas Becket, who combined singularly the worst political qualities of the three. But the importance of the Becket quarrel itself was greater in its indirect consequences than in its simple political issue, and its interest is rather moral or personal than constitutional.

The inter-
ests of
the king and
people were
now one
against that
of the
barons
Of the three temporal interests, those of the king, the barons, and the people, the first occupies the chief place in considering the external history of England, the third in the investigation of the internal ; but they had this in common, that their real aims were the same, the consolidation and good government of the country ; whilst the position of the barons, their selfish aims and foreign aspirations, were as dangerous to the crown as they were in effect oppressive to the people.

The Con-
queror did
not intend
to reproduce
in England
the state of
things that
existed in
France
One benefit which England gained from being conquered by a French vassal was doubtless this, that she was secured from ever falling into the condition in which France then was. The Conqueror, as a statesman, saw that it would never answer his purpose to suffer the existence in England of the class of vassals to which he himself belonged. The king of England should never be subject to the sort of influences which he himself and his fellow feudatories had exercised over the kings of France. In this stage of history every limitation of the power of the nobles was an extension of the liberty of the people. It became very different afterwards, when the power of the crown was established, and a new nobility sprang up under different conditions, with the will to be the leaders and to care for the interests of the nation ; but this belongs to a later period than the reign of Henry II.

What
amount of
feudalism
was intro-
duced by
William?
William the Conqueror may be said in a general way, with sufficient correctness to have introduced feudalism into England ; that is, he most probably reduced the land tenures to feudal principles universally, his military establishment in his later years was feudal, his ministers were chosen from among his great vassals, or were rewarded with great fiefs, and, so far as he allowed any legislative

action independent of or co-ordinate with his own, such legislative action, being exercised by men whose position was owing to their feudal rights, was of a feudal character.

But it was no part of his system that the executive power should be administered by feudal officers. This may be considered as proved by the common arguments : first, the fact that by dividing the possessions of those nobles whose services he was obliged to reward on feudal principles, and by requiring the oath of allegiance to himself to be taken by all freeholders throughout the country, he endeavoured to avoid raising up a class of vassals such as existed in France and Germany, where the sovereign was simply *primus inter pares*, or more truly the servant of his own servants. The second argument is based on the amount of subordinate organisation which he retained from the ancient Anglo-Saxon institutions. *His restrictions on the development of feudal tendencies*

The nobles who accompanied William were not likely to fall in with such a plan. For feudal reciprocity in its proper sense they might have had little or no favour, but they had existed for several generations under feudal principles, and they were in a manner acclimatised to the air of France. *The very different views of the barons. (1) Their feudal notions (2) Their pride of race*

But the root of the matter lay deeper far than the incrustation of feudalism. The pride of race was strong within them. It was a confederation of Norsemen that had placed Rollo and his successors on the throne of Normandy. It was a confederation of volunteer vassals, in whom the spirit of the Vikings had revived, that mustered the fleet and army which won the kingdom of England. William might be to the English the testamentary heir of the Confessor ; to to the French the mightiest vassal of the crown ; but to his own followers he was the head of the race, the duke of the Normans, rather than the king of England or the count of Rouen. If he was *primus*, they were *pares*, most of them of purer descent, many of them of equal origin : his actual primacy he owed chiefly to his personal character. *William's position due to his personal character ;*

Further, the early troubles of his reign in the duchy had considerably diminished the number of true Norman nobles, and this had the effect of concentrating the greater fiefs in the hands of his own relations. Both these things contributed to the maintenance of his personal authority, whilst they left the difficulties of the situation to his successors, with whom the bonds of influence and relationship were weaker, and who had to contend with a body of nobles who were becoming fiercer and prouder as they became fewer. *and to his family connexions ; causes which were less effective in the case of his successors*

These men were ready enough to take advantage of such points of feudalism as favoured their own independence. Why should they not occupy to the crown which had been won by their exertions the same position that they saw the counts of Champagne and

Pride of
race and
conquest in
the barons

Vermandois and the dukes of Normandy and Burgundy bearing to
the crown of France, whose wearer was their near kinsman, and far
less indebted to them for his position ?   Nor were they unworthy to
be the equals of kings, much less of French vassals, who counted
among their inferior members the house of Hauteville, which was
giving law to Italy and threatening the Eastern Empire.

(3) Their
pretensions
favoured by
the condi-
tion of the
conquered
country

There was much, however, in the condition of the conquered
country which might seem to favour the claims of the nobles to
feudal independence.   England under the Confessor had been
broken up into great earldoms or satrapies, each containing many
shires, and in fact representing in some measure one of the ancient
kingdoms of the Heptarchy.   Each earl governed by authority
directly delegated by the sovereign, and was supreme in his earldom,
both in war and in peace : but the dignity was not necessarily
hereditary, and although probably given in theory for the life of the
grantee, was subject to the conditions of promotion and degradation.
The exact parallel for this state of things must be sought in the
contemporary condition of Germany and in a much earlier condition
of France.   But the main point of separate independent jurisdiction
strongly resembled the feudal division of the latter country.   It
would have been the most natural thing in the world for Hugh of
Avranches, Roger Montgomery, or William FitzOsbern to have
taken the place of Tostig, Swegen, and Leofric.   The urgency with
which the local franchises of the Anglo-Saxon lords were pressed by
the Norman barons to the exaltation of their own privileges may
serve to show that had the chance been given them they would have
gladly claimed the greater jurisdictions on a like plea.   As it was,
they found themselves, in relation to the royal power, in a position
actually less influential than that which had been occupied by the
Anglo-Saxon earls.   They had conquered England for William, not
for themselves.   William's own measures show that he foresaw the
results of this ; but his sons had the first experience of its working.
In the attempt to set aside the male line of the ducal house in the
rebellion of 1095 may be traced the principle of the equality and
confederation of the race, as well as an attempt to assert for the
great vassals the independence of feudal princes.   Robert Mowbray
expiated his rebellion by a life-long captivity, but until the Norman
nobility became extinct he never lacked imitators.

(4) Their
jealousy of
the minis-
ters of the
crown

With this deeply-seated feeling of insubordination was closely
connected the jealousy with which the nobles regarded the king's
ministers.   Under the Conqueror, whose most faithful adherents
were men of his own blood, acknowledging in him the source of their
fortune and the pre-eminence of strength, we find few complaints of
the aggrandisement of insignificant officers.   William's servants were

in fact chosen either from the nobles themselves or from the clergy, whom the close union of secular and ecclesiastical supremacy in the friendship of the king and Lanfranc kept in their places, and from whose number the notoriously unworthy were for the most part excluded. Under William Rufus begin the complaints of unworthy favourites and ignoble ministers, and at the very same time the difficulties with the clergy, and the revolutionary attempts of the great vassals. Both the clergy, so far as Anselm represented them, and the vassals, aimed at a position to which, on the analogy of other countries, they felt themselves entitled, although they had never yet possessed it : the king's only possible agents in opposing their attempts were the ministers whom he had chosen, and whom gratitude and community of interest attached to him and his policy. If these men did not content themselves with hindering the aggrandisements of the nobles and clergy, but actually tried to drive them from the vantage-ground which in the exigencies of the Conquest had been accorded to them, there is nothing surprising in the fact that they were even more obnoxious to their opponents than was the king himself.

For to the difficulties which the very existence of the Norman feudatories, with their notions of race and of French feudalism, brought to the royal power, must be added certain weak points in the position of the crown itself. With the life of William I. ceased the unity of Norman feeling in England. Almost immediately on the accession of William Rufus the question of succession emerged, and with it division. Robert of Normandy had his adherents if he had had the will or energy to use them. Stephen of Aumale was the favourite of another, and that a very powerful, section of the barons. On the death of William Rufus the claims of Robert were asserted, and so far maintained as to compel Henry to enter into an alliance with the subject race. On Henry's death followed the divisions between the parties of Stephen of Blois and Matilda, and later on between the Norman and Angevin parties among Matilda's adherents. In all these divisions the nobles had ranged themselves sometimes on one side, sometimes on the other : they had contracted enmities and reconciled them, formed friendships and broken them : hardly any house had uniformly acted on the same principle, and consequently hardly any had not at some time found itself in opposition to the royal authority.[1] Thus the principle of attachment

(5) The disputes about the succession had shaken the attachment of the nobles to the king

[1] 'Heralds tell us that the shield of the traitorous knight is to be reversed. Had this law of chivalry been observed in Normandy, would not the beautiful stained glass glowing in the rich church windows have looked oddly? the majority of the emblazonments turned upside down, unless a double infidelity authorised Sir Knight to turn his shield right up again.' Palgrave, *Normandy and England*, iv. 256.

to the king had grown weaker and the love of independence stronger : the right of private war and of separate alliances had been exerted if not vindicated, and it was fortunate indeed for the royal power that it had been wielded by strong hands, or England

But they had also divided them among themselves

must have fallen altogether, as it did in Stephen's reign, into chronic anarchy. Fortunately also the internal feuds divided and weakened the nobles themselves and diminished their numbers, so that for Henry of Anjou there was left a not altogether hopeless prospect of consolidating a strong government.

Henry not bound to the Normans or their policy

Henry came to the destructive part of his work with great advantages. He was for the most part untrammeled by Norman traditions and associations. He did not owe his crown to the swords of Norman warriors, but to the support of the clergy given to the indisputable and undisputed claim which had been won for him by Earl Robert of Gloucester, the bastard son of his grandfather, who for all practical purposes was an Englishman. Henry himself was an Angevin, and the interests of his Angevin subjects were never likely to come into dangerous collision with his designs or prospects as king of England.

His struggle with the barons not embittered by personal feeling

The Normans had been indeed the enemies of his father and his paternal house, and but lukewarm supporters of his mother. But if there were few ties of personal friendship or of common natural feeling to be broken before the task of demolishing the rival interest was begun, there were also few incitements to personal hatred such as might embitter the contest or endanger the result. The struggle from the beginning was political rather than personal, and throughout it was rather the power than the estates or the persons of his enemies that Henry laboured to secure.[1] We read

No great forfeitures

during his reign of none of the great and startling confiscations which before the death of Henry I. had fallen on almost every one of the great families sprung from the companions of the Conqueror.[2]

He had at first an easy task in humbling the barons and dismantling the castles

The experience of the anarchy of the last reign had taught the nation generally to wish for a strong government, and the evils of it were so patent and indisputable that the policy of the new king, coinciding as it did for the most part with the provisions of the

[1] There is a very important passage in Ralph de Diceto, 570, too long to transcribe. He states that the partisans of the younger Henry were chiefly those on whom the hand of the father had fallen heavily, ' quia rex pater, regiæ titulos dignitatis ampliare procurans . . . castella patriæ suspecta vel everteret, vel in suam redigeret potestatem, bonorum occupatores quæ suam ad mensam quasi ad fiscum ab antiquo pertinere noscuntur, patrimonio proprio contentos esse debere assereret et etiam cogeret, &c.'

[2] ' Testantur hoc Normannorum proceres, alii capti, alii incarcerati, alii exhæredati in hodiernum diem.' Joh. Salisb. Policr. vi. 18.

treaty by which the crown was secured to him, was acquiesced in at first with very little difficulty. The castles of the smaller tyrants were speedily dismantled,[1] and with them their power of doing mischief was annihilated. It was only on the marches that resisttance was offered, and before the end of the first year of the reign Hugh de Mortimer was brought to submit [2] and William of Aumale deprived of his last stronghold. The Scots restored the northern provinces which had been won in the name of Matilda.[3] England welcomed peace and prepared to accept the reforms which alone could strengthen her internal union and enable her to defend and extend her borders. The king was at liberty to carry on alternately his measures of domestic legislation and his plans of foreign policy. His presence was for several years scarcely required in England, where he had shown both the strength of his hand and the real moderation of his aims.

He was thus enabled to legislate

But the shock which followed the quarrel and death of Thomas Becket gave the signal for the resuscitation of the slumbering elements of discord, and the rebellion of Henry and Richard in 1173 afforded occasion for the outbreak which nothing but the personal abilities of the king and his ministers prevented from becoming a revolution.

The rebellion of 1173 and 1174

It was still, if we may judge of it by the ordinary rules of evidence, far more a political than a personal conflict. Nearly all the great earls both in Normandy and in England were engaged on the side of the princes. Those of Chester, Leicester, Norfolk, Huntingdon, and Ferrers ; the king of Scotland, the great baron of Mowbray, Hamo de Masci, Richard de Morville, and Geoffrey of the Cotentin, representing the remnant of the party of the Conquest : men and families who had never before found themselves on the same side, united against the king.

Union of the great nobles against the king ; in England.

In Normandy the great feudatories of the duchy, many of whom had large estates in England, were bound up both in cause and in

and in Normandy

---

[1] 'Mox castella nova quæ in diebus avi sui nequaquam exstiterant complanari præcepit, præter pauca in locis opportunis sita quæ vel ipse retinere, vel a pacificis ad regni munimen retineri voluit.' W. Newb. ii. 1.

[2] Roger of Gloucester gave in about May ; Hugh de Mortimer on the 7th of July. R. de Monte, ad 1155 ; Gervase, 1378. Henry destroyed Cleobury Castle, the property of Mortimer, and on Roger's death retained the earldom of Hereford in his own hands. In the winter he seized the castles

belonging to the bishop of Winchester. On his return to England in 1157, he took into his hands the castles of Hugh Bigot, and the holdings which had been conferred on William the son of Stephen at Pevensey and in Norfolk by the treaty of Westminster. Brompton, 1038 ; R. de Monte, ad 1157.

[3] In 1157. R. de Monte, ad ann. "Aquilonales Angliæ regiones . . . nomine Matildis dictæ imperatricis et hæredis ejus olim a David Scottorum rege adquisitas." W. Newburgh, ii. 4.

kindred with the English rebels. The count of Meulan was the head of the Norman Beaumonts, as the earl of Leicester was of the English : the counts of Eu and Evreux [1] represented junior branches of the ducal house ; those of Alençon and Ponthieu the heirs of Robert of Bellesme. The earl of Chester held the hereditary viscounties of Bayeux and Avranches. All these were marshalled against king Henry. Arnulf, bishop and count of Lisieux, played in Normandy the same double game that his fellow count bishop Hugh of Puiset was doing in England. William of Aumale, who like Hugh of Puiset was closely connected with the house of Champagne, and had to revenge the loss of his almost regal power north of the Humber, after a mock defence yielded his whole continental possessions to the insurgents.[2]

Unfaithful vassals in Normandy

The king had a party of his own relations and a few nobles,

On Henry's side were the earls of Cornwall, Warren, Gloucester,[3] and Arundel, all closely connected with him by birth or marriage, and the earl of Essex, William de Mandeville, whose tie was that of simple honour and gratitude. Strongbow earl of Striguil,[4] the earls of Salisbury, Warwick, and Northampton were on the same side ; but Strongbow's chief interest now was in Ireland, and the others were, either in possessions or in character, insignificant. The strength of the royal party consisted first of those who had risen to importance as the ministers of Henry's reforms, and secondly of the people, who had benefited by them ; Ranulf Glanvill and Richard de Lucy at the head of the freemen of the country, supported by the Stutevilles, the Umfravilles, and others who had become more thoroughly English than the greater barons.

but its strength lay in the ministers and people

The whole of the bishops both in Normandy and in England remained loyal ; only Hugh [5] and Arnulf tried to be on both sides at once.

The bishops were faithful

The sources of disaffection in Aquitaine and Poictou were of the same sort as those in Normandy and England, but in those countries the cause owed, as in Brittany, somewhat of its character to the influences of nationality and to the personal popularity of the princes.

[1] The right of garrisoning the baronial castles was a chief prerogative of the dukes of Normandy, and a source of constant soreness with the great vassals. In 1161 Henry seized the castles of the count of Meulan and other Norman barons; in 1166 those of the counts of Ponthieu and Séez; those of the Lusignans in 1165 ; those of the Leonois in 1171. In the same year he doubled the revenues of the duchy of Normandy by resuming lands which had been detained since the death of Henry I. All the nobles who suffered this treatment are found in arms against Henry. Cf. R. de Monte, 1159, 1161, 1164, 1166.

[2] R. de Diceto, 571.

[3] Yet even the earl of Gloucester was suspected both now and in 1183, and his son-in-law, the earl of Clare. R. de Dic. 578.

[4] Strongbow was, however, present with Henry in France. R. de Dic. 572.

[5] R. de Dic. 573.

What pretexts were alleged by the barons as the cloak of the real causes of discontent does not appear.[1] In spite of the strength of their numbers and mass, and in spite of the real unity of their interest, they had no organisation, they had no bill of grievances, no head and no watchword. The whole rising bears the character of a simple reaction against the pressure of strong government; a reaction the opportunity of which was so obvious as to strike all alike, and to call even without concert all the subject forces into motion; but the only definite purpose of which was to create a confusion out of which the strongest hand might pluck advantage. The odds were apparently dead against the king. The rebels could hardly have calculated, considering the immense extent of the area of disaffection, the importance of the leaders, the alliance of the kings of France and Scotland, and the open adherence of Queen Eleanor and her sons, on a result which would strengthen the royal power and exalt beyond precedent the personal importance of Henry. *The rebels had no common cause*

The whole rebellion was crushed in a few months, and so thoroughly that the good fortune of the king seemed to his contemporaries more astonishing than even his skill and energy. The king of Scotland, the earls of Chester and Leicester were prisoners, the earls Ferrers and Bigot and Mowbray vying with one another, in haste to surrender, Henry found himself in firmer possession of the strongholds of the country than he had been even in 1156.[2] *The rebellion speedily crushed* *Henry's position strengthened*

It is difficult to say to what the barons owed their immunity from punishment, if it were not the certainty that it was safer to humble than to destroy them; safest of all, while disarming the system that upheld them[3] to win them by moderation, kindness, and confidence.[4] *He abstains from severe punishment;*

In the year 1176 the king took into his own hands all the castles of England and Normandy;[5] he did not even except the castle of

---

[1] Sir Francis Palgrave says of the rising of the Norman barons against Robert in 1087, 'Could the barons have patronised a chronicler of their own, this continued turbulence might have been described as a patriotic struggle to regain their lawful independence. Under William, however, they had really sustained no grievance except the necessity of submitting to the law.' *Normandy and England*, iv. 25. The same may be said almost exactly of this rebellion. Compare also the condition of Normandy under Robert (ib. 231) with that of England under Stephen.

[2] ' Sic in brevi pene rebelles omnes obtinuit, ut longe fortius quam prius ex eo quo infirmari debuit, confirmaretur in regno.' Dialogus de Scacc. p. 38.

[3] He immediately destroyed the castles of the rebels. R. de Dic. 585.

[4] Gir. Camb. De Inst. Pr. ll. 3. 'Inter ipsos triumphales eventus summam clementiam . . . conservavit.' William of Newburgh has a chapter on this, full as usual of good sense, ii. 38, ' Comprehensis insuper hostibus tam enormis sæculi incentoribus inaudita pepercit misericordia, ut eorum pauci rerum suarum, nulli vero status sui vel corporum dispendia sustinerent.' Dialogus, p. 38.

[5] R. de Diceto, 594. Cf. 600.

Ongar, which belonged to the faithful Richard de Lucy. Those of the earls of Chester, Leicester, and Norfolk, with those of Roger Mowbray, he dismantled. But early in the following year he restored the offending earls to their estates, the castles excepted, of which two only belonging to the earl of Leicester and one of the earl of Chester's remained standing.

That the policy of disarmament might not be evaded, the precautions of law were superadded. The justices *in itinere* were instructed in 1176 to take cognisance of the warderships of all the castles that were suffered to stand, and to enforce the complete demolition of the condemned ones. At the Council of Geddington in 1177, the custodians of all the Northern castles were removed, and from this time the maintenance of the royal grasp on these strongholds was regarded as a distinct object of policy. Gradually all the offenders were restored to their territories, but the custody of the castles was withheld. The visitation of the castellanships was made a regular article of the commission of the judges, and the governors were frequently changed, so as to vest the posts gradually and entirely in the hands of the king's officers. The result was that England enjoyed internal peace for the remainder of the reign, and when in 1183 the rebellion of the princes threatened abroad to renew the terrible scenes of 1174, the simple measure of securing the persons of the suspected earls was sufficient, and was regarded as more than sufficient, to guarantee the tranquillity of the kingdom.

Less stirring in incident but far more important in their effects on the life of the nation were the measures by which Henry built up the civil portions of his design of consolidation. They do not occupy the same space in the pages of the historians, and have yet to be investigated with the whole apparatus of archæological research : for they lie for the most part within the unpopular region of legal antiquities. But the most superficial view of the politics of the age would be not merely imperfect, but glaringly false, without some attempt to describe them.

In this respect as well as in the former Henry came to the crown with great advantages : he succeeded to the policy of the Conqueror and Henry I., and inherited the wisest and most faithful servants of the latter. It was in his favour also that, following on a period of anarchy, his reforms were not restricted to a simple restitution of the past, but with the restoration of government he might almost at will develop and extend its expedients. His general policy seems to have been a thorough development, in the direction of national life and unity, of the principles which had appeared in germ in the selfish policy of his predecessors.

It is, I think, strictly true to say that the actual alteration of the institutions of the country which took place at the Conquest has been *Overstatement of the effects of the Conquest. Two views of it* generally as much overstated on the one side as underrated on the other. One school of historical writers sees in the Norman policy very little more than a crystallisation of a process which was going on rapidly in the same direction during the last century of Anglo-Saxon rule ; the other regards it as a complete subversion of both persons and institutions. I believe the truth to be that the plan of *A third view* the Conqueror was simply to dovetail a feudal superstructure into the fundamental framework of the Anglo-Saxon polity.

That there was nothing radically inconsistent in the two systems *The feudal and allodial systems* is historically clear ; both sprang from the same home in the Teutonic forests. The allodial or Saxon system was that of the Germans at home ; the feudal or Frank system was their policy as settlers and conquerors.[1] William came with a band of feudal nobles to a free people ; his nobles might continue to be feudal and his people might continue to be free.

In the Anglo-Saxon system the strength of the fabric was, as I *Comparison of the two* have said before, in the lower ranges of the organism. The cohesion was weakest as the pyramid should have risen to an apex. In the feudal system the cohesion was the strongest above ; the principle of unity was fidelity to the superior, not the maintenance of the distinct freedom of the individual by voluntary association. At the foundation of the former was liberty, at that of the latter serfdom. The common medium was land, the possession of which was in the allodial system the proof of freedom, in the feudal the occasion of service. The feudal system was the exponent of the views of the rulers, the allodial of those of the nation.

To William the Conqueror, as indeed probably to the later Anglo-Saxon kings, the feudal system was doubtless the model system of government : to William it was the only one experimentally known. But it did not follow that it was to be forced in all its details on an unwilling people. He intended to be king of England, the king of the nation as well as the conqueror of the crown ; and whatever were the designs of William Rufus and Henry I., Henry II. followed in the steps of his greater ancestor. Why could not a system be devised which should unite the strength and unity of the higher institutions of feudalism with the strength and unity of the lower institutions of the ancient system ? True the principle of allodial tenure was to be extinguished : *William the Conqueror's treatment of feudalism*

---

[1] I do not mean by this remark to ignore the mixture of Roman usages in the feudal customs. The *beneficiary* principle, from which most of the peculiarities of feudalism rise, owed its origin to the German system of the ' gesiths ' of the princes, but its details and applications grew up after the conquerors had come within the influence of the civil law. Cf. Palgrave, *Commonwealth*, i. 77, 495, &c., who goes even further in ascribing it to the Roman law.

this had been done in a great measure before the Conquest, but the institutions of the system might be retained. The feudal tenure was to be universally enforced, but feudal jurisprudence was not inseparable from it. In Normandy itself the lower organisation of the feudal theory had never been carried into details or actually displaced the original institutions of the subject population.[1]

How to manage the baronage

Was it possible to raise up a great feudal nobility that would be all-powerful in dependence on and in defence of the crown, but unwieldy and unmanageable if an attempt should be be made to use it against the sovereign ? Would it be possible to maintain the characteristic institutions of the English nation in integrity for all purposes of peace, justice, and security ?

William creates a new nobility

By the forfeitures of the great Saxon earldoms in 1066 and 1070, William was enabled at once to secure the former object. By the distribution of their estates and dignities he created a new nobility on the ruins of the old, which would be collectively strong, but would have as its sole principle of union the maintenance of that central power from which it had received its existence. The same

He creates a new administrative system

event, by removing the cumbersome superstructure of the Anglo-Saxon system, enabled him to substitute for the ealdorman and sheriff ministers subject immediately to himself, and so to retain in his own hands the administration of justice and the sinews of war, the national revenue and the national militia. But could such a

Partial success of his plan

constitution be lasting ? The Norman kings tried the experiment and with partial success. They succeded in creating a feudal nobility, but not so far as to give the institution that unity and national spirit in which only it could become consolidated with the mass of the state. It was not until the Norman nobility was thoroughly humbled and disabled that internal peace was secured

Complete success of Henry II.'s

under the strong hand of Henry II. The same strong hand and active versatile mind must be traced in the administrative changes which at last brought the whole system of the country, judicial, military, and fiscal, under the control of the central government.

The Conqueror retained many of the Anglo-Saxon institutions

William the Conqueror retained in great measure both the laws and the judicial system of the earlier kings. He rather enforced than relaxed the observance of the frankpledge,[2] and the authority of the hundred and shire mote : trial by compurgation, the ordeal and the wergild. Merchenalage, Danelage, and Westseaxnalage still continued in their diversity ; the few Norman legal customs which he introduced were for the Normans only. But the sheriff ceased to be even in theory the elected president of the shiremote, and became

[1] Cf. Palgrave, *Commonwealth*, i. 549.
201, and *Normandy and England*, iii. 600, &c.

[2] Cf. Palgrave, *Commonwealth*, i.

the vicecount, as his superior the ealdorman had passed through the intermediate stage of earlship into the Norman count. The change in this point was indeed rather in name than in reality, for the sheriff had as well as the ealdorman become a royal officer long before the Conquest.[1] But the theory still was that he was an elective one, and some form of acceptance in the folkmote may have preserved the tradition of a time when it actually was so. But although the name of vicecomes now becomes the equivalent of scyrgerefa,[2] it signifies no real dependence on or derivation of authority from the earl. He was the king's representative, judicial, fiscal, and military, in the shire. The earl has his third penny, but the authority rests with the sheriff : the earl may be sheriff himself, but he administers the shire as sheriff, not as earl. So the magistrate of the hundred becomes a bailiff ; the court of the hundred with its pleas and profits is granted away to the feudal castellan ;[3] the view of frankpledge is severed from the sheriff's tourn and leet and made one of the rights of the feudal manor.

The retention of this lower machinery involved the retention of the ancient process of jurisdiction. In this, at least in its subordinate arrangements, the Conquest produced little change except in the substitution of Norman for English names and persons. But the position of the Norman baron in the office of sheriff differed from that of the Anglo-Saxon thane. The latter had his sak and sok, tol and them, outfangtheof, and infangtheof, and to these the Norman gladly put in the claim of succession : but the Norman had, besides, his barony in Normandy, which he governed by strict Norman law, to the process of which, as giving more power to himself, he naturally inclined to assimilate that of the English courts in which he held either a personal or a ministerial presidency. The office of sheriff was in many cases hereditary, and in almost all was vested in some important feudal noble.

There were thus co-existing in the country three distinct systems of lower jurisdiction, exclusive of the ecclesiastical courts. I. The ancient courts of the hundred and the shire, popular in origin and process and coeval probably with Anglo-Saxon civilisation ; presided over by magistrates whose election was claimed by the suitors, and which, although the claim was obsolete, were distinguished by the fact, and perhaps in some legal particulars, from those tribunals in which the king was recognised as the sole fountain of justice. II. There were secondly the jurisdictions of the ancient franchises, exercised by the lords who had succeeded to the estates whose ancient

Marginal notes:
The spirit of his changes

The sheriff in theory a popular, in fact a royal officer

Change of names

Lower courts and their process retained

Introduction of Norman processes

Three systems of co-ordinate jurisdictions

---

[1] Palgrave, *Commonwealth*, i. 128.
[2] On the relation between the earl and the sheriff, and the derivation of the word 'vicecomes,' see Madox's note on the Dialogus, p. 31.
[3] *Dialogus de Scaccario*, p. 42.

owners had possessed sak and sok. III. Thirdly there were the strictly feudal courts of the manors, organised by the new nobility of the Conquest.

Difficulty of obtaining and enforcing justice

The joint existence of these systems was a cause of perplexity to justice, for not only were their proper provinces and matters of litigation as yet far from being accurately divided, but their very existence afforded a basis for aggression, and a court which was intended as a resource in times of peace for civil disputes might easily, and did in the reign of Stephen, come in troublous times to be used for the purposes of oppression and exaction. That the persons who exercised these several jurisdictions were in many cases the same, added an element of uncertainty to the attainment of justice and a temptation to indiscriminate tyranny.

The means of obtaining equal and uniform justice

The natural and proper method of diminishing the evil was to retain in the popular courts as much as possible of the popular process, to limit the exercise of the old franchises,[1] and to hinder the extension of the new ones, regulating the whole by the appointment of superior judges and avoiding the nomination of those persons as sheriffs whose feudal position was such as to make it likely that they would import into their ministerial jurisdictions the principles they exercised in their feudal demesnes, to the detriment of justice and the furtherance of selfish aims.[2]

Henry II. as a legislator

To Henry II. we owe the framework of a uniform and equal judicial system, and a general and authoritative enunciation of the principles of the common law.

His judicial reforms I. Itinerant justices

There is no occasion to look for a precedent for the institution of itinerant justices in the missi dominici of Charles the Great, or in the measures of Lewis the Fat. The theory of a travelling

---

[1] On the limitations of the franchises, see Palgrave, *Commonwealth*, i. 211, &c.

[2] This preference of novi homines for offices of trust, and discarding of the great feudatories who had shown themselves unworthy of it, is a point on which Ralph Niger exaggerates greatly: ' Servos, spurios, caligatos, cubili, mensæ, regno præfecit, et ex iis quæstores, prætores, proconsules, tribunos, municipes, forestarios super provincias constituit.' By the word *spurios* Geoffrey is possibly referred to: the rest is false. The families from which Lucy, Glanville, and the other faithful ministers of Henry sprang, were equal in all but wealth to those of the great earls. Yet even Ordericus Vitalis speaks of the Bassets as upstarts, although the noblest of the Normans could hardly boast of a pedigree a century old. There was a great pride of race among them, but in their relations with one another wealth and power were the only real differences. Ralph continues, ' Illustres ignominiis oneratos, sed cæteris rebus vacuos, patrimoniis omnino privavit, vel subdole portionibus detractis decrustando sensim adnihilavit.' A punishment in most cases richly deserved, but by no means really inflicted. 'Ex cubiculariis et aulæ nugatoribus episcopos, abbates, factos auctoritate propria ad officium apparitorum revocavit, et quem præsulem crearat ex præside, in præsidatum recreavit ex præsule.' A statement, with the exception of his son Geoffrey, altogether false. R. Niger, ed. Anstruther, p. 167.

tribunal had been familiarised to the English by the judicial eyres of the Anglo-Saxon kings and by the three annual placita of the Conqueror. Nor was it merely the highest remedial jurisdiction in the person or court of the sovereign that had thus brought justice within reach of each region of the kingdom. Special commissions had been frequently issued for particular purposes.[1] The barons of the exchequer were also the judges of the king's court, and it might seem a simple step to add to the assessment of tallages, which was the object of their fiscal journeys, a portion of the judicial work which would otherwise come before them in the supreme court. Much obscurity hangs over the subject. It is certain that there were judicial eyres[2] early in the twelfth century, but the functions and exact status of the judges cannot be defined. We can only guess that they were the officers of the king's court, and that their functions were limited as much by the demand for their services as by the terms of their commission. Most suits must have been decided in the county courts before the sheriffs ; in some cases there seem to be traces of the establishment of provincial judges superior to the sheriffs :[3] but further litigation must have been expensive, laborious, and dilatory. We do not even know at what period the more important pleas of the crown were withdrawn from the jurisdiction of the sheriff, but as it was not later than the reign of Henry I. we may safely ascribe to him the mission of occasional judges who were superior to the sheriffs, and whose jurisdiction was to review both the judicial and fiscal proceedings of the shire. The thorough organisation of the details of this institution was one of the great works of his grandson.

Marginal notes:

Judicial eyres no novelty

Fiscal eyres

Early judicial eyres

The county courts

Henry I. employed justices in itinere

Henry II. perfected the system

---

[1] The famous assize of Huncote in 1124 must have been more than this : 'Thes ilces geares æfter S. Andreas messe toforen Christes messe held Raulf Basset and thes kinges thæines gewitene mot on Lethecæstre scire at Hunde-hoge and ahengen thær swa fela thefas swa næfre ær ne wæron.' Chr. Sax. ad ann. 1124.

[2] The languago of John of Salisbury, Policrat. v. 15, is obscure. ' Quæ vero de præsidibus aliisque judicibus dicta sunt, debent et apud proconsules, quos nostrates vulgariter dicunt justitias esse errantes, obtinere.' It may refer either to the sheriffs or to the fiscal journeys of the officers of the exchequer, as he goes on to charge them with extortion, This book was written between 1159 and 1162, too early, therefore, to refer to any of Henry's reformed institutions, unless we suppose it to have been re-written

at a latter period. William Fitz-Stephen mentions the justitiarii itinerantes as being at Dunstable before 1163. S. T. C. i. 214. Simon Fitz-Peter, who was the judge on that occasion, was the sheriff of Bedfordshire. Roger Pontign., S. T. C. i. 114. Cf. Grim, S. T. C. i. 23. Cf. R. de Dic. 536. Const. Clar.

[3] On this point the opinions of legal antiquaries give a uniform negative, but it is difficult to see what was the position of William Espec and Eustace FitzJohn (who were not itinerant judges but great resident barons and castellans), in Yorkshire, in the Pipe Roll of 31 Hen. I., if it were not of this sort : nor the meaning of the charter of the Empress Matilda, by which she makes Geoffrey de Mandeville not only sheriff but chief justice in Essex. Dugd. Baronage, i. 202.

The year 1166 must be fixed upon as the date, and the Assize of Clarendon as the act, which mark the first distinct appearance of this important reform.[1] The text of the assize was published first by Sir Francis Palgrave in the second volume of his history of the English Commonwealth,[2] from the royal manuscript of Hoveden, and is reprinted in a revised form in the appendix to this preface in the Rolls Series. I must be allowed to state my reasons for assigning it to the year 1166.

I. In the year 1176 Henry at a council at Northampton caused to be recorded and amended an assize called the Assize of Clarendon ; and this revised edition as given in the present chronicle agrees in so many particulars with the document in question that there can be no doubt that it was the one referred to.

II. In the year 1170[3] Henry made a visitation, by means of itinerant barons, of all the counties in England for the purpose of inquiry into the conduct of the sheriffs ; one of the articles of their commission was to examine into the disposition of the goods of felons and fugitives under the Assize of Clarendon. This assize was then of earlier date than 1170.

III. The assize itself contains in its last chapter a prohibition against the reception or protection of the heretics condemned in the Council of Oxford. This council was held in the king's presence in the January or February of 1166.[4]

IV. But at the beginning of Lent 1166 (March 3),[5] Henry left

---

[1] Various traces of earlier legislative acts in the same direction may be found in the loose language of the historians, especially William of Newburgh ; and, as I shall show below, Henry seems to have restored the eyres of the judges, as practised in his grandfather's time, as soon as he began to reign. The following notice, as early as 1160, refers only to his continental dominions, but something of the same kind may have been done in England. ' Anno 1160, rex Anglorum Henricus ad Natale Domini fuit apud Falesiam, et leges instituit ut nullus decanus aliquam personam accusaret sine testimonio vicinorum circum manentium qui bonæ vitæ fama laudabiles haberentur. De causis similiter quorum libet ventilandis instituit ut cum judices singularum provinciarum singulis mensibus ad minus simul convenirent, sine testimonio vicinorum nihil judicarent, injuriam nemini facerent, præjudicium non irrogarent, pacem tenerent, latrones cunctos statim punirent, quæque quiete tenerent ecclesiæ sua jura possiderent.' R. de Monte, Bouquet, xiii. 304. This looks very like an instruction to the county court.

[2] ii. clxviii.–clxxi.

[3] Gervase, 1410. S. T. C. ii. 262.

[4] R. de Diceto, 539. ' Quidam pravi dogmatis disseminatores tracti sunt in judicium apud Oxeneford, præsente rege præsentibus et episcopis. Quos a fide nostra devios et in examine superatos facies cauteriata notabiles cunctis exposuit expulsos a regno. Rex Angliæ transfretavit circa initium Quadragesimæ.' If this council be the same as that described by William of Newburgh, as held about 1160 or 1161 (and they appear to be the same) the fact that the king was present at it proves that he or his editor has given a wrong date. Henry was not in England from 1158 to 1163.

[5] R. de Dic., 539. Rot. Pip. A°. 12. Hamtona. See Madox's note on the Dialogus, p. 19.

England, and did not return until 1170, when he immediately issued the commission for the Inquest of Sheriffs.

The assembly at which this assize was enacted must be referred, therefore, to a date between New Year's day and the first day of Lent, 1166.

A Council of Clarendon is mentioned by Edward Grim and by Roger of Pontigny, in which an oath was exacted from the bishops that they would not appeal to the pope. This is very probably the identical council at which the assize was passed, and may be fixed to the year 1166 by Grim's statement, that 'per idem quoque tempus ' the pope wrote to Roger of York a letter, dated at Anagni, April 5, 1166.[1]

Historical notices of the council

For further confirmation of the date, we have recourse to the Pipe Rolls [2] as the only existing records for any indications of the royal movements at the time, and we are not disappointed, for the payments for the conveyance of the king's wine, venison, and harness show that he did in the twelfth year of his reign (therefore between Michaelmas 1165, from which date the roll of the twelfth year began to be made up, and the beginning of Lent) move from London to Oxford, from Oxford to Woodstock, from Woodstock to Clarendon, and from Clarendon or Woodstock to Shoreham, whence it would seem certain that he embarked. The mention of the conveyance to Clarendon of the king's provers, and of the payment for wax and for the delivery of summonses, point unmistakably to the holding of a court of justice at the same place. The mention of the Oxford heretics in the assize, which gives them an importance far from proportionate to the real danger arising from their exertions, is a proof that it must have been drawn up under the immediate pressure of the excitement caused by the council, and before the real insignificance of the heresy had been proved by results.

Evidence of the Pipe Rolls as to a council at Clarendon

That the Assize of Clarendon [3] really marks an important judicial

---

[1] S. T. C. i. 55, 156. Jaffé, 708.

[2] Pipe Roll, 12 Hen. II., WILTS. ' Pro conductu venationis regis de Chepeham ad Wudestoch, et pro conducendo vino regis de Clarendon ad Wudestoch.'

' Et pro conducendo crasso pisce de Lundonia ad Clarendon vi. s. pro Edw. Bl. et Rogero Ostiario xiii. s. iv. d., ad port. summon. et xii. d. pro cera ad summonit. et pro pannis ad opus Henrici filii regis xvi. li. xiii. s. et x. d. ; et pro custamento probatorum et pro conductu illorum ad Clarendon xlviii. s. ; et pro una hugia ad port. hernesium regis ad Shorham et pro ipso hernesio viii. s. et x. d.'

HANTS. ' Et pro vinis regis et ipsis conducendis de Hantona ad Clarendon et ad Wudestoch et ad Sarum et ad Chepeham, &c. In liberatione Eʃcccc quando rex transfretavit in Quadragesima, &c. In passagio regis Scotiæ, Gaufridi filii regis,' &c.

' Pro conduc. sell. et hernes. regis de Wudestoch ad Shoreham xiii. s. et iv. d., et pro feno conducendo ad Wudestoch.'

A reference to the Dialogus de Scaccario, pp. 10, 11, will show that these particulars belong to the holding of a court at Clarendon.

[3] The Assize of Clarendon seems to be identical with the ' arctior assisa

epoch, and is not merely a unique relic of a system which had been
in silent operation for some time, may appear from the following
considerations. In the first place the instructions have a retro-
spective view, and the point to which they look back is the commencement of the king's reign. They are not, as the famous
Constitutions of Clarendon were, an enunciation of 'consuetudines,'
but both in form and substance a new legislative act, and the first
chapter contains directions for an inquest into all cases of murder
and robbery that had occurred, not since the last *iter*, but 'postquam
dominus rex fuit rex.' The Inquest of Sheriffs in 1170,[1] on the
other hand, directs the barons errant to inquire into the receipts of
those officers since the king went abroad, a point of time coinciding
with our supposed date of the Assize of Clarendon,[2] and the
reference of the same inquest, and of the Assize of Northampton in
1176, to this assize, points to the inference that it was a distinctly
recognised measure of reform. The oblivion into which the assize
has fallen among the early historians may easily be accounted for
by the superior importance which the Council of Clarendon of 1164
held in common estimation. We have no real contemporary
historian of the year 1166, and those who wrote a few years later
very naturally may have supposed, as Gervase of Canterbury
certainly did, that the Assize of Clarendon had been enacted in
1164.[3]

The assize contains the instructions for itinerant justices holding
courts in the several shires. A further reference to the Pipe Rolls
at once confirms the supposed date of the assize, and throws light
on the functionaries to whom the execution was entrusted. We find

quam rex propter sceleratos constituit,'
of the Dialogus, p. 46, according to
which the goods of 'fugitives' were
confiscated to the king. See ch. 5
and 18 of the Assize, and the Assize
of Sheriffs, c. 6. It is called 'Regia
constitutio quæ est pro bono pacis.'
Dial. p. 48. It is well to observe that
the chattels of fugitives are accounted
for earlier than 1166 in some instances,
as in Northumberland, Rot. Pip. 10
& 11 Hen. II.; (and cf. Const. Clarendon, xiv., which shows that the confiscation of the goods of felons was
already in use), but that the chattels
of those 'qui perierunt in judicio
aquæ,' 'fugitivorum et eorum qui
perierunt ad aquam,' begin to be accounted for in the rolls of the 12th of
Henry II. The roll of the 15th mentions the Assize of Clarendon by name,
'Idem vicecomes reddit compotum de

catallis fugitivorum et suspensorum
per assisam de Clarendon.' Madox,
Hist. Exch. p. 236. And the Assize
of Northampton is named in exactly
the same terms in the rolls of the
22nd.
¹ Gervase, 1410.
² 'Et de catallis fugitivorum pro
assisa de Clarendune, et de catallis
eorum qui per assisam illam perierunt,'
&c. Gerv. 1411.
³ Gervase at least supposed that
the assize renewed at Northampton in
1176 was the *Constitutions* of Clarendon. 'A.D. 1176, rex Henricus
convocatis regni primoribus apud
Northamptoniam renovavit assisam
de Clarendonia eamque præcepit ob-
servari pro cujus exsecrandis institutis
beatus Thomas martyr Cantuariensis
usque in septennium exulavit.' c. 1433.

that it is from the year 1166 that the regular series of 'Nova Placita et Novæ Conventiones' before the justices in the several counties begins. The earlier rolls contain every year 'nova placita et novæ conventiones,'[1] but these were apparently transacted before the sheriffs, and contain fiscal rather than judicial accounts. They also contain the mention of occasional placita before the justiciar or the justice of the forest. The roll of the 31st Henry I. contains evidence of a nearly complete visitation of the kingdom by Geoffrey Clinton in association with other judges. In twenty-two counties out of the twenty-six whose accounts are recorded, he appears as judge, the persons associated with him being generally men of local as well as official importance. A few notices of a similar kind are found in the earlier rolls of Henry II.[2] In 1156 the constable Henry of Essex made a visitation of most of the southern counties, the chancellor holding pleas with him in Essex and Kent and the great justiciar in Lincolnshire.[3] Between the fifth and ninth years of the reign, William FitzJohn made a similar circuit, probably on forest business, and in the eighth year Richard de Lucy, the justiciar, held pleas in Cumberland, which seem to have been of much importance,

Earlier instances of eyres on the rolls

Eyres of the reign of Henry I.

Earlier eyres of the reign of Henry II.

---

[1] *Nova placita* are the pleas of the year to which the roll belongs. It is therefore only when we find *nova placita* held by the itinerating justices that we can infer that an *iter* was held in that year. Madox, of course, knew this, but in his lists of the itinerant justices he has neglected in the text to mark which judges belonged to previous *iters*, and which to the year in question. I have tried to make these matters clearer in the lists which I have given in the notes, which are taken from the Pipe Rolls themselves. Of these invaluable records there are in print those of the 31st of Henry I., 2, 3, and 4 Hen. II., 1 Rich. I., and 3 John; besides which the whole series of Northumberland accounts are published by Mr. Hodgson. Mr. Stapleton's wonderful Introductions to the kindred Norman rolls are full of interesting information: and Madox's work contains a mine of details in most elaborate order. Strictly speaking, the 'placita' were the fines inflicted by the judges; the 'conventiones,' the voluntary payments made by the parties to obtain a decision. Dialogus, p. 49.

[2] William of Newburgh refers to Henry II.'s judicial reforms as beginning early in his reign: 'ut legum vigor in Anglia revivisceret, qui sub rege Stephano exstinctus sepultusque videbatur, cura propensiore sategit.' Hist. ii. 1.

[3] In 1156 there are references to *placita*, which may have been held in 1155 or earlier by Henry of Essex in Somerset, Dorset, Devon, Hants, Wilts, and Sussex; by Gregory, the bishop of Chichester, and Ralph Picot in Middlesex, Surrey, Bucks and Beds: by the archbishop of York in Yorkshire, and by the chancellor as in the text. In the following year there are new pleas and conventions, but as no judges are mentioned they were probably held by the sheriffs. In the 6th year there are references to old pleas of the forest held by William FitzJohn in Devon, Somerset, and Hereford; in the 7th, to similar pleas by the same in Hereford and Yorkshire; in the 9th, to new pleas held by Richard de Lucy in Cumberland, he being then great justiciar; and by Alan de Nevill (of the forest) in Oxfordshire. In the 10th, there are no new pleas or conventions recorded. In the 11th, the references are only to the old pleas of William FitzJohn and Richard de Lucy.

K

probably as being the first legal settlement of the county after its restoration by the Scots.

Regular eyres from 1166
It is from the year 1166 that these placita are annual and general, the judges being, as in the earlier visitations, the chief officers of the court. In that year and the following the pleas in all the counties are held before Richard de Lucy, associated in seventeen out of eighteen with Geoffrey de Mandeville.[1] In 1168 a commission of four barons of the exchequer [2] was substituted for the justiciar and his companion. These visited, jointly or separately, the whole of England, and both assessed the aid for the marriage of the king's daughter, and heard pleas. The same judges repeated their visitation in 1169,[3] 1170,[4] and 1171. In the eighteenth year (1172) it does not appear whether the scutage for Ireland was levied by the sheriffs or by the justices, nor before whom the pleas were held ; but in the nineteenth year [5] a tallage on the demesne was assessed by six companies of the barons, and the principle of the circuits was for the first time introduced. The following year the business was transacted by the sheriffs in association with a clerk, and under the writ of the justiciar. It does not appear quite certainly whether these were judicial or merely fiscal *iters*.[6] In the 21st year the whole kingdom was visited by four of the judges, Ranulf Glanvill and Hugh de Cressi taking the north and east, William de Lanvallei and Thomas Basset the south and west.[7]

It would seem that these annual visitations of the justices proved

Justices *in itinere*, judicial and fiscal

Eyres of the justices

---

[1] Madox, *History of the Exchequer* (ed. 1711). Geoffrey de Mandeville died Oct. 21, 1167. Foss, *Judges*, i. 274. But as the fiscal year ended at Michaelmas he may have finished his eyre ; but the pleas recorded are in most cases (if not all) the arrears of 1166.

[2] A°. 14 Hen. II. Richard archdeacon of Poictiers, Wido dean of Waltham, Reginald Warenne, and William Basset held pleas and collected the aid *pur fille marier* in all the south and midland counties. Richard de Lucy held pleas in Yorkshire, Northumberland, and Cumberland ; and in Kent Henry FitzGerold was joined with the commission. These are criminal pleas as well as fiscal.

[3] A°. 15 Hen. II. The same four barons, with John Cumin and Gervase de Cornhill, in Dorset, Somerset, Devon, and Wilts.

[4] The inquest on the sheriffs of 1170 was not held by members of the

Curia Regis, but by a special commission of laymen and ecclesiastics ; they are, however, called *barones errantes*. Gervase, 1409.

[5] A°. 19. 1. In the Eastern counties, Seffrid the archdeacon, Wimar the chaplain, Adam de Gernemue, and Robert Mantell.

2. In Wessex, Wido the dean, Hugh de Bocland, Richard Wilton, Will. Ruffus.

3. In Kent, Bucks, and Beds, Richard the archdeacon, Reginald Warenne, and Nicolas the chaplain.

4. In West Mercia (Glouc., Heref., &c.), John Cumin, Walter Map, and Turstin FitzSimon.

5. East Mercia (Northants, Notts, &c.), William Basset, John Malduit, and John of Dover, clerk.

6. In Surrey and the home district, Reg. Warenne and Gervase de Cornhill.

[6] The list is different for each county, and is given in Madox, p. 84.

[7] See Madox, p. 85.

ineffectual to check the oppressions and exactions of the sheriffs. Inquests on the sheriffs in 1170 The judges were unable in the absence of the king, and in the disturbed state of public feeling, to put any check on the sheriffs, supported as they were by local influence and prescriptive authority. The complaints of the people became so loud that, in a great council held at London shortly after Easter 1170, the king sent a strong commission of barons errant, chosen from the clergy and nobles, and unconnected with the Exchequer or the Curia, to examine into the conduct of the sheriffs. The instructions for this inquiry, which have been several times referred to above, are given by Gervase in his chronicle.[1] They involve a strict scrutiny into the accounts and legal proceedings of the counties since the king's departure from England, and into the judgments passed under the Assize of Clarendon. The work was speedily completed : the commissioners brought in their returns on June 14,[2] in time for the coronation of the young king. Gervase does not state the result of the inquiry, but we find from our author that the king removed all the sheriffs and bailiffs from their offices. The Pipe Rolls furnish us with one Sheriffs fined and displaced or two cases of heavy fines imposed on the sheriffs under this inquest.[3] Henry, however, as we learn, did subsequently restore several of them, and they revenged themselves on the people by acting more tyrannically than ever.[4]

It is by looking carefully through the lists of the sheriffs who Legal officers substituted for the feudal magnates, in the office of sheriff went out of office and came into it in 1170 that we get the clearest notion of what was done.[5] It must be remembered that almost all the hereditary sheriffdoms had been abolished before this time ; probably before the 31st of Henry I., when we find the administration of large clusters of counties in the hands of a few great officers of state. Under Henry II., however, the several counties or pairs of counties had recovered their several sheriffs, and these officers were in most cases local magnates, and apparently held the position for life. A very clean sweep was made of these in 1170, and it is

[1] Gervase, 1409. Robert de Monte, ad 1170, and our author, R. S. ed. vol. i. p. 5. Henry seems to have contemplated a similar measure in Normandy in 1162. He collected a parliament at Rouen, ' querimoniam faciens de episcopis et eorum ministris et vicecomitibus suis.' R. de Monte, ad 1162. The oaths to be taken by the juries are given in S. T. C. ii. 262.

[2] Gervase, 1411. Gervase seems to think that this inquest was made merely to frighten the nobles and sheriffs into taking the oath to the young king, ' et sic timore culparum deposito omnes ad propria redierunt.'

[3] The case given in Madox is that of William Basset, who made a fine of 100 marks, ' pro fine quem fecit cum rege de jurata facta super eum de communi Inquisitione vicecomitum Angliæ per Walterum de Insula et Eustatium filium Stephani.' Pipe Rolls of 19 and 20 of Hen. II., Madox, p. 96. He must also have been dismissed from the sheriffalty.

[4] See our Chronicle, R. S. ed. i. p. 5.

[5] The following list will show this, the first column containing the names

K 2

most important to observe that, in the place of these unjust stewards, Henry substituted members of the Curia Regis and Exchequer, a

of the sheriffs who went out of office in the 16th year, the second those who continued, and the third those who were put in in the 16th.

—	Went out	Stayed in	Came in
Berks . .	Adam de Catmer .	. . . .	Hugh de Bocland
Oxon . .	Adam de Catmer .	. . . .	Alard Banastre
Beds and Bucks	Hugh de Leya and William FitzRichard	. . . .	David the archdeacon and William Fitz-Richard
Cambridge and Hunts	Philip de Daventry	. . . .	Ebrard de Beach and Waring de Bassing-bourn
Cumberland	. . . .	Robert FitzTroit .	
Derby and Notts	Robert FitzRalph	. . . .	William FitzRalph
Devon and Cornwall	. . . .	Robert FitzBernard	
Dorset and Somerset	Robert de Puckerell	. . . .	Alured de Lincoln
Essex and Herts	Nicolas, clerk, and Stephen de Beauchamp	. . . .	Robert Mantell
Hants . .	Richard FitzTurstin	. . . .	Hugh de Gundeville
Leicester & Warwick	William Basset .	. . . .	Bertram de Verdun
Lincoln .	Philip de Kyme .	. . . .	Walter de Grimsby
London and Middlesex	R. FitzBerengar and Will. Fitz Isabell	. . . .	John Bienvenutte and Baldwin clericus
Northumberland	William de Vesci .	. . . .	Roger Stuteville
Norfolk and Suffolk	Ogier dapifer .	. . . .	B. Glanvill, Wimar the chaplain, and Will. Bardulf
Northants .	Simon FitzPeter .	. . . .	Robert FitzSawin
Rutland .	. . . .	Richard Humet	
Salop . .	Geoffrey de Vere .	. . . .	Will. clericus
Stafford .	. . . .	Hervey Stratton	
Surrey .	. . . .	Gervase de Cornhill	
Sussex .	Roger Hai .	. . . .	Reginald Warren
Wilts . .	. . . .	Richard de Wilton	
Worcester .	William de Beauchamp	. . . .	Hugo Puhier
Lancashire .	W. de Vesci	. . . .	Roger de Herleberga
Gloucester .	. . . .	Gilb. Pipard	
Hereford .	William de Beauchamp	. . . .	Walter clericus
Yorkshire .	Ranulf Glanvill .	. . . .	Robert de Stuteville

Of those who were dismissed, Simon FitzPeter, Ogier, and Philip of Daventry had occupied inferior situations in the Curia Regis; William Basset had been and afterwards was a justice, but on this occasion was deposed and fined. Of the others (except Glanvill, to whom Robert de

measure which had the direct effect of placing the county courts under the royal influence and securing their administration by judges acquainted with the law. The itinerant judges who served between 1170 and 1176 were thus members of the same body which supplied the sheriffs, and all ought to have proceeded smoothly. The disturbed and disorganised condition of the country consequent on the rebellion and its suppression will account for the necessity of changes. The county courts are brought into better order

The year 1176, the 22nd of Henry II., is marked by a further step. In the great Council of Northampton, held January 25,[1] it was determined to add very considerably to the staff of the itinerating courts, and to adopt the principle of subdivision which had been found so useful in the collection of the tallage in 1173. The kingdom was accordingly divided into six circuits, to each of which were assigned three judges.[2] Most of these eighteen judges were at the same time sheriffs and barons of the Exchequer, representatives of the system which had been enforced in 1170. It is in reference to them that the title Justitiæ Itinerantes[3] first appears in the Pipe Rolls, although it was earlier given to the judges in eyre under the Assize of Clarendon. For their direction, a new recension of that statute was passed, and from this epoch the institution of itinerant justices is stated in the law books to date.[4] Assize of Northampton in 1176 / Regulation of the circuits of the justices

Notwithstanding the importance given to the Assize of Northampton, it is curious that the arrangement remained in force for only two years. The itinerant justices went their circuits in 1176 and apparently 1177, unless indeed it may have been that their visitation fell partly in the 22nd and partly in the 23rd year[5] of the reign, and Eyres under the Assize of Northampton

Stuteville was probably a deputy) no more is heard. Of the second column, only FitzTroit and Stratton were not members of the king's household ; of the third, sixteen out of the whole were employed at the Exchequer. Compare Foss's *Judges* and Fuller's *Worthies, passim.* In the cases of Worcester, Salop, and Hereford, the persons in the third column are the acting substitutes for the sheriffs.

[1] R. de Diceto, 588.

[2] 'Igitur post naufragum regni statum pace reformata studuit iterum rex avita tempora renovare, et eligens discretos viros, secuit regnum in sex partes, ut eas electi judices quos errantes vocamus perlustrarent et jura destituta restituerent. Facientes ergo sui copiam in singulis comitatibus, et iis qui se læsos putabant justitiæ plenitudinem exhibentes, pauperum laboribus et sumptibus pepercerunt.' Dialogus de Scaccario, p. 38. The pecuniary fines of these eyres were noted in a roll, which was transcribed into the Great Roll, with the names of the justices at the heading, p. 39.

[3] The name occurs in the Dialogus first in reference to the assessing justices : ' Fiunt interdum per comitatus communes assisæ a justitiis itinerantibus quos deambulatorios vel perlustrantes judices nominamus,' pp. 23, 44. They are called also, p. 36, ' Perambulantes judices.'

[4] The list of judges who actually went on circuit in 1176 will be found in Madox, p. 94, and agrees almost exactly with that given by our author, R. S. ed. vol. i. p. 107. It is in the roll of this year that the judges are first called ' justitiæ itinerantes.'

[5] The 22nd fiscal year would end at Michaelmas 1176. Dial. de Scacc. 37.

so appears on the roll for both years. In the 23rd year, the same judges were employed as barons of the Exchequer in levying an aid, and for this purpose they travelled in different combinations, and made only four circuits.[1]

New changes in 1178

In 1178, the king made inquiry into the proceedings of these judges, and finding, according to our chronicle, 'that the country and the men of the country were greatly oppressed by the multiplicity of the justices, for they were eighteen in number ; by the advice of the wise men of the realm chose five only, two clerks, and three

Reduction of the number of judges

laymen, all members of his private household. These five he ordered to hear all the complaints of the kingdom, and to do right, and that they should not depart from the king's court, but remain there to hear the complaints of the homines, so that if any question should come up amongst them, which could not be brought to an end by them, it should be presented to the royal hearing, and terminated as it should please the king and the wiser men of the kingdom.'[2]

Question as to the force of this act

It is by no means easy to determine the exact force of this measure. It seems impossible to doubt that the eighteen were identical with the judges of the year 1176, and that the intention was to prevent them from sitting in the Curia Regis. If the measure of 1176 really added largely to the number of the judges, and was not merely a rearrangement of their functions, there can be no doubt that the increased number was burdensome, and that the king intended to establish a new tribunal of five, to the exclusion of the rest. Accordingly the measure has been understood with great probability to imply the erection of a bank or bench in the Curia, to which the title of Curia Regis subsequently became restricted, and which is the original of the present Court of King's Bench.

Discarding of some of the old judges

But it seems probable that this act was attended by the deposition of most of the eighteen from their judicial functions altogether, or their relegation to subordinate places in the Exchequer, for the *iters* were served in 1178 and 1179 [2] by eight judges only,

[1] A°. 23. For assessing the aid.—
1. Ralph FitzStephen, Turstin Fitz-Simon, and William Ruffus in all the Western counties.
2. Robert Mantell and Ralph Brit in all the Eastern ones.
3. Roger FitzReinfrid and Gervase de Cornhill in Bucks, Beds, Sussex, and Kent.
4. William FitzRalph, William Basset, and Michael Belet in the North and Midland counties.
A°. 24. Justices.—1. Roger Fitz-Reinfrid, Ralph FitzStephen, Robert Mantell, and William FitzStephen in

all the Western counties.
2. William Basset, Robert de Valli-bus, and Michael Belet in the Northern counties.
[2] R. S. ed. vol. i. p. 207.
[3] A°. 25. The judges itinerant are Ralph FitzStephen, William Fitz-Stephen, Roger FitzReinfrid, and Robert Mantell, William Basset, Robert de Vaux, Michael Belet, and Bertram de Verdun ; the former four in the Eastern, and the latter in the Midland counties. Of these eight, Michael Belet and Robert Mantell were not in the list for 1176.

two of whom were new appointments; whilst on the redistribution of circuits, which was made in 1179 and carried out in 1180, Ranulf Glanvill alone of the eighteen judges of 1176 was reappointed. Many, however, of the itinerants of 1176 subsequently reappear in the transactions of the Exchequer.

The year 1179 is memorable on several grounds.[1] Soon after Easter Richard de Lucy, who had been justiciar since 1167, retired into his monastery at Lesnes,[2] and the king was left with his hands full of legal business. He almost immediately called a great council at Windsor, and in it the following important acts were transacted. The kingdom was rearranged into four new circuits for the eyres of the justices. The place of Richard de Lucy was not immediately supplied, but three bishops were chosen as chief justices, one of whom presided over each of the three southern circuits, in conjunction with one of the king's clerks and three other officers. To the fourth circuit, which included the whole of the north of England, were appointed six judges, one of whom was Ranulf Glanvill, who was probably already designated to the justiciarship; and these six judges of the northern circuit are stated apparently to be the six judges appointed to hear the complaints of the people in the Curia Regis, and answer to the five justices of the bench appointed in 1178, with Glanvill at their head. The business of the eyre was quickly transacted, and although the Council of Windsor was only held about Whitsuntide, the account of the kingdom was brought to the king at Westminster on the 27th of August.

With this act ends the series of measures taken by Henry II.[3] to

Legal measures of 1179

Rearrangement of circuits

Eyre of 1179

---

[1] The passage of Ralph de Diceto on the legal matters of this year deserves most attentive study. It is too long to be given entire, but I will note the principal facts. 1. It was in order to check the selfishness of the sheriffs that the king originally instituted the provincial visitations, 'certis in locis jurisdictiones aliis fidelibus suis in regno commisit.' 2. By-and-by, 'rursus aliquot temporum labente curriculo,' the king tried by what class of judges justice was most faith-iully administered. 'Abbates modo, comites modo, capitaneos modo, domesticos modo, familiarissimos modo, causis audiendis et examinandis præposuit.' Having done this, he determined to employ 'homines . . . qui licet viverent inter homines superintendentes hominibus, aliquid habebant, aliquid sentirent, aliquid auderent plus homine.' 3. In accord-ance with this resolution he appointed

the bishops of Winchester, Ely, and Norwich to be *archijustitiarios*. These ecclesiastics are not to be blamed for following the example of the great Roger of Salisbury. 4. 'Ab episcopis igitur supradictis et a con-judicibus eorundem querelis justitia mediante decisis, reservatis quibusdam ad principis audientiam, regi ratio redditur administrationis vi. kal. Sept. apud Westmonasterium' 5. The writer understands this as authorising bishops to preside in the county courts, *in comitiis*. 6. An investigation of the ecclesiastical courts took place the same year, and the archbishop of Canterbury had to swear that he would keep his hands free from bribes. R. de Dic. 605–607.

[2] He died in July. Gerv. 1456.

[3] For the names of the judges of this *iter* see Benedictus, vol. i. p. 238 (Rolls Series.) It will be seen that only five of the names are those of the judges of

Summary
of the pro-
ceedings of
Henry II.
as to the
eyres of the
judges
secure the administration of justice in the counties.[1] He had withdrawn the jurisdiction from the sheriffs and placed it in the hands of
a travelling court. When this failed he had removed the sheriffs
from their posts and substituted for them members of his own
council. He had further instituted an especial tribunal of itinerant
justices, and divided the kingdom into six circuits. He had superseded this arrangement by a special enactment, in which the judges
were associated with confidential members of the clerical and curial
bodies. From this time we lose sight of his direct agency in this
respect; but the four circuits of the king's judges were established,
the importance of the territorial franchises was broken down, the
character of the sheriff completely subordinated to that of the judge.
By the assize of Richard I. these measures were carried further, the
sheriffs were forbidden to act as justiciars in their own counties, and
by Magna Carta they were restrained from holding pleas of the
crown at all. The itinerant justices were restored by the same act,
but within a few years their visitations became septennial, and they
were gradually and finally superseded by the devolution of their
function on justices of assize.

Ranulf
Glanvill,
justiciar
The appointment of Ranulf Glanvill to the office of justiciar in
1180 probably relieved the king from the necessity of that constant
legislation on judicial matters which marks the previous ten years.
It is another important coincidence that this appointment syn-
chronises so nearly with our first clear indication of the existence of
a limited tribunal erected in the Curia Regis, to which very shortly
the name of Curia Regis became appropriated, and with which the
famous book of Glanvill has so important a connexion.

II. The
origin of
the Curia
Regis
The Curia Regis in its earlier and wider sense was doubtless the
Common Council of the nation, the assembly of feudal tenants of
the king which succeeded to the functions of the Witenagemote, and
which was held three times a year by the Conqueror. But although
this council acted on occasion as a court of justice, its judicial
functions and name were soon shared with that small portion of it
which remained continuously about the king's person. In this restricted sense it consisted of the great officers of the household, the
justiciar, chancellor, treasurer, and barons of the Exchequer, with
such of his clerks as the king might summon, and it probably in-

---

former years, viz. Ranulf Glanvill, of
ann. 15; Gilbert Pipard, of ann. 22
Thomas Basset, of ann. 21; John
Comin, of ann. 15; Michael Belet, of
ann. 24. Mr. Foss adds to these Richard
the treasurer, Ralph Brit, and Nicolas
the chaplain; but these had only acted
as assessors of the tallage in 1177.

See above, p. 134.
[1] Henry's personal share in these
reforms is noticed by the historians:
'Quoties autem judicibus mollius in-
digniusve agentius provincialium
querimoniis pulsabatur, provisionis
regiæ remedium adhibebat.' W. Newb.
ii. 1.

cluded the stewards of the honours and constables of the castles which were in the king's hands, or in demesne. It was on the justiciar and the officers of the Exchequer under him who bear the title of both justices and barons that the principal burden of judicial proceedings fell, and to them, as we have just seen, the commissions of provincial jurisdiction were entrusted.

We have seen that in 1178 Henry substituted a tribunal of five judges for the collective council of the Curia, with the direction, 'Quod illi quinque audirent omnes clamores regni et rectum facerent, et quod a Curia Regis non recederent'; and that this limitation has been very reasonably regarded as the institution of the Curia Regis in its third sense, in which it may be defined as a judicial committee of the king's judicial council, and which is probably the tribunal described by Glanvill as 'justiciarii sedentes in banco.'[1]

Henry substitutes a committee of five

Origin of the court of King's Bench

Previously to 1178 all the members of the Curia Regis seem to have exercised the judicial function in the Curia and in the Exchequer, as well as on the eyres generally as on the eyres, in committees of three or four.[2] Now it would appear that the central jurisdiction was entrusted to a single committee of five. As the six who were appointed in nearly the same words, the following year, to be justices of the Curia Regis, were apparently different persons from these five, with the exception of Glanvill, we may infer that the appointment of this committee was an annual or even a terminal one, and that the judges of the Curia, in this new form, or, as we may call them, the justices of the bench, were a temporary selection from the whole body of judges, who still discharged the offices of itinerant justices and barons of the Exchequer. That the itinerant justices did not lose their places in the Exchequer is clear, from the fact that their names appear in the lists of persons before whom fines were levied in the Curia Regis at a later period.[3]

Question as to the persons employed in the Curia Regis

We have unfortunately no account of further changes in the constitution of the Curia Regis during this reign, nor, when the existing records of that court begin,[4] can we see quite clearly who were the presiding judges. The origin of the bench of Common

Obscurity of the origin of the Three Courts

[1] Glanvill, ii. 6, viii. 1, and xi. 1.

[2] See examples from ann. 21 Hen. II., downwards, in Madox, pp. 64 and 65. The judges of 1176 held *placita curiæ* in quite different combinations from those on which they went their circuits; but the names are the same. The *placita curiæ*, given by Madox, are held in 1175 by William FitzRalph, Bertram de Verdun, and Thomas Basset; in 1176, by William Fitz-Ralph, Bertram de Verdun, and

William Basset; in 1177, by Walter FitzRobert, Hugh de Cressi, and Robert Mantell; but it is difficult to argue from such scanty data, and much information is not to be found in the rolls themselves.

[3] See the Fines published by Mr. Hunter for the Record Commission in 1835 and 1844.

[4] Edited by Sir Francis Palgrave, in two volumes, 1835.

Pleas is also very obscure. The final separation of the three courts originated in the direction of the 17th chapter of Magna Carta, but it does not appear that even then a distinct staff of judges was appointed to each tribunal. Probably until late in the reign of Henry III. the same persons continued as before to sit in the three different courts in distinct capacities.

III. The king's council

The same passage in our chronicle in which the original institution of this limited tribunal is traced, affords an indication of a still higher court of justice to which questions might be referred which demanded exceptional treatment ; that of the king in council, which contains the germ both of the equitable tribunals of the country, of the judicial power of the chancellor, and possibly of that of the Privy Council. The words are, 'ita ut si aliqua quæstio inter eos veniret quæ per eos in finem duci non posset, auditui regi præsentaretur, et sicut ei et sapientioribus regni placeret terminaretur.'

Composition of the king's council

According to this theory, which was first brought forward by Mr. Duffus Hardy,[1] this private concilium regis was, prior to the development of parliament, the highest tribunal in the kingdom. 'It was not only composed of the wisdom of the nation, but also the great officers of state ; the chancellor, treasurer, justices of either bench, and barons of the exchequer, were all active members of it.'[2] If this description is applicable to the earlier stages of its existence, it clearly was little more than a reappearance of the Curia Regis in

Number of councillors limited by circumstances

another shape. Considering the limited number of councillors whom the king could summon to such a court, we may suppose that it was really the whole body of the judges and ministers joined in the examination of points too knotty for the determination of the bench ; perhaps reviewing the decisions of their own committees.

The justiciar and the chancellor

It is probable that during the reign of Henry, who had a great aptitude for judicial functions, and was fond of administering justice in person, the king himself rather than the justiciar would preside in this court. During the reign of Richard, William Longchamp united the offices of regent, justiciar, and chancellor ; and from the time of his death the office of justiciar was political rather than judicial. John, like his father, occasionally administered justice in his own person, although the justiciarship possessed much the same character as it had under his father. But Hubert de Burgh was the last who possessed the proper status of the ancient justiciar ; with the division of the three courts emerges at once the increased importance of the chancellor, and the distinct equitable jurisdiction of the council. The chancellor was inferior to the justiciar as long as the old constitution of the Curia Regis remained. When the council

[1] Introduction to the Close Rolls, pp. 95–105, octavo edition.   [2] Hardy, from Sir M. Hale, Introduction, &c., p. 100.

succeeded to its place, the justiciar sank into the chief justice of a single court, and the chancellor became, in the absence of the king, the natural president of the council.[1]

The importance of the chancery, previous to the establishment of the independent judicature of the chancellor, was indirect, perhaps, but by no means insignificant. In its origin, it was the secretarial[2] department of the Curia Regis, and of that court the chancellor was a very important member; he kept the seal and originally drew up the writs. How great influence he might exercise on the mind of the king, so long as the latter took a personal share in the judicature, we may easily imagine; nor was this all: the chancellor might introduce modifications into the very terms of the decisions of the court. The theory that the importance of the chancellor owed something to the personal influence of Thomas Becket with Henry II. has, at different times, had able supporters; and a passage of John of Salisbury, in which the chancellor is said to have cancelled unjust decisions,[3] has been adduced in proof of his exercising a rudimentary equitable jurisdiction at this early time. The play on the word is not, however, peculiar to this case, and, if it means anything, must refer to the official rather than to the personal influence of the chancellor, the power of wording and recording the decisions of the sovereign.

Earlier character of the chancery

Accidental influence of the chancellor

Thomas Becket as chancellor

Another theory, turning on the same point, maintains that the chancellorship in Becket's person was advanced from the sixth to the second rank of precedence after the king; but of this I can find no definite proof. The functions of the chancellor were more strictly connected with the administration of justice than those of any other officer of the Curia, except the justiciar. The constable or the marshal or the chamberlain, merely as such, could hardly have taken precedence of the keeper of the great seal, and the chancellor was the second official in the kingdom before those offices had become attached to houses of first-rate baronial rank.

Did the chancellorship attain an increase of dignity in Becket?

Whether, after this was the case, the chancellor would have maintained his precedence, unless he had been also a bishop, may, I think, be doubted. From the very early date at which the title of second[4] from the king is given to Becket, it seems almost impossible

---

[1] Hardy, Introduction, &c., p. 105.

[2] Cf. Palgrave, *Commonwealth*, i. 177–179.

[3] Joh. Salisb. Enth. in Policr. 'Hic est qui regni leges cancellat iniquas et mandata pii principis æqua facit.'

[4] Becket is called 'secundus post regem in quatuor regnis,' by Peter of Celles. S. T. C. iv. 169. The chancellor was next in dignity to the justiciar, who was 'primus in regno.' Dialogus de Scaccario, 8, 9. No argument can be drawn from the signatures of charters, in which the name of the chancellor occupies the same place under Stephen as under Henry II. The names stand generally thus: (1) The bishops and abbots; (2) the chancellor and chaplains; (3) the earls and barons. The justiciar signs merely as a baron, and the chancellor in his position as a clergyman.

to suppose that the precedence was given him for personal reasons ; and the obscurity into which the office falls after his resignation seems to indicate that it gained nothing from him. Ralph de Warneville, the next on the list of chancellors, is scarcely known, except by the mention of his resignation. He lived away from court, in Normandy, and discharged his high function by means of a vice-chancellor.[1] Geoffrey, the king's son, received the seal as an endowment, the actual work being done as before. The office of chancellor was purchased by William Longchamp, for somewhat less than Geoffrey Rufus had paid for it to Henry I.[2] It is probably to William Longchamp, rather than to Becket, that the office was indebted for an increase of its practical influence. He was at once justiciar and chancellor, and, as under his tenure the chancery assumed a new and distinct character, so from this time the precedence and influence of the function was fully and permanently recognised.

Ralph de Warneville, chancellor

Geoffrey, chancellor

William Longchamp

But, however the honorary importance of the chancellor arose, it seems certain that his actual judicature sprang out of his office as president of the king's council.[3] It belongs to the investigator of our later legal history to examine how this took place, as well as to decide the steps by which, from the union of the council with the House of Lords in the Magnum Concilium, arose that confusion of powers which ended on the one hand in giving to the council legislative powers, and, on the other, in giving to the House of Lords that appellate jurisdiction which belonged more strictly to the council ; whilst the court of the council itself, after retaining its

Origin of the judicial power of the chancellor

---

[1] ' Radulfus de Warnevilla, Rothomagensis sacrista, thesaurarius Eboracensis, constitutus est Angliæ cancellarius ; qui modum vivendi parem a privato dissimilem, quem prius semper habuerat non immutavit, malens Waltero de Constanciis, canonico Rothomagensi, vices in Curia Regis committere, quam circa latus principis militantes expensis profusioribus cautioribus mensis, ad sui gloriam nominis propagandam per dies singulos invitare.' R. de Diceto, 567, ad 1173. Walter of Coutances ought to appear in the list of the Lords Keepers. He is called Sigillarius, Dic. 609.

[2] The price of the chancellorship of the younger king, in 1176, was 1,100 marks. R. de Diceto, 589. Our author says 11,000, i. 122; but it will be observed that the reading depends on only the inferior MS. The Julius MS. has a blank for the number of thousands, which the writer of the

Vitellius MS. may have filled up from R. de Diceto. If the reading be right the sum would be 7,333*l.* 6*s.* 8*d.* ; which seems as much beyond the mark as 733*l.* 6*s.* 8*d.* seems below it. The price of the treasurership in 1159 was 400*l.* On the statement of Foliot that Becket bought the chancellorship, see Robertson's *Becket*, p. 322. I think it most likely to be true ; and that although Henry chose him for his merits, he made him pay his price, as Richard did with William Longchamp under similar circumstances, allowing him to have it for 3,000*l.*, although there was another bid at 4,000*l.* Geoffrey Rufus bought it for 7,000*l.* (Ann. Margam, ad 1122), of which 3,006*l.* 13*s.* 4*d.* was unpaid in 31 Hen. I., Pipe Roll. William Longchamp paid 3,000*l.* for it in 1189. R. Devizes, p. 9.

[3] See Palgrave's *Essay on the Original Authority of the King's Council*, London, 1834.

original character in the court of Star Chamber, has, by various changes of law and circumstance, reached the present time in the shape of the Judicial Committee of the Privy Council. Modern develop-ments of the council

The loss of the original text of nearly all the measures by which Henry II. introduced his changes into the customs of the law, precludes the possibility of any such chronological arrangement of them as I have attempted in the foregoing sketch of his judicial innovations. It is on these measures for the most part that his right depends to the title of the founder of the common law. They were important and numerous, even if we exclude from the calculation those changes of custom which, appearing in his reign, and not being traceable in the remains of earlier legislation, are attributed to him as their author. To this latter class may belong the exchange of the ancient rule of inheritance for the feudal practice of primogeniture,[1] the disuse of the English language in charters, the depression of the lowest class of freemen into a state of villenage,[2] and the abolition of the invidious distinction between the English and the Norman freeman.[3] To these I might perhaps add the extinction of the provincial differences of the Mercian, Danish, and West Saxon customs, but the principle of money compensations for injuries,[4] on the carrying out of which most of the provincial distinctions depend, and which became obsolete at the same time, probably involved most of them in its abolition ; whilst others of the local usages continued long afterwards. IV. Legal enactments of Henry II. Probable consequences of his legislation

Henry's recognised acts of legislation are to be deduced from the text of the various assizes which have come down to us, and from the fragments of the lost ones which are imbedded in the work of Glanvill. The former class are of course as closely connected with his changes in the provincial jurisdictions, as the latter are with his institution or remodelling of the Curia Regis. Any attempt to evolve the particulars of the changes from a comparison between Glanvill and the Anglo-Saxon laws is, notwithstanding the apparent authority of Madox and Hallam,[5] entirely futile. The two are so far different in subject matter as to be incapable of direct comparison : Glanvill's work is simply a book of process ; the laws are for the most part the ·declarations of pains and penalties. Glanvill is a handbook for the Curia Regis, a court which he himself was chiefly instrumental in creating or developing. The Anglo-Saxon laws, so far as they are declaratory of process at all, Existing remains No comparison can be instituted between Glanvill and the early laws

---

[1] Geoffrey's assize of 1185, instituting the inheritance by primogeniture in Brittany, is printed in Palgrave's *Commonwealth*, ii. ccccxxxv., from Lobineau, ii. pp. 317, 318.

[2] Dialogus, p. 28, 'Ascriptitii de regni jure . . . licite vendantur.'

[3] Dialogus, p. 26 ; see above, p. 108, note.

[4] Palgrave, *Commonwealth*, i. 48.

[5] Middle Ages, ii. 339, &c.

are the rules of the courts which existed long before the Curia Regis, and the machinery of which, so far from being superseded by the machinery of Glanvill's formulas, existed for centuries afterwards. Hallam, in the form of a conjecture, has stated what is a self-evident fact to any one who will compare the two.[1]

Institution of juries

The same spirit in which Henry was determined, whilst retaining the machinery of the ancient courts of law, to substitute his own servants for the magistrates of the county and the lords of the franchises, appears in his amalgamation of English and Norman customs in criminal trials. By the first clause of the Assize of Clarendon, the justices are directed to make inquiry by twelve lawful men of the hundred, and by four lawful men of every township, by oath that they will speak the truth, if in the hundred or in their township there be any man who is publicly accounted or known to be guilty of robbery, murder, or theft, or a receiver of robbers, murderers, or thieves. Thus indicted, the criminal is to go at once to the ordeal of water, and if he fails, to undergo the legal punishment. In this direction the ancient system of the compurgatory oath is, except in the boroughs, *ipso facto* abolished;[2] but the presentment by twelve lawful men is retained from the Anglo-Saxon law.[3] Their verdict is that of witnesses according to the Anglo-Saxon fashion: but the process is an inquest under oath, according to the custom of the Normans.

Enforcement of frankpledge and the law of strangers

The enforcement of the law of frankpledge in the same assize is coupled with the direction to sheriffs to enter all franchises for the purpose of view.[4] The directions as to strangers are adapted closely from the old law. The court which is to be held before the itinerant justices is the court of the county under the presidency of the sheriff; the point of contact between the Curia Regis and the shiremote.

New institutions of Henry II.

It is from Glanvill that we learn the institution of the new process in civil trials; the enactment of the Great Assize,[5] and of the recognitions of Mortdancester[6] and Novel disseisin;[7] the system

---

[1] Middle Ages, ii. 341.

[2] On this very interesting question see Palgrave, *Commonwealth*, chap. vii., and on the whole subject, chap. viii. p. 259, &c.

[3] Palgrave, *Commonwealth*, i. 257. 'Assembled according to the Anglo-Saxon law and sworn according to the Norman law.'

[4] See Palgrave, *Commonwealth*, i. 118, 257, 297.

[5] The text of the Great Assize is lost. It is called by Glanvill, ii. 7, 'Regale quoddam beneficium clementia principis de consilio procerum populis

indultum.' And the provisions of it are quoted at ii. 17–19.

[6] The text of this assize is lost; it is referred to in Glanvill as 'constitutio regni quæ assisa nominatur.' Lib. xiii. 1. Glanvill mentions an 'Assisa Regni' (lib. x. c. 12) forbidding suits concerning the debts or tenements of laymen to be decided in a court Christian 'ratione fidei interpositæ.' This Assisa Regni is the Constitutions of Clarendon, c. 15.

[7] Lib. viii. 9., 'per assisam de consilio regni inde factam.' Compare, however, with that chapter the assize

of fines ; the distinctive character of courts of record ;[1] the inclusion of usury in the matters of presentment ;[2] the process of inquiry into purprestures.[3]

Side by side with these national jurisdictions and national juris- Forest
jurisdiction prudence was the administration of the forests : a department which was understood to be peculiarly, immediately and exclusively in the king's hands,[4] and in which Henry acted with more severity and in a more thoroughly tyrannical spirit than can be traced in any other of his acts, private or public.[5] I have given in the appendix (Rolls Series ed.) a copy of the Assize of the Forest made at Woodstock, pro- Assize of
Woodstock bably in 1184, of which the assize given in our Chronicle was an earlier form.

It would be presumptuous in me to attempt to enter on the fields General
tendency
of legal
reforms of investigation which are opened by the mention of these technical names. I have said, I think, sufficient to show the nature, extent, and purpose of the changes. It cannot be doubted that they contributed immensely and directly to the safety of life and property, the punishment of criminals, the limitation of dangerous privileges, the abolition of barbarous customs, the gradual assimilation of public usages, and the amalgamation of the different nationalities. These points must be worked out by the legal historian : but it requires no such investigation to assure us that they all contributed to the consolidation of the royal authority, the increase of the royal revenue, the directness of royal administration : nor, considering the part which both friends and foes ascribe to him, can we doubt the exercise of the king's personal agency, or refuse to trace his peculiar genius in these institutions.

of Northampton, c. 3, and of Clarendon, c. 18, and the laws of William the Conqueror, i. 48.

[1] Cf. Glanvill, vii. 16, with Dialog. de Scacc. p. 47.

[2] See D. de Scacc. pp. 44, 45. Glanvill, ix. 11.

[3] On these, see Palgrave, Commonwealth, i. 225, &c., 257, &c.

[4] ' Sane forestarum ratio pœna quoque vel absolutio delinquentium . . . seorsum ab aliis regni judiciis secernitur et solius regis arbitrio vel cujuslibet familiaris ad hoc specialiter deputati subjicitur. Legibus quidem propriis subsistit, quas non communi regni jure sed voluntaria principum institutione subnixas dicunt,' etc. Dialogus, p. 29.

[5] Frequent traces of this may be found in the present work. Ralph de Diceto seems to say that forest charges were trumped up against offenders against whom nothing could have been proved at law. Ralph Niger says, ' Avibus cœli, piscibus fluminum, bestiis terræ immunitatem dedit, et sata pauperum loca pascua fecit ' (p. 168), and ' legem quoque de forestis inauditam dedit, qua delicti alieni immunes perpetuo mulctabuntur quum decessores nulla linea sanguinis contigerit.' The enactment which was most odious was, however, this : ' Nulli infra metas forestæ habitanti in lucis propriis aut virgas colligendi aut sylvestria et invia in agriculturam agendi potestatem concessit sine forestariis.' Yet essarts were being made clearly throughout the reign. William of Newburgh (iii. 26) says that in his punishments for forest offences Henry was milder than his grandfather, who made no distinction between the man-slayer and the deer-slayer. Cf. Dial. de Scacc. p. 28.

Henry's fiscal measures

Although we would not, with Ralph Niger,[1] assert that the sole object of Henry's judicial and legal innovations was the accumulation of treasure, the connexion between these and his fiscal measures was very close. It could indeed hardly be otherwise, considering that both Curia Regis and Exchequer owed their organisation to the creative genius of one statesman, and that they were administered

Connexion between the law and the revenue

throughout the century by the same persons.[2] The sheriffs were both presidents of the county court and farmers of the revenue :[3] the judges were at once justices of the Curia and barons of the Exchequer ; their work in eyre was as much to assess the taxes as to decide the pleas ; the chief justiciar was both the principal judge and 'the first lord of the treasury.'

Light thrown on the origin of parliamentary institutions

It would be a most interesting task to attempt to trace the effects of this connexion of the two departments in constitutional history. Sir Francis Palgrave has pointed out the fact that the leading features of our parliamentary institutions are traceable to the judicial system of ancient times. The parliament is the highest court of judicature ; the representative principle is identical with that of the jury : and it may be added that the taxing power of parliament itself may be traced in the same way to the assessment by juries, of which vestiges may be found from the era of Domesday Book downwards, which existed in certain departments in the reign of Henry II., and was approved and recognised by law under Richard I.

Sources of ancient revenue

The revenue of the Anglo-Saxon kings arose principally from their demesnes, including both those which were kept in hand and those which were let at ferm at rents payable for the most part in kind. Besides this ordinary revenue, there were the Danegeld voted by the Witan for tribute or for the defence against the Danes, and certain other payments known generally under the name of geld or tax, which were probably derived from commutations of the trinoda necessitas, or special sums levied for the support of the shipping.

Norman system combining the feudal with the ancient taxes

The Norman sovereigns, proceeding on their general policy of combination, maintained these taxes, and added to them the feudal burdens. It is indeed uncertain whether the Conqueror and William Rufus took the trouble of defining the exact nature of the calls which they made on their subjects for money. With the reign of Henry I. our actual knowledge of the question begins, and before the end of

---

[1] 'Nullo quæstu satiatus, abolitis antiquis legibus, singulis annis novas leges, quas assisas vocavit, edidit.' p. 168.
[2] 'Illic enim resident capitalis domini regis justitia, primus post regem in regno ratione fori, et majores quique de regno qui familiarius regiis secretis

assistunt . . . verum quidam ex officio, quidam ex sola jussione principis resident.' Dial. p. 8.
[3] The author of the Dialogus compares the days of account at the Exchequer to a game at chess between the treasurer and the sheriff of each county. Dial. p. 4.

it we find the united burdens of the two systems pressing heavily on the nation at large. In the roll for the 31st year of his reign,[1] side by side with the fixed ferm of the counties and the Danegeld, two strictly national sources of revenue, appear the feudal payments for reliefs, marriages, and wardships ; talliages on the towns are a part of the annual account. From other sources we learn that the marriage portion of the Empress Maud was raised by a strictly feudal aid. A very considerable proportion of the revenue was already derived from the proceeds of placita, the profits arising from the administration of justice, enormous amercements for offences, and the sale of public offices.

Roger, bishop of Salisbury, was the founder of the organisation of the Exchequer, and by his family it was administered, except during Stephen's reign, during the whole of the century. Nigel, bishop of Ely, his nephew, presided at the treasury until the year 1159, when he was succeeded by his son Richard, who held the same position until his death in 1198. Roger le Poor,[2] the son of Bishop Roger, was at one time chancellor to Stephen ; the names of Herbert and Richard, successively bishops of the same see, and known by the same surname, probably carried on the family connexion with the Court and Exchequer far into the reign of Henry III. To the pen of Richard FitzNeal we owe the invaluable ' Dialogus de Scaccario ' ; to his father and great uncle the institution of the enrolments of the revenue known as the Pipe Rolls, which contain the only documentary evidence, strictly speaking, which exists for the illustration of the constitutional history of this reign. *Administration of the Exchequer*

Family of Roger le Poor

The business powers of Henry II. appear to great advantage in his dealings with the Exchequer. One of the first measures of his reign was to set up the old administration as it had been in his grandfather's time.[3] Bishop Nigel[4] was recalled to court and restored to his ancient place. The enrolment of receipts was at once *Henry II. restores the Exchequer*

---

[1] Published by the Record Commission in 1835. Edited by Mr. Hunter.

[2] Dial. p. 20. There can, I think, be no doubt that the name ' pauper ' was first applied to Bishop Roger, and descended from him to his son, the chancellor. It is proved by the application to the bishop of the line ' Paupertas tenuis quam sit fecunda virorum,' by the author of the Dialogus, who was his great nephew, p. 20. And the historians who give an account of his rise dwell much on his original poverty, although they do not give him the name. The son of such a

father was not likely to deserve the name of ' pauper ' in his youth, yet he has it universally. I am inclined to believe that Herbert ' pauper ' was son of Roger, the chancellor ; he was the offspring of a concubine. Ben. Pet. i. 352.

[3] ' Porro super his te vidimus quandoque sollicitum adeo ut missis a latere tuo viris discretis de eodem dominum tunc Eliensem conveneris.' Dial. de Scacc. p. 2 (ed. 1711).

[4] See Dialogus, &c., p. 24, where the author gives a glowing character of the bishop.

L

proceeded with, and although it was not for some years that the completeness of accounts which had existed under Henry I. was attained, the order and method of the rolls of Henry II. are in favourable contrast with the single remaining roll of the former reign. Besides Bishop Nigel and Richard of Ilchester, to whom he gave a special seat at the exchequer board,[1] Henry secured the services of Master Thomas Brunus or le Brun,[2] an old officer of king Roger of Sicily, whom he made his almoner,[3] and provided with a similar seat, and who kept a roll of the Exchequer, and other proceedings of the king and Curia, distinct from the counterpart enrolments of the treasurer and chancellor.

Exchequer accounts.
I. The ferm of the counties

The first item in the revenue rolls of each county is the firma comitatus ; the assized ferm or rent which the sheriff paid as commutation for the feorm-fultum of earlier times. This source of revenue amounted, if we are to believe Giraldus Cambrensis,[4] to 60,000 marks in the time of Edward the Confessor, but had fallen in the reign of Henry II. to 12,000 marks, in consequence of the heavy charges granted out of it by both Stephen and Henry to their followers. This statement cannot be strictly true. The ferms were assessed certainly before the reign of Stephen,[5] for in the 31st of Henry I. they had sunk to the amounts at which they continued

The ferms impoverished by Stephen

throughout the century, the aggregate in the gross not reaching to more than 12,000*l.* From this fund, which was the whole of the ordinary revenue of the crown, Stephen had drawn the endowments

---

[1] Dialogus, p. 13. He had risen from the ranks in the treasury ; being mentioned as a scriptor in the roll of the 2nd of Henry II., p. 30.

[2] Dialogus, p. 9.

[3] Froger, bishop of Séez, was almoner until 1159. Roger the Hospitaller took the office in 1177. Thomas Brunus was an Englishman who had been employed at the Sicilian court in high office. On the death of the king (probably Roger in 1154) he was invited to England. His name appears in the rolls from the 5th year to the 23rd. In the 15th year, 1169, he was almoner, so that he probably resigned that office in 1177. See Madox's note on the Dialogus, p. 17.

[4] De Inst. Pr. iii. 30. 'Annui fiscales redditus sicut in rotulo Wintoniæ reperitur ad sexaginta millia marcarum summam implebant. Tempore vero regis Henrici secundi, tot terris interim militibus tam a rege Stephano prius quam ab ipso postmodum . . . large utrinque datis, vix annui xii. millium marcarum redditus fiscales sunt in-

venti.' He adds that the German emperor has 300,000 marks per annum ; and that the city of Palermo alone yielded more to the king of Sicily than all England did to Henry. The use of the words *terris datis* in this passage is technical. See Dialogus, p. 14, and the Pipe Rolls, *passim*.

[5] Richard FitzNeal, writing in 1178, could remember the time when the ferms were partly paid in kind. Dialogus de Scaccario, p. 20. To remedy the oppression incident to the system, the king, Henry II., ' diffinito magnorum consilio destinavit per regnum quos ad id prudentiores et discretiores cognoverat, qui circueuntes et oculata fide fundos singulos perlustrantes, habita æstimatione victualium quæ de his solvebantur redegerunt in summam denariorum.' This writer states that part of the ferm of the county arose from *placita*, of which the earl had a third part, his third penny. But the whole ferm, and the third penny itself, had become a fixed charge before the reign of Henry II. Dial. p. 31.

of his fiscal or titular earls,[1] and the considerable sums which he spent on religious foundations. The crown was thereby so impoverished that it is difficult to see by what means during the middle and later years of the reign the royal state was supported, unless it were by a heavy Danegeld. One of Henry's first measures was to revoke these charges, and to restore them to their proper purpose. The lay grants were resumed, but the church endowments were beyond the king's reach; and as these, with the necessary provision made for his own family and followers, must be drawn from the same source, the sum of about 4,000*l.*, to which in the early years of the reigns the terræ datæ amounted, must be deducted from the gross sum of the ferms. This reduced sum continued the same throughout the reign, and agrees very nearly with the estimate of Giraldus, about 8,000*l.*[2]

Giraldus' statement

The Danegeld, which had been always an odious tax to the English, and which, from its impact on the cultivated lands of the country, by its very nature repressed any attempts at improvement, had been abolished by Edward the Confessor,[3] and restored by the Conqueror in an aggravated form. The ancient tax of two shillings on the hide had been on one occasion raised to six. It had not, however, become as before a part of the regular annual revenue, but was reserved by William for occasions of exceptional urgency,[4] so that it is possible that the gross amount so raised was not larger than it would have been if it had been collected annually, although in a time when money was scarce the accumulated pressure would be out of all proportion heavier. We are not informed by what

II. The Danegeld

The Danegeld under the Norman kings

---

[1] ' Quosdam imaginarios et pseudo-comites quibus rex Stephanus omnia pene ad fiscum pertinentia minus caute distribuerat.' R. de Monte, ad 1155. The reference is to the same in the passage of R. de Diceto quoted above, p. 116. ' Bonorum occupatores quæ suam ad mensam quasi ad fiscum ab antiquo pertinere noscuntur, patrimonio proprio contentos esse debere, assereret, et etiam cogeret,' c. 570. ' Considerans . . . quod regii redditus breves essent qui avito tempore uberes fuerant, eo quod regia dominica per mollitiem regis Stephani ad alios multosque dominos majori ex parte migrassent, præcepit ea cum omni integritate a quibuscunque detentoribus resignari.' W. Newb. ii. 2.

[2] These numbers are arrived at by adding up the gross receipts of the Pipe Rolls. I have been as careful as I could, but it is difficult to be sure

about the lower figures in a sum of fifty or sixty pages of Roman numerals, and I have preferred giving the result in round numbers.

[3] The Confessor is said to have seen the devil sitting on the money-bags. Brompton, 942, and Luard's *Lives*, p. 307. The author of the Dialogus says that it was an annual charge up to the Conquest, and that the Conqueror discontinued it; but see below. On the contrary, Stephen, in his charter of Oxford (Brompton, 1024), says that it had been levied annually, and this agrees with the Pipe Roll.

[4] Dialogus de Scaccario, p. 27. ' Noluit hoc ut annuum solvi quod fuerat urgente necessitate bellicæ tempestatis exactum, nec tamen omnino propter inopinatos casus dimitti. Raro igitur temporibus illius vel successorum ipsius solutus est.'

It becomes a fixed charge

influences this tax was modified [1] until we find it in the reign of Henry
I. a fixed and annual charge, bringing in the gross about 5,500*l.*,
but reduced by waste and by pardons to official persons to about
3,500*l.* It may be conjectured that this reduction was made in
consequence of the compact called the charter of Henry I., in which
he promises the abolition of all evil customs. If the number of
hides in the country was, as it is sometimes stated, 243,600, the
ancient Danegeld must have raised a sum of 24,360*l.* It is, however, more probable that the sums which appear under the head of
Danegeld in the rolls, and which were unquestionably all the produce
of the tax which reached the royal treasury, are simply the amounts
paid by the sheriffs as the ferm of the Danegeld. I am not aware
that this theory has ever been stated, but it would seem not improbable for several reasons. The great oppressiveness of the Danegeld of two shillings on the hide would render its collection a
matter of difficulty, and it would never be raised without considerable loss. A fixed sum, on the other hand, must be paid into
the treasury. It is possible that this sum was fixed on a low
average, and that the sheriffs collected as well as they could the
old tax, keeping for their own pay the difference between the sum
collected and the sum paid in. If this were so, we can account for
the fact that the Danegeld was still reputed in 1178 to be a tax of
two shillings on the hide, whilst the actual receipt of the Exchequer
was very small.

It may be questioned, however, further, whether the Danegeld
itself was not compounded before it reached the hands of the sheriff,
on the same principle on which forfeitures and reliefs were fixed at
an almost nominal sum in the reign of Henry I. A man who
owned twenty hides might be allowed to pay Danegeld for five, on
on the same principle that an abbot who owned twenty knights' fees
was allowed to pay scutage for a fourth part.

Some countenence for the theory may be derived from the
circumstances which are recorded by Becket's biographers as having
taken place in the council at Woodstock, on the first of July 1163.
On that occasion we are told that Henry wished to enter in the
Exchequer accounts, and add to his own revenues, a sum of 'two
shillings on the hide, which were given to the king's servants who
in the post of sheriffs kept the counties.' Thomas resisted this claim.
' We will not give this sum as revenue, saving your pleasure, but if the
sheriffs and the servants and ministers of the provinces serve us well

[1] As to the alleged revaluation of the lands by Ranulf Flambard, for the purpose of increasing the Dane-geld, see Orderic Vit. viii. 8; Pal-grave, *Normandy and England*, iv. 60–61; Lappenberg (ed. Thorpe), iii. 226.

and support our vassals, we will not be wanting in their assistance.'[1] This tax can be no other than the Danegeld, and Henry's object may have been to collect the entire sum into the treasury instead of the miserable fixed amounts which were paid in by the sheriffs. Whether Thomas appeared as the advocate of the sheriffs, who would be the first losers by the change, or of the people, is not clear, but the proposal to render 'auxilium' voluntarily to the sheriffs instead of payment does not favour the former supposition ; such a proposal, on the other hand, comes with an ill grace from the statesman who had substituted fixed payments for personal service in the case of the scutage. The subject is one of the most obscure in the whole of Becket's history. It is possible, however, that Henry's purpose was simply to revive the payment of Danegeld ; and if this were so, it was defeated by the primate's opposition, for no such tax was collected after the eighth year of Henry's reign,[2] the year preceding the Council of Woodstock.

Thomas Becket's resistance to the king at Woodstock

Notwithstanding Ralph Niger's assertion that Henry renewed the ancient Danegeld (a statement which may have been made in reference to the scene at Woodstock), it is certain that the abolition or permanent disuse of the tax is to be attributed to this king. It was collected in the second year of his reign, in very nearly if not exactly the same gross amount as in the 31st Henry I. From the third to the seventh years it was disused ; in the eighth it was collected in the same sums again, and after that it disappears until the 20th year,[3] when, although summonses were issued for the collection of it, there is no evidence to show that it was actually paid, unless the word is used simply as a synonym for talliage. It may be fairly a matter of conjecture whether this practical abrogation of the tax was owing to a wish on Henry's part to prove himself a worthy successor of the Confessor, or to a conviction that it was an unprofitable, unpopular, and impolitic impost, a small portion only of which reached the Exchequer ; or whether the facts that during the years of Becket's chancellorship the Danegeld was not exacted, that in the year of his resignation it reappears, that in the following year, after a stout resistance on his part, it was finally disused, point to the second martyr of Canterbury as the real deliverer from the tax, which in its first form the first martyr of Canterbury, St. Elphege

Danegeld comes to an end under Henry II.

Cause of the abolition of the tax

---

[1] This story is told by four of S. Thomas's biographers with a strong consensus. Grim, S. T. C. i. 21. Roger of Pontigny, S. T. C. i. 21. Garnier (quoted by Robertson, p. 329), p. 65. Will. Cantuar. S. T. C. ii. 5. Compare Robertson's *Becket*, App. IX.

[2] Madox thought that the accounts of Danegeld ceased after the second year ; but he did not see the roll of the eighth year, which has been recovered since his time, and in which the receipts for Danegeld are entered. Cf. *Hist. Exch.* p. 479, &c.

[3] Madox, *Hist. Exch.* p. 479.

had resisted to the death. The carucage which was levied by Richard I. in his eighth year was, however, to all intents and purposes a revival of this odious impost.

III. The donum and auxilium

The next item of ancient revenue was the donum, or auxilium, names which bear evidence to their original nature of contributions by the vassals to assist the necessities of their lords. The former term is applied to the sums raised by the counties, the latter to those by the towns. This impost varied in amount on occasion, and there is no reason to suppose that it was an annual tax. It seems to have answered to what was known somewhat later by the name of talliage, and in the thirty-first of Henry I. appears only in the form of auxilium burgorum, being probably intended to be to the towns what Danegeld was to the country.

Changes in 1156

The second year of Henry II. was marked by some variations from the older practice, which may be ascribed with tolerable certainty to the advice of Becket as chancellor. It was no doubt a year of extraordinary charges, and one in which the more elastic methods of raising a revenue by making up the arrears of legal proceedings could not be brought into effective working. We find in it accordingly the disappearance of Danegeld, coupled with the new arrangement of the donum, which brought all classes of the population under contribution.

Scutage, hidage, and talliage

From this time the donum may be taken as the general name of the irregular impost. It was called also *auxilium*, from the purpose which it was intended to serve, and hidage, scutage, or talliage, from the mode of collection or special character of the impost. The talliage or auxilium burgorum was levied on the towns, the scutage or donum militum on the knights' fees, and the hidage or donum simply on the tenants in socage. The peculiar measure of the second year was the collection of scutage from the

Scutage on the clergy in 1156

knights' fees holding of ecclesiastical superiors, a measure which met with much opposition from Archbishop Theobald at the time.[1] The amount actually accounted for on the roll, as raised by this scutage, was small, reaching altogether to not more that 500*l*. The donum comitatus and auxilium burgorum raised the same year about 2,700*l*. The whole sum accounted for on the year, with the addition of the profits of law proceedings and feudal incidents, is not much more than 22,000*l*. The donum of the fourth year was collected in a different form and in different relative proportions. It is possible

[1] This is the scutage referred to by John of Salisbury, ep. 128, in terms which would imply that it was really levied to enable Henry to make war on his brother Geoffrey. ' Verum interim scutagium remittere non potest, et a quibusdam exactionibus abstinere, quoniam fratris gratia male sarta nequidquam coiit, &c.

that we should connect with the scutage on the clergy in the second year the ordinance which, as we learn from Robert de Monte,[1] was made in the third year for the war in Wales, that every two knights or tenants in chivalry should join to equip a third, by which means, if we are to understand it literally, 90,000 knights would appear from 60,000 knights' fees. The scutage of 1156 was also for the war in Wales, and may have been the share borne by the dignified clergy of the increased burden borne by the knights in kind.

The term scutage, as is well known, acquired later the meaning of commutation for military service, and the tax imposed for the war of Toulouse[2] is commonly stated to have been the first occasion of its collection in this form. For this payment a general levy of revenue was made, and as this undoubtedly touched every knight's fee, as well as any other source of income, it is called by the contemporary historians a scutage. It does not appear from the Pipe Rolls to have differed materially from the tax of the second year; the whole sum accounted for under the head of donum is short of 11,000*l.*, of which the clergy and their knights' fees paid 3,700*l.*, the towns about 2,500*l.*, the rest falls under the head of donum militum, or scutage proper, with a few miscellaneous contributions. It is singular that the mention of the war of Toulouse, or of the commutation of service, does not occur in the rolls for this year, and that Alexander Swereford, the compiler of the Red Book of the Exchequer, supposed that the donum was raised for a war on the Welsh marches. A second scutage was raised in the seventh year (1161), probably for payment of debts incurred for the same war, the assessment being, in this as in the former case, two marks to the knight's fee. It is possibly to the joint sum of these two scutages that the words of Gervase are to be applied when he states that the whole scutage for the war of Toulouse raised in England was 180,000*l.* of silver.[3] If it was indeed so, the only conclusion we can come to is that the rolls are sadly incomplete; but there is a roundness in the sum that tempts a doubt. By Robert de Monte we are told that the scutage of the king's foreign dominions was sixty shillings Angevin[4]

Scutage as a commutation for military service

Scutages of the reign of Henry II.

Scutage of the war of Toulouse

---

[1] 'Ad ann. 1157. 'Circa festivitatem S. Johannis Baptistæ rex Henricus præparavit maximam expeditionem, ita ut duo milites de tota Anglia tertium pararent, ad opprimendum Gallensem terra et mari.'

[2] It was the scutage of Toulouse which was alleged against Thomas Becket by his enemies (Gilb. Foliot, ep. 194), and which his friends thought was the cause of his misfortunes. Joh. Salisb. ep. 145.

[3] Gervase, 1381. 'Hoc anno rex Henricus scotagium sive scutagium de Anglia recepit, cujus summa fuit centum millia et quaterviginti millia librarum argenti.' See Hume, Hist. Engl. i., note P.

[4] R. de Monte, ad 1159. 'Nolens vexare agrarios milites nec burgensem nec rusticorum multitudinem, sumptis 60 solidis Andegavensibus in Normannia de feudo uniuscujusque loricæ, et de reliquis omnibus tam in Nor-

Question as
to the
amount
raised for
the war of
Toulouse
to the knight's fee. If we suppose that Gervase had simply calculated the English scutage at sixty shillings sterling, the sum
raised on 60,000 knights' fees would of course be exactly 180,000*l.*
We know, however, that the sum was two contributions of two
marks, that is 2*l.* 13*s.* 4*d.* to the fee. This would raise 160,000*l.* in
the gross. But if the amount actually raised in the seventh year
corresponded with that of the fifth, the whole was not a fifth of that
sum. It is, however, impossible to come to an exact conclusion
without fuller data than exist even in the rolls themselves. We do
not know either the real number of knights' fees in England, or the
number on which the tax was levied.

Scutage of
Wales

Aid pur fille
marier
Another scutage was levied in the eleventh year for the army of
Wales, accompanied by a talliage on the towns. The aid pur fille
marier in the fourteenth year, a mark to the fee, was collected in
exactly the same manner by scutage and talliage, but owing to
several causes was much more productive than any former aid.
This particular description of aid requires no remark ; it had been
levied before for the marriage of the king's mother, and was not
imposed in addition to other taxes.

Scutage of
Ireland
It is in the eighteenth year that we find the scutage distinctly
taking the character of a commutation,[1] or perhaps it may be called
a fine in lieu of military service. It was for the Irish expedition,
and amounted to twenty shillings on the fee on those knights who
sent neither soldiers nor money for the expedition. The only other
Scutage of
Galloway
scutage of the reign was that for the Galloway expedition in the
thirty-third year, which was accompanied by a general talliage.

Talliages on
demesne
These imposts exhaust the list of the extraordinary taxes of the
reign, with the exception of the talliages on demesne, imposed in the
nineteenth, twentieth, and twenty-third years. The last of these
was probably expended on the preparations for war in France, which

mannia quam in Anglia, sive etiam
aliis terris suis, secundum hoc quod
ei visum fuit, capitales barones suos
cum paucis secum duxit, solidarios
vero milites innumeros.'
[1] The account given in the Dialogus is this : 'Fit interdum, ut
imminente vel insurgente in regnum
hostium machinatione, decernat rex
de singulis feodis militum summam
aliquam solvi, marcam scilicet vel
libram unam, unde militiis stipendia
vel donativa succedant. Mavult enim
princeps stipendiarios quam domesticos bellicis apponere casibus. Hæc
itaque summa, quia nomine scutorum
solvitur, scutagium nuncupatur.' It

had not yet acquired the restricted
sense exclusively, for the tax raised
for the redemption of Richard I.,
which was technically an aid, was
raised by a scutage. The goods of
knights or persons holding by knight
service of a superior lord might be
sold to pay their lord's scutage if he
was a defaulter, ' ratio namque scuta-
giorum milites suos magna pro parte
respicit, quia non nisi de militibus et
ratione militiæ regi debentur.' Dial.
p. 52. This law applied only to
scutage (in commutation of service),
not to a simple *donum*, and not to
tenants *in capite*, p. 54.

throughout the spring seemed imminent, the other two in repairing the damage done in the rebellion of the year 1173.

This brief review is enough to enable us to estimate the historical value of the statements of Ralph Niger and William of Newburgh. The former states that Henry II. renewed the Danegeld, enacted new laws annually for the purpose of gain, and depressed nearly all his subjects with scutages, recognitions, and other various forms of oppression. William of Newburgh,[1] on the contrary, affirms that he never laid a single heavy burden on either England or his foreign possessions until he imposed the Saladin tithe. The latter statement is undoubtedly nearer the truth. On the other hand, William of Newburgh acquits him of imposing tribute on the churches and monasteries, although he allows the truth of the accusation of Ralph, that he kept benefices vacant for the sake of the profits.[2] Possibly in William's estimation the consent of S. Thomas took from the scutage on church fees its sacrilegious character.

Statements of Ralph Niger and William of Newburgh

Henry's exactions from the church

The revenue raised from legal proceedings, on which Ralph Niger pours his especial vituperation, constitutes from the time of the Assize of Clarendon a very important item in the national accounts. It does not seem, however, in any year to have reached the amount raised by the same means in the thirty-first of Henry I. The placita of the itinerant justices and justices of the forest begin to appear in the rolls of 1166, the levies on purprestures emerging at the same time. From 1175 downwards we find entries of the placita Curiæ and of the Exchequer at uncertain intervals. Oblata Curiæ appear under distinct headings from the time of the establishment of the bench in the king's court, 1178 ; fines for the transfer of property from the twenty-eighth year.

IV. Profits of placita

The income arising from feudal incidents was, of course, so fluctuating that no calculation can be made to give even a fair idea of the average revenue derived from them. In a general view of the receipts it would appear that Henry II. never approached to the oppressive sums raised by his grandfather from this source. His reign is marked by no great forfeitures except those of William Peverel and Henry of Essex,[3] both of which were strictly legal. The escheats and seizures never remained long in the royal hands, whilst the regale in the case of ecclesiastical vacancies was pertinaciously and even illegally exerted.[4]

V. Income from feudal incidents

---

[1] iii. 26.

[2] William of Newburgh, iii. 26, gives Henry's own defence of himself. ' Nonne melius est ut pecuniæ istæ impendantur necessarii regni negotiis quam in episcoporum absumantur deliciis ? Nostri enim temporis præsules veterum in se formam minime exprimunt, sed circa officium remissi et languidi totis mundum brachiis amplectuntur.' A very bad argument, as the historian adds, considering who appointed the bishops.

[3] R. de Monte, ad 1155 and 1163. R. de Diceto, 531, 535.

[4] See, among innumerable proofs of this unconstitutional proceeding, S. T. C. iii. 23.

Henry's
measures
for securing
his feudal
revenues

It is clear, however, that Henry watched carefully for every opportunity of increasing this branch of his revenue. For this purpose was issued the commission of inquiry throughout England and Normandy into feudal services in 1168, which had so unfortunate an effect on Henry's relations with the archbishop, and the same was probably the cause of the inquiry entrusted to the sheriffs in 1177. A similar investigation in Normandy in 1171 is said by Robert de Monte to have had the effect of doubling the ducal revenue.

Moderate
amount
appearing
on the rolls

On a calm examination of the whole subject, it is difficult to affirm that the nation was oppressively taxed during any period of the reign. The amount of revenue accounted for in the last year of Henry, or as it is styled from the fact that the Michaelmas of 1189 fell in the next reign, the first of Richard I., is but 48,781*l.*, which stands in favourable contrast with the thirty-first of Henry I., when it reached the gross sum of 66,593*l.*[1]

Method of
assessing
and collect-
ing taxes

As to the mode in which the taxes were exacted and assessed we know too little to make any categorical statement. There can, however, be little doubt that the great council was consulted before the levying of any extraordinary impost, and that the assessment of the proportion to be paid by each individual was carried out in strictly legal form. The sheriffs were not at liberty to collect the donum of the county by oppressive means, but barons of the Exchequer made their circuits for the purpose of assessment.[2] It is certain that the knights assessed themselves by declaring their own assisable estate by a special carta stating the number of fees held by them of the

Possible
employment
of juries

Crown. In the case of socage tenants the assessment was probably made by inquest of jury, such as we find employed in the carrying out of the assize of arms and the levying of the Saladin tithe. It is possible, indeed, that this expedient was used only in the case of personal property to which these particular cases apply. When, however, in the reign of Richard I. we find a new assessment of

---

[1] 'Nullum grave regno Anglorum vel terris suis transmarinis onus unquam imposuit, usque ad illam novissimam decimationem, causa expeditionis Jerosolimitanæ, quæ nimirum decimatio in aliis æque fiebat regionibus.' W. Newb. iii. 26.

[2] Dial. p. 23. 'Cognita summa quæ de comitatu requiritur communiter ab iis qui in comitatu fundos habent, per hydas distribuitur ut nihil desit de illa cum ventum fuerit ad scaccarium solutionis.' In the case of towns the *donum* might be

settled in two ways, either by an apportionment to individuals made by the justices, or by an offer of the burgesses of a sufficient sum raised by themselves. If they tried to excuse themselves, inquiry was made, ' per fidem vicecomitis,' as to their solvency. Ib. p. 51. So we find the burgesses of Horncastle assessing themselves at a different sum from the assessment of the justices, and the latter accepting their decision. 14 Hen. II. Madox, *Hist. Exch.* p. 407.

carucage enacted,[1] the law orders it to be carried out by two servants of the king, a clerk and a knight, who, with the sheriff of the county and lawful men elected thereto, shall, after taking oath, call before them the stewards of the barons of the county, the lords of the townships, or their bailiffs or provosts, with four lawful men of the township, and two lawful knights of the hundred, who also are to swear that they will faithfully and without fraud tell what are the wainages of the carucates in each township : the moneys are to be collected by two lawful knights and the bailiff of the hundred, who are to account for them to the sheriff, and the sheriff to the Exchequer. This act took place in 1197, but there are traces of a similar proceeding at an earlier period. The inquisitions on which Domesday was founded were drawn up from inquests of two sorts : the first of the barons with the sheriff, the bailiff of the hundred, and the king's officers ; the second of the villenage, ' six ceorls being returned from every township, who, together with the parish priest and the town reeve, also made their statements on oath to the royal commissioners.'[2] This was, perhaps, an exceptional case, but it was a good precedent : as early as the reign of Henry I. the rights of the crown were ascertained by an inquisition or recognition by a sworn inquest. In the 14th of Henry II. we find the burghers of Horncastle, by permission of the justices, assessing their own contribution *pur fille marier*, and as this is incidentally mentioned the practice may have been general. It seems impossible for the justices to have acted without some such organisation as the jury. The form was as old as Domesday, and the machinery for legal matters in perfect working. The question is obscure, probably, only because the system was in regular operation and required no notice from contemporary writers. From its occasional use, we may infer its general applicability. The importance of the facts recorded on the question of self-taxation, representation, and the use of the jury can hardly be overstated, but they belong more distinctly to the two following reigns.

Among the minor matters of the Exchequer business the coinage received a large share of the king's attention. Twice, at least, during the reign a new currency was put into circulation, and very strict measures were taken to preserve its integrity. In this respect Henry no doubt felt himself to be carrying out the provisions of the treaty by which the throne was secured to him at Wallingford.

Marginal notes: Reason for the supposition; Earlier traces of juries for fiscal purposes; Coinage

---

[1] Palgrave, *Commonwealth*, i. 275, gives the following dates of the further development of the principle of assessment of personal property. I. 8 John. Every individual to swear to the amount of his income, II. 9 Hen. III. If the oath of the party was doubted or disputed, an inquest summoned. III. 16 Hen. III. Individual oaths discarded, and inquests impannelled for the township or hundred.

[2] Palgrave, *Commonwealth*, i. 272.

Restoration
of the coin-
age under
Henry II
We are to understand by this the restoration of the standard value of the coin, the debasement of which had been one of the charges laid by public opinion against Stephen : [1] and the abolition of the coinage of those usurping nobles who, among the other royal rights which they had arrogated, had each for himself coined money with his own mark. But Henry's measures went further still. He abolished the local differences of the coinage which had subsisted from the days of the Heptarchy, and instituted a uniform currency for the whole kingdom. Further, by insisting on the payment at the Exchequer of the lawful coin of the realm only,[2] he threw out of circulation the debased money which was still current in his foreign territories. His proceedings were not, indeed, altogether successful : the next reign witnessed another attempt to enforce a uniform system of weights and measures : even to the present day we are experiencing how powerful local customs in this respect are against law and common sense, as well as against the empirical innovations of financial theorists. But the reformation of the coinage was probably in a great measure completed, and it must have been in the first instance, at least, a welcome change to a nation weary of the debased, mutilated, and mongrel coin which had afforded so much room for exaction, cheatery, and litigation.

New coinage
in 1158
The new coinage was ready in 1158. It is referred by Hoveden to the year 1156, but it was probably a measure which required some time for general acceptance, and was accompanied by very severe measures against the fraudulent moneyers. These are mentioned in the rolls of the second year of the reign as punished by mutilation. The first notice in the accounts, of Commutatio Monetæ occurs in 1158 : the former proceedings were, therefore, in all probability preliminary to a general enforcement of the act, which, however generally welcome, would necessarily be attended with cases of individual hardship.

New coinage
in 1180
The new coinage of 1180 was not favourably received,[3] nor are we informed of the circumstances which rendered it necessary. It

---

[1] W. Malmesb. Hist. Nov. ii. p. 712.

[2] Dialogus de Scaccario, p. 5. 'Postquam rex illustris, cujus laus est in rebus magnis excellentior, sub monarchia sua per universum regnum unum pondus et unam monetam instituit, omnis comitatus una legis necessitate teneri et generalis commercii solutione cœpit obligari ; omnes itaque idem monetæ genus quomodocunque teneant solvunt.' Up to the time of Henry II. Northumberland and Cumberland paid in mixed money. Money in England might be pronounced false on three grounds, 'in falso scilicet pondere, in falsa lege, in falsa imagine.' Ib. p. 6. The second probably referred to coin discarded and withdrawn from circulation.

[3] William of Newburgh, iii. 5, states that it was owing to the debasement 'a falsariis,' but whether this means forgers or dishonest moneyers is not clear : probably the latter ; he adds, 'quod quidem ratione utilitatis publicæ pro tempore erat necessarium, sed regni pauperibus et colonis nimis onerosum.'

may, however, have been required owing to the fraudulent management of the moneyers,[1] who were very severely punished, being carted in fetters two and two to the king's court, where they were compelled to redeem themselves with a heavy fine. An assize was issued by which the payment of the old coin was declared unlawful after Martinmas, and a new coinage was struck under the superintendence of Philip Aymar, a native of Touraine. Philip unfortunately neglected to restrict himself to lawful transactions, and was discovered to be conniving at the villanies of the moneyers in the Exchequer. The fact that he escaped punishment on this occasion, whilst minor offenders were severely treated, is somewhat suspicious. He was pardoned, and escaped by the king's connivance to France.[2] But the same year, Idonea, a London lady,[3] probably a Jewess, was mutilated for clipping, and her chattels, to wit, 9*l.* 5*s.* 4*d.* in money, five marks in blank silver, nine small gold rings, and three gold fermailles, were paid into the Exchequer by the sheriffs. As late as 1184, one Richard of Stokes was in trouble for using the old coin in exchange contrary to the assize. And in 1189, the sheriff of Cumberland was under a fine for the same.[4] The whole proceeding was unpopular, and the leniency with which the principal offender was treated is possibly to be explained much to Henry's discredit. Ralph Niger, as usual, seizes on the opportunity for invective, and tells us that the king, 'being himself corrupted by Archbishop Richard, suffered the coinage to be corrupted, and, nevertheless, hanged the corrupters of it.'[5]

Punishment of the moneyers

Punishment for clipping

Charge against the king

Henry's management of military affairs savoured strongly of his favourite policy. Of the three possible systems, the ancient Anglo-Saxon plan of arming the whole nation for the common defence was not available for external war; the divided command and jealousy that pervaded a feudal host, and the short period of feudal service, rendered the profitable employment of such assemblages almost impossible; and the name of mercenaries was so abhorrent to the English people that an attempt to support a standing army of such materials would have been a signal for rebellion. Henry acted wisely in the way in which he dealt with these elements.

Henry's military system

The adoption of scutages in commutation of personal service enabled the king to call to his assistance only those feudal retainers

Use of scutage in commutation

---

[1] Even the carelessness of the moneyers was very heavily punished. Dial. p. 19. Although the writer allows that 'in moneta generaliter peccatur ab omnibus.'

[2] Cf. R. de Diceto, 611. Gervase,

1457. W. Newb. iii. 5.

[3] Madox, *Hist. Exch.* 189.

[4] Madox, *Hist. Exch.* 191, and note to Dial. de Scacc. 21. Pipe Roll of 1 Rich I., p. 137.

[5] R. Niger, p. 168.

on whom he might confidently rely; the others were glad to be excused attendance, and their contributions were more valuable than their presence.   The length of a campaign was no longer limited by the forty days of feudal obligation, and the payment of the force which consented to lengthen its term of service at the king's bidding was defrayed from this source, or the native population spared by the employment of Welshmen or Brabantines.   The war of Toulouse was thus conducted, the king leading to it his chief vassals in person with small retinues, but an innumerable host of soldiers, *solidarii.*[1] On one occasion, in 1177,[2] Henry did make a grand demonstration of the old sort, and collected the whole feudal force of the kingdom at Portsmouth for an invasion of France, but on almost every other occasion of foreign warfare he employed mercenaries.   The campaigns in Ireland and Galloway, which can hardly be looked on as foreign wars, were fought by feudal levies; but in the former, at least, of these cases there was a distinct intention of employing at a distance elements that were dangerous at home; it was a case of feudal colonisation and to be effected by feudal means.   It does not appear that Henry thought himself strong enough to interfere directly with the rights of the great vassals in this respect.   He could dismantle their castles, imprison their persons, and make it impossible for them to reclaim their longed-for capacity of making private war; but, supposing them to be at liberty and in possession of their estates, he would have been infringing the fundamental law of feudalism if he had attempted to meddle with their own relations to their vassals.

It was his interest, however, that England should be a military power; only the leading of that power must be in the king himself. It was necessary to foster a military spirit without giving it the opportunity of being used to the prejudice of the royal power. Happily, Henry saw a way, and had the means, of maintaining such a spirit in the heart of the nation.   If the national defence had been left to feudalism, the country must have relapsed into anarchy; if it had been entrusted to mercenaries, a military despotism must have resulted: if, on the other hand, the modern principle of creating a national military spirit had been forestalled, England might have become a nation of soldiers, a scourge of the western world.

The national militia, the legitimate successor of the Anglo-Saxon fyrd, seems to have subsisted in its integrity until the reign of Stephen.[3]   This force had helped to defeat the Scots at the

Marginal notes:
Soldiers hired with the produce of the scutage

Feudal muster in 1177

The feudal military system continues to exist

Henry's plan for training the nation to arms

Difficulties of the case

The remains of the old Anglo-Saxon military system

[1] R. de Monte. 'Capitales barones suos cum paucis, . . . solidarios vero innumeros." The king of Scotland, a Welsh king, and all the counts and barons of England, Normandy, Guienne, Anjou, and Gascony, were there in person.   Gerv. 1381.
[2] Ben. Pet. i. 168, 190.
[3] Cf. Palgrave, *Commonwealth*, ii., ccclxxiii.

battle of the Standard,[1] and chiefly contributed to the suppression of the rebellion of 1173.[2] On both these occasions the conquering army partook in great measure of the character of a tumultuary levy. It was in the latter case the *posse comitatus*, under the leading of the sheriffs whose fidelity the king had secured by the judicial measures of the preceding years. But although this doubtless contributed to the success of the organisation, it is clear from the history that the freemen of the nation, the body from which this force was drawn, were faithful to the king and instinctively hostile to the feudal rebels. The same feeling also pervaded the town populations, and united for patriotic purposes the two elements which were least likely to be deluded by the dreams of military glory, the traders and the cultivators of the land.

It was perhaps from this experience that Henry learned the real value of this force and the reliance to be placed upon them. And accordingly, when in 1181 he took measures for organising the defence of his whole dominions against the ambitious yearnings of Philip II., he included the whole free population in his famous assize of arms.[3] This legislative act was not confined to England,[4] and its importance in this respect must therefore not be exaggerated. It is the inclusion of the whole free population in the general measure, not their distinct organisation, that is important. The act enforced on all freemen the duty of providing arms according to their capacity, beginning with the landholders and descending to those who possessed ten marks in chattels, including indeed all burghers and freemen. The proper equipment of each rank was defined particularly, and means ordained for carrying out the statute. The sale and exportation of arms were forbidden, and the settlement of the legal status of every freeman is placed in the hands of justices, to be ascertained by the oath of lawful men of the hundred. By this ordinance was consolidated and organised a force which could be depended on to save the country from hostile invasion, and that class was trained in the use of arms from which in after times the conquerors of Creci and Agincourt were drawn. Subsequent legislation by Edward I. in the statute of Winchester, Henry IV., Philip and Mary, and James I., has served to maintain to our own day in the form of militia the primeval institution of our Anglo-Saxon forefathers.[5]

It is no wonder that Henry, whilst providing for the defence of

Henry's assize of arms

---

[1] Richard of Hexham, 321. The archbishop of York ordered every parish priest to attend with all the parishioners capable of fighting. Ailred, Bellum Standardii, Twysden, 338.

[2] B. Petr. i. 65, 68. R. de Diceto, 574.

[3] Ben. Pet. i. 278.

[4] Ben. Pet. i. 269, 270, shows that it was first published abroad.

[5] Cf. Palgrave, *Commonwealth*, i. 305, &c., and ii., ccclxviii., &c.

Henry's em-
ployment of
mercenaries
England by the militia, and having rid himself of the hazardous
services and precarious faithfulness of the feudal armies, should
have availed himself of the use of mercenaries in his foreign
wars. Some portion of those in his pay were Welshmen,[1] who had
taken service under him at the end of the Welsh war ; but the
greater part was composed of those fearful engines of slaughter, the
Brabançon and Basque mercenaries.[2] The use of paid foreign soldiers
had prevailed since the reign of the Conqueror, and these had been
generally drawn from the Low Countries which furnished so large
a portion of the first crusaders, and were known in England as
Character of
the merce-
naries
Flemings. In many cases they were doubtless soldiers formed and
trained amid the hardships of the crusades, who had concluded their
salvation and rid themselves of their conscience by the same service.
But about the mercenaries of the latter half of the twelfth century
there are features that can hardly be traced to this original. Sprung,
no doubt, in the first instance from the lands whose names they bore,
they had practised for generations, it would seem, a trade of war,
recruiting their numbers by the incorporation of criminals, and by
the children born to them in almost promiscuous concubinage.
The historians of the time seldom speak of them without horror, as
constituting a race by themselves, without nationality, country, or
religion.[3] The names they bore were not those of the Christian
saints ; they were excommunicated by the church ; they were
attached by no tie but pay to the leader who employed them, and
with him treachery and cruelty were the chief characteristics of
their relation. They were frequently led by banished or landless
lords, who, raising the sinews of war by means of plunder, were
eager to take advantage of any disturbance to obtain a settled position. Henry, abiding by the spirit of the treaty of Wallingford,
abstained, on all but one occasion during his reign, from introducing
these mercenaries into England ; and in this he was warranted by
their employment on the side of the rebels. In 1173 the Earl of
Leicester, and Hugh Bigot in the following year, had introduced a
large force of Flemings into the Eastern counties. The former was
defeated at Forneham, and lost ten thousand Flemings in the battle ;
the latter was forced to submit by Henry himself, and his mercenaries

---

[1] B. P. i. 74, ii. 46. R. de Monte,
915.

[2] Geoffrey of Vigeois (Labbe, ii.
328) enumerates the nations, ' Primo
Basculi, postmodum Teuthonici Flandrenses, et ut rustice loquar, Braban-
sons, Hannyers, Asperes, Pailler,
Navar, Turlau, Vales, Roma, Cotarel,
Catalans, Aragones.' Under several

of these names they were condemned
in the Lateran Council of 1179, in the
same canon with the heretics, the
Cathari and Publicani. Cf. R. de
Diceto, 590. R. de Monte, 923.

[3] See Gervase, 1461, who tells us
that their camp was a place of refuge
for profligate monks, canons, nuns,
outlaws of all sorts.

with reluctance suffered to return to Flanders. In this war the count of Flanders was in alliance with the rebels, and the mercenaries were, in a measure, protected by the character of belligerents from the fate of pirates. Henry himself was accompanied by his Brabançons;[1] but as they landed only on the 8th of July, and embarked for return on the 7th of August, they had not time to effect much mischief. It is here only that they touch English history during this reign.

In 1181, Hugh de Puiset, count of Bar on the Seine, an adventurer who had been instrumental in introducing the Flemings into England in 1173, proposed to lead a body of these troops on a crusade. The pope, however, seeing the disgrace to Christendom which would arise from the employment of such wretches, suggested that the Mahometans of Spain were fitter objects for his zeal, and directed him, as a work of penance, to lead his soldiers against them : but the proposition fell to the ground.[2] *Intended crusade of Hugh of Bar on the Seine*

It is unnecessary to pursue them through the reigns of Richard and John ; but it may be observed that they were undoubtedly the precursors of the famous free companies of the following centuries, which were known by the name of Catalans, or among the Greeks by the more heathenish name of Almugavares.[3] It may even be a question whether the mysterious proscribed races existing in some parts of Europe may not be the descendants of some of these detested bodies of men. *Free companies*

So many questions turn upon the character, status, and actual powers of the Great Council of the nation, that it would be presumptuous as well as useless to attempt an examination of the subject in this preface. It does, however, occupy so prominent a place in the annals of the reign that it is impossible to pass it over. Although in several respects our knowledge of the subject is complete, it is very difficult to draw from the facts any trustworthy conclusions. We know the character of the persons who composed the assembly, the manner of their deliberations, the times of their meetings, and the subjects of their discussions. But we do not know the actual importance attached to their proceedings, and we have a very faint knowledge of their real power in either legislation or taxation. *Henry's relations with the Great Council of the nation*

The persons who composed the assembly are described exactly enough, ' the archbishops, bishops, abbots, earls, barons, knights, and free tenants in chief of the king.' In this enumeration we trace a combination of the character of the Anglo-Saxon council with the *Composition of the Great Council in the reign of Henry II.*

[1] W. Newburgh, ii. 32. R. de Monte, 915. Gerv. 1427. R. de Diceto, 576.
[2] Ben. Pet. i. 276.

[3] Gibbon, *Decl. and Fall*, c. 62, vol. viii, p. 32.

M

feudal court. The archbishops, bishops, and abbots retained the
places they had held among the sapientes of the old system ; the
barons, knights, and free tenants in chief owe their position as clearly
to the land tenure of the new. The earls in theory fulfil both conditions ; they are at once the comites, the gesiths of the old, and the
most important of the barons of the new system ; but as earls their
position was purely that of the old sapientes: they were neither in theory
nor in fact representatives of their earldoms in any other sense than

Mixed
character,
feudal and
national, of
these assem-
blies

that in which every baron represented his own tenants. All these classes
were, however, feudal tenants of the king, for the few cases in which
foreign prelates and Norman barons sat in the English councils are
insufficient to prove that the king ever gave a place to one who had
not a right to it, either by his position in the church or by his tenure.
We can have no hesitation in identifying them with the proper
constituents of the feudal court of the king as Lord Paramount of
the land. But they are not the less the national council, the direct
successors of the Witenagemote ; the sapientes and sapientiores of
the nation. The two characters were perfectly compatible, and the
limited number of persons qualified to take part in either capacity,
and the abolition of any tenure which would allow of the existence
of a class of influential men not dependent directly on the king,
necessitated such a union. Whether, however, the legal status of
the assembly when it met was that of a feudal court or of a national
council, or both ; or whether the question of legal status ever
occurred to its members, or was clearer to them than it is to us, are
matters on which, as there are few grounds of argument, there will

Position of
the lords
spiritual

always be abundance of discussion.[1] The position of the spiritual
lords, who only could trace their right to seats to a period earlier
than the institution of the baronial tenure, and whose liberties only
were provided for in the national charters, saves the incipient parliament from the definite character of a feudal court. So long as they
sat in virtue of their spiritual office, the Great Council was a national
assembly. Of the other members there were none who did not both
theoretically and actually owe their places to the king, to their
position in his household, or to the tenure of their estates ; nor
could it be a question with them whether their place was due to
their personal, or to their official, or to their territorial qualification ;
the earls no longer represented their counties, the sheriffs, who
might in some measure have done so, sat, not as sheriffs, but as
tenants in chief of the crown.

It is not clear what proportion of the classes summoned actually
attended the councils. Except in the case of the higher members

---

[1] See Hallam, *Middle Ages*, ii., &c. Allen on the Prerogative, &c.

we have no data for a conjecture. The knights and free tenants in Attendance of the persons summoned chief were summoned, but in the indefinite language of the chroniclers we cannot find any basis for calculation. The immense multitudes who occasionally are mentioned as attending are evidence of the publicity of the whole transaction, not of the numbers of the councillors. It is probable that few of the inferior tenants attended, who neither were the ordinary suitors of the county where the parliament was held, nor had business of their own to transact. The theory, however, of a representative body was perfect; each tenant in chief representing and answering for his own mesne tenants, although the principles of delegation and election, already in use for other purposes, could not, so long as the council continued to be summoned in feudal terms, be made available for this. In this point the reign of Henry II. does not furnish us with details showing any process of change. The exclusion from the court, by the decree of Woodstock of 1175,[1] of those members who had been in rebellion during the previous years, unless called up by special summons, is construed to prove the adoption of summonses in this reign; but the argument is unnecessary, for the use of summonses, not as a matter of law so much as of necessity, is clear enough at an earlier period; whilst the character of the summons, its generality or speciality, is not touched by the case.

Henry began his reign with an attempt at least to maintain the Henry's frequent employment of councils forms of the old constitution in respect to these assemblies, and a similar feeling may be traced in the transactions of the years which he was able to devote without interruption to English business.[2] These years were indeed very few; out of the thirty-four which his Short periods of his visits to England reign contained, not more than twelve and a quarter altogether, and out of these only seven terms of twelve months consecutively, were spent in England. The proceedings of these years may be taken as specimens of what his notion of constitutional routine would have been had it been possible to carry it out.

I. In the year 1155 he traversed the whole of England, partly Councils in 1155 for political, partly for judicial purposes. He held great councils at London,[3] Wallingford,[4] Bridgnorth,[5] Winchester,[6] and Westminster.[7] We are not told whether on any of these occasions he wore his crown; but as they did not synchronise with any of the great festivals of the church, and as the military character of his

---

[1] Ben. Pet. i. 93. Cf. Hallam, *Middle Ages*, iii. 9.

[2] A general reference for authorities for the subject may be made to the Itinerary, given in the Appendix to this Preface in the Rolls Series.

[3] Gervase, 1377.

[4] Gervase, 1378. R. de Monte, 886.

[5] Chron. Battle, 75.

[6] R. de Monte, 887.

[7] Chron. Battle, 76.

movements probably decided the place of assembly more than the intention of reviving the old judicial placita of the three districts of the kingdom, it is likely that he did not.

In 1157 and 1158 Henry wears his crown

II. Between April 1157 and August 1158 was a year of internal peace. During this period, and this only, the king wore his crown and held his court *de more* on the great festivals : at Pentecost, 1157, at St. Edmund's,[1] at Christmas at Lincoln,[2] and at Easter, 1158, at Worcester ;[2] all either in the Danelage or the Merchenalage. After which, the chronicler tells us, he wore his crown no more.[3] On all these occasions Great Councils were held, archbishops, bishops, abbots, earls, barons, knights, free tenants, and people attending. A fourth council was held at Northampton[4] in July 1157, in which we are not told whether or no the ceremony was performed. But it was in all probability an important military gathering, and may have been assembled for the further purpose of levying a donum for the Welsh war.

Councils in 1163 and 1164

III. and IV. The years 1163 and 1164 were spent in England. Of the legislative importance of their transactions there can be no doubt; but we may notice, perhaps, as a feature of change, that the councils are not called only to the provincial capitals, but also to the *penetralia regum*, the forest palaces of Windsor, Woodstock, Marlborough, and Clarendon. In 1163 we have assemblies at Windsor,[5] Woodstock,[6] and Westminster ;[7] in 1164 at Clarendon,[8] Reading,[9] and Northampton.[10] Of these those of Woodstock and Clarendon were as clearly national councils as those of Westminster and Northampton.

Councils in 1175, 1176, and 1177

V. and VI. Between May 1175 and August 1177, councils were held at Reading at Pentecost,[11] at Gloucester,[12] Woodstock,[13] Nottingham,[14] and Windsor,[15] in 1175 ; in 1176 at Northampton,[16] London,[17] Winchester,[18] and Westminster ;[19] in 1177 at Northampton,[20] London,[21] Oxford,[22] and Winchester,[23] the latter a military levy and council of war ; moreover during this period the king made two circuits of the southern and one of the northern counties.

VII. Between July 1178 and April 1180 we have less satisfactory

---

[1] Chron. Battle, 85.
[2] Hoveden, 281.
[3] R. de Diceto, 531. See Sir H. Ellis's pref. to John of Oxenedes, p. xviii.
[4] Gervase, 1380.
[5] R. de Anesty, ap. Palgrave, *Commonwealth*, ii. xxiii.
[6] R. de Diceto, 536.
[7] Gervase, 1384.
[8] R. de Diceto, 536.
[9] R. de Monte, 899.
[10] R. de Diceto, 537.

[11] B. P. i. 91.
[12] B. P. i. 92.
[13] B. P. i. 93.
[14] B. P. i. 94.
[15] B. P. i. 103.
[16] B. P. i. 107.
[17] B. P. i. 116.
[18] B. P. i. 118.
[19] B. P. i. 124.
[20] B. P. i. 132.
[21] B. P. i. 154.
[22] B. P. i. 162.
[23] B. P. i. 178.

evidence; but courts were certainly held at Christmas and Easter at Winchester,[1] again at Pentecost;[2] at Nottingham[3] at Christmas, 1179, and at Reading,[4] in Lent, 1180. Councils in 1178, 1179, and 1180

Nearly all, if not all, of the assemblies here enumerated were meetings of the Great Council of the nation. To many of them the attendance of the kings of Scotland, with their barons and bishops, and of the princes of Wales, gave the character of an imperial parliament. In particular Malcolm, king of Scotland, attended a court at Chester in 1157, at which he did homage, and another at Carlisle in 1158.[5] During great part of the former year he was in attendance on Henry and he followed him to the war of Toulouse.[6] In 1163 he was present again and did homage to father and son at Woodstock, in the council at which the Danegeld was debated.[7] William the Lion, who succeeded to the crown in 1165, attended the Easter council at Windsor in 1170,[8] and with his barons did homage to the younger king at Westminster the day after the coronation. After his release from captivity in 1175 he was more frequently in attendance at the royal councils. He was present at the Great Council of Northampton in January 1176,[9] and again at court in October at Feckenham, and in June 1177 at Winchester. At Christmas 1179 he was at court at Nottingham. He paid the king a long visit in Normandy in 1181, in obedience to a peremptory summons to appear in court to answer the complaints of his bishops. In 1185 he was summoned to the council at Clerkenwell and attended in person; and in 1186 he was firmly attached to Henry by a royal marriage; four days after his marriage he sent his wife to Scotland, but himself stayed for a council at Marlborough.[10] He was not, however, at the Council of Geddington, when the Saladin tithe was granted, and probably never saw Henry again. The Scottish barons refused to join in the payment, and defeated an arrangement between Henry and William by which the latter was to recover his castles.[11] One of the first measures of Richard I. was to release William from his feudal dependence, and to restore the castles, in return for a sum of money to be spent on the crusade. The attendance of the Welsh princes at the court was less easily obtained, and Henry had generally to make an expedition into the west to receive their homage.

Most of these strictly national councils

Attendances of the kings of Scotland

The Scottish barons refuse to pay the Saladin tithe

Fealty of Scotland released

Henry seems to have taken every opportunity to assemble these

[1] B. P. i. 221, 228.
[2] B. P. i. 246.
[3] B. P. i. 244.
[4] R. de Diceto, 610.
[5] Hoveden, 281.
[6] R. de Monte, ap. Bouquet, xiii. 300.
[7] R. de Diceto, 536.
[8] B. P. i. 4.
[9] B. P. i. 111.
[10] B. P. i. 351.
[11] B. P. ii. 44.

More impor-
tant na-
tional busi-
ness : legal,
financial,
feudal, and
military councils, and to have asked their advice on every possible subject.
The most important of them are described as 'concilium de statu
regni et pace reformanda,' or ' de statutis regni.'   Of this sort were
those of Bermondsey in 1155,[1] of London and Wallingford in
1156,[2] of Clarendon and Northampton in 1164, of London in 1170,
of Northampton in 1176, and Windsor in 1177.   Financial business
was treated in others, especially in that of Woodstock in 1163, and
in the Council of Geddington in 1188.   Others seem to have been
held chiefly for the reception of fealties, others for the inquiry into
feudal services, others for the organisation of the army.   In all these
we can trace the proper character of a national as well as of a feudal
assembly, although the subjects were treated, no doubt, indiscrimin-
ately ; and they are constitutionally important.

Complimen-
tary consul-
tations   Besides these, however, there were many in which matters were
canvassed on which even in the present day the voice of parliament
would not be consulted.   The arbitration between the kings of
Navarre and Castile, the application of William of Sicily for the
Private
questions
debated hand of Johanna, and the reconciliation of the archbishops of
Canterbury and York, were referred by Henry to the Great Council,
and decided by him on their recommendation.   In one particular we
gain a glimpse of an important constitutional point, when we find
the king asking of his council leave to quit the kingdom ; the cases
in which it is recorded may be merely complimentary, but the form
itself has considerable significance.

Did Henry
really ask
advice ?   These details are in themselves quite insufficient to be the
groundwork of a theory, but they afford a strong presumption as to
the real relations between Henry and his council, the king and the
parliament.   If he could have dispensed with it, his calling it together
on so many occasions shows that he wished to maintain constitutional
forms : if he could not, the fact that these assemblies were held so
regularly proves that he was able to carry on his government either
through them or in the most friendly relations with them.   It is
probable that he could have acted without them, for the baronage
was thoroughly humbled, and the adherence of the people was
secured.   We may infer from this that when he asked advice he
wanted it, and gladly availed himself of constitutional forms for
He might
do it with-
out jealousy eliciting it.   On the business of the kingdom it may be fairly said
that a strong government such as Henry's was is always amenable
to advice.   Where there was no room for jealousy, good counsel was
much more likely to be taken than under a balanced constitution,
where each constituent is afraid to accept advice lest it should grant
too much authority to the giver.   The difficulties of limited monarchy
arise from the indefinable limits of regal and parliamentary power.

[1] Gervase, 1377.   [2] Gervase, 1378.

Henry was wise enough to know his own strength, and strong enough to take good advice from whatever quarter it came.

Matters did not, however, always work smoothly. The question of Danegeld at Woodstock, and of the acceptance of the written Consuetudines at Clarendon, are proof that the voice of constitutional independence, at all events on the church side, could still make itself heard. It is needless to analyse the history of these contests. They are important as isolated constitutional phenomena, but they were not decided on constitutional principle, nor directly conducive to the development of constitutional liberty. Without Thomas Becket, it is true, we might never have had a Hubert Walter, a Langton, or a Winchelsey; but these men, when their time came, sought their precedents not from the days of Becket, but from the earlier times when the consent of the English people was deemed as necessary for the election of a king as for the concession of a tax. *Occasional difficulties*

Attempts at constitutional resistance

But however much the participation of the council in legislation and taxation may have depended on the will of the king, Henry did not assume the title or style of an absolute sovereign. His legal enactments were passed in the presence of his bishops, earls, and barons, and ' by the advice of his son, the king, and by the advice of the earls, knights, and vassals,' or ' by the common counsel of the realm,' or ' by the advice of the archbishops, bishops, abbots, and the rest of the barons of the kingdom.' There was a well-drawn line between the ' commune jus regni ' and the forest jurisdiction, which was the arbitrary will of the sovereign: the very maintenance of such a form was a protest against despotism. It was indeed a form which had been retained during the most oppressive periods of Norman tyranny, and when it was really only a form; but under Henry, in compliance with constitutional usage, advice was asked and given, though not always taken. *Henry acted with respect to constitutional forms*

The process of taxation was not often brought forward as a subject of debate, so far at least as our chroniclers tell us: it must indeed have resembled the making of a parochial rate in the present day, far more than the granting of a tax in the imperial parliament. Men know that they must pay, and in what proportions; direct resistance is useless: the notice of a rate is sufficient without assembling a vestry. So in the twelfth century, the barons and people knew that they were legally liable to certain calls and customarily liable to certain others. These bore the names of gifts and aids, but were really taxes as irresistible as the demand for a poor's rate. They were levied at certain periods and in ascertained amounts fixed by law, charter, or custom. When they became oppressive the people complained or rebelled, but their only means of redress was to bind the king by new oaths, and to keep him to *Process of making or granting a tax*

Process of taxation carried on apparently without the action of the council

them by force. The command of the purse-strings was not yet acquired, and an extravagant king could not be set on one side like an extravagant guardian or an improvident churchwarden. The Great Council at its best, or on the theory of its most enthusiastic admirers, was a very different thing from a constitutional parliament.

Sir Francis Palgrave's view of the reign ;

In this review of the internal policy of Henry II., I have, as may easily be seen, inclined to follow the old-fashioned view of the position of his reign in our history, and not the more modern one propounded but not demonstrated by Sir Francis Palgrave.[1] It is not without much thought and study that I have ventured to differ from so great an authority, from one who combined so many of the qualifications of the perfect historian—student, lawyer, and philosopher. But I must distinctly refuse to acknowledge in Henry's measures anything that should entitle his reign to be called a second conquest, or to allow that any great revolution was effected by him.

as a period of revolution

In the following passage the great historian gives some of the grounds of his theory. 'It is most certain that after the accession of the Plantagenets we find a very great similarity between the laws of Normandy and the laws of England. Both belonged to one active Sir Francis Palgrave's theory of the reign of Henry II. and powerful sovereign, one system of administration prevailed. It was after one and the same course of business that the money was counted on the Exchequer table on either side of the sea : the bailiffs in the Norman bailliages passed their accounts just as the sheriffs to whom the bailiwicks of the shires were granted in England ; and the breves by which the king administered the law, whether in the kingdom or the duchy, are most evidently germane to each other. In all these circumstances I can find the most evident and cogent proof that a great revolution was effected, not by William, but by Henry Plantagenet.'

His view accounted for

This is not an isolated passage, but a specimen of a theory into which its illustrious author was drawn by under-estimating the actual changes introduced at the Conquest, and the formal character of the portions of the old system which were retained. It was necessary to account for the phenomena of the later age by supposing a period of rapid change, and for that later date the power and genius of Henry II. seemed to account. But the arguments of the passage here quoted amount to very little, and for the most part the indications apply equally to the reign of Henry I. In his reign the laws His arguments apply equally to the reign of Henry I. of England had become so impregnated with feudalism that the element could not be eliminated even in the attempt to recall and codify the laws of the older race. We cannot say that they had

[1] *Normandy and England*, iii. 601.

become Norman, because there are so few vestiges of Norman customs with which they can be compared, and because the probability is great that the kings, having developed a system of law or custom in their insular dominions, rather assimilated the Norman practice to the English than the reverse. The Exchequer was governed on exactly the same principles in Henry I.'s reign as in Henry II.'s ; and the Norman Exchequer and the English were under Henry I. administered on the same plan and by members of the same family. The actual forms of judicial procedure which were established under Henry II. are distinctly traceable under his grandfather, and although the legal reforms of Henry II. run into details and have peculiarities which distinguish them, and even give them a true claim to the title of original conceptions, they do, at least the most important of them, distinctly retain as strong features of Anglo-Saxon as of Norman parentage. And this Sir Francis Palgrave has himself shown even whilst he ascribes to the heir of the Anglo-Saxon kings the final abolition of the Anglo-Saxon legislation. There cannot be in the mere application to novel disseisin and mortdauncester of the mode of procedure which had been long in use for other matters, nor in Henry's extending to his English subjects forms of process which had been the privilege of his Norman ones, grounds for so sweeping a charge. *Henry II.'s reforms not revolutionary*

Henry's genius as a legislator is exemplified rather in the application and combination of principles than in the origination of them. That his reign witnessed the amalgamation of the free of both nations is an evident fact. That it was the period of the more complete depression of the unfree is a theory that depends chiefly on our ignorance of their status, not only in the preceding, but in the following reigns. *Character of his legislation not originative. Question of slavery in England most obscure*

A *priori* a period of despotic oppression, a reign of terror, like that of Rufus, thirty years of rigorous systematic discipline like that of Henry I., or twenty years of anarchy such as had existed under Stephen, might seem a much more likely occasion for such a revolu-tion as that of which Sir Francis Palgrave writes. But for the revolution itself proof is wanting, and even if the phenomena which are ascribed to its effects are granted to have such an origin, it seems strange justice to fix for the period of its occurrence a reign in which every recorded measure tended to peace and to the perfect equality of the two nationalities. As for serfdom, far too little is known to enable us to say what was the actual condition of the lowest class of the people before our formal records begin. We cannot practically distinguish between the freedom of a ceorl under the Confessor and the slavery of the nativus under Henry II. : the former was in certain senses bound ; in certain senses the latter was free. We are not *Obscurity of the origin of villenage* sure of the distinction between the villein regardant and the villein in gross : we know that the mediæval serf was never so low in condition as the Anglo-Saxon theow. It may with some show of proof be denied that personal slavery, or any slavery apart from land services, ever existed in England after the Conquest. As soon as the villein class really emerges in history, it is as a class whose very disabilities imply corresponding privileges. But whatever were the

No sufficient reason for charging it on Henry II.

disabilities, and whatever were the privileges, the fact of their legal position first appearing in the work of Glanvill is a very insufficient argument for ascribing the depression of the class to the measures of Henry II.

What did Henry really abolish ?

If the constitution of England had become so feudalised before the Conquest that William had in the first instance little else to do than to take the place of Edward, what is meant by saying that Henry II. created a revolution by abolishing Anglo-Saxon legislation? What was it that he set aside ? The system of Alfred or that of Edward ? If that of Alfred, then the theory of the feudalism of Edward falls to the ground ; if that of Edward, then was it really his feudalism or his remnant of the old polity that was now abolished ? Sir Francis Palgrave might mean the latter ; I should be inclined

The feudal influence in government

to say the former. But whatever Henry abolished, he put in the place of it a system compounded of the wisest parts of both laws ; he developed and applied the principles on which the Conqueror might have acted had the revolt of 1067 and 1068 never taken place.

Consolidation the great feature of the reign ;

The length of Henry's reign, the comparative peace which the country enjoyed during it ; the uniform direction of his measures, the actual consensus of his counsellors, the ready acceptance of his reforms, all combine to give it a character of consolidation, and of power which, however highly we may be inclined to estimate it, we shall overrate if we ascribe to it features which it did not possess. It has every mark of a period of progress, of organic growth, of

not revolution

steady development. It has none of a period of revolution. It was destructive of Norman usurpation, constructive of English freedom.

Construction, not destruction

Historically, it raised the people by annihilating their oppressors ; made their interests for the time one with the interests of the crown ; gave to the fabric of society a stability, and to the constituent elements of society a distinctness of character and definiteness, which enabled them to recognise their relations to each other ; and when

Combination without confusion

the time came for further change, to distinguish friend from foe, to combine without confusion. The nobility that Henry humbled was that of Normandy ; the nobility that he founded was that of England ; nor is it a mere ingenious calculation, but a proof of the real tendency of his government, that whilst of the allies of the Conqueror every one, either by himself or by his heirs, had incurred forfeiture before the end of the reign of Henry I., of the signatories of the Great Charter nearly every one owed his position in the country to the fact that he or his fathers had been among the servants of Henry II.

¹ [1] If Henry's character as a constitutional sovereign is to be estimated by his observance of the compact under which he came to the throne, the considerations into which I have gone in the foregoing preface ought to enable us to define it pretty clearly. He was faithful to the letter of his engagements. He recovered the demesne rights of the crown, so that his royal dignity did not depend for maintenance on constant taxation. He restored the usurped estates ; he destroyed the illegal castles, and the system which they typified ; he maintained the royal hold on the lawful ones, and the equality and uniformity of justice, which their usurpers had subverted : he restored internal peace, and with it plenty, as the riches of England in the following reign amply testify. He arranged the administration of justice by enacting good laws and appointing faithful judges. He restored the currency ; he encouraged commerce, he maintained

Creation of a new nobility

Conclusion Henry observed the terms on which he was raised to the throne

Beneficial results of his policy

---

[1] The text of the agreement by which the barons bound Stephen to rule, and also bound Henry before assenting to his arrangement with Stephen, does not seem to exist. The treaty between Stephen and Henry makes no mention of the compact, and is simply a contract for the succession. (Fœd. i. 18.) The compact is described by Robert de Monte (Bouquet), xiii. 296) thus : ' Quod dux post mortem regis, si ipse eum superviveret, pacifice et absque contradictione regnum haberet ; juratum est etiam quod possessiones quæ direptæ erant ab invasoribus ad antiquos et legitimos possessores revocarentur quorum fuerant tempore Henrici optimi regis. De castellis etiam quæ post mortem prædicti regis facta fuerant, ut everterentur, quorum multitudo ad ccclxxv. summam excreverat.' Ralph de Diceto (527) has the following : ' Regalia passim a proceribus usurpata recipiet : munitiones suis [Stephani] fundatæ temporibus diruentur, quarum numerus usque ad undecies centum quindecim excrevit . . . Prædiis assignabit colonos, insularios ædificiis, nemoribus saltuarios, feris ditabit indagines, ovibus decorabit montana, pascua replebit armentis. Clerus nunc demum dominabitur, pacis tranquilli-

tatem indicet, muneribus sordidis non gravabitur, ab extraordinariis vacationem habebit. Defensivæ locorum seu vicecomites locis statuentur statutis, non in votum exercendæ cupiditatis abibunt ; non quenquam ex odio persequentur ; non gratificabuntur amicis ; non indulgentiis crimina sublevabunt, suum cuique reservabunt ex integro : metu pœnarum nonnullos afficient ; præmiorum exhortatione plurimos excitabunt. Fures terrebuntur in furca, prædones sententia capitali plectentur. Milites caligati gladios suos in usum vomeris ligonisque convertent. A castris ad aratra, a tentoriis ad ergasteria, Flandrensium plurimi revocabuntur, et quas nostratibus operas indixerunt dominis suis ex necessitate persolvent. Quid multis ? Ab excubiis fatigati a communi lætitia respirabunt. Innocens et quieta rusticitas otio relevabitur. Negotiatores commerciorum vicissitudo locupletabit. Forma publica percussa eadem in regno celebris erit ubique moneta.' In this passage the legal compact takes the form of a prophecy or joyful anticipation. Matthew Paris (p. 86) places the treaty at Wallingford, but there is much obscurity as to both the time and place.

the privileges of the towns; and, without encouraging an aggressive spirit, armed his people for self-defence.   He sustained the form, and somewhat of the spirit, of national representation.   The clergy had grounds of complaint against him for very important reasons; but their chief complaints were caused by their preference of the immunities of their class to the common safeguard of justice. Henry's personal character, his ultimate aims, his principles of policy, the very means which he used to carry out these desirable ends, are matters of a different kind, to be judged on other principles, and to be acquitted or condemned by a more competent tribunal than distant posterity.

THE CHRONICLE OF ROGER OF HOVEDEN. Vol. II.

[ROGER OF HOVEDEN was a clerk or chaplain of Henry II.; he was connected with the North of England; he was at one time a justice of the forests. A considerable part of his work is devoted to the history of the See of York, and to the history of Hugh of Puiset and of his family. It is supposed that Roger took his name from the town of Howden. His work is of great value to the historian, and was for centuries the principal store of facts for the reign of Henry II. In the ensuing pages will be found (1) an account of the death of Henry II., and (2) a sketch of the relations of England with the Continent during that king's reign. Henry II. was 'the greatest monarch of the time, the most cautious politician, and the wealthiest man, practised in all the arts of the warrior and the statesman, a man who never gave way, never truckled, never missed his aim before, falls before the rising fortunes of an enemy whom he despised as a boy, and the arms of a son whom he had trained to his own humiliation.' Such is Bishop Stubbs's picture of Henry II. After describing in eloquent terms the last scenes of the great king's life, the Bishop shows how the foreign policy of England dates from this time, explains the French, German, Spanish, and Italian policy of Henry II., and traces through English history the effects of the relations then entered upon.]

*   *   *   *   *   *

HENRY had been in France since July 1188. Early in that year he had concluded his arrangements to join Philip in a crusade, and had returned to England to make preparations there. From England he was recalled by the outbreak of war. Philip had made a protext of the quarrel between Richard and the count of Toulouse, to invade Berry and take possession of Châteauroux. His expedition was anything but glorious, for he fled at the very news of Richard's approach, and did not attempt a battle. As the territories which he ravaged were the property of Henry, the old king, after an ineffectual attempt at peace, defied Philip and invaded his states. Several efforts for pacification having been defeated by the inveterate mistrust which was mutual between Philip and Henry, a truce was concluded for the Christmas holidays, to end, as was usual, on the feast

Sketch of the last days of Henry II.

The winter of 1188

of St. Hilary. At the expiration of the truce war was renewed, but in the meantime Richard had deserted his father and joined Philip.

Henry's illness in the spring of 1189

Henry seems to have lost hope and energy. He was suffering from a fistula, and depressed in both body and mind. He continued at Le Mans with his court,[1] but with no great force, during the spring of 1189, the allies in the meantime devastating the border territories, and the papal legate, John of Anagni, attempting to mediate. But Philip believed that the legate was in Henry's pay, and took advantage of his arrogance to refuse his arbitration. At Whitsuntide a last attempt at peace was frustrated, and from that date the stream of events ran rapidly.

Last attempt at peace, June 4

Philip conquers Maine and approaches Le Mans

Burning of Le Mans

The conference was held on Trinity Sunday. It broke up in a more determined quarrel than ever. Yet Henry returned to Le Mans and took no overt action. Within a week [2] Philip had overrun Maine, and announced his determination to attack Tours. Still Henry did not move. On the Monday week [3] after the conference Philip suddenly appeared before Le Mans, and the royal forces prepared for a siege, or at least for an assault. Stephen of Turnham, steward of Anjou, in attempting to burn a suburb that might otherwise give shelter to the besiegers, set fire to the city itself. A struggle ensued for the possession of the bridges, and between the fire and the French Henry found his position untenable. Unable to keep the oath he had sworn to the Manceaux that he would never leave them, he was compelled to fly, and leave his birthplace and his father's tomb in the hands of the enemy. The few of his knights who could threw themselves into the citadel, and held out until the third day; but Henry with 700 horsemen fled in panic before Philip and Richard, and had it not been for the breaking down of the bridge over a stream that the pursuers could not ford, they must inevitably have been taken.[4] It is here that Giraldus takes up the story.[5]

Flight of Henry

The king's companions

Besides Geoffrey the chancellor, Henry had with him William Fitz-Ralph, the steward of Normandy, and William de Mandeville, earl of Essex, and in his wife's right count of Aumale, two of the small number of nobles who had been faithful to him

[1] Gir. Camb. De Inst. Pr. iii. 13, ed. Brewer, p. 115. There were three archbishops at court, Baldwin of Canterbury, Walter of Rouen, and Bartholomew of Tours, whom Giraldus, in common with Benedict and Hoveden, calls William. It does not appear which of the prelates was with him at his death, but he was buried by the archbishops Bartholomew of Tours and Fulmar of Treves. R. de Diceto, 645. Baldwin remained in France until the end of July, and it is strange if he was not with his old friend until the last. But I have no evidence to prove that he was (Gervase, 1546); and he certainly was at Rouen when the king was at Azai two or three days before he died. Epp. Cantuar. 296.

[2] Between Trinity Sunday, June 4, and S. Barnabas's day.

[3] June 12.

[4] Benedict, ii. 68.

[5] Vita Galfridi, Angl. Sac. ii. 381.

during all the treasons and struggles of his reign. John was not there, but his father had not yet learned his treason, and the rebellion of Richard had probably strengthened his determination to make him his successor. It would appear that the fugitives left Le Mans by the northern of the two bridges over the Sarthe; it was defended by a strong fortification, which held out against the French for some days after the citadel had surrendered. They fled towards Normandy.[1] The day was extremely hot, the roads narrow and heavy:[2] the flight had all the circumstances of a rout. The pursuit indeed was not carried far. The horse of Richard, who was leading it, was wounded by the lance of one of his knights, and he was thrown.[3] Perhaps the stoppage gave him time to think, and he turned back. At a distance of two miles[4] Henry was able to draw rein, look back on the burning city, and bid it his last farewell. The farewell was, as Giraldus reports it, uttered in the very spirit of blasphemous defiance which was so characteristic of the Plantagenet temper. 'My God, since, to crown my confusion and increase my disgrace, thou hast taken from me so vilely the town which on earth I have loved best, where I was born and bred, and where my father lies buried, and the body of S. Julian too, I will have my revenge on thee also; I will of a surety withdraw from thee that thing which thou lovest best in me.' He said more still, which Giraldus thought safer not to record; then he continued his flight. Twenty miles[5] they rode that day, and towards night reached La Frenaye,[6] a castle of Henry's kinsman, the viscount of Beaumont, lying on the left bank of the Sarthe, on the road to Alençon. The castle was too small for the whole retinue, and the chancellor wished to remain outside in the village, in case of an attack being made by the enemy in pursuit. But Henry seems to have clung to him with the earnestness of despair; he insisted on his coming in, and they passed the night together. Geoffrey had lost all his baggage in Le Mans; the king was a little better provided, and furnished his son with a change of linen.[7] The discomfort of the journey had

They fly northwards

The flight from Le Mans, June 12

Henry's farewell to his native city

Arrival at La Frenaye

The king spends the night there

[1] The words of the *Philippis* are clear as to the direction of his flight, although he did not, according to Giraldus, go so far as Alençon; 'dum fugit oblitus famæ et regalis honoris, Donec Alençonis tuta se clausit in arce, Continuo fugiens viginti millia cursu.' *Philippis*, ap. Pithœum, p. 266.

[2] Gir. Camb. Vita Galfridi; in Anglia Sacra, ii. 381.

[3] Gir. Camb. De Inst. Pr. iii. 24, ed. Brewer, 140.

[4] Gir. Camb. De Inst. Pr. iii. 24, ed. Brewer, 138.

[5] *Philippis*, p. 266.

[6] 'Frenellas,' Gir. Camb. De Inst. Pr. iii. 25, ed. Brewer, 140; and Vita Galfridi, in Ang. Sac. ii. 381. I suppose the place to be La Frenaye. Giraldus describes it as containing a castle, a municipium, and a 'villa modica.' It is at the right distance and in the right direction from Le Mans. See Stapleton's *Norman Rolls*, ii. p. xxxii.

[7] 'Interulam propriam et vestimenta,' Gir. Camb. V. Galfr. 381.

been very great; many of the knights had perished from heat and fatigue before they reached the place of safety.

They took supper together; but after supper, Henry, with that passionate waywardness which marks his failing powers, refused to be undressed. He lay down on a couch, and Geoffrey spread his own cloak over him.

In the morning, Tuesday, June the 13th, the king had changed his mind. He would not desert his native province; he would return to Anjou, and if he must die he would die there. In vain his counsellors argued that his strength lay all to the north, that the Norman castles were out of the reach and above the strength of Philip. Geoffrey might lead the army, the scanty force that still mustered round him; he would go back; he could go to Chinon.[1] The nobles were forced to obey. William Fitz-Ralph and William de Mandeville swore that, if anything unlucky befell the king, they would surrender the castles of Normandy only to John. The chancellor was to see the force in safety to Alençon; then he might rejoin his father. How Henry reached Anjou we are not told. It must have been an adventure equal in secrecy and rapidity to those of his best days, for all the roads were beset by Philip's forces. Henry, however, knew the country, both as a soldier and as a hunts-

man. Geoffrey hurried to Alençon, and then, having assured him-self of the safety of the place, took a hundred chosen and well-equipped knights, and set off to seek the king. He overtook him at

a place called Savigny,[2] thence they proceeded to Chinon, and a few days later to Saumur.

Of the acts of Henry during the following fortnight we have no record. He was probably suffering from his disease, aggravated by the heat of the weather and the loss of rest. In the meantime Philip was possessing himself one by one of the fortresses of Maine, and announcing his intention not to rest until he had taken Tours.

There were on both sides many counsellors of peace, and it is probable that several interviews were held between the subordinates in the last week of June, for otherwise it is difficult to account for the differences of the date of the final agreement, as given by the several historians. But it is not probable that Henry, Richard, and Philip met more than once again. An interview was arranged, as

---

[1] 'Versus Andegaviam,' Gir. Camb. V. Galfr. Ang. Sac. ii. 381; Hoveden, ii. 364; Benedict, ii. 68; Rigord, 185, who, however, makes Henry fly direct to Chinon.

[2] 'Savigniacum.' There are so many places in Maine of this and similar names that I cannot venture on deciding which is the one referred to. As the western part of the county was less in Philip's hands than the eastern, I should look for it in that direction. But possibly it is the village on the Vienne, between Chinon and Cande.

Giraldus states, to be held at Azai on the 30th of June,[1] but Henry was too ill to attend. On that very day he was seized with fever. Henry seized with fever Philip and Richard refused to believe that this was anything but an excuse for delay, and although the terms of peace were proposed, and probably accepted on both sides, no formal armistice was made. Philip was determined to take Tours before he laid down his arms.

On the same day, the 30th of June, on a Friday,[2] Philip appeared Philip approaches Tours, Friday, June 30 before Tours ; Henry being at Saumur, and knowing himself to lie at his enemy's mercy. The young conqueror announced his intention of attacking the city on the Monday, whether or no Henry should in the meantime determine on submission. One more attempt was made to end the war. With Philip were his uncle, archbishop William of Rheims, Philip count of Flanders, and Hugh duke of Burgundy. Visit of the French nobles to Henry at Saumur, July 2 The two former were now growing old men, and were better able to estimate Henry's character and position than they had been twenty years before, when they had been the chief supporters of Becket. The count of Flanders and the duke of Burgundy were earnest and sincere crusaders ; they both perished two years afterwards in Palestine, They were inclined to mediate Philip on his second pilgrimage. If the holy city were to be recovered, peace must be made before Henry was crushed and Christendom maimed of one of its mightiest members. Gratitude as well as piety, and prudence as well as gratitude, may have swayed

[1] There is a consensus of historians as to the festival of S. Peter and S. Paul as marking the date of the drawing up of the treaty. R. de Diceto, 645. Giraldus speaks of the conference as held in Henry's absence : 'sumpto inter reges colloquio non procul ab oppidulo Turoniæ, cui nomen erat Azai, feria sexta, rex Anglorum eodem quo convenire debuerant die, apud Azai, lethaliter acuta febri correptus accubuit.' R. de Diceto places it on the eve, June 28, Wednesday ; Giraldus on the Friday, June 30.

[2] The French historian, Rigord, 185, places the assault of Tours on the 23rd of June, and the death of Henry twelve days after. But the evidence of Benedict, Hoveden, and of Giraldus also, is clearly against this. It is true that the earlier date would give more room for the otherwise crowded action of the week ; but Rigord is not so exact a chronicler, nor so nearly contemporary, as the others. It is impossible altogether to reconcile the statements of the different writers. Hoveden and Benedict place Henry at Saumur on Sunday

July 2 ; Giraldus makes him fall ill at Azai on the Friday before ; William the Breton makes him come from Chinon to Colombières on the Tuesday. Again Hoveden seems to suppose that he was present at the conference at which the terms of the treaty were drawn up ; Giraldus says that although he was at Azai he was sick, and disappointed Philip and Richard, who refused to believe the excuse. I have tried to follow the sequence of facts, arranging the localities as I found the authority of the historians confirmed by the relative position of the towns where the events happened. Chinon lies about halfway between Saumur and Azai, Azai about halfway between Chinon and Tours, and Colombières halfway between Tours and Azai. If Henry were at Azai on the Friday, he could hardly have gone back, ill as he was, to Saumur for Sunday ; he would rather have gone to Chinon. To harmonise the statements is impossible, for Giraldus clearly believed that he was at Azai from Friday to Tuesday ; Hoveden as clearly says that he was at Saumur on the Sunday.

them. Henry had more than once interfered to save them; it would not be well that Philip should become too powerful. The year before they had mediated successfully, and vowed to desert Philip if he would not agree to peace. Against his will they visited Henry on the Sunday at Saumur. We have no record of the conversation; they had no authority to make terms other than were determined on the Friday before.

Philip takes Tours, Monday, July 3

On the Monday Philip assaulted Tours: it was defended by a scanty force, and its natural strength was not sufficient to counterbalance the deficiency. The Loire was half dried up by the continued heat, and on the river-side the ladders of the besiegers were planted. It surrendered the same day.

Henry goes to Azai

And now Henry nerved himself for an interview which he knew could have but one issue. Ill as he was, he moved from Saumur to Azai, and in the plain of Colombières [1] met Philip and Richard on the day after the capture of Tours.[2]

Conference at Colombières, Tuesday, July 4

Henry, notwithstanding his fistula and his fever, was able to sit on horseback. His son Geoffrey had begged leave of absence, that he might not see the humiliation of his father; [3] but many of his other nobles, and probably two of his three archbishops, rode beside him.[4] The terms which he had come to ratify had been settled beforehand. He had but to signify his acceptance of them by word of mouth. They met face to face, the unhappy father and the undutiful son. It was a clear sultry day, a cloudless sky and still air.[5] As the kings advanced towards one another a clap of thunder was heard, and each drew back. Again they advanced, and again it thundered louder than before. Henry, wearied and excited, was ready to faint.

Henry's submission.

His attendants held him up on his horse, and so he made his submission. He had but one request to make; it was for a list of the conspirators who had joined with Richard to forsake and betray him. The list was promised, and he returned to Azai. Before he parted with Richard he had to give him the kiss of peace; he did so, but

---

[1] 'Anglicus interea pacem rogat, et licet ægra
Febre laboraret, calida Chinone relicta
Usque Columbare pro pacis amore venire
Sustinuit.'
Philippis, ap. Pith. p. 268.

[2] At p. 365 of this volume (Rolls Series), and, I am sorry to say, twice in the second volume of Benedict of Peterborough, I have given Rigord as the authority for this statement. Both place and day are derived from the *Philippis* of William the Breton, which occurs in the same volume with Rigord.

He mentions Colombières expressly as the place. The day is fixed by the statement 'post triduum,' which is confirmed by Matthew Paris. I quoted Rigord by memory, and forgot to verify the reference. *Philippis*, p. 268; M. Paris (ed. Wats), p. 151. According to Giraldus, the conference between Philip and Henry took place on the day after the capture of Tours.

[3] Gir. Camb. Vita Galfr., Ang. Sac. ii. 381.

[4] Archbishop Baldwin was at Rouen: Epp. Cantuar. 296.

[5] Hoveden, Rolls Series, vol. ii. p. 366.

the rebellious son heard his father whisper, and was not ashamed to repeat it as a jest to Philip's ribald courtiers, ' May God not let me die until I have taken my due vengeance on thee.' [1]

But not even his submission and humiliation procured him rest. Among the minor vexations of the last months had been the pertinacious refusal of the monks of Canterbury [2] to obey the archbishop in certain matters in which they believed their privileges to be infringed. Henry had, as usual with him in questions of ecclesiastical law, taken a personal interest in the matter, and had not scrupled to back the archbishop with arms at Canterbury and support of a still more effective kind at Rome. A deputation from the convent, sent out in the vain idea that Henry's present misfortunes would soften his heart towards them, had been looking for him for some days. They found him at Azai,[3] most probably on his return from the field of Colombières. ' The convent of Canterbury salute you as their lord,' was the greeting of the monks. ' Their lord I have been, and am still, and will be yet,' was the king's answer; ' small thanks to you, ye traitors,' he added below his breath.[4] One of his clerks prevented him from adding more invective. He bethought himself probably that even now the justiciar was asking the convent for money towards the expenses of the war; he would temporise, as he had always seemed to do with them. ' Go away, and I will speak with my faithful,' he said when he had heard their plea. He called William of S. Mere l'Eglise, one of the chiefs of the chancery, and ordered him to write in his name. The letter is extant,[5] and is dated at Azai. It is probably the last document he ever issued. It begins, ' Henry, by the grace of God king of England, duke of Normandy and Aquitaine, and count of Anjou, to the convent of Christ Church, Canterbury, greeting, and by God's mercy on his return to England, peace.' The substance of the letter is, that the monks should take advantage of the delay in his return to reconsider their position, and the things that make for

Visit of the monks of Canterbury to Henry at Azai

The king's letter to Canterbury

---

[1] Gir. Camb. De Inst. Pr. iii. 26, ed. Brewer, p. 150.

[2] The whole story of the dispute is in Gervase; and the letters written on the subject are in the *Epistolæ Cantuarienses*, which form the second volume of my *Memorials of Richard I.*

[3] This is certain from the date of the letter issued by the king, and from Gervase, c. 1544. The latter author distinctly says that he died and was buried within a week of his interview with the monks. He died on Thursday July 6th, and on the following day the funeral started for

Fontevraud. We are not told the exact day of the burial, but it could scarcely have been before Saturday, on which day Giraldus seems to place it, V. Galfr. p. 382. If I am wrong in supposing the king to have gone from Saumur to Azai on Monday, or early on Tuesday, the interview with the monks may have taken place two or three days earlier.

[4] Epp. Cantuar. p. 295.

[5] Epp. Cantuar. p. 297; Gervase, c. 1545. Gervase omits the peculiar words of the salutation.

peace, that they might find an easier way out of their difficulties when he should come. The monks, delighted with their success, retired, and the king lay down to rest. It was then, probably, that the fatal schedule was brought him,[1] which he had so unwisely

He receives the list of the traitors: and hears the name of John

demanded at Colombières. It was drawn up in the form of a release from allegiance; all who had adhered to Richard were allowed to attach themselves henceforth to him, in renunciation of the father's right over them.[2] He ordered the names to be read. The first on the list was that of John. The sound of the beloved name startled him at once. He leaped up from his bed as one beside himself, and looking round him with a quick troubled glance exclaimed, 'Is it true that John, my very heart, the best beloved of all my sons, for whose advancement I have brought upon me all this misery, has forsaken me?' The reader had no other answer to make than to repeat the name. Henry saw that it was on the list, and threw himself back on the couch. He turned his face to the wall, and

His despair

groaned deeply. 'Now,' he said, 'let all things go what way they may; I care no more for myself nor for the world.' His heart was broken, and his death-blow struck.

He moves from Azai to Chinon

He could not, however, remain at Azai. His people carried him in a litter to Chinon,[3] where Geoffrey was waiting for him. It was the fifth day of the fever, and in all probability he was delirious with the excitement of the morning. It was remembered and reported in England that after he was brought to Chinon he cursed the day

Stories of his cursing his sons

on which he was born,[4] and invoked God's malison on his sons: the bishops and priests about him implored him to revoke the curse, but he refused. But Giraldus, bitter enemy as he was, somewhat softened by his misfortune, tells a different tale. He draws the picture of the dying king leaning on Geoffrey's[5] shoulder whilst one of his knights held his feet in his lap. Geoffrey was fanning the flies from the king's face, as he seemed to be sleeping. As they

Giraldus's account of the last days

watched, the king revived and opened his eyes. He looked at Geoffrey and blessed him. 'My son,' he said, 'my dearest, for that thou hast ever striven to show towards me such faithfulness and gratitude as son could show to father, if by God's mercy I shall recover of this sickness, I will of a surety do to thee the duty of the best of fathers, and I will set thee among the greatest and mightiest men of my dominion. But if I am to die without requiting thee, may God, who is the author and rewarder of all good, reward thee, because in

---

[1] He was still at Azai, Hoveden, p. 366. Cf. Gir. Camb. De Inst. Pr. iii. 25, ed. Brewer, p. 148.
[2] Gir. Camb. l.c.
[3] Hoveden, 366; Gir. Camb. V.

Galfr., Ang. Sac. ii. 381.
[4] Hoveden, ii. 366; M. Paris, 151.
[5] Gir. Camb. V. Galfr., Ang. Sac., ii. 381

every fortune alike thou hast shown thyself to me so true a son. Geoffrey, of whose sincere sorrow there can be no doubt, was overwhelmed with tears. He could but reply that all he prayed for was his father's health and prosperity. Another day passed, and the king's strength visibly waned. He kept crying at intervals, ' Shame, shame on a conquered king.' [1] At last, when Geoffrey was again by his side, the poor king kept telling him how he had destined him for the see of York, or, if not York, Winchester; [2] but now he knew that he was dying. He drew off his best gold ring with the device of the panther, and bade him send it to his son-in-law, the king of Castile; and another very precious ring, with a sapphire of great price and virtue, he ordered to be delivered out of his treasure. Then he desired that his bed should be carried into the chapel, and placed before the altar.[3] He had strength still to say some words of confession, and received ' the Communion of the Body and Blood of the Lord with devotion.' And so he died, on the seventh day of the fever,[4] on the sixth of July, the octave of the apostles Peter and Paul.

Geoffrey's conversations with his father

The king's confession and death, July 6

*   *   *   *   *   *

There is a branch of politics without some consideration of which our view of the reign and of the value of its historians would be very imperfect. I will point out very briefly the ways in which the foreign policy of England during the middle ages was affected by the circumstances, the acts, and the alliances of the first king of the house of Anjou.

The foreign policy of England dates from this time

It is scarcely an exaggeration to say that England owes her introduction into the family of European nations to the Norman Conquest. Almost all her previous intercourse with the continent had been of that personal and occasional sort which, although it helps to increase acquaintance, has little in common either with the dynastic policy of kings or the political action of nations. It is the first step indeed, but only a step towards it. The early intermarriages of the house of Wessex with the Karlings, and the later ones with the families of the Saxon and Franconian emperors; the momentary jealousy of Charles and Offa, that of Lewis and Kenulf [5] (if it were more than a mere verbal bravado); the travels of Ethelwulf and Alfred; the wanderings of the children and grandchildren of Ethelred; the long list of pilgrimages to Rome and Jerusalem

Isolation of England before the Conquest

Englishmen and transactions abroad before the Conquest

[1] Gir. Camb. De Inst. Pr. iii. 26, ed. Brewer, p. 150.
[2] Gir. Camb. V. Galfr., Ang. Sac. ii. 382.
[3] This is mentioned, I think, only by Hoveden, ii. 367.
[4] 'feria quinta, et a quo decubuit septima; die videlicet quem physici criticum vocant.' Gir. Camb. De Inst. Pr. iii. 26, ed. Brewer, p. 150.
[5] Kemble, Codex Dipl. i. 281. Compare this with the letters of Leo III. to Charles, in Mansi, xiii. 969, 974.

that stretches through the whole of the Anglo-Saxon annals from Willibald to Ealdred and Sweyn, from Ina to Harold and Tostig : all these had done little more than remind the struggling powers of the 'dark' ages, that in the Northern Sea, separated in language and laws from the races that had fallen and risen under the spell of Rome, lay two islands full of Christian men and churches, that had their wars and peace, their councils and policy, almost entirely to themselves.

In one respect indeed there was an apparent and an obvious exception to this general severance : from the first ages of the Conversion some sort of intercourse had been maintained between the churches. But even this was scanty, interrupted, and exceptional. Northumbria by her missions to Friesland, Wessex by the gift of Boniface to Germany, had done something to fulfil the duty of children to the parent land. Alcuin had more than repaid the debt under which, two centuries before, the Franco-Gallican church had laid the infant Christianity of the Heptarchy. One or two literary friendships continued to throw a ray of light across the gloom of the ninth century. Once or twice a legate is admitted from Rome, but as an inquirer or an ambassador, not yet as a judge ; from time to time an archbishop crosses the Alps and is entertained at the Lateran. From Fleury and S. Omer we had imported an unwelcome and unseasonable monachism ; and later on had even drawn a new system of education from the colleges of Lorraine. But there was

little in common between the ascetic prelates and pious witan of England and the secularised bishops and disloyal politicians of France and Germany ; little harmony of feeling between the scholars of Bede, Alcuin, Alfred, and Elfric, and the schools, moral, political, or intellectual, that produced a Hildebrand or an Adalbert. English bishops were a greater novelty in a council of France or Rome than their British predecessors had been at Arles and Rimini, or the names of Anglo-Saxon saints in the calendar of Lanfranc. From the Conquest this isolation ceases.

Like many other features of our national character, this, in the age immediately preceding the Conquest, seemed to be undergoing a change. The reign of Canute had put his English kingdom in close connexion with Northern Europe ; a relation which, beginning under a prince who possessed a larger stake on the continent than any other who ever ruled in England, might have resulted in some such effects as followed the union with Normandy. But in this case the duration of the connexion was so short, and the point of conjunction so far removed from the focus of political life, both in religion and in secular matters, and the English policy of Canute was so English, that, in spite of his statesmanlike and cosmopolitan instincts, no such results followed. Again under Edward the Confessor England seemed first to advance towards and then to retire from intimacy with her foreign sisters. Edward's wandering life had made him familiar with the manners and cities of many men ; and although he came back to his island throne little wiser than when he left it, having learned only what had better have been forgotten, his people were awakened somewhat rudely to the fact that there were other nations than Danes and Norsemen who felt a vivid interest in their fertile lands and cunning goldsmiths' work. From Lorraine and Saxony poured in strange bishops ; from Normandy and Flanders came noble adventurers with old Teutonic names, but Frenchmen in manners and intrigue ; now each political party at home sought allies and a fulcrum in some foreign court : one in Normandy, one in Flanders, one in Denmark ; the king himself most naturally in the imperial house. It was from Germany perhaps that he had learned to admire the relations of Henry II. and Cunegunda,[1] and to see in their Bamberg a pattern for his own Westminster.[2] But just as feudalism itself, although matters had been verging upon it so long, came on England at last *per saltum*, the result of sudden invasion, not the outgrowth of natural causes regularly developed ; so, when the time came for her to step into the whirlpool of European interests, the impulse came from without, the step was taken at the time and as a consequence of the Conquest. Henceforth, instead of associating with other nations in casual, personal, or occasional interests only, she was to take her place as a player in the great game.

Not less than by the mere fact of the Conquest, this result was affected by the character of the conquering house, by the condition of Europe itself, and by the nature of the great enterprise which had for its chief consequence the bringing the nations face to face with each other—the first Crusade. Of this latter influence it is almost as difficult to overrate the importance as it is that of the Conquest itself ; but whether or no England would without the Norman dynasty be drawn into the Crusade—and throughout the Crusades, in their whole duration, there is a thread of English distinct from Norman or Angevin interest—it was by that connexion that it was in fact so involved. It is a consequence of the Conquest, not one of a set of co-ordinate causes.

It might seem more natural to fix our date at the reign of Henry I. It was nearest to the Crusade ; it was the earliest point at which the

And Edward likewise

Political alliances of the English parties under Edward

The Conquest the real starting-point

Importance of the Crusades in this view

English as contrasted with Norman exploits in the Crusades

[1] Vita Henrici, Canis, Lect. iii. p. 2, p. 31.

[2] I dare not venture to affirm that Edward ever was in Germany, but the evidence for his political connexion with that country is abundant.

Gunhilda, the first wife of Henry III. is called by the biographer of Edward (ed. Luard, 395) Edward's sister. She was the daughter of Canute and Emma.

public mind of England could have been consulted on foreign politics, for under the Williams national thought in Norman as in Englishman was in abeyance, and Henry by his relations with France and Flanders, by the marriage of his daughter with Henry V., and that influence over his son-in-law which led to the belief that by his advice the emperor was about to tax the empire on the plan of Domesday Book,[1] clearly exercised an important weight in continental politics. But Henry's position in Europe, dignified as it was, resulted in great measure from his father's policy, and sprang altogether from that startling success which had roused France into terrified jealousy, and spread into further Europe the panic fear that William Bostar, the chosen of Alexander and Hildebrand, was going to descend upon the empire like Alaric or Attila, or as a little later the Normans did on Apulia, at the papal invitation, a scourge at

once of schism and civilisation. But it is to the Conquest itself, as including all the other secondary impulses, that we may trace everything distinctive in the change. By it the church is brought into close connexion with Rome, and the nation in its political aspect, after a short apprenticeship in the quarrels of French and Flemish provincial sovereigns, takes that place in European parties which, for good or evil, it has retained with little change of attitude for seven hundred years, and more or less to the present day.

It would, I am aware, be more in accordance with the philosophy of history to base the relations which subsisted between England and France during the latter middle ages upon general principles, by a reference to those general laws which are so convenient a revelation in the ignorance of facts : by adducing the natural antagonism between insular and continental nations, between Teutons and Celts, between trading and agricultural peoples ; or the jealous rivalry which is of course the normal condition of states which, having no common object of ambition, are always in active competition ; or any of the elaborately ingenious arguments which are so apt to show that all things would have been exactly as they are if everything had been diametrically opposite to what it was. All this may be quite true ; it may be a fair experiment for the reconstruction of the moral government of the world ; but it is not history, and whatever the philosopher may do, the student may not pretend to view matters from that high standing point at which facts and individualities become invisible. As a matter of fact it was from the Norman Conquest that England as a state was brought into relation with the powers of Europe, and from its initial relations with those powers, as the events of the twelfth century defined them, that its political position was determined down to the period of the

[1] Otto Frising, ap. Urstis. i. 148.

second French revolution. And this definition was owing, not to antipathies or sympathies of races, not to physical geography, nor to distinctions in the development of feudal institutions, but to the varying personal relations of the rulers of the kingdoms, and to the second nature of peoples educated for twenty generations in the wars, and identifying themselves through good and evil with the interests, and accumulating six centuries' experience of the rights and wrongs of kings.

But although it was by the Conquest that England was forced into the participation of European politics, it is to the complications of the following century that the determination of her exact position with regard to them is to be ascribed. There were during the mediæval period three distinct crises which defined the relations of England with France, out of which most of her external history resulted : the Conquest, the reign of Henry II., and the reign of Edward III. Of these three the second is from this point of view the most decisively important. The French and Norman quarrels might indeed have produced the same results as did the marriage of Henry and Eleanor, but their operation was merged in the larger questions opened by the personal hatred between the Angevin princes and the house of Lewis VII., and by the jealousies accumulated by the transfer of Guienne and Poictou. The wars of Edward III. and Henry V. would have been impossible without that training in the hatred of foreigners which had been growing upon the English since the Conquest, but had reached its maximum during the internal and external quarrels of the thirteenth century. Not that it was by any means an indiscriminating hatred. England accepted the alien Stephen rather than the alien Geoffrey ; and by the alien Simon de Montfort wrought her deliverance from the tyranny based on and aggravated by foreign favouritism. The king as a general rule was accepted as the national leader, and, so long as his barons remained foreigners in spirit, the heart of the nation was with him against them. When the amalgamation between the barons and the people was completed, and by a singular coincidence the king brought his friends and ministers from abroad, it was time indeed to limit the power of the crown, but there was no thought of changing the dynasty ; and the political alliances of the king, unlike mere matrimonial ones, seem to have commanded the full sympathy of the nation generally. To the English of the twelfth century, delivered by Henry II. from the feudal tyranny of the Norman baronage, France was the great stay and support of the common enemies of themselves and their king : to those of the thirteenth, from the accession at least of Henry III., France was the source and home of men and measures which, as sustaining the royal faithlessness,

Relations of England and France during the middle ages

They take their colour from the reign of Henry II.

The origin of the national feeling towards France

France the great object of English antipathy

were alike hateful to nobles and people: from the reign of
Edward III. downwards, king, nobles, and people joined heart and
soul in a war which lasted as long as the middle ages themselves.

Balance of
power in
Europe in
the twelfth
century
The state of 'the balance of power in Europe,' in the twelfth
century, was this briefly: there were certain great bundles of states,
connected by a dynastic or by a national unity; the kingdom of
France, the empire in Germany, the Christian states of Spain, the
territories of the house of Plantagenet, the still solid remnant of the
Byzantine empire, the well-compacted dominions of the Normans in
Apulia and Sicily. Of these, France, Germany, and Spain were
busily striving either for consolidation or against dissolution; the
estates of the Plantagenets were bound only by the personal tie;
Constantinople was far removed from the interests of Christendom,
her face set always eastward, in church and state; the Norman state
in Sicily and Apulia was the best organised and most united kingdom,
and this, taken in conjunction with the wealth, splendour, ability,
and maritime superiority of the kings, gave it an importance much
greater than was due to its extent. All these great powers, with the
exception of the last, had their energies for the most part employed
on domestic struggles, and were prevented by the interposition of
small semi-neutral territories from any extensive or critical collision,
whilst much of their natural aggressive spirit was carried off to the
East. Between the Normans and the *de facto* empire lay the
debatable and unmanageable estates of the papacy, and the bulwark
of Lombardy, itself a task for the whole imperial energies. Between
the same empire and France lay the remains of the ancient
Divisions of
Europe
Lotharingian and Burgundian kingdoms, from the North Sea to the
Mediterranean, hardly ever more than nominally imperial; a region
destined to be the battlefield of many generations, as soon as the
rival nations should have consolidated themselves and girt up their
strength, but at present acting as a barrier over which it was useless
to fight, and far safer to shake hands. Between France and Spain,
neither of which had time for foreign war, lay the southern inheritance of Eleanor and her vassals, whilst, although between Lewis VII.
and Henry II. there lay no such convenient welcome borderland,
there existed in France a class of vassals whose interest was at once
to keep the two kings asunder and to prevent either from overwhelming the other. The welfare of Champagne and Flanders
depended on the balance of power between the two successive
husbands of Eleanor of Guienne.

No general
wars
By broad intervening barriers, and by constant occupation at
home, now in the humiliation of aspiring vassals, now in the struggle
for existence against the overwhelming power of the greater
feudatories, now in the maintenance of peace between rivals, the

two great representatives of the resurrection of European life, the
kingdoms of France and Germany, were kept at arm's length from
each other, and, as being at arm's length, in an attitude something
like friendship. So for the most part they continued until the
consolidation of France by Lewis XI., and the great accumulation
of territory in the hands of Charles V., produced what is now the
recognised clue to modern politics, the balance of power properly so
called : the days when the borderlands became, instead of a
guarantee of peace, a battlefield of annual wars. The only real
question between them at this time was the papacy ; and it was not
yet time for a European war to be produced by the intrigues of rival
popes. The emperor found no sympathy in France for his claim   French
to nominate or influence the election of a pontiff: France was   policy as
                                                                       regards the
always the open asylum of the exiled champions of ecclesiastical   papacy and
independence. But France was yet a long way from Italy, and her   Italy
assistance was given more readily in the applause of councils, and
in the material support of board, lodging, and preferment, than in
either armies or embassies. Italy could fight her own battles, and
her innate life and passionate vigour was more than a match for
the strength of Germany removed far from home to a land of
strange air and unfamiliar food. Beyond Germany lay towards the
East a wide field for imperial energies, whether they took the line
of conquest or that of conversion. But the typical dominion of
Italy was an object far too dear, even to the wise head and the strong
heart of the great Frederick, to allow him to look elsewhere, until
the time came for the united effort of the Christian world to recover
Jerusalem, lost by their divisions and apathy.

Into such a Europe was England, or I should rather say the English   Eleanor's
people under their foreign lord, introduced in the twelfth century.   inheritance
                                                                          places
The Conquest had taught them what foreigners were ; the reign of   Henry in
                                                                          close neigh-
Henry II. placed them in the closest relation to France, and through   bourhood
it in a position to affect the rest of the continent. By the possession with the
                                                                          chief
of the insular kingdom the monarchs of the Norman house had   European
made at once the presence of a new influence felt. When Henry   powers
had successfully vindicated his claims to the domains and superior-
ities united in Eleanor's inheritance, he found himself in one part
or another of his estates in contact as close as was convenient with all
the great powers. Gascony brought him to the borders of Aragon,
and to the disputed frontier of Castile and Navarre. The homage   His early
                                                                          policy cal-
of Toulouse [1] placed him in condition to affect the outlying pro-   culated to
                                                                          encroach on
vinces of the empire in the south, from which in the north he was   France by
separated by the line, geographically and politically thin, of the   securing
                                                                          border terri-
county of Flanders. Between north and south he bordered on a   tories

[1] Hoveden, ii. 45.

land French by law and right, but quite willing to be debatable. His earliest measures were taken to make this debatable land his own. By marrying his son Henry to the daughter of Lewis VII., he possessed himself of the Vexin, and left the French king with no defensible line, in case of war, between Rouen and Paris ; by the marriage of Geoffrey he obtained immediate possession of Brittany, to which he had already a feudal claim, as to the Vexin he had some show of an hereditary one ; [1] by the betrothal of Richard to a princess of Aragon,[2] he seemed for a moment inclined to attempt an intrusion into Spain, but it was really a momentary expedient intended to affect the great claim to Toulouse, and when no longer necessary was suffered to drop, preference being given to another French match which would secure Bourges and Berry for the future lord of Guienne and Poictou.

His general conduct with regard to France

In these few circumstances we have the whole of the French policy of Henry II. They point, if not to a high ambition, certainly not to a mischievous one ; and they indicate a mind far more desirous of peace than of war. By these measures, and by a policy of peace, Henry managed to put himself in the right in all disputes with Lewis VII. ; and during the early years of Philip II. he acted with singular unselfishness as an arbiter in the quarrels of the French vassals.[3] In the former reign the difficulties always arose from the interference of Lewis in the domestic affairs of his ex-wife ; and in the latter Henry repaid good for evil, acting as a pacificator in disputes which originated in the domestic jealousies of the maternal and

Henry's French wars fought by mercenaries

matrimonal connexions of the young king. In these transactions the English did not often find themselves engaged hand to hand with their French foes. The few campaigns in which battles were really fought Henry carried on by mercenaries. It was rather by sympathy with a sovereign who spared both the blood and money of his own people,[4] who utilised and consumed for the fighting of his battles the objects of their most intense antipathy, that the English hatred of the French originated and grew, until they met to fight side by side under the walls of Acre. The policy of Henry in France was simply a family policy—Angevin it may perhaps be called, but Angevin in two senses, a bad one and a good one : bad in the inherited feature of petty aggrandisement and unscrupulous chicanery, good in the point that England's men and treasure were not exhausted in a great war or in a large political struggle.

Had the state of Europe been other than what it was, his

[1] Ord. Vit. vii. 14, x. 5. Gir. Camb. De Inst. Pr. (ed. Brewer), p. 13.
[2] Robert de Monte, ad 1159, ed. Pistorius, i. 892.

[3] Benedict, i. 277, 312.
[4] Dialogus de Scaccario, p. 25. ' Mavult enim princeps stipendiarios quam domesticos bellicis apponere casibus.'

intensifying and unintermitting feud with France must have driven Henry II. to seek alliances with such of the great powers as might feel the same apprehensions from the same quarter. Spain, Germany, and Italy would be the natural resource in such circumstances. But no two powerful states, as has been remarked already, felt themselves at this time in immediate contact or in immediate rivalry. Eleanor's inheritance had placed England nearer to France than any other two states capable of independent policy yet lay to each other. The *rapprochement* between Henry and the more distant powers was brought about by other means, more especially by the struggle with Thomas Becket, which from a mere personal quarrel became, owing to the pertinacity of both parties, a topic of intense interest throughout Europe. Henry's three daughters were married into Germany, Spain, and Italy ; in two at least out of three cases the alliance was suggested by the political circumstances arising from this contest. In all three we trace the beginning of a connexion which runs, with come changes of colour, but in an unbroken thread, throughout the middle ages. These marriages, however, were not of Henry's seeking ; they were the result of earnest application from the royal suitors, and they were concluded after careful consideration of the eligibility of the husband in the royal or national councils.[1]   It is as clear that the goodwill of the nation was consulted in the case of the daughters, as it is that neither its interests nor its wishes were regarded in the case of the sons ; and thus that they were married as English, not as Angevin princesses, and into countries where the English were well pleased to place them. Although I should not venture to say that these marriages afford a clue to anything like a comprehensive foreign policy on Henry's part, they do mark the commencement of close relations with European states which considerably affected later combinations. I will take them briefly in order.

Germany had been since the year 1152, nominally at least, under the sway of Frederick Barbarossa, who seemed at the beginning of his reign to have united in a family alliance the Northern and Southern, the Saxon and Franconian interests, which had been in their rivalry so pregnant of trouble to Henry IV., and which were to divide the world in the parties of Guelf and Ghibelin. In the strength of this union Frederick had set up his own pope, and kept Alexander III. for some years in exile ; he had maintained a strong hold on the Italian cities, and had curbed or intimidated into quietness the too rapidly degenerating Normans of Apulia. Frederick

Marginal notes:
Henry's relations with France not immediately connected with his other foreign relations

The Becket quarrel a cause or occasion for foreign alliances

Germany during the reign of Henry II.

Strength of Frederick Barbarossa

---

[1] The marriage of Matilda with Henry the Lion was the occasion of an aid *pur fille marier*, as to which see Madox, *Hist. Exch.*, p. 398. That of Johanna with William the Good was the subject of a deliberation in council : Hoveden, ii. 94 ; Benedict, i. 115, 117.

Barbarossa inherited the blood of the emperor Charles the Great, by the same stream that brought it into the veins of Henry Beauclerc and Henry Plantagenet. Judith, the widow of Tostig, son of Godwin,[1] had taken as her second husband duke Welf of Bavaria, the common ancestor of Frederick and his cousin and ally Henry the Lion. Her sister Matilda was the wife of William the Conqueror.

Connexion of the English royal family with Germany

The German connexion, begun by the children of Ethelred [2] and Edmund, had been maintained by the marriage of Matilda the daughter of Henry I., the heir ultimately of the line of Cedric, with the emperor Henry V. Much English gold had flown thenceforth into Germany. German princes visited and revisited the Norman court; an Austrian duke or margrave had perished in the White Ship.[3] The imperial hold on the Belgian provinces, which was vindicated by Henry V.,[4] brought the empire into close contact with the coveted Flemish inheritance of his father-in-law. Henry I. had

Henry I. and Henry V.

the reputation of greatly influencing the policy of the later years of Henry V.: on the emperor's death the imperial jewels found their way into the English treasury; it was not altogether impossible that Henry V. intended the empire to go with them to either Matilda or her father.[5] The prompt action, however, of the Saxon party had defeated the designs of both Matilda and the Franconian and Swabian dukes. Lothar had subverted for the time the old imperial policy, and the reign of Stephen had in England centred all men's thoughts on their own safety.

Proposals for marriages in 116b

It was apparently the similarity of circumstances and a craving for political sympathy and alliance in ecclesiastical difficulties that brought Henry II. and Frederick Barbarossa together. In 1165 Frederick found himself inextricably entangled with the pope, and saw Henry in the same predicament with Becket, whom the pope was warily and Lewis VII. enthusiastically supporting. It became an object of importance with Frederick to' obtain the adhesion of England to the antipope. The emperor proposed two marriages ; [6]

---

[1] 'Accepit autem reginam Angliæ tunc viduam, filiam scilicet Balduini nobilissimi comitis Flandriæ, Judith-am, in uxorem; ex qua duos filios, Guelfonem et Heinricum, . . . progenuit.'—Monachus Weingartensis, De Gwelfis Principibus (scr. cir. 1188), ap. Canis, Lectiones, vol. iii. p. 2, p. 582.

[2] See the curious passage in Hoveden's legal Appendix, R.S. vol. ii. 236, where the protector of the etheling Edward is called Malescoldus, rex Dogorum. Other copies have Rugorum, others Hunnorum, from which

perhaps our author freely translated, Dogorum *quasi* Hundorum. Malescoldus's kingdom was also called Russia. The passage is generally explained of Stephen king of Hungary, but it is surely very obscure. Is there confusion with Godescalc, prince of the Wends? See Freeman, *Norman Conquest*, i. 649.

[3] Ord. Vit. xii. 26. He must have been a son of Agnes of Swabia, by her second husband, Leopold of Austria.

[4] Otto Frising, ap. Urtisium, i. 148.

[5] Hoveden, i. 181. Ord. Vit. xii. 43.

[6] R. de Monte, ed. Pist., i. 900.

asked two of Henry's daughters, one for his son, the other for his cousin Henry the Lion. The proposal was favourably received by the king, although his prime minister, the earl of Leicester, refused to hold any intercourse with the imperial ambassador, the archbishop of Cologne,[1] and the altars on which he had celebrated were thrown down by the indignant clergy. Two English ministers attended the diet of Würzburg, in which Alexander III. was renounced, whether with or without their assent is uncertain.[2] One of the royal marriages passed off; the other, between Henry the Lion and Matilda, was carried out three years later.[3] The ecclesiastical importance of the negotiation turned out *nil*. If Henry ever really thought of committing himself to the antipope, the thought was transient. Far more probably he had determined by negotiation with the enemy, to frighten the wavering pope into compliance with his demands. His mother was still alive,[4] and she had, if not experience, at least warning in the case of her first husband of the danger of dealing with antipopes.[5] The time was not yet come for England and Germany to take the same side heartily on such a question.

Henry the Lion, the husband of Matilda, is one of the most interesting characters in mediæval history, and in the period before us is second in importance to Frederick alone. He was heir of the imperial duchies of Bavaria and Saxony, which had been held by his father, and from his mother he inherited, with the vast allodial estates of the Billung dukes and the counts of Nordheim and Brunswick, the right or claim as the representative of Saxon nationality to the affection and obedience of the whole of the people of Lower Saxony. He had family claims as descended from Azzo and Cunegunda to the domains of the house of Este in Lombardy, and by expectancy, from his uncle Welf of Tuscany, to the allodial estates of the great countess Matilda. He had come to this vast inheritance as a child, and, after the usual vicissitudes of a minority, had received from his cousin full investiture of his German estates. His best years were spent in the subjugation of the Wends and Slavs. His success in consolidating and Christianising his conquests entitled him to the character of a national hero, which he still possesses in North Germany. A few years after his marriage he made a splendid pilgrimage to Jerusalem, and on his return governed his vast estates in peace for three or four years. At the end of that time occurred the

Marginal notes:
The English suspect the envoys

Marriage of Matilda with Henry the Lion

Career of Henry the Lion

Quarrel of Henry the Lion with the emperor

---

[1] R. de Diceto, c. 539. Becket was of course opposed to this proposal, and made it the ground of the excommunication of Richard of Ilchester: Ep. 5; S. T. C. iii. 12.
[2] See Robertson's *Becket*, p. 176.
[3] R. de Monte, ad 1168, ed. Pistorius.

i. 903.
[4] See a letter of Rotrou of Rouen to cardinal Henry, S.T.C. iv. 148. She refused to see the German embassy.
[5] Albert, 1102. Silvester IV. 1105–1111.

quarrel with the emperor, which resulted from the defeat of Legnano. It is not now the time to attempt to unravel that mysterious business ; all that is certain is that Frederick attributed his defeat to Henry's lukewarm support, and in consequence determined on his downfall. Summoned before an imperial court, scorning or fearing to obey the summons, by one sentence the lord of half of Germany found himself a landless man. His wife's dower alone was spared out of respect to her father. The unhappy couple took refuge in Normandy and England, and there their children were born and brought up as English princes. After four years' exile Henry was restored to his Brunswick estates on the intercession of his father-in-law ; but in 1188 he was again banished, and was only permitted to return after the death of Frederick. He died in 1195, and lies with his faithful wife in his great church in Brunswick, hard by the ancient picture of the Martyrdom of S. Thomas, whose controversies had brought them together.[1]

His death

On a connexion like this it may seem crotchety or pedantic to lay much weight ; but it points, to say the least, to matters of considerable importance. It illustrates forcibly the characteristic policy of Henry II., to interfere in foreign matters, even those most closely connected with the interests of his own family, only so far as he saw that his interference was likely to be effective. He spent his money liberally, he sent ambassadors, he stirred up all his political interest with France, Flanders, and Rome to obtain his son-in-law's restoration ; but he did not go to war : nay, he admitted a proposal for the marriage of his son Richard with a daughter of the emperor.[2] But further, the connexion itself was very fruitful of effects. One of the sons of Henry the Lion and Matilda, in England earl of York,[3] in France invested with the county of Poictou,[4] the inheritance of his grandmother, in Scotland regarded as the probable heir of William the Lion,[5] and the not impossible successor of Richard himself,[6] achieved by his uncle's aid a higher destiny still, and became emperor as Otto IV. Another son, William of Winchester, carried on the line of Brunswick [7] princes, which after

Character of Henry II.'s policy in Germany

Otto IV.

William of Winchester

---

[1] The monks of Canterbury appealed to Henry and Matilda, by their regard to the martyr, to intercede for them with the king in 1188. Epp. Cant. 158.

[2] Benedict, i. 319, 322.

[3] Hoveden, ad ann. 1190 (f. 390).

[4] Hoveden, ad ann. 1190 (f. 390 v°).

[5] Hoveden, ad ann. 1195 (f. 430), and ad 1196 (fo. 432, Savile).

[6] Hoveden, 449 (Savile).

[7] Henry the Wonderful, duke of

Brunswick, writes to Edward I. as his cousin in 1280 ; and his mother, Adelheid of Montferrat, cousin of Edward on the mother's side, consults him as to the guardianship of her children. Fœdera, i. 580, 581. Relationship was probably forgotten before 1352, when John, king of France, arbitrated on a challenge to single combat, sent by Otto of Brunswick to Henry duke of Lancaster.—Leibnitz, *Scr. Rer. Bruns.* ii. pref. 8-10.

THE CHRONICLE OF ROGER OF HOVEDEN

the lapse of five centuries slid into the throne of the Plantagenets. But the chief point of interest lies in the fact that the connexion with Germany continued to subsist throughout the succeeding centuries as a national rather than a merely dynastic one. England was successively the ally of Otto IV. the Welf, of Frederick II. the Ghibelin, and of the papal or Welfic party which achieved his downfall. From England came king Richard of Almain ; and in England Rudolf of Hapsburg sought a bride for his son Hartmann. Adolf of Nassau, king of the Romans, fought against France as a mercenary of Edward I. Edward III. was brother-in-law of Lewis of Bavaria, his successor was son-in-law of Charles IV.[1] No sooner was the title of each successive house to the empire established, than the English alliance was sought as the complement of imperial authority. The house of Lancaster acted cordially with the house of Luxemburg. Henry IV. had fought with the German Crusaders ; his brother, cardinal Beaufort, waged war on the Hussites. Henry V. and Henry VI. supported the plans of Sigismund at Constance and Basel. During the schism the German pope was the English pope. English Wycliffe gave the colour to German Protestantism. Until the male line of Plantagenet ended, and the Burgundian inheritance falling to the imperial house added the Burgundian to the imperial traditions of alliance, and at the same time changed the face of Europe : from the Reformation to the year 1830, if not to 1854, this traditionary alliance was still one of those forces of modern Europe whose workings constitute modern history.

Rudolf of Hapsburg

Relations of English kings with Germany

The precise transaction which placed Henry II. in direct political contact with Italy was, as in the case of Germany, the Becket quarrel.[2] In the year 1169 he offered the cities of the Lombard league a large sum of money for their fortifications, and proposed a marriage with one of his daughters to the young king of Sicily, if they would use their influence with the pope to procure the deposition or translation of the archbishop.[3] Italian affairs had, however,

Relations with Italy begin from the Becket quarrel

---

[1] I only mention here the imperial alliances. The *Fœdera* contain a vast number of treaties with the several princes. The importance of these transactions should not be exaggerated ; for, continuous as they are, the advantages derived from the alliances seem to be exclusively on the side of the Germans. Although the connexion was national, there was not much love lost between the nations. I am inclined to place the restoration of a cordial feeling between Germany and England as late as the fourteenth century, when different circumstances combined to make Charles IV. and Richard II. support the pope of Rome against the pope of Avignon, in the great schism. A great deal, religiously as well as politically important, resulted from this accident.

[2] Spicilegium Liberianum, p. 548, S.T.C. iii. 122.

[3] Baronius ad ann. 1169. 'Confugit ad Italiæ civitates promittens Mediolanensibus 3000 marcarum ad murorum suorum validissimam reparationem, ut cum aliis civitatibus quas corrumpere moliebatur, impetrarent a papa et ecclesia Romana

o

194   THE CHRONICLE OF ROGER OF HOVEDEN

Englishmen in Italy and Italians in England

long before this been an object of interest in England. The Norman conquest of Apulia occupied a place in the common histories hardly less important than the Crusades; many Englishmen, such as Robert of Salisbury, the chancellor of Sicily,[1] Herbert of Middlesex, the bishop of Cosenza,[2] and Richard archbishop of Syracuse,[3] had sought and obtained high preferment in the south. English physicians studied like Athelard[4] at Salerno, English canonists like S. Thomas himself at Bologna.[5] Rome had been a kind Alma Mater to Nicolas Breakspear and Robert Pullanus.[6] From North Italy had come to England Lanfranc and the two Anselms; from the court of king Roger, Thomas le Brun, the minister of the English exchequer.[7] Peter of Blois was the intimate friend of both Henry II. and William the Good. The constant missions to and from Rome had made Italians and Englishmen pretty well acquainted. Henry's political exigencies, however, brought them still nearer. William the Good was connected by blood very closely with the Beaumonts of Leicester and Warwick, a family which supplied Henry II. with several ministers in his early years. Many of his principal clergy were Englishmen or Normans, and he seems to have been an enthusiastic admirer of Henry II. What action was taken in consequence of Henry's proposition to him is not known: probably none; but we find him in 1173 writing to console the king on the rebellion of his sons, and, as soon as the princess Johanna was old enough to be asked for, petitioning for her as a wife.[8] The proposal was referred to the national council, and

Alliance between William the Good and Henry II

dejectionem vel translationem Cantuariensis archiepiscopi. Nam ob eandem causam Cremonensibus duo millia marcarum promiserat, Papiensibus mille, et totidem Bononiensibus . . . At quod per se impetrare non poterat, regis Siculi viribus conatus est extorquere. Sed nec ille licet ad hoc toto nisu Syracusanus episcopus . . "—From a letter addressed to 'Alexander III.

[1] John of Hexham, ap. Twysden, 275. He was chancellor to king Roger in 1147.

[2] R. de Diceto, 628.

[3] Richard Palmer, bp. of Syracuse, elect. 1155, a candidate for the see of Lincoln, S.T.C. iii. 123; translated to Messina, in 1183, Græv. Sicil. ii. 293, 613. He entertained S. Thomas's relations in exile: S.T.C. iii. 319, 320. Walter, archbishop of Palermo, 1169–1187: R. de Diceto. His brother Bartholomew succeeded him: Græv. Sicil. ii. 77. He was bp. of Agri-

gentum, 1172–1187.

[4] Wright, Biogr. Lit. ii. 95.

[5] W. FitzStephen, S.T.C. i. 185.

[6] Chancellor of the Apostolic see under Lucius II. and Eugenius III.; he was a cardinal priest, but of what title I cannot find. J. Hexham, 275; Jaffé, Regesta Pontificum, pp. 609, 616.

[7] Dialogus de Scaccario, p. 17.

[8] See vol. ii. in Rolls Series, p. 94, note 2. In that note I have argued a little rashly, from the words of William's letter to Henry, Fœdera, i. 32, that the renewal of the proposition came from Henry. The date of the letter is too late to show this. It appears from Benedict and Hoveden that the Sicilian ambassadors came to England about April 1176; they received the oath taken for Henry by three of his counsellors, for the marriage, and reported to their master that the king of England demanded his oath in return. His

accepted. Johanna was sent to Palermo, and received a magnificent dower.[1] In that splendid court she reigned supreme during her husband's life. His fleet covered the Levant, and although the loss of Jerusalem was sometimes laid to his charge in consequence of his disabling the Byzantine empire from action, the last two years of his life were devoted to the equipment of the Crusade. As his health failed he made a will, by which he left to Henry not only all the provisions collected for the expedition,[2] but a vast treasure besides, going moreover so far as to offer the succession to his crown to him or one of his sons.[3] This proposal Henry wisely declined, as he did also the thorny crown of Palestine. His moderation was hardly appreciated by his contemporaries, whose idea of his ambition transcended all probability. This close connexion with William the Good, coupled with Henry's attempt to marry John to the heiress of Savoy, a measure which would have put the Alpine passes at his disposal, and some rumour of his promises to the Lombard league, perhaps formed the basis of the story that, looking at the unsettled condition of Italy, he was disposed to become a candidate for the suffrages of the Roman citizens with a view to the empire.[4]

William leaves his stores to Henry

Story of Henry's Italian designs

More substantial results than this followed. The dowry of Johanna was the ground, first of the quarrel and then of the alliance of Richard I. with Tancred, an alliance that was to be cemented by the marriage of Arthur as heir of England with a daughter of the Sicilian king. This agreement led to the captivity of Richard, and subsequently to his alliance with Henry VI., an alliance broken indeed by the events of the next reign, but bearing fruit in time in the English marriage of Frederick II., and in the repeated offer of the Sicilian kingdom to Henry III., an event which, however unimportant as regards Italy, was fraught with abundant interest to English constitutional history. It is unnecessary to mention the later acts of England in North and South Italy, matters certainly of antiquarian and minor historical interest, but—with a few insignificant

Results of Johanna's marriage

English chronicles rich in Italian history

letter to Henry is to excuse himself from taking the oath personally, as beneath his royal dignity; it is to be taken by proxy. This is dated Palermo, August 23. Before receiving it Henry's preparations were made for Johanna's journey (Benedict, i. 119), on the 15th of August.

[1] Benedict, i. 116.
[2] Benedict, ii. 132.
[3] Pet. Blesens., ep. cxiii. (ed. Busæus), p. 204.
[4] Giraldus Cambrensis, De Instr. Pr. ii. 1, p. 13, 'verum etiam ad Romanum imperium, occasione werræ diutinæ et inexorabilis discordiæ inter

imperatorem Fredericum et suos obortæ, tam ab Italia quam urbe Romulca cœpius invitatus; comparata quidem sibi ad hoc Morianæ vallis et Alpium via, sed non efficaciter obtenta.' If we may judge from the particulars preserved by Ralph de Diceto, English sympathy was rather on the side of the Italian cities, c. 584, 585, 590, 591. I fear that nothing can be pleaded but necessity in favour of Henry, who at the same time was allying himself with Frederick and contributing to the fortification of the Lombard cities against him.

exceptions, as regards political history, of little serious import —secondary in all respects and subsidiary to the more prominent personal interests of the empire and France. It is enough to say that from the time of Frederick Barbarossa to that of the Visconti and the Sforze, Italian politics are faithfully reported in English chronicles, sometimes with more precision and with more verisimilitude than in their own ; a fact that shows the existence of constant private as well as public intercourse.

English interest in Spain begins through the Normans

With Spain the English as English had little or no connexion. Before the Conquest I do not find record of even a pilgrimage to Compostella. The national intercourse began under the Normans, was greatly increased by the Crusades, and when the inheritance of Eleanor had made the territories of the ruling houses conterminous, ripened into a friendship which lasted until the Reformation. Spain was the earliest, as it was the latest and the most prosperous, battle-ground for those crusading energies which were so natural to the Norman spirit of adventure. Roger de Toëny, the standard-bearer of Normandy, had won his laurels there while duke William was still a baby, and had taught the sagacious Castilians the value of Norman swords. Alfonso the Valiant had petitioned for the hand

Normans in Spain

of a daughter of the Conqueror. Count Rotrou of Perche and Robert Burdet had been the heroes of the war which finally delivered Aragon from the infidels.[1] Norman as well as French and Burgundian valour had helped to found the kingdom of Portugal.

Conquest of Portugal

Norman piety found and Norman valour kept up the route of pilgrimage to St. James. By the time of Stephen English sympathies were enlisted on the side of the Christian powers. The coast of Portugal lay most convenient for the crusading fleets ; there the ships might take in water and horses, the crews stretch their cramped limbs, and the warriors flesh their maiden swords on infidels by way of prelude to the great battle. So the English in conjunction with the Flemings had taken Lisbon in the second crusade ;[2] the English strictly so called, without a single great Norman baron among them : the East Anglians under Hervey Glanville, the Kentish men under Simon of Canterbury, the Londoners under Andrew of London, the Hampshire and Hastings men under William Calf. Gilbert of Hastings, an Englishman, was the first bishop of Lisbon. This was done when Stephen and the Norman nobles had not a finger to raise but in their own quarrels. What was then done was the first link in a chain that bound Portugal to England ; and it was followed up by the similar capture

---

[1] See Orderic. Vit. xiii. 3, 4 ; for the exploits of Robert Burdet, xiii. 5, 6, &c. ; and the history of Spain generally, xiii. 1–10.

[2] Itin. R. Ricardi, pref., pp. cxliv-clxxxii (Rolls Series).

of Silvia in the year 1188,[1] a conquest which very nearly completed the coast-line of the existing kingdom. In the north of Spain, however, the more immediate interest lies. As early as 1158, Henry II., as we have seen,[2] negotiated a marriage for his infant son Richard with a daughter of queen Petronilla of Aragon; in 1170 he married his daughter Eleanor to Alfonso III. of Castile. This latter alliance produced a close intercourse. In 1177 Henry was chosen to arbitrate between the kings of Navarre and Castile, gave audience in a public council of his barons,[3] consulted them as to the verdict, and in their name and his own pronounced the decision. Spanish bishops took part in the services of the English church. Compostella became a favourite place of pilgrimage. Thither Henry himself proposed to go;[4] Henry the younger offered to do the same in atonement for his rebellion;[5] Henry the Lion actually visited the famous shrine during his exile.[6] It was on his way from Compostella that earl Patrick of Salisbury was slain by Guy of Lusignan,[7] a sin which caused the banishment of the latter, and tended in no remote way to the loss of Palestine. The vicissitudes of Moorish warfare during this period are carefully recorded by English historians.[8] Was it altogether impossible that the king might fulfil his vow as a crusader, and find a fit field for his ambition, in the recovery of Spain for the Christians? From the same association sprang the marriage of Richard I. with Berengaria; but we cannot afford now to trace the line of connexion in detail. Let it suffice to point out the results of the first Spanish marriage, in the claims of Lewis VIII. of France on the kingdom of John; in the relations of Edward I. to Alfonso the Wise, from whom he received an exemplary wife, the gift of knighthood, and the curious resignation of the duchy of Gascony, which it was said had been given by Henry II. to his daughter Eleanor.[9] By this second match Ponthieu came to the English crown, and gave Edward III. in his turn a foothold in France; whilst the marriages of his sons, the dukes of Lancaster and York, together with the warlike spirit of the Black Prince, involved the kingdom in the complications of Spanish warfare, and made Edward the ancestor of the emperor Charles V. In the particulars of all these transactions there are opened to us details of great personal and antiquarian interest. The connexion of the De Montforts with Aragon is another point of importance, which bears more remotely on the present subject, and yet may have exercised

Marginal notes:
Marriage of Eleanor and Alfonso

Intercourse between England and Spain

Marriage of Richard and Berengaria:

Edward I. and Eleanor:

John of Gaunt and Edward of Langley:

Possible results from the intercourse of England and Spain

[1] See Roll Series, vol. ii. p. lviii.
[2] P. 188.
[3] Benedict, i. 139. Hoveden, ii. 120.
[4] Benedict, i. 157.
[5] Ibid. i. 114.
[6] Benedict, i. 288.
[7] R. de Monte, ad 1168. Hoveden, i. 273. Gervase, 1403.
[8] E.g. R. de Diceto, 623, 624.
[9] Fœdera, i. 310.

some considerable influence on the growth of the English constitution ; but it may be we are not yet in possession of materials that may enable us to determine the amount of credit to be ascribed to Simon and to Edward respectively, or, through their education, to Aragon and Castile ; to determine in what measure and through what line of events we can connect the Great Charter of England with the Great Privilege of Aragon, or the summoning of borough representatives in England with the like usage across the Pyrenees.

Interest of these particulars

Whatever we may think of the sagacity of the great prince from whose designs so important results followed, and however much we may be inclined to see in these details but the occasions for combinations which must have taken place in the natural course of things, it is by no means the least interesting part of the work of the historical student to trace the connexion of the facts, and to group them in such a way as may display them, if not as the conscious work of politic heads, at least as the strivings of a family of nations after a social organisation : the attempts of the individual peoples to realise their personal identity, if I may so speak, in the exercise of national memory, national affections, national intimacy with each other. I trust that I have pointed out, however sketchily, the way in which England, under dynastic influences, did this. To show how those dynastic influences leavened the nation with kindred sentiment would be a longer and far more difficult task : it might be done ; it would be interesting ; but as we already know the result, the process of investigation would be less important. We do know

Actual results from these small causes

that England stood on terms of close friendship with the empire, and through it with Spain and Italy, and in immemorial enmity with France, when the Reformation introduced a new element of political life, and at the same time the balance of power in Europe became the leading idea in politics. Nay, we see how, notwithstanding the differences of religion and throughout the reign of the political idea, England retained for the most part her old affinities : [1] how, in spite of the Spanish armada, Charles I. sought a bride in Spain ; how, in spite of the Palatinate marriage, England abstained from taking an active part in the thirty years' war ; and how in spite of all that might have drawn England and France together, for the space of six hundred years, from the siege of Acre and the

---

[1] In the history of the seventeenth century as in that of the thirteenth, the dynastic policy of the king may have differed, sometimes widely, from the political wishes of the people so far as they had any. The Spanish match was an idea of the king; the people would have gone to war for the Palatine; the French under Henry IV. were probably more popular in England than ever before or afterwards. But the older feeling was revived and more than justified by the events that followed the Restoration; and the end of the century saw the old combinations stronger than ever.

battle of Arsouf to the siege of Sebastopol and the battles of the Crimea, English and French armies never met except as enemies.

To descend again to particulars. The books on which we are here employed were written by men living in the court, and in daily intercourse with the kings from whose designs such long-continued effects have flowed. In the preceding sketch I have drawn only the greater and more important outlines, those which have political connexion and historical consequences. More antiquarian research would, I am aware, reveal equally interesting, though less significant, series of details in other relations besides those to France, Italy, Germany, and Spain. Palestine, Constantinople, Norway, the Moors of Spain and Africa, all contribute their quota of incidents to the annals, and their documents to the illustration of the politics of the period. The extreme value of the contemporary histories of this reign is shown by this among other proofs, that in one or other of them is contained every important document, on every important transaction, national, dynastic, political, or diplomatic, that has been preserved at all. There are few such records in existence older than the date of the manuscripts of the historians, and of those few hardly one that is not enrolled by them in their most precious storehouses, attesting by its faithfulness to the original the conscientious honesty as well as the unwearied industry of their way of working.

These things written by contemporaries, rich in documentary evidences

THE CHRONICLE OF ROGER OF HOVEDEN. VOL. III.

[The Preface to this volume deals with sundry events in Richard I.'s reign from 1189 to 1196 ; Richard's policy on his accession is described, and the history of Longchamp's administration receives careful treatment. The characters and policy of Hugh de Puiset, of Hugh of Nunant, and of Geoffrey Plantagenet are also sketched. But the main interest of this Preface centres round Longchamp, of whose fall a full account is given.]

*   *   *   *   *   *

Sketch of the early history of Richard I.'s reign

THE interest of the internal history of Richard's reign is only very slightly indebted to the personal action of the king. His influence is felt only as a remote and varying pressure, affecting the amount and impact of taxation, the placing and displacing of ministers. The island kingdom, irrespective of its function as

His personal interest in England

supplying revenue, lies very much out of the sphere of his political plans, and owes nothing to any paternal care or special exercise of sagacity on its behalf. He originated no reforms ; he did not even interest himself in such things so far as to reverse the measures of his father. He had no policy of government, and for his policy of aggression England satisfied him by contributing money.

Early education of Henry's sons

Henry's early idea of dividing his dominions among his sons had this among other indirect effects : Henry, Richard, and Geoffrey were exposed to all the temptations of a sovereign position without the absolute liberty of action which would have left them free to find work for themselves. Whilst other princes of their age were learning experience and sowing wild oats in the Crusades, they were exercising substantial power as the colleagues or vassals of their father in England, Normandy, Aquitaine, and Brittany. Their

Provincial influence on their characters

education, such as it was, was carried on amidst the people whom they were to govern, and, as is usual in such cases, their characters were formed by the moral and political tone of their provincial courts. Henry became the ally, the hero and the victim of the feudal party in England and Normandy ; Geoffrey developed the Angevinity —the dishonesty, turbulence, and general want of principle—which marked his grandfather's line; Richard, the faults and the brilliancy of the Poictevin. Throughout his life he is amenable in a remarkable way to the personal authority and national influences of his mother. Richard was born in England,[1] and nursed by an Englishwoman;[2] but there his personal interest in England seems to determine. At a very early age he was marked out as the heir of Eleanor.[3] When he was two years old his father planned for him a marriage with the daughter of the queen of Aragon, one of the terms of which was the settlement of the duchy of Aquitaine on the infant couple.[4] In 1165 his mother brought him from England into Normandy.[5] At Epiphany 1169 he did homage to Lewis VII. for the duchy of Aquitaine;[6] the following year he received it as his share of his father's dominions, when, in the expectation of death, Henry, at Mote de Ger, divided them among his elder sons.[7] In 1171 he joined with his mother in laying the foundation of the church of S. Augustine at Limoges.[8] On Trinity Sunday the same year he was installed as duke in the abbatial seat of S. Hilary at Poictiers, receiving the lance and banner from the bishop John of Poictiers and the archbishop of Bordeaux, and having the hymn, ' O princeps egregie,' sung in procession. The same year he was invested at Limoges with the ring of S. Valeria, the protomartyr of the Gauls;[9]

Richard's birth, nurture, and early prospects

He becomes Duke of Aquitaine in 1171

---

[1] His birth at Oxford is asserted by Ralph de Diceto, c. 531. The event is placed at Windsor by the author of the chronicle quoted in the next note, but Oxford is more likely. Windsor might easily be substituted for Oxford by one ignorant of the circumstances; not so Oxford for Windsor. The month September, 1157, is mentioned by Robert de Monte, 890 (ed. Struve), and the day ' Sexto Idus Septembris ' is given in the Chronicon Andegavense published by Labbe, Bibliotheca MSS. i. 276, from a MS. of the monastery of S. Albinus at Angers.

[2] ' Mense Septembri natus est anno MCLVII°, regi filius Ricardus nomine apud Windleshore ; eadem nocte natus est Alexander Necham apud Sanctum Albanum ; cujus mater fovit Ricardum ex mamilla dextra, sed Alexandrum fovit ex mamilla sua sinistra.' MS. in the Lord Arundel's collection, quoted by James in his collections now in the Bodleian, vol. vii. 34. The name of Richard's nurse, whether she was Alexander Neckham's mother or no, was Hodierna. She had an estate in land of seven pounds a year at Chippenham, and the parish of Knoyle Hodierne in Wiltshire still preserves

her name. Rot. Claus. Hen. III. (ed. Hardy) i. 416. This could not have been the whole of her property, for her land in 30 Hen. III. was talliaged at 40s.

[3] Gir. Camb. De Inst. Pr. lib. iii. c. 8.

[4] Rob. de Monte (ed. Struve), 892.

[5] Ibid. 900.   [6] Ibid. 905.

[7] Ben. Pet. i. 7.

[8] Geoff. Vigeois, Labbe, Bibl. MSS. ii. 318: ' Monasterium Sancti Augustini Lemovicis inceptum est construi. Tempore illo Regina Alienor cum filio Ricardo Lemovicæ forte cum esset, lapides in fundamento primos jecerunt.'

[9] Geoff. Vigeois, Labbe, ii. 318: ' Tempore illo rex Henricus senior filio Ricardo ex voluntate matris Aquitanorum tradidit ducatum. Post hæc apud Sanctum Hilarium Pictavis Dominica post Pentecosten, juxta consuetudinem, in abbatis sedem elevatur, sed a Bertramo Burdegalensi et Johanne Pictavensi præsulibus lancea ei cum vexillo præbetur, et ad processionem cantatur O princeps egregie . . . Procedenti tempore Ricardus Lemovicas veniens in urbe cum processione suscipitur, annulo Sanctæ Valeriæ decoratur, novusque dux ab omnibus proclamatur.'

and in 1173 he received the homage of the count of Toulouse, being then sixteen.[1]

By that unhappy fate which attended his family, he fought his first campaign as duke of Aquitaine, against his father, under the influence of his mother and her advisers Ralph de Fai and Lewis VII.[2] From the time of the pacification Richard, unlike his elder brother, recovered his hold on his share of the inheritance, and from his eighteenth year administered Aquitaine with very slight control from

his father.[3] In the apparently conflicting statements of Giraldus that during this period he showed great powers of organisation, reducing the disorderly nobles to subjection, extending the boundaries and improving the laws of his states ;[4] and those of Benedict and Thomas Agnellus,[5] that he governed capriciously and tyrannically, that he was 'malus omnibus, suis pejor, pessimus sibi,'[6] we trace an element of agreement. His policy was, like his father's, directed to the humiliation of the barons who had enjoyed under the weak and luxurious princes who preceded Eleanor an almost unbridled licence, and to the creation of a really independent sovereignty. The complaints of his treatment of the wives and daughters of the nobles show, if they were true, that he followed in other respects the traditions of his mother's house too faithfully. By the barons of Aquitaine the younger Henry, who had been the stalking-horse of the baronage in Normandy and England, was called in against Richard. His death opened the way for his brother to higher honours, but Richard's relations with the great vassals of the duchy were throughout his life the same ; and the stand which during his father's life he made against them without help from abroad abundantly vindicates his character for perseverance and military skill. The lords of Saintonge, the counts of Angoulême, the viscounts of Limoges,[7] with a wide network of alliances among

---

[1] Ben. Pet. i. 36. Geoff. Vig. (ap. Labbe, ii. 319) gives the day Feb. 25.

[2] Ben. Pet. i. 42.

[3] In 1175, Ben. Pet. i. 81. Ralph de Diceto places the date of his creation as duke of Aquitaine in his 23rd year, 1179 (R. Dic. 675) ; but he was in active employment there long before.

[4] De Inst. Pr. iii. 8 : 'Terram hactenus indomitam in tenera ætate tanta virtute rexit et domuit, ut non tantum ipsam per omnes ejus anfractus longe plenius et tranquillius solito pacificaret, verum etiam mutilata dudum et dispersa reintegrans, strenua virtute pristinos in status singula revocaret. In formam igitur informia redigens, in normam enormia quæque

reducens, fortia confundens et aspera complanans, antiquos Aquitaniæ terminos et jura reformavit.'

[5] See the passage quoted in the preface to Hoveden, R. S. vol. ii. p. lvii.

[6] Ben. Pet. i. 292.

[7] Richard's enemies are the same throughout his career. They are enumerated by Benedict, i. 115, and much of their history may be learned from Geoffrey of Vigeois. The barons of Poictou seem to have had an admitted right of making private war ; at least Richard on one occasion alleged it to Philip as an excuse for not using compulsion with them (Hoveden, iii. 255) ; but this must be distinguished from the constant trouble

the almost inaccessible lordships of the Pyrenees, afforded him work and discipline enough, not to speak of the claims on Auvergne and Toulouse, which could, if enforced, have brought only an empty homage. Two short visits, one in 1176,[1] and another in 1184,[2] seem to be the sum of his opportunities for making acquaintance with England, during the twenty years that preceded his accession to the crown. He visits England only twice before his accession

Untrained to English ways, and exempt for the most part from the influence of English factions, Richard must have seen that his best policy was to leave the kingdom alone, to be governed on his father's principles, and to develop resources which might enrich him without giving him trouble. But he must have underrated the personal influence of his father if he trusted that the institutions which he had created would act by themselves, or answer to the handling of new, inexperienced workmen. Henry's influence had been felt directly everywhere, and his servants had been educated under him, or had grown with him into the knowledge of their work. Richard's first attempt was to manage by new men a system which was far from maturity, and would not bear rough or indiscriminate usage. The elements which had supplied Henry's early difficulties survived, although weakened and disarmed. Much of the influence which his great ministers exercised over the baronage was personal quite as much as official. It might be a question whether, after his guiding hand was removed, the old administrators could have successfully maintained their position and his policy. Richard's initial measures, and the results which followed them during the years which he spent on crusade and in captivity, were such as to try very cruelly the fabric which his father had raised. He attempts to rule the kingdom by new ministers His system was a rude test of his father's policy

The English history of the reign is, then, the history not of Richard, but of his ministers; of the administrations of his four successive justiciars, William Longchamp,[3] Walter of Coutances, Hubert Walter, and Geoffrey FitzPeter. The importance of the The history of the reign is really the history of the ministers

which the *malæ consuetudines* of the Pyrenean counts and barons gave him, who were really patrons of banditti who lived on the plunder of pilgrims to Compostella. See Ben. Pet. i. 132; Ric. Devizes, p. 12; Hoveden, iii. 35, 36.

[1] In 1176 he landed on Good Friday at Southampton, spent Easter at Winchester, and almost immediately returned to Poictou. Ben. Pet. i. 115, 120.

[2] In 1184 he came to England in November, stayed over Christmas, which he spent at Windsor with the king, and sailed from Dover before

New Year's Day 1185. Ben. Pet. i. 319, 333, 334. [Richard paid Henry II. a short visit in England soon after Whitsuntide 1179.]

[3] William Longchamp was chief justiciar either solely or with colleagues from Dec. 11, the day of Richard's departure, to October 10, 1191, when he was compelled to vacate the post. Walter of Coutances held the office from Oct. 10, 1191, to the time of his departure to Germany in January 1194; Hubert Walter from January 1194 to July 31, 1198; Geoffrey FitzPeter from that time to his death in 1213.

first two of these is of a political, that of the latter of a constitutional character. But the survey of a period which, coming between Henry II. and John, must necessarily have witnessed a great growth of national life, and which contains other elements of interest which have engrossed the attention of contemporaneous and later historians, to the exclusion of the less romantic topics, deserves examination in detail.

His imprudent choice of ministers, and provision for John and Geoffrey

The seeds of the difficulties of the first three years of the reign were sown by Richard himself during the few months that followed his coronation, in the choice of the ministers who were to govern England during the crusade, and in the measures taken for securing the good behaviour of John and Geoffrey. In neither of these respects can Richard be charged with any greater fault than political short-sightedness. The events that illustrate them begin from the very moment of his father's funeral.

Richard's treatment of his father's friends and enemies

No sooner was the body of Henry consigned to the tomb at Fontevraud than the question arose how were the new and old relations of his successor to be reconciled ; how was he to treat those who had been faithful to his father on principles which would make them not less faithful to himself, and how to reward those who had been his friends on principles which would from the moment of his succession make them his enemies. First and foremost of these classes came his brothers, the faithful Geoffrey and the faithless John ; after them the whole roll of the baronage ; on the one side, Ranulf Glanvill and Stephen of Turnham, with the rest of Henry's servants ; on the other, Ralph of Fougères, Juell of Mayenne,[1] and the rest who had deserted the father to make capital in the service of the son. Richard's first thought was to revenge himself on his father's friends ; but it was a short-lived idea, and gave way so soon to better feelings that the two on whom the first brunt of his hasty anger fell seem to have become, as soon as their punishment was

He exacts money from the former,

over, his most faithful friends.[2] Stephen Turnham[3] and Ranulf Glanvill[4] were compelled to purchase his goodwill by heavy fines ; but those paid, the former was restored to his post as steward of Anjou, and Glanvill, although he was not suffered to retain the justiciarship, attended the court as a counsellor until his departure

and punishes the latter

for the crusade, on which he died. Towards those who had deserted Henry in his last difficulties, Richard adopted different conduct : dispossessed them of their estates, and treated them as his own enemies. The lords of Fougères and Mayenne continued during his

---

[1] Ben. Pet. ii. 72.
[2] See Ben. Pet. ii. 76.
[3] Ric. Devizes, pp. 5-8. See also Ben. Pet. ii. 71, 72, where the king is said to have broken off the marriage

of Stephen's son on account of the inferiority of his birth. The question of Stephen's identity is, however, still unsettled.
[4] Ric. Deviz. pp. 6-8.

reign, as they and their ancestors had done constantly before, to Opposition in Anjou lead the baronial opposition in Brittany, Maine, and Anjou.

The requirements of revenge and justice being satisfied, the new He attempts to make peace the interest of all parties : sovereign seems to have determined to bind to himself by gifts and promises all the leaders, or would-be leaders, of the parties which his own quarrels with his father had, if not created, at least furnished with opportunities for organisation. As soon as he was invested provides for John and Geoffrey : with the duchy of Normandy he began to make a lavish provision for John ; he renewed the promise of the archbishopric of York to Geoffrey, and he proposed to pay to Philip not only the 20,000*l.* with and pays money to Philip which Henry had purchased peace, but 4,000*l.* more to indemnify him for the expenses of the war.; this done, the two undertook to meet early in 1190, and proceed to the crusade together. The Liberality to John provision made for John on this occasion was the bestowal of the county of Mortain, in Normandy, which had been the property of king Stephen, and had escheated on the death of his son William in 1159,[1] and the promise of a revenue of 4,000*l.* a year [2] from lands in England with the completion of the marriage contract with the daughter of John's marriage the last earl of Gloucester, the son of Robert, who had been betrothed to John in 1176, and who brought with her by way of dowry the honour of the earldom of Gloucester.

To all this were added, as soon as the brothers arrived in England, Bestowal of honours and castles on John the several castles and honours of Marlborough, Lancaster, Ludgarshall, and the Peak, the castle of Bolsover, the town and honour of Nottingham, the honours of Wallingford and Tickhill, and the county of Derby with the Peverell fee.[3] It is to be observed

---

[1] I have remarked (vol. ii. p. 6, Rolls Series) on the difficulties attending the statement that John had the county of Mortain before his father's death, made by Hoveden (as an addition to Benedict), and also by Richard of Devizes, who says, ' præter comitatum de Moritonio, quem dono patris pridem perceperat,' p. 7. William of Newburgh (iv. 8) describes Richard as ratifying his father's gift. The truth seems to be that Henry had promised the county and that Richard actually bestowed it. Although count William died in 1159, his sister, who married Matthew of Boulogne, carried the claim on the county to him. He died in 1173, and his daughters do not seem to have made any claim ; it was in the king's hands in 1180, and he had in fact bought off count Matthew's claim in 1168. See Stapleton, Norman Rolls, i. pp. lxiii, cxxiii. Benedict distinctly says that the county was given by Richard to John on the occasion of his investiture as duke of Normandy, July 20, 1189. Ben. Pet. ii. 73.

[2] Ben. Pet. ii. 73 ; M. Paris, 152. This promise of 4,000*l.* a year in land was not regarded as fulfilled by the bestowal of the counties shortly after mentioned, although it is nearly the sum at which their revenues may be valued ; we find that in 1195, when John had been removed from the government of the counties, his income from the exchequer was 8,000*l.* Hoveden, iii. 286. But unfortunately for Richard's character as a liberal brother, the 8,000*l.* are in Angevin money and only equal to 2,000*l.* sterling. However, it is clear that whilst he was in charge of the counties, he was receiving a large sum from the exchequer. R. Devizes, p. 26.

[3] These honours were given before the coronation, Ben. Pet. ii. 78. The money value may be estimated roughly by reference to the roll of the 3rd of

that this enumeration of the endowments should be construed exactly
as detailed by Benedict and abridged by Hoveden. In a few cases
the castle and honour are given together, but in the more important
ones, Tickhill, Wallingford, and the impregnable one of Nottingham,[1]
the honour is given without the castle ; the hold of the crown is
maintained on these castles as well as that of Gloucester, a matter
that has much significance in its relation to later events.[2] Not content with this enormous accession of territory, John received in addition, before Richard's departure from England, the counties of Devon,
Dorset, Somerset, and Cornwall.[3]

Immediately after the coronation Richard held a Great Council at
Pipewell, at which he filled up the vacant church preferments, and
changed the sheriffs of the counties in contemplation of the Michaelmas session of the Exchequer. In the former class of appointments
we trace the working of several natural influences. His father's
servants, Hubert Walter, the nephew of Glanvill ; Richard FitzNeal,
the treasurer of the Exchequer ; Godfrey, the son of Richard of Lucy
the loyal,[4] were secured by bishoprics ; and William of S. Mere
l'Eglise, the prothonotary, by a rich stall at York. To his own
personal servant, William Longchamp, he gives a bishopric ; to the
brother of William Marshall, who had been the intimate friend and
companion of his brother Henry, the deanery of York. The old
bishop of Durham is propitiated by the bestowal of the treasurership of the same church, which had been held by his cousin S.
William and himself in succession, on his nephew Bouchard de
Puiset ; and the services of the Champagne connexion, still so

Marginal notes:
Castles of the honours withheld

Bestowal of counties

Appointments made at the Council of Pipewell, to propitiate all sides

Church appointments

John, when Wallingford is worth 80*l*.,
Tickhill 85*l*., the Peverell fee 232*l*.
10*s*. ; and to the Pipe Roll of 1
Richard I., when the honour of Gloucester is worth 548*l*. 17*s*. 11*d*., and
Lancaster, 251*l*. 5*s*. 10*d*.
   [1] R. Devizes, 30.

[2] It is especially noted by Hoveden,
iii. 6.
   [3] Bestowed in December. Ben.
Pet. ii. 99. The gross values of all
these counties, for Richard bestows
not only the ferms, but all the profits
of administration, were in 1 Rich. I.
as follows :—

	£	s.	d.
Devonshire . . .	2,041	12	11
Dorset and Somerset .	1,153	15	1
Cornwall . . .	512	3	11
Notts and Derbyshire	373	17	9

In all 4,081*l*. 9*s*. 8*d*.

or if the ferms alone be counted,—

	£	s.	d.
Devonshire . .	312	7	0
Cornwall . . .	233	4	1
Dorset and Somerset .	480	0	0
Notts and Derby .	319	15	11

In all, 1,345*l*. 7*s*.

[4] Jordan Fantosme, p. 71. 'Godefridus filius memorandi Ricardi illius de
Luci.' R. Devizes, 9.

strong both in France and in England, were further secured by the
nomination of Henry de Soilli,[1] to the abbacy of Glastonbury. In
all these, a prudent regard to existing personal or political interests
is distinguishable.

The secular appointments were not bestowed with similar circum- *Secular preferments*
spection, although the marriages and wardships in the hands of the
crown were distributed on much the same principle. Among the
latter class of preferments, William Marshall got the heiress of the
earldom of Strigul; the son of Roger FitzRainfrai, the heiress of the
barony of Kendal;[2] William Longchamp, the wardship of Stephen
Beauchamp.[3] But with the official posts it was otherwise. The
place of Ranulf Glanvill was filled by two old statesmen, Hugh de *New justiciars*
Puiset, bishop of Durham, and William Mandeville, earl of Essex and
count, in the right of his wife, of Aumale, the most faithful servant of
Henry II.;[4] and this change of the head of the administration was
followed by a clean sweep in the sheriffdoms. It is not clear whether *New sheriffs*
this was done at Pipewell, or a fortnight later at the Michaelmas
exchequer; probably it was arranged at the former place, and carried
into execution in the latter. The changes seem to imply an im-
prudent desire on Richard's part to carry with him most of the leading *Most of the barons were under vow of crusade*
members of his father's government; a desire that was aided by the
fact that most of these were already under a vow of crusade, which
under a king who was himself an ardent crusader, and who had
obtained from the pope the privilege of commuting the vows of his
subjects for a money payment, was not likely to be redeemed with-
out enormous cost.[5] In a few cases some method may be traced. *The old king's friends displaced for new*
In Yorkshire Ranulf Glanvill gives way to John Marshall, the old
king's friend to the new;[6] in Herefordshire Ralph Arden, Glanvill's

[1] Ben. Pet. ii. 85; Hoveden, iii. 15, note 5.

[2] Ben. Pet. ii. 73, 76.

[3] I mention this because it seems to have been a lucrative piece of prefer-ment. It had been bought by Bertram de Verdun for 200 marks; he sold it to Longchamp for 20 marks' profit. Madox, *Hist. Exch.* 691. After the chancellor's death his brother Henry had the wardship of the heir of Stephen, and paid 100*l.* for it in the first year of John. Possibly it was in this way that he became sheriff of Wor-cestershire, the hereditary sheriffdom of which belonged to the Beauchamps. Rot. de Finibus, 1st John, p. 15.

[4] Hoveden adds to Benedict's infor-mation that Geoffrey FitzPeter, William Briewere, Robert de Wihtefeld, and Roger FitzRainfrai were asso-

ciated in the office. See Ben. Pet. ii. 87; Hoveden, iii. 16.

[5] Of the barons and justices of Henry II.'s reign, Ranulf Glanvill, Bertram de Verdun, Roger Glanvill, Gilbert Pipard, and others, went with the king. Geoffrey FitzPeter, William Briewere, and Hugh Bardolf bought of the king a licence to stay at home. R. Dev. p. 8. Hugh Bardolf is men-tioned as being at Messina in Novem-ber, 1190; Hoveden, iii. 62; and even William Marshall must have been there early in 1191, if we are to take literally the words of Benedict, ii. 158, Hoveden, iii. 96. Yet he was acting as a judge in England very shortly before (Mon. Angl. i. 391); perhaps he accom-panied and returned with Eleanor.

[6] Glanvill had administered York-shire by his steward Reiner, who went

son-in-law, is replaced by Henry Longchamp, the chancellor's brother. Such appointments strengthened, no doubt, the hands of the king's personal friends. Others, however, must have seriously weakened the administration. Among these the foremost are the purchase of sheriffdoms by three of the bishops : Hugh de Puiset, of Durham, buys Northumberland for 2,000 marks ;[1] Godfrey de Lucy, by a single fine, obtained for himself the county of Hampshire, with the castles of Winchester and Porchester, his own inheritance, and indemnity for the treasure of his church ;[2] Hugh of Nunant, bishop of Coventry, was allowed to take for a smaller fine the sheriffdoms of Leicestershire, Staffordshire and Warwickshire.[3] The counties bestowed on John were withdrawn from the ordinary administration of the government. Gerard Camville, one of his sworn followers, for 700 marks, entered on the sheriffdom of Lincolnshire ;[4] Hugh of Nunant was also his personal adherent. Of the other counties, only seven or eight retained their old sheriffs, and only five of the old sheriffs[5] found places in the same capacity : these were old servants of the state, not likely to become politically dangerous. But the changes in the sheriffdoms are not to be imputed solely to Richard's wish to carry with him to Palestine all the men of mark ; in some cases the office was doubtless bought. Those officers who were removed were not disgraced, for out of them, after making them pay heavily for the commutation of their vows, Richard chose the chief advisers of the regency. The great offices of state were, moreover, paid for by their fortunate holders ; Hugh de Puiset paid at least a thousand marks for his share of the justiciarship,[6] and William Longchamp, although the king's confidant, paid three thousand for the chancery, notwithstanding that the bishop of Bath bid a thousand more.[7] Other very large sums were levied on the barons and bishops for the ratification of rights and confirmation of their tenure of estates, the greatest bargain being that made by the king

Marginal notes:
Purchase of sheriffdoms and castles

Weakening of the government in consequence

Sale of the justiciarship and chancellorship

---

with him on crusade, and died in Cyprus. Ben. Pet. ii. 150. He had rendered account of a fine of 1,000 marks on his own accunt in the second of Richard I. (Pipe Roll); another proof of the way in which as Richard of Devizes describes, the Glanvill connexion was plundered at this time.

[1] Pipe Roll, 2 Ric. I. :—'Hugo episcopus Dunelm. debet MM. marcas pro comitatu Northumbriæ habendo.' He gave 1,000 marks for the justiciarship, Ben. Pet. ii. 90 ; 600 for Sadberge, Hoveden, iii. 39. Richard of Devizes raises the sum of money invested by him to 10,000l., p. 8.

[2] For 3,000l., R. Devizes, p. 10.

Another 3,000l. he paid for the restoration of Meon and Wargrave, Rot. Pip. 2 R. I.

[3] For 300 marks, Madox, *Hist. Exch.* 316.

[4] 'Gerardus de Camvilla reddit computum de 700 marcis pro vicecomitatu Lincoln. et castello civitatis habendis.' Rot. Pip. 2 Ric. I.

[5] Oger Fitz-Oger, Henry de Cornhell, William Ruffus, William FitzHervey, Robert de la Mara ; others, however, probably acted under John in his counties.

[6] See above, note 1.

[7] R. Devizes, p. 9.

of Scots, who, for a payment of 10,000*l.*, emancipated himself from the conditions imposed on him by Henry II. in 1175. But the object of these latter sales was merely the raising of money.

By such means Richard endeavoured to secure peace during his absence from Europe; his policy was to work the governmental machinery by men who were not likely to be dangerous, to bribe by large benefactions those whose claims might have made them so, to bind those who had invested their treasure so largely in public appointments to the maintenance of public security, to carry away with him as much as possible of the money which might have sustained private wars, and as many as possible of those members of the feudal baronage whose possessions were so large or their traditions so continuous as to render them jealous of royal authority. But before he left England he had reason to see that all this would be futile. The death of William Mandeville in November left the justiciarship vacant, for Hugh de Puiset could not be trusted to act alone—nay, it was a question whether the king ever seriously intended him to act in this capacity at all. The archbishop elect of York had quarrelled with his clergy and fallen into disgrace with Richard, and it was found necessary to secure John with further gifts. The king was, however, in a hurry to embark, and perhaps not unwilling to leave matters to settle themselves. The bishop of Durham was left as justiciar, but with the chancellor, Hugh Bardulf, and William Briewere as colleagues.[1] Further questions were to be settled at a council in Normandy before the pilgrimage to the East began.

Richard left England on the 11th of December. Almost immediately after his departure the chancellor and justiciar quarrelled. The bishop of Durham saw that the bishop of Ely was intended to hold the substance of power, whilst, even if faith were to be kept with himself, there would be left him only the shadow, the expense, and the responsibility. To him the castle of Windsor had been intrusted; but to the chancellor the Tower of London.[2] Longchamp was not indisposed for a struggle; he declined to admit the presence of the bishop of Durham at the Exchequer,[3] or to recognise him as in charge of the county of Northumberland. No reason is given for this, but the probable one is that the bishop had not actually paid the money offered for the county,[4] and that the chancellor acted under Richard's orders. At the same time, however, he dispossessed

Margin notes:
Theory of Richard's policy

Early indications of its failure

The justiciars quarrel

The seemingly arbitrary conduct of the chancellor dictated by policy, perhaps prescribed by Richard

---

[1] Ben. Pet. ii. 101. Hoveden makes the chancellor co-justiciar, and Hugh Bardulf, William Marshall, Geoffrey FitzPeter, and William Briewere, associates; a different committee from that appointed at Pipewell. It is not improbable that Hugh was really the chief justiciar for the short time that

intervened between the king's departure and his summons to Normandy.

[2] Benedict, ii. 101. Hoveden, iii. 28.

[3] R. Devizes, p. 11.

[4] The money is still a debt in the P pe Roll of 2 Rich. II.; that is, at Michaelmas 1190.

the bishop of Winchester of the honours he had purchased, and even of his own inheritance, on which he had so lately entered.[1] In this case the desire of getting both the sheriffdom and the castles into the hands of the government probably operated. As for the bishop of Coventry, it was thought sufficient to proceed against him in the ecclesastical court, and obtain an injunction from the archbishop of Canterbury against his holding a sheriffdom.[2]

When in the month of February or early in March the king held his council in Normandy, complaints on all these grounds were laid before him. Most of the leading men in England attended ; the
chief business done was the appointment of the chancellor as justiciar of England, the bishop of Durham's jurisdiction being confined to the north of the Humber ;[3] John and Geoffrey were sworn not to return to England for three years. Hugh of Nunant undertook before the archbishop to give up his secular office.
Measures were also taken to obtain for the chancellor the office of legate in the absence of Archbishop Baldwin.

Notwithstanding the great powers with which Longchamp was now invested, the task which he undertook was probably as difficult a one as ever fell to the lot of any minister. He was, indeed, trusted by his master, but he could have hardly trusted Richard out of his sight, knowing how uncertain were the expedients of his fickle policy, how easily he was imposed upon, and how his inveterate extravagance laid him open to intrigues in which money would be too powerful a temptation for him to resist. The condition of England was anything but bettered by Richard's policy. The great earls of
Chester and Leicester, the great minister Glanvill, and his colleagues Bertram de Verdun, Gilbert Pipard, and others, the great bishops Hubert of Salisbury, and Walter of Rouen, were indeed gone ; and John and Geoffrey were sworn to stay away. But the uneasiness was not removed with them ; the sources of disturbance were in the very atmosphere of society. The removal of the great men made the country more difficult to manage, the balance more difficult to
adjust. Hugh de Puiset had made himself a comfortable principality in the north, where the justiciarship of the whole province was added

---

[1] R. Devizes, 11.
[2] See the letter from Archbishop Baldwin to the bishop of London, in R. de Diceto, 652: Hugh had at Rouen promised to resign his sheriffdom within a fortnight after Easter. In the Roll of the 2nd of Richard I., he renders account for Warwickshire and Leicestershire for half a year, and Hugh Bardulf for the second half, and in 1191 Hugh Bardulf accounts for the whole year in Warwickshire and Leicestershire, while the bishop has had Staffordshire for a whole year. It would seem, then, that he had obeyed the archbishop's command as long as he lived. In 1192 he accounts for all the three counties.

[3] Ben. Pet. ii. 106. Hoveden, iii. 32. Longchamp is now 'summus justitiarius.' R. Devizes, 14.

to his ordinary and palatine jurisdiction as bishop, and the newly-purchased earldom or sheriffdom of Northumberland. John had an equally compact, though less extensive, dominion in the west; and in the middle of England, he and his friends possessed a band of jurisdictions and castles reaching through the counties of Lincoln, Nottingham, Derby, Leicester, Warwick, and Stafford. Although of the towns of this midland territory many, if not all, were faithful to the crown, and some of the castles were still retained by the king as a check on his brother, the whole of the ordinary jurisdiction was withdrawn from the direct action of the justiciar. John's own counties rendered no account at the Exchequer, and their judicial business was managed by his own justiciar; in the shires under Hugh of Nunant and Gerard Camville, the influence of the justiciar could not be available without the co-operation of the sheriff. The chancellor could regard only the east and south-east of England as really amenable to his authority. Any attempt to exert it beyond these limits would necessarily lead to a complication with one or all of his rivals.

Localisation of parties

Withdrawal of John's counties from the ordinary jurisdiction of the justiciar

Hugh de Puiset was a man whose ancestors had been accustomed to deal on an equality with kings, and to give them no small trouble. He was, in all probability, the son of that Hugh de Puiset,[1] viscount

Ancestry of Hugh de Puiset

---

[1] It is impossible to speak with entire certainty of the parentage of Hugh de Puiset, but I believe the following to be the truth. I should say that the whole pedigree of the Puisets is difficult to make out. The Puisets were lords of the castle of that name near Chartres, and the head of the family was hereditary viscount of Chartres. I. Ebrard, viscount of Chartres, and his wife Hunbergis were the parents of Hugh de Puiset, viscount of Chartres, and Adelaide the wife of Roger Montgomery the ally of William the Conqueror. (*Cartulaire de S. Pierre de Chartres*, 159. Ord. Vit. v. 13.) II. Hugh de Puiset, viscount of Chartres, married Adelaide of Montlheri, sister of Guy de Rochfort, dapifer to the king of France. He was viscount in 1096 and had three sons, Ebrard, Hugh, and Guy, and a daughter Hunbergis. (*Cartulaire*, &c. p. 240.) III. Of these three sons, Guy was viscount of Etampes; Hugh married Mamilia de Roucy and went to the Holy Land about 1106. (Will. Tyr. xiv. 15.) Ebrard went on the first crusade and took part in the siege of Antioch in 1097. (W. Tyr. vi. 4; Alb. Aq. 236, 255.) IV. The next viscount

of Chartres is Hugh de Puiset, the enemy of Lewis VI., who is described by Abbot Suger as the nephew of Guy of Etampes, and son of the countess Adelaide of Corbeil. (*Opp. Suger.* ed. Le Coy de la Marche, p. 70.) His father had gone on the first crusade. He was, then, the son of Ebrard who died at Antioch, and, as viscount, agrees with the abbot of S. Pierre for the commemoration of his father Ebrard as soon as the day of his death is known. (*Cartulaire* &c. 452.) V. This Hugh had a wife Agnes, and two sons, Ebrard and Bouchard (*Cart.* p. 412), of whom Ebrard was viscount of Chartres 1143. (*Cart.* 644; Bouquet, xv. 493.) VI. The next viscount is Hugh de Puiset, count of Bar, son of Ebrard (Ben. Pet. i. 278), and nephew of Hugh de Puiset bishop of Durham. Therefore bishop Hugh must have been a younger son of Hugh and Agnes, and Agnes must have been an unknown daughter of Count Stephen of Blois and Adela the daughter of William the Conqueror. This pedigree, which has given me a good deal of trouble, will be found to agree with the charters and historians, but not with the deductions of the French genealogists, who rather

P 2

Inheritance
of turbulent
traditions of Chartres, who had for many years defied the power of Lewis VI.
Another Hugh de Puiset, his cousin,[1] had nearly produced a revolution
in Palestine; another ancestor, Bouchard of Corbeil, had attempted to
wrest the crown of France from Philip I.[2] Hugh himself was a
Family of
Bishop Hugh great-grandson of William the Conqueror; nephew of Stephen, of
Henry of Winchester, and Theobald of Champagne; cousin to both
Richard I. and Philip II. Adelidis, the mother of one at least of
the bishop's children, was a lady of the great house of Percy,[3] and
this connexion added the influence of her family to the other sources
of the bishop's strength. One of his sons, also Hugh de Puiset, had
been chancellor to Lewis VII.[4] Hugh had had now a longer tenure
of power than any man of his mark in Europe. At an early age he
His early
promotion,
versatility,
and ex-
perience had been made treasurer of York, in which capacity he had styled
himself Hugh, 'by the grace of God, treasurer and archdeacon';
had fought the battles in court, council and chapter, of his cousin
S. William, and had headed the garrisons and trained the soldiers of
Henry of Winchester when Henry II. was yet a child.[5] He had

ignore bishop Hugh. In addition to
the references given above, compare
Martene and Durand, *Amplissima
Coll.*, i. 774; Bouquet, xv. 493; Du-
chesne, iv. 528. The identification
of Hugh the viscount, as the son of
Ebrard, is proved by the charter of the
abbey of S. Pierre, in which he refers
to his imprisonment; *Cart.* &c. 452;
Suger, pp. 73, 76; and that of his son
Ebrard by the letter of Lewis VII.
Cart., &c., 644.

[1] Hugh the younger, son of Hugh
and Mamilia de Roucy, count of Joppa.
See W. Tyr. xiv. 15.

[2] Suger, V. Ludov. VI. p. 80. He
was slain by Stephen of Blois. Ib. 81.
He was father of Adelaide the wife of
Ebrard, and grandmother of the
bishop.

[3] According to William of Newburgh, v. 11, the bishop was father of
three sons by three different ladies
before he took priest's orders, but as one
of the persons called by the historian
his sons was his nephew Bouchard,
archdeacon of Durham, the rest of the
story may be apocryphal. Two sons
he is known to have had, of both
of whom Adelaide may have been the
mother, as she certainly was of his son
Henry. This Henry gave Stockdale
to Sallay Abbey ' pro salute animæ meæ
et Adelidis de Perci matris meæ et
Dionysiæ sponsæ meæ . . . . sicut in
cartis Ricardi de Morevill et Willelmi

de Perci continentur.' Mon. Angl. v.
510. Adelidis de Percy had another
son named Alan de Morvill, who confirmed a donation which Adelidis de
Percy his mother had made to Henry
de Puiset his brother, of all the land of
Settle and the church of Giggleswick.
Whitaker, *History of Craven*, p. 111.
She probably had married a Morvill
after Hugh became a bishop. Henry
de Puiset's wife Dionysia was a
daughter of Odo de Thilli, of the
family to which Randulf de Thilli, archbishop Roger's constable, belonged.
Madox, *Hist. Exch.* p. 356, from
Pipe Roll of 31 Hen. II. It is clear
that the connexion of the Puisets and
Percies was very close, and that the
former had gained a strong position in
Yorkshire. Henry de Puiset was a
great benefactor of Finchale priory.

[4] See Ben. Pet. i. 241; W. Newb. v.
11. He is to be distinguished from
Hugh the count of Bar on the Seine,
the bishop's nephew, who comes more
into English history and was buried in
the Galilee at Durham, Ben. Pet. ii. 92.
The bishop's son, who was chancellor
in 1180, died before 1185. He was the
youngest of the family.

[5] John of Hexham, ed. Raine, p. 155.
' Qui Hugo thesaurarius interim epi-
scopales possessiones Wintoniæ et
castra cum militari manu ipse militans
defensabat.' Ibid. p. 158. Mon. Angl.
v. 494.

every opportunity and many qualifications for becoming a very great man, and in spite of his failures he left a mark upon the north of England which is not yet effaced. He was a man of grand stature, and singularly noble face,[1] eloquent, energetic, a mighty hunter,[2] a great shipmaster,[3] a magnificent builder, an able defender and besieger, a consummate intriguer, and a very wary politician.[4] Against great odds he had retained his position through all the struggles of Henry's reign. Of the Becket quarrel he kept himself comparatively clear, sympathising, doubtless, as his uncle of Winchester and his cousin of Sens did, with the ecclesiastical principles of the martyr, but unwilling to risk anything by taking a decided part against the king. The death of the bishop of Winchester in 1171, and his own close connexion with the French court, induced him in 1173 to take a more hazardous part, and although not actually to rebel, to attempt the position of mediator which had been held by his uncle in the contest between Stephen and Matilda, but which Matilda's son was little likely to regard as loyal. His temporising policy on this occasion drew down on him the severe animadversion of Henry,[5] but he was not, like Arnulf of Lisieux, a prelate who could be driven into resignation. Henry doubtless saw that his own policy was to make it the bishop's interest to be faithful, and not to risk on the side of Scotland the substitution of a weaker, even if more trustworthy, champion. By every turn of affairs, then, he had gained power, and could he have realised the authority apparently intrusted to him by Richard, he would have exercised during the remaining years of his life a rule more exactly resembling that of the great ecclesiastical princes of Germany than anything that has ever existed in England. We

Margin notes: Character and policy of Hugh de Puiset — His earlier career — Hugh de Puiset the nearest approach in English history to the imperial type of prelate

---

[1] Geoff. Coldingham, *Scr. Dunelm.* p. 4. This writer makes bishop Hugh only 25 at the time of his election to Durham in 1152; if this is right he must have been trained early to the use of arms, as he was early preferred in the church. But he was probably older.

[2] On his 'caza' or chase in the forest of Weardale, which was quite on a royal scale, like everything else about him, see *Boldon Buke*, ed. Greenwell, pp. liv, lv. His hunting hall, built for each chase by the villeins of Auckland, was 60 feet long, chapel and kitchen, &c., in proportion.

[3] On his ships see Surtees' account of him in the *Hist. of Durham*, Coldingham, p. 13 :—" Naves pulcherrimas . . . ut majorum episcoporum sive ducum gloriam superaret.' Also

Madox, *Hist. Exch.* 493.
[4] His character is drawn by William of Newburgh, v. 10.
[5] Ben. Pet. i. 64, 67. His policy is, I think, quite that of the Champagne counts and bishops: resistance to the royal authority on ecclesiastical grounds; in all other matters,thoroughly secular. Hugh is always found on the clerical side, although he had very little that was clerical about him; and so helped to thwart Archbishop Geoffrey, and was always on the best terms with the popes. Without being a great man, he was always in a great position, and seldom unequal to the occasion. His biography, if it could be written in detail, would be a diplomatic or political history of at least fifty eventful years of English national life.

picture him as like one of those grand stern figures that look down in stone from the walls and piers of the cathedrals of Mentz, Würzburg, and Bamberg. He was very ambitious, not more than commonly unprincipled or unscrupulous, and, with the exception of the shortsightedness inseparable from a narrow personal selfishness, an able, as he was a very experienced, man. He seems to have possessed strong affections, and, notwithstanding their constant ill-usage of him, to have been personally a friend of both Henry [1] and his sons. His charm of manner and good nature, perhaps, did as much for the permanence of his power as did the versatility of his policy.

Contrast of Hugh de Puiset with William Longchamp

Such was the first enemy, for he was an enemy by the very necessity of the case, whom William Longchamp had to encounter ; a man whose position, character, and history stood in the most marked contrast with his own. William Longchamp was a *novus homo*.

Family history of William Longchamp

Without crediting the ill-natured statement of Hugh of Nunant [2] and Giraldus [3] that his grandfather was a runaway serf who had escaped from the Beauvaisis into Normandy, it may be considered as certain that that grandfather was the founder of the family. William was a son of Hugh de Longchamp, [4] who, so far as we can see, was the person to whom, early in the reign of Henry II., lands in Herefordshire had been given by the king ; [5] who held in the same county a knight's fee under the house of Lacy, [6] and in Normandy the office of fermer of the Honour of Conches. [7] He took his name from the ducal demesne and castle of Longchamp, one of

---

[1] So far as Henry is concerned this is an inference from the treatment he received from him. Richard, although he sometimes made a jest of him, and certainly plundered him cruelly, seems to have been as fond of him as of any one ; interfered promptly when Longchamp went beyond his orders, and treated him personally with great regard. See Hoveden, iii. 239. Coldingham mentions that Richard used to call him his father, p. 14; and both he and John always recognised the near relationship. John even carried it on to the next generation, calling Henry de Puiset his cousin. Rot. Cart. (ed. Hardy), p. 126.

[2] See Ben. Pet. ii. 216; Hoveden, iii. 142.

[3] Gir. Camb. V. Galfr. in Ang. Sac. ii. 404.

[4] 'VIII. kal. Nov. obiit Hugo de Longocampo, et Willelmus filius ejus Ehelyensis episcopus.' Necrology of Rouen, among the Rolls' Transcripts :

'Archives of Normandy, No. 412, excerpta ex necrologio ecclesiæ Rothomagensis de obitu principum Angliæ.'

[5] 'In terris datis Hugoni de Longocampo 16 l. 10 s. in Lintuna et in Wiltuna.' Rot. Pip. 3 Hen. II. p. 93, also pp. 51, 144. 1 am aware that Dugdale decidedly denies the connexion of the chancellor with this family, but the following notes will probably be thought to be proof enough.

[6] Liber Niger Scaccarii (ed. Hearne), p. 155: Among the knight's fees of Hugh de Lacy, 'et feodum unius militis de feodo antiquo quod oblitus sum, feodum Willelmi de Burehopa quod tenet Hugo de Longo Campo in maritagio' ; and p. 159 : 'Henricus de Longocampo tenet Wilton per unum feodum.' 'Rex pater regis Johannis dedit Wilton Hugoni ob gen.' Testa de Nevill, p. 70.

[7] Stapleton, *Rolls of the Norman Exchequer*, i. 74, &c.

the four castles in the forest of Lions, in which he occupied a small holding. He seems to have married a Lacy,[1] and perhaps was one of those knights who made their fortunes in the service of the younger Henry. In the year 1180 he was in disgrace, being greatly in debt to the exchequer of the duchy, and having failed to present himself before the justiciar when he was summoned. His balance of account unpaid for the honour of Conches was upwards of 700*l.*, and he owed besides for purprestures in the forest, for the rents of the carpenters of Longchamp, and an amercement of 100*l.* for non-appearance and waste.[2] That his difficulties were the result of political misconduct appears from the statement of Giraldus, that the chancellor had been spoken of by Henry II. as a traitor on both father's and mother's side.[3] The date of his appointment to Conches would tally very nearly with the period of the younger Henry's ascendency in Normandy. That he was a man of mark may be inferred from the fact that Ralph Tesson, Reginald of Pavilly, and Richard Vernon, three of the great barons of Normandy, were among the sureties for the payment of his debt, a fourth being his son, Hugh de Longchamp the younger.[4] To this Hugh the estate of Wilton in Herefordshire is stated to have been given by his father,[5] although the person whom we first find administering it was named Henry. The elder Hugh must have had a large family; among his sons were, besides the chancellor and the second Hugh,[6]

Difficulties of Hugh Longchamp

Brothers of the chancellor

[1] See note 6, p. 214.

[2] 'Rob. de Stoteville debet 23 s. 4 d. de censibus porpresturarum in Longo Campo recuperatis per juream, quas Hugo de Longo Campo tenebat . . . . Præter hæc li acræ et dim. virgata terræ quas Hugo et homines ejus tenebant sunt recuperatæ per jueam . . . Hugo de Long Campo debet 706 l. 17 s. vi d. de rem. computi sui de honore de Conches. Et 8 l. 8 s. de porpresturis forestæ de Leons de septem annis et unoquoque anno 24 s. Et 66 l. 10 s. de censibus carpentariorum de Longo Campo de septem annis et xi. mensibus. Et de hoc anno 7 l. 10 s. Et 100 l. de misericordia sua pro prædictis porpresturis et quia non venit ad submonitionem justitiarii. Et pro wasto de districto de Longo Campo.' R. Stapleton, Rolls &c. i. 74.

[3] V. Galfr. p. 390. 'Improperabat enim eidem pluries quod proditorem suum et proditionis hæredem ex utroque parente familiarem habebat.' See also p. 405. It would appear

from the Pipe Roll, 1 Ric. I., that both Walter de Lacy and Henry Longchamp had been kept out of their Herefordshire estates by Henry II., and only restored to them on his death, pp. 141, 145.

[4] Stapleton, Rolls, &c., i. 64, 80, 96, &c.

[5] Rot. Cart. R. Joh. p. 146:— 'Sciatis nos concessisse . . . Henrico de Longo Campo, assensu et concessione Gaufridi fratris sui primogeniti, Wilton in Herefordsiria cum castello . . . quæ Hugo avus suus dedit Hugoni patri ejusdem Henrici.' Mar. 7, 1205.

[6] This Hugh, if he was the father of Geoffrey Longchamp, son of Emma of S. Leger, who afterwards married Walter Baskerville, must have died before 1195, as in that year Geoffrey fines as his mother's heir. Anyhow, Geoffrey was one of the family, for Osbert Longchamp is his pledge. Madox, Hist. Exch., 356. See more of Geoffrey below, p. 258, note 4.

Brothers
and sisters
of thé
chancellor
Stephen, steward of Normandy,[1] Henry,[2] sheriff of Herefordshire,
Osbert,[3] sheriff of Yorkshire, and afterwards of Norfolk and Suffolk,
and Robert, who was abbot of S. Mary's at York. Of his daughters,
one, Richenda, was married to Mathew de Cleres, castellan of Lions
and Dover; and another to the head of the Herefordshire house of
Evreux.[4]

Description
of Long-
champ's
person
At its best the origin of the chancellor was very humble compared
with that of the bishop of Durham. His personal qualifications
were scarcely less so. That he was the monster of ugliness that
Giraldus depicts,[5] more like an ape than a man, deformed and lame,
we may safely set down as an exaggeration ; but the utmost that a
tolerant critic could say for him was that his person was respectable,[6]
and that it required all the greatness of his mind to compensate for
the shortness of his body. And the careers of the two statesmen
Career of
William
Longchamp
were in strong contrast ; whilst Hugh de Puiset had been plotting
and warring, William had been working as a clerk in the chancery,
first under Geoffrey, who had made him his official in the archdeaconry of Rouen,[7] then under Richard, who had made him his
confidant and chaplain before he came to the crown.[8] His rise from
such a post to that of chancellor, justiciar, and legate was very
sudden, and shows that he possessed in an extreme degree the confidence of his master as well as great ambition and confidence in himself.
The horrid accusations of immorality brought against him by
Giraldus [9] defeat themselves ; they are the utterance of a spiteful

[1] Stephen Longchamp had Frome
Herbert in Herefordshire of the gift of
Walter de Lacy, and Mutford in Suffolk
in right of his wife Petronilla, daughter
of Osbert de Cailly and Hildeburga,
lady of Baudemont. This connexion
accounts for the mention of him in
the treaty between Philip and Richard
in 1195, and for his relations with
Henry de Vere. See below, p. 240.
Stapleton, Rolls, &c. II. cxi. &c. Rot.
Pip. 3 John, &c.
[2] Henry, the chancellor's brother,
is identified with the sheriff of
Herefordshire by the mention of his
imprisonment at Cardiff. Gir. Camb.
V. Galfr. p. 399. The sheriff was
prevented by imprisonment from
rendering his accounts in 1192, and
released before the Exchequer session
of 1193.
[3] Osbert's career will be found
worked out further on, and Robert's
also.
[4] Stephen Devereux in 1205 had
Frome Herbert by the gift of his
uncle Stephen Longchamp. Rot.

Cart. R. Joh. p. 156. He was a
nephew also of the chancellor. See
Eyton's Hist. Shropshire, v. 21.
[5] V. Galfr. part ii. 19, p. 405:—
'Statura exigua despectaque . . .
claudus . . . capite grosso . . .
simiam simulans . . . facie canina
. . . mento reflexo . . . collo con-
tracto, pectore gibboso, ventre præam-
bulo, renibus retrogradis, tibiis tortis,
et in modico corpore pes immensus.'
[6] R. Devizes, p. 11:—'Persona
spectabilis, brevitatem corporis animo
recompensans.'
[7] Gir. Camb. V. Galfr. p. 390.
[8] R. Devizes, p. 6:—'Ante coronam
comitis Pictavorum fuerat cancellarius.'
[9] V. Galfr. p. 406. It is impossible, if there were any truth in such
charges, that John should have
charged him, as his most offensive
crime, with introducing into England
the foreign custom of serving on the
knee : R. Devizes, p. 31. The whole
may be based on the story of Eleanor's
refusal to intrust her grandson to his

and defeated antagonist, one, moreover, whose words on a question of personal interest are never worthy of consideration. All that we really gather from his description is, that William was a plain, short, lame man, who did not understand English, and who was very imprudent in showing his dislike to the nation that he had to govern.[1] Against the charges of immorality, so easy to bring and so hard to repel, which both his chief assailants allege against him, we must set the panegyrics of the monks of Canterbury, who dared not have taken as their patron a bishop of notoriously evil life ;[2] of Peter of Blois, who had nothing in common with the monks,[3] but was a sincerely pious man ; Nigel Wireker, of whose sincerity and desire of reform there can be no doubt, and who actually dedicated to him his satire on the manners of the age.[4] It is, however, simply impossible that such a man as Giraldus describes should have been tolerated in an age and country in which S. Hugh of Lincoln was religiously all-powerful. S. Hugh does not seem to have liked the chancellor's policy ; their political principles were opposed, and the Saint took part in the proceedings against Longchamp in defence of Archbishop Geoffrey ; but their personal relations were not unkind, and the chancellor seems to have trusted implicitly to the bishop's good will.[5] The man who would not tolerate the dead bones of Fair Rosamond within the choir of Godstow would not have hesitated to denounce a profligate in the sacred offices of legate and bishop.[6] Setting aside, then, these calumnies, his character seems to have been this :—He was a strong-minded, ambitious, self-confident, resolute man ; faithful to his master, ready and active in his service ; unsparing of labour, energetic, and unwearied ; relentless in exactions

Improbability of his being a vicious man

Theory of his character

care (ibid. p. 403), and on the mere insinuations of Hugh of Nunant in his letter against him. Hoved. iii. 142, &c.

[1] Although there is no reason whatever to believe Giraldus, he states this in a circumstantial way ; and it is at all events important, as showing that although the leading men in England were still all of Norman blood, it was beginning to be regarded as an unwise thing to despise the English. He is arguing so as to excite odium among a people who felt themselves English : 'Anglos autem cum tota curia sua tanto et tam in exorabili est odio persecutus, ut usuali verbo in eorum opprobrium et improperium dicere consueverint : "Anglicus fiam, si hoc fecero. Pejor sum Anglico si illud admisero." Ad injuriarum quoque cumulum, et dedecoris argumentum cum ad exquisita naturæ pergere parabant, dicere

solebant "Eamus facere Anglicum." ' V. Galfr. p. 407.

[2] Epp. Cantuar. p. 354 ; and see the introduction to that book, pp. lxxxv, lxxxvi, &c. ; also Wharton's note in Anglia Sacra, i. 632.

[3] Hoveden, iii. 148–150.

[4] Leyser, Hist. Poetarum, p. 754 ; and compare the note in Epp. Cantuar. pp. lxxxv, lxxxvi.

[5] Hoveden, iii. 152–154. Bened. ii. 223, 224.

[6] The same argument is available in defence of Richard himself, against whom the like charges are insinuated. S. Hugh of Lincoln heard his confessions and declared that his most crying sins were his unfaithfulness to his wife, which was notorious, and his carelessness in the use of church patronage. Magna Vita S. Hugonis, p. 255.

and oppressions where his master's interests could be advanced by such means; fearless to rashness in his undertakings; greedy of advancement for his family; intolerant of opposition or equality; devoid of tact in dealing with his peers and of sympathy with his inferiors; probably, as appears from the general tone of his history as told by neutrals as well as by enemies, elated by the greatness of his position beyond the ordinary exultation of the upstart. He was thus a man whose nobler as well as meaner qualities would lay him open to attack from the king's enemies and his own competitors for power.

Character of Longchamp

William Longchamp had been consecrated to the see of Ely on the last day of 1189, and enthroned with great pomp on the feast of the Epiphany 1190.[1] Before the end of February,[2] having quarrelled with the co-justiciar, he joined the king in Normandy, where he stayed till Easter, and immediately after the festival returned to England with full powers; the bishop of Durham remaining behind to secure his grant of the justiciarship of the north, and the bishop of Winchester to obtain the restitution of his purchased honours.[3] The first event of the chancellor's government was untoward. The Jews of York, alarmed by the riot which had taken place at London on the occasion of the coronation, and was followed by similar outbreaks at Norwich in February, at Stamford in March, at Bury St. Edmund's on Palm Sunday, and at almost every large town except Winchester,[4] had obtained, in expectation of a general rising, permission from John Marshall, the sheriff of Yorkshire, to occupy a tower in the castle of York. Thither they had removed their families. Before the alarm had blown over, the sheriff ordered the Jews to quit the tower, and on their demurring called out the force of the county against them. The knights of Yorkshire besieged the castle, and the Jews, on the Friday before Palm Sunday, slew their wives and children, shut themselves up in the tower, set it on fire, and perished in it. The citizens and knights thereupon seized the Jews' houses in York and burned them, destroying with them the bonds by which the debts due to them were secured, and on which the whole banking business of the north depended.[5] The leaders of

After the council in Normandy he returns to England

Panic of the Jews at York

Frightful catastrophe of the Jews at York

---

[1] Anglia Sacra, i. 632.
[2] Benedict, ii. 106. He was at Westminster on the 24th of January, where he attested a charter together with the bishops of London, Durham, and Coventry, with the other justices. Eyton, Hist. Shropshire, vii. 12. In Normandy, on the 14th of March, John of Alençon, the vice-chancellor, was acting for him, but on the 20th he is at Rouen with the king, also on the 22nd and 23rd; on the 27th he was at

Lions. Fœd. i. 51.
[3] R. Devizes, p.11–13. Ben. P. ii. 109.
[4] R. Devizes, p. 5. W. Newb. lib. iv. cc. 7–11. It is a curious coincidence that whilst the Jews were being persecuted in the towns, Richard was issuing charters of protection for them, especially on March 22. See Fœd. i. 51.
[5] Benedict, ii. 107; Hoveden, iii. 33.

the knights in this exploit were Philip of Falconberge, Richard Malebysse, William Percy, and Marmaduke Darrell.[1]

Immediately on the chancellor's return from Normandy, early in May,[2] he visited York with a military force under his brother Henry.[3] The citizens denied all complicity with the persecutors, several of whom had fled to Scotland.[4] Longchamp, unable or unwilling to use harsh measures, accepted a fine from the citizens,[5] and took hostages of them, who were sent in custody to Northampton.[6] He inflicted, however, severe penalties on the knights who had taken the lead in the transaction. John Marshall he removed from the sheriffdom, appointing his own brother Osbert [7] in his place. It was unfortunate that, whether justly or not, the punishment fell most heavily on the adherents of the Percies, the relations and allies of the bishop of Durham. The lands of William Percy and Richard Malebysse, his kinsman,[8] with those of their squires, were seized to the king's use : the entire property of the fugitives was also confiscated, and the money due to the Jews was collected where it

Marginal notes: Conduct of the Yorkshire knights. Longchamp visits York, and punishes the knights. The punishment falls heavily on the adherents of the bishop of Durham

[1] Chron. de Melsa, i. 251.

[2] 'Circa Dominicæ Ascensionis solemnia.' W. Newb. iv. 11.

[3] 'Henrico de Longo Campo et aliis militibus qui abierunt Eboracum propter occisionem Judæorum, lx. li. per breve Cancellarii.' Rot. Pip. 2 Ric. I., Lincolnshire.

[4] 'De exitu terrarum et catallorum hominum qui aufugerunt pro assultu Judæorum in civitate Eboracensi.' Rot. Pip. 2 Ric. I.; W. Newb. iv. 11.

[5] W. Newb. iv. 11.

[6] Rot. Pip. 5 Ric. I. :—' Cives Eboraci reddunt computum de x marcis pro habendis obsidibus suis qui fuerunt Norhantoniæ propter occisionem Judæorum.' This was in 1193, when Longchamp was out of the way and the affair had blown over.

[7] Hoveden, iii. 34. In the Pipe Roll, 2 Rich. I. John Marshall accounts for Yorkshire for half a year, and Osbert for the other half. Osbert had also Westmoreland, which had been held, like York, by Ranulf Glanvill.

[8] Rot. Pip. 4 Ric. I. :—' Ricardus Malebysse reddit computum de xx marcis pro rehabenda terra sua usque ad adventum domini regis, quæ seisita fuit in manu regis propter occisionem Judæorum Eboraci; et ut ipse et Walterus de Carton et Ricardus de Kukeneia, armigeri ejus, habeant pacem regis usque ad adventum ejus.' Madox, 334. Also William de Percy,

knight, and Picot, Roger de Ripun and Alan Malckake 'debent v marcas pro eodem.' These are probably nominal compositions made after Longchamp's deposition. Richard Malebysse, the ancestor of the Yorkshire clan of Beckwith, is called nephew of Agnes Percy in a charter of Sallay; Mon. Angl. vi. 513. Picot is a family name among the Percies; Mon. Angl. vi. 93. Picot the sheriff was grandfather of William Percy, whose charter is attested by Henry de Puiset. Alan Malekake and Picot de Percy are found attesting a grant of Henry de Puiset to the monastery at Bakestanforde, in Raine's *Priory of Finchale*, p. 10, and Henry de Puiset and Richard Malebysse sign another together, p. 15. On the other hand, the Fauconbergs and Cukeneys were closely connected and were fellow benefactors of Welbeck; Mon. Angl. vi. 873. Marmaduke Darrell also attests a charter of William Percy; Mon. Angl. vi. 1190. I should not like to accuse the Puiset and Percy connexion of a deliberate attempt to get rid of the evidence of their debts on this occasion, but so it may have been. These details are not unimportant, if we consider Roger Hoveden's own relation to Hugh de Puiset, and that many of these charters are attested by William of Hoveden.

could be by the king's officers. On the same occasion the cathedral was put under interdict and the clergy suspended, because they declined to receive Longchamp as legate, although he had not yet received his commission.[1] It was clear to the bishop of Durham and his friends, both in the county and in the chapter, that the chancellor had jumped at an opportunity of infringing his jurisdiction as justiciar, and that his sense of right had been quickened by his desire of injuring the supporters of his rival.

Interview of the bishops of Durham and Ely, ending in the arrest of the former

As soon as the examination was over, William Longchamp set out towards Lincoln, where he had a like work to do ; but he had only reached Blythe,[2] in Nottinghamshire, when he met Bishop Hugh bearing his commission, and hastening to secure himself in the territory in which he was now scarcely less than sovereign. Hugh was not without suspicion of the chancellor's double-dealing, for in passing through London he had presented himself to the barons of the Exchequer and suffered a rebuff at their hands.[3] Now he delivered his credentials. Longchamp professed himself most happy to obey the directions of the king : Hugh talked largely of his new powers : the chancellor was more reserved. At last the commission was read and proved to be less formidable than he expected.[4] He agreed to meet the bishop a week later at Tickhill.[5] On the appointed day he received him alone in the castle there, and, to the bishop's disgust, produced a commission to himself dated some days later than his rival's. Hugh felt that he had been shamefully treated, but he had no chance of retreating. The chancellor arrested him, and swore by the life of Richard that until the old bishop surrendered everything that he had purchased of the king—castles, justiciarship, earldom, and sheriffdom—he should remain a prisoner.[6] In vain he protested ; he was taken back to London and there compelled to surrender all, and to give up, moreover, his son Henry and another knight, Gilbert de la Leya,[7] as hostages for his good behaviour. This done, he was allowed to return northwards ; but when he reached

He is kept under bond at Howden

his manor of Howden he was stopped by the sheriff Osbert and William Stuteville,[8] and obliged to give security for residing there during the chancellor's pleasure. He forwarded his complaints immediately to the king, who was now at Marseilles. Richard, thinking, perhaps, that his minister had been too zealous, and that it was hard treatment for so old and dignified a man, wrote to

---

[1] Ben. Pet. ii. 108, 109.
[2] Ben. Pet. ii. 109.
[3] R. Devizes, p. 12.
[4] R. Devizes, p. 13.
[5] R. Devizes, p. 13.
[6] R. Devizes, p. 13. Benedict, ii. 109.

[7] Benedict, ii. 109. Gilbert de la Leya held a fief in Craven under the Percies, as did Henry de Puiset, Bolton in Bolland. Whitaker, *Hist. Craven*, p. 110.
[8] Ben. Pet. ii. 109.

Longchamp, ordering him to restore fhe manor of Sadberge and the castle of Newcastle-on-Tyne.[1] But Hugh was kept still at Howden. The fruits of victory remained with the chancellor. He had effectually rid himself of his chief competitor : and in this matter his appointed counsellors in the Exchequer were at one with him. He saw himself at the summit of his ambition : and he now received the legatine commission from Clement III., which made him supreme in church and state ; a letter of Richard, from Bayonne, dated June 6, which was perhaps the document which had confounded Hugh de Puiset, gave him full power to act in all things as the king's lieutenant.[2]

The barons of the Exchequer connive at Longchamp's treatment of him

The measures which he next took were dictated partly by the king and partly by his own instinct of self-defence. His brother Stephen accompanied the king ; but Osbert and Henry remained with him : to Osbert he intrusted the sheriffdoms of Yorkshire and Westmoreland—he had already received from the king the keeping of the palace of Westminter and the prison of London.[3] He himself undertook the fortifying of the Tower, which he intrusted to one of his dependents, William Puinctel, as constable, and on the repairs of which he laid out 2,881*l*. 1*s*. 10*d*.[4] On Dover Castle, which was held by his brother-in-law, Matthew de Cleres, he expended 1,068*l*. 3*s*. 8*d*., through the hands of William Maunsel.[5] The ten months which followed were the heyday of the chancellor's prosperity. He traversed the country with a large retinue, levying contributions from the barons as justiciar, and as legate exacting procurations from the clergy. He was attended by a court of clerks and knights, the latter anxious to connect themselves with so successful a man by marriages with his kinsfolk, and the former singing his praises as a liberal and magnificent patron.[6] It was probably at this time that he secured for the son of Henry Longchamp the heiress of the great family of Croun :[7] he placed in his brother's hands also

Longchamp strengthens his hold on the royal fortresses

His proceedings at the Tower and at Dover

Character of his administration

---

[1] Hoveden, iii. 38, 39.

[2] R. de Diceto, 655. The letter of legation is dated June 5 ; that of the king, June 6.

[3] That is, the Fleet prison. The appointment is printed in the Fœdera. i. 50, dated Nov. 30, 1189, Canterbury. That the prison in question was that ' de Ponte de Fliet ' appears from an entry in the Pipe Roll of the 9th Ric. I., Madox, *Hist. Exch.* 356. Osbert has 10*l*. 12*s*. 11*d*. for his trouble at Westminster and 7*l*. 12*s*. 1*d*. for the charge of the gaol in 2 Ric. I. See the Pipe Roll of that year.

[4] Ben. Pet. ii. 101, 106. Rot. Pip. 2 Ric. I. This William Puinctel is doubtless a relation of Alexander Puinctel who captured Archbishop Geoffrey at Dover.

[5] Rot. Pip. 2 Ric. I.

[6] Benedict, ii. 143 ; and see Hugh of Nunant's account. Hoveden, iii. 142, &c.

[7] William, son of Henry Longchamp, married Petronilla, daughter of Guy de Croun, and got through her large estates in Lincolnshire. He died before 1207, and she afterwards married Henry de Mara and Oliver de Vaux. The identity of her father-in-law is established by the suit which she and her second husband brought against the lord of Wilton for dower. Rot. Fin, 9 John, p. 410.

He strength-
ens his posi-
tion by new
alliances
among the
barons
Stephen Beauchamp, whose wardship he had purchased from Bertram de Verdun : for another brother, Robert, he intrigued that the monks of Westminster might choose him as their abbot.[1] He made use of his position also to strengthen himself in the good graces of his colleagues. By a transaction which seems scarcely less than fraudulent, he allowed Geoffrey FitzPeter to be received as heir, in right of his wife, of William Mandeville, earl of Essex.[2] He formed a strict

Alliance
with the earl
of Arundel
and William
de Braiose
alliance with the earl of Arundel, to whom, for 2,000 marks, he restored the honour of his earldom, which had been for sixteen years retained in hand by the crown ;[3] and with William de Braiose[4] and others who had the power to serve and defend his family on the Welsh border, where the family estates lay.

Conduct of
the co-justi-
ciars
The country was at peace, and only troubled with those heavy exactions which, as being a part of Richard's necessary policy under all his ministries, cannot be ascribed to the influence of the chancellor, although they tended doubtless to make him unpopular. Complaints from the co-justiciars that their advice was systematically neglected are said to have been conveyed to the king ; but they continued to act with him, and Richard gave no sign of believing them, or of a design to modify his minister's commission to please men whom he less trusted. Longchamp found time to hold solemn

Council at
Gloucester
meetings of the clergy. On the 1st of August he held a council at Gloucester, the object of which may not have been entirely ecclesiastical, as Richard of Devizes ascribes his presence there to a wish to besiege the castle.[5] It is not clear, however, who could be holding the castle against him. Here the bishop of Winchester met him, and received back his patrimony, but not the purchased sheriffdom. The reconciliation seemed to be perfect. Longchamp took the bishop's advice in not pressing for entrance into the castle. This is the

Council at
Westminster
first sign of difficulties to come. On October 13 he held a legatine assembly at Westminster,[6] in which the bishop of London sat on his

---

[1] R. Devizes, p. 34.

[2] Beatrice de Say was aunt of William Mandeville, last earl of Essex, and his heiress. She had two sons, William and Geoffrey. William died, leaving two daughters, one of whom married Geoffrey FitzPeter. The inheritance was disputed between this lady and her uncle Geoffrey de Say. Longchamp first adjudged the whole to Geoffrey de Say, at his mother's wish, for 7,000 marks, and gave him seisin. There was some difficulty about the payment, and in consequence the chancellor, for 3,000 marks down, transferred the barony to Geoffrey FitzPeter. See Mon. Angl.

iv. 145, and the Pipe Roll of the 2nd of Richard I.

[3] Dugdale's Baronage, 120. This was done by Richard's order, dated at Montrichard, June 27. See Fœd. i. 48.

[4] Gir. Camb. V. Galf. p. 396, an *affinity* with William de Braiose the younger. Can this refer to the marriage of Walter de Lacy with Margaret de Braiose, which took place a few years later, but may have been arranged now ? Dugdale's Baronage, p. 98.

[5] R. Devizes, p. 13 ; R. de Diceto, 655.

[6] R. de Diceto, 656 ; R. Devizes, 14. Gervase, 1566.

right hand and the bishop of Winchester on his left. In November, on the 18th, he visited Canterbury and was entertained with great honour by the monks of Christ Church.[1] Little is known of the business transacted on these occasions. Gervase, the Canterbury Chronicler, preserves an account of a discussion relative to the consecration of the bishop-elect of Worcester, and Richard of Devizes mentions the quarrels of the bishop and monks of Coventry as a topic at Westminster; but there is no trace of any important act of constitutional policy during this time; and the sole political move which is mentioned is the negotiation with the King of Scots, carried on, doubtless, with Richard's sanction, for the recognition of Arthur of Brittany as heir in case of the king's dying childless.[2] The charters of towns granted so freely by Richard at a later period, which form the mark of his reign on domestic history, are scarce under this administration;[3] and although the chancellor acted as judge in the courts both in London and in the country, there is no trace of any improvement introduced by him, such as had distinguished year after year the rule of his predecessor. Obscurity transactions at these councils

The few notices we have of his acts during this period show that he was in constant progress, and confirm the statements of the historians as to the burden of entertaining him. A visit of a single night cost the house which received him three years' savings.[4] He entertained a train of a thousand horsemen.[5] He moved through the kingdom, Richard of Devizes says, like a flash of lightning.[6] Unhappily, the collection of revenue to satisfy the ever-increasing demands of Richard seems to have been his principal occupation. Longchamp's rapid movements in 1190

His occupations

So the year 1190 ends. Early in 1191 we find him at Northampton witnessing, with the other judges of the Curia, a final concord between the abbot of Peterborough and one Roger de Torpel, relative to the advowson of the church of Maxey.[7] This seems to have been about the last peaceful transaction in which he was engaged.

His misfortunes came upon him all at once. Complaints had been carried to Richard, who was now at Messina, in unbroken succession, and he had refused to listen; now the queen-mother herself undertook the task of remonstrance. She started on her journey to Sicily in February;[8] one part of her errand was to forward the Complaints forwarded to Richard

[1] Gervase, 1566.

[2] Will. Newb. iv. 14.

[3] One to Winchester is printed in the Fœdera, i. 50, 51, dated at Nonancourt, March 14, 1190.

[4] Bened. ii. 143.

[5] Will. Newb. iv. 14. 'Procedebat cum mille equis.'

[6] R. Devizes, p. 14, 'in similitudinem fulguris coruscantis.'

[7] Mon. Angl. i. 391:—'Coram W. Elyensi episcopo, domini regis cancellario, et Willelmo Comite Arundel et W. Marescallo, Galfrido filio Petri, Hugone Bardulf, W. Briwerre, Simone de Pateshill, Roberto de Whitefeld, justitiis domini regis.' Thursday after S. Vincent's day, i.e. Jan. 24.

[8] R. de Diceto, 654.

Vacancy of
the see of
Canterbury

consecration of the archbishop of York. The same month brought
from Messina the news of the death of the archbishop of Canterbury.[1]
As soon as the two metropolitan sees should be filled up, the legatine
power would almost to a certainty be withdrawn from the bishop of
Ely, and with it a large part of the influence which made him for
the time invulnerable.

Eleanor's
visit to
Sicily

But Eleanor's journey to Messina seems to have had another
more speedy and more fatal consequence. Unfortunately the want
of exact dates prevents us from ascertaining the period of John's
return to England ; but if it was before February 1191, his mother's
influence, whilst she was within reach, must have kept him within

John begins
to move
John had
tasted the
sweets of
power

bounds. As soon as she departs, we find him in active mischief.
John was not inclined to wait for his succession ; the foolish
policy of Richard in attempting to conciliate by the gift of real
power an enemy whom he knew to be faithless and whose weakness
of character he despised too much for his own safety, had given John
a taste, too tempting by far, of substantial sovereignty. After he had
returned to England he set up his own court in the castles which
had been given him, with scarcely less than royal pretension. He

His court
and minis-
ters

had his own justiciar, Roger de Plasnes,[2] lord of Eastthorpe and
Birch in Essex ; his chancellor, Stephen Ridell,[3] afterwards archdeacon of Ely and always a thorn in Longchamp's side ; a member
of one of the great ministerial houses of Henry. I.'s reign, nephew to
the archbishop of Canterbury : his seal bearer was Master Benedict,[4]
probably the same who became in after years the bishop of Rochester ;
William of Kahannes was his seneschal;[5] Theobald Walter his
butler.[6] With these ministers he taxed and judged the tenants of
his estates and the inhabitants of his franchises. The counties under
his control were administered by his own sheriffs, and their revenues

His wealth
and magnifi-
cence

were a loss to the exchequer of the king. Extravagant as he was, he
was rich enough to dispense with the oppressive measures taken by
the chancellor ; his magnificence made him popular, and his court

---

[1] The letters containing the news
are given in the Epp. Cantuar. pp.
329, 330 ; one of them dated Messina,
Jan. 25.

[2] R. de Diceto, 664.

[3] Ben. Pet. ii. 224. Ang. Sac. i.
634. Longchamp deprived him of his
preferments after Richard's return,
Gir. Camb. V. Galf. 404. The date of
his appointment to the archdeaconry is
not settled, but it was probably after
this. He was many years later the
papal candidate for the see of Ely. A
letter from the pope's chamberlain,
Stephen, to John is in existence,

asking for his promotion. 4th Report
of the Deputy-Keeper of the Records,
App. ii. p. 141. This must have been
in 1215. He died before the see was
filled up.

[4] Ben. Pet. ii. 224.

[5] Fœdera, i. 55.

[6] Fœdera, i. 55. This is the brother of Hubert Walter, chief butler to
John as Lord of Ireland, and ancestor
of the Butlers of Ormond. He was
also constable of Lancaster castle, and
fermer of the honour. Madox, Hist.
Exch. 412.

became the headquarters of all who had grounds of complaint against Longchamp. He lived at Lancaster, where Theobald Walter was his castellan, or at Marlborough, and waited for a chance of supplanting the minister. The leading man in his counsels was Hugh of Nunant, bishop of Coventry, who, much as he hated Longchamp, had not yet quarrelled with him. John himself, until the outbreak, seems to have been on good terms with him, and it was from him as legate that he had received absolution from his vow of absence from England for three years.[1]

He waits for his oppor- tunity

Hugh of Nunant his chief ad- viser

Hugh of Nunant was sprung from a family the head of which held the barony of Totness by gift of King William Rufus. He was sister's son and adopted child of Arnulf of Lisieux,[2] the pertinacious schemer of Henry II.'s reign, and had inherited from him the diplomatic abilities of his race. He had travelled and negotiated, and under Henry II. had been ambassador to Frederick I. and Alexander III.[3] He had tried his hand also at the work of a legate; had been sent in that capacity to Ireland for John's corona- tion, in 1187;[4] and on his way had insulted the church of Canterbury by carrying a cross and wearing a mitre whilst yet unconsecrated, in the presence of Archbishop Baldwin. Since his consecration, on the other hand, his aim had been to play the part of a temporal lord; he had bought, as we have seen, the sheriffdoms in three counties. He was possessed with an extreme hatred of monachism, which was amply repaid by the monks. He was a thoroughly unprincipled man; very vain and ambitious; clever, eloquent, and adroit, but jealous of all pre-eminence and unscrupulous in word and deed. Gervase of Canterbury, with some discrimination, represents him as an able and spirited man of business; captious in word; ready to curse when a curse would frighten; apt enough with soft words where the object was to subvert the strong.[5] I have already referred to him as the author of the vile charges brought by Giraldus against Longchamp. If the monks might be believed, his own character was no better. It was said that when, lying on his death-bed, he recounted the sins of his life, he found no confessor who would venture to appoint him a penance.[6] Giraldus[7] adduces this as a proof of the greatness of his penitence; but the story proceeds to say that he sentenced himself to purgatory until the day of judgment. It was he who advised Richard to send the monks to the devil; 'devils' was the best name he ever found for the fraternity; and the great object of his episcopal policy was to substitute for them

Character and career of Hugh of Nunant

His death- bed confes- sion and repentance

[1] Gir. Camb. De Rebus a se gestis; Ang. Sac. ii. 496.
[2] Arn. Lexov. ep. cxxvii.
[3] Ben. Pet. i. 322.
[4] Ben. Pet. ii. 4; Gervase, 1486.
[5] Gervase, 1487.
[6] M. Paris, 192; Chron. de Melsa, i. 249, from Higden.
[7] Gir. Camb. De Vita H. Nonant; Ang. Sac. ii. 353, 354.

canons, not only at Coventry but in the other conventual cathedrals.

His quarrel with the monks

The whole details of his contest with his own monks, which was as long and lively as that of the archbishop with those of Christ Church, are not preserved ; but it is not unlikely that part at least of his hatred of Longchamp was caused by the conduct of the latter in this respect. Longchamp was a favourite with the monks, and possibly exerted himself on their behalf with a view to the promotion of his brother Robert. Before Baldwin's departure, in a council at Westminster on October 22, 1189,[1] Hugh had shown himself to the bishops black and blue with the blows the monks had given him ; and Baldwin, whose feelings were easily excited, and who had no love of monks who were not Cistercians, had joined in a sentence of excommunication against the assailants. The chancellor had so far

Longchamp at first connives at his treatment of the monks for a time

yielded to the same pressure as to order, in the council at Westminster in October 1190,[2] the removal of the monks ; but it is probable that he hesitated to sanction the oppressive means by which the change was carried out, or that, when the see of Canterbury became vacant, he adopted the more promising policy. Whether Hugh had kept terms with him until he gained his object, or had quarrelled with him on the subject, does not appear ; but now the close friendship which the world had seen between the two bishops broke up suddenly,[3] and Hugh of Nunant became the intimate friend of John.

Causes of John's hostility to Longchamp

Subsequent events showed the line of argument by which John's fears and mistrust of the chancellor were aroused. Richard whilst at home had avoided any recognition of John as his heir, and the very liberality with which he had dealt with him was clogged with restrictions that showed his mistrust. The prospect of the succession of Arthur was intolerable ; yet it was understood that that was a settled thing between Richard and his minister. The king had, in the November just past, arranged for a marriage between Arthur

The probability of Arthur's succession

and a daughter of King Tancred, and had written to the pope about Arthur as his heir.[4] Possibly the news of this negotiation may have prompted Eleanor's visit to her elder son, and her anxiety for his speedy marriage. She cared little for Arthur, and her love for John probably made her desirous that his state of suspense should be terminated by the birth of a direct heir. In pursuance of the king's plan, Longchamp had negotiated with William the Lion,[5] who was the nearest kinsman, on the side of his mother, to the young duke. Besides, the vacancy of the see of Canterbury laid open to the legate the highest constitutional position in the realm : if Richard were to die on the crusade, there could be no doubt whose voice would be most potent in the nomination of his successor ; there could be no

---

[1] R. Devizes, p. 9.   [2] R. Devizes, p. 14.   [3] Will. Newb., iv. 18.
[4] Ben. Pet. ii. 137. Hoveden, iii. 65.   [5] Will. Newb., iv. 14.

doubt either that the chancellor was tampering with the monks to obtain the election for himself.   The bishops as a body were sure to accept the king's nominee, and the king was certain to nominate the chancellor ; the monks, who alone could impede or delay such a consummation, were being prepared to look to him as their protector ; he would soon be archbishop ; then John's chance of the crown would be gone.   Richard's object in nominating the archbishop of Montreal [1] could only be guessed.   It might be that he had sold the appointment, or that he had sold the promise; or that he merely wished to waste time and shut out other competitors.   It could be scarcely thought that he intended the nomination to be sustained.   In the meantime some blow must be struck that would disgrace or disable Longchamp ; nor would it be difficult to find an occasion.   He had offended all classes and all parts of England by his exactions, his arrogance, and his contempt for the nation at large.   He had rejected the advice of John himself, had virtually imprisoned his fellow justiciar the bishop of Durham ; he had shown a provoking disregard of the counsel of the barons whom Richard had associated with him in the regency.   There is so much truth unquestionably in these accusations that we cannot be surprised that John acted upon them.   And an opportunity soon presented itself.

The immediate cause of the outbreak was this :—Gerard Camville, son of that Richard who commanded the English fleet on the crusade and was afterwards viceroy of Cyprus, had married Nicolaa of Hay, the heiress of the castellanship of Lincoln, and shortly before the king's departure had bought the sheriffdom of Lincolnshire, with a promise of seven hundred marks.   The impolicy of allowing the sheriff's jurisdiction and the possession of the castle to be in the same hands was an admitted principle of administration ; even John himself had not been suffered to hold both castles and provincial jurisdictions together : but Gerard Camville's position was not in itself illegal.   He had, however, allowed his castle to become a den of robbers, and then, to avoid judicial inquiries, had done homage to John.[2]   On hearing of this, the chancellor ordered him to give up both castle and sheriffdom.   This he refused to do and prepared for resistance.   Nearly at the same time Roger Mortimer, lord of Wigmore, got into difficulties with the government and held his castle against the chancellor's men.[3]

Side notes:
The probability of Longchamp becoming archbishop

Influence of the archbishop in the determination of the succession to the kingdom

Longchamp had offended all classes

Behaviour of Gerard Camville

He does homage to John and defies Longchamp

[1] See below, p. 329.
[2] R. Devizes, p. 30 ; Will. Newb. iv. 16. Hoveden, iii. 242 :—' retatus fuit de receptatione prædonum :' the sum of the charges only appears after the king's return, when they were heard before him at Nottingham.

[3] R. Devizes, p. 30.   The charge against Roger was that he was contriving rebellion against the king with the Welsh.   I believe this fact is noticed by no other writer than Richard.

Interview
between
John and
Longchamp
(March 24,
1191)

It is impossible to say whether the interview which was held between John and Longchamp on Mid-Lent Sunday at Winchester preceded or followed this outbreak of revolt.[1]   But it is certain that an estrangement had by this time taken place, and that the two had then and there a serious discussion as to the tenure of certain castles belonging to the honours which John enjoyed, that were yet withheld from him, and as to the pensions settled upon him out of the exchequer.   Unless, however, events followed very rapidly, we may place the revolt of Lincoln after this meeting ; and it was probably a result of it.   If John had not quarrelled with Longchamp, Gerard Camville would not have dared to put himself into his power on the

chance of being protected.   The interview certainly settled nothing, and John, for once in his life prompt to action, hastened to the north.   Longchamp had to go first to Wigmore ; long before he could reach Lincoln the castle was in a state of defence, and, worse still, the castles of Tickhill and Nottingham, which had been purposely withheld from John, had been surprised by him.[2]   John de Lacy, the

constable of Chester, who had undertaken to hold them for the chancellor, had intrusted them to Robert of Croxton and Eudo Deiville, and had gone to the crusade, during which he died at Tyre.[3]   Roger, his son, had placed two other knights as companions of these two, and all four had turned traitors.   John won the first move of the game, and when Longchamp arrived in Lincolnshire, after taking Wigmore and sentencing Roger Mortimer to three years of

exile,[4] he found his forces weary and an attack impossible.   At the same time two other pieces of news reached him.[5]   Clement III. was dead, and his legation would require the confirmation of the new pope ; and Walter of Coutances, archbishop of Rouen, the trusted minister of Henry II., who had accompanied Richard to Messina, was returning to England with unknown instructions.   A proposal for pacification was only too welcome : the legate returned to Winchester, and there, on the 25th of April, an agreement was drawn up for an arbitration.

The management of this was intrusted to three bishops, Winchester, London, and Bath.   The bishops summoned three barons to represent each side : for the chancellor, the earls of Warren, Arundel, and Clare; for John, his chancellor, Stephen Ridell, William of Wenneval, and Reginald of Wasseville ; and in addition to these each party chose eight other knights.   The choice of the three earls—old Hamelin of Warren, the brother of Henry II. ;

¹ R. Devizes, p. 26.
² Hoveden, iii. 134.   Benedict, ii. 207.   Will. Newb. iv. 16.   R. Devizes, p. 30.

³ Ben. Pet. ii. 232. Hoveden, iii. 172.
⁴ R. Devizes, p. 30.
⁵ Will. Newb. |iv. 16 (ed. Hamilton, p. 46).

William of Albini, son of Queen Adeliza, and his stepson Richard of Clare—shows that the chancellor's position still recommended itself to those who might be supposed to have the king's interest most at heart. They had been among the most faithful friends of Henry II.; John's representatives, on the contrary, were three of his own creatures. Both parties swore to act fairly, and the arbitration was pronounced, as follows :—Gerard Camville is reconciled with the chancellor and allowed to retain the castle of Lincoln. John is formally to restore the castles of Tickhill and Nottingham, but the chancellor is to intrust the command of them to Richard of Wasseville and William of Wenneval, liegemen of the king, but partisans of John ; each of whom is to give security for the surrender of them to the king, if he shall return ; if not, to John. As for the other castles belonging to the honours of John, the chancellor is to change the wardens if John can show due cause for such a measure. In case of the king's death the chancellor is to do his best to secure the succession for John. All the articles, it will be seen, are decided in favour of John—a proof either that his cause was regarded as superior, or that the chancellor's fortunes were sinking in the estimation of his friends ; for the two main points of his policy, so far as we can discover, were the maintenance of the king's hold on the castles and of the succession of Arthur.[1] Two days after the pacification, the archbishop of Rouen landed at Shoreham, furnished with a batch of instructions from the king.[2]

Articles of arbitration

Its practical meaning

Walter of Coutances, ' the Pilate of Rouen,'[3] was a man of fair abilities, noble birth,[4] sound religious character, and great experience. He was, however, somewhat wanting in resolution, and scarcely strong enough to be intrusted with the almost unlimited discretion with which Richard accredited him. He left Messina with Queen Eleanor on the 2nd of April,[5] glad to escape, by the sacrifice of his treasure, the further perils of the crusade. Richard, in a characteristic way, although in the utmost need of his services, made him pay heavily for the relaxation of his vow.[6] But hastily as he had made his way home, his commissions were dated as far back as the 23rd of February.[7] It would seem that the king had not been able to make up his mind to discard the chancellor until the arrival of

Arrival of Walter of Coutances

Instructions given by Richard to Walter of Coutances

---

[1] R. Devizes, pp. 32, 33. See also the notes to Benedict, ii. 208. Hoveden, iii. 135.

[2] R. de Diceto, 659. Gervase places the arrival of the archbishop two months later, about midsummer, c. 1571.

[3] This is the name given him by Longchamp after his deposition ; Ben. Pet. ii. 224 ; Hoveden ; iii. 155.

[4] Gir. Camb. V. Galfr. ii. 10, p. 399 : ' Galterius iste ab antiqua et authentica Britonum prosapia Trojanæ nobilitatis apicem præferente originem trahens.'

[5] Itin. R. R. 176; Hoveden, iii. 100; Ben. Pet. ii. 158, 161.

[6] R. Devizes, p. 27.

[7] R. de Diceto, 659; Gir. Camb. V. Galfr. p. 396.

Eleanor ; and that even when, in consequence, we may suppose, of her representations, he at last confided the instructions to the archbishop, it must have been with a verbal command to use them as the occasion might seem to warrant. Unless there were some such private direction the conduct of the archbishop is inexplicable. He was far too honest a man to conceal an order given peremptorily by the king; unquestionably his mission was in the first place to investigate, although after investigation he had full power to act.

It must, however, be considered that Richard's conduct was puzzling to all parties ; at the very moment he was intrusting the widest powers to the archbishop, he was writing to urge John and others to

act in unison with the chancellor.[1] On his arrival he found that John had gained a decided advantage over the chancellor, and that to produce the letters which superseded the latter would be to throw all power into the hands of the man whom his master most

reasonably distrusted.[2] He saw also, it seems likely, that the humiliation ;which Longchamp had gone through would be enough to cut him off from the hope of the primacy, and his legation had already expired. John was at the moment the more dangerous of the two, and Longchamp's authority must be sustained.

The chancellor, on the other hand, finding that the archbishop produced no new instructions, and that the mercenary force which he had introduced into the country was daily increasing,[3] took heart and prepared for another struggle. Before attempting this, however, he had to visit Canterbury, where the bishop-elect of Worcester was waiting for consecration. There on May 5 he met the bishops of

---

[1] R. Devizes, 29. This may account for his hesitation in acting. Longchamp had utterly foiled the bishop of Durham by producing instructions of later date than his own. Walter of Coutances' letters were dated in February. Many letters of later date must have reached England before the end of April ; and these were favourable to the chancellor.

[2] The letters subsequently produced by the archbishop are given in part or entire by R. de Diceto and Giraldus Cambrensis. Of these, one is a fragment of a letter addressed to William Marshall, Hugh Bardulf, Geoffrey FitzPeter and William Briewere ; placing in their hands the supreme power, in case the chancellor shall have not acted faithfully ; it is not dated and contains no mention of the archbishop. R. de Diceto, 659. A second, also given by R. de Diceto, is dated Feb. 23 at Messina, addressed

to the chancellor and the four barons above mentioned, associating the archbishop in the government of the kingdom, and speaking of an especial commission given to him relative to the see of Canterbury. A third, dated Feb. 20, and addressed to William Marshall alone, contains words nearly identical with those of R. de Diceto's first fragment, but directing that, in case of the chancellor's unfaithfulness, the justices are to act ' secundum prædicti archiepiscopi dispositionem.' Richard of Devizes mentions other instructions, no doubt addressed to the convent of Canterbury, and one in particular giving Longchamp leave to manage by himself the election to the abbacy of Westminster. R. Dev. p. 29. See notes on Benedict, ii. 157, 158 ; Hoveden, iii. 96.

[3] W. Newb. iv. 16, p. 46.

Winchester, Bath, Chichester, and Rochester,[1] and his great enemy Hugh of Nunant; and by these the consecration was performed. On the following day the legate, for so he still called himself, presented to the monks of Christ Church the king's letters, recommending them to elect the archbishop of Montreal.[2] The monks expressed surprise at the urgency of the legate's behaviour, and asked leave to present their answer to the council of bishops which was to sit a few days later at Northampton. The permission was granted by Longchamp readily enough, for although he might have preferred the election of a stranger to the translation of any of his brethren, he was better pleased that the archbishopric should be vacant still. It is to be suspected that on this occasion there was some underhand dealing between Longchamp and the monks, for immediately on the departure of the legate[3] they displaced their prior, Osbert, whom Baldwin had appointed against their will, an act for which they were never called to order by Longchamp : from this moment also the idea recovered ground that he himself intended to be the new archbishop. The report reached John, who wrote urgently against him to the convent,[4] and the archbishop of Rouen allowed so much of his instructions to transpire that it was known that one part of them at least was to settle the business of the election.

He visits Canterbury

Long- champ's transactions with the monks of Canterbury

Fear of his being elected archbishop

The meeting at Northampton followed shortly,[5] and a further postponement of the election. The monks required further evidence of Baldwin's death and of the qualifications of the aspirant. The justices urged that the election should be proceeded with instantly, but the monks as usual contrived to gain their point, this time probably with the direct support of the chancellor.

Successive postpone- ments of the election

Shortly after this arrangement was made, the hostilities between the chancellor and Gerard Camville were resumed. Immediately after midsummer,[6] having taken measures to secure his reappointment as legate, one of which was the forwarding of urgent letters in his favour from the bishops and from Walter of Coutances among them,[8] he brought together his forces and again advanced on Lincoln, this time taking permanent possession of the sheriffdom, which he handed over to William Stuteville.[8] The castle, however, still held out, and on the first report of the chancellor's march the garrisons of Tickhill and Nottingham, as might be expected, opened their gates

Hostilities resumed

Longchamp marches against Lincoln

[1] Gervase, 1568.
[2] Gervase, 1569. See below, p. 329.
[3] Gervase, 1570.
[4] Epp. Cantuar. 330, 346.
[5] Gervase, 1570.
[6] 'Post festum Sancti Johannis Baptistæ.' Ben. Pet. ii. 207.
[7] So Pope Celestine III. states dis-

tinctly : ' omnes Anglicani episcopi pro eodem legationis officio confirmando *mihi* proprias litteras transmiserunt.' Ben. Pet. ii. 242, 243 ; Hoveden, iii. 190.
[8] Hoveden, iii. 134; Ben. Pet. ii. 207.

to John. But again both parties avoided a battle, although Longchamp had called up a third of the feudal levy of England for his

Second pacification at Winchester defence.[1] The moderate counsels of the archbishop of Rouen prevailed, and at another conference, at Winchester on July 28, a somewhat fairer arbitration was arranged.[2] In this the bishop of Durham also took part, having, it would seem, been liberated from his forced inactivity by the arrival of Walter of Coutances ; and besides the three who had arbitrated in April, the bishops of Coventry and Chichester were present. Preserving in some measure the lines of the former agreement, they decided that John was to place Tickhill in the hands of William of Wenneval,[3] and Nottingham in those of William Marshall, to be held by them for the king, but in the event of his death, or of a further attack on John by the chancellor, to be surrendered to the former. The other castles of John's honours are intrusted to the archbishop of Rouen, the bishop of London, and others, to be surrendered to him in case of the king's death. The castle of Windsor is handed over to the earl of Arundel, Winchester to Gilbert de Lacy,[4] and Northampton to Simon Pateshull, all

Result of the second arbitration partisans of the chancellor. Gerard Camville is to be replaced in the sheriffdom. In all these points the chancellor gave way somewhat more than was wise, but less than he had done in April. When these arrangements should be completed, the complaints of the chancellor against Gerard Camville were to be heard and John was

Sureties on both sides bound not to interfere. Oaths were taken on both sides, for Longchamp, by the earls of Arundel, Salisbury, Norfolk, and Clare, William FitzRobert, William de Braiose, and Roger FitzRainfrai : for John, by his chancellor Stephen Ridell, William of Wenneval, Robert de Mara, Philip of Worcester, William of Kahannes, Gilbert Basset, and William of Montacute. Among Longchamp's jurors were some who very shortly showed themselves to be his enemies, especially the earl of Salisbury and Roger FitzRainfrai.[5] It is possible that his interests were intentionally betrayed, and it was certainly a puerile piece of lawyer's work to pretend to regard the main question as one between Gerard Camville and the chancellor.

Influence of the archbishop of Rouen But the archbishop of Rouen probably sacrificed other considerations to the maintenance of his own position as mediator, and to the obtaining the omission of any terms which would have openly asserted John's claim to the succession.

---

[1] R. Devizes, 32.

[2] Hoveden, iii. 135.

[3] He had held Nottingham under the earlier treaty (R. Devizes, 33), and he was constable there again in 1194. Hoveden, iii. 240.

[4] Another of the numerous proofs of the connexion of Longchamp with the Lacies ; as indeed was the fact that he intrusted Nottingham and Tickhill to the constable of Chester (above, p. 228).

[5] These were both excommunicated by him after his exile. Ben. Pet. ii. 223 ; Hoveden, iii. 153.

After the party broke up the chancellor returned to London,[1] and John removed to Marlborough,[2] whence a little later he went to Lancaster.[3] The archbishop of Rouen now again attempted to carry out the king's directions as to the election at Canterbury, but was met by a positive prohibition from Longchamp.[4]

Another cloud was rising, not now in the distance. After two years of struggling, the archbishop-elect of York had received permission and an order to be consecrated by the archbishop of Tours.[5] Immediately on his consecration, urged by John and perhaps not discountenanced by Eleanor,[6] he gave out that he was determined to proceed to his see, and that he, as well as John, had been allowed by their brother to withdraw his promise to absent himself for three years from England. The chancellor had received no such instructions ; it was his duty to prevent his return, or at least to compel him to swear fealty to the king : as early as July 30,[7] he had ordered the sheriff of Sussex to arrest him if he should attempt to land within his jurisdiction,[8] and about the same time had obtained a promise from the countesses of Boulogne and Flanders to forbid his embarkation. Having satisfied himself with these precautions he moved northwards, and having visited probably Ely and S. Edmund's,[9] he is next found at Norwich.[10]

Geoffrey Plantagenet, the eldest surviving son, if not the first-born of Henry II.,[11] is not, like William Longchamp and Hugh of Nunant, a man of whom his contemporaries could deliver contradictory characters. His virtues and faults are clearly the same in the mouths of friends and enemies. His faithfulness to his father when his legitimate children had forsaken him is no recommendation to those who hated

Marginal notes: Break-up of the conference

Return of Geoffrey, archbishop of York

Precautions of Longchamp

Character of Geoffrey

[1] Two days after the pacification, July 30, the chancellor writes from Preston to the sheriff of Sussex to secure Geoffrey of York. Gir. Camb. V. Galfr. p. 390. On the 2nd of August he writes to the bishop of Bath from the Tower of London ; ' teste Radulfo archidiacono Herefordiæ.'

[2] Hence he dates his letter to the monks of Canterbury against the chancellor. Epp. Cantuar. 346.

[3] Gir. Camb. V. Galfr. p. 393.

[4] R. de Diceto, 660, 661 ; Gir. Camb. 395. The letter is dated August 25, ' apud Releiam.'

[5] Gir. Camb. V. Galfr. p. 388.

[6] Benedict, ii. 210. I cannot go so far as to say that Geoffrey's visit was the result of a deliberate plot on John's behalf, any more than the revolt of Gerard Camville had been ; but in both cases he grasped with avidity the

opportunity of damaging Longchamp and strengthening his own position.

[7] Gir. Camb. V. Galfr. p. 390 ; R. de Diceto, 660.

[8] Ibid.

[9] Jocelin of Brakelond mentions his visit to S. Edmund's, which it is difficult to place at any earlier period after the date of his legation.

[10] Gir. Camb. V. Galfr. p. 392.

[11] He was born in 1151, if Giraldus is right in stating that he was forty at the time of his consecration. V. Galfr. p. 388. He must have been born, therefore, six years before Richard. If his mother were indeed Fair Rosamond, who is described as a girl in 1176, she must have been the king's mistress for six-and-twenty years, and he must be credited with constancy at least. See Ben. Pet. ii. pref. xxxi.

his father, but it is not less a virtue. His skill in arms, his energy, his high and generous spirit, are apparent even when adduced as an argument of his unfitness for high spiritual office. His secular ambition calls for the animadversions both of his rivals and of those who would condemn such a feeling in an ecclesiastic altogether, neither choosing to remember that his ecclesiastical character was forced upon him. He had been for many years the close companion of his father as chancellor, and it was Henry's last expressed wish that he should be archbishop of York ; probably he saw that in such a character only would his life be safe against his brothers, or any share of the power which he had enjoyed so long remain to him.

His strange ambition

His own ambition, Giraldus tells us, pointed [1] another way : to his chance of surviving his childless brothers and becoming king of England. The idea is so strange that we might almost suspect that Giraldus did not invent it. Such a thought, however, explains in some measure the conduct of both Geoffrey and Richard. The king was anxious to have him ordained, as the tonsure would be a bar to the crown ; Geoffrey held back from ordination himself, as he had done before when elected to the see of Lincoln ; nor did he receive consecration until he had seen both Richard and John married. But

His many enemies and rivals for power

on Giraldus's word alone it cannot be taken for truth, and there were plenty of people whose interests were concerned in hindering his acquisition of the full rights of his position. Hugh de Puiset had no wish to be placed under an ecclesiastical superior from whom, although he had by papal privilege obtained the right of refusing him formal submission,[2] he might look for constant canonical as well as constitutional interference. Richard was anxious, for a long time at least, to keep Geoffrey out of England, and to retain in the hands of the Exchequer the great revenues of the see of York. The chapter of York was filled with turbulent and secular men, a large proportion of whom Geoffrey had offended immediately after his election by refusing to confirm their titles. These were in constant strife with him before and after his consecration, and during the whole of his pontificate, misinterpreting and perverting every action of his, and catching at every chance which his undeniable talent for quarrelling with everyone gave them of attempting his deposition. John could have nothing in common with Geoffrey, although he anxiously pressed upon him his duty of taking charge of his church, with the intention, no doubt, of preparing fresh difficulties for the chancellor. William Longchamp seems to have been fully persuaded that the king had

---

[1] ' Sperabat enim si de rege fratre suo in peregrinatione tam periculosa quicquid forte sinistre contigerit, se regnum universun et regni partem non modicam assecuturum.' Gir. Camb. V. G. p. 383.

[2] Ben. Pet. ii. 146 ; Hoveden, iii. 74.

made no concession in respect of the oath, and that he was perfectly justified in forbidding his return. He might, however, have seen that Geoffrey, if he could make him a friend, would be a counterpoise to John in the north of England.

It was probably the news brought from England by Eleanor that induced Richard to stir at last in the matter; he saw, perhaps, that Geoffrey might be harmless, or even useful in the case of a struggle between the bishops of Durham and Ely. Eleanor, on her visit to Rome, laid the circumstances before Pope Celestine;[1] all difficulties were obviated; the letters of Clement III., by which Hugh de Puiset was authorised to refuse the profession of obedience, were set aside; and the archbishop of Tours, Bartholomew of Vendôme, under whose eye Geoffrey had studied in the schools,[2] was ordered to consecrate him. This was done on the 18th of August; the same day he received the pall, and immediately set out for England. On his arrival at Guisnes[3] he learned that the countess of Flanders had forbidden her men to convey him across the straits, and that the countess of Boulogne had done the same at Whitsand. On remonstrating, however, he was told that the prohibition extended only to him personally, that the Whitsand boatmen would carry his equipage, and that he might cross in an English vessel. The hint was taken; the retinue, under Simon of Apulia, crossed in Flemish vessels on Friday the 13th of September;[4] Geoffrey followed in an English boat and reached Dover on the following day about nine in the morning. The authorities were prepared for him; before he had time to land, the messengers of the lady of the castle, Richenda, the chancellor's sister, boarded the vessel, and insisted on his proceeding straight to the castle, where the day before his baggage had been deposited. Geoffrey declined the invitation, hastily disguised himself,[5] and mounting the horse which was prepared for him on the beach, started at full speed for the priory of S. Martin. One of Richenda's men rode after him, and caught the horse by the bridle; but Geoffrey

Marginal notes:
Eleanor's influence used in Geoffrey's favour

Geoffrey's consecration

He is forbidden to sail to England

He crosses to Dover; and an attempt to arrest him is made

He takes refuge at S. Martin's

---

[1] Hoveden, iii. 100. It was probably a result of this intercession of Eleanor that Celestine III. on the 11th of May issued the letter to Geoffrey which is printed in the Mon. Angl. vi. 1188, and contains the following statement: 'quod licet personam venerabilis fratris nostri Hugonis Dunelmensis episcopi . . . sedes apostolica providerit et duxerit honorandum, quia tamen juri et statui Eboracensis ecclesiæ nos oportuit et decuit providere . . . ei dedimus in mandatis atque præcepimus, tibi sicut suo metropolitano, exemptione qualibet obtenta pro eo a Romana ecclesia non obstante, et ante consecrationem et cum fueris consecratus assistat . . . et . . . debitam tibi obedientiam et reverentiam, sublato cujuslibet contradictionis et appellationis obstaculo, impendere non postponat.' The letter is printed unintelligibly in the Monasticon.
[2] Benedict, i. 93.
[3] Gir. Camb. V. Galfr. p. 390. Benedict, ii. 210.
[4] Gir. Camb. V. Galfr. p. 390.
[5] 'Mutavit vestes.' Benedict, ii. 210. Hoveden, iii. 138. Giraldus does not mention this undignified act of his hero.

was equal to the occasion, struck out with his right leg, and hit his adversary's horse full on the side with his armed heel. The horse plunged, and compelled the rider to relax his hold.[1] The archbishop, after this exploit, proceeded unmolested to the priory, where he found the monks beginning mass; the epistle was being read: the words (so the story went) in the reader's mouth were, 'He that troubleth you shall bear his judgment, whosoever he be,' and 'I would they were even cut off that trouble you.'[2] The soldiers who followed did not venture to lay hands on him, but took possession of the monastery. When the mass was over, the archbishop sent to ask Richenda whether the outrage were authorised by her. She replied that she had the chancellor's order, and that if he bade her to burn both Dover Castle and London town,[3] she would obey. The knights of Kent, under William Auberville, son-in-law of Ranulf Glanvill, entreated the archbishop to take the oath of fealty to the king and chancellor at once. Geoffrey, with his usual impetuosity, replied that to the king he had already sworn fealty, and would not do it again upon compulsion; as for the chancellor, he would do nothing for him but what should be done for a traitor. The state of siege continued for four days; on the Sunday, Geoffrey excommunicated Richenda;[4] thereupon the soldiers took possession of the church. By the evening Matthew de Cleres, the constable, arrived in person, a little shocked by his wife's zeal, but his entreaties failed to persuade Geoffrey to take the oath. At last, on the Wednesday, he was arrested by a band of mercenary soldiers, under Aubrey Marney, an Essex knight, and Alexander Puinctel, a hanger-on of the chancellor.[5] He was dragged from the altar, where he had been assisting at mass, and brought on foot, for he refused to mount a horse, carrying his archiepiscopal cross, to the castle.

The news of the outrage spread like wildfire; the few parallels which presented themselves with the sufferings of S. Thomas invested Geoffrey for the time with the character of a church champion.[6] S. Hugh of Lincoln, who was at Oxford, excommunicated with lighted candles[7] the castellan and his wife, with all their aiders and abettors. The bishop of London hastened to Norwich to remonstrate with the

Marginal notes:
Negotiations with the lady of the castle

Geoffrey refuses to swear fealty

Geoffrey excommunicates his enemies

He is taken from S. Martin's to the castle

Public excitement at the news

---

[1] Gir. Camb. V. Galfr. p. 390.
[2] This is mentioned by Benedict, ii. 210, and Hoveden, iii. 138. Yet the day was the feast of the Exaltation of the Cross, and the epistle for that day does not contain these words; nor does that for the week (the 13th Sunday after Trinity, although it is taken from the same epistle, that of S. Paul to the Galatians. Either the historians have imagined a coincidence, or the missal of the monks of S. Martin's had a peculiar rite for the day.
[3] Gir. Camb. V. Galfr. p. 390.
[4] Gir. Camb. V. Galfr. p. 391.
[5] R. de Diceto, 663.
[6] Gir. Camb. V. Galfr. 391. R. de Diceto, 663. Gervase, 1576. W. Newb. iv. 17, p. 48.
[7] Gir. Camb. V. Galfr. p. 392.

chancellor : [1] the bishop of Norwich, that old John of Oxford, who had known so long the dangerous waters on which Longchamp was launching, forgot his failing health,[2] and urged the immediate liberation of the archbishop in very brisk argument. The prior and convent of Canterbury, on whose goodwill he had so much reason to depend, wrote more in sorrow than in anger.[3] In vain the chancellor cursed the zeal of his friends and the fickleness of his master.[4] He lamented the outrage. He had given no such orders ; he had simply directed that the archbishop should take the oath of fealty to the king, which he had not yet done since his consecration, and that if he refused he should be sent, bag and baggage, to Whitsand. In vain he showed the letters-patent in which Geoffrey had promised to stay away for three years.[5] His blunder was more fatal to him than his crimes. His enemies had at last secured a charge which would unite all classes against him ; or, for all classes were already against him, would give them a common excuse for action.

The bishops remonstrate with Long-champ

The charge against him taken up by all his rivals

Hugh of Nunant drew together the strings of the plot.[6] As soon as the arrest was known he hastened to John at Lancaster, and pointed out to him the greatness of the opportunity. Together they came immediately to Marlborough,[7] whither John invited the chief men on whom he could depend, either as personally attached to himself, or as likely, for the sake of keeping order in the country, to take part against the chancellor. Longchamp, in compliance with the remonstrances of his friends, sent a hurried order for the archbishop's release.[8] He was obeyed ; Geoffrey was conducted back to S. Martin's after eight days of restraint,[9] for it had not been an un-courteous captivity, on the 26th of September ; he stayed there until the 28th, and then proceeded to London, where the bishop Richard FitzNeal received him with a solemn procession at S. Paul's on Wednesday the 2nd of October.[10] The chancellor was now assembling his friends and preparing for the first new move that John and his party might take.

Hugh of Nunant works upon John.

Release of Geoffrey He goes to London

We inquire in vain what the justices had been doing all this time. Richard had appointed, at various times, William Marshall, William Briwere, Hugh Bardulf, Geoffrey FitzPeter, Robert de Wihtefeld and Roger FitzRainfrai, as assessors to the chancellor. We do not find a trace of opposition on their part to the oppressions

Inactivity of the justices

[1] R. de Diceto, 663.
[2] Gir. Camb. V. Galf., p. 392.
[3] Epp. Cantuar. 344.   Gervase, 1576.
[4] Epp. Cantuar. 344, 345.   Gerv. 1577. R. Devizes, 36.
[5] Epp. Cantuar. 345.
[6] Gir. Camb. V. Galf. p. 393. It is

not too harsh to call it a plot. See R. Devizes, 37.
[7] Gir. Camb. 393.
[8] W. Newb. p. 49.   R. Devizes, 36.
[9] Triduanus, R. Devizes, 36. Die septima, Gervase, 1577. Sept. 26th, R. de Diceto, 663.
[10] R. de Diceto, 663.

charged against Longchamp ; they had joined in his refusal to admit
Hugh de Puiset as justiciar ; [1] they had not resigned their seats, or
stood aloof when he treated them with neglect. Yet they joined
immediately in John's proposal for his overthrow.[2] It was, perhaps,
the sight of Hugh de Puiset's unlucky attempt to resist him that
intimidated them, but it is more probable that, although they disliked their chief and were glad of an opportunity to get rid of him,
they could not disown his acts, and perhaps saw nothing enormous
about them. William Marshall was a brave soldier, but he had
been hand and glove with the younger Henry in his treason,[3] and
his wisdom had yet twenty years to ripen before he became governor
of England and her king. Geoffrey FitzPeter also was an able and
moderate minister, whose character was to develop under the discipline of the next reign. Of William Briwere [4] we know little that
is distinctive, but he was certainly a trusted man of business. Roger
FitzRainfrai we have seen apparently on the chancellor's side in
the quarrel with John.[5] None of them were yet marked men.
Richard had done foolishly in taking away those of their own class
who could have led them and kept them together. Just now, if
Giraldus is right, they were scattered through the country, preparing perhaps for the Michaelmas audit of the Exchequer. William
Marshall was in Gloucestershire, William Briwere in Oxfordshire,
The justices,
bishops, and
barons meet
John at
Marlbo-
rough
Geoffrey FitzPeter in Northamptonshire.[6] One by one they received
John's invitation, and one by one they accepted it. The bishop of
Winchester, who had suffered so much from Longchamp, the bishop
of Bath, who had hitherto been his friend,[7] who had negotiated for
him the business of the legation, followed. They met at Marlborough,
and the arrival of the archbishop of Rouen gave a head and authority
to their proceedings. The time was clearly come for him to act up
to his fullest powers. The chancellor must be sacrificed before John
had time to bind to himself, by complicity in revolution, the barons
who were now loyal enough to Richard, although they hated and
had just grounds of complaint against his representative.

Longchamp could not at first see the difficulty of his situation ;
he saw that the muster at Marlborough was a step to revolution, but

---

[1] R. Devizes, p. 12.
[2] Gir. Camb. V. Galfr. 393.
[3] Ben. Pet. i. 46.
[4] Notwithstanding the English
sound of his name, William was a
Norman by extraction, and his family
name in full is Brieguerre. It is
frequently spelled by Hoveden, in MS.
A, Brigwere, and is softened down
gradually through Briewere, Briwere,
Bruere, &c.

[5] Hoveden, iii. 137.
[6] Gir. Camb. V. Galfr., 393. William
Marshall was sheriff of Gloucestershire
this year, and William Briwere of
Oxfordshire. Geoffrey FitzPeter had
been so in Northamptonshire in 1189 ;
but Richard of Engaine had paid 300
marks for three years' tenure of the
office and was now sheriff. Rot. Pip.
3 Rich. I.
[7] W. Newb. iv. 17, p. 49.

he could not see the enormity of the offence that he had given, and above all he was ignorant of the policy, and even of the commission, of the archbishop of Rouen.   He issued orders to Geoffrey to appear in London before the barons of the kingdom, and to the bishops and justices who had joined John to leave him immediately as a traitor.[1] He was, however, so far in the dark that he allowed Geoffrey[2] to leave London and join the party of malcontents, who had now advanced by Oxford, where they had picked up S. Hugh of Lincoln, to Reading.   He himself proceeded from Norwich to London, and thence to Windsor,[3] to watch the movements of the other side. There he was met by a summons to attend a conference or parliament of the barons which was to be held on the 5th of October at the bridge over the Loddon, about four miles from Reading and twelve from Windsor.[4]

The 5th of October was a Saturday—an unlucky day for oaths and contracts, as men thought—and the chancellor, much against his will, set out from Windsor with the bishops of London, and the earls of Arundel, Norfolk, and Warren, who seem to have stuck to him until now.   But at the fourth mile from Windsor his heart failed him ; he saw that his companions were without spirit to support him, and that his policy was not to endanger his own liberty.   He sent on his friends, and complaining of illness, returned to the castle.   They, not rendered more enthusiastic by his desertion, proceeded to the place of meeting.[5]

There were assembled the two archbishops, the bishops of London, Winchester, Bath, Lincoln, and Coventry ; John earl of Mortain, William of Arundel, Roger Bigod of Norfolk, Hamelin of Warren, and William Marshall of Strigul ; Geoffrey FitzPeter, William Briwere, and many other barons, with their retainers.   As soon as the assembly was got together and order proclaimed, the archbishop of York stood up and exhibited his complaints ; the documents by which the king had authorised his return and his participation in public business were read and explained by Hugh of Nunant to the barons.[6]   The archbishop of Rouen followed ; he had been sent by the king to arrange the election at Canterbury, with the fullest powers and the most private instructions, yet the chancellor had forbidden him to proceed on his mission—nay, he had sent him word that he would cross London Bridge at his peril ; further, he had never once since he landed in April been consulted by the chancellor on any matter whatever.[7]   In the third place the justices,

[1] Gir. Camb. pp. 393, 394.
[2] Ibid. p. 394.
[3] Ibid. p. 394.
[4] Ibid. p. 394.

[5] Gir. Camb. p. 395.   Bened. ii. p. 212.
[6] Gir. Camb., p. 395.
[7] Ibid. p. 395.

Complaints
of Long-
champ's
special
foes

especially William Marshall, William Briwere, and Geoffrey Fitz Peter asserted that their counsels, which he was obliged by the king's express orders to respect, were never attended to. Even the earl of Arundel, who seems to have wished to say what he could for him, could not deny this.[1] There were other complaints of a less general character. Hugh of Durham and his son Henry sent in the tale of their wrongs.[2] Henry de Vere in particular, who had been deprived of his estates through the chancellor's agency, probably in favour of Stephen Longchamp, who was his brother-in-law, was bitterly urgent against him ;[3] Roger FitzRainfrai forsook him completely. The conclusion of the whole deliberation was put by the archbishop of Rouen ; he pledged the barons present to rise against the chancellor, to depose him, as useless to the king and kingdom, from the office of justiciar, and to appoint another in his place.[4] Whether on

Walter of
Coutances
shows his
hand at last

this occasion Walter of Coutances produced his commission cannot be quite ascertained, but he clearly left the assembly assured that he had good authority for his proceedings. The bishops of London, Lincoln, and Coventry were deputed to fetch the chancellor at once to hear his fate, but before they had gone far they met his messengers reporting that he had returned to Windsor.[5]

Negotiations
between
Longchamp
and John

Sunday, October 6, was a busy day. Very early, messengers began to pass between Windsor and Reading. The chancellor sent two of his confidential servants to persuade John to intercede for him ; knowing John's weakness, they were to promise any amount of money to him and his like. Personal mediation, as in the case of William de Braiose, who had the courage to make a move for his friend, was also employed. But all that was attained was an invita-

He fails to
make friends.

tion to meet the barons at the old place on the morrow ; if the chancellor declined to appear there and give account of his misdeeds, he was to expect no more consideration from the barons.[6] By the arguments of his friends he was prevailed upon to promise to attend and so pledge himself. The bishops lost no time. At High Mass in the morning the bishop of Bath acted as celebrant, and Hugh of Nunant preached ; the point of application of his sermon was the excommunication of all aiders and abettors of the outrage on the

and is ex-
communi-
cated

archbishop of York. Not only Aubrey Marney and Alexander Puinctel, but the chancellor himself was named in the anathema, and denounced as excommunicate.[7]

Probably the news of this act diminished still further Long-

[1] Gir. Camb. 359.
[2] Benedict, ii. 212.
[3] R. de Diceto, 664.   Henry de Vere married a daughter of Osbert de Cailly, and co-heiress with Stephen's wife, of Mutford in Suffolk ; see Stapleton,

Norman Rolls, ii. cxv.   There may have been other grounds of quarrel.
[4] Gir. Camb. 395, 396.
[5] Ibid.
[6] Ibid. 396.
[7] R. de Diceto, 664.

champ's inclination for a parley. The postponed meeting did not Both parties hasten to London, on the Monday Oct. 7. take place; both parties dreaded treachery. The barons, on the Monday morning, after marching in order out of Reading, crossed the Loddon and sent their baggage under the charge of a strong guard through the forest to Staines, whilst they themselves proceeded on the highway towards Windsor.[1] The chancellor on his part advanced about two miles to meet them, when he was met by one of his knights, Henry Biset,[2] who had seen the division of the forces and the larger part taking the London road. He immediately gave the alarm ; the malcontents were going to seize the capital. Longchamp hastily returned to the castle, and, having made a hurried arrangement for its defence, started, as he supposed, in pursuit ; crossed the Thames and took the northern as the shorter road, in order to intercept the enemy. The barons, hearing of his departure, pursued him at full speed, and it became a race who should reach London first ; the chancellor's retinue, having the start, arrived a little before the others, but not in time to avoid a skirmish in which Roger de Skirmish on the road Plasnes, John's justiciar, was killed [3] by Ralph Beauchamp, one of the chancellor's knights. This must have occurred somewhere near Hounslow, where the direct road from Windsor meets that from Staines, which the barons had taken.

As soon as Longchamp arrived in London, he called together the Longchamp meets the citizens in the Guild-hall citizens in the Guildhall,[4] and entreated them to defend the king's right against the attacks of John, who, according to his view, had thrown away every scruple, and was now plainly aiming at the crown.[5] To his dismay, his words seemed without effect. Archbishop Geoffrey, in his passage through the capital the week before, had made too good use of his time ; he had taught his friends to regard the struggle as merely an attempt to unseat the justiciar, no treason being contemplated towards the king.[6] The magnates of the city were divided— Richard FitzReiner, the head of one party, took the side of John. Henry of Cornhell was faithful to the chancellor.[7] These two knights Two parties in the city had been sheriffs at Richard's coronation, and both represented the ancient burgher aristocracy : Reiner, the father of Richard, the son of Berenger, had filled the same office ; [8] and Henry was the son of Gervase of Cornhell, who had held the sheriffdom of Kent, which, with that of Surrey, the son now held. It is probable that Richard headed the party of change, and Henry, who was more closely

[1] Benedict, ii. 211, 212.
[2] Gir. Camb. 396, 97. R. Devizes, p. 37.
[3] R. de Diceto, 664. Benedict, ii. 212.
[4] R. Devizes, 38. Gir. Camb. 397 :—'In aula publica quæ a potorum conventu nomen accepit.'

[5] Gir. Camb. 397.
[6] R. Devizes, 38.
[7] Gir. Camb. 397.
[8] Madox, Hist. Exch. p. 476, 194. Rot. Pip. 2, 3, 4 Hen. II. pp. 17, 18, 27, 112. Rot. Pip. 1 Rich. I. p. 223. Liber de Antiquis Legibus, p. 1.

connected with the country interest, and, through his office of fermer

of the Mint, with the Exchequer, that of order.[1] The division in council was so even that the chancellor thought it his safest plan to take up his quarters in the Tower. This he had scarcely done when John arrived. He was welcomed by Richard FitzReiner with open arms, and entertained in his house, where he learned the terms on which he was to expect the adherence of the city.[2] The burghers had long been anxious to obtain for themselves the royal recognition of their corporate character, or *communa*. This had been opposed to the theory of Henry II., who instead of conferring political or municipal nidependence on towns by· charter, preferred to deal out his benefactions by the medium of fines, keeping thus the power of withdrawing them in his own hands. Henry knew and probably disliked the foreign idea of the commune : ' tumor plebis, timor regni, tepor

sacerdotii." [3] John, however, had no scruples. He was ready to promise for the whole party that they would swear to observe the rights and customs of the citizens, and accordingly in the morning of Tuesday, when the assembly met at S. Paul's, this large and aristocratic body was fully represented.[4] The city had, indeed, quarrelled with Longchamp by refusing, at his request, to shut the gates against John, and a large proportion of the burghers was prepared to take extreme measures against him.[5]

The scene in S. Paul's seems to have been a repetition of that of the Loddon. First Geoffrey, then Hugh of Nunant, told the story of the chancellor's misdeeds ; the wrongs of Hugh de Puiset and the ignominy heaped on the justices were not forgotten.[6] Then, for the

first time, Walter of Coutances produced the commission dated in February, addressed to William Marshall and his fellow justices, and directing that in case of the chancellor's misconduct he should be superseded by the archbishop.[7] The barons, at John's instigation, at once recognised the letter as genuine, and declared by acclamation that the chancellor was no longer the governor of the kingdom, that the archbishop of Rouen was now the king's chief justiciar. John himself should be regarded as regent, ' summus rector

---

[1] Madox, *Hist. Exch.* p. 631.
This year Henry de Cornhell renders account of 1,200*l*. which he has received of the treasure, by the brief of the chancellor, to sustain the Mint of all England, except Winchester, and of 400*l*. the profit of the Mint for a year, in all 1,600*l*. He must have been closely connected in this way with the chancellor, and his connexion with the court may have set him in opposition to the supporters of the guild or communa. This theory

seems to be supported by the fact of his marriage with Alice de Courcy, and that of his daughter with Hugh Nevill, the master forester of England. See Mr. Stapleton's preface to the Liber de Antiquis Legibus, p. 11.
[2] R. de Diceto, 664. Gir. Camb. V. Galfr. 397, 398.
[3] R. Devizes, 53, 54.
[4] Gir. Camb. 398 ; Bened. ii. 213.
[5] R. Devizes, 38.
[6] Bened. ii. 213.
[7] Bened. ii. 213 ; ' tunc primum.'

totius regni ' ;[1] next under him should be the archbishop as The barons welcome him as chief justiciar; and salute John as regent justiciar; under him the other justices would have no difficulty in acting, and again the whole administration of the country would be able to work. In this recognition of John the assembly went beyond anything that had been contemplated by Richard or even by Walter of Coutances ; the office of regent, if it existed formally at all, being filled already by the queen-mother, whose absence from England had thrown considerable additional weight into the scale against Longchamp. This done, oaths were largely taken : John, the justiciar, Oaths taken to the communa; and the barons, swore to maintain the *communa* of London ;[2] the oath of fealty to Richard was then sworn, John taking it first, then fealty sworn to Richard the two archbishops, the bishops, the barons, and last the burghers, with the express understanding that, should the king die without issue, they would receive John as his successor.[3]

The sentence had still to be enforced on Longchamp, and the Longchamp shut up in the Tower citizens willingly joined in besieging the Tower. Unfortunately for the chancellor, it was not victualled for a siege, or, with time on his side, he might still have won.[4] Henry of Cornhell was ready to divide His chances of success the city in his favour ; John, having got all that he wanted, might be bought over, especially as his object now would be to undermine the authority of the new justiciar. The party had been brought together by an accident, and any accident might dissolve it. But the state of the stores would not admit of Longchamp standing a siege, and both Geoffrey and Hugh of Nunant saw that their only safety was in his downfall. He was obliged to offer terms to the new He applies for reconciliation and is visited by four bishops, on Wednesday, Oct. 9 powers, and early on the Wednesday the four bishops of London, Lincoln, Winchester, and Coventry,[5] were sent in answer to his application, and to declare at the same time the resolution of the assembly. According to Giraldus, they found him in an abject state of prostration, mental and physical ; he knelt before them—he swooned away from the violence of his agitation. Richard of Devizes confirms the story of his fainting, and adds that he was recovered by the sprinkling of cold water on his face ; he ascribes the swoon to angry excitement and not to fear.[6] He was told that he must resign the seal and surrender the king's castles. He declared that he He refuses to resign would do neither ; he charged the barons with disloyalty to Richard ; already they had given the kingdom to John. He threatened them with the king's anger, if he should ever live to see him. As for the castles, how could he surrender them ? None of his house had ever

---

[1] R. Devizes. p. 38.
[2] Gir. Camb. 398. Bened. ii. 214.
R. Devizes, 53, 54. R. de Diceto, 664.
[3] R. de Diceto, 664. Bened. ii. 214.
[4] W. Newb. p. 50.
[5] Gir. Camb. 398.

[6] R. Devizes, 39. As this writer is anything but favourable to Longchamp, I think his statements may be accepted always in mitigation of Giraldus's language,

yet been a traitor.   Hugh of Nunant argued like a brute : 'Do not
talk to us about your house, but do what you ought to do ; what
cannot be avoided, it is of no use to dally over.   Depend on it, your
house, young as it is, cannot account you its first traitor.'[1]   Prostrate

In the
evening he
agrees to
appear
next day
before the
justices

as Longchamp was, he held his ground in argument until evening,
when, having tried to bribe John,[2] and found that if he were successful with him there were, besides, more enemies than he could purchase, he yielded at nightfall to the entreaties of his servants, and
allowed one of his brothers to go to John to say that he agreed to
give hostages for his appearance before the justices the next day.[3]
The hostages were his brother Osbert and Matthew de Cleres.[4]
Whilst this was being done, or perhaps, earlier in the day, the bishops
executed one little piece of spite against him, by procuring the election of William Postard as abbot of Westminster, to the destruction
of the chancellor's scheme of promoting his brother Robert.[5]

The barons met in great force early on the morning of Thursday,
October 10th, in the fields to the east of the Tower, and there at last
William Longchamp stood face to face with his accusers.[6]   With
singular ill-feeling, Hugh of Nunant undertook to declare the charges
and the ultimatum of the barons.   For justiciar they would have
him no longer ; bishop he might be still, but justiciar he was not,

and as chancellor they would do their best to strip him.   He might
keep three castles, Dover, Cambridge, and Hereford ; but the rest he
must resign ; he must give pledges to keep the peace, and might
then go where he liked.   Longchamp could scarcely have entertained
any hope of changing the mood of his enemies by a speech, but he
seems to have been overwhelmed by the volubility of the bishop, at
once declaring the indictment and pronouncing the sentence.

When he found words he declared himself innocent of every charge.
His fellow justices could,[7] he said, if they were questioned, justify all
that he had done to raise revenue for the king, and for every farthing

He consents
to give
pledges for
the surren-
der of his
castles

he had so raised he could render an account.   For the surrender of
the castles, as he was in their power, he would give pledges, but his
offices he could not resign, nor would he recognise the act of his
enemies in deposing him.   'I am one, you are many, and you are
stronger than I.   I, the chancellor of the king and justiciar of the
kingdom, sentenced contrary to the form of all law, yield to the
stronger, for yield I must.'[8]   So much said, and the words were true
and not deficient in dignity, the meeting closed.   That night Long-

[1] Giraldus, p. 398.
[2] Ibid. 'Comitem Moritoniæ adeo
ab incepto fere Cancellarius avertit.'
[3] R. Devizes, 40. Gir. Camb. 398.
[4] Gir. Camb. 398.
[5] R. de Diceto, 664.
[6] R. Devizes, 40. Gir. Camb. 398
R. de Diceto, 665.
[7] R. Devizes, 41.
[8] Ibid. 41, 42.

champ slept in the Tower ;[1] on the Friday he gave up both that and
Windsor, and moved with his baggage to Bermondsey.[2] On the
Saturday he proceeded, in company with Bishop Gilbert of Rochester
and Henry of Cornhell, to Dover.[3] His reason for going into Kent
was said to be that he might lay down at Canterbury the cross of
his legation, which had expired on the death of Clement III. ; but the
events that followed showed that this was a mere pretext.[4] He had
been compelled to swear to surrender all the king's castles and to leave
the appointment of constables for his own three to the justices ;[5]
until this was completed he was not to quit the country. Windsor
and the Tower he had given up, but he could not bear to do more.
Neglectful of the safety of his pledges, his brothers Henry and
Osbert,[6] as well as of his own oath, he attempted, in the dress of a
woman, to escape on board ship, on the Thursday after his arrival at
Dover.[7] This was prevented ; he was dragged into the town and imprisoned with great ignominy in a cellar. The justices, on hearing
of his discomfiture, issued immediate orders for his release, and
having compelled him to yield in every point, let him go his way.
He crossed over to Whitsand on the 29th of October. His misfortunes did not end here ; he was seized, plundered, and put to ransom
by the Flemish nobles.[8]

This little crisis occupies in our histories a place more proportionate to the interests of its personal incidents than to its
constitutional importance.[9] The proceedings of the barons were
revolutionary. Although the question of allegiance to the king does
not enter formally into the complication, the insurrection must be
regarded as of the same character as those by which from time to
time the king's tenure of power has been directly attacked—the
machinery which has the power to make laws interposes with
effect to meet a case and to overcome difficulties for which the laws
have failed to provide ; to punish the offences of a person who by
circumstances, as in this case, or on theory as in the case of the
monarch, is above the ordinary process of the law. The accused,
when such a consummation is imminent, cannot expect to secure
the benefit of legal treatment ; rightfully or wrongfully he must be
condemned ; for he whom in such a position it is possible to bring
to trial has fallen too low to be able to resist, although not so low

[1] R. de Diceto, 665.
[2] Gir. Camb. 399. R. de Diceto, 665.
[3] R. de Diceto, 665.
[4] Benedict, ii. 219. Hoveden, iii. 145.
[5] Gir. Camb. 398.
[6] R. de Diceto, 665.
[7] Benedict, ii. 219, 220. Hoveden,

iii. 146. R. Devizes, p. 42. R. Diceto, 665.
[8] R. de Diceto, 665. Hoveden, iii. 150. Ben. Pet. ii. 220. R. Devizes, 42.
[9] Sir Francis Palgrave has given a recension of it in the preface to the first volume of the Rotuli Curiæ Regis, which is very valuable.

Revolution made possible by Longchamp's misconduct, but produced by John's intrigues
as to be safely spared. Nor does our history present us with a case in which the wrong-doings of such a person have by themselves provoked the revolution which overwhelms him. He falls under the accumulation of hatred, not because of it; it is because there is some one ready to take his place, who cannot afford to wait. So it

Opportunity and cause of revolution
may often be that the pretexts of revolution are out of all harmony with its real justification, and have nothing whatever to do with its definite causes. Longchamp's position was unrighteous and tyrannical; the hatred he had inspired was widely spread and not unwarranted; the movement by which he fell was of the nature of a conspiracy; the real objects which his enemies had in view were strictly selfish aims after personal or political aggrandisement. It was, however, a good precedent against John himself in after years.

Conduct of the archbishop of Rouen at the crisis
The man who appears to the most advantage in the matter is the new minister, the Pilate of Rouen, who, if not a strong man, was an honest one, and in the main gave himself as thoroughly as Longchamp had done to the king's interests. If we consider that he was sent by Richard to England to hold the balance of power between John and Longchamp; to humour John as long as he could do so without encouraging him in his disaffection; to strengthen the chancellor unless he found it was no longer possible to keep peace between him and the barons; that he knew all the time that Longchamp was trusted by Richard, and that John only lacked the power to be a traitor; and if we consider further that in the motley band of malcontents with whom he had to work there were not two who had the same object in view; that John was striving for the increase of his own power and the right of succession, that Geoffrey was struggling for the see of York, whilst Hugh de Puiset, who for the moment was working with him, was bent on vindicating his personal independence of his metropolitan; that the barons cared far more to get rid of Longchamp than to administer the kingdom under himself, also a foreigner, and scarcely less suspected than Longchamp: we we may, I think, regard his conduct of the crisis as skilful and

His success in the crisis
complete. He managed to get rid, by John's aid, of the chancellor who could govern no more, and yet to keep the substance of power as far as ever out of John's reach.

His comparative failure as a minister
But his own administration was not very successful. Although strengthened by the support of the queen, he was unable to meet the manœuvres of John aided by Philip of France. The result was that from the moment of Richard's captivity he lost his grasp on the reins of government, and the country was only saved from anarchy by the management of Hubert Walter, who superseded him after two years and three months of office in the opening of the year 1194.

The archbishop's first piece of work was a failure. The day of

Longchamp's surrender, October 10, letters were issued for a meeting of the bishops at Westminster on the 22nd, and for the election of a successor to Baldwin.[1] The king had not yet withdrawn his nomination of the archbishop of Montreal; the monks were suspected of wishing to elect the chancellor; the archbishop of Rouen, who was supposed to have the king's instructions, was also suspected of wishing to exchange a poor archbishopric for a rich one.[2] The monks were really inclined to a delay which prolonged the day of their own independence and would increase the chances of their patron. But the justiciar was pressing, and they could resist no longer. After a preliminary meeting on October 22, they made the election on December 2. The bishop of Bath, whom no one seems to have thought of before, was elected. He died a few weeks after, but his election had satisfied the occasion.[3] No new one could be made before the king had been consulted, and leave to elect granted. The primacy continued for a year and a half longer unfilled.

As a matter of course, Longchamp's more offensive acts were now remedied; the bishop of Winchester was reinstated in the castle of which he had been deprived; the county of Northumberland was delivered over to Hugh de Puiset;[4] Osbert and Henry Longchamp were removed from their sheriffdoms, and the latter imprisoned at Cardiff.[5] The Yorkshiremen who had got into trouble about the Jews were restored to their estates.[6] The bishops were instructed to take no notice of the legate's letters. Geoffrey returned to his see, and before Christmas had time to excommunicate his late ally the bishop of Durham.[7] Hugh bore the sentence with equanimity, and met it by contriving new difficulties for the metropolitan, for whose sanctity he had been so lately ready to fight. The archbishop of Rouen regarded the chancellor as lying still under the Reading anathema. Longchamp, as soon as his legation was renewed, issued an excommunication, in which he included the whole ministry. Not content with this, he named *seriatim* all his great enemies—the bishop of Winchester, Hugh of Nunant, the four co-justices;[8] Richard Malbysse, the persecutor of the Jews and ally of Hugh de Puiset; Roger FitzRainfrai who had deserted him at the last; Henry de Vere,

Marginal notes: Business of the election to Canterbury. Election of Reginald FitzJocelin. Longchamp's acts reversed. Cross-fire of excommunications.

[1] Epp. Cantuar. 348.
[2] Gervase, 1580.
[3] See Epp. Cantuar. pref. pp. lxxxvi–xc.
[4] R. Devizes, 39.
[5] Gir. Camb., 399.
[6] See above, p. 219, note. Richard Malbysse did not keep long out of mischief; in 1194 we find 'Ricardus de Malbysse reddit computum de 300 marcis pro habenda benevolentia regis, quia dicebatur fuisse cum comite Johanne; et ut sit quietus de forisfacto occisionis Judæorum Eboraci, et pro habendis terris et wardis et forestaria sua sicut habuit quando rex iter arripuit Jerusalem.' Rot. Pip. 6 Rich. I.
[7] Ben. Pet. ii. 225.
[8] Ben. Pet. ii. 223. Hoveden, ii. 153, 154.

his brother Stephen's competitor for the Baudemont heritage; Gerard
Camville, the delinquent of Lincoln ; Stephen Ridell, the chancellor
of John, and the best endowed clerk in the diocese of Ely ; Master
Benedict, who pretended to bear the king's seal; the earl of Salisbury and the count of Meulan ; two of the Bassets, and Simon of
Avranches, lord of Folkestone, are thrown in, perhaps as having
taken part in the Dover outrage; Earl John himself is spared, and
Hugh Bardulf ; but the latter is ordered to give up the sheriffdom
of Yorkshire to William Stuteville, and John, if he does not take care,
will find himself excommunicated on the next Quinquagesima
Sunday.

Before the chancellor ventured on this act he had received very
encouraging news from Rome. The pope had not yet renewed his
legation, but addressed him as if it had never been interrupted.[1] The
savage attack made upon him by the bishop of Coventry had caused
some little reaction in his favour. Peter of Blois wrote manfully for
him ; [2] Celestine III. would hear nothing from the other side ; he
argued, in fact, from his knowledge of Richard's trust in Longchamp
and the obsequiousness of the bishops and barons in the days of his
prosperity, that the attack on him was more prompted by envy and
jealousy than it really was.[3] The chancellor's steadfast purpose was
to make his way back to England. After his expulsion he had passed
through Flanders to Paris, where he had been received with processions, at his own expense, by the bishop at Notre Dame.[4]
Returning to Normandy he found himself treated everywhere as
excommunicate ; neither the office of chancellor nor the title of
legate spared him this humiliation.[5] Whilst he was there, Philip
returned from Palestine.

Historians have recorded of the early events of 1192 little more
than the cross-fire of excommunications ; the interest of the period
is in the crusade. John's plots and Longchamp's counter-plots lie
below the surface. But we can see that Philip's return has introduced a new element into the calculations of both ; that Philip's
object is to injure Richard wherever he has the chance, by stirring
up war on the Continent and persuading John to unsettle England.

John spent Christmas at Howden, with Bishop Hugh, learning
how to behave under excommunication.[6] Early in the year he
received two communications. Philip invited him to France to a
conference, offering him his brother's French possessions with the

---

[1] Benedict, ii. 221. Hoveden. iii.
151.
[2] Hoveden, iii. 148–150.
[3] Hoveden, iii. 190, 191. Bened. ii.

242–244. W. Newb. iv. 18, p. 53.
[4] Benedict, ii. 220.
[5] Ibid. ii. 221.
[6] Hoveden, iii. 179. Bened. ii. 235.

hand of the precious Alais ;[1] William Longchamp offered him a round sum in money if he would contrive his restoration.[2] John listened to both the tempters, contrary as their purposes were. He had found by this time that the archbishop of Rouen was not inclined to give way to him, and that the title of ruler of all England which he had assumed was less effective than the more constitutional rule of the justiciar. He promised to visit Philip ; he also promised to do his best for Longchamp. It would seem that Eleanor was the first to hear of these negotiations, and the news quickly brought her to England. The chancellor had visited Philip in order to lay before him a complaint of the seizure of his property by the Flemish nobles ;[3] and the juxtaposition of two such men was not a little alarming. The queen landed at Portsmouth on February 11,[4] and found John ready to sail to France. Very determined he proved himself. Between Sexagesima Sunday and Easter the queen held four councils of the barons, at Windsor, London, Oxford, and Winchester.[5] John showed himself more obdurate than was conceived. He not only persisted but plotted. He actually succeeded in persuading the constables of Windsor and Wallingford to hand over their castles to him.[6] It was only by the severest remonstrances that he was prevailed upon to give up his projected visit. The archbishop, with Eleanor and the justices, threatened that the moment he embarked they would seize, in the king's name, every castle and manor that he possessed.[7]

In the midst of the excitement caused by these discussions, the bishop of Ely landed at Dover and took up his quarters with his sister in the castle.[8] John had listened to his overtures, and now that he and the archbishop of Rouen had quarrelled, the support of the chancellor would be very important to him. Accordingly, about the fifth week in Lent, Longchamp wrote from Dover to the heads of the government—the queen, John, and the justices—offering to stand his trial and demanding the restoration of his property. Now, Eleanor as well as John would have listened. She had prevailed already on the archbishop to release the estates of the see and withdraw the excommunication ;[9] Longchamp also withdrew his sentence against the justices. But even if these could have safely admitted his return, the barons were implacable. Little news came

Marginal notes: Proposals of Philip and Longchamp to John. Longchamp visits Philip. Eleanor returns to England and compels John to renounce his projects. Determined opposition of the queen to John. Longchamp lands at Dover in March. His proposals to the queen, John, and the justices.

[1] Benedict, ii. 236. R. Devizes, 56.
[2] Bened. ii. 239. R. Devizes, 57.
[3] R. Devizes, 55.
[4] R. Devizes, 55. Gervase, 1580.
[5] R. Devizes, 57.
[6] Ibid.
[7] Benedict. ii. 257.
[8] In the middle of March, Gervase,

1580. R. Devizes, 57, 58. W. Newb. iv. 18, p. 54. Benedict, ii. 239. Gir. Camb. V. Galfr. 402 (circa kalendas Aprilis).
[9] R. Devizes, 56. Gir. Camb. V. Galfr. 402. According to Gervase he came to England by the queen's invitation, c. 1580.

The barons refuse to listen to him

from Palestine. John's succession seemed more than imminent, and with Longchamp they would have nothing to do. John pleaded the cause of his new friend; he saw, in fact, that his arrival gave him the opportunity of making new terms for himself. One of the subjects marked out for consultation in the sitting of the barons was, what notice should be taken of John's treasonable conduct in corrupting the constables of Windsor and Wallingford.[1] By holding out a threat to side with the chancellor, he entirely escaped inquiry into this. And this was, perhaps, all he wanted. He made no secret of the price at which Longchamp had bought him. 'Within a week,' he told the justices, 'the chancellor will pay me 700l. of silver if I abstain from interference between him and you. Money is what you see I want. You know what I mean; you are wise men.'[2] The justices saw that they must buy him. They offered him 2,000 marks, 500l. of which were to be raised from the chancellor's estates.[3] John graciously accepted the sum, and peremptory letters were at once written by all parties to the common enemy, directing him, if he cared for his life, to quit England. He obeyed; sailed on the Thursday in Holy Week; landed again at Whitsand, and, as the English believed, betook himself at once to the court of Philip as a traitor.[4] It is probable that his occupation was rather that of a spy; but we lose sight of him entirely for nearly a year. His envoy, the prior of Hereford, had already made his way to Palestine and poured into the king's ears the complaints which had so impressed the pope.[5] He found Richard at Ascalon in April. The king was, as might be expected, disturbed at the news, but the distressed state of the crusade at the moment prevented his leaving. Six weeks afterwards, in May, at the Canebrake of Starlings, John of Alençon, the vice-chancellor, whom he had left in Normandy, reached him with new complaints; this time, probably, from the archbishop of Rouen:[6] but just now it was out of his power to leave with honour. The break-up of the crusade was, however, imminent, and after a bold but destructive march on Jerusalem in the height of summer, the three years' truce with Saladin was concluded, and in October Richard embarked for home. The next news of him is in January 1193, when he is reported to be in prison in Austria.

During these months the history of England is nearly a blank. Eleanor had succeeded in producing a temporary lull in the political strife. Hugh of Nunant had time to persecute his monks; Geoffrey

John accepts a bribe from the justices and forsakes his new ally

Longchamp ordered to quit England

He sends complaints to Richard

Mission of John of Alençon

Capture of the king

The queen's pacific influence in England

---

[1] R. Devizes, 57, ' de præsumptione castellorum.'
[2] R. Devizes, 57, 58. W. Newb. iv. 18, p. 55.
[3] Benedict, ii. 239. R. Devizes 59.

Hoveden, iii. 188.
[4] Benedict, ii. 240, 241. Hoveden, iii. 188.
[5] Itin. R.R. 333.
[6] Itin. R. R. 358.

of York to offend the dignity of the southern as well as to quarrel to
the point of anathema with the clergy of the northern province.   The
justiciar had his hands full of Norman business.   Whilst he was
acting as the king's lieutenant in England, his own unhappy province
was laid under interdict by the legates sent in consequence of Longchamp's complaints.[1]   Philip was in arms, and only prevented by
a resolute remonstrance of his barons from entering Richard's
territories.   Old Bishop Hugh de Puiset had to be recalled from his
retirement and sent into France to negotiate.

Eleanor seems to have continued in England during this time, *Minor acts of 1192*
and her presence was a pledge of peace.   Longchamp lurked in
Normandy and Aquitaine.[2]   John nursed his grievances at Marlborough and Lancaster.   At the Michaelmas exchequer, Richard
Malbysse and William Percy were admitted to the possession of their
lands until the king's return, for a fine of 20 marks.   Gerard
Camville was still in possession of Lincolnshire ; Hugh of Nunant
was sheriff of Warwickshire, Leicestershire, and Staffordshire ; Henry
Longchamp at Cardiff in prison.[3]

Towards Christmas, great uneasiness began to be felt in England *Rumours of Richard's capture*
as to the fate of the king.   The pilgrims who had stayed behind him
in Palestine were flocking home, and the last that had been heard of
him was that the ship in which he had left Acre had been seen at
Brundusium.[4]   Rumours of his being in trouble reached the country.
Soon after Christmas, John received from Philip the news of the
capture and went over to Normandy in consequence.[5]   After *Intrigues of Philip and John*
attempting to prevail on the Norman barons to swear fealty to
himself, he joined Philip and agreed, according to the proposal of
the last year, to become his vassal for his brother's dominions,
including, as rumour said, England as well as Normandy.[6]   He
then returned to England, got possession of Windsor and Wallingford,

[1] It was not in consequence of Longchamp's complaints that Normandy
was laid under interdict, but because
the steward had refused to receive the
legates without the king's licence.
Ben. Pet. ii. 247. R. Devizes, p. 43.
[2] Gir. Camb. V. Galfr. 403.
[3] Rot. Pip. 4 Rich. I. Herefordsh.:
'Willelmus de Braiose non reddidit
computum hoc anno de firma comitatus neque de summonitionibus, quia
Henricus de Longocampo, qui anno
proximo præcedente comitatum tenue-
rat, propter captionem suam computum
non reddidit. Cujus computus oportuit computum Willelmi præcedere.'
[4] Hoveden, iii. 194.

[5] Hoveden, ii. 204.
[6] The treaty made with Philip on
this occasion is printed in the Fœdera,
i. 57 ; it is dated at Paris in January,
and amounts to a partition of the inheritance of Richard.   It is most
curious, in our present question, as
containing a special provision for the
securing to Hugh 'Constan' episcopo'
safety and restoration in case of peace
being made with Richard.   This Hugh
can be none other than Hugh of
Nunant, and Constan' is a misprint
for Coventren'.   The bishop of Coutances at this time was William of
Tournebu, who presided from 1179 to
1199.

and demanded of the barons their recognition of him as king, now
that his brother, as he said, was dead.

Communi-
cations
opened with
the captive
king

The archbishop of Rouen behaved with great circumspection and
moderation. The first step was to discover where the king was ; for
this purpose the abbots of Boxley and Robertsbridge were sent to
Germany.[1] To open communications with him when found, William
of S. Mere l'Eglise, the prothonotary,[2] was directed to follow, and
he was joined by Hubert Walter, who, returning after Richard from
Palestine, had heard in Sicily of his misfortunes.[3] Savaric, bishop

Embassy to
Henry VI.

of Bath, was directed to the imperial court to make the best terms
he could.[4] Savaric was the emperor's kinsman and friend. The
abbots met the king in Franconia in March, and from that time he
was in regular communication with the government at home.[5]

Longchamp
visits
Richard

The chancellor was one of the first to find his way to him.
Richard received him with unreserved delight, and sent him back to
England with powers to raise or to treat for the raising of the ransom,
and a general commission to do his best for him.[6] But the urgent
business of the kingdom took precedence even of the king's deliver-

John in
rebellion

ance. John, as soon as the barons had definitely refused to listen
to his proposals, took up arms. Windsor and Wallingford he had
secured before his visit to France ; they were now surrendered to him
in form ;[7] Nottingham and Tickhill had been in his hands since the
year 1191 ; Lancaster and the Peak were fortified, and enabled to
resist. He had hired a large force of Welsh mercenaries, whom he

His friends
and allies

placed in Windsor.[8] He had increased the number of his friends ;
Hugh Bardulf, and even William Stuteville, had become his men.[9]
A great fleet of French and Flemish vessels appeared off the coast
to co-operate with him,[10] whilst Philip was using both force and fraud

Resistance
of the arch-
bishop of
Rouen

to gain a strong hold on Normandy. But the archbishop of Rouen
was equal to the occasion ; he gladly showed that there was no
complicity between himself and John, and all the divided parties
flocked to his standard. By a hasty call of the whole population
capable of bearing arms, he prepared to defend the coast,[11] and

Capture of
John's
castles

utterly defeated the design of invasion. Wallingford, Windsor, and
the castle of the Peak fell before the justices.[12] Archbishop Geoffrey
and Bishop Hugh laid aside their spiritual weapons and joined to

---

[1] Hoveden, iii. 198.
[2] Ibid. iii. 209.
[3] Will. Newb. iv. 33, p. 98 ; Hoveden,
ii. 209.
[4] Hoveden, iii. 197. On Savaric,
see Epp. Cantuar. pref. pp. lxxxvii
&c.
[5] Hoveden, iii. 198.
[6] Hoveden, iii. 209. Gir. Camb.
V. Galfr. 403. W. Newb. iv. 33,

p. 97.
[7] Hoveden, iii. 204. W. Newb. iv.
33, p. 98.
[8] Gervase, 1582.
[9] Hoveden, iii. 206.
[10] Gervase, 1581. Hoveden, iii. 205.
[11] Gervase, 1581.
[12] Hoveden, iii. 207, 208. Gervase,
1582. W. Newb. iv. 34, p. 100.

besiege Tickhill.[1]   But it was not the purpose of the government to reduce to extremity one who might any day become king.   The news of Richard was too uncertain ; and, much against the will of the barons, Eleanor persuaded the justiciar to conclude a truce with John from May to November.[2]

By this measure time and peace were gained for the compassing of the king's redemption.   This had been, of course, the earliest thought in the archbishop's mind.   Before John had begun hostilities, he had called a council of bishops and barons to Oxford for the 28th of February,[3] whilst Savaric was on his way to the imperial court, and before it was actually known that Henry VI. would require a ransom.   What was done at this assembly we are not told ; probably the difficulties occasioned by John's behaviour may have prevented its being held, or anything else of the kind being contemplated before the arrival of the ministers who had been in communication with the king.   On the 20th of April Hubert Walter landed with authentic news,[4] and it was his mediating influence, probably, that induced the contending parties to make the six months' truce.   A few days later arrived a letter from the king, dated April 19th, stating that the sum of 70,000 marks was required for his liberation.[5]   To raise this the justices demanded an aid of a fourth part of all revenue, lay and clerical, with an equal sum to be levied on personal property, and a scutage of 20 shillings on the knight's fee : all the wool of the Gilbertines and the gold and silver of the churches.[6]   Whilst this was in process of collection—for no time was lost about it—arrived the golden bull of the emperor, brought by William Longchamp, and delivered by him to the queen and justiciar at S. Alban's.[7]

Notwithstanding his high credentials and the assurance given by the king's letter that he still possessed his confidence, his very approach revived all the angry feelings of the barons.   Before landing he had been obliged to swear that he would attempt to transact no business but that of the king's release.   During his stay in London he had, however, ordered the seizure of some houses belonging to the bishop of Coventry, who was in open rebellion, and this produced such an outcry against him on the part of the citizens that the interview between him and the court could not be held in the capital.[8]   At S. Alban's he was not more welcome.   'I come,' he said, 'not as a justice, not as chancellor, not as legate, simply as

Marginal notes:
- Measures for securing Richard's release
- Return of Hubert Walter
- Money raised for the ransom
- Arrival of Longchamp as the king's envoy
- His behaviour in London
- His treatment at S. Alban's

---

[1] Hoveden, iii. 206, 207.
[2] Gervase, 1582.
[3] Hoveden, iii. 197.
[4] Gervase, 1582.
[5] Hoveden, iii. 209. W. Newb. iv.
31, p. 109.
[6] Hoveden, iii. 210.
[7] Gir. Camb. V. Galfr. 403. Hoveden, iii. 211, 212.
[8] Gir. Camb. 403.

bishop and the king's messenger.'[1]   But the chief justiciar refused
him the kiss of peace ; when he demanded the hostages, as he was
specially accredited to do, the queen refused to intrust to him her
grandson William of Winchester,[2] and the principal nobles declined

He retires in
disgust

to put their children in his power.   Intensely chagrined, he contented
himself with declaring the king's message and summoning the barons
whose presence was required by Richard in Germany.[3]

Longchamp
recalled by
Richard

Richard had empowered his chancellor to undertake this task,
probably as a demonstration of his own confidence in him, but he
was not inclined to risk anything more ; and fearing that his conduct might offend the barons, summoned him hastily to his side
again.   He was present with him at Worms on the 29th of
June,[4] and a few days after negotiated a truce with Philip at Mantes,

He nego-
tiates peace
with Philip

July 9.[5]   A meeting had been arranged between Philip and Henry
for June 24, at Vaucouleurs, the usual trysting-place for the emperors
and kings of France,[6] but many circumstances happened to prevent it, and this truce, which was observed no better than the engagement to meet, was probably a substitute for it.

Hubert
Walter and
others ap-
pointed to
collect the
ransom

In the meantime Hubert Walter had, on the 30th of May, been
elected archbishop of Canterbury,[7] and to him, the bishop of London
the treasurer, and the mayor Henry FitzAylwin, with William of
Arundel and Hameline of Warren [8]—two men who had never
wavered in their support of the chancellor—the care of the money
to be raised for the ransom was committed.   The date of the assembly at S. Alban's cannot be fixed, but it was probably early in June.
In the treaty of Worms, at the end of the same month, the emperor

Ransom
raised to
150,000
marks

raised his terms.   The sum required now was more than doubled ;
150,000 marks were to be paid, of which 20,000 were to be the share
of Duke Leopold.[9]   A new budget was therefore necessary, but
100,000 marks being paid and hostages given, the arrangement of the
new taxes was left until the king's arrival.   Under the skilful hand
of Hubert Walter everything was now concluded with facility ; the
autumn was devoted to the collection of the subsidies.[10]   John was

Turn of
affairs in
Long-
champ's
favour

away in France, whither he had gone again as soon as he had heard
from Philip that the 'devil was unloosed.'[11]   Philip himself was
busy with his matrimonial difficulties.   The chancellor was in attendance on his master, who had, moreover, summoned to him most of

[1] Hoveden, iii. 212.   Longchamp
seems to have been fond of distinguishing his own several capacities.
We may compare his speech when he
arrested Hugh de Puiset as given by
Richard of Devizes : ' ego te capio,
non præsul præsulem, sed cancellarius
cancellarium.' R. Dev. 13.

[2] Son of Henry the Lion.   Gir.
Camb. 403.
[3] Hoveden, iii. 212.
[4] Ibid. iii. 215.   [5] Ibid. iii. 217.
[6] Ibid. iii. 212.   [7] Gervase, 1584.
[8] Hoveden, iii. 212.
[9] Ibid. iii. p. 215, 216.
[10] Ibid. iii. 225.   [11] Ibid. iii. 216.

the other uneasy spirits, the ambitious and officious Savaric, and even Hugh of Nunant, among the number.[1] The hopes of Long-champ's party began to revive; his brother Henry was released from prison,[2] and, by a zealous attempt at poetic justice, Matthew de Cleres ventured to arrest and imprison the bishop of Coventry on his way to the continent with bags crammed with peace-offerings for Richard.[3] The process of excommunication had to be resorted to again to obtain his release.

The negotiations between Richard and John were carried on, strange to say, through the chancellor,[4] who seems to have done his best to effect a reconciliation. John was prevailed upon to swear fealty to his brother, but the arrangement was defeated by the barons of Normandy, who refused to give up the castles of his honours in that province, and he returned in disgust to Philip to plot with him the longer detention of the king.[5] Before the end of the year Richard summoned his mother, the justiciar, and the chancellor to Mentz, and as the absence of the justiciar from England practi-cally vacated his office, he nominated the archbishop of Canterbury in his place.[6] Hubert had indeed been at the head of the govern-ment since his return in April; he maintained the royal authority until the king's return against the frantic opposition of John's supporters, and had recovered all the castles except Nottingham and Tickhill before Richard's arrival. *He negotiates between Richard and John*

Hubert Walter made chief justiciar

Here, however, the administration of Walter of Coutances, and the period of political and personal strife, end. The interest of the remainder of the reign is constitutional rather than political, and I shall attempt in the preface to the fourth volume of this chronicle to give a brief survey of it. At present it may not be uninteresting to state the later fortunes of some of the actors who appear no more after the conclusion of the period. *End of the administra-tion of Walter of Coutances*

Hugh de Puiset, after the capture of Tickhill, presented himself to Richard at Nottingham, and was received with great show of affection.[7] A few days later he attended the royal council at Not-tingham, and after quarrelling at Selston with the King of Scots about lodgings—a thing which he had done once before with Henry II.—he drew down on himself a sharp rebuke from Richard.[8] Partly in consequence of the king's coolness, he surrendered the county *Later his-tory of Hugh de Puiset*

[1] Hoveden, iii. 226.
[2] Rot. Pip. 5 Ric. I.:—'Henricus de Longocampo reddit computum de anno tertio Regis Ricardi, qui dilatus fuit propter captionem.'
[3] R. de Diceto, 671. Gir. Camb. 404.
[4] Hoveden, iii. 227.
[5] Hoveden, iii. 228.
[6] R. de Diceto, 671. Hoveden, iii. 226.
[7] Hoveden, iii. 239.
[8] V. S. Godrici, p. 178. Hoveden, iii. 246.

of Northumberland.[1] Scarcely, however, had he done this when he repented, and offered the king, as soon as he had gone to Normandy, two thousand marks for its restoration. When Hugh Bardulf demanded possession, the bishop declined to surrender until he had his answer from Richard. Hugh Bardulf, having consulted the king, took possession of the county and exacted, moreover, the 2,000 marks as well as the surrender of the manor of Sadberge.[2] In September we find him at York annulling the archbishop's sentence against the canons.[3] On Ash Wednesday 1195, he was there again, confirming the sentence passed by the dean against Geoffrey's party.[4] This was his last public act. On leaving York he fell ill at Crayke,[5]

Death of Hugh de Puiset but persevered in riding on to Doncaster; from Doncaster he was taken in a boat to Howden, where, on the 3rd of March, he closed his uneasy although magnificent career.[6] His son Henry survived

Fortunes of his son him several years. He was in difficulties in 1198.[7] In 1201 he went, as so many of his forefathers had done, to Palestine,[8] but, unlike them, he lived to return. He died in or before 1212, and as his estates escheated to the crown, we may conclude that he left no issue.[9]

Later history of Hugh of Nunant Hugh of Nunant despaired, as well he might, of Richard's clemency; not only was he known to be in the secret of all John's schemes, but his brother Robert had actually been the emissary who proposed the continuance of the king's imprisonment and refused to be a hostage for him on the ground of his being John's liegeman.[10] One of Richard's first acts after his liberation was to arrest Robert and order Hugh to stand his trial in the clerical as well as in the secular courts, as bishop as well as sheriff. In the council of Nottingham he failed to appear, and was summoned again on the 31st of March 1194.[11] The suit of the monks against him was being prosecuted in the Curia Regis. He was allowed by the king to purchase his pardon and restoration for 5,000 marks,[12] in March 1195; but Robert was still imprisoned, under the careful superintendence the lady Richenda, at Dover, where he died.[13] The bishop sinks into obscurity from henceforth; although his suit with the monks lasted his life, it is uncertain whether he ever returned to England. He seems to have hung about the court until his death. In February 1198, Archbishop Hubert restored the monks of Coventry, and' in

[1] Hoveden, iii. 249.
[2] Ibid. iii. 261.
[3] Ibid. iii. 272, 273.
[4] Ibid. iii. 284.
[5] W. Newb. v. 310, p. 145.
[6] Hoveden, iii. 284. W. Newb., p. 146.
[7] Madox, *Hist. Exch.* p. 366.
[8] Pat. 3 John, p. 3:—' Concessimus quod Henricus de Puteaco, qui crusiatus est, possit invadiare quas voluerit terrarum suarum.'
[9] Cart. 5 John, p. 126. He has a confirmation of the manor of Witton from the king in 1204.
[10] Rot. Claus. 14 John, p. 124.
[11] Hoveden, iii. 233.
[12] Ibid. iii. 241, 242.
[13] Ibid. iii. 287.

March Bishop Hugh died at Bec Hellouin, condemning himself to **His death** purgatory until doomsday.

Of Longchamp's other opponents it is satisfactory to find that **Richard's treatment** they were treated by Richard exactly as his minister had intended, **of Longchamp's** and this, perhaps, shows that the king had exercised over his move- **enemies** ments a closer supervision than was suspected. The bishop of Winchester was, after the council of Nottingham, disseized of his castle and county, and lost with them a large part of his inheritance.[1] Gerard Camville was deprived at the same time of Lincoln Castle and county, and put on his defence for the charges brought against him by the chancellor. He recovered the king's favour for 2,000 marks, and on John's accession became a greater man than ever.[2] His wife Nicolaa stood also so high in John's estimation that on her husband's death she was appointed sheriff or custos of Lincolnshire in 1216.[3] The Yorkshire knights also had to raise much larger sums than they expected, to recover the king's goodwill.[4]

The fates of the several members of the Longchamp family were **Fate of Stephen** various. Stephen, the steward of Normandy, the friend and companion **Longchamp** of Richard, survived his master, and on the loss of Normandy by John, after some attempts to maintain his possessions in both countries, went over to Philip.[5] He was slain, fighting for Philip, at the battle of Bouvines.[6] Henry, the sheriff of Herefordshire, after his release from **Henry Longchamp** prison, appears as sheriff of Worcestershire from 1195 to 1198; but after the death of the chancellor both he and his sons seem to have fallen under the king's displeasure.[7] The last we hear certainly of him is during the fourth crusade. He had placed his estates, before his departure, in the king's keeping,[8] and is mentioned by Villehardouin[9] as joining the Flemish knights who passed through Piacenza and took the route of Apulia, instead of starting from Venice. He died in 1204,[10] and the next year the king confirmed the gift of the castle of Wilton to another Henry the son of Hugh;[11] of his two sons, William, the **His sons**

[1] Hoveden, iii. 246.
[2] Hoveden, iii. 242.
[3] Rot. Pat. 18 John, p. 199.
[4] The citizens of York had to pay 200 marks to prove their joy at the king's return. 'Cives Eboracenses r. c. de cc. marcis de dono suo pro gaudio adventus domini regis de Alemannia.' Rot. Pip. 6 Ric. I.
[5] Stapleton, *Norman Rolls*, ii. cxv.
[6] Rigord, ed. Pithou, 217; he is called 'miles probus et fidei integræ,' p. 219. Fighting, besides him, was William des Barres, Richard's companion in the crusade: 'Willelmus Barrensis flos militum.'
[7] Rot. Pip. 9 Rich. I. Dugdale's

Baronage, 594.
[8] Rot. Pat. 4 John, p. 11.
[9] Villehardouin (ed. Du Cange), p. 21.
[10] On the 23rd of March 1204, Matilda, his widow, had from the king an allowance of 10*l.* out of the manor of Wilton. Rot. de Liberate, pp. 84, 106.
[11] Rot. Cart. 6 John, p. 146. The charter especially names the grantee of Wilton, Henry the son of Hugh, We may ask how it was that Henry's own sons did not succeed him. In answer, I can only suggest either that he himself held Wilton only as guardian of his nephew, or that his

Osbert
Longchamp

husband of the heiress of Croun, died before him. Osbert, after being sheriff of Norfolk and Suffolk in 1194, was, with his brother, in disgrace in 1198,[1] and no more is heard of him, except in private charters, until his death in 1207, when his wife Avellina paid a fine not to be compelled to marry again, and for the wardship of his heirs.[2]

Robert
Longchamp

His family continued in Kent until the end of the century.[3] Robert, the monk of Caen, whom the chancellor made prior of Ely, and to whom the king, after his death, in grateful remembance gave the abbey of S. Mary at York, survived until 1239. A nephew named

Geoffrey
Longchamp

Geoffrey, son of Hugh and brother of the lord of Wilton, was among the barons who compelled John to grant the charter.[4] The lord of Wilton died in 1212,[5] and his grand-daughter brought the castle of the Longchamps into the house of Grey.[6]

Later years
of the
chancellor

The chancellor seems to have retained or regained Richard's full confidence and kept his office until his death. During the few years that succeeded Richard's return, he was in constant attendance upon him. Richard had reconciled him with his most formidable enemies before they quitted England, and it is probable that he never

sons, if he had any surviving, had lost their title by joining Philip, as their uncle Stephen had done. His daughter-in-law Petronilla had claims of dower on the Wilton estate, which seems to prove to a certainty that he himself had held it. William his son was dead in 1203. Rot. Pat. 37. Madox, *Hist. Exch.* p. 68.

[1] In the 3rd of John, Gilbert Fitz-Rainfrai was in trouble, 'quia ivit in foresta cum Osberto de Longocampo.' Rot. Canc. 3 John, p. 119, 218. Rot. Pip. 10 Rich. I., Kent. 'Osbertus de Longocampo reddit compotum pro habenda gratia regis et saisina omnium terrarum et catallorum de quibus dissaisitus fuit per praeceptum regis secundum judicium curiæ regis, si quis cum eo inde loqui voluerit, sed respondit infra partes Herefordiæ in Wallia.'

[2] Rot. Pip. 9, 10 John. Walter Tiwe had bought the marriage for 400 marks; Avellina bid 500 and was relieved from the obligation to marry him.

[3] Osbert de Longchamp held the manor of Ovenhelle in Kent by serjeanty in the reign of Edward I. Hasted, ii. 129. And his name occurs in the parliamentary writs, vol. i.

[4] This Geoffrey was the husband of Isabella, daughter of Henry de Mineriis of Westbury in Gloucestershire, Rot.

Claus. 345. His estate was at Eston. He was with John's enemies in 1216 (Rot. Claus. 279). His land was of the fee of Walter de Lacy (Rot. Claus. 241).

[5] He married Maud, the sister of William Cantelupe, who had the wardship of the heirs. He was with John's army in Ireland in 1210. Rot. Liberate, anno 12 Joh.

[6] To make an end of the Longchamps. The identity of the family with that of Wilton I have, I think, established in the notes. It would be a most extraordinary thing if Herefordshire contained two families of exactly the same names and both holding lands under the Lacies. It is of Hugh de Lacy that Hugh de Longchamp held in Wilton in 1168; from Walter de Lacy that Stephen held Frome Herbert, and Geoffrey his land at Kempley; and in close connexion with them he was a benefactor of Acornbury. (8th Report of Dep. Keeper, App. ii. pp. 136, 137.) Again Hugh, the nephew of William the chancellor, is closely connected with the Watervilles and Dives. (Eyton, Shropshire, ix. 77.) This Hugh was son of Henry (Rot. Fin. 6 John), and brother therefore of William; both of them had lands in Lincolnshire. Hugh married Georgia, daughter of Henry de Columbariis, Rot. Pip. 3 John.

returned to the country where he had suffered so much. Anyhow, he passes away entirely from English history. He died at Poictiers in 1196, whilst on a journey to Rome to defend the king against the archbishop of Rouen. At Poictiers he was not unpopular, if we may believe that the cross of S. Martial wept a flood of tears at the moment of his death. He was buried in the abbey of S. Mary du Pin, whose abbot Miles had been his fellow courtier for many years.[1]

His death, in 1196

The restless career of Geoffrey of York cannot be here even entered on. The process by which he was being developed from his early quarrelsome violence into the character of a defender cf constitutional liberties must have been now advancing, but its ripening belongs to the age of John.

Geoffrey of York

Walter of Coutances remains. He also, as he advanced in years, sank the character of a statesman in that of an ecclesiastic. In 1196 he had a terrible quarrel with Richard and laid Normandy under an interdict, which the king bought off by an exchange of lands, giving for the land at Andely on which his Château Gaillard was built, an estate which suited the archbishop better. Walter of Coutances acquiesced readily in the transfer of allegiance to Philip, and died the ' pater patriæ ' in 1207.

Walter of Coutances

[1] Hoveden. Itin. R. R. pref. xxxiii, xxxiv.

THE CHRONICLE OF ROGER OF HOVEDEN. VOL. IV.

[IN this Preface the reign of Richard I. is again dealt with. Special attention is given to 'the history of Archbishop Geoffrey of York, the legal and political administration of Hubert Walter and Geoffrey FitzPeter.' Light is also thrown upon 'foreign history by the more careful notices of events which took place during the period in Italy, Germany, Norway, and Spain.' In all of his writings Hoveden devotes considerable attention to the history of the See of York. In the present Preface Bishop Stubbs gives a very valuable account of the constitutional policy of Hubert Walter. The Judicial Iter of 1194 and the Carucage of 1198 are fully described, and their relation to the measures of Henry II. explained.]

* * * * * *

Condition of the province of York in the twelfth and thirteenth centuries

I. The religious and ecclesiastical condition of the province of York during the twelfth century was anomalous and extremely critical. The country had never recovered the savage cruelties to which it was subjected by the Conqueror. Northumbria had been one of the best and earliest consolidated kingdoms of the Heptarchy, her kings the bravest and holiest, her missionaries the most devoted ; her monasteries had kept up European learning in the darkest age, her mariners and merchants were enterprising, her population equally and abundantly diffused. Archæological discovery testifies to a populousness and a civilisation that history seems almost to have forgotten. Under the Danish invasion Yorkshire had gone through no more severe experiences than Middle England ; the Angle population coalesced with the Danish immigrants ; the lands changed their owners and the villages their names, but the changes were in analogy and in proportion to the usual rule. The conquerors were converted and civilised ; but whilst they presented in some respect a marked contrast with the men of the south, the social condition of the country was not very different from what it had been, or from the rest of England. The phantom kings of Danish Northumbria rose and fell under the alternate pressure of West Saxon suzerainty, or recurring invasion from Scandinavia. The archbishop, by far the more permanent institution of the two, vindicated in practice his independence of his southern brother, and not unfrequently represented his province as a distinct nationality from that of Canterbury.

During the century before the Conquest the political condition of the northern primacy had been materially varied. The inclusion of Nottinghamshire, a Mercian county, within the diocese of York, made the archbishop a regular member of the Witenagemot of the West Saxon dynasty, and the hold thus given was, by the royal policy, strengthened by suffering the archbishop to hold the extensive bishopric of Worcester *in commendam*.[1] The adhesion of Yorkshire to the West Saxon race of kings was secured far more by the archbishops of York than by the ealdormen of Northumbria; and notwithstanding many drawbacks from internal quarrels, and the threatening growth of the power of the Scots, the district enjoyed an average tranquillity and comparative wealth and prosperity until the terrible invasion of 1069. What William then left undone was completed by Malcolm and Cospatric in 1070. The ambition and turbulence of the Norman earls and the savage inroads of the Scots prolonged the desolation until the accession of Henry I. Henry put an end to the ravages of the Scots, took advantage of the forfeitures the Mowbrays to endow a less dangerous body of nobles and attempted to restore here as elsewhere so much of the ancient political system as was capable of resuscitation.

But the ecclesiastical organisation had suffered as deeply as the social, and in the process of restoration neither church nor state had much choice of means and instruments. The old border sees of Whithern and Hexham had been extinct for centuries. The archbishop exercised, or rather claimed to exercise, his jurisdiction in the north-western counties through the archdeacons of Richmond, under whose ineffective rule the church was impoverished and demoralised. Nearer the centre the work of restoration was undertaken by the Cistercians; but of the prelates to whom the Norman kings intrusted the see of York, the first Thomas was mainly occupied in

Marginal notes: Previous condition of Northumbria

Desolation under William the Conqueror

Restoration of order by Henry I.

Injuries to the church organisation

---

[1] The connexion of Worcester and York seems to have begun with S. Oswald, who retained the former see, to which he had been consecrated, on his promotion to York in 972. Aldulf, his successor, held the two together until his death in 1002; and Wulfstan, the next archbishop, retained Worcester until 1016, when Leofsi was appointed as bishop. On Leofsi's death Brihteage, nephew of archbishop Wulfstan, was appointed, in 1033; his successor Living and Archbishop Elfric then contested the possession of the see. Aldred, who succeeded Living in 1045, became archbishop of York in 1061; Sampson, the first Norman bishop of Worcester, was brother of Thomas I., archbishop of York; Thomas II., archbishop of York, was son of Sampson, bishop of Worcester. The church of S. Oswald at Gloucester was a peculiar of York, and the cause of one of the quarrels of Richard of Canterbury with Archbishop Roger. The close connexion subsisted in one shape or another for at least 150 years.

The arch-
bishops
from the
Conquest
onwards
a struggle with Canterbury, and seems to have lived most frequently
at Gloucester; Gerard, his successor, was a mere courtier, and
Thomas II., a pious man, did not live long enough to produce any
marked result. Thurstan, the fourth archbishop after the Conquest,
devoted himself heart and soul to the revival of religion and of the
arts of peace. Thurstan was the great patron of the Cistercians, on
whom likewise the nobles, rich in land if poor in money, lavished
enormous territorial grants, and the Cistercians, not only by their
devotion to the religious improvement of their dependents, but
by their attention to sheep-farming and grazing, which only could
make their estates remunerative in the thinness of the reduced
population, laid posterity under a double debt.   It was under
Thurstan's primacy, moreover, that the see of Carlisle was founded
and that of Whithern revived ; the former to undertake a substan-
tive share in church government ; the latter perhaps to enable the
primate to extend the benefit of episcopal work to the remoter portions of his enormous diocese.

Relapse
under Ste-
phen
No sooner, however, was this measure of policy adopted than it
was defeated, and the work thrown back for twenty years. The
occupation of Northumberland and Cumberland by the Scots coincided in point of time with the paralysis of church government at
Disputed
election of
archbishop
York, arising from the disputed election of S. William and Henry
Murdac. During these years the lands in Scottish hands had no
effective spiritual supervision. The Scottish church was disabled
for the work by deficiencies of organisation, which, already apparent,
went on increasing in importance until it fell before the comparative
life and order of the Calvinistic reformation. The bishop of Carlisle
was only occasionally allowed to visit his diocese, and after his death
sixty-two years elapsed before a successor could be prevailed on to
accept the see. In Yorkshire S. William was supported by the
party of Stephen and his brother the legate ; Henry Murdac by the
Cistercian interest, backed not only by the archbishop of Canterbury
but by S. Bernard himself, and all-powerful at Rome. The better
title and the wiser influence were arrayed against each other. Murdac held the see as long as he lived. The restoration of S. William,
and the promotion of Hugh de Puiset, who was, like himself, a
nephew of Stephen, were probably parts of the general scheme of
pacification that belongs to the year 1153. But whilst the princes
were struggling the church was perishing, and the degradation of
the latter was accomplished when Osbert of Bayeux, who had been
archdeacon to Thurstan [1] and Murdac, having poisoned the arch-

---

[1] Osbert was of Bayeux, Thurstan's
own town. Mon. Angl. vi. 205. He
had a son called William of Bayeux,
who was at law with the canons of
York in 1191. Rot. Pip. 3 Rich. I.

bishop in the Eucharistic chalice, claimed and obtained immunity as a clergyman from the vengeance of the outraged law.

The reign of Henry II. witnessed the restoration of the lost counties and of the territorial completeness of the province. It was, with the exception of one considerable struggle, a period of peace for the north country. The chair of Paulinus was filled by the active and clever Roger of Pont l'Evêque, and that of Durham by Hugh de Puiset, of whom his worst enemies could not say that he was either indolent or avaricious. Both these prelates showed much zeal and considerable constructive power in their administration : both, however, were builders of castles rather than of churches, and church-builders rather than missionaries.[1] The distant portions of Roger's diocese scarcely felt his rule at all ; the nearer were planted with prebendal churches, and brought up to the ordinary standard of the southern dioceses. Craven was, however, still left to the Cistercians ; Richmondshire, Lancashire, and Westmoreland to the absentee archdeacons ; the North Riding was full of peculiars of the church of Durham, ancient demesnes of S. Cuthbert, which had been reclaimed from the prevailing desolation. And Roger, moreover, was a courtier and a lawyer ; he had his quarrels with Becket to carry to their wretched end ; he was the greatest power in Yorkshire, and on him the organisation of defence depended as much as that of Durham and Northumberland on the palatine earl-bishop. The importance of the sheriffdom of Yorkshire was so great that it was generally intrusted to the prime minister of the Crown, the chief justiciar, as the most trusty of the baronage, and in his constant absence the real burden of counsel, if not of authority, fell on the primate.

The close connexion of the archbishop with the court had the further effect of filling all the posts of importance in the northern church with royal officials, who were absentees and unpriestly, if not irreligious, men. And this evil was aggravated during the long vacancy that followed the death of Archbishop Roger in 1181. Henry's reasons for prolonging this vacancy can only be guessed at ; but it seems probable that he was influenced partly by the large revenue which he was enabled to draw into the exchequer,[2] partly by an

Marginal notes: Restoration of order under Henry II. — Archbishop Roger — Secular occupations of the primate — Appointments of absentees — Long vacancy of the see after Roger's death

---

[1] William of Newburgh's sketch of Archbishop Roger is admirable ; it is, however, too long to quote. He, like his successor Geoffrey, is charged with appointing beardless boys to prebends; with speaking contemptuously of monks ; he was a good husband to his see, but with wonderful blindness thought that he could 'obsequium præstare Deo ' by posthumous benefactions, when he had neglected to lay up treasure in heaven. Lib. iii. cap. 3.

[2] The proceeds of the archiepiscopal estates were let at ferm in 1189 for 1,056*l*. 9*s*. 4*d*.; the amount of synodals was 29*l*. 18*s*. 8*d*. besides, and there were other windfalls. The ferm in 1185 was 1,112*l*. 2*s*. 10*d*. The see was vacant for eight years, so that the benefit accruing to the exchequer from the vacancy must have been nearly 10,000*l*. Madox, *Hist. Exch.* 211 ; Pipe Roll of Rich. I. p. 9.

aversion to bestow upon any of his clerical ministers a preferment which might involve a second struggle, such as that with Becket had been; partly by an indistinct intention of somehow providing for his faithful son Geoffrey. The course of action adopted was, however, very prejudicial to Geoffrey's interests; the prolongation of the vacancy being itself a great source of disturbance to the province, and the ecclesiastics who were promoted being of the class most likely to be jealous of a new archbishop, and especially of such a one as Geoffrey. Geoffrey's troubles were thus created for him long before he had any certain prospect of the archiepiscopate, and the circumstances under which he was promoted to it were untoward in an extreme degree.

Attempts at an election In September 1186, Henry II., in a court at Marlborough,[1] proposed to the assembled canons of York the election of a new archbishop; and they nominated five persons for royal approval. These were Hubert Walter the dean, Hamo the precentor, Bernard prior of Newburgh, Laurence archdeacon of Bedford, and Master Roger Arundel; the two last were ministers of the Exchequer, who had at the time the management of the archiepiscopal revenue.[2]

The king's reasons for refusing to ratify the election Henry refused all five, as he had in the preceding May declined to sanction the election of Richard FitzNeal, Godfrey de Lucy, and Herbert the Poor to the see of Lincoln; on that occasion alleging that all these candidates were rich enough already, and that for the future he would never give a bishopric to any one for love or relationship, counsel, prayer, or price, but to those whom the Lord should choose.[3] It was no doubt from something like a religious sense of right that he promoted Hugh of Lincoln and Archbishop Baldwin, but his other nominations both before and after this date can scarcely be reconciled with this declaration.

Nomination of Geoffrey to the see of York Nothing more was done in the matter until the king's last illness, when he nominated his son Geoffrey. During this time the ministers of the Exchequer received the temporalities of the see, Hubert Walter as dean had the care of the spiritualities,[4] and the episcopal functions were discharged by the bishop of Durham, who as a principal member of the church of York seems to have claimed certain undefined rights in the cathedral body, if not also a voice in the election of the metropolitan analogous with that which the southern bishops still occasionally exercised in the elections to Canterbury.[5]

Composition of the chapter at this time Very much of the interest of the subsequent history depends on the character and position of the canons of the chapter at this time.

---

[1] Ben. Pet. i. 352.
[2] William le Vavassur was joined in the commission with them. Madox, *Hist. Exch.* 211; Pipe Roll of Rich. 1.

p. 9.
[3] Ben. Pet. i. 346.
[4] Hoveden, iii. 7. Ben. Pet. ii. 78.
[5] Hoveden, iii. 7. Ben. Pet. ii. 77.

At the head of it was Hubert Walter, the nephew and chaplain of Ranulf Glanvill, justiciar of England and sheriff of Yorkshire. He of course was non-resident, having been generally in attendance on the king, either as the representative of the justiciar who remained in England whilst Henry was abroad, or in some capacity connected with the business of the Chancery.[1] Hubert was a man, as his later history showed, of great ability in affairs, a well-trained and most practical statesman, and a thoroughly English minister to a thoroughly un-English king. It is in his relationship to Archbishop Geoffrey that the worst side of his character comes out. As having been elected to the see in 1186, and being in possession, as dean, of the spiritualities, he seems to have regarded himself as having a claim upon the archiepiscopate which the promotion of Geoffrey of course would disappoint. The power which he had in the chapter and diocese in these two capacities was exercised in his absence by his official, Master Bartholomew.[2] Next in importance, though not in dignity, after the dean, were the archdeacons ; Ralph, of the West Riding, of whom we know no more than transpires from his subsequent conduct to Geoffrey ; Geoffrey Muschamp,[3] of Cleveland, who afterwards was bishop of Lichfield ; and William Testard, of Nottingham. The archdeaconry of the East Riding was annexed, it would seem, to the treasurership.[4] The archdeaconry of Richmond, one of the most wealthy and influential posts in the English church, was filled by Godfrey de Lucy, the son of the late justiciar Richard de Lucy,[5] whom we find to have been in constant

Hubert Walter the dean

The archdeacons

The great dignities of the chapter

[1] Hubert was made dean on the death of Robert Butevilein in 1186; only a short time before he was elected to the archbishopric. He attests the king's letters dated at Guildford early in 1187 (Epp. Cant. p. 28). In 1189 he was in attendance on the king in Maine, and apparently had the royal seal at his disposal (Epp. Cant. pp. 282, 283, 284). William of S. Mere l'Eglise, who succeeded to his prebend at York in 1189, is called the king's protonotary, and it is possible that Hubert held the office before him, or that he acted as vice-chancellor under Geoffrey, as Walter of Coutances had done. His connexion with the chancery under whatever title must have brought him into early intercourse with Geoffrey, and probably produced the personal jealousy which so much affects their later relations.

[2] Hoveden. iii. 7. Benedict, ii. 77.

[3] Geoffrey Muschamp was probably appointed by Henry II. just before his death, as his nomination is one of those said to be fraudulently sealed by Geoffrey as chancellor, and as his predecessor Jeremiah is mentioned in the Pipe Roll of 1 Rich. I. Hoveden, iii. 274.

[4] This is an inference from the fact that no archdeacon of the East Riding is mentioned in these disputes, and that the churches which are specified by Hoveden as being in the treasurer's archdeaconry are situated in the East Riding. Hugh de Puiset seems to have held it with the treasurership, and, as Hoveden was locally within it, it was no doubt an additional reason for his wish to strengthen the family interest there, by obtaining it for his nephew Bouchard. The first person known as archdeacon of the East Riding by that name is Walter of Wisbech, in 1218. Hoveden, ii. 70. Le Neve, ed. Hardy, iii. 141.

[5] Ben. Pet. i. 334.

employment during Henry's reign in the judicial and financial work of the Exchequer, and who is known to us under Richard as bishop of Winchester, alternately the friend and victim of William Longchamp. Of the great dignities of the chapter, the treasurership was held by Geoffrey himself, the king's son; he had received it on the promotion of Ralph Warneville, his predecessor in the chancellorship, together with the archdeaconry of Rouen, and probably other important preferment.[1] The treasurership was a very valuable post, next in wealth to the deanery, and very far beyond the other dignities. It had been held in succession by S. William, afterwards archbishop; Hugh de Puiset; John of Poictiers, afterwards archbishop of Lyons; and Ralph of Warneville, the chancellor. It was properly in the gift of the archbishop, and in fact Roger, who died whilst the promotion of Ralph de Warneville was in contemplation, had promised the reversion of it to the precentor Hamo,[2] thus preparing a new rival and a pertinacious one for his unlucky successor. The chancellorship of the church was vacant. The precentor Hamo was the only dignitary in constant residence. He had filled the office for many years, had been nominated, as we have just seen, by Roger to the treasurership, had been also proposed to the king for election to the see in 1186, and seems from the later history to have embodied all the traditions of the chapter, as well as to have wielded all its local influence. Of the other canons only a few names have reached us, and those are of local interest only.[3] But it seems not improbable that the hereditary principle in the tenure of these preferments still retained some vitality. The most important ecclesiastics in Yorkshire after these seem to have been Peter de Ros, archdeacon of Carlisle, and Roger Arundel, a canon of Southwell and custos of the temporalities of the see. It must not be forgotten that the archbishop had, at Ripon, Beverley, and Southwell, three other chapters of canons well endowed and largely leavened with influential public men. Among these it would be strange if Roger Hoveden were not provided for; that he was so, however, we have no proof.

The news of Geoffrey's nomination to the archbishopric must

Margin notes: Geoffrey the treasurer — Hamo the precentor — Permanence of hereditary interest among the canons — Other chapters of canons

---

[1] Gir. Camb. (Ang. Sac. vol. ii.), V. Galfr. p. 380.

[2] Ben. Pet. ii. 88. It is added that Henry II. had confirmed the appointment.

[3] There is a difficulty in drawing up a regular list, because of the several that present themselves; it is not certain whether they held the stalls in succession or contemporaneously. Master Erard, William of Stigandby,

and Geoffrey Muschamp seem to have been nominated by Henry shortly before his death; William of S. Mere l'Eglise, William of Chimeli, and Bouchard de Puiset by Richard at the council of Pipewell; Simon of Apulia and Master Honorius by Archbishop Geoffrey. Besides these, Peter of Flanders held the prebend of Husthwaite, Hugh Murdac was another canon, Adam of Thornovere another.

have reached England with the news of Henry's death; and it was afterwards said that he turned the fact of his holding the great seal to advantage, by sealing letters of collation to vacant prebends after his father's decease [1] and before the seal of the new king was made. If the charge is true, his purpose probably was to insure himself a certain party among the canons. Hoveden very justly remarks upon the act as disgraceful if true; [2] but it does not follow that anything was done without the direction of Henry, whose death was sudden and whose last commands were confided to Geoffrey. Richard seems to have had no fault to find with the nomination at first; Henry's promise made on the 4th or 5th of July at Chinon was confirmed by the new sovereign at Rouen, on the occasion of his investiture with the duchy of Normandy on the 20th of the same month,[3] and Geoffrey immediately despatched his officers with royal letters to York to replace those of the king and the dean, and to transact the business of the election, which must necessarily be conducted in canonical form. So little time was lost in doing this, that on the 10th of August the chapter assembled to make the election.

The prospect of having such an archbishop as Geoffrey after a long interval of quasi-independence was not very welcome to the York clergy; but at first they seem to have made the best of it. The archdeacon of Richmond, who probably saw the way to promotion open elsewhere, sent a letter of proxy to assent to it; [4] and a sufficient number of canons present followed the lead; but the act was not completed without a strong protest on the part of Master Bartholomew, the dean's official, who appealed to the pope against the election as invalid, in consequence of the absence of his principal, and of the bishop of Durham the only surviving suffragan. William of Newburgh tells us that the precentor was frightened into taking part; [5] but as we find him a little later good friends with Geoffrey, on whose support he may have reckoned in his pursuit of the treasurership, it is probable that he joined willingly in the election.

Geoffrey seems to have considered that his promptness in obtaining canonical election superseded the necessity of further watchfulness.

Marginal notes:
Geoffrey's misuse of his father's seal

The vacancies probably filled up by Henry before his death

Geoffrey's nomination confirmed by Richard

Election of Geoffrey by the chapter

Time lost by Geoffrey after the election

---

[1] Hoveden, iii. 274.
[2] That the accusation was rife seems to be shown by Giraldus, who mentions that Geoffrey immediately on his father's death sealed up the great seal with the seals of the barons who were present, and sent it to Richard (V. Galfr. p. 382). Richard himself believed or found it convenient to believe

the charge, and Geoffrey seems to have admitted or not to have contradicted it. Hoveden, iii. 274.
[3] Benedict, ii. 73.
[4] Benedict, ii. 77. Hoveden, iii. 7.
[5] W. Newb. lib. iv. cap. 2. Ralph de Diceto also mentions that Hamo published the election in place of the absent dean, c. 653.

He neglected to keep Richard in sight, and instead of following the court to England at once, spent some weeks in visiting his estates in Anjou and Touraine. Giraldus Cambrensis [1] alleges that he was reluctant to take orders, and so to cut himself off from a remote chance of succession to the throne. It is possible that there may be a grain of truth in the assertion ; that he was anxious to retain his hold on the see of York without taking orders until it was absolutely necessary ; it is also possible that Richard's design was to draw him into Holy Orders by the hope of the archiepiscopate, intending, as was afterwards done, that by means of pecuniary exactions and enforced exile he should be disarmed of any power that the position entitled him to. All this is, however, conjectural. The fact was that from the very moment that his promotion was announced a large

Opposition to his appointment by the queen, bishop Hugh, and the ministers

number of influences were set to work against him. Queen Eleanor naturally disliked her husband's natural son, whose behaviour to his father was in such strong contrast with that of her own children. Bishop Hugh de Puiset was very much disinclined to accept as his superior so energetic a person as Geoffrey, and was not without hope of obtaining the see of York for his nephew Bouchard.[2] The ministerial party, moved by Hubert Walter and represented by Ranulf Glanvill, remonstrated against the appointment ; and the canons who had been absent or in the minority at the election, moved also

Appeal of Hubert Walter

by Hubert Walter, pushed their appeal. This appeal was formally renewed by Hubert in the presence of five bishops, a few days after Richard's landing, at Winchester ; and the result was the issuing of a mandate from that place that the property, both temporal and

Geoffrey's servants displaced

spiritual, of the see should remain as it was at the death of the late king. In consequence of this Geoffrey's servants were displaced by those of the dean and the exchequer.[3]

He makes good his position with Richard

Geoffrey, finding that he was quickly losing the hold on his brother which the remorse consequent on his father's death had given him, now hastened to England, met the representatives of the chapter at London, and after a show of reluctance gave his formal consent to the election.[4] Thence he proceeded to Windsor, where after considerable difficulties he seems to have made good his position against all opponents, or perhaps to have outbid them in promises made to secure the fickle favour of Richard. He appeared at the coronation as elect of York ; [5] but the appeal probably rendered it necessary that the process of election should be renewed, or at all events receive papal confirmation.

At the council of Pipewell Richard attempted, by his distribution

[1] V. Galfr. pp. 382, 383.
[2] Ibid. p. 384.
[3] Ben. Pet. ii. 77.
[4] Gir. Camb. pp. 382, 333.
[5] Benedict, ii. 79.

of ecclesiastical patronage, to satisfy all the opposing interests involved   Promotions at the council of Pipewell
in this question.   To Geoffrey he gave the archbishopric ; Hubert
Walter was reconciled by his appointment to Salisbury ; Godfrey de
Lucy got his expected promotion at Winchester ; the bishop of
Durham obtained for Bouchard the treasurership of York, vacated
by Geoffrey, and gave his formal assent to the election of Geoffrey.[1]
The difficulties of the appointment were, however, complicated by the
conduct of Archbishop Baldwin, who, remembering the old strife
between York and Canterbury, forbade the consecration of Geoffrey
by any other bishop than himself.   This was especially unreasonable,   Appeal of Archbishop Baldwin
as Baldwin was now starting for the Crusade ; Geoffrey's confirma-
tion at Rome could not be transacted before he departed, and the
king had determined that Geoffrey should not set foot in England
during his absence.   Geoffrey does not seem to have been aware of   Geoffrey is ordained priest
this, for a week after the council he obtained priest's orders from the
bishop of Whithern at Southwell, and sent Adam of Thornovere to
Rome to apply for his pall ; [2] the king, however, forbade his sailing at
this time.

   At this juncture a little common sense and self-restraint might   His want of ordinary prudence
have stood Geoffrey in good stead.   He was eminently impracticable.
He had for the moment got rid of his most formidable difficulties ;
his rivals were provided for by promotion, and he himself was almost
in possession.   Richard had allowed him to visit his see, and had
commissioned him to go as far as the Tweed at the head of the
baronage of Yorkshire to meet William the Lion, whom he was to
conduct to Canterbury to do homage.   From Southwell he made
his way to York, where he speedily involved himself in new
troubles.

   Geoffrey had been at York sixteen years before, when as elect of   His visit to York
Lincoln he had headed the king's forces against the Mowbrays in
the great rebellion of 1174, and having beaten them had been
received in the ancient city in triumph.[3]   In that struggle he had
shown qualities that seemed beyond his years ; now, a man of
mature age, he showed a want of tact that would have been
remarkable in a boy.   The promotion of Hubert Walter had vacated   The new dignitaries there
the deanery, and the king had given it to Henry, brother of the great
William Marshall ; he and Bouchard de Puiset were now at York
waiting to be installed.   Although the king's right to fill up the
places, which became vacant during the vacancy of the see, seems to
have been fully recognised, Geoffrey was vexed to see himself deprived
of the two best preferments in his gift ; the precentor Hamo had
already, acting in the interest of the archbishop, refused to install

[1] Gir. Camb. p. 383.   [2] Benedict, ii. 92.
[3] Gir. Camb. V. Galfr. p. 379.

the new dignitaries on the ground that the right belonged to the
Geoffrey refuses to install them archbishop only. Geoffrey himself refused on the excuse that until
he was confirmed by the pope his acts would be liable to be invalidated.
The dean and treasurer hastened off to complain to the king.
Geoffrey was solemnly received in the minster, but as soon as the
news reached Richard he ordered all the lay estates of his brother
in England and France to be seized. He does not, however, seem to
have threatened his tenure of his canonical rights.

He conducts the king of Scots to Canterbury
From York Geoffrey proceeded northwards, met the king of Scots,
and brought him to Canterbury, where he found Richard's attitude
extremely threatening. His enemies had improved their opportunities. Hubert Walter, although now bishop of Salisbury, renewed
his claim ; Hugh de Puiset vouched for the uncanonical character
of Geoffrey's election ; stories of Geoffrey's private behaviour were
Renewed efforts of his enemies
invented and brought to Richard ; he had been used to put the cover
of a gold bowl on his head and say, 'Is not this head fit to wear a
crown ? ' and he had trodden underfoot a portrait of Richard, saying
that such a king as he ought so to be treated.[1] And now the
disappointed dean and treasurer put in their word ; the man was a
murderer, the son of an adulterer and a whore,[2] unworthy to be
promoted to the priesthood.

He goes to the legate and offends the king
Geoffrey, again unwisely, betook himself to John of Anagni, the
papal legate, who was then at Dover, and obtained from him
confirmation in defiance of these appeals ;[3] so little did he understand the nature of his brother. Richard was extremely indignant,
but there was a way in which his indignation could at any time be
assuaged. He extorted a promise from Geoffrey to pay him 2,000*l.* ;
the appeals were then withdrawn, the legate's confirmation recognised,
Richard is reconciled
and Geoffrey's possessions, personal and official, restored. He in
his turn had to confirm the appointments of the king's nominees,
and promised to renew the covenants which his predecessor had made
with the bishop of Durham.

Geoffrey goes again to York in January 1190
Again Geoffrey started for the north. The king left Dover on
December 11. Early in January the archbishop elect, the dean, and
the treasurer were at York ; and before the twelve days of Christmas
were over they were in a thicker fray than ever. On the eve of the
Epiphany the archbishop proposed to attend vespers in the minster
in state. The precentor Hamo and the other canons who were on
his side waited to receive him in procession. Whether Geoffrey was
behind time or not does not appear ; but when the procession reached
the choir they found that the candles were lighted and that the dean

---

[1] 'Suppeditari et subjici;' the
former word certainly implying a pun.
Gir. Camb. V. Galfr. p. 385.

[2] Benedict, ii. 99.
[3] Gir. Camb. 384, 385. Benedict,
ii. 99.

and treasurer had begun the service. So marked and gratuitous an insult roused Geoffrey at once, he commanded the choir to be silent, and the precentor in a more constitutional way seconded the command. The order was obeyed and Geoffrey himself began to sing the service; thereupon the treasurer ordered the candles to be extinguished: the management of the lights belonged to the treasurer as much as that of the singing did to the precentor; his command also was obeyed, and Geoffrey finished the vespers in the dark. When the service was over he protested loudly against the insult, and suspended the church from Divine service until an apology should be made him.[1]

He is insulted in the minster by the dean and treasurer

Geoffrey, although impracticable, was placable enough; on the following day he offered to meet the dean and treasurer and to receive amends. The church was full of clergy and citizens anxious, no doubt, to see the new archbishop and canons, as well as to witness the issue of the struggle. The two parties met in the choir, and Geoffrey was ready to be reconciled; but the two dignitaries not only refused an apology but tried to get up a demonstration against him. A riot followed; the citizens took Geoffrey's part, and were with difficulty restrained by him from falling on his opponents. Dismayed at the result, they had recourse to flight; one took refuge in the tomb of S. William, the other in the deanery. Unhappily Geoffrey was not now content with their discomfiture; he excommunicated them both and closed the church.[2]

He offers to be reconciled

Riot in the minster and flight of the dean

This unfortunate affray defeated one of the main objects of Geoffrey's visit. It offended Hugh de Puiset, who, as justiciar, forbade the tenants of the see to pay any money to the elect;[3] and it opened the eyes of the citizens to his uncertain tenure of his office, so that it was impossible to raise a loan. He had to follow Richard to France without the money that he had promised. He found him at Lions,[4] about Easter, told his story, and found himself again disseised. Not content with this, the king now sent the bishop of Bath, Reginald Fitz-Jocelin; Nicolas, dean of S. Julian's at Le Mans; and Bouchard de Puiset, to Rome to forbid his recognition by the pope.[5] For this, however, they were too late; Clement III. had already on March 7 confirmed the election and sent the pall.[6] After another tedious negotiation with Richard, in the course of which he offered to surrender the estates of the see for a yearly pension, he obtained grace. At Vézelai he paid 800 marks down;

Unfortunate consequences

Richard again offended

The pope confirms the election

[1] Hoveden, iii. 31, 32.
[2] Hoveden, iii. 32.
[3] Gir. Camb. p. 386.
[4] Gir. Camb. p. 386. Richard was at Lions in Easter week. Fœdera, i. 51.

[5] Gir. Camb. p. 386.
[6] Ralph de Diceto, 653. The pope mentions that Alexander III. had already granted Geoffrey a dispensation; from the bar, no doubt, of illegitimacy.

1,000*l.* the king forgave him ; the balance of the debt he was to account for at the Exchequer.[1]   Before he parted with Richard he had to swear that he would not return to England within three years.

Geoffrey retired to Tours, whence he sent his agents to Rome to watch the proceedings of his adversaries, and, if they could not obtain an order for his speedy consecration, to procure the cancelling of the letters which Hugh de Puiset had obtained releasing him from his dependence on the see of York.   Geoffrey's agents on this occasion were Simon of Apulia, an Italian lawyer, who had served Henry II., and whom he now, or a little later, made chancellor of York ; his friend Hamo the precentor ; William Testard, archdeacon of Nottingham, and Ralph Wigetoft, canon of Ripon ; all of whom, except the last, afterwards took a decided part against him.[2]

For a year and a quarter Geoffrey stayed at Tours.   During this time Longchamp was supreme in England ; Hugh de Puiset reduced to insignificance, and living at Howden ; the dean and treasurer allpowerful in York.   What little action was taken in his concerns was carried on at Rome and Messina.   In April 1191 Eleanor was instructed by Richard to inform the pope that the objections to his brother's consecration were removed.[3]   Celestine III., within a month of his own elevation to the papacy, issued an order to the archbishop of Tours to consecrate him, and on the 11th of May authorised him to exact from Bishop Hugh de Puiset the profession of obedience

which Clement III. had allowed him to decline.[4]   Of this Hugh was immediately informed by his agents, and forthwith appealed against it as involving a grievance to his church, placing his own person and church, with all its members, under the special protection of the Holy See.[5]

According to Giraldus, the archbishop had been released from his promise to stay away from England for three years, before he parted from Richard ; but the exact truth or falsehood of this statement has never been cleared up.[6]   He now prepared for his consecration and for his return home as soon as it should be completed.

He was consecrated by the archbishop of Tours in the church of S. Maurice at Tours on the 18th of August, and received the pall the same day from the abbot of Marmoutier.[7]   That done, he issued

a letter to the bishop of Durham to attend a synod of the province of York on the Monday after Michaelmas, in which he should both

[1] Gir. Camb. p. 387.
[2] Gir. Camb. p. 387.   William of Newburgh also mentions Simon of Apulia as the principal agent of the archbishop at Rome, lib. iv. cap. 17.
[3] Hoveden, iii. 100.
[4] This letter is printed in the Monasticon, vi. 1188.   The privilege

which Hugh had obtained from Clement III. is described by William of Newburgh, lib. iv. cap. 27.
[5] Hoveden, iii. 169.   Benedict, ii. 225.
[6] Gir. Camb. p. 387.
[7] Gir. Camb. p. 388.   Ralph de Diceto, c. 663.

renew his profession and give an account of his conduct in detaining
the procurations due to the see of York from the jurisdictions of
Allertonshire and Howdenshire.[1] On the receipt of this summons
Hugh again appealed to Rome.

The story of the landing of Geoffrey, his imprisonment and release, His landing,
the part he took in the humiliation of Longchamp, and the revolution imprison-
that followed, need not be told here.[2] He joined for a moment with share in the
Hugh de Puiset and William Marshall in this business, but almost Longchamp
before it was over the quarrel broke out again. Longchamp's deposition took place on the 10th of October. That done, Hugh laid
his case before the bishops. Geoffrey hastened by Northampton,
where he had studied in earlier years, and was still sufficiently popular
to be welcomed with a procession, to York, where he was enthroned He goes to
with great solemnity on All Saints' day.[3] Bishop Hugh failed to excommuni-
make his appearance, and after three citations,[4] to which he replied Hugh
by three appeals, was excommunicated, Geoffrey so far disregarding
moderate counsels as to direct that the sacred vessels in which Holy
Communion was celebrated in the bishop's presence should be broken
up, as polluted.[5] Hugh took up his residence again at Howden, Hugh con-
where John visited him at Christmas ; he also urged his appeal at sentence
Rome. Exasperated by this contempt, Geoffrey excommunicated him excommuni-
a second time in more violent terms than before, on Candlemas day cated, Feb. 2,
1192.[6]

Not content, apparently, with making one inveterate and powerful Appeal of
enemy, and involving himself in one suit at Rome, Geoffrey soon of Clemen-
after this excommunicated the prioress of Clementhorpe for resisting thorpe
his command to reduce her little nunnery to dependence on the
distant abbey of Godstow.[7] She also carried her wrongs to the pope.
The heavy hand of Geoffrey fell also on the chapter. Henry Marshall New appeals
and Bouchard de Puiset were stimulated by the bishop of Durham to canons, and
renew their appeals, and a new quarrel emerged, the causes of which munications
are obscure, but which alienated from the archbishop his old servant
Adam of Thornovere, Peter de Ros, the archdeacon of Carlisle, and
Hugh Murdac, another of the canons. As usual, Geoffrey excommunicated them, and as usual, they appealed.[8] Matters looked so
threatening that at Mid-Lent the queen summoned the two prelates to
London to compel them to keep the peace. They obeyed the sum- Failure of
mons ; Hugh offered to submit to the arbitration of the bishops, but attempt at a
Geoffrey insisted that he should sue to him for absolution and promise tion
obedience. Hugh answered that if that was the archbishop's view

---

[1] Hoveden, iii. 168, 169.
[2] See above, pp. 233–245.
[3] Gir. Camb. p. 400.
[4] Benedict, ii. 225, 226.
[5] Hoveden, iii. 169.

[6] Benedict, ii. 237.
[7] Hoveden, iii. 188.   Benedict, ii.
240.
[8] Benedict, ii. 248.

T

he would make no peace with him unless he would publicly confess

Geoffrey offends the bishops

that his sentence of excommunication was null. Geoffrey would not hear of this, and having added to the number of his enemies the bishop of London and other suffragans of Canterbury, whom he had outraged by having his cross borne erect at the Temple, returned somewhat discomfited to his own province.[1]

Commission of delegates on the quarrel with the bishop of Durham

It was just at this juncture that a commission was brought from Rome, directed to the bishops of Lincoln and Rochester and the abbot of Peterborough, ordering them to declare that the pope had annulled the sentence against Bishop Hugh ; [2] and further enjoining on them that, if on inquiry they found that the archbishop had issued the orders for destroying the sacred vessels, the bishop should no longer be bound to make his profession of obedience. The judges

Sittings of the delegates

delegate undertook to arrange this quarrel. After a hearing early in the spring they adjourned to Midsummer day, and from Midsummer day, as the bishop of Durham was absent from England, to the feast of S. Calixtus.[3] The other disputes Queen Eleanor and the justiciar, Walter of Coutances, took in hand. It was necessary to send Hugh de Puiset to France on important business ; he refused to go unless the questions were settled. Under this stimulus they issued per- emptory letters to Geoffrey to satisfy his discontented chapter, and directed William Stuteville, in case of his non-compliance, to seize the whole estates of the see.[4]

Apologies of the canons

It would have been madness to disobey such a monition ; for- tunately for Geoffrey, his opponents were growing tired of the contest.

Reconcilia- tion of all the digni- taries except the dean

Bouchard de Puiset, Adam of Thornovere, Hugh Murdac, and Peter de Ros consented to ask formally for absolution, and Geoffrey, in return for the concession, reinstated them in their stalls and emolu- ments.[5] Hamo and Bouchard also under his auspices patched up an agreement, by which they divided the revenue of the treasurership. Bouchard was to hold it for life, unless he changed his profession or received higher promotion ; Hamo in such case to have the re- version of the dignity. Only the dean held out, and against him the archbishop hurled an avalanche of curses, going so far as to place his metropolitan city under interdict so long as it was polluted by Henry Marshall's presence.[6]

---

[1] Benedict, ii. 238.

[2] Hoveden, iii. 170, 171. Benedict, ii. 245. The latter chronicle enu- merates here the privileges which Bishop Hugh acquired from Celestine III. No one was to have power to excommunicate him without special mandate from Rome. He was not to be required to make his profession at all. Hugh was not satisfied with this ;

he sent back his agents to demand entire independence of Geoffrey. The same conclusion is inferred from the language of William of Newburgh, lib. iv. cap. 27.

[3] Hoveden, iii. 172.

[4] Benedict, ii. 247.

[5] Benedict, ii. 248.

[6] Benedict, ii. 249.

At this point we lose the guidance of the Chronicle of Benedict, and Hoveden does not immediately take up the thread of the story; but it would appear from a scanty notice preserved by Gervase of Canterbury,[1] that the judges delegate arranged a reconciliation between Geoffrey and Hugh at Northampton in October, the old bishop consenting at last to recognise his canonical superior. The reconciliation lasted for some time, being no doubt strengthened by the union which was effected throughout the north against John, who had taken up arms on the news of his brother's imprisonment. The most obdurate of Geoffrey's opponents was also got rid of soon after. Richard whilst in Germany nominated the dean of York to the see of Exeter.

Up to this time we may fairly regard Geoffrey as not more sinned against than sinning. All the difficulties of his position, the provoking attitude of his opponents, the low standard of ecclesiastical morality, are insufficient to excuse the wanton exercise of the awful weapon of excommunication. Henceforth we see him the victim, not only of grossly unfair treatment by Richard, but of the less obvious persistent hostility of Hubert Walter, and of cruel ingratitude on the part of his own servants. His own conduct is as far as ever from being impeccable; he is still a violent, intemperate, impracticable man of the world, but he has no longer to contend with opponents whose party principles and prejudices palliate the guilt of their conduct towards him; his enemies are now the men whose fortunes he has founded, and for whom in great measure the actions have been done which gave an excuse for the enmity of his earlier foes.

The news of Richard's imprisonment reconciled him for a time with Hugh de Puiset, and the promotion of Henry Marshall delivered him from his greatest personal enemy in the chapter. But the necessities of Richard's ransom compelled him to take measures which alienated all his friends at York, whilst the negotiations for the appointment of a new dean resulted in the conversion of his oldest and most confidential servant into a bitter and inveterate personal enemy, whose conduct became a precedent and excuse for a long series of desertions. The promotion of Hubert Walter to the archbishopric of Canterbury, shortly followed by his nomination to the justiciarship, and a year later by his appointment as legate, placed the unfortunate and imprudent Geoffrey at the mercy of an old and honourable but still determined enemy.

Among the first persons in England to whom Richard in his great emergency applied for help in raising the ransom money was Geoffrey,[2] on whom, notwithstanding his treatment of him, he felt he

Marginal notes:
Reconciliation of the archbishop with Bishop Hugh in October 1192

Promotion of the dean

Geoffrey victimised by Richard, Hubert Walter, and his own servants

Geoffrey's impracticable character

Alienation of his friends in the chapter

Promotion of Hubert Walter

Richard asks Geoffrey's aid in the raising of his ransom

---

[1] Gervase, c. 1580, 1581.   [2] Hoveden, iii. 222.

could depend, both as his father's son, as an ally who had everything
to fear from John, and as a source of revenue which if fairly
managed would not be soon exhausted. Geoffrey showed the greatest
alacrity in taking up arms for the defence of Richard's rights ; and
with scarcely less zeal, tempered however by no slight misgivings,
he undertook to negotiate for supplies. He laid the matter of the
ransom before the Chapter of York ; [1] throughout the kingdom, he said,
it had been agreed that a very great sacrifice should be made, it was
necessary that they should offer a fourth part of their annual revenue.
Hoveden, in telling the story, rises in tone for the moment to dilate
on the ingratitude of the clergy. He called, counselled, entreated
those canons with whom he had had the most friendly relations,
whom he had enriched and promoted, to do this. They at once turned
round upon him, declared that he was attempting to destroy the
liberties of his church, and that from henceforth they would have
nothing more to do with him. The threat seems to have been
literally carried out. They left him to the company of his household
servants, closed the minster, forbade the ringing of the bells, stripped
the altars, locked up the archbishop's stall in the choir, and blocked
up the door by which he entered the church from his palace. Co-
incident with this unseemly state of things arose the quarrel with
Simon of Apulia.

This unprincipled adventurer we have already seen acting as
Geoffrey's confidential servant. He had been his agent at Rome in
1190 ; he it was who commanded the archbishop's retinue when he
returned to England : [2] and Geoffrey had rewarded him with the gift
of the chancellorship of York, and even promised him the reversion
of the provostship of Beverley. In gratitude and hope alike he might
have been patient with a master whose difficulties he knew better
than anyone else. The news of Henry Marshall's appointment to
Exeter reached Geoffrey whilst he was staying at Ripon,[3] and he
prepared to fill up the deanery. He had a brother named Peter,
probably, as he is not called son of Henry II., the son of his mother
by one of her other lovers. Peter had been made archdeacon of
Lincoln some years before. Geoffrey now proposed to make him dean
of York. He was, however, at Paris, and Richard had sent from
Germany an urgent letter desiring that John of Bethune, provost of
Douay and brother to the advocate Baldwin, who had accompanied
him on his return from Palestine and shared his captivity, should be
appointed. In order to avoid doing this, or leaving the preferment
open, Geoffrey consulted his two friends, Simon and Hamo, who
were with him at Ripon, and the result of the deliberation was

Marginal notes:
Refusal of the York clergy to submit to the exactions

They close the minster and block out the archbishop

Simon of Apulia deserts him and joins the enemies

Dispute as to the filling up the deanery

[1] Hoveden, iii. 222.   [2] Gir. Camb. p. 390.
[3] Hoveden, iii. 221.

that Simon was nominated. Shortly after, when the dread of Richard's interference had blown over, Geoffrey declared that he intended him merely as a stopgap for his brother Peter. Simon insisted that the appointment was *bona fide*, and threw himself on the sympathy of the discontented canons, helping, no doubt, to organise the opposition on the subject of the money grant. The chapter elected him to the deanery, and then Geoffrey, attempting to disarm Richard's anger, named to the same office Philip of Poictiers, the king's favourite chaplain and clerk, who became afterwards bishop of Durham. Simon of Apulia elected by the chapter

Both parties now appealed to Rome, and both took the precaution of laying the circumstances before the king in Germany. Simon visited Richard in person, and so got the first word. The king at first contented himself with forbidding the appeals and summoning Geoffrey into his presence; but finding that Geoffrey did not obey the summons, he allowed the canons free action against him.[1] Appeals on the subject of the deanery Richard connives

The archbishop's delay or disobedience was thus accounted for. He had started on the receipt of the king's order and had reached the coast, when the received the intelligence of the closing of the minster and the other outrageous doings of the chapter.[2] He immediately sent to York by his clerks a peremptory command to the clergy of the cathedral to return to their duties; this they treated with contempt, and the archbishop found that he must return in person. He did so, arrived at York on the first of January 1194, and found the church deserted.[3] Taking counsel, as Hoveden tells us, with prudent men, he substituted for the contumacious clerks another body of chaplains, and excommunicated the canons. The latter, determined to lose no time, sent four of their number to the king. These four were Hamo the precentor, who henceforth throws his influence into the scale against Geoffrey; Geoffrey Muschamp, archdeacon of Cleveland, for whom the archbishop had in earlier years obtained his prebend; William Testard, archdeacon of Nottingham, who, like Hamo, had in 1190 acted as his agent in Rome; and the archdeacon of the West Riding.[4] They reached Richard before he heard from his brother, took advantage of his momentary irritation, and obtained leave to carry their appeal to Rome. Simon of Apulia was allowed at the same time to prosecute his claim to the deanery, and the whole party proceeded to lay their complaints before Celestine III. A few Geoffrey fails to obey the king's summons He visits York and places his own clerks in the minster, in January 1194 Hamo and others now take part against him Simon goes to Rome

[1] Hoveden, iii. 229, 230.
[2] Hoveden, iii. 223. Gervase says that he had got a good way towards the sea, going by cross-country roads in order to carry his cross erect in the province of Canterbury; but was ordered back by the archdeacon of Canterbury, and returned to York, c. 1586. That was perhaps the Canterbury view of the story.
[3] Hoveden, iii. 229, 230.
[4] Hoveden, iii. 272.

days after, Richard's liberation was arranged, and in March he
returned to England.

Richard's
return to
England
With Richard's return began new complications for Geoffrey.
Nottingham, the first place to which Richard directed his way after
landing, was in Geoffrey's diocese. There Geoffrey met his brother
Prudence of
Geoffrey on
this occa-
sion
and was not unkindly received. He had the good sense even to
avoid giving new offence to Hubert Walter ; and, by not carrying
his cross erect, showed that he had placed himself under strong
restraint.[1]   Unfortunately this was not met with like moderation on
Hubert's part. He insisted on having his cross carried erect, and,
when Geoffrey remonstrated, somewhat insolently threw doubts on
his right to be regarded as archbishop, winding up with an appeal to
Rome against him.   Geoffrey complained to the king, who declined
to arbitrate, and recommended him not to appear with his cross at the
approaching coronation for fear of a quarrel.[2]   This caused Geoffrey
to absent himself from the coronation, but, anxious to maintain his
right, he presented himself to the king at Waltham, near Portsmouth,
with cross erect. It was now Hubert's turn to remonstrate, but
Richard refused to settle the dispute ; it was, he said, the pope's
duty, not his. Hubert nursed his anger till the king was gone.

He buys the
sheriffdom
of Yorkshire
Notwithstanding this rising cloud, the archbishop and the king
were on the best terms during Richard's visit. Geoffrey sat on the
king's left hand in the great council of Nottingham,[3] was allowed to
purchase the sheriffdom of Yorkshire for 3,000 marks,[4] and to treat
with contempt the complaints made against him by clerks and laymen of his diocese for pecuniary exactions, the secret of which was
well enough known to the king.[5] He attended the king also at Winchester and Portsmouth ; although he absented himself from the coro-
Richard re-
stores his
French
estates
nation, it was partly at the king's request.[6] Richard showed his sense
of this behaviour by restoring to him his estates in Anjou and Touraine,
and by compelling Longchamp to apologise for, or disavow in legal
form, the ill-treatment that Geoffrey had been subjected to at Dover
in 1191.[7]

His enemies
silenced
only for a
time
But although Richard may have been sincere in his desire of
peace and goodwill to the unfortunate Geoffrey, every glimpse of
good luck only served to enhance the disappointment which uniformly
followed. Hoveden himself exclaims against his folly in undertaking
the sheriffdom, and throwing himself into the power of the king in a
lay office. The complaints, which at Nottingham and in his brother's
presence he was strong enough to ignore, were only silenced for a

---

[1] Hoveden, iii. 239.
[2] Hoveden, iii. 246, 247, 250.
[3] Hoveden, iii. 240.
[4] Hoveden, iii. 241.

[5] Hoveden, iii. 242.
[6] Hoveden, iii. 246, 247.
[7] Hoveden, iii. 250, 251.

time. The ear of the justiciar was quick, where the king had been willingly deaf. The news from Rome also was untoward, and the dean and canons were on their way home.

The archbishop of Canterbury waited some months before he took the first step in accomplishing the ruin of the rival primate. In August or September, however, when Richard had got as far as Guienne, Hubert, in his character of justiciar, sent to York a commission of the royal judges, Earl Roger Bigot, William of Warenne, William Stuteville, Hugh Bardolf, William Briwere, Geoffrey Haget, and William FitzRichard, to hear the complaints of the canons. These barons carried matters with a high hand. The archbishop's servants who were accused of robbery they took and imprisoned ; they then summoned Geoffrey himself to appear before them.[1] He refused, took refuge in his manor at Ripon, and was declared contumacious. The whole estates of the see, with the exception of Ripon, were then taken possession of by the king's officers ; the canons were replaced in their stalls ; and although the justiciar did not venture to assume the sheriffdom or to remove Geoffrey's subsheriff, Roger of Batvent, he placed over them both, as *custodes*, William Stuteville and Geoffrey Haget.[2] This was one of the most arbitrary and high-handed proceedings of Hubert's ministry ; and hardly anything, either on moral, legal, or constitutional grounds, can be said in excuse for it. The restoration of the canons by force to the places which they had deserted, and to which they had refused to return at the orders of the archbishop, was extremely irregular ; and the whole transaction is a serious blot on Hubert's fame.

Scarcely had Geoffrey realised the blow that personal enmity had directed, when the appellants arrived in triumph from Rome. The same month, before Michaelmas, Hamo and the archdeacons of Cleveland and Nottingham presented themselves with papal letters.[3] They had had indeed signal success. Simon of Apulia had been confirmed in the deanery by the pope, the sentences of excommunication issued against the canons had been annulled, and a mandate issued for the restoration of their ecclesiastical rights and properties, which had been already effected by the authority of the justiciar. But this was not all : Celestine III. by letters dated May 31 had commissioned the dean of Lincoln and the archdeacons of Leicester and Northampton to compel the archbishop not merely to restore the property, but to give satisfaction for the loss involved in the

Side notes:
Visitation of the justices at York

They take possession of the lands of the see, and restore the canons

Unjustifiable conduct of the ministers

Return of the appellants from Rome, September 1194

Two commissions on the archbishop's acts issued by Celestine III.

---

[1] Hoveden, iii. 261, 262.
[2] Roger de Batvent acts as undersheriff to Geoffrey to the end of Richard's reign, as may be ascertained from the Pipe Rolls ; at the same time it seems very probable that Geoffrey never paid the 3,000 marks which he had bid for the office. This sum was still due in 1200. Hoveden, iv. 140.
[3] Hoveden, iii. 272.

seizure of it, and empowered them to assess the damages ; [1] a week
after, he issued a second commission to the bishop of Lincoln, the
archdeacon of Northampton, and the prior of Pomfret,[2] in which
he rehearsed the heavy charges laid by the clergy of the province
and confirmed by the evidence of thirteen abbots, eleven of them

Charges
against him

Premonstratensian, against Geoffrey. In these the archbishop is
described as neglecting all the duties of his high office, as spending
his time in hunting and hawking ; he never holds ordinations or
synods or consecrates churches ; the only spiritual function he

Points to be
examined
by the dele-
gates

discharges is excommunication ; he destroys the liberties of the
Church, prevents appeals to the Holy See, and frustrates by violence
the execution of its commands ; he misuses his patronage in the
most shameless way, shows a marked contempt of the religious
orders, and has robbed and maltreated his own canons. The delegates
are empowered to hear evidence and send it sealed to Rome. If
there be a lack of evidence the archbishop is to be made to find
compurgators, three bishops and three abbots : if he fail to do that,
notwithstanding the lack of evidence, he is to be deposed. If, however, he has before receiving their citation appealed to Rome, they
are to give him three months' notice, at the expiration of which he
must appear at Rome. A more outrageous sentence on an ex-parte
statement was never issued, nor is it to be supposed that Celestine,
arbitrary and violent as he was, would have condescended to such
injustice except under strong pressure. It is to be feared that the
measure was pressed by the whole force of the royal agents acting
under Hubert Walter's direction. The fact that the eleven complaining abbots were Premonstratensians, members of an order
specially affected by Hubert,[3] looks like a strong confirmation of this
conjecture.

Privileges
granted at
Rome to the
chapter of
York

But the canons had not been content with this : they had procured
a privilege which was to preserve them against all attacks, not only
of Geoffrey but of any other archbishop ; this is dated on the 16th of
June. It first confirms the dean and chapter in the possession of all
their estates, customs, and liberties in the ordinary form of charters,
but then goes on to direct that the archbishop shall not have the
power to issue sentence against any member of the chapter without
the consent of the whole body, nor to relax sentences issued by them

---

[1] Hoveden, iii. 285, 286.
[2] Hoveden, iii. 279–281.
[3] Hubert's abbey, founded at West
Dereham, was Premonstratensian, and
in his final concord with the monks of
Canterbury he proposed to erect a
similar house at Lambeth. Ranulf
Glanvill, his uncle, founded another,

Leystone, in Suffolk ; Glanvill's son-
in-law, William of Auberville, founded
Langdon, in Kent ; Helewisia, daughter
of Glanvill, founded Coverham Abbey
in Yorkshire. A large proportion of
the Premonstratensian houses in
England were thus founded by Hubert's
kinsfolk.

against their enemies ; that the dean shall not do homage to the archbishop ; that the archbishop's nominees to the vacant stalls shall be made to take an oath to the dean and chapter, and be installed by the precentor under the mandate of that body, and that if the archbishop shall fail to fill up the vacancies within the time prescribed by the Lateran Council, the chapter shall do it in his place by apostolic authority and without appeal.[1]   The last of these powers they intended to use with unscrupulous pertinacity against the archbishop.

We are not to suppose that all these letters were produced at once, although probably the archbishop's agents would be able to guard him against a surprise.   The mandate for the restoration of the canons was, however, published on Michaelmas day by Hugh de Puiset,[2] and the report of the further measures in contemplation had the effect of hurrying Geoffrey to Normandy.   He first appealed against the papal sentence and then betook himself to the king, who for a payment of 2,000 marks ordered him to be reinstated in all his rights and properties, and to be no longer molested by lay power in the exercise of his spiritual functions.   This decision of Richard, dated at Mamers on the 3rd of November,[3] had the affect of annulling the proceedings taken by the justiciar in September.   At the same time the king, at Geoffrey's instigation, directed that the estates of three of the canons, Geoffrey archdeacon of Cleveland, William of Stigandby, and Master Erard, should be seized, as their title to the preferment was insufficient.   These were the men whose collations had been sealed by Geoffrey as chancellor after his father's death ; they had turned against him the power which his carelessness or chicanery had placed in their hands.[4]   Having gained these advantages Geoffrey determined to continue by his brother's side at least until the first violence of the papal procedure should have broken, or more favourable terms could be obtained from Rome.   He appointed as his officials at York Master Honorius and Gerard de Rowell,[5] on whom devolved the burden of defending his interests in his absence.   He himself did not return to England until after Richard's death.

The year 1195 opened with a tardy attempt on the part of the judges delegate to examine into the charges against the archbishop. The bishop of Lincoln and his colleagues had given Geoffrey ample time to appeal.   On the 15th of January they formally began proceedings at York, heard evidence on both sides, and in accordance with their instructions directed both parties to present themselves at Rome on the 1st of June.[6]   About the same time, apparently, the

Marginal notes:
Restoration of the canons, Sept. 29

Geoffrey goes to Normandy and purchases Richard's goodwill in November

Geoffrey stays at court

He appoints Honorius as his official

Proceedings of the delegates at York in January 1195

---

[1] It is printed in Wilkins, *Concilia*, i. 503.
[2] Hoveden, iii. 272, 273.
[3] Hoveden, iii. 274.
[4] Hoveden, iii. 274.
[5] Hoveden, iii. 298.
[6] Hoveden, iii. 230, 231, 278–282.

other commission which was directed to assess the damages of the canons held two sittings, one at Torksey, the other at Ancaster, and having heard the claims of the injured parties adjudged the archbishop to pay them a thousand marks.[1]

A month after the opening of the commission, the new dean, Simon of Apulia, made his appearance at York ; before he reached the gates he was met by a large party of citizens and clergy ; he produced letters of confirmation from both the pope and the king, and insisted on being received as dean. Two of the archbishop's adherents, Master John Otui and William de Bonneville, protested against this being done until the whole controversy was settled, and in their intemperate zeal laid hands on Simon. He, in the usual way, replied by excommunication. The citizens thereupon gave way and deserted the assailants. He made his way to the minster and was received by the canons in procession on the 12th of February, and on the 15th the bishop of Durham visited the church and confirmed the sentence issued by him against the archbishop's friends.

This was Hugh de Puiset's last public act ; he was taken ill, on his way from York to London, at Doncaster, and died at Howden on the 3rd of March.[2]

Although Hugh de Puiset had not taken an overt part against Geoffrey since Richard's return, he had generally been found ready to help the other side. His death, no doubt, delivered the archbishop from a dangerous rival. It would, however, have been absurd in Hugh to have joined in the accusations made against Geoffrey at Rome, as nearly all of them might have been brought with much greater plausibility against himself.

The absence of Geoffrey and the death of Hugh de Puiset left the north of England without a resident bishop. The approach of Easter made it an important question to what source the clergy should look for the supply of chrism, the consecration of which ought to take place on Maundy Thursday. Geoffrey's suffragan, Bishop John of Whithern, came to York a few days before, and offered to perform the ceremony, but the dean and chapter refused his services ; he went on to Southwell and did it there, the archbishop's officials undertaking the distribution of it. It is a sign of

---

[1] Hoveden,iii. 286. William Testard, in 1197, paid 300 marks into the Exchequer, ' pro habendo archidiaconatu suo, secundum quod ei adjudicatus fuit a judicibus delegatis.' Madox, *Hist. Exch.* 336. Simon of Apulia, in 1195, paid 666*l*. 13*s*. 4*d*., ' de dono suo ' (Rot. Pip. 7 Rich. I.), and in the eighth year, 1196, Master Erard, the archdeacon of Cleveland, and William of Stigandby owed 100*l*. for recovering the king's favour. In this case Simon's payment at least must have been equivalent to a purchase of his preferments, but it was perhaps dictated by a sense of prospective favours.

[2] Hoveden, iii. 283–285.

the prevalent spirit that the archdeacon of Cleveland on the receipt of the sacred substance threw it on a dunghill. The York clergy applied to Hugh of Lincoln for a supply, but here Archdeacon Peter, the archbishop's brother, interposed and forbade the bishop to grant their request, appealing to Rome on his behalf.[1] Contempt of the chrism

Hubert Walter had now an opportunity of showing his contempt for Geoffrey. The pope had made him on the 18th of March legate of all England. His first measure under his new powers was to come and hold a visitation at York. He came as justiciar as well as legate, on the 11th of June; on the 12th his officers held assizes; on the 13th he visited St. Mary's and deposed the abbot; and on the two following days held a council at which the leading members of the chapter, Simon, Hamo, and the archdeacons of Cleveland and Nottingham attended.[2] The canons passed at his council are important, but they cannot be shown to have any special bearing on the state of the Church in the province, or on the quarrels with Geoffrey. Although the act of visitation was one of ostentatious contempt, it could hardly have done any harm to the latter; the legate was morally restrained from any substantial injustice; and the only question touching Geoffrey's interests which arose on the occasion was left undecided. The archdeaconry of the West Riding, vacant by death, had been given by Geoffrey first to his brother Peter, who wisely kept out of the hornet's nest, and then to Peter of Dinan, chancellor of Brittany. Peter of Dinan on this occasion demanded installation; the dean and chapter insisted that the appointment under Pope Celestine's recent charter had lapsed to them; Geoffrey's officials appealed, and Hubert, not seeing his way to a decision, allowed their appeal to stand.[3] Hubert paid a second visit to York at Christmas, but nothing seems to have been done affecting the main question. On one of these two occasions the archbishop's officials refused to receive him as legate, and were in consequence removed by him; but on consideration he restored them, and they retained their authority until the arrival of the sentence from Rome.[4] Hubert becomes legate He visits York as legate and justiciar, June 1195 Results unimportant Hubert avoids involving himself in the local quarrel

In the meantime Geoffrey, in attendance on his brother, was letting matters go against him by default at both York and Rome. The 1st of June came, and he did not present himself to the pope. Proceedings at Rome

[1] Hoveden, iii. 286, 287.

[2] Hoveden, iii. 292–298. W. Newb. lib. v. cap. 12. The latter writer accounts for the conduct of the canons in attending this visitation thus: 'legato potius, quem amicum et patronum optabat, maluit subjici, quam illius [sc. Gaufridi] non frænandam potentiam experiri.' He mentions a privilege acquired by the church of York a few years before, exempting the archbishop and the church from legatine visitation. This must have been the privilege overruled by Celestine III. in his commission to Hubert. Hoveden, iii. 291.

[3] Hoveden, iii. 297, 298.

[4] Hoveden, iii. 316, 317.

Celestine, unwilling to be harsh with him, prolonged the day of grace until the 18th of November. No appearance was entered then, and, a month after, definite sentence was issued ; Geoffrey, as contumacious, was suspended from his spiritual functions, and the administration of the diocese was committed to the dean. Three sets of letters were despatched on the 23rd of December, to the dean, to the clergy, and to the judges delegate ; the last enjoining the continuation of the inquiry and the furthering of additional evidence to Rome.[1]

The archbishop is suspended, December 1195

This last injunction was probably the result of an application of the canons who were offended at the remissness of the judges delegate ; they had applied for a decree of suspension against Geoffrey, which S. Hugh had refused, declaring that he would rather be suspended himself than suspend the archbishop.[2] Richard was now growing tired of his brother's company. More than once they had had to renew their reconciliation ; but Geofrey, as imprudent as ever, bethought himself at last of rebuking Richard for his sins. This was more than the king at the moment would stand. He went into a violent passion, and directing that he should be disseised both of his archiepiscopal estates and of the sheriffdom.[3]

S. Hugh of Lincoln refuses to deprive Geoffrey

Geoffrey offends the king again

The papal mandates reached York early in 1196 ; the archbishop's officials were removed, the dean undertook the spiritual jurisdiction, and for the time had reached the summit of his ambition. Geoffrey, on hearing the news, made his way at last to Rome, where he appears to have arrived in the spring. With some difficulty he obtained a hearing from Celestine, who was justly provoked at his contumacy ; that hearing, however, served materially to alter the complexion of affairs. The accusers admitted that they were unable to prove the charges, and a complete acquittal followed. New letters were issued declaring the innocence of Geoffrey, and ' insinuating ' that the accusations were false and fictitious.[4]

He goes to Rome early in 1196

The pope issues letters in his favour

Richard's indignation at this news seems to prove that his previous show of reconciliation, however often repeated, was insincere, and that his sole purpose throughout the struggle was to wring money from Geoffrey ; whilst they were friends he extorted it in one way, when they quarrelled he confiscated the estates of the see. He now saw that the papal acquittal would make Geoffrey practically independent of him ; he immediately directed that the sentence should be ignored, and took upon himself the bestowal of the vacant preferments. Geoffrey, hearing this, returned from France, which he had already reached on his way home, and retired to Rome.[5] We lose

Richard opposes the restoration of the archbishop

Geoffrey goes again to Rome

---

[1] Hoveden, iii. 231, 281, 309–319.
[2] Hoveden, iii. 305, 306.
[3] Hoveden, iii. 287.
[4] Hoveden, iv. 7.
[5] Hoveden, iv. 8.

sight of him for some time : he probably remained, if not at Rome, out of Richard's reach for more than a year. During this time very untoward reports were brought to England. Ralph of Wigetoft, Geoffrey's agent at Rome, being on his deathbed, confessed to the pope that he had sent forged letters to England. Celestine warned Hubert Walter of this, and by his commands Roger of Ripon, the bearer of Ralph's letters, was arrested, and a quantity of poison found upon him. This he declared his master had given him to poison Dean Simon, who accordingly was summoned to London ; the poison, in the shape of gold rings and a belt, was presented to him, and, with the letters, burnt at Tothill fields. The bearer of them was imprisoned. The story, of which the details are very suspicious, was made a ground for new charges against Geoffrey.[1]

Rumours of poison and forged letters

The peremptory action of Richard decided the struggle for the York preferments against the archbishop, whose absence in 1196 lost him some very fine windfalls. Bouchard de Puiset died, and poor Hamo was again disappointed of the treasurership ; the king gave it to Master Eustace, the keeper of his seal ; William de Chimeli was made a bishop, and the archdeaconry of Richmond was likewise bestowed on Eustace. Peter de Ros, archdeacon of Carlisle, died and his stall was given to Aimeri Thebert, nephew of the new bishop of Durham, who had succeeded Bouchard in his Durham preferment.[2] In all these cases Geoffrey's claims were passed over, and the chapter did not venture to assert their right against the king. Richard further nominated Adam of Thornovere, Geoffrey's old servant and recent opponent, to the archdeaconry of the West Riding ; but Peter of Dinan, whom the archbishop himself had appointed, managed also to obtain a nomination from the king. The two claimants thereupon agreed to divide the revenues of the office, and to occupy the archdeacon's stall, when they both happened to be in York, on alternate days.[3]

New appointments to the York dignities

Matters languished on until the spring of 1198, and Richard then set himself in earnest to remedy the disgraceful state of anarchy which had so long prevailed. Early in the year he summoned Geoffrey to court, to meet the dean and canons. Geoffrey arrived first, found Richard placable, and made his peace with him once more, Richard on this occasion promising that he would not again interfere with the bestowal of his patronage. He also granted him full restitution, and sent one of his clerks with Honorius, Geoffrey's official, to England to enforce it. Geoffrey was not to return immediately to England, but to go to Rome on the king's business ; he set off for Rome ; two days after his departure the dean and canons arrived at court, and so worked on the king that he delayed the restitution of

Richard's attempts in 1198 to reconcile the archbishop and the canons

Defeated by Dean Simon.

---

[1] Hoveden, iv. 15, 16.   [2] Hoveden, iv. 12, 14.   [3] Hoveden, iv. 8, 9.

the archbishopric until Geoffrey's return ; and this done, not being anxious to face the archbishop, they hastened back in triumph to York.[1]

New attempt on the king's part.

Several events were now making it extremely necessary that a decision should be come to. Celestine III. was dead, and Innocent III. was likely to look upon matters with much clearer eyes than his predecessor. Hubert Walter's influence with Richard was becoming smaller, and within a few months he had to resign the justiciarship. The promotion of Eustace the chancellor, and Geoffrey Muschamp, opened again the question of the preferments.[2] The news of the pope's death seems to have stopped Geoffrey on his way to Rome ; he returned to the king at Andely, and Simon and the canons were

He proposes an arbitration.

The negotiations again broken off by the chapter.

recalled to meet him.[3] Richard proposed an arbitration : the archbishop of Rouen and the bishops of Winchester and Worcester would act as umpires. Geoffrey consented ; the dean and canons refused ; they demanded a tribunal consisting of secular canons only, and insisted that before the general question was discussed the archbishop should confirm them all in the preferments which the king had given them. Their arguments weighed with Richard more than can be accounted for, if he were moved by argument alone. He broke off the negotiation and sent back the canons more jubilant than ever.[4]

The treasurership and archdeaconries of Richmond and Cleveland were now vacant. The first of these was at last handed over to Hamo, and the precentorship vacated by his promotion was given to Reginald Arundel. The archdeaconry of Richmond Geoffrey bestowed

Geoffrey bestows the archdeaconry of Richmond on Honorius

on his official Honorius, exacting from him, however, the concession of the right of institution to benefices, a peculiar right of the archdeaconry given in the time of Henry I. as compensation for the loss of the jurisdiction in the new diocese of Carlisle.[5] Honorius had been until now a faithful servant of Geoffrey ; on his promotion he, like Simon of Apulia and with a somewhat similar excuse, turned against him and involved him in another long litigation. He now hastened into Yorkshire, received the submission of the clergy, and presented his letters of appointment at York.[6] But Simon was ready

Opposition of the dean.

for him. The letters were informal, they did not mention the dean ; moreover, the king had nominated Roger of S. Edmund, and by virtue of the privilege of Pope Celestine Roger was installed ;

One canon only takes Geoffrey's side.

Honorius appealed, but was sent about his business. Hoveden adds that but one of the canons, Hugh Murdac, who on a previous occasion had taken part against Geoffrey, now refused to join in the conspiracy

---

[1] Hoveden, iv. 44, 45.
[2] Hoveden, iv. 41, 45.
[3] Hoveden, iv. 51, 52.
[4] Hoveden, iv. 53.
[5] Hoveden, iv. 177–180.
[6] Hoveden, iv. 52.

against him, and was excommunicated by the dean.[1] He had appealed before the sentence, but the violent and unscrupulous Italian showed no regard to this, and on Hugh's presenting himself in the choir he ordered the candles to be extinguished and stopped the service.

He is excommunicated

On the failure of the negotiations at Andely, Geoffrey proceeded to Rome and laid his case before the new pope. Innocent III. saw through the duplicity of the king, the unscrupulous craft of Simon, and the wrong-headedness of Geoffrey; he wrote to Richard begging him to be reconciled with his brother, and holding out an indistinct threat of interdict if he should not. Richard thereupon made a last attempt at compromise; he sent the bishops of Durham, Ely, Winchester, Worcester, and Bath to propose peace; Geoffrey was to confirm the king's gifts; the king would then restore him to his see.[2] Geoffrey demurred; would the mediating bishops put their advice on record that it might go sealed to the pope? They refused, and the treaty was again broken off. Geoffrey returned to Rome and obtained a decision in his favour on all points. The king's agents reported to him that this was to be enforced by interdict. Before, however, the letters were issued, April 28, 1199, Richard was dead. Geoffrey had advanced eight days' journey from Rome when he heard of it; he returned, to make assurance doubly sure, to the holy city.[3]

Return of Geoffrey to Rome : Innocent III. writes in his favour

Failure of a new attempt at compromise

Letters of restoration

Death of the king

Much of the interest of the contest now terminates. John, at all events at this period of his life, did not dislike Geoffrey so much as Richard had done. The difference in their age, probably, precluded the feeling of personal rivalry, which had embittered the relations of Richard with a brother whose early exploits and military accomplishments were little inferior to his own. In the great struggle of 1191 John had taken the part of Geoffrey, and before the papal sentence in his favour reached England the change of sovereign had had the effect of improving the archbishop's prospects. Honorius was immediately received as archdeacon of Richmond;[4] Simon thereupon excommunicated him, and John was obliged peremptorily to direct the status quo to be observed until he should be able to decide. His decision, promulgated a few weeks after his coronation, was in Geoffrey's favour. Whilst still in England he ordered that the archbishop's manors should be restored as soon as he returned. The brothers met at Rouen on the 24th of June; several of the canons placed their presentations in the hands of Geoffrey as having been illegally acquired, and he proceeded to readjust them as equitably as he could. Adam of Thornovere, the dean Simon, the new precentor, and others still held out.[5]

Relations of John and Geoffrey

Improvement in Geoffrey's prospects

Restoration of Geoffrey

---

[1] Hoveden, iv. 53.   [2] Hoveden, iv. 66, 67.   [3] Hoveden, iv. 67, 92.
        [4] Hoveden, iv. 89.   [5] Hoveden, iv. 93.

Mediation of Peter of Capua

Cardinal Peter of Capua had been sent by Innocent to arrange, if possible, the many causes of discontent and trouble now operating in both England and France, and so pave the way to a new crusade. Under his influence the two parties agreed to accept as arbitrators the bishop of Lincoln and Master Columb, the pope's subdeacon ; but the influence of Hubert Walter and Geoffrey FitzPeter was used to prevent the completion of any arangement, and mutual recriminations at first seemed the only result.[1]

Formal peace concluded in 1200

At last, towards the end of the year 1200, a formal peace was concluded at Westminster. Bishop Herbert of Salisbury and Abbot Alan of Tewkesbury, the last judges delegate appointed by the pope, were accepted as arbitrators ; after long discussion Geoffrey received to the kiss of peace, first his old ungrateful servant William Testard, then Reginald Arundel the precentor, and at last Dean Simon himself. Personal enmity being at an end, all further questions were to be settled in the chapter-house at York.[2]

Quarrel of Geoffrey with John

The great ecclesiastical dispute ends here. The peace settled no principle, for no principle was involved in the quarrel. It would be well if we could assert that Geoffrey had learned wisdom and moderation by it. But this was not the case. A month was scarcely over when he rushed into a quarrel with John. The king had summoned him to go to France ; he had neglected to obey ; he had refused to let his tenants pay the carucage ; John was provoked ; Geoffrey was again dispossessed by the sheriff of Yorkshire, his own tenure of the sheriffdom having at last expired ; and he retaliated by excommunicating, not only the sheriff and all his abettors, but all those who had irritated the king against him. At the same time he excommunicated the townsmen of Beverley for breaking into his park.[3]

Moderation of John on this occasion

John, acting under good advice, tried to avoid another struggle. The archbishop, in resisting the royal exactions, would have a strong party on his side, the same party, in fact, that he had formerly alienated by the exactions he had made in the interest of Richard ; the king ordered his estates to be restored on the understanding that he should give an account of himself before the Curia Regis, and pay a sum of three thousand marks which he owed king Richard.[4] Some insults offered by his servants to John, on his visit to Beverley in January 1201, embittered matters still further, but at

Geoffrey purchases his favour

Mid-Lent he received his brother at York and made peace again with a pecuniary fine ; and in May John issued a full charter of restitution in return for a promise of a thousand pounds sterling, for the payment of which the archbishop pledged his barony to the king.[5]

[1] Hoveden, iv. 99.   [2] Hoveden, iv. 126.   [3] Hoveden, iv. 139, 140.
[4] Hoveden, iv. 140.   [5] Hoveden, iv. 157, 163.

At this point Hoveden's chronicle ends ; but we leave Geoffrey, although reconciled with John, again engaged in a struggle with the chapter. The suit of Honorius was still being prosecuted.[1] Reginald of Arundel the precentor was dead ; Geoffrey nominated a new one ; the dean objected. Geoffrey appointed his official, Ralph of Kyme, to the archdeaconry of Cleveland, which he had unwisely left unclaimed since 1198 ; the dean declared that it had lapsed, and that the chapter had presented Hugh Murdac. Geoffrey insisted on installing Ralph ; Simon insisted that only the precentor could lawfully install, and now there was no precentor. So Geoffrey excommunicated Hugh Murdac, whom two years before the dean had excommunicated as his partisan.[2] Next the provost of Beverley died. Geoffrey appointed his brother Morgan ; Simon appealed against this on the ground that the archbishop had promised the reversion of the provostship to himself, the bitterest, most ungrateful, most unscrupulous of his foes ![3]

Such was the atmosphere in which the last days of Roger Hoveden were spent ; an atmosphere so redolent of curses that one cannot wonder at his belief that the devil was just then unloosed. Reflexions on the story are needless.

Archbishop Geoffrey lived for more than ten years after our chronicle closes. His struggles with the dean and canons continue, but they are lost sight of in the more important contests into which he was forced by John's unconstitutional demands for money. He never again was brought so low as he had been under Richard, but in 1207 he was compelled to choose between unconditional submission to John and exile. He chose the latter ; left England, rather than pay the sums demanded by the king, and never returned. He died in 1212, and was buried in the church of the order of Grandmont, Notre Dame du Parc, in the neighbourhood of Rouen.[4] His character has been variously read ; all things considered he seems to have resembled Richard in his nobler traits and

Marginal notes: New quarrels with the chapter — Constant quarrels of the dean and archbishop — Atmosphere of Hoveden's last days — Conclusion of Geoffrey's adventures — Character of Archbishop Geoffrey

[1] Hoveden, iv. 177–184.
[2] Hoveden, iv. 158.
[3] Hoveden, iv. 174.
[4] Dr. Ducarel saw his monument with this epitaph :—

 'Regis erat natus, meritis et honore
   probatus,
 'Vermibus esca datus, his qui jacet
   incineratus.
 'Hic quid opes sequeris, quid, homo,
   fugientia quæris ?
 'Hoc speculo quid eris, finemque
   tuum mediteris.

 'Cur fundum fundo cumulas, quadrasque rotundum ?
 'Stercus in immundum tandem restat tibi fundum.
 'Sed vivas mundo ut sis salvus a morte secundo.'

Ducarel, *Anglo-Norman Antiquities*, p. 38. It is interesting to observe that he was buried in a church of the Good Men of Grandmont, as his father had wished to be. The day of his death was Dec. 18. Stapleton, *Norman Rolls*, ii. clxx.

in his least repulsive faults ; to have been generous, impulsive, and open-hearted ; his sufferings were the result, firstly, of his unhappy position, laying him open to insult and extortion, and increasing his natural irritability ; secondly, of that thoughtless, violent, impracticable temperament, which made him the victim of unscrupulous opponents, and which seemed to justify the oppressiveness of his brothers and the ingratitude of his servants. Like Ishmael, his hand was against every man, and every man's hand against him. Otherwise he left behind him the reputation of personal temperance and a pure life.

II. The special importance of the ministerial career of Archbishop Hubert Walter arises from the facts, first, that being the nephew, pupil, and confidential friend of Ranulf Glanvill, the prime minister of Henry II., and having occupied a position involving constant and close intercourse with that king during the latter years of his life, he must be regarded as the most likely person to have had a thorough acquaintance with the principles that guided the reforms of Henry's reign, and as probably developing those principles in the changes or improvements which he adopted when he was himself practically supreme ; and, secondly, that the period during which he either exercised the authority of the crown as justiciar, or in his offices of chancellor, archbishop, and legate brought his powerful influence to

bear on the sovereign as well as the people, was the last period of orderly government that preceded the granting of Magna Carta. On Hubert's death the regular administration of the country was thrown out of gear by the tyrannical conduct of John, who had felt himself under the influence of his minister, as long as he lived, to a degree which mere gratitude and the sense of his usefulness can only insufficiently explain.

Hubert's advice had been with Richard all-powerful ; with John it had a certain weight, sufficient to modify if not to overrule his self-willed behaviour ; he exercised a control, the removal of which was felt by the king as a great relief, whilst the nation, with whom, as his master's servant, he had never been popular, found almost immediately that in him they had lost their best friend, the only bulwark strong enough to resist or to break the attack of royal despotism.

In tracing, through the measures of Hubert and the men of his school, certain steps of growth and development which connect the legal reforms of Henry II. with the improved sense of public law and national right that find their expression in the Great Charter, I am not so rash as to claim for him the character of a great politician, or even a consciously intentional programme for the education of the people for the exercise of self-government. The utmost that could be predicated of him in that direction would be that he was wise enough to see that an extension of self-agency on the part of the people, in the lines in which they were accustomed to act for local business, was a pledge of peace and good behaviour ; that the more they could be made to perceive that every man has a stake in the public weal, and may take a share in the maintenance of the public peace, the more certain would be the dependence of the commonwealth on the people ; the more thorough and lasting the peace, the safer and quieter the country, the more ready and the more able it would be to supply the wants of the crown.

The growth of our constitution was never, at least during the middle ages, sensibly affected by philosophical or doctrinaire views. The several steps of growth have been almost always of a character that might seem accidental, were it not that even in their most experimental forms they testify to an increasing confidence on the part of the rulers in the wisdom of trusting to the people, and a corresponding sense on the people's part of the wisdom of a just and moderate use of their powers, as the surest way to retain and increase them. For example, in the process by which the custom of county representation—itself being, as the concentration of all local machinery, the basis of English self-government—reached its growth, no step is more certain or important than that by which the principle of electing knights representative to choose the grand juries and recognitors of the assizes was introduced. Yet no one will for a moment think of asserting that that custom was introduced in order to make a conscious advance towards the working out of the principles of liberty. Neither, when we regard the custom of assessment by jury as a step in the education of the people towards taking the command of the national purse, do we for a moment contemplate that education as a purpose in the mind of the ministers who originated the plan. The result is not accidental, because it sprang from the increase of confidence between the governors and the governed, and proceeded by the evolution of principles the working of which we can trace in measures which suggested themselves as the readiest for the moment and occasion ; but were it not for this, it might seem as if the end and the means had only the most casual connexion. And so throughout the whole story. The English constitution owes all in it that is peculiar to itself to the accumulation of precedents that were found to answer other ends than those for which they were originally devised ; it is full of anomalies and abounds in checks and counterchecks which would be intolerable in an ideal polity ; its history is a very chapter of accidents and experiments until it is read in the light of this truth.

As law took the place of despotism, and organisation succeeded to routine ; as peace and security increased wealth, and the conscious-ness of wealth made peace and security more precious ; as the people educated themselves, by the exercise of their judicial and economical powers on a small scale, for the exercise of the same powers on a great scale ; the advance towards a more or less perfect system of self-government was found to be rapidly accelerating. The source of the advance was in the deeper current to which the outward and visible signs of it were ascribable : signs the relation of which to the main result was on a superficial view little else than accidental. But the actual result was shaped by those signs. In the strong conservatism of English politics every such sign is incorporated and perpetu-ated. The expedient of to-day is a precedent for all time ; if it fails it is not cast aside and a new one devised, but its failure is remedied by some new and special contrivance which in its turn is incorpo-rated, is found to answer some other end, and is perpetuated too. The structure, however inconvenient, is not demolished and rebuilt, but a room is added here and a passage there ; the chapel of the old house becomes the muniment-room of the new ; the presence-chamber of the old palace, a mere passage to the halls and courts of the full-grown edifice ; but every original chamber remains, and without it the structure would not be, as it would not have become, what it is. With the superficial student and the empiric politician it is too common to relegate the investigation of such changes to the domain of archæology. I shall not attempt to rebut the imputation ; only if such things are archæology, then archæology is history ; and that is as much as its most fervent students would ask for it. If by archæology is meant the science of the obsolete, I deny that they are archæological ; it is only to the plucked flower that the root is archæologically related. The healthy nation has a memory as well as aspirations involved in the consciousness of its identity ; it has a past no less living than its future. Even the energy that is based on reform and repentance cannot afford to think of that past as the dead burying its dead.

Hubert Walter undertook the office of Great Justiciar at the beginning of the year 1194, and retained it until the middle of the year 1198. On John's accession he became chancellor, and con-tinued in that post until his death, exercising, however, through his important position as legate and archbishop, an amount of authority that no chancellor before him had enjoyed, and scarcely inferior to what he had possessed as justiciar. It is to his career, however, as justiciar that the following remarks chiefly apply. That portion of his history is the one illustrated by Hoveden, and it is also the one in which such principles of administration as he had find their freest expression.

Constitutional history not archæological

Hubert's career as justiciar and chancellor

The principal events of this administration were, in the first year of it, the collecting of the large sum to be paid for Richard's ransom, the management of the king himself during his visit to England, and the judicial iter of 1194. The year 1195 is marked by the archbishop's appointment as legate, and the circumstances which attended his first exercise of his new powers. Hoveden's pages are filled with the troubles of Archbishop Geoffrey, and the only significant constitutional measures are those taken for the maintenance of the public peace. - In the year 1196 come the design of remodelling the Exchequer administration, the riot of William FitzOsbert, and Hubert's first threat of resignation. The assize of measures is the only important act of the year 1197. The following year is remarkable for the successful opposition of S. Hugh of Lincoln to an unconstitutional demand of Richard ; for the elaborate scheme devised for the assessment and collection of the carucage ; and for the withdrawal of the archbishop from the office of justiciar. As all these events are given by Hoveden in detail, and as his account of them is not to any important extent complicated by the statements of contemporaries, it is not necessary to reproduce it in this place. It will be sufficient if I attempt, under the two heads of judicial and financial business, to point out the bearings of Hubert's policy, and to show the way in which his measures were tending to the end of self-government.

Magna Carta being the translation into the language of the thirteenth century of the ideas of the eleventh, through the forms of the twelfth, we may naturally look for some significant transitional data in the policy of a minister with such antecedents as those of Hubert Walter.

The financial history comes first both in place and importance. The effort that England made for the ransom of Richard far transcended anything of the kind that had taken place before. It comprised all the ancient devices for procuring supplies, and formed a precedent for new ones. The proceedings by which it was carried out fall partly in the year 1193 and partly in 1194, for the aids demanded by Richard in person in the latter year were probably intended to complete the sum required of him, although it cannot be said with any certainty that they were so applied ; and it is not quite clear, from either the language of the chroniclers or the public records, how the disposal of the funds levied in 1193 is to be distinguished from that of 1194.[1]

---

[1] The measures taken are described by Hoveden in more places than one. In vol. iii. p. 210 he mentions first the demand of a fourth part of revenue and mobilia, of the scutage, and of the wool, and the treasure of the churches. At p. 225, after recapitulating these in different order, he adds that some of

The sum to be raised was after some negotiation fixed at 150,000 marks, 100,000*l.* sterling : an amount more than twice as large as the whole revenue of the country accounted for in the last year's exchequer of Henry II. Unprecedented as the occasion was, it does not appear to have led the way to any national deliberation on ways and means. Richard wrote urgently to his principal barons and prelates, but the responsibility of the budget was undertaken by Queen Eleanor and the justices : they demanded a scutage from the

tenants by knight service, a hidage or carucage from all tenants in socage, a grant of a fourth part of revenue and goods from all persons whatsoever, by way of donum or aid ; the wool of the Cistercians and Gilbertines, and the gold, silver, and jewels of the churches. The ' communis assensus ' [1] which admitted the demand must be attributed, not to the vote of any general assembly, but to the feeling of common helplessness. The aid was one of the three customary aids, and even under Magna Carta might be taken without reference to the common council of the realm.

(1) In demanding a scutage of 20*s.* on the knight's fee the justices did not go beyond the average rate of scutage. The rate in the 33rd of Henry II. was the same, and the three other scutages raised in Richard's reign were also 20*s.* on the knight's fee. John's first scutage was raised to two marks. The sum thus levied must have amounted to not less than 25,000*l.* if rigorously collected ; but

the bishops took a fourth, some a tenth, of the revenue of the clergy. At p. 222 he says that Archbishop Geoffrey demanded a fourth part of the revenue of the canons of York. In the history of the Council of Nottingham in 1194 he specifies the king's demand of the carucage, iii. 242. Yet the mention of the scutage and carucage occurs first in the Pipe Roll of 1194. Is it possible that the imposts raised in 1193 were collected by some process different from the ordinary one of the Exchequer ? It was certainly intrusted to special officers (vol. iii. 212), but it is more probable that the measures of 1194 were merely the legal carrying out of the plan devised in 1193 than that two scutages should be collected for the same purpose in two successive years, of which only one should be mentioned in the national accounts. William of Newburgh expatiates on the disappointment that was felt at the insufficiency of the sums first raised : ' Putabatur quidem tanta pecuniarum

coacervatio redemptionis regiæ sum-mam excedere, quam tamen non attigit, cum universæ particulæ Lundoniis convenissent ad summam ;. quod accidisse creditur per fraudem executorum. Denique, propter hanc primæ collationis insufficientiam, ministri regii secundam tertiamque instaurant, quosque locupletiores pecuniis spoliant, manifestum rapinarum dedecus honesto redemptionis regiæ nomine palliant.' After mentioning the collection of the treasures of the churches, he proceeds : ' Tota tamen illa opum coacervatio, ut dicitur, ad complendam regiæ redemptionis atque expensarum ejus summam minus sufficere potuit.' Lib. iv. cap. 38.

[1] ' Statutum est communi assensu.' R. de Diceto, 670. This writer does not mention the scutage or carucage under the year 1193, an additional presumption that Hoveden's statements refer generally to the imposts raised in the two years for the purpose. See the last note.

it was probably assessed on the old system, and if so would not amount to more than 12,000*l.*[1]

(2) The hidage or carucage, if levied at 2*s.* on the hide or caru- cate, must have been nearly the same in amount as the ancient Danegeld,[2] and produced a sum of about 5,000*l.* This sort of impost had been levied during Henry II.'s reign, generally under the name of *donum*, and as supplementary to the scutage.

The hidage or carucage

(3) The grant of a fourth part of revenue and mobilia may be contrasted with the two particulars just mentioned. It no doubt took this form in consequence of the urgency of the occasion, and was the source of the largest portion of the sum achieved. Although revenue and personal property had been long liable to taxation in the shape of talliage and donum, this appears to be the first occasion on which they were subjected directly to central taxation. The Dialogus de Scaccario describes the two methods of determining the incidence of talliage : *per capita*,[3] poll-tax, or local assessment. Here, however, we have a direct demand of the central authority on the individual. The principle was, nevertheless, not quite a novelty, although the form was so. The assize of the Saladin tithe formed the precedent for demanding a fixed portion of each man's goods, and the assize of arms brought personal property under direct contribution for the national defence. Either of these ordinances would also have afforded a precedent for an equitable method of assessment by a jury of the venue ; but we have no authority that shows it to have been followed on this occasion. This impost is the precedent for the grants of subsidies in the shape of tithes, sevenths, thirteenths, fifteenths, and

The grant of a fourth of revenue and mobilia

Precedents for this impost, and its importance as a precedent

[1] If we compare the account given by Madox from the Pipe Rolls of the sum paid as scutage in 1172 with those paid in 1194, we shall find them nearly identical; *e.g.* in both cases the archbishop of York pays 20*l.* for his knights, William Fossard 31*l.* 10*s.*, and so on. If the same sums were paid, no doubt the same deductions were made, and the same compositions held good. The scutage of 1194 would thus produce no more than those of Henry II.'s reign. This enables us to understand the relief given by the 44th article of the Magna Carta of 1217, 'Scutagium capiatur de cetero sicut capi consuevit tempore Henrici regis avi nostri;' John's scutages having been larger in amount and arbitrarily imposed. Madox, *Hist. Exch.* pp. 411, 441.

[2] On the hypothesis stated in the last note. For instance, the hidage of 1194 was in Somerset 293*l.* 18*s.* 2*d.*; in Dorset, 241*l.* 3*s.* 9*d.* The Danegeld levied in 1156 was, in Somerset, 277*l.* 10*s.* 4*d.* ; and in Dorset, 228*l.* 5*s.* The difference may be accounted for by either the reclaiming of waste or the varying number of persons excused. Madox, *Hist. Exch.* pp. 411, 412, 476, 477, &c.

[3] *Per capita* may mean rather a household or family tax than a poll-tax ; it was the arrangement by which all the payers paid equally, without respect to the difference of their ability. To alter this and substitute an assessment by which each man would pay in proportion to his wealth was the pretext of the riot of William FitzOsbert. Hoveden, iv. 5. See Dialogus de Scaccario, lib. ii. cap. 13.

other proportions, which in the next century largely supersede the earlier methods of taxation.

Demand of wool

(4) The demand of the wool of the Cistercians and Gilbertines is án important precedent also for the raising of revenue on and through the staple article of English production.

Demand of the treasures of churches

(5) The demand of the treasures of the churches, an expedient which, although occasionally threatened by our other sovereigns,[1] was not actually repeated until the days of Henry VIII., is a sign of the enormous effort made by the government on this occasion, too enormous to be taken as a safe precedent. Unfortunately, we have no clue whatever to the actual proportions of the required sum made up from these last three sources. The country endured the united pressure of taxes which had never been imposed before at the same moment, and of some that were never proposed again. England, although the largest and wealthiest part, was far from being the whole of the area to be taxed ;[2] and yet, either because the money was not honestly applied, or because the produce fell short of the estimates, considerable arrears of the ransom were unpaid in 1195.

Payments in 1194

In the Council of Nottingham in 1194 Richard demanded a carucage of 2s. on the carucate ; as the mention of hidage comes into the Pipe Rolls only in this year, we must conclude that this was the occasion on which this portion of the revenue applied to the ransom was granted. The language of Hoveden leads to the conclusion that in form it was an innovation.[3] On the same occasion he asked for the wool of the Cistercians, who compounded for it with a fine.

Their supplementary character

Probably in this case also the negotiation was supplementary to that of the year 1193. The king further demanded a third of the military service of the country to go with him to Normandy. If I am right in supposing that both the scutage and the carucage were collected on the ancient assessments which had been in use in

---

[1] This is illustrated, as well as the demand of the wool, by the measures taken by Edward I. when in severe financial difficulties in 1294. Hemingb. Chron. ii. 53, 54.

[2] The Norman Exchequer Roll of 1194 is lost. In that of 1195 is an entry stating that Geoffrey the Exchanger (Cambitor) renders account of 22,891l. 7s. 4d. Angevin, for 5,722l. 16s. 10d. sterling; and 4,600l. and 400l. Angevin ; altogether 27,891l. 7s. 4d. Angevin, of which 16,000l. Angevin, answering to 6,000 marks of silver, was paid to Ruffus de Volto and Everard the chamberlain, the emperor's messengers for the delivery of the hostages. Stapleton,

vol. i. p. 136. This may have been, however, only the English contribution in transitu. Further on, p. 172, William Poignart renders account of the receipt of 4,000 marks raised by talliage on the town of Caen for the king's ransom, an enormous sum. The citizens of London in 1194 owed 1,500 marks of donum, 'pro benevolentia domini regis et pro libertatibus suis conservandis et de auxilio suo ad redemptionem domini regis' (Madox, 412), a statement which shows that they were determined to get all they could for their money. It is very unfortunate that all our information on this important business is fragmentary.

[3] Hoveden, iii. 242.

Henry II.'s reign, the largest part of the burden of the ransom must have been defrayed from the donum of the fourth part of revenue and personal property, the most oppressive and general of the imposts ; and we may attribute to the inquisitorial and universal pressure of this exaction the discontent with the fiscal administration which seems to have followed, as well as the urgent measure of reform which the justiciar attempted later in the year.

The judicial iter of 1194 was the necessary consequence of Richard's return and of the restoration of the governmental machinery. Like the similar proceedings under Henry II., it was directed with a view to fiscal advantage ; the Inquest of Sheriffs of 1170 [1] was followed as a precedent ; exact inquiry was made into the escheats, patronage, wardships, and other feudal incidents, and into the debts and available property of John. Strict directions were given for the re-stocking of the lands in the royal possession, and for the supervision of the commercial and monetary dealings of the Jews. A talliage of cities, towns, and demesne lands was also ordered.[2] A measure, however, of far greater importance which the justiciar proposed, the examination into the accounts of receipts taken by the sheriffs, bailiffs, foresters, and other servants of the Exchequer, since the beginning of the reign, was deferred.[3] Such an examination would no doubt have shown the very great discrepancy between the sums collected by the local officers and those which were paid into the treasury ; would have proved the often suspected fact that the system of ferm or composition was ruinous to the Exchequer, which lost the benefits of such increments as would arise from the extension of cultivated lands and improvement in agriculture ; and would have demonstrated the necessity of a new and general system of assessment. It was defeated, however, probably by the influence of the fiscal officers ; although Richard was in the greatest straits for money, and even raising funds by granting licences for tournaments which had the year before been forbidden by the pope.[4]

The Pipe Rolls of 1195 testify to the collection of a scutage for the army of Normandy imposed in the seventh year of Richard, and those of 1196 to a third scutage imposed in the eighth year ; both of these were of the same amount, 20s. on the knight's fee.[5]

Margin notes:
Fiscal measures involved in the iter of 1194

A talliage ordered

Examination of the sheriffs' accounts threatened, but postponed

Scutages of 1195 and 1196

---

[1] See Benedict, vol. iii. pref. lxvi, clv.–clviii.

[2] This talliage, cruel enough after the enormous exactions of the year, is accounted for in the Pipe Roll of 1195, Madox, p. 486, and partly probably in that of 1196.

[3] Hoveden, iii. 267.

[4] Hoveden, iii. 268.

[5] Madox, 443, 444. These are not

to be supposed to be collections of arrears ; they are distinctly called, the first, ' Secundum Scutagium exercitus Normanniæ assisum anno præterito,' *i.e.* 1195, Rot. Pip. 8 Rich. I. ; the second, ' Tertium Scutagium exercitus Normanniæ assisum hoc anno,' *i.e.* 1196, ibid. The first scutage of Richard being apparently one for Wales, levied in 1189 or 1190, and

Renewal of
a project of
Exchequer
reform in
1196
Neither of these is noticed directly by Hoveden. In the latter year the king was so much dissatisfied with his receipts from England that he renewed the proposition for a visitation of the Exchequer, and, greatly against the archbishop's wishes, sent over the abbot of Caen, a clerk well versed in the method of business pursued in the Norman Exchequer, to make inquiry into the receipts of the royal

It is again
defeated
officers.[1] The carrying out of a measure which, however necessary, would be very distasteful to the officials, was again impeded, this time by the death of the commissioner to whom it was confided. The abbot died at London a few days after his arrival.

Discontent
of the people
and of the
king at the
state of the
finances
We may conjecture that Richard was prompted to this proposition chiefly by his own necessities, but he may partly have been influenced by the condition of popular opinion, which insisted that whilst the nation was heavily burdened the crown was poor, and that the fault must be laid upon the ministry. This feeling found its expression

William
FitzOsbert's
movement
in the revolt of William FitzOsbert or Longbeard,[2] which broke out shortly after the death of the abbot of Caen. The ostensible reason of the disturbance was the unfairness of the assessment for the taxes payable by the citizens of London. Hoveden, who seems to have regarded the grievance as a real one, distinctly states that it was caused first by the frequency of the imposts, and secondly by the fact that, owing to the craft of the richer citizens, the main part of the burden fell on the poor. That the higher rank of citizens had the power of doing this, either by raising the sums demanded per capita,[3]

Probable
explanation
of William
FitzOsbert's
movement
or by unfairly assessing the poorer people, is indeed clear. It is probable, moreover, that the ruling body was in close connexion with the Exchequer,[4] the monetary dealings of which brought them in

---

accounted for in the latter year. These three were scutages in the restricted sense of commutation of service, and the sum raised in the same way for the ransom, although called also a scutage, is not numbered among them, but regarded as an aid.

[1] Hoveden, iv. 5. W. Newburgh, lib. v. cap. 19. The latter authority states that the abbot obtained the commission by assuring the king that he was cheated of half his revenue by the officials of the Exchequer: 'fraude officialium regiorum ærario plurimum deperire; qua nimirum deprehensa et castigata, absque omni provincialium gravamine duplicia posse fisco accedere.'

[2] William of Newburgh (v. 20), although expressing an opinion condemnatory of William FitzOsbert, distinctly connects the two events:

'Similitudine vel causæ vel proposit consonare videbantur. Abbas enim, ut commoda regia cum quiete provincialium quæreret, fraudem atque effrenem avaritiam officialium regiorum castigandam esse censebat. Iste autem . . . allegans . . . quod ad omne edictum regium divites, propriis fortunis parcentes, pauperibus per potentiam omne onus imponerent, et ærarium principis multa summa fraudarent.' Nearly the same words as Hoveden uses.

[3] See on this Madox, 506.

[4] For instance, Henry of Cornhell, the head of one of the two great parties of the citizens, was manager of the Mint in 1191, and Reginald of Cornhell after him, apparently during the whole reign of Richard. Madox, 631, 632, 666.

contact ; and that the justiciar, on interfering in the dispute, took
their side too strongly. That William Longbeard was an ordinary
demagogue, a deserter of the ranks with which his birth naturally
associated him, may also be true ; [1] but the fact of the grievance is
not impugned by such a consideration. The archbishop, after he
had raised enormous sums for Richard, found that he was discontented ; the people refused to believe that all the money raised reached
the royal coffers ; the system of the Exchequer and the vested interests
of the sheriffs were too strong to be broken down, and the method
of taxation was becoming obsolete. The archbishop, weary with Hubert
the odious work, teased to death by his monks, who had now appealed offers to
to Rome against him on account of the pollution of Bow church, resign
where William Longbeard was seized, offered to resign the justiciarship. After urgent remonstrance from Richard he withdrew the
offer. Hoveden tells us that during the two preceding years he had
collected for the king not less than 1,100,000 marks of silver, a
statement which must be erroneous,[2] but the belief in which shows
that the oppression by way of taxation must have been unprece-
dentedly heavy.

The Assize of Measures is the only fiscal act that marks the year Assize of
1197.[3] Its chief importance lies in the fact that the wording of Measures
Magna Carta, in the clauses that touch this question, is borrowed in 1197
from it. It was found too severe for the commercial spirit of the
country to bear, and was set aside by the justices early in the reign
of John.[4]

We come thus to the year 1198, a year signalised by at least two
highly important events. In the Great Council of the nation assembled

---

[1] See the sketch of his history given
by Sir Francis Palgrave in the preface
to the first volume of the Rotuli
Curiæ Regis.
[2] Hoveden, iv. 13. I think the sum
is incredible. At the same time it is
clear from the extracts given by Madox
from the Pipe Rolls that the sums of
money passing backwards and forwards
at the Exchequer were much larger
than they had been during the previous reigns. The sum of 1,100,000
marks is said to be computed as of
silver of the realm of England : no
deduction can be made from it, therefore, as being of foreign coin : it represents a sum of 733,333l. 6s. 8d., or
366,666l. 13s. 4d. per annum ; a sum
curiously approximating to Ordericus'
statement of William the Conqueror's
daily income of 1,061l. 10s. 1½d., on
which see Maseres, p. 258. According

to the computation of the learned
baron, the sum must be multiplied by
three to find the present value in
silver, and then by twenty to ascertain
its value in exchange for produce.
This would make the sum annually
raised by Hubert equal to 22,000,000l.
of our money, which is quite inconceivable. If the sum had been given
in figures we might suspect that a
cipher too many was inserted, and
that we should read 110,000 marks, or
73,333l. 6s. 8d., but this would be
much less than would be probable.
Altogether the passage defies explanation, except on the ground that
mediæval statements of number, except
in strictly legal documents, cannot be
interpreted with any approach to
exactness.
[3] Hoveden, iv. pp. 33, 34.
[4] Hoveden, iv. 172.

Opposition of Hugh of Lincoln to Hubert's demands on the king's behalf

at Oxford early in the year,[1] Hubert announced a demand of the king that the barons should furnish him with a force of 300 knights, to be paid three shillings a day each. Two of the bishops—S. Hugh of Lincoln, who represented at the time the religious party in England, and the old school of liberty for which S. Anselm and Thomas Becket

Opposition in the National Council to a new impost

had contended ; and Herbert of Salisbury,[2] who represented the older traditions of the Exchequer—opposed the grant, and the archbishop was obliged in chagrin to withdraw his proposition, although it was supported by the bishop of London, the treasurer. Whatever were the grounds of the opposition of S. Hugh, ecclesiastical or constitutional, this occurrence is a landmark in English constitutional history. It may be placed on a par with S. Thomas's opposition to Henry II. in 1163 at Woodstock, but it is the first clear case of the refusal of a money grant demanded directly by the crown, and a most valuable precedent for future times.

The carucage of 1198

The other mark of the year is the plan devised for the collection of a carucage.[3] This impost was probably intended to redress the balance between the tenants in knight service, who had lately paid two scutages, and the tenants in socage, who had not been taxed for four years ; and this may account for the fact that it was fixed at five shillings on the carucate, more than double the rate collected in 1194. A still more important innovation was the determination that

Substitution of a uniform for a variable measurement

every hundred acres should be regarded as a carucate.[4] Formerly the word was strictly interpreted to mean the land that could be cultivated with a single plough, and of course, according to the character of the soil, the extent varied indefinitely. The substitution of a uniform for a variable carucate [5] was a great advantage to the

---

[1] Magna Vita S. Hugonis, pp. 248, 249. Hoveden, iv. 40.

[2] Herbert of Salisbury, called le Poor, was the son of Richard, archdeacon of Poictiers, that is, Richard of Ilchester, the clerk of the Exchequer to Henry II., and afterwards bishop of Winchester. This is, I think, proved by the documents printed in Madox's Formulare Anglicanum, pp. 47, 52. It is curious that he should be known by the name of Poor, a name which certainly seems to imply some connexion with Roger le Poor of Salisbury, and so with Nigel of Ely, Richard FitzNeal, and the chancellor, Roger le Poor. If this be so, then we have the family exercising a sort of hereditary judicial and fiscal influence for nearly a century and a half, Richard le Poor, bishop of Durham, dying in 1257.

[3] Hoveden, iv. 46, 47.

[4] According to the Dialogus de

Scaccario, i. 17, the *hide* was a hundred acres : that is, it was regarded by the time of Henry II. as of that extent. This act of Hubert, then, identifies the carucate henceforth with the hide, as far as concerns extension. In the same spirit of definition the prices of cows, pigs, sheep, &c., the 'animalia pacabilia,' are fixed, instead of being allowed to vary according to the size or condition of the animal. See the seventh clause of the XXIII[d] article of the assize of 1194. Hoveden, iii. 265, 266.

[5] A parallel case to the variable carucate is the variable oxgang which subsisted in the last century : ' Each field [of the common fields of Pickering] consisted of 22 oxgangs, each of which, on one side of the township, contained 24 acres, on the other, 12.' Marshall's *Rural Economy of Yorkshire*, i. 51.

Exchequer, and the allowance of a hundred acres to the plough was not an illiberal measure towards the cultivators. Remeasurement contemplated

But a consequence of greater importance resulted from the change ; the land in cultivation must be remeasured. The old hidage measurement of Domesday must be given up, with all its machinery of deductions and excuses ; and for this purpose was to be employed the plan of assessment by jury, of which the Domesday record was the most valuable precedent, but which since Domesday [1] had been used only for the assessment of income and personal property. To collect this tax the king sent through each county of England a clerk and a knight, who, with the sheriff and lawful knights chosen for the purpose, sworn to fulfil the king's business faithfully, caused to come before them the stewards of the barons of the county, and from every township the lord or bailiff of the township, and the reeve with four men of the township, whether free or villein, and two lawful knights of the hundred, who swore that they would faithfully and without fraud declare how many wainages of ploughs there were in each township, how many in demesne, how many in villenage, how many in alms ; and on the wainage of each plough they imposed first two shillings and afterwards three. The account was written in four rolls, kept by the clerk, the knight, the sheriff, and the stewards of the barons respectively. The money was received by two knights and the bailiff of each hundred ; they accounted for it to the sheriff, and the sheriff accounted for it at the Exchequer.[2] Method of assessing the carucage

The plan contains several other minute directions, but the above are enough to show that the principle of representation for the purpose of assessment was fully recognised as applicable to real property, whilst the mention of the chosen knights, who in each county were to superintend the proceeding, points to the speedy approach of a time when the ideas of representation and election were to be permanently united. The setting aside the great and venerable assessment book of William the Conqueror for a new valuation to be made by the representatives of the taxpayers was surely a long step towards the exercise by the taxpayers of a direct hold on the determination of taxation. When the elected knights who now superintended the valuation should be called to the royal councils, and there take part in the voting of the impost, the constitutional fabric would come not far off its rough completion. Within less than twenty years the principle which involved this result was to be admitted. Application of principles of representation and election

Unfortunately, the records of the Exchequer do not enable us to say whether this elaborate plan was carried out in its integrity ; but Importance of this act

[1] See the title of the Ely Domesday. Domesday, iii. 497.
[2] Hoveden, iv. 46, 47.

Importance
of the modes
of assess-
ment

it remains a singular link between Domesday Book and Magna Carta, and a most important precedent. An examination of the documents contained in the *Fœdera* and *Parliamentary Writs*,[1] on the question of assessment and collection of taxes, carucages, thirteenths, fifteenths, and the like, shows how from time to time the main principle was varied, until, a hundred years exactly from this date, the right of the commons to representation, and the right of the parliament to regulate taxation, being admitted, the details of the arrangement by which men's minds were prepared and educated for the work sank into secondary importance.

Resignation
of Hubert
Walter

If we suppose that the difficulties of the task thus undertaken were greater than Hubert Walter was able to meet, we may be not very far wrong. The day fixed for the return of the new valuation was the 31st of May; before the 14th of July he had resigned, and his successor was appointed. The first act of the new administration was to order a new iter of the judges, and this was accompanied by a

Stringent
action of the
new admi-
nistration

new and more stringent publication of the forest assize. The impost of the carucage was resisted by a portion of the monastic clergy, and a measure of practical outlawry against the whole clerical body was

Character of
the policy of
John

needed to enforce the payment. This severe act was the first sign of the change in the spirit of the government.[2] Another was the augmentation of the scutage and carucage at the beginning of the reign of John,[3] followed by the speedy and heavy increase of taxation which in 1207 culminated in the demand of a thirteenth, and caused the exile of Archbishop Geoffrey; by the substitution, for the system of jury assessment, of the direct valuation of the justices; and by the great expansion of the system of fines, which drove the barons into rebellion. Some of these measures Hubert might have connived at, but we can scarcely suppose that he would have taken the chief

---

[1] I have put together the chief documents illustrative of this process in *Select Charters* (Oxford, 1870), pp 274, 342, 345, 351, 355, 357, 491. In the first, in 1207, for the assessment of the thirteenth, the use of jury is not mentioned; in the second, the carucage of 1220, election in full county is used; in the third, the fifteenth of 1225, both election and jury are employed; in the fourth, the fortieth of 1232, the townships are represented by four *elected* men and the reeve in each case; in the fifth, the scutage of 1235, the arrangement is simply feudal, the collection is by the stewards of the barons; in the sixth, the thirtieth of 1237, the knights collectors are nominated, the local assessors, the reeve

and four *elected* men. In the last case, the talliage of 1304, the collection is made simply by the king's officers. The comparison shows the maintenance of the royal authority in cases of strictly feudal taxation, such as scutage and talliage; and the employment of election and representation in both the collection and assessment of the non-feudal or national, such as carucage and the taxes by rate of tenth, thirteenth, &c.

[2] Hoveden, iv. 63.

[3] The scutage was raised to two marks on the knight's fee in 1199, Madox, p. 444; and the carucage from two to three shillings on the carucate in 1200. Hoveden, iv. 107. R. Coggeshale, c. 860.

part in originating them. He had probably held the supreme financial authority as long as he could conscientiously exercise it. He resigned it by express command of Innocent III.

Hubert's resignation of the justiciarship

The minutiæ of the judicial measures of Hubert's administration are not less important than those of the fiscal ; but they are simpler and more distinctly indicative of progress. The first act to be noted is the direction for the judicial iter of 1194, which has been several times referred to already.[1] The first clause of this document directs the process of electing the grand jury of each county. Four knights are to be chosen from the whole county, who by their oath are to choose two lawful knights of each hundred or wapentake, and those two are to choose ten knights of each hundred and wapentake ; or, if there be a lack of knights, ten lawful and free men ; so that those twelve may together answer, on all heads, for their whole hundred or wapentake. It is necessary for the understanding of this direction to recur to two points in the legislation of Henry II. : the Assizes of Clarendon and Northampton,[2] and the institution of the Great Assize.[3] The two former measures constitute what may be called by anticipation the grand jury, the inquest by twelve lawful knights of each hundred, and four men and the reeve from each township, into cases of reputed criminals in the hundred, with a view to the presentment of the guilty to the itinerant justices. Such is the character of the body instituted in 1194, but its functions are extended to all the business of the judicial visitation. How this representative body was under the assizes of 1166 and 1176 constituted we are not told ; but it is most probable that the lawful knights were simply nominated by the sheriff in the same way as the recognitors for the assizes of mort d'ancestor and darrein presentment ;[4] it is, however, just possible that they were elected[5] in the local assemblies, in which case the reform now adopted must be referred to earlier practice. But it is in the ordinance of the Great Assize that the closer parallel to the direction of 1194 is to be found. According to that institution the twelve recognitors are to be nominated by four summoned knights of the shire in which the disputed property lies.[6] In that case the selection is removed by one step from an arbitrary selection by the sheriff and placed in the hands of a body of four. In the direction of 1194 then, first, the practice of electing through four representatives

II. Judicial measures

Election of grand jury

Extension of its powers

Introduction of the elective principle into shire offices

---

[1] Hoveden, iii. 262.
[2] Hoveden, ii. 248, for the assize of Clarendon ; ii. 89, for that of Northampton.
[3] Glanvill, De Legibus Angliæ, lib. ii. c. 7.
[4] Glanvill, xiii. 3. ' Summone, per bonos summonitores, duodecim liberos et legales homines de visineto.' They were probably nominated by the reeve from a list, or at his or their convenience, as jurors for an inquest are at the present day.
[5] The word *eligendi* is used. Glanvill, xiii. 3.
[6] Glanvill, ii. 7.

is extended from the Great Assize to the grand jury; secondly,
by the interposition of a second act of selection, the four knights are
to choose two who are to co-opt ten ; that is, the selection is placed
two steps instead of one only from a simple nomination. A further
point, which is of importance, is the recognition of four knights as
a sort of representative quorum of the county court for these
purposes.

The use of the word 'election' for the process by which these four
knights were singled out leads to a further question. Are we
to understand that they were chosen in the court of the wapentake and county, or that they were mere nominees of the sheriff? I
have already said that the probability is that in the selection of lawful men to act as recognitors in assizes of mort d'ancestor and darrein presentment, although the word *eligendi* is used, we are to
understand that the choice was made by the sheriff only. Those

recognitors were required only for the particular case for which they
were summoned, and there seems to be no reason to suppose that
the shiremoot or hundredmoot was called together on purpose to elect
them. The sheriff had a list of the knights, and ways of ascertaining the names of the lawful men of the district, and summoned out
of them those most likely to be well informed as to the matter in
hand. And the same course was probably, if not certainly, adopted
in the selection of the four knights who nominated the recognitors
of a Great Assize. We may conclude that the great balance of
probability is in favour of the practice of simple nomination as in use
under Henry II.

If, however, we look on to Magna Carta, we shall find that the
principle of election in and by the county court was in 1215 the rule
in all cases of the sort. By the 18th clause, recognitions of novel
disseisin, mort d'ancestor, and darrein presentment are to be taken
in the county courts only, on a particular day, and in a special place,
four times a year : that is, instead of having a special nomination of
recognitors at the discretion of the sheriff for each case, all such
business is to be concentrated in quarterly courts of the whole shire.
But further, these assizes are to be taken by the king's itinerant
justices, with the assistance of *four knights of each county chosen by
the county court*. Here, then, the principle of election is clearly
stated, and the concentration of the assizes at the county court of
course made that plan of election as certainly feasible as the earlier
practice of holding them at the discretion of the sheriff, or of the
curia regis, made it difficult. A similar rule is laid down in clause
48 of Magna Carta for the inquiry into forest grievances by twelve
sworn knights of each county, to be chosen *per probos homines ejusdem comitatus.*

This being so, at what period between 1176 and 1215 are we to look for the transition from the principle of nomination to that of election? We naturally should fix it at the point of time at which the special assizes for which the knights representative were required were concentrated in the county court; and that appears definitely to be the assize of 1194 now before us, the second chapter of which specifies among the capitula for which the grand jury is to answer all recognitions and all pleas which have been summoned before the justices by writ of the king or chief justice, or sent before them from the chief court of the king ; whilst the 18th article includes the cases of Great Assize also, where the land in dispute is below a certain value.   Not only is there no extant assize earlier than this in which the principle is laid down, but there is the strongest possible ground for believing that no such document was issued between 1176 and 1194.   I think then we may with great probability conclude that when the word *eligendi* is used for the appointment of the four knights of the shire, for the purpose of nominating the grand juries of the hundreds, it means that they were elected by the county court, as the 18th clause of Magna Carta describes, and as the later parliamentary representatives were chosen.

A further argument in the same direction may be drawn from the 20th article of the assize of 1194, which directs that in every county shall be chosen three knights and a clerk, guardians of the pleas of the Crown.   This direction is the origin of the institution of coroners, who have always been and still are elected by the whole body of the freeholders.

The creation of this new office, an elective office, and one which relieved the sheriff from a considerable portion of his work, indicates a disposition on the part of the justiciar to limit the sheriff's direct exercise of judicial functions, which is in strict accordance with the proposed examination into his fiscal exactions, to which reference has been already made more than once, and which was intended to be carried out this very year.   It would appear that the tendency of the local magnates to use the sheriff's office for their own purposes was too strong to be overcome by the more personal and official changes carried out by Henry II., and that it was necessary to introduce an organic modification of the functions of this ancient magistrate.   The time was not come at which the county court could be trusted to elect the sheriff ; [1] the only alternative was to limit his functions. It will be seen, on a general survey of the whole history of local administration, that as the elective principle gained ground the powers of the sheriffs were limited.   The present assize not merely

Margin notes:
Point of transition from nomination to election

This point may be fixed to the year 1194

Institution of coroners

Institution of the coronership, a step in the progress of the elective principle

Functions of the sheriffs limited as the elective principle gains ground

[1] Art. Super Cartas, cc. viii. and ix.   Statutes of the Realm, i. 139, 140.

throws a large part of their duties on the elective coroners, but forbids that the sheriff should be justiciar in his own sheriffwick, or any county in which he has been sheriff since the coronation of Richard. Magna Carta forbids that any sheriff, constable, coroners, or other royal bailiffs, shall hold pleas of the Crown.

Oath of the peace, in 1195

The oath for the conservation of the peace ordered by Hubert in 1195 to be taken by all men throughout the kingdom[1] is a valuable illustration of the permanence and adaptability of one of the very ancient legal customs of the country. The laws of Canute direct that every man above twelve years shall make oath that he will neither be a thief nor cognisant of one ;[2] the Assize of Clarendon was based upon the obligation of this oath, although it devolved the execution of it upon a select body of knights and lawful men. It

Revival of an earlier custom

is now revived in the earlier form : they shall swear that they will keep the peace of our lord the king to the best of their ability ; that they will not be thieves, or robbers, or receivers of them, nor in any matter consent to them ; that when they learn the existence of such criminals, they will do their best to take them and deliver them to the sheriff ; that when hue and cry is raised they will follow, and will deliver to the sheriff those who refuse or avoid the duty. This

Knights assigned for the conservation of the peace

oath is to be taken by all over the age of fifteen before knights assigned for the purpose. These knights assigned appear to be the lineal predecessors of the more modern justices of the peace. The legislation of the reign of Henry III. incorporated the system of the assize of arms with that of watch and ward and hue and cry, and the whole of the measures existing for the conservation of the peace were codified in Edward I.'s statute of Winchester. The assigned knights of whom we read here for the first time become under Edward III. able to try felonies, and are called justices of the peace. There does not seem to be any ground for the assertion that these were at any period elective functionaries.

Iter of 1198

These are, then, the judicial measures of Hubert Walter's justiciarship. The directions for the iter of 1198, issued soon after his resignation, contain no important change, unless the order that the elections for the Great Assize shall be taken before the itinerant justices may be regarded as a repromulgation or extension of the application of the elective principle to that process, which is unnecessary. The forest assize, reissued at the same time, varies but little from the assize of Woodstock of 1184.

Summary of the constitutional measures of Hubert's administration

The principles which may be regarded as definitely worked out for the first time in the archbishop's general administration are, the application of direct taxation to personal estate and revenue ; the employ-

---

[1] Hoveden, iii. 299.　　　　[2] Secular Dooms, cap. 21.

ment of assessment by jury to determine the obligation of the cultivated lands to carucage; the introduction of the representative
principle into the county administration on a scale hitherto unprecedented; and the application of the elective process to the selection
of judicial representatives. That the last was not a mere accident Town
or coincidence may be shown, I think, from the fact that the first charters
extant charter of a town which contains the provision for the
election of its ruling magistrate is that of Lincoln, of 1194.[1] This
privilege, which had been at an earlier period purchaseable by fine
for the particular occasion, is now made perpetual, and a precedent
for a large class of similar charters in the early years of the next
reign, during which the archbishop's influence with the king was
the strongest. But this opens up a subject far too complex and
extensive to be touched here.

III. The light shed by Hoveden, following the direction taken by Illustra-
his predecessor, on questions of foreign history, was the subject of foreign
several pages of the preface to the second volume of this edition history
(Rolls Series).[2] The general statements made there I shall not repeat,
but content myself with pointing out the passages which especially
illustrate the value of the work in this regard.

1. The places which touch upon the history of the Emperor History of
Henry VI. are numerous, and though not of first-rate importance, family in
decidedly valuable in the comparative barrenness of the continental Sicily
authorities of the period. The chief of these are, the account of the
coronation by Celestine III.[3] and of the consequent destruction of
Tusculum,[4] derived probably from the canons of York who were
then at Rome, or from the members of Eleanor's retinue who had
visited the city at that time; the particulars of the internal dissen-
sions of the German princes, which are brought out in the history of
the negotiations of Richard for his release;[5] the hostile attitude of
the emperor towards France, which partly resulted from Richard's
release, and was partly the purposed effect of his diplomacy;[6] the
cruelties and outrages committed by Henry in the Sicilian kingdom in
1194;[7] the German crusade of 1197;[8] the reverses of the imperial
arms in Sicily the same year;[9] and the illness and death of Henry
himself, followed by the collapse for the moment of all his dynastic
plans in both Germany and Italy.[10]

2. The history of the empire, as distinct from the personal History of
history of Henry VI., is illustrated by the account of the election of of Otho IV.

---

[1] *Fœdera*, i. 52.
[2] See above, pp. 181–199.
[3] Vol. iii. p. 101.
[4] Vol. iii. pp. 102–105.
[5] Vol. iii. pp. 214, 232, 234.
[6] Vol. iii. pp. 300, 302, 303.
[7] Vol. iii. 268–270.
[8] Vol. iv. pp. 25–27, 28, 29.
[9] Vol. iv. pp. 27, 30.
[10] Vol. iv. pp. 30, 31, 32.

the Emperor Otho IV.,[1] and his subsequent struggle with Philip of Swabia, as well as by the precedent notices of the adventures of the children of Henry the Lion. As William of Winchester, the younger brother of Otho, was brought up in England, and resided at the court of Richard during a part at least of the later years [2] of our chronicler ; as the intercourse, moreover, between Otho and Richard, although not between Otho and John, was continuous and friendly, it is easy to account for the special value of these particulars in the prevailing barrenness of the foreign writers of the time. The details of Otho's election, although not above legal and antiquarian criticism, are of great authority. Of the commissioners who attended on Richard's behalf, the bishop of Durham, Philip of Poictiers, was, in all probability, in constant intercourse with Roger of Hoveden, living at Howden, and having been as a royal clerk or chaplain acquainted with him in earlier years ; another, William de Chimeli, was archdeacon of Richmond ; another, the count of Aumale, was the great potentate of the East Riding. From one of these, or from some person in the retinue of one of them, our author must have received his information ; it is even possible that he himself attended the bishop of Durham on the occasion.[3]

History of the papacy

3. Hoveden's contributions to the history of the papacy are not so large as might be expected from the continuous communication existing during his period between York and Rome ; the most important, perhaps, are the accounts of the attempt made by Celestine III. to influence the choice of his successor,[4] and of the early reforms of Innocent III.[5] He has, however, preserved one

Illustration of the history of Rome

detail of considerable importance touching the municipal condition of the city of Rome, the history of the change in the senatorship in 1194, with the short review of the previous condition of that magistracy.[6]

History of France

4. French history is so closely connected with English during the whole reign of Richard and the portion of John's reign which is embraced by the chronicle, that it is unnecessary to point out any special passages that throw light upon it. The measures taken by Philip to obtain a divorce,[7] his dealings with the Jews,[8] and his conduct of the quarrel between the university and citizens of Paris,[9] are the best instances of our author's contribution to the separate history of France.

History of Scotland

5. The same may be said of Scotland. Of incidents of purely Scottish history, the transactions of William the Lion with Harold

[1] Vol. iv. pp. 37–39, 95, 122.
[2] Vol. iv. pp. 79, 116.
[3] Vol. iv. p. 37.
[4] Vol. iv. pp. 32, 33.
[5] Vol. iv. pp. 41, 44, 45.
[6] Vol. iii. p. 270.
[7] Vol. iii. pp. 224, 306, 307 ; vol. iv. p. 112.
[8] Vol. iv. pp. 118, 119.
[9] Vol. iv. pp. 120, 121.

MacMadit,[1] and his negotiations for the marriage of his daughter with Otho of Saxony,[2] are specially noticeable. Hoveden's exact details on the subject of the homage at Lincoln in 1200 and the negotiations that led to it are very valuable.[3] So is also his story about William's intention of invading England at the beginning of John's reign, an intention which he gave up in consequence of a dream or vision which he had when spending the night at Dunfermline, the burial-place of his great-grandmother, S. Margaret.[4] The statement of our author[5] that in the year 1197 the king of Scots introduced into his dominions the oath for conservation of the peace which had been prescribed in England in 1195 may seem startling to those antiquaries who insist that the English reforms in law and police had been anticipated by King David, and were in fact borrowed from him by Henry II.; but there can be no doubt that it is a statement that throws light on a very obscure subject, and affords a glimpse of the process of imitation by which Scotland was assimilating herself to England in matters of the sort: a process which continued until the wars of Edward I. threw her upon the French alliance, and caused her to adopt the French in preference to the English constitutional principles of law and government. *Imitation of English institutions by the Scots*

6. The few obscure notices given by Hoveden of the affairs of Norway under Swerre Birkbain,[6] are important chiefly as showing a certain amount of national intercourse, and of the interest that still existed in England as to the history of the northern kingdoms. *Scandinavian history*

These instances will be, I think, sufficient to show both the value of our Chronicle, the painstaking exactness of its author, the soundness of his means of information, and the amount of intelligence as to foreign affairs which prevailed around him. The notices of Spanish and Oriental history are of less importance, and have, although recorded within a very few years of the time at which the events occurred, acquired from distance a tinge of the legendary character which diminishes their value. *Other historical illustrations*

*　　*　　*　　*　　*　　*

[1] Vol. iv. pp. 10–12.
[2] Vol. iii. pp. 298, 299, 308.
[3] Vol. iv. pp. 88, 91.
[4] Vol. iv. p. 100.
[5] Vol. iv. p. 93.
[6] Vol. iii. pp. 270, 272 ; vol. iv. p. 25.

MEMORIALS OF THE REIGN OF RICHARD I.

I.

ITINERARIUM.

[THE *Itinerarium Regis Ricardi* was probably the work of Richard the Canon of the Holy Trinity in Aldgate. Richard the Canon may have been in the service of the Templars, and may have become prior of the House. Whoever the author may have been, the work was early regarded as one of taste and beauty. It is superior in style to that of Matthew of Paris, though inferior in matter and method. In the *Itinerarium* Richard I.'s part in the Third Crusade is fully described by a writer who was evidently well acquainted with the Holy Scriptures. In the Preface Bishop Stubbs draws an admirable picture of Richard I., comparing his character with that of Saladin. He then sketches the history of the Crusades.]

THERE are periods in the history of all nations which are neither seed-times of great principles nor harvests of great results. They are the seasons during which the institutions of earlier policy are spreading wide and striking deep below the surface of society, its spirit working into the heart and life of the people, and its fruits growing and ripening before the beginning of a new development. These periods may be longer or shorter, as the growth of principles is retarded or fostered : accordingly as rulers force their propagation by repressing them, or moderate it by training and guidance. If they are longer they have a series of heroes of a type of character peculiar to themselves. If they are shorter they have at least the old age of the men who have established the principles, and the youth and training of those who are to work out the further steps of progress. But anyhow they are richer in materials for the student of national and personal character than in topics for the constitutional historian. The former will find abundant details of adventure and elucidations of manners : the latter, unless he is well supplied with records, in which he may trace the workings of the institutions that are not less a part of the nation's life because they are uninteresting to the superficial reader, can only guess here and there at what is going on amongst those whose lives are not written, and is tempted to indulge in the visions of a speculative philosophy of history.

The short reign of Richard the First shares in some measure the character of these periods, for it falls between the initiation of good principles of law under Henry II., and the development of good principles of government in the reign of John : it is barren of incidents for the constitutional historian, partly because the working of the institutions of the former reign was impeded, as it had been during the last years of Henry's life, by domestic strife and anarchy, partly because the character and occupations of the king were not such as to produce any striking effect in the acceleration or retarding of progress. If John had succeeded his father immediately, Magna Carta might have dated ten years earlier than it did ; or if Richard had reigned twice as long as he did, it might have dated ten years later ; but in the latter case it would have been rather the absence than the presence of any policy cn the king's part that made the difference.

Short, however, as the reign was, its peculiar circumstances rob it of the proper interest that belongs to shorter periods of transition. It did not witness the declining glories of the statesmen of Henry, nor form a school of training for those who were to resist King John. The former were spent and worn out in the very beginning of it. Of the latter it would be difficult to mention any, except William Marshall, who occupy even a secondary place of interest in the reign of Richard. It has its warriors and politicians all to itself. The roll of the latter is not a long one. Hubert Walter, William Longchamp, Walter of Coutances, Geoffrey FitzPeter, and William Marshall were about all. In the class of warriors the king himself throws all others into second rank : few of his companions in arms were native Englishmen, or even Anglicised Normans. The chief field of their exploits was too remote, and the time of their adventures too short, for them to produce any effect on the national character, and that produced by the character of Richard himself was neither immediate nor direct. The siege of Acre used up the brave men that his father had left him, and his French wars those whom he had himself formed in the triumphs and troubles of the Holy Land. He was the creation and impersonation of his own age ;[1] and that, though full of character and adventure, was short and transitory in its very essence ; but it was by a rare fatality that the lives of the men of the transition were as short and transient as itself.

Still, although it furnishes little that is of interest to the investi-

---

[1] 'Cum quo, multorum judicio, decus et honor militiæ pariter sepulta sunt.' M. Paris, ed. Wats, p. 196.   'Proh dolor in tanto funere mundus obit.' Hoveden, 450. 'Rex tuus est speculum, quo te speculata superbis.'

gator of domestic legislation,[1] it is not to the mere details of adventure or of character that it owes the charm it possesses for those who study history for its own sake.

Anyone who will follow King Richard carefully through the ten years of his reign will be brought into contact with a variety of men, and complications of politics unequalled in interest by those of many longer and more important reigns. The Crusade brings East and West together. The family connexions of the king involved him in the conflicting interests of Italy, France, Germany, and Spain. His personal adventures open up the whole political history of the age. The dominions in which he exercised real or nominal sway were more diversified in character and circumstances than those of any prince of his time. King of England, lord of Ireland, Scotland, and Wales, duke of Normandy, Aquitaine, and Gascony, count of Maine, Anjou, and Poictou, and superior lord of Brittany, Auvergne, and Toulouse ; king of Arles, conqueror of Cyprus, and for a time the ruler of the kingdom of Palestine, he was brought into collision with almost every potentate in Christendom. In his continental dominions he had an unwearied enemy in Philip of France ; in Sicily he involved himself in quarrels with both the Norman Tancred and the German Henry ; in Cyprus he not only startled the fitful lethargy of the Eastern empire, which almost thought that the yellow-haired king from the West was coming,[2] before whom the golden gate of Constantinople was to open of its own accord, but afforded a ground of accusation to enemies who might be thought far enough removed from the interests of the Comneni.[3] In Palestine he managed either by his superior prowess to draw on himself the envy, or by his utter want of tact to alienate the goodwill and sympathy, of every prince of East or West with whom he had to do. He had no policy abroad any more than

Galf. Vinsauf, *Ars Poetica*, ed. Leyser, Helmstadt, 1724, p. 16.

[1] Palgrave, preface to the *Rotuli Curiæ Regis*, i. lxx. This introduction contains the clearest account I know of the domestic history of Richard's reign.

[2] Ralph de Diceto, 642 ; Hoveden, 370.

[3] Isaac Comnenus, emperor of Cyprus, was sister's son to the Emperor Manuel. Hoveden, 340. Theodora, the mother of Leopold of Austria, was a niece of Manuel. Ansbert, the Austrian chronicler, calls this connexion the ' efficiens causa ' of Richard's captivity (ed. Dobrowsky, p. 114). The affinity between the Emperor Henry and Isaac Comnenus must have been very distant ; Henry's father and Leopold's grandfather were half-brothers. Conrad of Montferrat's mother was sister to the one and half-sister to the other. Richard's conduct to Leopold stirred up the whole race sprung from Agnes of Suabia : in Germany, Italy, and Sicily. The affair of Cyprus was only a pretext. Isaac was a usurper and a rebel : and Richard was welcomed by the Cypriots as a deliverer. Yet, when a charge against him was wanted, Leopold and Henry took up the cause of Isaac as a family matter. Cf. R. Coggeshall, ad 1193 ; Hoveden, 414 v° ; where Leopold is called *uncle* to Isaac's daughter. Agnes, sister of Philip of France, was married to Alexius II. Comnenus, who died in 1183.

at home, and his foreign relations were as anomalous and unquiet as his domestic ones. And with all this, besides the undoubted influence which his personal character gave him in his own dominions, he had power to place one of his nephews on the throne of Godfrey of Bouillon, and other on that of Charles the Great.[1]

Brought thus into contact with so many and diverse interests, and occupying, by his own position and choice, a central place in the history of his times, Richard has been portrayed for us, if not from more distinct points of view, at least by a greater number of historians than any sovereign of his age or any king of England before him. We know what Englishman, Norman, Frenchman, German, Greek, and Mussulman thought about him; and it is no wonder, considering the number of princes whom he either outshone by his exploits, or offended by his pride, or injured by active aggression, or who, having injured him, hated him with the pertinacity of injustice, that his character has fared badly in the hands of foreign chroniclers.

The descriptions given by the French and German writers are frequently inconsistent with each other, and are based upon proofs that will not bear historical inquiry ;[2] but they are rather exaggerations and misrepresentations of existing facts than accusations altogether false. There is indeed a contrast between the writers of the two nations that is of some interest and importance as illustrating the source and growth of national prejudice, while at the same time it vouches for their own sincerity. The German historians describe Richard as a monster of pride and arrogance,[3] the French

---

[1] The steps of the promotion of Henry of Champagne to the kingdom of Jerusalem are detailed in the fifth book of this history. He was half-nephew to both Philip and Richard, being grandson of Lewis and Eleanor ; but he had attached himself throughout to Richard's party in Palestine. The election of Otto IV., who was son of Henry the Lion, and Matilda, sister of Richard, and made count of Poictou by his uncle, is stated to have been carried either by Richard's influence or in hopes of his support : ' Ricardus vero rex cum multis expensis eum ad imperium transmisit. O laudabilis viri laudabile factum, qui totum mundi imperium nepoti suo comparavit.' Robertde Monte, App. ad Sigebertum ; ap. Pistorium, ed. Struve, i. 939. Cf. Conrad Ursperg. (ed. 1540), p. cccxxi ; Hoveden, 441 v°, &c. Otto was not crowned emperor until 1209.

[2] For example, the capture of Messina from Tancred is construed

into an act of hostility to the Emperor Henry VI. Annales Marbacenses, Pertz, xvii. 164. Richard is charged with selling Ascalon to the Saracens ; Ansbert, 112.

[3] Otto of St. Blaise, a partisan of the emperor and Duke Leopold, inveighs against Richard on the most curiously imaginary grounds. He says of Richard after the surrender of Acre, ' Præter hæc [the insult offered to the duke's flag] præda communi universorum sudore acquisita, inter suos tantum distributa, reliquos privavit, in seque odia omnium concitavit. Omnibus enim fortiori militum robore præstabat, et ideo pro velle sua cuncta disponens, reliquos principes parvipendebat. Attamen Teutonica militia cum Italica his admodum exasperata, regi in faciem restitisset nisi auctoritate militum Templi repressa fuisset. Anglicam itaque perfidiam detestantes, Angliæque subdi dedignantes, ascensis navibus simul

as the most perfidious of men. But the Germans have envenomed
their calumny with a hatred that is absent altogether from the
French historians ; and what is more to the point, they look upon him
as an Englishman and involve his country in his condemnation.
The ancient friendship between Germany and England, which
dated from the times of Boniface and Charles the Great, had reached
its point of closest connexion in the time of Edward the Confessor,
and had been resuscitated for a time by the marriage of Henry V.
with Matilda of England. But the tie between the house of Anjou
and that of Brunswick, which, originating in the marriage of Henry
the Lion with Matilda the daughter of Henry II., was drawn tighter
by the misfortunes of the Welfic family, was not looked upon in
Germany in the same light in which the old national friendship had
been. The English name shared the unpopularity of the defeated
party of the Welfs even before the conduct of Richard in Sicily
and Palestine had given umbrage to Henry of Hohenstaufen and
Leopold of Austria.[1] Offence once given, a long score was soon
recollected for revenge, and a hope succeeded that some of the
English gold which hitherto had been spent in support of Henry the
Lion might be diverted without dangerous violence into the coffers of
the imperial house. National alienation on the one hand, party
animosity and personal enmity on the other, were fruitful causes of
hatred. Then, when malice had its worst, there was the consciousness of wrong done and the desire of national justification to induce
the writers of Germany to represent Richard as they have done.

With the French it was otherwise. Richard was to them a
perfidious and faithless vassal.[2] But that was all. They knew he
was no Englishman : and, if it is not an anachronism to speak of

cum Duce Leopaldo repatriaverunt,
rege cum suis adhuc remanente,
quotidieque paganos impugnante.'
Urstisius, Germaniæ Hist. Illustr. ed.
1670, vol. i. p. 216. A similar view of
Richard's character is taken by
Ansbert, though with more moderation : ' Idem itaque rex Angliæ primus
et præcipuus in tota militia Christiana, eo quod in facultatibus et in
omnibus opibus alios præcedebat, et
eos aspernatus postponebat, dominium
sibi super omnes usurpabat,' p. 111 ;
and further on, ' Rex Angliæ Richar-
dus, qui gloria omnes anteire voluit,
et omnium indignationem meruit,'
&c., p. 113. The English historians
seem to have been peculiarly offended
with the German ones for representing
Richard's capture to have taken place
whilst he was cooking. Chron. Petro-

burg. ed. Giles, p. 108. The story is
thus told by several of their writers,
who show the same spiteful pleasure
in telling it that the English writers
show in the details of the matrimonial disappointments of Philip of
France.
[1] Henry II.'s policy in Germany
was not altogether unlike that of
James I. in similar circumstances.
His political sympathies were doubtless with the emperor, but his family
connexion went the other way. He
contented himself with pecuniary
support, and that to no great extent,
and so was no favourite with either
party.
[2]   '—— et quo
' Anglorum sceptris melior non præfuit
        unquam
' Si regi servare fidem cui subditus esse

any national feeling in a Frenchman of that age, to accuse him of national faults would have been to accuse themselves. He was, according to their reading of his character, a brave and most noble king; the most glorious of the kings of the earth if he would but have kept faith with Philip : and that was the concern of Philip, not of France. He was jealous of Philip's glories and faithless to Philip's allegiance. The former charge is not brought in so many words by any contemporary historian, and we may easily guess why. Philip's laurels were yet to be won, when Richard's career was closed, and such as they were, they were won in the far different field of feudal chicanery. But the charge of perfidy is freely brought, and, so far as the facts go, cannot be rebutted. The moral and political guilt, however, of such perfidy was infinitesimal. The relation of suzerain and vassal was at this period antiquated, and indeed extinct, except where it served the purpose of the moment to drag it into a legal procedure, or where the suzerain was strong enough to enforce rights which were supported rather by his own strong hand than by the 'main et bouche' of his vassal. Between a mighty prince like Richard and the venerable imposture of the French monarchy there could be no real tie of homage and fealty; nor probably would the plea have been brought against Richard had not he himself taught Philip the use of it in his struggles with his father and his brothers. Any war waged by the duke of Normandy or the count of Anjou against the king of France was construed into perfidy, and the craft and cunning of war, as it was then practised, into fraud and treachery. Richard was not a king who would have encouraged rebellion in the dominions of an ally, at the same time disavowing his share in it : but he was not like Frederick Barbarossa, one who would send a cartel of defiance to an infidel foe before he waged war ; much less would he have denied himself any advantage that craft or speed could give him over an enemy who hated him, and whom he despised so heartily as Philip. They were at war, open or secret, during the whole of Richard's reign, and neither ever scrupled to steal a march upon the other.

Richard has suffered hardly less from the exaggerated praise of English writers, who, while they have honestly recorded the crimes and excesses which on the face of it refute their views of his general character, seem to have thought it possible to show that, although

---

'Lege tenebatur, Regemque timere
   supremum
'Cura fuisset ei.'
   '―― succedit ei quo pejor in orbe
'Non fuit, omnimoda vacuus virtute
   Johannes.'―(W. Brito, *Philippis*,
   v. p. 292, ed. Pithœus.)

It is clear that Philip had craft enough to put Richard legally in the wrong. Compare his intolerable teasing of Richard at Messina, as told by Rigord, ed. Pithœus, p. 189, and at Acre. Ibid.

in every relation of life he was found grievously wanting, he was, on the whole, a great and glorious king, to be defended against the calumnies of all the world. Those of them who lived under John may be excused for taking a flattering view of the past in contrast with the miserable and disgraceful present. Those who remembered his father's government wondered, but could not deny, that the foolish people bore Richard's scorpions more willingly than they had done his father's rods.[1] A bad son, a bad husband, a selfish ruler, and a vicious man, he yet possessed some qualities which the men of the time accepted as better than the wicked wisdom of his father, and which made his tyranny less intolerable than his brother's weakness ; besides that, his glory and renown reached thousands of homes too humble to suffer from his exactions : he himself, with his oppressive hirelings, was far away from England, but fame had its myriad tongues. With John there was no glory, and not even the enchantment of distance to modify the bitter sense of national shame and personal suffering. Surely the historians were not so very far wrong, as modern thinkers, judging on high moral principles, might suppose. Judged according to the standard of his own time, he was acquitted of much for which we must condemn him ; judged by that of ours, he carries with him in his condemnation the age that tolerated or admired him. Still there were a few redeeming points in him that should mitigate the censure of the moralist, and may force him to grant that in a better age Richard might have been a better and as great a man.

Richard was no Englishman that we should be concerned to defend him on national grounds, if it were right to argue to a foregone conclusion. Nothing in regard of national character or glory depends on his vindication or condemnation. He had very little English blood in his veins ; most of his prominent characteristics were inherited, and are traceable with little obscurity to his Norman, Angevin, and Poictevin ancestors. His strength of will, his love of war, his unscrupulousness in means and money, his recklessness of human life, seem to have been his indefeasible inheritance from the Red King [2] and Henry I. His eloquence, such as it was, may have come to him with his troubadour tastes from his mother. We have to go back to his great-grandfather, King Fulk of Jerusalem, to find

---

[1] William of Newburgh (ed. Hamilton), i. 285, comparing the reign of Henry with that of Richard, under whom he wrote, says, ' Et tamen populus insipiens cum minori nunc querela scorpionibus cæditur, quam ante annos aliquot flagellis cædebatur.'
[2] Cf. Giraldus's remarks on Rich-

ard's death, De Instr. Princ. p. 176. (ed. Brewer, 1846). There is a good deal of likeness between the worst points of Richard's character and that of William Rufus ; but William seems to have been quite devoid of Richard's nobler traits.

the source of the spirit of knight-errantry which is so strongly exemplified in the work before us. This was not the whole of Richard's character. His power of winning the love of better men,[1] his wonderful facility in pardoning personal injuries, his tact in the choice of ministers, so inconsistent with his want of it in the rest of his conduct ; a certain blundering faith in human nature, slow to suspect evil in the worst of men ; and the heroic side as contrasted with the merely adventurous side of his character, came to him certainly from no ancestor nearer than the good Queen Maud : if they were not inherited from her, they were his own especial gifts : he was the first of his family who possessed them.[2]

The leading feature in Richard's character was the love of war,[3] and that not for the sake of glory or acquisition of territory, but as other men love science or poetry, for the mere delight of the struggle and the charm of victory. By this his whole temperament was toned : united with the genius for military affairs which he undoubtedly possessed, it called forth all the powers of his mind and body. It brought into play the few virtues which alone can save such heroes from being scourges of mankind. It was the occasion of most of the sins that were laid to his charge, and of most of the miseries that oppressed his people during his reign. For this ruling passion he condescended to the meanest tricks of avarice,[4] the most

---

[1] See Mr. Dimock's *Metrical Life of S. Hugh*; Lincoln, 1860, p. vii.

[2] The favourable characters of Richard are by Gervase of Tilbury, *Otia Imperialia*, ap. Leibnitz, *Scriptores Rerum Brunsvicensium*, i. 947. ' Post hunc genitus floruit ille rex regum terrenorum Ricardus in strenuitate, magnanimitate, militia, scientia, et omnis generis virtutibus nulli secundus ; sacri patrimonii Jesu Christi, Terræque Sanctæ strenuus defensor ; timor Gentilium, mors hostium, gladius et tutamen Christianorum : cui mundus ad largitiones non sufficeret, et orbis velut pugillus crat ad dimicandum : ' in the Chronicle of Tours (Martene and Durand, *Amplissima Collectio*, v. 1037), ' Vir quidem animosus ac bellicosus, donis largissimus, armis strenuissimus, militari negotio circumspectus, a militibus dilectus et a clero et populo honoratus, ecclesiæ patronus et divini officii auditor indefessus ; ' Giraldus, De Instructione Principum, p. 105, ' Inter varias quibus præeminet virtutes peculiari quadam prærogativa, trina hunc insignia incomparabiliter reddunt illus-

trem, strenuitas et animositas eximia, largitas et dapsilitas immensa semper laudabilis in principe, cæterasque adornans virtutes, tam animi quam verbi firma constantia.' See also the last chapter of these Memorials, Rolls Series ; and Matthew Paris, p. 373, 374.

[3] This characteristic he shared with his elder brother. ' Erat eis mens una, videlicet, plus cæteris posse in armis.' Hoveden, 331. It is needless to multiply references.

[4] Richard was not avaricious in the proper sense of the word, but as most extravagant people are. Sir Francis Palgrave (pref. to Rot. Cur. Reg. i. p. xli) is much too hard upon him. And the reproach taken by Giraldus from an epigram (De Inst. Princ. p. 176, Brompton 1280), that he embezzled the money of the Crusade, is absurd. The amount of money that he had spent on the Crusade must have been immense, including the spoils of Sicily and Cyprus. Rigord coolly praises Philip's generosity in accepting a third of the money extorted from Tancred, when he had no right to a single Angevin, p. 188. The story

unscrupulous violence of oppression ; for this he incurred the imputation of wanton cruelty and causeless perfidy, and for this he
squandered with the most fatuous prodigality the treasures which he
had amassed at the sacrifice of honour and faith.

In such a man we do not expect to find much self-restraint or
consideration for other men's weakness. We dare not assert that
Richard was free from the more sordid vices that defiled the
character of his father and brother. The standard of morality was
indeed so low that even if the historians were altogether, as they are
for the most part, silent as to his personal vices, their silence could
not be taken for a negation. Had he been in any considerable
degree free from such, the praises of his chastity and temperance
could not fail to have been sung by some one or other of his
admirers. Unhappily, what little is said is dark and condemnatory.[1]
His sins were such as called for open rebuke and bitter penitence.
On two occasions before his last confession on his death-bed,[2] he is
recorded to have publicly exhibited an extreme agony of remorse,
and to have done open penance for the foulness of his life. Coming,
however, as he does between Henry and John, to whose history their
personal vices give so strong a colouring, he may at least plead that
his sins in this respect, whatever they may have been, were neither
so heinous as theirs, nor, what is more to the point, were allowed to
influence his public life. We do not read that he ever, for the mere
gratification of passion, either lost a friend or made an enemy, or
broke any of the laws of honour which the times recognised, or even
risked the smallest advantage. He was a soldier, and his vices were
the common vices of the camp, set off with no garnish of romance,
glaring in their own foulness and leaving us with no suspicion of
anything worse behind.

told of his attacking the castle of
Chaluz in search of a treasure, on the
occasion on which he met his death, is
curious, and, if it is to be believed,
should be taken as a whole. The
treasure was, according to Rigord (p.
200), 'Imperator quidam de auro
purissimo, cum uxore et filiis et filia-
bus, ad mensam auream residentibus.'
See also Hoveden, 449 v°; Trivet, 160.
It is probable that the difficulties in
which he found himself after his imprisonment had the effect of increasing his unscrupulousness in exacting
money. See the curious passage in
John of Oxenedes, pp. 94, 95.

[1] The passages are, Hoveden, 428
v°; W. Newburgh, ii. 56 ; Heming-
burgh, i. 229 (where the history of
Richard's death-bed reads like a

chapter from the *Gesta Romanorum*).
These must be read with the recollection that they are not to be interpreted
in pessimam partem. The language
of the monkish writers is often indiscriminate and exaggerated upon such
points.

[2] First at Messina, in 1190, Hoveden, 388 ; secondly, on the Tuesday in
Easter week, 1195, Hoveden, 428 ;
and thirdly on his death-bed. See
the curious story of his release from
purgatory, in Matthew Paris, p. 373.
He had professed on his death-bed
that he would gladly endure the pains
of purgatory until the day of judgment : Trivet, 161. According to the
story by M. Paris, he was released the
same day with Stephen Langton and
one of his chaplains.

He was a man of blood, and his crimes were those of one whom long use of warfare had made too familiar with slaughter to be very chary or sparing of it when the cost was his own ; much less would the scruples of humanity occur to him when the blood to be shed was that of an open enemy or an infidel. But he was too impetuous to be either treacherous or habitually cruel ; nor can any well-founded charge of either vice be brought against him. The sacrifice of the prisoners or hostages at Acre cannot be excused on any principle of morality, but it was in strict agreement with the letter of the law. It was no ebullition of savage passion, but a judicial cruelty which had almost become a necessity, and which was not executed until some weeks after it fell due and was seen to be necessary. The prisoners had been spared subject to terms and ransom. The terms might have been easily kept if Saladin had chosen. The massacre was, moreover, a sort of reprisal on Saladin for his murder of the Templars after the battle of Hittin.[1]

There is no evidence that connects the assassination of Conrad of Montferrat with any proceeding of Richard ; such a crime implies a fault of which all the rest of his life proves him guiltless, and an amount of imprudence beyond even his political incapacity. He might, had he compassed such a design, have certainly foreseen that it would be charged upon himself ; and he might assuredly have effected the purpose by much simpler means. It was perpetrated at a moment when he was fast losing his interest in the Crusade, and anxious to go home ; at a time, therefore, when the old complications hung light upon him, and he would be particularly careful about entangling himself in new ones. The charge was never made in a more tangible form than as a rumour or a suspicion : it is impossible to suppose that, had the family of Conrad believed it, his brother should have taken service under Richard as he did ;[2] in fine,

---

[1] The account given by Bohadin (*Vita Saladini*, ed. Schultens), pp. 181–183, is important, as illustrating Saladin's policy and the Oriental view of Richard's conduct ; and may be compared with the details of our author, iv. 2, 3, 4. On the expiration of the first month from the surrender of Acre, the true cross was to be restored with 100,000 pieces of gold and six hundred captives. Saladin was unable to make up the number of captives, and endeavoured to gain time by proposing that the Saracen prisoners should be restored to him before the ransom was paid, on condition of his giving hostages and pledges for the performance of the conditions. Richard re-

fused, insisting that the Saracen captives should not be surrendered until all was paid. Saladin, suspecting that Richard intended to keep both prisoners and ransom, refused to trust to his honour ; and hence the miserable result. This is probably the truth, and it explains why the Saracen princes looked on Saladin as, in a measure, answerable for the massacre. Hoveden says that Saladin massacred all his Christian prisoners two days before the slaughter by Richard, but it is impossible that he should have been guilty of so suicidal an act. Hoveden, 397.

[2] Boniface of Montferrat in 1197 received of King Richard 800*l.* as his

the character of Conrad was such, and the persons whom he had
injured so many and various, that it is a wonder he was not disposed
of earlier than he was. His chief enemies were among the Greeks
and Pullani, the most likely of all enemies to seek a remedy by the
swords of the Assassins.

Richard's indomitable pride [1] and his carelessness of expressing
the contempt he felt for those beneath him in fame or strength
are constantly alleged against him by foreign writers, and are not
denied by his own panegyrists ; they were, indeed, the fruitful
causes of his misfortunes. Still it must have been a difficult thing
for the Lion-heart to have shown respect for one whom he knew so
well, and despised so justly, as he did Philip of France, or to have
pretended a regard for one so faithless and selfish as Conrad of
Montferrat. His conduct to so enthusiastic a pilgrim as Leopold of
Austria was, however, as indefensible as the meanness which avenged
it, and which leads us to suspect that Richard may have known
Leopold better than we do. Certainly the other instances may be
referred rather to a want of political tact. He was not so far wrong in
the contempt he felt as rash and headstrong in his way of showing it.

If he had the vices of an unscrupulous and impetuous soldier,
he had also the virtues of a brave man. His very impetuosity prevented him from being selfishly cold-blooded, or employing the
artifices of falsehood and treachery. He was ready to forgive as he
was hasty to offend ; neither revengeful himself, nor suspicious
of such a fault in others ; he never forsook or betrayed a friend.
He was open-handed and magnificent to excess, a virtue which, by
itself, accounts for much of his popularity. He shared, in common
with many other great warriors, in that sincere yet formal attention
and attachment to ceremonial religion [2] which, considering the

fee, and 26*l.* 13*s.* 4*d.* as a present
from the king. Stapleton's *Rotuli
Scaccarii Normanniæ*, ii. pref. xiv,
and 301.

[1] See Giraldus, De Instr. Prin. 107.
He was ' ferocissimus ad ultionem,'
Newburgh, ii. 31: ' rex vero propter
magnitudinem animi ac virium, quos
forte per mansuetudinem unire sibi
poterat, indignantis animi monens
exasperabat.' Ibid. ii. 72, and the passages from the German writers above.

[2] He heard mass every day. R.
Coggeshall. His care in collecting
relics is spoken of by Matthew Paris,
p. 374. He was on good terms with
the clergy. See note from the Chronicle of Tours above, p. 317 ; also p.
447 of the Memorials in the Rolls

Series. That he was very popular
with such of the clergy as he had not
cheated of their money is clear from
the honourable mention made of
him in the Obituary of Fontevraud :
in the notes of the French editors
of R. Coggeshall, Bouquet, xviii. 85.
He was greatly honoured among
the Cistercians. See Martene and
Durand, *Thesaurus*, iv. 1281, 1307,
1324, &c. The day of his death was
also kept at Canterbury Cathedral,
to which he had granted Boughton-
Blean in Kent, as a pledge of which he
sent his gloves to be hung up before
the altar. His anniversary was kept
solemnly in choir and refectory ; each
priest said a mass for him ; the rest
of the monks said the proper psalms.

circumstances of a soldier's life, must be accepted by the moralist, in default of any higher development, as the expression of a mind which willingly and humbly recognises the source of all power and might.

As a warrior, Richard was by no means a mere headstrong and headlong combatant. He had that rare prerogative of true genius, to be able to see the best plan of operations to be the best, even when it did not proceed from his own brain. He was circumspect in design and swift in execution ;[1] ready to seek and take the best advice, to yield his own schemes and accept a subordinate position when the decision of the majority was against him.

Skilful as he was in the designing, and earnest in the execution of military combinations, he was the veriest tyro in politics. He had none of the tact of a wise prince ; he showed none of the self-restraint in the camp that he practised in the council-chamber. His political alliances were formed on the merest grounds of likes and dislikes ; he had no scheme of territorial aggrandisement, such as gave a unity to the whole life of his father and of his competitor Philip. His dangerous dalliance with Saladin and Saphadin, purposeless in itself, was madness when persisted in, in defiance of the advice and public opinion of the Crusaders. When Messina was won, solely by his arms, he was easily persuaded to share the fruits of victory with his faithless ally, although he might far more wisely have used them to counteract his schemes. The rich and tenable acquisition of Cyprus was cast away even more easily than it was won. The whole history of his connexion with the Lusignans shows that he was as ready to forgive old injuries as he was to shut his eyes to future disadvantages, provided he could carry out the fancy of the moment, whether it was founded on prejudice alone, or, as in that particular case, on a prejudice that happened to be on the side of right.

He was eloquent after a rude and effective fashion. Being consciously unfit to govern men in peace, he did his best to choose good ministers.[2] Hence he cannot be looked on as a mere tyrant,

---

The expense was defrayed from the revenue of the said estate. Martyro-log. Cantuar. ad 8 id. April. MS. Lambeth, 20.

[1] Bohadin (p. 161) says of him : 'The king of England, strenuous before all, magnanimous, of strong courage, ennobled by glorious battles, of fearless boldness in war. He was counted less than the king of France in respect of his kingdom and dignity, but both more flourishing in riches and much

more celebrated in the might of war.' P. 185 ; 'He was old in war, excellent in counsel.' The proof of what is said in the text may be seen at large throughout the present work.

The praise which our author (p. 447) gives Richard for loving the society of good men, whether deserved or not, is confirmed by Giraldus, De Inst. Pr. 106, who, comparing him with his brother Henry, points out some characteristics which he un-

although his designs could not be and were not carried out without
the use of means that amount in effect to tyranny. If he cannot be
acquitted on modern principles of deserting his direct and immediate
duty as a king for the chimerical honours of a Crusader, it may be
pleaded on his behalf that the means which he took to secure the
peace and happiness of his subjects before he left were such as would
have held good if he had had to deal with men of ordinary honesty.
The anarchy of his reign is rather to be ascribed to the ingratitude
and faithlessness of his brothers, and to the perfidy of Philip, than
to his own neglect. When he started on the Crusade, he bound his
brothers with an oath not to enter England for three years during
his absence ; and to the tie of honour he added that of interest,
loading them both with benefits, which might have shown them that
they had everything to lose and nothing to gain by breaking their
oath. He did not leave home until he could be accompanied by that
faithless ally from whom his most serious evils were to be appre-
hended. He could not have calculated on the desertion of Philip,
the perfidy of John, or his own imprisonment in Germany. If he
might have foreseen that the scum of the nobility who were left at
home would murmur against the humble origin of his minister, he
stands excused for his too great faith in men's honour. He might
have known, however, that he was taking with him to the East those
whose presence at home would have been his best safeguard. Had
he taken John, and Geoffrey, and Hugh of Puiset with him to the
Crusade, and left Ranulf Glanvill and Hubert Walter at home, it
would probably have changed the whole character of his reign. Nor
should it be forgotten that the personal presence of a Norman prince
had never been any guarantee of the happiness of England, whilst,
if it had, his dominions were so wide that the fulfilment of the
duty to one part of them involved the dereliction of it to the rest.

But all allowances being made for him, he was a bad ruler ; his
energy, or rather restlessness,[1] his love of war, and his genius for it,
effectually disqualified him from being a peaceful one ; his utter
want of political common sense from being a prudent one. And
thus in this capacity he stands as far below the Norman princes as

doubtedly possessed. ' Strenuitas illis
et animi magnitudo fere par, sed via
virtutis valde dispar. Ille [Henry]
lenitate laudabilis et liberalitate ; iste
severitate spectabilis et stabilitate.
Ille suavitate commendabilis, hic
gravitate. Illi facilitas, huic constantia laudem peperit. Ille misericordia
conspicuus, iste justitia. Ille misero-
rum et male meritorum refugium, iste
supplicium. Ille malorum clypeus,
iste malleus. Martiis ille ludis ad-
dictus, hic seriis; ille extraneis, iste
suis; ille omnibus, iste bonis. Ille
magnanimitate mundum ambiebat,
iste sibi de jure competentia non in-
efficaciter appetebat.'
[1] 'Regnavit autem satis laboriose
annis decem.' Rob. de Monte, 939 ;
R. Coggeshall, c. 857. ' Magnanimitas
nullo tempore sustinuit esse non
actuosa '; p. 447, in vol. R. S.

he does in other respects above them.   The delight of victory, as a
ruling passion, is less degrading to a king, and a cause of less shame
and suffering to his subjects, than the sordid passions of avarice and
lust, to which the first two Henries, in spite of their sagacity and
superior mental power, were wretchedly enslaved.

The great blot on Richard's character, as a ruler, was his wanton
disregard of good faith in regard to money, for which his military
exigencies gave occasion, but of which they afford no excuse.   The
engagement that he would not have dreamed of forfeiting with a
brother warrior sat light upon him when it involved his faith to a
powerful bishop or a rich abbey, or a promise to an urgent influential
suitor.   The bargains that he made before the Crusade, for the sale
of office and dignity,[1] were not in themselves more disgraceful than
much else that prevailed in the public administration of the times ;
but the utter unscrupulousness exhibited in the repudiation of
promises and agreements after the money was received reminds one
of nothing more honourable than the dealings of the Turkish
government with its pashas, and of the pashas with their subjects.[2]

The relations of Richard with Henry II. can hardly be looked
upon as those of a son with his father.   He was brought up as the
heir of his mother's house,[3] and among a people more alive to her
wrongs than to her crimes.   He had to endure what of all things is
most intolerable to an impetuous mind, to be made a tool of by his
father for purposes in which he had himself no interest.   Alternately
the puppet and the victim of Henry's policy, betrothed for a political
purpose to a wife whom he was not allowed to marry,[4] credibly
certified that his father had not scrupled to sacrifice her to his own
lust,[5] as he had sacrificed his son's happiness to the mere desire of
acquiring territory, he might with reason look on Henry as the
source of constant misfortune and misery to him ; the persecutor of
his mother, the seducer of his betrothed wife, the instigator of the

---

[1] Cf. Palgrave, preface to the *Rotuli
Curiæ Regis*, i. xli, and the authorities there quoted : Benedict of Peterborough and Richard of Devizes.

[2] His conduct to Stephen de Marzai
and Ranulf Glanvill, as recorded by
Richard of Devizes, are capital illustrations ; ed. Stephenson, pp. 6, 7.

[3] 'Provida patris dispositione, pa-
ternæ nomen renuens, maternæ stirpis
honorem statim adeptus.'   Girald.
De Inst. Pr., 104.

[4] Besides the wretched betrothment
to Alesia of France, in 1168 (Joh.
Salisb. ep. 244), which was the burden
of his life from 1174 to 1191, and pro-

bably the cause of his vices, he was
twice betrothed by his father, first in
1159 to a daughter of Raymond
Berenger, count of Barcelona (Rob. do
Monte, p. 892), to whom Trivet gives
perhaps confusedly the name of Berengaria (p. 46), and again in 1183 to
a daughter of Frederick Barbarossa,
who died shortly after.   Hoveden,
355 v°.

[5] Hoveden, 392 : ' In uxorem ducere
nulla ratione possit, quia rex Angliæ
pater suus eam cognoverat et filium
ex ea genuerat, et ad hoc probandum
multos produxit testes, qui parati
erant modis omnibus hoc probare.'

Y 2

hostility of his brothers could claim indeed the allegiance of a feudal inferior, but had little right to the affection of a son. Nor was the tempter wanting. Philip was shrewd enough to take advantage of the character and circumstances of his neighbour, and to use him as the instrument of his own unscrupulous enmity against his father. If all this cannot be regarded as an excuse for Richard's unfilial conduct, it may, coupled with the consideration of his youth at the time when he was first led into the attitude which, during Henry's life, he more or less maintained, and with the sincerity of his repentance, be allowed in mitigation of that condemnation which has generally been visited upon his fault.

To such a man as Richard a new Crusade offered a prospect full of charm : countless battles to fight and fortresses to take ; enemies ready to hand in endless plenty, and those enemies worth conquering, in the view of temporal and spiritual glory : a sovereign of mature age and acknowledged reputation to humble ; a knight,[1] moreover, and one who prided himself on not being outdone by the Christian chivalry in their own favourite virtues of honour and courtesy : a quarrel long ago inveterate and which need never be reconciled ; a battle-field whose associations of holiness and reverence were, perhaps, to Richard's mind equalled by its fame in romance and in the true history of its knightly conquerors : great fame to rival, and, perhaps, greater yet to gain ; and with the persuasion all the while that he was at once winning salvation by fighting God's battles and following the occupation he loved best—in all this there was temptation to the Lion-heart. Now he might put to proof the knowledge that he had all his life been gaining, without having his triumph shortened by the intrigues of politicians or by the obligation of taking fair terms as from a Christian foe. For the feud between Christ and Mahomet was an eternal one, and the limits that usage and mutual forbearance placed on struggles between Christian princes had no existence when the adversary to be humbled was an enemy of both God and man. It was a struggle in which there could be no failure, for he was on

[1] See p. 9 (vol. R. S.), where it is said that Saladin was knighted by the Constable Henfrid of Toron. The French romance in which Saladin is made the son of the countess of Ponthieu, and which is followed by the *Chronique d'Outremer*, makes him apply for knighthood to Hugh of S. Omer, lord of Tiberias. *Histoire Littéraire de la France*, xxi. 681. But Hugh of S. Omer died in 1107. Will. Tyr. p. 798. He was the founder of Toron, which fact perhaps misled the romancer. Why Saladin applied for knighthood to a Chistian does not appear, as some institution of the kind seems to have existed among the Moslems. The Emir Karakoush, by an anachronism equal to that of the French romance, is said by R. de Diceto, 654, to have been knighted by Kerbogha at the siege of Antioch. We find a son of Saphadin knighted by King Richard (vol. R. S. p. 325) ; so that probably the value attached by the Saracens depended rather on the character of the bestower than on the nature of the rite.

the side of the God of battles, in Whose service is perfect freedom, and for Whom to perish is itself a most glorious victory. How very different an undertaking he found really awaited him, and how soon he was undeceived, we learn from a comparison of the work before us with Bohadin's Life of Saladin.

Viewed side by side with the Saladin of history, Richard does not appear to advantage, though doubtless the inferiority is less than when he is compared with the hero of romance or the figment of historical unfairness. The superiority of Saladin seems to have been rather in his character as a man than as a warrior or a ruler. Richard was a Christian, Saladin a Moslem ; and we must judge the latter by a more lenient standard, although the example of S. Lewis and Edward I. had not yet taught the Western princes that a good man may be a good king. In many respects there was a likeness between the two ; both were generous, liberal, and honourable ; both were famous captains, although Richard's exploits in war were far above Saladin's ; both were men of more cultivated mind than were most of their fellows. The extravagances and cruelties of both were on a like scale, and on the same principles. But we look in vain in Richard for the profound love of truth and justice which were in Saladin. Otherwise most of the differences were such as are attributable to the different temperaments of East and West. Richard used force where Saladin used contrivance. Richard was rude where Saladin was courteous. Richard was haughty and impatient where Saladin was patient and prudent. The circumstances in which these differences were exemplified were similar ; both had to deal with great hosts of divided and jealous warriors. The result showed that Saladin's treatment of his allies was wiser than Richard's, and that decided the struggle between them. Saladin was a good heathen, Richard a bad Christian ; set side by side there is not much to choose between them ; judged each by his own standard there is very much. Could they have changed faith and place, Saladin would have made a better Christian than Richard, and Richard, perhaps, no worse heathen than Saladin ; but Saladin's possible Christianity would have been as far above his actual heathenism as Richard's possible heathenism would have been above his actual Christianity.

* * * * * *

The condition of Palestine had been a source of sorrow and shame to Christendom for more than four hundred years before the first Crusade.[1] The capture of Jerusalem by Chosroes in 614 was

[1] Jerusalem was taken by Chosroes in 614 ; recovered by Heraclius in 628 ; taken by Omar in 637 ; fell into the hands of the Fatimite Caliphs about 969 ; was taken by the Turks about 1077 ; covered by the Fatimite Caliph, 1096 ; taken by Godfrey, July 15, 1099. Our author, at p. 22 (R. S.), states that

the decisive sign that told the East what had been long known in the West, that the power of the Roman Empire had come to an end. It had shared the fate of all empires founded and built up as it had been by warlike aggression. It was not luxury alone that destroyed it, for the period of its greatest licence was also that of its widest sway ; but the energies that had been strong, so long as new worlds remained to be conquered, became weak and ineffective in triumphant peace. The time came for defence, but no power of defence was found, only the walls that the sons of the builders were too weak to man, and engines which answered to no hands less skilful or less mighty than theirs who framed them. The Moslem power was victorious, not because it was irresistible, but because there was nothing to resist it. The spasmodic effort by which Heraclius was enabled to recover Palestine from the Persians was over when the greater foe came, and the fanatical hosts before whom the Persian himself had fallen.

During those four centuries it had been almost an impossibility for either East or West to attempt a rescue. The Byzantine state had had more than enough to do to maintain its existence against external enemies ; and the West was passing through that Medean caldron from which it was to rise renewed and strengthened for fresh strifes. Meanwhile the city of God lay waste, and the abomination of desolation standing in the holy place seemed to be a sign of the approaching end of the world. When the tenth century closed without the expected arrival of the judgment day, and Christendom saw before it a long prospect of extension and glory under its new lease of life, the thoughts of men turned quickly towards Palestine. Pilgrimages began to multiply. It was no longer here and there that a stray palmer, a monk or bishop from the West, having overcome strange difficulties and undergone strange adventures, returned, one out of a thousand, to tell of the sad state of the ' Land of Pilgrimage.' Great bands organised their expeditions together ; and when they came home they reported that, although the conduct of the pagans to strangers was as cruel and oppressive as ever, their power, for the same reason that the power of Rome had fallen, was approaching its fall, and what had been

it had been in the hands of the Turks for forty years when Godfrey took it ; William of Tyre (p. 633) says 38 ; either this is a mistake, or refers to some short unrecorded occupation by the Turks about 1060. It is to be observed, however, that the word used is not *Turks* but *Gentiles*, which leads to a suspicion that for ' quadraginta '

quadringentos should be read. The passage is otherwise confused in all the MSS.: two of them make the occupation by the Christians to have lasted 96 years instead of 89 ; and the other two place the date of the capture in 1188 instead of 1187. The same confusion of the well-known date is found at p. 5 (R. S.).

lost in the paralysis of imperial energy might be regained by a united effort of Western feudalism.

At the time, however, that the East was ripe for conquest the West was not ready to reap it. Jerusalem changed masters, but it fell into the hands of the Turks, not of the Christians. And it was not until nearly thirty years after that the Western powers were roused to united action, or even able to entertain the idea of a joint expedition. The European states had by that time emerged from chaos. The quarrels of Henry IV. with the popes had not availed to shatter the sturdy strength of the German Cæsarship. England and Normandy were powerful under the policy of the Conqueror, and the French kings were not strong enough as yet to initiate that system of aggression which has created modern France. The popular fervour seconded the politic designs of the princes : the circumstances of the Holy City, which had for a moment been rescued from the Turks by its old tyrants the Fatimite Caliphs, were exceptionally favourable ; and the careful wisdom and chivalrous prowess of Godfrey of Bouillon guided the warriors of the first Crusade to their goal. Jerusalem once more became Christian, and the reproach of four centuries was wiped away.

Unfortunately, Godfrey did not live to consolidate the state that he had founded, and his successors, although brave and accomplished warriors, were quite incompetent to fill a place that required its occupants to be heirs of his statesmanship even more than of his prowess. Circumstances were so far favourable that for half the term of its allotted life no Saracen leader appeared strong enough, or sufficiently supported by the tribes of the East, to demolish the fabric that was being erected by the Frank powers, as quickly as it was raised. Although the impulse of the first Crusade was sufficient to maintain the little colony so long, it was not free from the natural process of relaxation ; and the very forces from which it resulted contained the elements of disruption. But the actual fall of the Frank kingdom is chiefly to be attributed to the evils inherent in an attempt to colonise Palestine on feudal principles, although the determination of the time of its fall was due to the cessation of those divisions among the Mahometan nations which had rendered its existence possible. It is necessary for the understanding of the book before us to go briefly into detail as to these internal defects, which reached their climax of injurious operation in the history here recorded.

The conquest of Palestine did not immediately result from the capture of Jerusalem ; it had to be occupied city by city, and when so occupied to be kept in order by the erection throughout its extent of a system of strong forts. Under ordinary circumstances and in the face of a united resistance, such a tenure would have been impossible. How wonderful it was that the kingdom lasted so long as it did appears from the way in which the whole fabric, raised with such pains, fell before Saladin after the battle of Hittin. One victory then decided the fate of the colony, but it was almost the only regular victory which the Saracens gained during the century. They could occasionally by overpowering numbers or by surprise humble and disperse the Frank armies ; but it almost seems that a consciousness of their inability to fight a pitched battle with any chance of victory was, as much as their disunited and disorganised condition, the reason why they preferred an inch by inch defence of their strongholds.

At the time of Godfrey's death (July 18, 1100) very little besides the city of Jerusalem and the communications with the coast and the Imperial dominions were in the hands of the Franks. The principality of Antioch was held by Bohemond, and Baldwin was in possession of Edessa ; the proper defences of Palestine were, however, in the hands of independent Moslem emirs. The city of Ramlah had fallen before Godfrey on his way to Jerusalem ; the Christians of Bethlehem had made common cause with him before the siege ; but after the capture of the capital, Ascalon, the key of Syria towards the south, had successfully resisted his arms, and the city of Arsûf had been made tributary only after three sieges. Hebron, Tiberias, Naplous (which had been occupied by Tancred), and Joppa, had been rebuilt and fortified ; and Haipha was being besieged at the time of Godfrey's death. The limits of his conquests were thus circumscribed, partly because of his wish to remain as long as possible on friendly terms with the emirs on the coast, and partly in consequence of the jealousies of his fellow leaders ; but the great reason was undoubtedly the insufficiency of the force at his command to conquer and hold the cities. It was imperatively necessary that he should be able to maintain himself in the field : the acquisition of further territories must be left until the news of the conquest had brought from Europe fresh hosts of crusaders whose zeal for the cause or for their own interests could be utilised in that direction. Godfrey died before this took place, and the task fell to his two immediate successors.

Baldwin I. (1100–1118) availed himself of the help of those pilgrims whom either commercial enterprise or more exalted motives brought to Palestine, to extend the conquest. With the aid of the Venetians Haipha was taken 1100 ; in 1101 the fleets of Genoa and Pisa co-operated in the capture of Arsûf and Cæsarea ; Acre fell before the Genoese in 1104, Byblus [1] and Tripoli in 1109 ; the

---

[1] The city of Byblus or Biblium, *Jebeil*, which was made by the Genoese into a lordship for the family of the Ebriaci, must not be confounded with

Pisans took Berytus in 1110, and Sidon was captured the same year by the aid of King Sigurd and the Norwegians. Tancred in the meantime was seizing the towns of Antioch and Cilicia, Adana, Mamistra, Tarsus, Laodicea, Atsareb, and Sardana. The conquests of Baldwin II. were chiefly in the north of Syria ; but his reign was marked by the capture of Tyre by the forces of the kingdom whilst he himself was in captivity, in 1124, and by that of Paneas in 1128. Ascalon did not yield before 1153, when the tide had already turned against the Crusaders ; Edessa had been taken by Emadeddin Zenghi in the year 1143, which, as it was in point of time the central year of the Christian occupation, marks also the moment at which their good fortune began to decline.

During this period of progress the defence of the country had been secured by the erection of fortresses at Scandalion [1] and Toron,[2] in the north of the kingdom, and at Montreal [3] in the south, under Baldwin I. ; and at Beit-Nûba,[4] Beit-Gebrin,[5] Kerak,[6] Ibelin,[7] and Tel-es-safieh [8] under Fulk. The military orders had several other strongholds, of the precise date of whose erection we have no record, especially Merkeb [9] in the north of Syria, Kaukab [10] and Latroon [11] belonging to the Hospitallers ; and Safed,[12] Merle,[13] and the Cave of

Gabala, or Jebleh, in the principality of Antioch, which is mentioned below, p. 333. They seem to be the *Gabelct magnum* and *parvum* of Benedict of Peterborough.

[1] Scandalion, *Iskanderûna*, under the Ladder of Tyre, was fortified by Baldwin I. in 1116. W. Tyr. 815 ; Fulcher of Chartres, 427.

[2] Toron, the ancient and modern *Tibnin*, was founded by Hugh of S. Omer, lord of Tiberias, in 1107, and soon after became the fief of Henfrid, father of the Constable. W. Tyr. 798. It is about 13 miles to the east of the Ladder of Tyre.

[3] Montreal. See below, p. 333, note 7.

[4] Beit-Nûba, the fort of which, Castel Arnald, was founded by the Patriarch William (1130–1144) in 1132, lies on the direct way from Joppa to Jerusalem. It was identified by the Crusaders with Nob. W. Tyr. p. 856.

[5] Beit-Gebrin, or Ibelin of the Hospitallers, anciently Eleutheropolis, was founded by the patriarch in 1134. W. Tyrt 865. See in vol. R. S. p. 360, note 9. Pauli, Codice Diplomatico, i. 18, 46.

[6] Kerak, see below, p. 333, note 7.

[7] Ibelin, anciently Jabneh, now *Yebna*, 11 miles S.W. of Joppa, was founded in 1142, and given to Balian the old. W. Tyr. 886.

[8] Tel-es safieh, or Blancheguard, founded in 1143. W. Tyr. 886.

[9] Merkeb, or Margat, was on the northern frontier of the county of Tripoli, on the coast. W. Tyr. 738 ; Ansbert, p. 5. Crach of the Hospitallers, in the same region (W. Tyr. 1017), is now *Hesn-al-Akrad*. See Robinson, Later Bibl. Researches, p. 565.

[10] Kaukab, called by the Crusaders Coquet, Coket, Cuschet, and more commonly Beauvoir or Belvoir, now Kaukab-el-Hawa, lies among the mountains, near Jordan, between Bethshan and Tiberias. W. Tyr. 1027 ; Pauli, Codice Diplomatico &c., i. 4, 7, 32 ; Bohadin, pp. 76, 88 ; Fulch. Chart. 381 ; Cartulary of the Holy Sepulchre, ed. Rozière, pp. 226, 228.

[11] Latroon, see in vol. R. S. p. 368, note 1.

[12] Safed, 7 miles N.W. of the sea of Galilee. W. Tyr. 1027 ; Ansbert, p. 6.

[13] Merle, see in vol. R. S. p. 255. Not far from Merle was the Castle of Pil-

the Temple [1] to the Templars. That which had hitherto been a matter of precaution became now a necessity; Gaza [2] was restored by Baldwin III., Darum [3] on the Egyptian frontier by Amalric, and Castel-neuf [4] and Jacob's Ford under Baldwin IV. The lord of Sidon also had built himself a fortress at Belfort,[5] and the lord of Ibelin at Mirabel.[6]

From the year 1164, in which Paneas fell for the third time into the hands of Noureddin, the Christian power quickly waned. The brilliant victories of Amalric and Baldwin the leper, the astuteness of Reginald of Châtillon, the veteran wisdom of Henfrid the constable, the devoted valour of the military orders, staved off for a time but could not hinder the inevitable end.   Europe had proved

grims, also belonging to the Temple, now *Athlit*. Ben. Peterb. ii. 488; Assizes, i. 420.

[1] Cava or Spelunca Templariorum lay beyond Jordan, on the confines of Arabia. W. Tyr. 962. Bohadin, p. 32, calls it Acapha in the desert.

[2] Gaza was fortified in 1152 and given to the Templars. W. Tyr. 917.

[3] Darum, see in vol. R. S. p. 318.

[4] Castel-neuf, or Nigra Guarda (perhaps *Kulat-Hunin*, near Paneas), was built by the Constable Henfrid shortly before his death. W. Tyr. 942, 1014.

[5] Belfort now *Shakif-Arnun*, 8 miles N.W. of Paneas; belonged to the lord of Sidon. Assizes, i. 420; W. Tyr. 1015; in vol. R. S. p. 63; Bohadin, p. 89, &c.

[6] Mirabel (cf. W. Tyr. 918, 1009; in vol. R. S. pp. 307, 324, below; Pauli, Codice Dipl. i. 236; Bohadin, pp. 187, 228; Ansbert, p. 4; Cartulary of the Holy Sepulchre, p. 132) was identified by Wilken in his 'Comment. de Bell. Cruciat.' with the Masjdeljaba of Bohadin, from a comparison of the mention of the capture of the two places as given in Abulfeda, Excerpta, p. 41, and in the Chron. Terræ Sanctæ, p. 559; but as the circumstances are so discrepant, he does not seem to have approved on afterthoughts of the conjecture. It is impossible, however, to find another place that answers as well. It would seem from a grant of Balian I. to the Hospitallers that Mirabel was north of Ramlah and Ibelin (at least the other places specified in the same grant were so,) and from an exchange between Hugh of Ibelin, the Church of the Holy

Sepulchre, and the abbot of SS. Joseph and Habakkuk, that it was near the latter monasteries. (See in vol. R. S. p. 285, note 2; Cartulary of the Holy Sepulchre, ed. Rozière, pp. 132, 133) Masjdeljaba also is mentioned by Bohadin, as Mirabel is by our author, in vol. R. S. p. 324, as not demolished after the battle of Arsûf.

Besides these there were among the less famous castles of Palestine, Faba or la Fève, now El-Fuleh, in the plain of Esdraelon, held by the Templars and Hospitallers jointly: Cont. W. Tyr. p. 598. Caco, or Chaccahu, now *Kakoun*, 11 miles S.E. of Cæsarea, a castle of the Templars: Cont. W. Tyr. 598: W. Tyr. 828. Calenzun, now *Kalansaweh*, 4 miles S. of Kakoun: Pauli, Codice Diplomatico, i. 32. Caimount, or Laqueimont, *Kaimoun*; Cont. W. Tyr. 640: Assizes, i. 420, Galatia, *Kuratiyeh* (see in vol. R. S. p. 384). Rouges Cistern, in the wilderness of Adummim, now *Ed-dem*, between Jerusalem and Jericho. Le Quarantayne, in the wilderness of the Temptation. Ben. Pet. ii. 488. Cartulary of the Sepulchre, pp. 222, 235. Castrum Beroardi, near Azotus : cf. Albert of Aix, 349, and Marino Sanuto, 87. In the north were Caphar Mundel, a little N. of Nazareth; Montfort near *Kerain*, 7 miles E. of Achzib; Cavea de Tyrum, now *Mughara*, 10 miles due E. of Sidon. Cf. W. Tyr. 962; Ansbert, p. 4.

The list of the castles of the Holy Land is given by Benedict of Peterborough, ii. 488, and Hoveden, 362, vº. Assizes of Jerusalem (ed. Beugnot), i. 419, &c.

itself, by the abortive crusade of 1147, unable to furnish the zeal and strength required to sustain the fainting colony ; the constant appeals for help for Jerusalem were unavailing. The great name of Saladin carried with it the sound of conquest. Still the Christian state might possibly have survived many years, by sufferance of the Sultan, had it not been forced by the fatal development of its own internal sources of decay to the sad catastrophe which was crowned by the battle of Hittin.

Feudalism [1] was verging towards decrepitude in Europe when it was transplanted with all its mechanism into Palestine ; and as the old system perished in Europe, so almost contemporaneously, although from widely different causes, the new offshoots languished and died in Syria. And yet the feudalism of Godfrey was by no means, as it would have been in the hands of a constitution-monger, the same system at the same point of growth at which he had left it at home. It was the system of a century earlier, or perhaps of a still remoter period. In this respect Godfrey as a lawgiver stands in an attitude strongly contrasted with that of William the Conqueror, who had a few years before introduced into England an arrangement which the kings of France spent a century and a half in trying to imitate. Each was certainly wise and long-sighted in the course he took, considering the circumstances in which he had to act. Godfrey's first and only object was the occupation of a hostile country ; William's first object was the same, but hardly second to it was his purpose of rendering impossible in England a relation of the great feudatories towards their suzerain such as he had known in France. And the lapse of time and growth of nations justified

[1] Lest I should seem to have used this expression wrongly, I should say that I understand by feudalism the feudal system whilst it still retained life and some sort of energy, before it was reduced to a mere matter of legal rights and payments. In this sense it went through four stages before it became extinct :—1. That in which the rights and obligations of the great feudatories were observed. 2. When the superiority of the suzerain had become merely nominal. 3. When the king had succeeded in reducing his vassals into order and obedience. 4. When the vassals with the church and commons had imposed constitutional (not feudal) obligations on the king. England never went through the first two stages, for feudalism was introduced in its third stage by William the Conqueror. France was still in the second stage when the kingdom of Palestine was founded, and continued in it until the reign of Philip Augustus. Godfrey introduced his system in the first stage, which may be considered to have lasted until the death of King Fulk. England seems to have arrived at the fourth stage, in which the principle of feudalism, that had lingered since the invention of scutage, was almost entirely eliminated, about the time of the confirmation of the charters by Edward I., a few years after the loss of Acre. In France the third stage may be considered to have been permanent ; the power of the king increasing until the theory of mutual obligation on which the feudal bond depended was exchanged for servility on the one hand, and selfish isolation on the other.

the policy of William, and condemned that of Godfrey. Feudalism
in England was a step towards the development of constitutional
government : in Palestine it was a brilliant pageant, an unsuccessful
experiment in colonisation ; it had neither adequate basis nor
practical result.

The collection of usages known as the Assizes of Jerusalem [1]
gives us a very perfect picture of a feudal state, but it is no description of any that actually existed. Parts of it may be certainly
looked upon as embodying Godfrey's policy, but the greater portion
of the laws was drawn up at least 130 years after his death. We
trace his hand in the prescribing constant military service [2] (not
definite or merely for a certain period of each year), in the non-
recognition of representation [3] in inheritance, in the rules designed
to prevent the accumulation of fiefs in a single hand,[4] in the
stringent regulations for the marriages of widows and heiresses.[5]
These features all belonged to an earlier age, to a time when every
knight represented a knight's fee, and when no fee could be suffered
to neglect its duty ; when the maintenance of the conquered country
was deemed more important than the inheritances of minors or the
will of widows and heiresses. That these provisions were wise is
amply proved by the fact that it was in these very points that the
hazard of the Frank kingdom lay ; to say that they were not enough
to remedy the evils they were aimed at is but to state a truism—no
legislation can counteract old age or death. Other portions of the
Assizes are to be ascribed to the necessities of the state of things
that followed the recovery of Palestine by the Saracens; such,
for instance, as the decision how far deforcement by the Turks
defeats seisin ; [6] and were of importance only in the event of a
reconquest. It was in the kingdom of Cyprus and the conquests of
the Crusade of Villehardouin, or possibly in Palestine during the
short period that followed the visit of the Emperor Frederick II.,
that the system of the Assizes was more generally exhibited.

The kingdom of Jerusalem [7] can hardly be said to have ever
subsisted actually in the integrity in which it is described in the

---

[1] The edition of the Assizes which
I have used and quote in this preface
is that of the Count Beugnot, Paris,
1841, which contains also the *Lignages d'Outremer*.

[2] Assizes, preface to vol. i. pp. xix,
345, 346.

[3] Assizes, i. pp. 108, 109, 276, 637.

[4] Assizes, i. p. 225.

[5] Assizes, i. 279, 264, &c.

[6] Assizes, i. 107. ' En quel cas force
de Turs tolt saisine.'

[7] The kingdom of Jerusalem extended from Darum on the Egyptian
frontier to the little river Lycus,
between Byblus and Berytus. The
county of Tripoli from the Lycus to
Merkeb. The Antiochene territory
from Merkeb to Tarsus. The county of
Edessa, east of Antioch, reached from
the forest of Marith to Maredin in
Mesopotamia. W. Tyr. 908; J. de
Vitry, 1068 ; Wilken, ii. 596.

Assizes; for the principality of Edessa had been lopped off before the royal demesne had been completed by the acquisition of Ascalon. In its idea, however, it contained four great fiefs ;[1] the principality of Jerusalem as Godfrey had held it ;[2] that of Antioch, which was claimed also by the Byzantine emperor as a fief, but was secured to the monarchy by Baldwin II. ;[3] the county of Edessa, which having nominally become part of the kingdom by the accession of two of its counts successively to the throne, had afterwards been bestowed on Jocelin of Courtenay by investiture and the gift of a standard ;[4] and that of Tripoli, which was from the conquest dependent on the kingdom.

The principality of Jerusalem contained four principal baronies,[5] the county of Joppa and Ascalon, the principalities of Galilee[6] and Hebron,[7] and the lordship of Sidon and Cæsarea.[8] In the royal demesne were included among other places Tyre, Naplous, and Acre ; and from the time of Fulk and Baldwin III. the county of Joppa and Ascalon was the appanage of the member of the royal house who was nearest to the succession: the position, however, of the great house of Ibelin, who were lords of Ramlah, Mirabel, and Ibelin,[9] and

[1] Assizes, i. 417, 418.

[2] Godfrey did homage to the patriarch : W. Tyr. 771.

[3] The patriarch also claimed fealty from the prince : W. Tyr. 864. The patriarch of Jerusalem invested Bohemond with Antioch, and Godfrey with Jerusalem at the same time. W. Tyr. 771.

[4] W. Tyr. 817. The same author, p. 871, speaks of Edessa as a fief of Antioch.

[5] Assizes, i. 417, 418.

[6] The principality of Galilee, having been held by Tancred, Hugh of Falkenberg, castellan of S. Omer (1101–1107), Jocelin of Courtenay (1113–1118), William de Bures the Constable (1118–1130), returned apparently to the family of Falkenberg in the time of Baldwin III. (W. Tyr. 921), and came by marriage to the Ibelin family in the 13th century; Lignages d'Outremer, Assizes, ii. 455. Hugh of Tiberias, mentioned p. 23, was son of Walter of Falkenberg by Eschiva, who afterwards married Raymond of Tripoli : W. Tyr. 998.

[7] The principality of Hebron or S. Abraham, given first to Gerard of Champ d'Avesnes, then successively to Rorgius of Haipha, Walter Mahomet, and Hugh of Rebecq, was a fief of no great importance until it was joined

with the lordship of the country on the other side of Jordan which contained Kerak and Montreal. This lordship passed first through the hands of Romanus and Ralph du Puy (W. Tyr. 884). Having been forfeited by the latter, it was given in exchange for Naplous, to Payn the butler of the kingdom, brother to Guy de Milli, and uncle of Philip of Naplous. Philip of Naplous, who ultimately succeeded (W. Tyr. 1039), left a daughter Stephanie, who married first Henfrid II. of Toron, then Miles of Plancy, and last Reginald of Châtillon. Lign. d'Out. 452 ; Albert. Aquens. pp. 293, 329, 342, 352, &c.

[8] The lords of Sidon and Cæsarea descended from Eustace Grenier, the Constable, d. 1123. Reginald lord of Sidon mentioned in vol. R. S. pp. 121 and 445, was his grandson, the son of Gerard. Cæsarea was held as a fief of Sidon by a branch of the same family. Lignages d'Outr. 455. There are some verses in Martene and Durand, Ampl. Coll. v. 540, which claim Hugh of Rebecq, Hugh of Falkenberg, Eustace Grenier, and 'Harbel of Rames,' all as natives of the diocese of Terouanne.

[9] The origin of the house of Ibelin is obscure. According to the Lignages, which were probably drawn up by

subsequently engrossed nearly all the fiefs of Jerusalem and Cyprus, intrenched very materially on the power of the counts of Joppa. To the prince of Galilee belonged Tiberias and the north-east ; the lord of Sidon had the coast from Sidon to Arsûf, with the strongholds of Belfort and Bethshan ; the prince of Hebron or S. Abraham held the south, with the exception of the territory of Ascalon, on both sides of Jordan, including the impregnable fortresses of Montreal and Kerak. These four baronies contained in their turn inferior fiefs, of which the most important were, in the county of Joppa, those of the house of Ibelin ; in the lordship of Sidon, those of Cæsarea, Arsûf, and Haipha ;[1] in Galilee, those of the house of Toron, Paneas, and Castel-neuf. In all these lordships there were high courts of justice, and in thirty-seven towns of the Holy Land were as many courts of *bourgeoisie,* presided over by viscounts,[2] who were often hereditary fief-holders and related by blood to the greater barons.[3] Side by side with this elaborate system, and partially incorporated with it, was the administration of the fortresses intrusted to the military orders and of the ports belonging to the Italian republics : there were also different tribunals for the Syrian Christians.[4]

This organisation, which might in favourable circumstances have been a sufficient defence to the throne of Jerusalem, and at least would have formed the nucleus of a strong occupying force, the body of which would have been furnished by the successions of warlike pilgrims, was, on the contrary, a fatal source of

a member of the family, ' Balian le François fu frere au conte Guilin de Chartres, et vint deçà mer soi dizième de chevaliers, et le roi Fouques avoit fermé Ibelin, si li dona et Mirabel.' He married Helvis, the heiress of Ramlah, and had three sons, Baldwin of Rames or Ramlah, Hugh of Ibelin, and Balian II. Of these, Hugh married Agnes of Edessa, and Balian, Mary of Byzantium, the wives of King Amalric. The difficulty is about Balian I. William count of Chartres was the eldest and disinherited son of Stephen of Blois and Adela, daughter of William the Conqueror. But Adela certainly had no son named Balian ; possibly he may have been an illegitimate son of Stephen. He makes his appearance in the Holy Land as constable of Joppa, having been appointed by Hugh de Puiset count of Joppa, and *viscount of Chartres.* Strangely, the connexion between the family of Puiset and the counts of Blois is in the same

obscurity ; for Hugh de Puiset, bishop of Durham, was nephew to King Stephen, and his mother must have stood to Stephen of Blois in the same relation that Balian did if the *Lignage* is correct. The family of Puiset were early in the Holy Land ; two of them were successively counts of Joppa, and one, Stephen, who had himself been viscount of Chartres, became patriarch of Jerusalem (W. Tyr. 848). The town of Ramlah was given by Baldwin I. to Baldwin of Ramlah, the father of Helvis, Balian's wife. Cf. *Lignages d'Outremer,* p. 448, &c. *Gesta Dei, &c.* i. pp. 685, 699, 714, 860, &c.

[1] Payn of Haipha, mentioned in vol. R. S. pp. 121, 199, seems to have been an inveterate enemy of Guy of Lusignan.

[2] Assizes, i. 419.

[3] Thus at least were the viscounts of Naplous. Pauli, Codice Dipl. i. 61, 64.

[4] Called ' Corts de la Fonde.' Assizes, ii. 171.

decay. The feudal principle was not strong enough to hold it together. The families of Antioch, Edessa, and Tripoli were younger branches of great European houses, who, having found a splendid provision in the East, were inclined, like the great feudatories in France, to look forward to an independence for themselves, instead of taking their places as constituent parts of a noble but most hazardously situated colony: they held themselves competent to wage war on their own behalf, and to treat for peace and alliance with sovereign princes, even such as were at war with their suzerain. In the same way the great barons of the principality, as in France, were eager to increase their domains, and aspired to the position of the great feudatories with whom they were closely connected by marriage. Jerusalem was to all of them only a secondary consideration ; the zeal that set Europe from time to time in a blaze found no answer in the land for which so much was being sacrificed. The fresh hordes of Crusaders who disembarked, full of energy and ambitious of victory, were drawn off by their settled countrymen for their own separate purposes ; and the force that should have secured Egypt and Damascus was wasted on unconnected enterprises.

The process of decay and dissolution was hastened by local and incidental circumstances. The original settlers did not live long in their new possessions, and their children born in the land were a degenerate race. There were eleven kings[1] of Jerusalem in the twelfth century : under the first four, who were all of European birth, the state was acquired and strengthened ; under the second four, who were born in Palestine, the effects of the climate and the infection of Oriental habits were sadly apparent ; of these four three were minors at the time of their accession, and one was a leper. The noble houses which were not recruited, as the royal family was, with fresh members from Europe, fell more early into weakness and corruption. The general character of the native Franks united the faults of their European ancestry with those of the nations among whom they lived. Personally brave, for the heritage of Godfrey and Bohemond was not to be forfeited in a single generation, they were at once ferocious and effeminate, violent and faithless, luxurious and avaricious ; far more likely, therefore, by their example to betray the

---

[1] Godfrey, 1099–1100; Baldwin I., 1100–1118; Baldwin II., 1118–1131; Fulk, 1131–1142 (W. Tyr. 888 ; 1143, Wilken, *Gesch. d. Kreuzzüge*, ii. 717 ; 1144, Beugnot, Assizes, i. 428) ; Baldwin III., 1143–1162 ; Amalric, 1162–1173 ; Baldwin IV., 1173–1185 ; Baldwin V., 1185–1186 ; Guy, 1186–1192 ; Conrad, 1192 ; Henry, 1192–1197. In the same period there were four kings of England, four kings of France, six emperors, and sixteen popes. The life of Fulk of Anjou curiously joins the pedigrees of the kings of England and Jerusalem. The princess Isabel or Elizabeth, whose four marriages are the key to the history of the later Crusades, stood in exactly the same relation to Fulk as our King Henry II. did.

new pilgrims into dishonour and degradation than to lead them
to victory, or to direct their fresh energies into channels in
which their own experience should have taught them that the
course of Western empire, if it were ever to be a reality, must be
made to run.

The moral degradation of the Franks need not have entailed destruction from enemies not less degraded; and their inferiority
in numbers would have been more than compensated by the
successions of pilgrims, which, although they came but for a
time and special purpose, were constant; and every one of which
might have signalised its visit by some great exploit of conquest, if
there had been a strong policy or any fixed principles of administration to guide it. But the shortness and precariousness of life was
an evil without remedy, and in its effects irreparable. Of these the
most noticeable was perhaps one which would have arisen under any
system—the difficulty of carrying on a fixed policy whilst the
administrators were perpetually changing; but scarcely second to
this was the influence in successions which was thrown into the
hands of women. The European women were less exposed than the
men to the injurious climate, or to the fatigues of military service;
and many of them, having been born in Palestine, were in a measure
acclimatised. The feudal rights and burdens of heiress-ship,
marriage, and dower were strictly observed; consequently most of
the heiresses lived to have two or three husbands and two or three
families. To prove this in detail would involve the recapitulation of
all the *Lignages d'Outremer*. The principality of Antioch was in
wardship from 1111 to 1126, and from 1130 to 1136. From 1136
to 1163, or later, it was held by Constance and her two successive
husbands. During the regency of Roger of Apulia the chance of
gaining Aleppo was lost; and the folly or vice of Raymond of
Poictiers was the ruin of the second Crusade. In the kingdom
itself, out of eleven descents in the century, only two were from
father to son, and both of these were under questionable circumstances. The principality of Galilee, having come by marriage to
William de Bures, was carried by Eschiva to two or three successive
husbands. That of Hebron in the same way passed to the three
husbands of Stephanie. The lordship of Sidon alone descended
directly in the male line.[1] The fiefs were all heritable by females;
the widows of the lords had half their husbands' lands in dower, and
the other half in bailliage or guardianship for their children.[2] The

---

[1] For similar examples in the sequel
of the Crusade of Villehardouin, the
conquest of Romania, &c., refer to the
History of Mediæval Greece and
Trebizond, by Mr. Finlay, and the
genealogical details in his appendix.
[2] Assizes, i. 261–267, 280, 281, &c.
If the ward was a sovereign prince or

result of all this was that the great estates were for the greater part
of the century vested either in women or in minors ; and the administration of them, and the political influence attached to their
possession, fell into the hands of men who had at the best but a
terminable or short life-interest in them, and were either adventurers,
or, if possessed of a stake in the country, likely to sacrifice their
terminable estates to their nearest interests. Palestine was, moreover, thus overrun with a race of nobles closely connected by the
half-blood, and with all the family likenesses and jealousies that such
a connexion engenders.[1]

Still, among the adventurers and fortune-hunters of the Crusades
there were some who sustained by their prowess the fabric that had
in itself no trustworthy principle of cohesion. Such were Henfrid
of Toron,[2] the chivalrous constable of Jerusalem, from whose hand
Saladin received the girdle of knighthood, and who was the prop of
the kingdom for six-and-thirty years ; and Reginald of Châtillon,
the fox of Antioch, who, having been for many years a great support
of the state by strength and craft, precipitated by one act of perfidy
the ruin in which he himself so signally perished. The history of
Reginald illustrates what has been said above of the tendency of
circumstances to throw supreme power into the hands of irresponsible men.

Reginald, although the son of a great French noble, Henry, lord

suzerain, the guardians of his person
and lands were chosen by the court of
his vassals, p. 261. Only a father or
mother could have ' bailliage enterin,'
that is of both person and fief ; in
other cases the nearest relation to
whom the fief might descend had
charge of the fief, and the nearest
relation to whom it could not descend
had charge of the person of the ward.
These usages were exemplified in the
case of Baldwin IV. and V. Later on
it was ruled that the queen-mother
was the lawful guardian of a king in
his minority Assizes, ii. 397.

[1] One famous *Matron* of the Cru-
sades was Madame Estefenie la
Flamengue, who by her first husband,
Gui de Milli, was ancestor of the
princes of Kerak, and by her second,
Baldwin of Ramlah, of the lords of
Ibelin. Her daughter Helvis was
twice married : 1, to Balian of Ibelin ;
and 2, to Manassier the Constable.
Her grand-daughter Stephanie of
Hebron was three times married.
Constance, princess of Antioch, gave
that principality to her two husbands,

Raymond of Poictiers and Reginald
of Châtillon. Queen Sibylla was
three times promised or given in marriage, and her half-sister four times.
Agnes of Edessa, mother of Baldwin
IV., was three times married.

[2] There were four Henfrids of
Toron : the second, called Henfrid I.
(see below, p. 9) was constable from
1147 to 1179 ; his son Henfrid II. was
the first husband of Stephanie of Kerak
and died before his father ; Henfrid
III. was the first husband of the
princess Isabel or Elizabeth, who
divorced him to marry Conrad of
Montferrat (vol. in R. S. pp. 120, &c.) ;
Henfrid III., although slightingly
spoken of by our author, was a brave
man, and very useful in the negotiations between Richard and Saladin.
Bohadin (p. 193) describes him as a
fine young man, with shaven cheeks.
He had been married to Isabel in
1183, when she was twelve years old, the
age for the marriage of heiresses in
Palestine ; and they had lived together until 1191.

of Châtillon-sur-Marne in Champagne,[1] came to the Holy Land in 1147, according to William of Tyre, as 'stipendiarius' or 'gregarius miles,' probably being too poor to maintain a following of his own. In 1154 he was chosen by the young widow Constance of Antioch for her second husband, and in her right exercised supreme power in Antioch for many years, retaining until his death the title, and probably some of the privileges, of prince. The vigour and unscrupulousness with which he exercised his authority drew on him the peculiar enmity of his Saracen neighbours, whilst among the Christian nobles he was viewed as an adventurer. Having been taken captive by Megedin the governor of Aleppo, in 1160, he was kept in prison for sixteen years, either by the vindictiveness of his enemies, or, as is more probable, by the lukewarmness of his friends. In 1175 he was released on payment of an immense ransom, and to mend his fortunes married Stephanie, princess of Hebron, daughter of Philip of Naplous, and widow first of Henfrid II. of Toron, and secondly of Miles of Plancy, the late seneschal of the kingdom. This marriage placed him in a position even more important, as regards Palestine, than he had while prince of Antioch ; for Stephanie's own inheritance was the principality of Hebron, and the south country on both sides of Jordan, whilst as guardian to her son by her first husband, Henfrid III., she placed him, after the death of the constable, in possession of the fiefs of the family of Toron in the region of Galilee. One of her children was married to the Christian prince of Armenia, Rupin of the Mountain, and the other to the princess Isabel of Jerusalem. She was cousin to the lords of Ibelin, two of whom had married the two wives of king Amalric. In 1177, as lieutenant of the kingdom under Baldwin the Leper, Reginald won the famous battle of Ramlah over Saladin ; in 1181 he ravaged Arabia ; in 1183 he compelled the invincible Sultan to raise the siege of Kerak. Notwithstanding his great marriage and important position he was loaded with debt,[2] perhaps contracted for the payment of his ransom ; and this is said to have been the cause of his attacking, in 1187, the Egyptian caravan during the truce,[3] which was the ruin of the Holy Land, and drew down upon him the special

---

[1] The authors of the *Histoire Littéraire de la France*, xxi. 681, quote a MS. of the Chronique d'Outremer in which Reginald is described as brother of the lord of Gien on the Loire, which would seem to them more probable than that a member of the great house of Châtillon should be spoken of by William of Tyre as a common soldier. But either the authors of the *Histoire* or the writer of the MS. must have confused Reginald of Châtillon with

Reginald of Montmirail, who was one of the heroes of the Crusade of 1200, and brother to Hervey of Donzi, lord of Gien. Cf. Duchesne, *Histoire de la Maison de Chastillon*, p. 70.

[2] *Expeditio Asiatica Imp. Frid.* :— Canisius, vol. iii. pt. ii. p. 500.

[3] A truce had been concluded with Saladin, by Raymond of Tripoli as regent, in 1184, for three years ; and at Easter 1187 was renewed for three years more by King Guy.

vengeance of Saladin. The history of his cruel murder after the battle of Hittin is told by our author as well as by the Arabic writers. It is a blot on the fame of Saladin. The conqueror's hatred of perjury may have been an excuse in the eyes of his admirers for such an unworthy deed, but we cannot doubt that his indignation was further inflamed by the recollection of the defeat of Ramlah, and his own precipitous flight into Egypt.

If the kingdom of Jerusalem had fallen by inheritance, marriage, or election, to a man gifted with the energy and vitality of Reginald of Châtillon, the evil day might perhaps have been averted. The three minorities of Baldwin III., Baldwin IV., and Baldwin V. hastened the end.

It would have been very difficult under the most favourable circumstances to devise a law of succession for such a colony as Palestine, which required from its very nature to have at its head a man of mature years and statesmanship, with a sound title and definite authority. It fared ill under a line of sovereigns hardly one of whom came without opposition to the throne, whose powers were limited by closest feudal usage, and whose position was rivalled in wealth and influence by that of their own vassals. Possibly a strong government might have been secured by making the throne of Jerusalem dependent on some well-founded European power, such as the empire was under Frederick Barbarossa. But such a thought seems never to have entered the heads of the Crusaders ; the succession was left very much to chance, or to be the prey of the first comer. Had a proper election been made on Godfrey's death, Tancred would perhaps have been found his fittest successor ; but whilst the princes were delaying decided measures, Baldwin of Edessa succeeded as his brother's heir. No better successor to Baldwin could be found than his cousin Baldwin de Bourg, who had grown old in the wars of the Holy Land ; nor could any objection be made to the devolution of the throne to Fulk of Anjou, his son-in-law. By these expedients (for no principle of succession was established) a series of four princes of ripe years and martial experience was obtained, and as long as they lived prosperity lasted. The attempt to reconcile election with a certain regard for hereditary succession had been hitherto beneficial. From the death of Fulk began a series of disputes touching the rights of guardianship and succession. The first of these was between Milesende and her son Baldwin the Third. He was a minor at the time of his father's death, but was recognised as his successor by the nobles. Milesende, however, as the heiress of the kingdom, had a right to the honours of queen regnant. Accordingly, mother and son were crowned together, and during Baldwin's minority it made no difference whether the queen exercised supreme authority as guardian of the

z 2

king or as herself the sovereign.   As soon as he came of age a quarrel broke out, the nobles ranged themselves on different sides, and the schism was only closed by a division of the demesne of the crown : the evil example, however, was set, and followed at the beginning of each succeeding reign.   Amalric, whose manners were offensive to some of the great nobles, did not gain recognition as his brother's heir without some trouble, but no competitor for the crown seems to have been proposed.   His unfortunate marriages produced another crisis.   By his first wife, Agnes of Edessa, he had Baldwin IV. and Sibylla ;   having divorced her on grounds of consanguinity, he married Mary of Constantinople.   On his death, Baldwin was hailed as his successor, ' consonante omnium desiderio.'   But Baldwin was a minor ; if he was not illegitimate, still his mother was not under the circumstances a fit guardian for him.   Miles of Plancy, the seneschal of the kingdom, to whom Baldwin seems to have been intrusted by his father, was a French adventurer, and disliked by the nobles.   The regency was therefore claimed by Raymond of Tripoli.   This was granted by the nobles, but it was another case of compromise.   The law of the kingdom was that if the sovereign was a minor his guardian should be appointed by his vassals ; their choice was quite free.   But the usage amongst the vassals themselves was that the wardship of the person of the minor should belong to the nearest relation incapable of inheriting, whilst the guardianship of the fief should belong to the next heir ; in case, however, of one of the parents being alive, he or she had a right to the ' bailliage enterin '—of both person and fief.   Raymond, in claiming the wardship, set aside altogether the rights of the mother, and alleged himself as the nearest relation on both sides, a connexion which would by itself cancel his legal claims.   He was, however, chosen by the vassals, and filled the place not only during the minority but during several occasions of Baldwin's illness.   This unhappy prince could not escape the conviction that his death would be a signal for the disruption of the kingdom.   If Raymond were suffered to engross the supreme power during his life, the rights of his sisters Sibylla and Isabel would be defeated.   He therefore married Sibylla to William Longaspata, marquis of Montferrat, and intrusted his brother-in-law with the administration of the kingdom.   William unhappily died very soon after his marriage, and a successor was sought for Sibylla's hand.   After an ineffectual negotiation with the duke of Burgundy, she married Guy of Lusignan, who very soon encountered such determined hatred from the native nobles that Baldwin deposed him from the regency,[1] and is said to have con-

---

[1] Raymond was especially hated by the Patriarch Heraclius, Jocelin of   Edessa, the king's uncle, and Gerard of Bideford, the Grand Master of the

templated a divorce.   Before this was effected he died, and Baldwin V., the son of Sibylla and the marquis, succeeded by his will.   Again Raymond of Tripoli claimed the regency, this time by nomination of Baldwin IV.; and Jocelin of Edessa was admitted as guardian of the person of the king.   The death of Baldwin V. put an end to the legal power of Raymond, but he seems to have hoped to be chosen king.   But the old compromise was adhered to ; Raymond had made bitter enemies ; Sibylla was chosen to succeed her son, and immediately bestowed the crown on her husband.   The result of her choice was the loss of the Holy Land.   The two children of Sibylla and Guy died with their mother at the siege of Acre, and the heiress-ship devolved on Isabel or Elizabeth, daughter of King Amalric by his second wife, Mary of Byzantium, who had been married to Henfrid III. of Toron and Hebron, and was divorced from him by the intrigues of Conrad of Montferrat, to whom she gave her hand. It is needless to follow further the details of the pedigree.   Isabel was four times married, and thrice conferred the title of king on her husbands.   The last of them was Amalric of Lusignan, king of Cyprus, brother of Guy, in whose line the titular crown of Jerusalem subsisted until it came to the dukes of Savoy.[1]

The line of succession here exhibited was doubtless a mere series of expedients meant to remedy the defects of hereditary succession by a sort of election.   Intended to secure the benefits of both methods, it incurred the dangers incidental to both, the weakness of hereditary right, and the jealousies of the elective system.   The crown was inheritable by females, but the husband of the queen had to be elected by the states ; a minor might succeed, but the regency must be provided for by a special act.   When Sibylla bestowed the crown on her husband, she acted as a true wife, and her

Temple.   It was probably at this juncture that Heraclius and the Grand Master of the Hospital were sent to offer the sovereignty of Palestine to Henry II.

[1] Isabel had no children by Henfrid. By Conrad of Montferrat she had Mary, wife of John of Brienne, king of Jerusalem, by whom she had Yolande, wife of Frederick II., through whom the crown descended to Conrad and Conradin.   By Henry of Champagne, Isabel had three daughters, of whom Mary died young; Alice married Hugh I. of Lusignan, king of Cyprus ; and Philippina married Erard of Brienne.   From the second of these the title descended to the kings of Cyprus, and through them to the

dukes of Savoy, now (1864) represented by the emperor of the French.   By her fourth husband, Amalric of Cyprus, she had two daughters, Sibylla, wife of Leo king of Armenia, and Milesende, wife of Bohemond IV. of Antioch. Mary, the daughter of Milesende and Bohemond, sold her rights to the kingdom of Jerusalem to Charles of Anjou, king of Sicily.   The title descended with the kingdom of Sicily to the Angevin kings, and also to those of the house of Aragon.   In right of the latter the title is (1864) borne by the king of Naples, the queen of Spain, and the emperor of Austria, the last of whom has also the rights of the house of Lorraine to the inheritance of the Angevin kings.

choice under ordinary circumstances might have been a wise one. But she must have known the prejudice against him which existed in the country, and ought either to have renounced the succession or to have accepted the responsibility of making a fresh choice. The nobles of Palestine would not submit to a French adventurer ; the coronation of Guy practically sealed the fate of the colony. The choice immediately alienated the count of Tripoli, who, besides his own great fief, held, in consequence of his marriage with Eschiva, the widow of Walter of Tiberias, supreme influence in the principality of Galilee. The great house of Ibelin was also offended. Baldwin of Rames refused to do homage to Guy, and renounced his estates in preference. Balian of Ibelin, his brother, who had married Amalric's queen Mary, and was with her guardian of the legitimate heiress Isabel, took a prospective view of the power he would have if she were on the throne. Reginald of Sidon was closely connected with the same family, having married after the death of Sibylla's mother, Agnes of Edessa, Helvis, daughter of Balian of Ibelin by Queen Mary. Henfrid of Hebron, however, probably acting under the influence of his stepfather, sacrificed his own interest as Isabel's husband to the feeling of loyalty. Guy and Sibylla were thus little more than titular sovereigns ; the great fiefs and baronies were, with one exception, opposed to them by interest and ambition ; the best part of their own county of Joppa and Ascalon was in the hands of the house of Ibelin ; and the royal demesne was impaired by the settlement of Naplous as the dowry of Queen Mary, and thus made available for the aggrandisement of the same family. The land which had been won by the labour and blood of all Europe was become the property of a close corporation of native-born Franks, who would be contented rather to serve Saladin than to be shorn of their power by European supremacy. Within a year of the coronation of Guy, the battles of Nazareth and Hittin were lost, the former because Balian of Ibelin stayed on his way to hear mass,[1] the latter by reason of the treachery or irresolution of count Raymond. Guy, with the True Cross, fell into Saladin's hands. During his captivity Balian and Reginald of Sidon surrendered Jerusalem. All the strongholds had fallen before the capture of the city, or were taken shortly after, except Ascalon, which was given up by Sibylla for her husband's ransom, Tyre, which was relieved by Conrad of Montferrat, and two or three mountain fortresses which were compelled to surrender in 1189, shortly before the opening of the siege of Acre.

[1] Cont. W. Tyr. p. 599. ' Quant il ot erre deux milles, il vint a une cité qui a nom le Sabat. Il se pensa qu'il estoit beau jor, et qu'il n'iroit avant jusque qu'il auroit oi messe. . . . Et saches que si Beleen ne fust torne au Sabat, per oir messe, il fut bien venu a point a la bataille.'

The only sound element in the country was the organisation of the military orders.[1] These procured a constant succession of fresh and healthy blood from Europe, they were not liable to the evils of minorities, their selfish interests were bound up with the strength of the kingdom. If one Grand Master fell, another of equal experience and dignity took his place ; if estates accumulated in their hands, they were not applied to the strengthening of faction against faction or family against family, but for the aggrandisement of the body in sustaining the welfare of the Holy City and Palestine. It was probably for this reason, their character as corporations, undying and free from the evils of old age and infancy, and perhaps from a trust, not misplaced, in the virtue and honour of the knights, that Henry II. chose them as the depositories of his treasure devoted to the purpose of a crusade. It was certainly for the same reason, and not for any real pretext of faithlessness, that they fell under the especial vengeance of Saladin. It may be safely said that if Palestine could have been recovered and maintained by the Western powers it would have been by the knights of the Temple and the Hospital.[2] If their system had been adopted Palestine might have been still in Christian hands, or at least have continued so as long as Cyprus. Even the Venetian system, by which the Levantine states were afterwards governed, might have insured a longer measure of life ; for it was secured by the constant infusion of fresh blood, and by the avoidance of the evils of which the history of Palestine was sufficient warning ; nor did it fall until Venice was too decrepit to support it.

I have already pointed out some of the reasons why the second Crusade and the constant successions of minor expeditions failed to secure their object. The pilgrims were drawn in to ally themselves with the divided interests, and to subserve the petty purposes of the Frank

[1] Yet the catastrophe of the kingdom was due partially to the quarrel between Raymond of Tripoli and Gerard of Bideford, the Grand Master of the Temple. This arose from the fact that Raymond had refused Gerard, before he took his vows, the hand of the heiress of Botron, in the county of Tripoli. Hence the Templars had a hand in the elevation of Guy of Lusignan to the throne. Is it possible that the hostility of Raymond to Gerard and the Templars should throw any light on the authorship of this book ? The most ancient MS. contains the account of the treachery of Raymond at Hittin, and of the martyrdom of Gerard at Acre. Of these, the former is altogether omitted and the latter abridged in the later MSS. The

language of the Cotton MS. is just what we might expect if Richard the canon and Richard the prior were identical.

[2] I do not of course forget the charges of ambition and faithlessness generally received against the military orders, on the faith of the *Chronique d'Outremer*. It is of the machinery of their government that I speak ; such charges are always made against bodies of men who will not serve the private interests of the accusers. Precisely the same charges are brought against the Patriarchs, the Legates, the Syrian Christians, the European Crusaders, in fact everybody except the native Frank nobles, who, if facts are to speak, were far the most guilty in the loss of Palestine.

settlers. The agency that was so well employed by Baldwin I. in capturing the fortresses of the coast was diverted and wasted when the native families had established their separate interests. The strife between the parties of Guy and Conrad before Acre was the climax of what had been going on ever since the death of King Fulk. But there was a further reason, which perhaps is still more fully exemplified in the history of the crusade of Richard. The heterogeneous composition of the crusading armies; their want of common or uniform organisation, and the presence with them of immense crowds of warlike pilgrims ready to serve any master for wages, and dependent on very precarious means for subsistence at all. Ill provided and unattached, they were a constant encumbrance, a constant source of famine and disease.

So long as the princes were followed by their knights, and they by their own retainers, discipline and united action could be insured, but even then the allied forces required the guidance either of a general council of command, or, better still, of one commander. The former plan was adopted at the siege of Acre with some degree of success, and the latter during the subsequent campaigns under Richard, but only in a measure; the army was still encumbered with an immense mass of followers, who were generally their own masters. In illustration of this defect, I may refer to the very curious tract in the appendix to the preface to these memorials (in R. S.) The event it describes was an episode in the second Crusade, the siege and capture of Lisbon in 1147, but the same proceedings were repeated with similar results by several of the other crusading fleets, and especially on the occasion of the capture of Silvia by the English and Flemish warriors on their way to Acre.

A kingdom thus divided against itself, under a powerless stranger, filled with feudal nobles who feared and hated the Christians of Europe more than the Moslems themselves, might have fallen long before the battle of Hittin. It may be said indeed to owe not only its continued existence but even its origin to the divisions between the Saracens of Egypt and the Turks in Mesopotamia and Syria. So long as they were kept asunder, the kingdom maintained itself. But no sooner had Noureddin founded a strong power in Syria than the decay began. Wars might be alternately waged against Egypt and Damascus, but the pressure of war was continual. When Egypt and Damascus were united by Saladin the end was imminent; [1]

[1] Although it is almost impossible to identify all the names of the allies of Saladin as given in the earliest MS. of this work, pp. 12 and 13, vol. in R. S., we may make out sufficient to show that by report at least he had united in his service all the tribes of his empire. Noureddin the emir of Amiza was Noureddin the son of Kara Arslan; his presence in the army is mentioned

there was no seeking peace at Damascus to gain time for a war in Egypt, nor aid in Egypt against an upstart sultan at Damascus. Saladin had abolished the Fatimite Caliphate, which had rendered this state of things feasible. The enemy was one, on all sides, watchful, unwearied ; without a succession of help from Europe, however often defeated, he must be at last victorious. The Frank nobles saw themselves perishing for a cause with which they had little sympathy ; under Saladin they might still be powerful, as refugees in Europe they could be reduced to the insignificance from which they sprung. Hence to all the evils of the perishing kingdom the native Franks added the want of faith in their own cause, and consequently either actual treachery towards their allies, or a lukewarmness in support of them that was not less fatal.

The crusade of Richard was, then, an experiment tried with the very best intentions to restore and maintain the existence of a state that possessed but one element of life, and that not a part of its own organisation, and overborne by the general process of decay. An indefensible territory, for all the approaches to Palestine were in the hands of Saladin ; the native population either annihilated, or, where it existed, in active hostility ; a royal succession dependent on the caprices of a girl ; the hereditary nobility degenerate and divided, more attached to their own interests than to their nationality or their character as Christians, and preferring subjection to a pagan suzerain to the constant uncertainty and harass of a defensive organisation ; a vast and unmanageable host of allies, carrying with them to Palestine all their jealousies, and accumulating fresh causes

by Bohadin, pp. 51, 58, 104 ; he was accompanied by the emirs of Mesopotamia—Roob, Rakka, Nisibis, Myafarekin, Edessa, Samosata, Bireh, and Turbessel. Among the Syrian allies we recognise the emirs of Gibel, Kerak, Antilibanus, Bozrah or Buseireh, Aleppo, and Damascus ; among the Egyptian those of Damietta, Cairo, and Alexandria. From Asia Minor the sultan of Iconium, the lord of Khelat (Acalatinus), Bohadin 61, and Shemseddin of the Mountains. The caliph of Bagdad and sultan of Iconium are not likely to have been present in person ; the latter, however, was closely connected by marriage with Saladin (vol. in R. S. p. 51) ; and the former, under the name of ' Muleina,' seems to be referred to ibid. p. 230, as under the orders of Saladin. The ' dux Serbeth de Harengo,' if it is meant for Serchak the governor

of Harem (Abulf. p. 5), who was deposed in 1183 (Abulf. 34), is an anachronism ; and some of the other names were only picked up by hearsay. There are some that can be identified with Saladin's personal attendants and councillors, Bellegeminus, Mestoch, Baffadinus (either Bohadin or Saphadin) of Arka ; Aias de Stoi (Ijaz-et tawil), the emir Carracoensis (Karakoush) ; dux Dordcrinus Hedredinus Bedreddin Duldurn (vol. in R. S. p. 434). The forms Sanscous and Sanguinus seem both to represent Zenghi. The emir Cassachius is probably the person called, by Bohadin, Hassan the son of Kipjak ; or the emir of the Caffechaks (Chron. Terræ Sanctæ, p. 548). Jebedinus is Saladin's uncle Shebeddin Mahmoud (Abulfeda, Exc. p. 9) ; Megedinus, Muhjoddin (Bohadin, 57) ; Jerafaradinus, Sjerphoddin (Bohadin, 50)

of strife at every step of their journey; the impossibility of uniting in even one effort a sufficient force of different nations; the division of the Christian camp into two irreconcilable parties; the unhealthiness of the country; the difficulty of communications; the scarcity of provisions; the unwearied aggressions of a most able adversary; the certainty that treachery was lurking on every side; and the distraction of conflicting claims on his time and thoughts, were causes surely enough to account for any failure on Richard's part to carry out his hopes of conquest. Yet his expedition, such as it was, and coming at the moment it did, was the means of prolonging the existence of the kingdom for another century, and, in its consequences, of maintaining the social and mercantile communication between Europe and the Levant throughout the middle ages. Venice and Genoa, with all that resulted from their colonial system in the eastern Mediterranean, owed their opportunity and some part of their prestige to the conquest of Cyprus, and the other exploits of the pilgrims of the third Crusade.

Although the increasing helplessness of Baldwin IV., and the imminent prospect of a disputed succession or an unpopular regency, scarcely aroused the Franks of Palestine to a sense of the danger of their divided condition, the rapid advance of Saladin in power and resources warned them unmistakably that, unless they were helped from the West, their continued existence as a nation would soon depend on the sufferance of the Saracens. From none of the princes of Europe had they greater right to expect aid than from Henry of England. Personally, he was the nearest kinsman of the royal house, and in right of his wife he was head of the family to which the prince of Antioch belonged.[1] He had been for many years under a vow of pilgrimage. Very early in his disputes with Archbishop Thomas he had declared himself anxious to take the cross. In 1166 he had tried to raise money by placing in all the English churches an alms-box to receive contributions for Jerusalem.[2] When in 1168 he had declared himself ready to go down into Egypt to the aid of his uncle Amalric,[3] the fulfilment of his expressed intention had been so long delayed that Lewis VII. refused to believe that he would ever fulfil it. In 1169 the Archbishop Frederick of Tyre had found in him the only prince of Europe who

[1] Raymond of Poictiers, father of Bohemond III., the reigning prince, was brother to Eleanor's father. She also claimed to be head of the family of Toulouse, to which the count of Tripoli belonged, her grandmother

Philippa being daughter and heiress of Count William IV.
[2] R. de Diceto, 547.
[3] John of Salisbury, ep. 244, c. ed. Migne.

held out even a promise. He would, he said, if the pressure of his difficulties with Becket were removed, start for Jerusalem the next Easter ; calling his uncle, the king of Jerusalem, to witness that he had forgiven his enemy.[1] He was absolved from the guilt of his share in Becket's death, in consideration of a vow to go for three years on a crusade, and to perform his pilgrimage the very next summer ; he was also to maintain two hundred knights for a whole year for the defence of Palestine.[2] When his vow fell due, it was

[1] Joh. Salisb. ep. 293.

[2] Hoveden, 303; Gir. Camb. De Instr. Prin. 26, 27. It is just possible that to this vow was remotely due the establishment of an order of knights of S. Thomas of Acre, which was in existence early in the next century, and which, if the Chronicle of the Teutonic Order is to be believed, possessed in 1291 no less than 5,000 soldiers, Chron. Ord. Teut. in Matthæus, Vet. Ævi Analect. x. 182 (ed. 1710); Hermann Corner, ap. Eccard, i. 942.

The origin of the order is also attributed to William, the chaplain of Ralph de Diceto. Matthew Paris (p. 427) asserts that the knights were originally seculars, but that the order was remodelled and affiliated to the Templars, by Peter des Roches, bishop of Winchester, during his visit to Palestine from 1227 to 1232. Newcourt (Repertorium, i. 553) quotes from the *Theatre of Honour*, Lit. 9, c. 11 : 'The order of Saint Thomas was instituted by the king of England, Richard surnamed Cœur de Lyon, after the surprizal of Acres, and being of the English nation, they held the rule of S. Augustine, wore a white habit, and a full red cross charged in the middle with a white scallop.' The house of S. Thomas of Acre in London was founded in connexion with this order by Thomas Fitz Theobald of Helles, and Agnes his wife, sister of Thomas Becket, which points to an earlier origin than the siege of Acre. Cf. Newcourt, l.c., and *Monast. Angl.*, vi. 646, &c. The Patent Rolls of the ninth year of John contain a protection of the messengers of the House of S. Thomas at Acre, being canons, who had come to England seeking alms for the redemption of captives. Rot. Pat. i. 76 (ed. Hardy), Oct. 13, 1207 It is to be observed that Henry's

200 knights were to be regulated by the customs of the Templars. The order of S. Thomas survived the capture of Acre, and even the ruin of the Templars. The master of the hospital of S. Thomas of Acre in London is called, in 1279, ' frater militiæ ' (Reg. Peckham, fo. 158 b). Besides this hospital, the order had possessions in Wapping, Coulsdon, Stepney, Westbury, Hertford, and the hospital of S. James, at Doncaster. It had a preceptory in Ireland, founded by benefactions of Fulk de Villars, in 1219, and Gilbert, earl marshal. I have not been unable to recover the names of any of the masters of the order before the capture of Acre, unless William de Huntyngfeud, who was master of the house in London in 1267, was one. In 1279 the master was in England, and the brethren begging for their church. After the capture of Acre, the seat of the master was at Nicosia, in Cyprus, where he possessed a church, 'S. Nicolai Anglicorum.' In 1323 Henry de Bedeford, knight and master of the order, was in England, having made over the hospital in Nicosia to Brother John de Parys : the brethren at Nicosia refused to recognise Henry de Bedeforde as master, and William de Glastonbury, the preceptor, was at the head of the order there. In 1344 Robert de Kendale was the master, with the title ' Totius ordinis militiæ S. Thomæ Martyris in regno Cypri, Apuliæ, Siciliæ, Calabriæ, Brundusii, Angliæ, Flandriæ, Brabantiæ, Scotiæ, Walliæ, Hiberniæ, et Cornubiæ, &c. &c. generalis præceptor.' In 1357 Hugh Curteys was preceptor in Cyprus. In 1379, and after that date, the mastership of the order seems to have been held by the 'master of the hospital of S. Thomas in London, which gradually fell into the status of an ordinary Augustinian hospital. See the

not renounced, but delayed; and the delay was purchased by a promise to found three abbeys, which he fulfilled in a characteristic way,[1] by displacing (in 1177) the canons of Waltham and the nuns of Amesbury, to make way for establishments of the stricter orders of Austin canons and nuns of Fontevraud. In the same year he had agreed with Lewis VII. to take the cross; in 1181 he had made the same arrangement with Philip. He had given a further proof of sincerity in the annual payment of money, which had accumulated in the coffers of the Templars and Hospitallers, in 1187, to 30,000 marks. Something also might reasonably be expected from the English and Norman chivalry, who had never since the first Crusade drawn a sword in the cause of the Sepulchre. The conquest of Lisbon, the sole fruits of the Crusade of 1147, was indeed accomplished, for the most part, by English valour, but it was the work of the burgher and poorer pilgrims, not of the feudal nobles.

Accordingly, the Patriarch Heraclius, in 1185, betook himself especially to Henry, demanding of him more than pecuniary assistance, either the fulfilment of his vow, or the mission of one of the young princes to take the government of the Holy Land.[2] He went so far as even to recognise him as the heir and lord of Palestine.[3] But this bribe had no charms for Henry: any little town in France would have been more inviting. He called a council at Clerkenwell to decide for him, and there his coronation oath was alleged as an excuse for refusing personal aid; nor would he venture to bind his sons in their absence. Heraclius, after an angry remonstrance, ended his mission by applying to the young princes the words that Saint Bernard had used of their father; ' From the devil they came : to the

Register of the house, MS. Cotton. Tiberius C.V. Report of Deputy Keeper of Records, vii. 272, 293, &c. Taxation of P. Nicolas, 47, 52, &c.

[1] Gir. Camb. De Instr. Prin. 27.

[2] Peter of Blois declares that he was present, ' ubi regnum Palæstinæ, regnum etiam Italiæ, patri vestro, aut uni filiorum suorum, quem ad hoc eligeret, ab utriusque regni magnatibus et populis est oblatum.' Ep. cxiii. ad G. Eboracensem archiepiscopum, Opp. (ed. Busæus, Mentz, 1600) p. 204; cf. Giraldus Camb. De Instr. Prin. 59; R. de Diceto, 626; Hoveden, 358.

[3] The importance of this point appears greater when it is remembered that the kingdom of Jerusalem was looked upon as a fief of the Holy Sepulchre; that Godfrey himself had done homage and fealty to the patri-

arch. In case of the extinction of the family of King Baldwin, much might be made to depend on such a title, especially if the possessor was strong enough and rich enough to maintain it. But it is also possible that Baldwin IV., seeing the danger of a female succession, commissioned Heraclius to make the offer. The MS. Continuation of William of Tyre, Reg. 14, c. 10, has this : ' Erat et specialis causa quare eum in regni illius tuitionem vocare disponerent, quoniam si quid humanitus iis qui erant contingeret hæredibus, ad ipsum vel liberos ejus universa devolverentur jure agnationis. Erat sane Amaurici patruelis, et Fulconis quondam regis nepos.' Lib. i. c. 2. The statement of relationship is wrong; but the error is a common one.

devil they will go.'[1] He returned in despair to Palestine, followed,
however, by a large company of pilgrims, who, finding on their
arrival that Guy had just concluded the truce of Easter 1187,
returned home. Two English knights, Hugh de Beauchamp and
Roger de Mulbrai, remained to share the fortunes of the Franks ;
the former of these was slain and the latter taken captive at the
battle of Hittin.[2]

The terrible news of the loss of the Holy Cross, the capture of
the king, and the murder of the Templars was brought to Europe
in letters from the chiefs of the Temple and the Hospital, early in
October 1187. Pope Urban III. died of grief at receipt of the tidings,
on the 20th of that month : and in November, perhaps before the
capture of Jerusalem was known, Richard, count of Poictou, received
the cross from the hands of the archbishop of Tours.[3] William of
Tyre, the historian of the kingdom, arrived soon after. The Crusade
was preached in England, France, and Germany. In January 1188
Henry and Philip were reconciled, and took the cross ; in March
Frederick Barbarossa held his great council at Mentz for the same
purpose, and fixed the time for setting out for the March of the
following year. It is impossible to say whether Henry would have
fulfilled his vow ; he went, however, so far as to enter into negotiations with the king of Hungary and the emperor of Constantinople,
for a passage for his forces through their dominions. A fresh quarrel
with Richard, almost immediately after, put a stop to his preparations,
and the contest continued until a short time before his death, on the
6th of July, 1189.

Frederick, in pursuance of his vow, marched from Ratisbon in
1189,[4] and after proceeding through the Byzantine dominions, beset

[1] Giraldus, De Inst. Princ. p. 67.
The story of S. Bernard's prophecy is
told in Bromton, coll. 1045–6.

[2] Hoveden, 361 v°, 361 r°.

[3] The news which induced Richard
to take the cross reached the West
about the calends of November : Gir.
Camb. De Instr. Princ. p. 98 ; and he
took it the very morning after he received the news. Bromton, 1148. He
was the first to take the cross. Itinerarium, p. 32. So that he may have
waited until the news of the capture
of Jerusalem arrived. A month was
quite sufficient time for the news to be
brought from Palestine to France, the
voyage from Acre to Marseilles occupying only 15 days with a fair wind :
Hoveden, 382 v° ; yet it would seem,
from the arrangement of the letters in
the different chronicles, that the

account of the battle of Hittin did not
arrive before October. The loss of
Jerusalem seems to have been a less
shock generally than the capture of
the True Cross.

[4] The writer of this work is an independent authority on the march of
Frederick, and agrees so closely with
the details of Ansbert and the other
authorities referred to later on,
that it is clear he received his information from eye-witnesses. The
letter of Saladin to Frederick, as given
by him in the longer version, is probably authentic ; the enumeration of
the Sultan's titles, in the conclusion,
agreeing closely with the summary of
them given by Bohadin, *Vit. Sal.* p.
1. ' I essay to write the history of the
victorious king, defender of the faith,
subduer of the servants of the cross,

at every step with both violence and treachery, perished in the Caly-
cadnus in June 1190. The shattered remnant of his army, under
his son Frederick of Suabia, arrived in the Antiochene territory on
the 21st June, and at Acre in August. The English and French
crusaders, under Philip and Richard, had not at that time left Europe.
Whilst the princes were delaying, the humbler and more independent pilgrims were hurrying to Palestine. Geoffrey of Lusignan,
brother of the king, was compelled by a quarrel with Richard to leave
France, and hastened to the East, arriving at Tripoli in the summer
of 1188. The fleet of Londoners, Norsemen, and Frisians left Dartmouth in company on the 18th of May the following year, and, having
afforded the king of Portugal material aid in his war with the Moors,
arrived at Acre in September 1189. A strong detachment of French
nobles, including the bishop of Beauvais, Counts Henry of Bar and
Erard of Brienne, James of Avesnes, the hero of the siege of Acre, at
the head of the Flemings, and Lewis, landgrave of Thuringia, with a
company of German pilgrims, started at the same time. These were
followed at a short interval by a mixed company of English, French,
and German knights.[1] The counts of Blois and Champagne, with
strong reinforcements, reached Acre in July 1190.[2]

The main body of the English and French armies was still lagging
behind, with the kings : and did not move from home until a whole
year after Frederick Barbarossa had left Ratisbon. In March 1190
an English, Norman, and Gascon squadron, under Richard de
Camville, Robert de Sabloel, William de Forz of Oléron, the archbishop
of Auch, and the bishop of Bayonne, sailed from Dartmouth ; they
reached Marseilles, where they expected to meet Richard, on the 22nd
of August, and not finding him there sailed to Messina, where they
arrived on the 14th of September.[3]

lifter up of the standard of justice and
equity, health of the world and of
religion, Saladin, the sultan of the Moslems and of Islam itself, deliverer of
the holy house of God from the hands
of idolaters, the servant of the two holy
cities, Abulmodaffer Saladin, the son of
Job.' Compare with this p. 40, vol. in
R. S. The letter of Frederick to Saladin
is evidently corrupt in its present state,
in all the versions, so that it is hardly
fair to condemn it without more information : judged, however, by the side
of the manifestoes of modern heroes,
it contains nothing, *prima facie*, inconsistent with authenticity.

[1] In this company were William of
Perche-Goeth and Hervey of Gien,
the sons of Hervey of Donzi, or the
latter may have been Hervey of Donzi

the father, see pp. 28 and 74, vol. in
R. S., also Theobald of Bar, brother and
successor of Count Henry.

[2] In this party were, besides the
count of Blois and his brother Stephen
count of Sancerre, Count Ralph of
Clermont, with his nephew William
the Butler, in Senlis, who was taken
prisoner on the day of Conrad's
marriage, see p. 122, vol. in R. S.; Guy
and Lionel of Châtillon, Gobert of
Aspromont, Bernard of S. Valery,
Clarembald of Noyers, and the Count
William of Châlons. Most of the
minor nobles may be identified in the
various heraldic and genealogical
memoirs of the French families, or in
Du Cange's notes to Villehardouin.

[3] Hoveden, 380 v°, 383 r°.

Richard, having assembled his forces at Tours, and Philip, having rendezvoused at Paris, met at Vezelai on the 11th of July. Thence they proceeded to Lyons, where the kings separated, Philip hastening to Genoa, and Richard to Marseilles. There the English army divided. Richard and his suite, the chief of whom was the archbishop of Rouen, left on the 7th of August, coasted along the Italian shore,[1] and, after a leisurely tour, arrived at Messina on the 23rd of September.[2] Baldwin, archbishop of Canterbury, with Hubert Walter and Ranulf Glanvill proceeded directly to Palestine : they arrived at Tyre on the 16th of September, and at Acre on the 12th of October.[3] The third division, to which the author of the *Itinerarium* was attached, and which was to rejoin the king at Messina, left Marseilles on the 16th of August, and reached the place of meeting a few days later ; being followed by the fleet, which had sailed round by Portugal.[4] Philip, who had taken advantage of an illness which attacked him at Genoa, to secure the friendship of the republic, arrived at Messina on September 16th. At Messina the two armies stayed until the spring of 1191, and it was not before June, four years after the battle of Hittin, and two from the opening of the siege of Acre, that the crusade was completed by the arrival of Richard at Acre, the first to take the cross, and the last to fulfil his vow.

The occasion of this delay[5] was said to be the necessity for providing money and food for so large a force ; and this was probably the true reason. The delay was an unhappy one, so far as it touched the reputation of the kings, who had time not only to waste in unhappy bickerings, but actually to aggravate the animosity, that was already too strong to be concealed, into deadly hatred. But in estimating the evil consequences of this waste of time and power it should be considered that, if it tended to prolong the distress of the army before Acre, labouring, as it did, under famine and pestilence, surrounded by enemies, and destroyed by internal corruption, it saved from a like destruction the hosts of Richard and Philip. The defenders of Acre were worn out with a siege of two years when they surrendered, although the force of the besiegers was numerically an overwhelming one. If mere numbers or skill could have captured the city, it must have fallen long before Richard came ; and if the

---

[1] He made his appearance off Genoa, with fifteen galleys, on the 13th of August. Ottoboni Annales ; Pertz, xviii. 101.

[2] Hoveden, 380.

[3] Letter from Baldwin to the convent of Canterbury ; MS. Lambeth, 415, fo. 85.

[4] See p. 153, vol. in R. S.

[5] It is clear, however, that as late

as September 23rd the kings intended to proceed direct to Acre. Archbishop Baldwin, when he reached Tyre, believed that Richard was following close behind him : and according to Hoveden, 383 vº, Philip sailed for Acre the very day that Richard reached Messina, but was forced to put back into port by the weather.

difficulty of providing food and shelter for the existing army was so
great as it appears, it would have been madness to increase it during
the winter with the hosts of England, Normandy, Poictou, Anjou,
and France.

The object of the third Crusade was nothing less than the
reconquest of the whole kingdom of Jerusalem, and that under the
most unfavourable circumstances. When the first Crusaders undertook the same task, the country was in an unsettled state, the towns
governed by Emirs, who were practically independent, the Mahometan
powers of Egypt and Syria arrayed in both temporal and spiritual
rivalry against each other, and the sovereignty of Jerusalem itself in
dispute between them. Godfrey found, from the cities he passed on
his march from Antioch to Jerusalem, at least neutrality, from some
even hospitality. He had no difficulty in reaching Jerusalem, and
it soon fell before him. Now, on the contrary, the garrisons of
Saladin, experienced and valiant soldiers, trained to Frank warfare
and clad in Frank armour, occupied all the strongholds from Sidon
to Darum, Tyre only excepted. Saladin was lord of Damascus and
Aleppo and Bagdad, and had abolished the prayer for the Fatimite
Caliph in the mosques of Cairo. The fortresses which it had taken
the Frank kings ninety years to build and fortify were, every one of
them, in the hands of the enemy. The Sultan had followed up the
defeat of Hittin with energy. Within the month of July 1187 he
had taken Tiberias, Acre, Naplous, Haipha, Cæsarea, Sepphoris,
Nazareth, Toron, and Sidon. In August he took Byblus and Berytus.[1]
Saphadin, whom he had summoned from Egypt to meet him at
Masjdeljaba,[2] laid waste the plain of Ramlah and the south country,
Darum, Ibelin, Joppa, Ramlah, Mirabel and Arsûf. Ascalon was
surrendered in September, and in consequence Gaza, Beit-Gebrin, and
Latroon yielded without a blow. The Holy City was taken in
October. Early the next year the few remaining fortresses were
besieged, Kaukab or Belvoir, the stronghold of the Hospitallers,
Kerak, Shobek, Belfort, and Safed. Whilst they were holding out,
the victorious Sultan overran the territory of Antioch and Tripoli.
He took in succession Laodicea, Jebleh, Sehjoun, Bacasus, Burzia,
Derbasac,[3] and reduced the prince of Antioch to promise that he
would surrender that city, the firstfruits of the first Crusade, if it
were not succoured within seven months. Safed and Kerak were
taken in November 1188,[4] Kaukab in January 1189,[5] and Shobek in

---

[1] Tiberias, July 5; Acre, July 9;
Toron, July 20 Sidon, July 27; Bery-
tus, July 30–Aug. 6 ; all the rest before
September 7 ; Bohadin, 73. Abulfeda,
Excerpta, 41, gives the captures in
slightly different order, as does the

Chronicon Terræ Sanctæ. Cf. Hoveden, 362 vᵒ.
[2] Abulfeda, 41.
[3] Ansbert, 5.
[4] Bohadin, 88.
[5] Bohadin, 88.

the following May.[1]   Against all this was to be set only Tyre, which
was relieved by Conrad of Montferrat in July, and had successfully
held out against Saladin in the winter of 1187.   Tripoli had been
saved by Margarit, the admiral of William of Sicily, who had also
destroyed the fortifications of Byblus and Joppa in a descent upon
the coast.[2]   Hervey of Donzi, in the principality of Antioch, was at
the head of a small but well-trained army.[3]   Merkeb and Hesn-al-
akrad were still held by the Hospitallers[4], Reginald of Sidon
maintained Belfort against Saladin ; and Hugh of Tiberias,[5] in a
hasty raid, had destroyed the garrison and defences of Arsûf.   Belfort
held out until April 1190.[6]

When King Guy, with his 700 knights and 9,000 serving-men,
encamped before Acre, Tyre and Belfort were the only towns in the
territory of Jerusalem that were held by the Christians.   Richard
and Philip had not begun their preparations.   Frederick Barbarossa,
far off in Macedonia, was struggling against the savage auxiliaries of
the Byzantine empire.   There was division in the remnant that
remained in the country.   The marquis had refused to allow the
king to enter Tyre.   The Genoese had attached themselves to the
former, and the Pisans to the latter ; and the quickly-arriving
companies of pilgrims attached themselves, according to their
national alliances, to the one or the other.   What Guy proposed,
Conrad objected to ; the count of Tripoli was dead ; the prince of
Antioch a helpless neutral.   It was an act of no small faith and
energy in King Guy, with so small a force and so few powerful
European connexions, to undertake a task which proved too great
for all the chivalry of Christendom.   ' The king, the Templars, the
Hospitallers, the archbishop of Pisa and the Pisans, against the will
of the marquis and of the archbishop of Ravenna, came down
against Acre to besiege it, four days before the end of August
1189.' [7]

It does not appear why Conrad opposed this measure ; perhaps it
was only because he himself was not placed in command.   It was a
matter of necessity that Acre should be recovered before anything
else was attempted ; for it was the only safe harbour on the coast of
Palestine, except Tyre ; and its position was such as to enable its
holders to open or close, at will, the communications between Tyre
and Jerusalem.

There were three possible ways of proceeding to the conquest :

[1] Bohadin, 90.
[2] R. de Diceto, 641.
[2] See Roger Niger, ed. Anstruther,
p. 94.
[4] Hoveden, 368 ; Ansbert, 5.
[5] Expeditio Asiatica Friderici, in

Canisius, iii. pt. ii. p. 502.
[6] It was closely besieged from April
21, 1189, to April 22, 1190. Bohadin,
89, 113 ; cf. Itinerarium, vol. R. S.
p. 63.
[7] R. de Diceto, 648.

A A

to bring an army by land through Asia Minor, Armenia, and Antioch ; to seize the Damietta mouth of the Nile, and occupy the isthmus ; or to land an army on the coast, and open the shortest line of communication between Jerusalem and the Mediterranean. By the first route the German Crusaders were expected ; but they would not be able to pass Acre, even if they could bring with them their own provisions. An Egyptian campaign was very hopeless whilst Saladin was in possession of Ascalon, and the experience of the later Crusades shows us that it was impracticable. The third plan was the most feasible every way. The besieging force might be supplied both from Tyre and from the sea : if Acre was taken the line of coast from thence to Joppa was easily to be overrun, and after that the route to Jerusalem was open.

A few days after the siege began, Saladin brought up an immense force to crush the besieging army, and occupied the range of hills that surround the plain of Acre. The month of September, however, brought up the Northern fleet ; the Flemings, under James of Avesnes, quickly followed ; next came the counts of Dreux, Bar, and Brienne, and the warlike Philip of Beauvais. The nobles of Champagne came next, then the landgrave of Thuringia, who persuaded the marquis, with 1,000 knights and 20,000 serving-men, to join the siege.[1] The battle of the fourth of October, in which Gerard of Bideford perished, seems to have convinced the princes that there was no hope of driving away the forces of the Sultan, and they proceeded to intrench their own camp and to invest the city. The struggle for the possession of the harbour was decided in favour of the Crusaders in a battle fought in March 1190. In the July of that year they were reinforced by a large army of French pilgrims, and Archbishop Baldwin, with the English contingent, followed in October. The great increase in numbers, the scarcity and badness of the provisions, the despairing impatience of the soldiers, produced almost directly after a terrible demoralisation in the army. Pestilence followed ; and at that moment the jealousies of the leaders broke out into open quarrels.

Guy of Lusignan was a brave soldier, a good commander, an honourable and generous enemy, and a faithful friend ; [2] but he had

---

[1] R. de Diceto, 648 ; and p. 61, vol. R. S.

[2] Guy was obliged by Henry II. to fly from Poictou in 1168, for his share in the death of Patrick earl of Salisbury. Hoveden, 294 v°. ; Gervase, 1403; Trivet, 62, from R. de Monte, 904. Henry had just before burned the Lusignan country and the castle of the lord ; R. de Monte, 903. There is nothing to show that Patrick was not killed in fair fight, but, as he was returning from Compostella, the sacrilege was punished by Guy's exile. Unfortunately for the character of the family, Geoffrey the brother of Guy was obliged to fly in 1188 on a similar occasion : he had killed a great friend of Richard in an ambuscade. Our author, at p. 350, vol. R.S., gives a

two great faults in the eyes of the native Franks : he was without wealth or powerful connexions, and he was devoid of that craft which in them took the place of strength and honest dealing. Conrad of Montferrat,[1] although at first objected to as an adventurer, soon convinced them that his character was much more to their liking. He was strong in the relationship of the emperors of both East and West; whilst Guy came of a family which, though honourable for antiquity, possessed as yet only a third-rate fief, and that by a very questionable title : he was rich, ruthless in enmity, faithless in friendship, cunning and unscrupulous enough to pass for an Italian of a later age ; and withal, a famous captain by sea and land.[2]

Guy had never been able to gain possession of his kingdom, and Conrad was determined that he never should. As the master of Tyre, he was able to get the first word with every convoy of pilgrims that landed there on their way to Acre ; and his success in this direction, from the very opening of the siege, may be calculated by comparing, with the 700 knights and 9,000 serving-men with whom Guy sat down before Acre, the thousand knights and 20,000 followers whom the marquis brought up a month after.[3]

Guy, however, remained at the head of the besieging force only a very short time. James of Avesnes, a knight of great valour and

character of Guy, to whom, as a partisan of Richard, he was attached : at p. 71, however, he gives a story of his saving the life of the Marquis Conrad, which counterbalances all that is said against him. William of Newburgh, ii. 88, calls him 'vir strenuissimus.' He belonged to a family which was not only personally hostile to Richard, but whose interests were opposed to his own. His brother Hugh of Lusignan had contrived to secure the county of La Marche, the reversion of which had been purchased by Henry II. in 1177. Hoveden, 326. Geoffrey had been one of the tools of Henry in his hostility to his son. Diceto, 639. Under these circumstances Richard's support of Guy as king of Jerusalem is curious, and still more his anxiety to provide him with the kingdom of Cyprus. Hugh X., count of La Marche, who married the widow of King John, was a nephew of Guy.

[1] Conrad is described by Richard of Devizes, p. 52, as 'vir leviannigena,' a son of Leviathan, the crooked serpent. Bohadin in several places celebrates both his craft and prowess, pp. 91, 135, 170, 214. He had gained

a great reputation in both empires, but lost both his credit and life by his selfish conduct in Palestine. Yet the levying of the Crusade was in great measure done by his exertions. Bohadin, 91. He had some difficulty in overcoming the dislike of the native Franks. Diceto, 642. Three marquises of Montferrat are mentioned in this book : William the old marquis (called in the *Chronique d'Outremer*, c. 588, Boniface, and confounded by the author of the *Expeditio Asiatica Friderici*, Canisius, v. 501, with his son Reiner, king of Thessalonica), who was taken prisoner at Hittin (see vol. R. S. p. 23); William Longaspata, his son, and brother of Conrad, Reiner, and Boniface ; and Conrad himself.

[2] 'Fuit autem Conradus armis strenuus, ingenio et scientia sagacissimus, animo et facto amabilis, cunctis mundanis virtutibus præditus, in omni consilio supremus, spes blanda suorum et hostium fulmen ignitum, simulator et dissimulator in omni re, omnibus signis instructus ; respectu cujus facundissimi reputabantur elingues.' Historia Terræ Sanctæ, Eccard, ii. 1353.

[3] R. de Diceto, 648.

A A 2

experience, very early superseded him, and he was shortly after obliged to share the command with the landgrave, whose only title to it seems to have been his rank and influence. In July 1190, Henry of Champagne, who represented both his uncles, Richard and Philip, succeeded James. Two months after, the duke of Suabia, who had been induced by Conrad to come to Acre, was put forward by him as a candidate for the command. But this minor contest was soon merged in the more important struggle for the kingdom between Guy and Conrad. Queen Sibylla and her children died about October 1190, and left the succession to her sister Isabel, who was divorced from Henfrid of Kerak and married to the marquis immediately after, in spite of the excommunication pronounced against them by Archbishop Baldwin, the vicegerent of the patri-arch.[1] The duke of Suabia died in January 1191.

Immediately after his wedding Conrad left for Tyre, and although he had bought the consent of many of the princes to the marriage, by liberal promises of provisions to be sent to the besiegers, he seems to have troubled himself very little more about Acre, until the arrival of Philip in the following April. The famine and pestilence lasted from November to February.[2]

Philip immediately on his arrival threw himself into Conrad's party, probably having been already engaged by the Genoese. Guy, in order to avoid being summarily dispossessed of his throne, was compelled to seek Richard in Cyprus, and to beg his aid. This was readily given ; Richard never flinched in his support of the king. Conrad, as soon as he heard of the approach of the English king, prepared to return to Tyre.[3] He had already lost the confidence of the Frank nobles ; and the princes of Antioch and Tripoli,[4] as well as the luckless Henfrid, were on the side of Guy. Conrad ordered Tyre to be closed against Richard, and on his arrival at Acre did not venture to answer the complaints laid against him by Guy, and enforced with wager of battle by his brother Geoffrey. Philip, how-ever, not content with recalling Conrad and placing him at the head of his household and council, further alienated Richard by claiming a half of Cyprus, according to the letter of their original alliance. Richard answered by demanding half of the county of Flanders,

---

[1] The important point that Sibylla's death preceded the marriage of Conrad and Isabel seems to be proved by an unpublished letter in the Lambeth MS. 415, from a chaplain of Bald-win to the convent of Canterbury. This letter is dated Oct. 21st; Sibylla was then dead. Baldwin had only arrived at Acre on the 10th. The marriage was not concluded for some time after his arrival, and the negotia-tions that preceded it took place at Acre.

[2] Hoveden, 387 v°.

[3] Bohadin, 170 ; Hoveden, 394 v°.

[4] Hoveden, 393 v°. The new prince of Tripoli, Raymond III., was the son of Bohemond III. of Antioch.

which Philip had claimed as an escheat a few days before. The dispute was, however, reconciled, and a new agreement made for the future.

Acre surrendered on the 12th of July : the True Cross was to be restored, and a ransom paid for the prisoners of 200,000 Saracenic talents : according to Bohadin the marquis was to have, over and above, 10,000 talents for his share in the capitulation, and his knights 4,000 more.[1] A few days later the princes came to an agreement, by which Conrad waived his claim to the present possession of the kingdom, and was confirmed in his tenure of Tyre, and right of succession. He then withdrew to Tyre : Philip returned home : the duke of Burgundy took the command of the French. The whole of the expense, and most of the labour of the last year of the Crusade, fell on Richard ; and Conrad from that moment set himself in determined opposition to him, adopting a course which completely frustrated the purpose of the expedition.

Richard was not yet awake to the difficulty of his position. His health had failed almost immediately after his arrival, and his allies had deserted him ; yet on the 6th of August he wrote from Acre to the justiciar that the Holy Land would soon be restored to its former state, and by the next Lent he should set out on his return.[2] As late as the first of October he retained this hope.[3]

The plan of Richard and the Frank princes was to carry out the programme begun by Guy with the siege of Acre. That city was to be for the time the headquarters of the Crusade : the line of coast from thence to Joppa was to be secured, and then the road from Joppa to Jerusalem. Richard accordingly, marching past Haipha, which had been burned by Saladin four days before Acre was surrendered, proceeded to Cæsarea, which he found deserted ; and thence, harassed at every step by Saladin, who followed in a parallel line of march, towards Arsûf or Arsur, the ancient Apollonia. Before he reached this city Saladin compelled him to fight a general battle, which ended in so decided a victory for the Crusaders that Saladin, in a panic, ordered the demolition of all the strongholds except Jerusalem, Kerak, and Darum. From Arsûf, where James of Avesnes was slain, the army went on to Joppa, which they reached on the 10th of September, having occupied nearly three weeks in marching less than 60 miles. Seven weeks were spent in fortifying Joppa and two villages on the road to Ramlah ; on the 31st of

---

[1] Bohadin, 179.
[2] ' Sed quam citius terram Suriæ in pristinum statum revocaverimus, tunc in terram nostram revertemur. Itaque pro certo scias quod ad proximam Quadragesimam mare intrabimus.' Richard to the Justiciar, MS. Lambeth, 415, fo. 90 v°.
[3] Letter from Richard to the abbot of Clairvaux. Hoveden, 398.

October they set out for Jerusalem, Saladin retreating step by step before them, and dismantling the fortresses on the road. Richard moved first from Joppa to Yazour,[1] Saladin, who had destroyed Ramlah, being then at Latroon ; on the 15th of November [2] Richard marched from Yazour towards Ramlah, and Saladin dismantled Latroon and retired to Tel-al-sjusour. Three weeks after, the vanguard of the army reached Latroon,[3] and Saladin almost directly retired into Jerusalem. After Christmas the Crusaders proceeded to Beit-Nûba, enduring the utmost misery from the weather and want of provisions, which were intercepted by predatory detachments of Turks, who came down from the mountains and from the garrison of Masjdeljaba. After perils of every sort, the available force being impeded and embarrassed with crowds of useless pilgrims, they were compelled to halt. Having come almost within sight of Jerusalem, the leaders found their council divided. There is no doubt that, had they proceeded at once, they might have taken the Holy City. But the object of the native Franks was not to recover Jerusalem : only to keep the pilgrims in Palestine until they had recovered their own possessions. Jerusalem once taken, the pilgrims would go home, and Saladin come back more terrible than ever ; the city could not be held, if it were taken, without garrisoning all the forts along the line of route ; and for this there was not sufficient force in the country : the hundreds of thousands who were to have done it had perished by famine and pestilence before Acre. The French, it was said, jealous of the leadership of Richard, began to straggle back from Ramlah to Joppa. At last, on Saint Hilary's day, the council determined to retreat,[4] and to occupy Ascalon, or even to invade

[1] Bohadin, 211. Saladin retreated from Ramlah to Latroon on the 5th of October; Ramlah and Lydda were condemned on the 25th Sept. Bohadin, 202, 204.

[2] Bohadin, 220. The destruction of Latroon was begun as early as October 5. Ibid. 204.

[3] Hoveden, 406; pp. 298, 299, vol. R. S.

[4] It is to this point of time that the story told by Joinville (ed. Didot, Paris, 1859, p. 172) is to be referred, if it is true. It should be compared with the false report told by Benedict of Peterborough, ii. 721. 'Il atirèrent leur gent, et fist le roy d'Angleterre la première bataille, et le duc de Bourgoingne l'autre après, à tout les gens le roy de France. Tandis que il estoient à esme de prendre la ville, en li manda de l'ost le duc que il n'alast

avant ; car le duc de Bourgoingne s'en retournoit arière, pour ce sanz, plus, que l'en ne deist que les Anglois n'eussent pris Jerusalem. Tandis que il estoient en ces paroles un sien chevalier li escria : "Sire, Sire, venez jusques ci, et je vous mousterrai Jerusalem." Et quant il oy ce, il geta sa cote à armer devant ses yex tout en plorant, et dit a Nostre-Seigneur : "Biau Sire Diex, je te pri que tu ne seuffres que je voie ta sainte cite, puisque je ne la puis délivrer des mains de tes ennemis."' The latter part of the story applies better to the second retreat : see vol. R. S. p. 369. I do not see how the circumstances can be true, but it is certain that the desertion of the French on the first occasion prevented the capture of Jerusalem. Bohadin, pp. 8, 9.

Egypt, before proceeding to take Jerusalem. Richard, in compliance with this decision, immediately moved southwards, the French lending him a very feeble support : after two days' march, unimpeded by the Saracens, he came to Ascalon. The spring was spent in the rebuilding the walls of Ascalon, the occupation of Gaza, Beit-Gebrin, and Tel-es-safieh, which were deserted, and the capture of Darum from the garrison placed there by Saladin.

The death of the Marquis Conrad, in April, reunited the contending parties under Henry of Champagne : Guy gave up his claims to the crown, and another march to Jerusalem was projected. As the first had been undertaken in the depth of winter, the second fell at a still more unfortunate time, the height of summer. Richard going north from Ascalon, and the other princes south from Acre, the two armies met at Beit-Nûba, and there again they stayed. Again the council was divided, the same arguments were brought forward, the impossibility of an advance was proved, Richard himself being convinced of it ; the French, on the principle of contradiction, now insisting on the capture of Jerusalem. The armies had hardly met when they were separated, and this time finally. Richard, broken down in health and distracted with the conflicting messages that reached him from home, proceeded to Acre on his way to Europe. Thence he was recalled by the attack of Saladin on Joppa ; he added one more splendid victory to the list of his fruitless glories, and then made peace.

Such is, in a few words, the record of the Crusade given us in the book before us, and the other Christian histories. From the Saracen writers we learn the details of the diplomatic struggle that was going on during the entire course of it, and which only emerges from time to time in the narrative of our author.

Saladin was at no point of the Crusade secure of victory. The armies he had to manage were almost as intractable and soluble as those of the pilgrims ; he himself had no violent hatred against the Christians : nay, if we may believe the story told by Hoveden, he would have gladly purchased their friendship and alliance against the rebellious princes of Mesopotamia, by the surrender of Jerusalem, and the restoration of most of the strongholds of Palestine.[1]

---

[1] July 6, 1191 : Hoveden, f. 395, and Bromton, col. 1204. Also July 14, Bromton, 1206 ; Hoveden, 396. Saladin wanted aid against Kothbeddin, the son of Noureddin, whom these writers call the lord of Musse, by which they perhaps meant Mosul. He was lord of Diarbeker. On the 16th of July, Kothbeddin proposed to them an alliance against Saladin. I may as well mention here that I have quoted Bromton's compilation generally, only in those passages in which his account represents Benedict of Peterborough, as being more easily referred to than Hearne's very scarce edition of the latter author.

But whether he was sincere in this offer or not, he thought it advisable to temporise, and, being well acquainted with the divided counsels of his enemies, to play them off one against another. During the siege of Acre, intercourse more or less friendly had taken place between the Sultan and Richard, and on one occasion an interview was arranged between Richard and Saphadin, which the council interfered to prevent.[1] Still, presents were exchanged ; Saladin sent snow and fruit for the sick king,[2] and the messengers went to and fro until the massacre of the Saracen prisoners put a stop for the time to proceedings of more than doubtful consequence. The only result seems to have been to create a suspicion against Richard in the mind of his allies.

Richard's misgivings as to the final success of the expedition clearly originated during the march to Joppa : both parties then measured each other's strength. On the 3rd of September, four days before the battle of Arsûf, Richard opened negotiations with Saphadin. The two heroes met on that day,[3] Henfrid of Toron acting as interpreter. Saphadin inquired on what terms peace would be accepted. Richard demanded the immediate possession of the whole country. This was at once refused. The same demand was made on the 12th of September,[4] two days after the arrival of the army at Joppa ; and this time the Sultan was in such a panic that, although in words he flatly refused to entertain the proposal, he constituted his brother Saphadin plenipotentiary, for the conclusion of a treaty.

Conrad of Monferrat, seeing his downfall certain in the event of a peace concluded by Richard, now began to communicate with

---

[1] June 17, Richard asked an interview with Saladin ; the answer was, ' Kings do not meet for conversation, unless they have first made a treaty ; and it would not be decorous for them, having talked and eaten together, to stir up war. If King Richard desires this, the terms of peace must be settled first. Moreover, we must have an interpreter in whom we can both trust. If these conditions can be fulfilled, by God's will we will meet.' Bohadin, 169. After this, frequent messages were exchanged, but without effect. At the end of the month, the Sultan agreed that Saphadin should meet Richard in the plain, in the presence of both armies. The Christian princes having interfered to prevent this (p. 171), Richard excused himself on the ground of illness, proffering a present to the Sultan.

Saphadin accepted the present on condition of being allowed to make one in return. The messenger then explained that the present destined for Saladin was some hawks ; these were sick, and required to be fed on poultry, which he asked Saphadin to send. Saphadin laughed, and said, ' The king wants the poultry for himself.' On the first of July he sent a Moslem captive as a present to Saladin ; Saladin returned him with a rich dress and presents, p. 172.

[2] July 4 : Bohadin, 176. On the 15th of July Richard sent some hawks and harriers to the Sultan : Bromton, c. 1206. On the 31st of July Saladin requested information about the Christian faith, pretending that he might be converted. Ibid. 1210.

[3] Bohadin, 193.

[4] Ibid. 200.

Saladin.[1] He offered, if Sidon and Berytus were secured to him, to join Saladin, proclaim war against the Franks, and besiege Acre. Saladin replied that if he would give proof of his sincerity by joining the Moslem forces at once, Sidon and Berytus should be given him, but not otherwise. The lord of Sidon, who acted as Conrad's ambassador, was magnificently received by the Sultan in November ; [2] he brought the news that Conrad was willing immediately to break with the Christians on the specified conditions.

Side by side with this intrigue, the negotiations for peace proceeded between Richard and Saphadin. They were renewed early in October ; [3] on the 16th Saphadin accepted a horse from Richard ; [4] and on the 18th we find Richard considerably abating his terms, and in fact almost appealing *ad misericordiam*. He said that Moslems and Franks were alike perishing ; the country was utterly wasted ; the prize for which they were contending was perishing from both of them. They had both done their duty as warriors for religion ; nothing remained to be decided but the possession of the Holy City and the True Cross, and the division of the country. Jerusalem, as the mother of the Christian faith, ought to belong to the Christians ; the wood of the Cross was valueless in the sight of the Moslems : both might easily be given up. As for the country, let Jordan be the frontier between the two powers ; only let there be peace.[5] Saladin replied that the Holy City was as dear to the Moslems as to the Christians : nay, more so, for thence the Prophet took his night-ride, and there the angels were wont to meet. He would not, therefore, retire from the city or surrender the country, which naturally belonged to his nation, and had only fallen into Christian hands in consequence of the weakness of the Moslems. As for the Cross, it was indeed a scandal, and an offence to God, and could not be surrendered except to gain some great end for the true faith.[6]

On the 21st Richard made a new proposition to Saphadin.[7] He offered him his sister, Queen Joanna, in marriage : she might be queen of Jerusalem, and Saphadin king, if Saladin would endow his brother with Palestine, give up the Cross to the king of England, and leave the military orders in possession of their strongholds. This message was sent on to Saladin, who doubted Richard's good faith, and thought it a good plan to pretend acquiescence, throwing the onus of the next move upon the Franks. The result was as he

---

[1] Bohadin, 204. Saladin's answer was given on the 4th of October.

[2] November 3: Bohadin, 214. His interview with Saladin took place on the 9th : Bohadin, 217.

[3] Oct. 5. : Bohadin, 204.

[4] Bohadin, 207.

[5] Ibid. 207.

[6] Ibid. 208.

[7] Ibid. 209. This author was himself the messenger who brought the report of this offer to Saladin.

expected.[1] The lady refused to marry a Moslem ; Saphadin must become a Christian ; the question of peace might remain open until a decided answer could be given. Saphadin, however, did not look on these negotiations as binding him to pacific conduct. On the 6th of November [2] we find Richard remonstrating with him on account of the ambuscade laid for his forces at Bombrac. An interview between the two princes resulted from this. They met on the 8th,[3] but with no other issue than to increase the odium against Richard among the princes of the Crusade. Saladin refused to see him, and his demands were further abated to a request that the country should be divided between himself and Saphadin.[4]

On the 11th of November [5] the Sultan laid the rival proposals of Conrad and Richard before his council, and those of the king were accepted. Saphadin might marry Joanna, and the two should have the whole kingdom between them. Richard, alarmed at the acceptance of an offer which could not be carried out without covering him with shame, and of the feasibility of which he was by no means sure, informed the Sultan that the question must be referred to the pope. Joanna was a widow, and could not be remarried without the apostolic sanction ; but if consent were refused, Eleanor of Brittany, his niece, would be a fair bride for Saphadin, and as she was a maiden in his ward no papal consent need be sued for. Saladin, on the 15th,[6] replied to this that he could listen to no such proposition : his brother would have the queen of Sicily or none at all. He at the same time renewed the plenipotentiary authority of Saphadin, and gave him instructions to temporise. No more was said after this about the marriage.[7]

During the winter months the intercourse seems to have been broken off. Saladin disbanded his forces, and remained in panic at Jerusalem ; the Crusaders were perishing at Ramlah. Early in the spring Richard made a new bid for peace.

On the 20th of March, 1192,[8] Henfrid of Toron, and Abubeker the gatekeeper, reopened negotiations in behalf of Richard. ' It has been agreed,' they stated, ' that we should divide Palestine ; so be it : let Jerusalem be ours ; you can keep, if you like, the mosque Es-Sakra.' A week later Saladin answered that, reversing the

---

[1] Saladin's acceptance was notified on the 25th of October, and the refusal of Joanna was reported to the Sultan the same day. Bohadin, 210.
[2] Bohadin, 216.
[3] Bohadin, 216; Itinerarium, vol. R. S. p. 296.
[4] Bohadin, 217.
[5] Ibid. 219.
[6] Ibid. 230. On this day the

Franks saw Reginald of Sidon riding out with Saphadin.
[7] Nothing is said about this marriage by our author, who believed that the negotiations were broken off because the Sultan would not restore Montreal : vol. R. S. p. 297. Abulfeda also mentions the proposal : Excerpta, p. 51.
[8] Bohadin, 222.

conditions, he was willing to treat. 'You may have the church of the Resurrection, but the city and citadel of Jerusalem must be ours.' This was inadmissible, and the matter again dropped. Saladin was besieged by the messengers of Conrad, and at the same time pressed with an insurrection in Mesopotamia. He agreed on a peace with the marquis,[1] and left Richard to the conquest of the south. If Conrad would break with the Franks, he should have a treaty on the terms that Richard had refused, Ascalon not being included in the surrender. A week after this Conrad was assassinated.

After the second retreat from Beit-Nûba, Richard again lowered his demands. He was now convinced of the hopelessness of the Crusade, and anxious to return home. The Franks of the kingdom were neither desirous of his aid nor worth his trouble : if he could but get an honourable peace he would be content. He declared himself ready to accept Saladin's terms ; Count Henry, the newly-chosen king, should be his friend and ally ; the Christians should have the Holy Sepulchre, the coast, and the plain, of which they were now in possession ; the Saracens might keep the city of Jerusalem and the hill country. These were Saladin's own proposals of the last March, but the Christians were now much stronger in the south, and Ascalon was a new bone of contention. Ascalon, Saladin answered, must be destroyed. Richard would not hear of this ; but, seeing it was impossible for him to retain his conquests in the south, he ordered Darum to be dismantled, and all the remaining strength of the Crusaders to be devoted to the maintenance of Ascalon.[2] The Sultan resumed hostilities, and the contest of Joppa followed. Richard now saw the bitter truth : he was, in fact, at Saladin's mercy. After an ignominious entreaty[3] for compensation for the

---

[1] Bohadin, 223, 224. Saladin received the last proposal of Conrad on the 21st of April ; returned his answer on the 24th ; and received the news of his death on the 1st of May. On the 15th of May Saladin received an embassy from the Emperor Isaac Angelus, proposing that the True Cross should be given up to the Greeks, as well as the Church of the Holy Sepulchre and other holy places : on these terms he was ready to make an alliance, offensive and defensive, with the Sultan, and join him in invading Cyprus. Two days after, the Sultan returned answer, rejecting utterly the imperial proposition, and adding that he had refused to sell the Cross to the king of Georgia for 200,000 pieces of gold. Bohadin, 226. The same emperor had, in 1190, offered to open a mosque in Constantinople, and informed Saladin in triumph of the destruction of the German Crusaders. Ibid. p. 130. Diceto, 642.

[2] The chronology and authorities for this negotiation are given in vol. R. S. p. 398, note 1.

[3] Aug. 27. 'Abubeker related that he had had a private conversation with the king, and that he had said to him, " Entreat my brother, Al Malek Al Adil (Saphadin), to see how he can procure for me and conclude a peace with the Sultan, so that he shall not grudge to yield Ascalon to me ; for then I shall immediately depart. After that he will have to do only with a small handful, from whom he will easily take away these countries. I, for my part, have no other object than to save my own reputation among

expenses of Ascalon, he was compelled to agree to the sacrifice of that place, next in importance to Acre itself. A truce for three years, so purchased, was the lame and impotent conclusion of this great and costly undertaking.[1]

By this agreement the Christians remained in possession of Tyre, Casal Ymbert, Acre, Haipha, Cæsarea, Arsûf, and Joppa ; but their occupation was strictly confined to the coast. The inland appurtenances of those lordships were withheld by the Sultan : Nazareth and Sepphoris were excepted from the cession of Acre, Yebna (Ibelin) and Masjdeljaba (Mirabel) from that of Joppa.[2] The casal of Maen, on the road from Joppa to Jerusalem, was the utmost limit of inland occupation allowed by Saladin ; and it was not until the day on which the treaty was signed that he consented to the retention of Lydda and Ramlah as compensation for the walls of Ascalon.[3] To these concessions he afterwards added the gift of Kaimoun to Balian and his wife Queen Mary, and that of Sarepta to Reginald of Sidon.[4]

These towns represented the fruit of the whole labour of Europe during five years, of the expenditure of an unparalleled amount of life and treasure, of the several intrigues in the conflicting interests of the native and foreign Franks, and of the extraordinary prowess of the greatest soldiers of Christendom. The West threw itself with all its strength upon the East, and recoiled broken and dispirited, more by its own divisions than by any irresistible barrier. All except Tyre and Acre was won by Richard.

The length to which these remarks have run must be my excuse for not having discussed the two important questions, what were the causes and what were the consequences of the Crusades in Europe, and more especially in England. The scene, however, of the whole action of the present book is external to England, whilst the treatment of those subjects belongs more properly to a work connected

---

the Franks. But if the Sultan will not give up Ascalon, at least let him refund the money I have spent on the fortifications." ' Bohadin, 258. These words, which were doubtless the true expression of Richard's feelings, are made by Michaud the ground of a charge of deliberate dishonesty against him.

[1] For the details of this negotiation, see vol. R. S. p. 427, note 7. The truce was to be, according to R. de Diceto, c. 668, and W. Newburgh, ii. 87, for three years, three months, three weeks, three days, and three hours, to begin from the following Easter ; and Hoveden, f. 408, says that it was to last

three years from the same date. But Bohadin, p. 259, dates the beginning of the truce from the day of signing, September 2.

[2] Aug. 29. Bohadin, 258 ; Diceto, c. 667 ; Abulfeda, *Excerpta*, 56.

[3] Sept. 2 : Bohadin, 261. According to Hoveden, 408, and Abulfarajius (Bruns' *Excerpta*, Oxford, 1780), Saladin paid in money for the walls of Ascalon. This doubtless gave occasion for the reproach of the German writers that Richard had sold Ascalon to the Turks.

[4] Cont. W. Tyr. ap. Martene et Durand ; *Amplissima Collectio*, v. 640.

immediately with the internal history of the kingdom. I may be allowed, however, to say that I believe the Crusades to have been caused by a movement as religious as the Reformation, and much less connected with political objects, and to have shared, with almost all purely religious movements, in the baneful results which seem inseparable from any source of popular excitement. As to the direct consequences of the Crusades, a generation which has witnessed the Crimean war, and traced in its causes and course no indistinct parallel with the events of the third Crusade, cannot suppose that they have ceased directly to affect the history of the Christian world, although the state of Palestine at the present day differs little from what it was when Godfrey of Bouillon undertook the conquest.

As for the indirect consequences of these great undertakings, it is not too much to say that they have affected, and still remotely do affect, almost every political and social question. To treat of them in all their bearings would require a great work, and no satisfactory sketch of them could be compressed into the bulk of a Preface.

* * * * * *

CHRONICLES AND MEMORIALS OF THE
REIGN OF RICHARD I. Vol. II.

EPISTOLÆ CANTUARIENSES. A.D. 1187-1199.

[THE above volume contains letters of the Prior and Convent of Christ Church, Canterbury, during Richard I.'s reign. The history of the Church of England during that reign ' is a record of five great disputes and appeals ' which are connected with the ecclesiastical quarrels of Henry II. They are also valuable as throwing light on the relations of Church and State in the reign of John. Bishop Stubbs in the following Preface sketches the history of Monasticism in England, and lays special stress upon the struggles which in Norman and Angevin times arose between Popes and English kings. The contrast which he draws between the tactics of the Courts of Rome and England in Henry II.'s reign is illuminating, and the whole Preface will be read with great interest.]

*   *   *   *   *   *

Peculiar prestige of early monachism in England

THE history of monastic and other religious establishments in England differs in very many respects from that of similar institutions among those nations which had been civilised and settled subjects of the Roman empire. Whatever remains of such civilisation or settlement existed in Britain after the departure of the Romans were swept away by the Anglo-Saxon invasion, and the work of civilisation and Christianity had to be begun from the beginning in the sixth and seventh centuries. The conversion of England was accomplished principally, if not entirely, by monks either of the

Monachism coeval with Christianity in England

Roman or of the Irish school; and thus the monastic institution was not, as among the earlier converted nations, an innovation which rested its claims for reverence on the sanctity or asceticism of its professors : it was coeval with Christianity itself : it was the herald of the Gospel to kings and people, and added the right of gratitude to that of religious respect or superstitious awe. Hence the system occupied in England and in the countries converted by English missionaries a position more really honourable and better maintained than elsewhere. Although the monasteries of France and Italy were larger and politically more powerful than those of England, they did not enjoy the same place in the affections of the people, nor were *Its connexion with national life, and its comparative purity* they either so purely national, or nurseries of patriotic spirit in the same way. It may be added that whilst in the Latin speaking countries the history of monachism is one long record of corruptions and reforms, in which constant changes and the institutions of new rules were insufficient to counteract increasing decline, the English monasteries were free from most of the evils that prevailed abroad. The fact that no important new rule of monastic life was indigenous in a country so famous for the number of its monastic houses seems to prove that no crying necessity for moral reformation was ever made out. The new foreign rules were at times freely adopted ; the Cistercian rule in particular was extremely popular almost from its foundation, but the more ancient monasteries continued to call themselves Benedictine without a difference ; and although the Cluniac reformation was coeval with the monastic revival under Odo,[1] and probably exercised some influence upon it, there is no instance of the formal introduction of that rule before the Norman Conquest. The great influx of foreign monachism that then set in was one of the smallest effects of that event on the character of the English convents.

The apostles of England, Augustine and Mellitus, Aidan, Finnan *Character of primitive English monasticism, missionary and ascetic* and Fursey, Chad and Cedd, Wilfrid and Egwin, although the fashion of their tonsures differed, all professed the threefold obligation of humility, chastity, and poverty. In the best of these and of their immediate followers, the ascetic and the missionary characters were happily blended. Their devout retirement was a means of gaining rest and strength of body, mind, and spirit for new work. Every good missionary must be an ascetic ; so for the first century of the conversion every monastery was a mission station, and every mission station a monastery. As the country became more thickly peopled, and the people more generally Christianised, a settled clergy took the place of the missionaries. The settled clergy were not bound by monastic rule, but were allowed to hold property, and probably to marry, although the marriage of the Anglo-Saxon clergy at so early a period is not so well ascertained as it is later on, and in the ages immediately before and after the Conquest. The characters and status of clerk and monk were not so sharply separated as they afterwards became ; the Benedictine was but a lax follower of the

---

[1] Odo sought the tonsure and his monastic education at Fleury in or about the year 942, the last year of the life of Odo of Cluny, who was engaged in reforming that monastery. Ang. Sac. ii. 82. Mabillon, *Acta Sanct.* sæc. v. p. 131. Oswald of Worcester was educated at, and Æthelwold of Winchester learned discipline from, the same famous house. Mab. *Act. SS.* sæc. v. pp. 601, 709, &c., and *Hist. Rams.* ap. Gale, pp. 391, 392.

rule of S. Benedict, the priest had not yet arrived at the comforts and luxuries of an independent life and definite position.

As, however, the needs of mission work became less exigent, and the established clergy further removed from monachism, a change necessarily took place in the character of the monasteries. Some became the cells of anchorites, as Lindisfarne, Crowland, and Glastonbury : some became schools of learning, as Canterbury and

Malmesbury. The spirit brought by Theodore and Adrian into the south, and by Benedict Biscop into the north of England, combined a stricter rule of life with the love of learning, cultivation of manners, and tact in association with the world. Theodore was the great administrative founder of the Church, and his introduction of learning into the country fell most fortunately at a moment when the zeal of missionary adventure began to look abroad for fresh fields of work, and but for this the monasteries would have sunk, one and all, into the follies of a stupid and mischievous asceticism. This learned period may be considered to have extended from the year 669 to the middle of the following century in the south of England ; and about fifty years longer in the north, where the example of Bede, and the munificence of Archbishop Egbert and his successors, had an influence on the cultivation of letters which at once culminated and expired in the glories of Alcuin.

The better portion of the monastic spirit, which was neither devoted to learned pursuits nor lost in the asceticism of the marshlands, found abundance of missionary work in Germany and Friesland. Boniface and his companions, although personally and in principle far more self-denying than the monks they left at home, and in theory quite as much devoted to the monastic ideal, were practically guided by earnest Christian zeal, and showed unwearied industry in their great work. No man saw more clearly than Boniface, or spoke more plainly of, the evils inherent in the monastic system where it depends on asceticism alone : the utter worthlessness of the prayers of men whose hands do not work for the things they pray for.

The middle of the eighth century witnessed a rapid degeneration in monastic discipline ; and at the same time we begin to see more clearly the demarcation between the character of the monastic and

that of the secular priest : the monastery becomes distinguished from the college of clerks and the cathedral minster. The Council of Clovesho, of 747,[1] marks both the increase of selfishness and exclusiveness in the monks, and the release of the clergy generally from the monastic bond. An attempt seems to have been made, probably originating in the remonstrances of Bede and Boniface, to reduce

[1] Spelman, Conc. i. 242, &c.

the true monasteries to the Benedictine model, and to put an end to the fraudulent perversions of religious foundations to serve the ends of secular avarice. Almost at the same time the institution of a new rule for priests living in community, a measure the credit of which is due to Chrodegang, archbishop of Metz, gave to the clergy who were not under monastic vows a dignified and creditable status which they had not before possessed. This system, although never introduced in detail into England,[1] served as a model on which colleges of clerks or canons were incorporated, and quickly commended itself to those who wished the clergy to do a good work in the world, and to retain the advantage of monastic superintendence and corporate feeling, without the trammels of a rule which hindered their practical efficiency. The monks and priests, who had until now lived together, separated. Their rival churches began to rise side by side in the larger cities : disputes arose as to ancient gifts of property, whether they belonged to the clergy as clergy, or to the monks, the successors of those who had been both monks and clergymen ; and whether the original foundations of particular houses were or were not monastic. The popularity of monachism began to decline, and the charms of the secular life to draw away many from the stricter rule. In 787 the legatine Council ordered by special canon[2] that monks should live monastically and canons canonically. The dark age of monastic history had already set in, and the veil drawn forcibly by the cruel ravages of the Northmen and Danes from 790 to 870 closed on a state of things so obscure as to be unable to reveal its own condition.

Institution of canons

Decay of monachism, followed up by the destruction of monasteries

The ninth century in England, until the reign of Alfred, is a blank as to learning, sanctity, or practical activity. Swithun, the one saint of the period, is vastly more mythical than the most obscure of the heroes of the two preceding centuries. Learning had reached the point at which, south of Humber, it was hard to find a man who could read Latin.[3] Devout men spent their active energies in pilgrimages to Rome rather than in doing their duty ; and when the Danes came in force, they fell on an enervated and almost defenceless people. Monachism, for good or for evil, had become (so far as the scanty notices of the chronicle teach us) extinct before the reign of Alfred.[4]

Very few of the religious houses which perished during the Danish wars ever rose again from their ashes. The cathedrals and

Period at which monachism became extinct

---

[1] W. Malmesb. Gesta Pontificum, lib. ii. p. 1548 (ed. Migne).
[2] Spelman, Conc. i. 294.
[3] King Alfred in Camden's *Scriptores*, p. 27.
[4] Asser : Camden's *Scr.* p. 18.

There were many monasteries standing empty in Asser's time ; either owing to the ravages of war, or the contempt into which the regular life had fallen. Alfred's attempts to revive it were failures ; ib. 19.

city monasteries were almost the only exceptions. Alfred's foundation at Athelney bore the name of a monastery, and some pains were taken by him to introduce into England learned monks from France, Flanders, and Germany. The attempt, however, to restore monachism against the sense of the nation was premature, and its issue was so discouraging that his son Edward gave the New Minster of Winchester to clerks instead of monks. It is certain that in 942 there were no real Benedictines in England ; [1] Odo, Oswald and probably Dunstan, sought the knowledge of true discipline at Fleury, which had been just reformed under the spirit, if not under the name, of the Cluniac revival.

Revival of monachism under different circumstances and character in the tenth century

Monachism, as introduced by Dunstan and worked by his disciples, was a very different thing from what it had been before the invasion. It was aggressive and self-asserting in an extreme degree. It claimed the rights and territories of the ancient houses, and introduced a spirit of persecution and tyranny altogether foreign to the ancient character. Although it had no real pretension to represent the system under which the country had been converted, it took to itself at once the prerogative right to national gratitude. Not content with claiming the property of the old monasteries which had fallen out of cultivation, or got into the hands of the secular clergy, it insisted on the removal of the latter from foundations to which they had at least an equal claim. It spared neither spiritual terrors nor the commanding temporal influence which it had obtained rather from the superstition of the kings than from the ambition of the prelates. And yet it had its bright side ; for it helped to cure great defects of moral discipline ; it prevented the Church property from becoming the inheritance of a distinct priestly caste ; it produced a revival of national learning ; and it still maintained, notwithstanding an occasional influx of foreign zealots, a thoroughly national spirit. The bishops were the agents of the change, and they acted on their own inherent authority, not at the dictation of the court of Rome. This new movement lasted as long as the supremacy of the family of Edgar. Cnut and Harold, as practical men, founded colleges. Edward the Confessor revived the monastic spirit with which he was himself pervaded ; and the system which was extended and consolidated by Lanfranc was inaugurated in his reign by the new foundation of Westminster.

It still retained its national spirit

The policy of Lanfranc and the Conqueror with regard to monasteries

The effect of the Norman Conquest in this matter was peculiar and important. It owed its character indirectly to the two powerful minds that were at the head of the Church and State. Lanfranc saw, in the monasteries, societies of degenerate Benedictines ; William, nests of anti-Norman feeling. Lanfranc tried to reform the

---

[1] Anglia Sacra, ii. 91, 194, &c.

abuses by drawing closer the rules of discipline ; William sought to stifle the patriotic spirit by setting over them the tools of his strong policy. But turbulent and worldly foreign abbots were not more likely to improve the tone of religious society than rigorous reformers to soften the asperities of national antipathy. The two forces did not exactly neutralise one another, because they were neither equal nor opposed in direction ; but the combination produced a result that neither William nor Lanfranc could have calculated on.

For a long time the English spirit in the monasteries maintained itself against both tyranny and reform. They hated the Norman invaders, but they had no inclination towards Rome, under whose auspices the Norman invasion had succeeded. At the time, however, that the Normans were taking deep root in England and becoming amalgamated with the natives of the soil ; as their interests became insular, and their policy influenced by their insular interests ; at this very time also, the royal and the papal politics were diverging ; during the whole period of the amalgamation the influence of the court of Rome was declining, partly from the failure of goodwill in England, partly from its own weakness. *Results of that policy*

As the Normans became Anglicised, and the royal policy, internally at least, English, the monasteries, still in opposition, lost their distinctive characteristic of patriotism. As the State ceased to be influenced by the court of Rome, the monks looked to the court of Rome for sympathy and assistance. As the bishops and secular clergy opposed themselves to Roman centralisation, the monasteries became colonies of Roman partisans. Their sympathies and antipathies were all in common with Rome, and their national spirit evaporated altogether to find a fitter and more permanent abode in the necessary organism of the church. So long as the pope and the king were on the same side, the monks and the nation were opposed to both alike ; when the pope and the king quarrelled, the nation sided with the king, the monks with the pope ; hence the monasteries became more papal as the State become more national, and the same series of events made them less English without becoming more Norman, and more papal without becoming more loyal. Matters had reached this point in the latter years of Henry II. *Alienation of the monastic system from the national life*

The monastic cathedral was an institution almost peculiar to England.[1] The missionary bishop, himself a monk, accompanied by a staff of priests who were also monks, settled in the chief city of a kingdom or province. He built his church ; his staff of missionary monks became the clergy of that church ; the church itself was *Origin of the two classes of cathedrals*

---

[1] There were, I believe, a few abroad : when the abbey of Monreale in Sicily was made an archiepiscopal see, Lucius III. ordered that the monastic order should be preserved.

called a monastery. As the mission work prospered the populations
of the larger towns were converted, and settled clergy who were not
monks undertook the spiritual charge of them. In time the over-
grown dioceses were divided. The principal church of the district
became the seat of a bishop, who might or might not be a monk, but
who found his episcopal chair placed for him in a church which was
of older foundation than itself, and which possessed a character that
he ought not and perhaps had not power to infringe. The longer
the subdivision of the original diocese was delayed, the more certain
was the new bishop to find himself surrounded by a staff of secular
city clergy. His cathedral continued to be an establishment of
secular clerks, and when the name and usage of canonical life came
into fashion they took, as a matter of course, the name of canons.
In this way it happened that, whilst the newly-founded sees of
Anglo-Saxon bishops were placed in secular churches, the original
settlements of the first missionary bishops retained a monastic
character. Canterbury was thus monastic, although Rochester and
London, founded as episcopal sees within seven years, were secular
cathedrals. Lindisfarne continued monastic, but York was a minster
of clerks. The mother church of Mercia was the monastery of
Diuma, but Lichfield and Hereford, and, as far as we know,
Leicester, Dorchester, and Worcester, were from the beginning in
the hands of clerks.[1]

During the early stages of monasticism, briefly characterised
above, this distinction was practically of little importance ; monks
and clerks lived together comfortably enough. Later on the secular
bishop in a monastic cathedral kept his clerks in his palace ; the
monks served the church ; the monastic bishop in a secular cathedral
lived as abbot in his own house and presided as bishop in the
church.[2] In the further stage of the decline of monachism the
churches came almost entirely into the possession of the bishops'
clerks. As restored monachism developed its more aggressive
character, the monastic bishops in some cases edged out the secular
clergy from the cathedrals. At Worcester the bishop's chair and the
cathedral property were transferred from the college of S. Peter to

The newer cathedrals secular

Cathedrals in the early period of monachism

Relation of later monachism to the cathedrals

---

[1] According to Rudburne, Ang. Sac.
i, 190, Birinus was a Benedictine monk,
and the church of Winchester originally
monastic ; but there is no proof of
either statement. The monastic order
became extinct there, according to the
same author, in 870.

[2] I believe that this is still the case
with the Greek, or at least the Rus-
sian bishops. They are necessarily
monks or celibates, and their staff is
composed of monks or celibates : but

the cathedrals are served by secular
clergy under an archpriest. The
Scoto-Irish system, in which the
bishop was an officer of the monastery
governed by an abbot, in whom, and
not in the bishop, the jurisdiction
was vested, is, of course, completely
different. But it is possible that the
monastic system, as it existed at Lindisfarne, was influenced by the Irish
connexion quite as much as by the
pattern of Canterbury.

the monastery of S. Mary; at Sherborne and Winchester the clerks were compelled to embrace the monastic life or to retire from the churches. At the time of the Conquest York, London, Hereford, Selsey, Wells, Exeter, Rochester, Lichfield, Dorchester, and Thetford were secular; Winchester, Worcester, and Sherborne were monastic; the mother churches of the north and south had retained from the beginning the monastic profession. The chair of Augustine had never been removed from Canterbury, and Durham had inherited the original character of Lindisfarne.[1] In the former, as early as the time of Bede,[2] the monastic character of the church was based on the authority of S. Gregory, and before the Conquest this was understood to have been confirmed by a rescript of Pope Boniface IV.[3] Durham, according to its own historian Simeon, had been continuously tenanted by a society of mixed character.

The cathedral church of Canterbury was not, however, a monastery in the same sense as that of S. Augustine's in the same city; the latter was founded for monastic purposes; the other was the mother church of the whole kingdom, its monastic character being almost accidental. Hence, even in the strictest days of regular discipline, it had contained many clergy who were not monks, and many monks who were so only in name. As at the first the essential character of its inmates was priestly, not monastic, so, as time went on, their successors included both priests and monks. It continued a monastery in name, but of its clergy some were and some were not under monastic vows. Although the later monkish historians contended that all the archbishops up to the Conquest were monks, it is certain from Bede and from the Chronicle that they were not uniformly so. Under variations in the characters of the rulers of the church, the double character of the archiepiscopal *familia* may well have been maintained, so long as no jealousies sprang up between the two constituents, and there was work enough for both. It is not easy to say at what period the monastic discipline at Christ Church became extinct. Early, however, in the ninth century we find Archbishop Wulfred allowing his *familia* to possess houses of their own within the monastery,[4] and to dispose of them by will among their brethren, a state of things quite incompatible with the rigour of Benedictine rule. The pontificate of Ceolnoth (833 to 870) is the date fixed by the monastic historians for the so-called usurpation of the cathedral by secular clerks.

Marginal notes: Monastic character of Christ Church, Canterbury

Sketch of monachism there

[1] Simeon of Durham (Twysden), c. 49, 50.
[2] *H. E.* iv. 27.
[3] W. Malmesb., *G. P.* i. c. 1464 (ed. Migne).
[4] Kemble, Codex Dipl. 200. This privilege was granted on the understanding that the brethren were still to frequent the refectory and the dormitory: so that they were not yet quite secularised.

According to this story, the number of the monks having been reduced by sickness to five, the archbishop ordered his chaplains and the priests of the city to assist in divine service until he could properly supply the vacancies.[1] This the continuance of war prevented him from doing, and Æthelred his successor was defeated in a like purpose. After nearly two centuries of secular occupation Archbishop Ælfric succeeded in restoring the monks, but of these all but four are said to have shared the martyrdom of S. Ælphege.[2]

Cathedral system at Canterbury in the 11th century a compromise between secular and regular professions

From 1012 to 1070 a curious compromise between theory and fact seems to have prevailed. The church was a monastery, and the inmates bore the name of monks, but they did not keep the monastic rule, and moreover assumed the titles of a secular chapter; their president was called a dean, the monks were also cathedral canons.[3] The exact truth of these details it is of course impossible to test, but they contain nothing that is either improbable or inconsistent with ascertained facts. The subject has been rendered obscure both by the partisans and by the enemies of monachism. The former have never allowed the most positive evidence where it clashed with their claims of superiority and antiquity; the latter have been almost as unscrupulous. But it would seem, on a careful consideration of what is said and what is left unsaid in trustworthy records, that the body which Lanfranc undertook to reform was in name monastic, whether it became distinctively so under Ælfric or had borne the title through various fluctuations of discipline from the earliest times.

Aggressive policy of monachism

It was unfortunately the policy of the monks and their advocates to claim an original right to all monastic churches, and to aggrandise themselves whenever they could with the occupation of those to which they had not the original claim, on the ground of their sanctity. In this way no prescription against them was allowed to defeat their existing claims, and the shortest prescription in their favour was pressed against the most just claim of the seculars. To turn a church of clerks into a monastery was a merit of great efficiency for the remission of sins, but to turn a monastery into a secular church was an unheard-of impiety. On this principle Worcester and Winchester changed their discipline under Oswald and Æthelwold ; and although there were probably other reasons for the changes introduced shortly before and after the Conquest, the rule that a claim to superior ascetic sanctity entirely superseded all the rights of property and prescription was acted upon, if not by those Norman and Lotharingian bishops [4] who attempted to force

---

[1] Chron. Sax. ad ann. 870, 995. Gervase, c. 1643.

[2] Gervase, 1650, 1654.

[3] ' Æthelnoth munuc ┐ decanus æt

Christes cyrcan.' Chron. Sax. 1020. Gervase, 1650.

[4] Giso at Wells, Leofric at Exeter, Thomas at York. W. Malmesb. *G. P.*

the use of a common dormitory and refectory on their reluctant canons, certainly by Gundulf in his reforms at Rochester and William of S. Carileph at Durham.

It may be, however, that the measures of Lanfranc and his followers in the reform of the cathedrals were not altogether spontaneous. It is even possible that the original design was, not to turn the secular ones into monasteries, but to reduce the monastic cathedrals into the form common throughout the Western Church.[1] At Winchester Bishop Walkelin made a vigorous effort to expel the monks, which was only defeated by a papal letter forbidding him to molest them.[2] A similar letter [3] is extant, addressed to Lanfranc in reference to changes reported to be in contemplation at Canterbury. It was probably in consequence of this admonition that he organised the cathedral establishment on the footing which it maintained down to the dissolution. The alteration was quietly effected, the dean becoming the prior and the rest of the unmarried canons accepting the profession and position of monks.

Lanfranc's reformation of his cathedral insti-gated by Alexander II.

Notwithstanding the great prestige of the monastic order in the early Anglo-Saxon Church, and in spite of the fact that the episcopal superintendence was exercised by men who were in many cases monks, and in all imbued with extreme respect for the sanctity of the institution, the real inherent antipathy between the two ideas developed very early. It is certain that in the Council of Hertford, which was held by Archbishop Theodore in 673, to reduce to order the religious organisation of the southern kingdoms, this was a matter of consideration. The third canon of that assembly [4] provided, ' that as all monasteries are consecrated to God, it shall be lawful for no bishop to disquiet them in anything, or to abstract any of their property by violence.' It would seem from this that difficulties had already arisen. It is a question whether any of the papal exemptions which claim so early a date as the eighth century are genuine. Bede, however, records a privilege of Pope Agatho to Benedict Biscop,[5] by which the monastery which he had built was rendered safe and free for ever from any interference from without. The monks of Peterborough alleged that they had a still earlier one, in which Pope Vitalian exempted them from all subjection except to the pope of Rome and the archbishop of Canterbury.[6] Evesham

Origin of exemptions of monas-teries

Inherent antipathy between the episcopal and monas-tic systems

Character of early exemptions

ii. c. 1548. Stubbs, in Twysden, 1708, 1709. Hunter's *Ecclesiastical Documents*, pp. 17, 22. *Foundation of Waltham Abbey*, pref. p. xi. It is curious that in the only places in the Anglo-Saxon laws in which canons are mentioned it is in connexion with the dormitory and refectory. Thorpe,

Ancient Laws, &c. pp. 130, 134.
[1] Eadmer, p. 10.
[2] Anglia Sacra, i. 321.
[3] Eadmer (ed. Selden), pp. 10, 11.
[4] Bede, *H. E.* iv. 5.
[5] Historia Abbatum, c. 6, p. 320 (ed. Hussey).
[6] Chron. Sax. 657. Cf. 675.

possessed two letters of Pope Constantine conferring liberties of the same character in language more grandiloquent than precise.[1] The famous exemptions of S. Augustine's at Canterbury bear the names of Popes Adeodatus and Agatho,[2] but their authenticity was a matter of question in the twelfth century. In all these cases except the first there is great room for doubt. The chartulary of Chertsey[3]

Moderate character of early genuine exemptions contains a bull of Pope Agatho to S. Erkenwald, which, although not free from suspicious characteristics, has greater claim to be received as genuine. There is also a similar grant of Pope Constantine to the monasteries of Bermondsey and Woking, which is found in the Black Book of Peterborough,[4] and which, as no monasteries are known from other sources to have existed at those places before the Conquest, is exposed to very slight presumption of forgery. The two last-mentioned privileges are in strong contrast with the lavish bestowals of independence that appear in the later and forged charters of exemption. The convents are to elect their own abbots, but the canonical power of the bishop of the diocese is not to be infringed : the episcopal examination must be passed before the abbot can receive benediction. The bishop is carefully excluded from interfering with the administration of the monastic property. The exemption was supposed to make the monastery independent of the diocesan, but did not make it dependent on the court of Rome. It is probable that to this extent, and no further, the independence of the monasteries reached before the Conquest. After that event the

Later exemptions foreign system of exemptions was occasionally introduced ; the greater abbeys, by either forged or genuine privileges, actually acquired independence ; and the smaller ones, by affiliating themselves to one of the new orders, such as those of Cluny or Cîteaux, which were dependent on a chief abbot or on a general chapter, and through them on the pope alone, placed themselves and were frequently strong enough to maintain themselves in a similar position. These houses neither were in obedience to the bishops nor contributed to their revenues in synodals and procurations, nor could the bishop celebrate mass or hold synod in them without permission.

Attempts of the cathedral monasteries to acquire independence The cathedral monasteries looked with a jealous eye upon their privileged sisters. In them the bishop claimed the place of abbot, the right of presiding in the election of the officers, or of actually nominating them, and the abbot's share in the management of the estates. He was the *persona* of his cathedral, and through him as tenant in chief of the Crown the tenure of the monastic property

[1] Hist. Evesham (ed. Macray), pp. 171, 172.
[2] Elmham (ed. Hardwicke), pp. 244–247.
[3] MS. Cotton. Vitellius A. xiii. fol. 24.
[4] MS. Soc. Antiq. No. 60, folio 50.

was defined. Such at least was the episcopal claim, confirmed by the language of Lanfranc and Anselm.[1] The monks, unable to emancipate themselves by papal privilege, could only gain an equality with the exempt monasteries either by occasionally influencing a pious bishop to defeat the rights of his successors, or by procuring from the Crown charters of confirmation to the prior and convent, instead of, as they had hitherto run, to the bishop and his monks, the bishop and his family, or the bishop and his flock. The vigilance of the prelates generally prevented the latter expedient from succeeding, but advantage was frequently taken of the piety or weakness of those who had been monks before their consecration to effect the former. Hence the eagerness of the cathedral monasteries to elect none but monks as their bishops. The see of Canterbury was filled by monks for one hundred and twenty years, from Lanfranc to Baldwin, with only two exceptions, William of Corbeuil, who was a canon regular, and S. Thomas, whose monastic profession was assumed long after his consecration. During this time the power of the prior and monks, to the exclusion of the archbishop, increased with more or less rapidity. Lanfranc had either actually separated the estates of the archbishop from those of the monks, or had confirmed the separation. They appear under different heads in the Domesday survey. Anselm bestowed on the prior and convent the power of administering these separate estates and of despatching in common council all the business of the house ; in this was included the right of holding the manorial courts on their estates.[2] To him also the convent owed, besides liberal gifts in money, furniture, and land, the settlement of the whole oblations of the high altar,[3] of which Lanfranc had retained half, and of the xenia, or Easter and Christmas offerings from their manors, which were settled on the cellarer for the use of the sick and strangers.[4] By these sacrifices he left himself little more than a nominal supremacy in the chapter, and renounced all interest in the revenues of the house of which he was theoretically abbot. His object, however, was not to exempt the monks from the authority of the archbishops, but, as is expressly stated by Eadmer, to prevent the estates from falling into the king's hands during the vacancies of the see.[5] This policy was easily interpreted by the monks as freeing them from subjection to either king or primate.

The example of Anselm was followed by S. Thomas,[6] and Arch-

The convent of Canterbury made almost independent by Anselm

[1] Lanfranc, Decreta, pref. Anselm, ep. 78, p. 396 (ed. Migne).
[2] Eadmer, p. 108.
[3] Battely's Canterbury, p. 103. MS. Lambeth, 1212. Battely, App. p. 49. Eadmer, 108.

[4] Gervase, 1478. Anselm appropriated these Easter pence to the work of the church. Eadmer, 108.
[5] Eadmer, 109.
[6] Battely, pp. 18, 19.

bishop Richard, who had been prior of Dover, a monastery in the gift and under the dominion of the cathedral. Both of these had surrendered the oblations of the church, which during the time of Richard included the immense treasures offered at the tomb of his predecessor. Richard had further appropriated four churches, with their dependent chapels,[1] to the uses of the almonry. One privilege, however, seems to have been retained by the archbishops, the right

of presenting to the churches on the estates of the convent. This was supposed by the monks to be a usurpation of Archbishop Theobald ; but it is by no means certain that the right had ever been exercised by the convent without the nomination of the archbishop. S. Thomas retained the presentations in his own hands,[2] and although Richard, in the first year of his consecration, professed to restore them, Gervase the chronicler admits that the restoration was defeated by the intrigues of the archbishop's clerks, and that the convent did not enjoy its rights.

It is no wonder that under these circumstances, and owing to the frequent long absences of the archbishops, the obedience formerly due to them came to be looked upon as a voluntary thing. The claim of the convent to elect their head was put forward on every occasion, and yet when the archbishop was elected he was hardly recognised as a member of his own church. Although he was the rector and *persona* of the cathedral, the prior and monks claimed to be the church of Canterbury. To the convent, according to their absurd interpretation of the oath of profession, every newly-consecrated bishop swore fidelity ; the archbishop was little more than their minister and mouthpiece, and when his voice was not in accord with theirs he was directly disowned. The martyrdom of S. Thomas, which, if it was an offering at all, was certainly an offering for the immunities of the whole of the clergy, was looked on as the redemption of the church of Canterbury ; the church of Canterbury was the mother church of England, a declaration which, however true in one sense, was pressed now into a meaning that was false both in law and in fact.

The influx of wealth produced a corresponding lavish and luxurious outlay. The hospitality of the convent became famous in all the Western Church, from the crowds of pilgrims who returned from the shrine of the martyr. The internal expenditure was also immense. The refectory was the scene of the most abundant and

---

[1] He also restored the xenia, which must have been kept back by the archbishop since Theobald's time. Gerv. 1675. The churches were Eynesford, Eastry, Monkton, and Mepeham. Somner, 112. Battely, 97.

The first three had been appropriated before, and were really restored by Richard.

[2] W. Fitz-Stephen, ed. Giles, p. 208. Gerv. 1667, 1675. See also p. 532, vol. R. S.

tasteful feasting. Seventeen dishes were served up at the prior's table.[1] The servants and equipages of a hundred and forty brethren [2] were numerous and splendid. The monastery had become a little town, in which the prior was supreme both temporally and spiritually. The example of Canterbury was followed by some of the other cathedral monasteries, and the struggle recorded in the following pages was the result of an attempt of the archbishop and bishops to remedy the evils and discomforts of such a relation.

The first tokens of the strife may be discovered in the history of the pontificate of Theobald, in 1150.[3] At that time the revenues of the convent were so much diminished by the demands of hospitality and by the ravages of war that the prior restored to the archbishop the administration of the conventual property, which had been granted by Anselm, begging him to manage it, and to maintain the brethren until better times came. Theobald began by exercising severe economy; he closed the convent against all but the poorest guests, and fed the monks, to their great disgust, on coarse bread and vegetables, sometimes allowing only one loaf to two. The monastic temperament would endure none but voluntary fasting; speedy repentance followed the exercise of stricter discipline, and the archbishop was roundly charged with nursing his own estates at the expense of his flock. Theobald, who had undertaken the stewardship with great reluctance, was justly provoked at this absurd accusation, and refused to listen to the complaint of the prior; the convent appealed to Rome; the archbishop closed the monastery and restrained the monks from egress, stopped divine service, seized the prior's horses, carried off the charters of the church, and arrested and imprisoned the brethren who had been chosen to prosecute the appeal. Adding insult to injury, he compared the monks to dogs. The mediation of the prelates was shortly afterwards successful in inducing the convent to renounce the appeal and the archbishop to

Margin note: Struggle between Archbishop Theobald and the convent

---

[1] Giraldus, Ang. Sacr. ii. 480.

[2] Gervase, 1654. The number of monks expelled in 1207 was sixty-four (John of Oxenedes, *ad annum*); thirteen more were sick; there were therefore not more than seventy-seven at that time; at the dissolution there were fifty-three. Of the number of servants it is difficult to form an idea. The cellarer in 1322 had thirty-eight servants under him; and the chamberlain and sacrist had large numbers of people employed as tailors, furriers, launderers, &c., and in the service of the church. See Somner, pp. 108, 109; and Appendix 35, vol. R. S.

[3] Gervase, 1367–1369. Gervase records two other quarrels between the archbishop and the convent, one in the time of William of Corbeuil, about the church of Dover; and a second, between Theobald and Prior Jeremiah, whom he compelled to resign. Both, no doubt, helped to embitter the feeling between the parties, but they have no particular bearing on the present controversy. Peter of Blois (ep. 216) states that there had been a continual hostility of the monks to the archbishop since Anselm's time: the days of Thomas not excepted: one of the brethren refers to the ill will shown by the convent to the martyr in No. cclxviii.

restore the estates. He insisted, however, on the resignation of the prior, which he effected after three years' litigation, the contest being a drawn game, except so far as his personal enmity to the prior was gratified by the result.

Character of Archbishop Baldwin

Archbishop Baldwin, whose misfortune it was to renew the struggle after the position of the monks had been strengthened and their resources increased during the pontificates of Thomas and Richard, was a man of singular sanctity, courage, and honesty. He was one of the most distinguished scholars of his, time, and has left behind him works which attest his proficiency in the studies of the day.[1] According to Giraldus Cambrensis,[2] who knew him well, although it is not easy to say how far he speaks the truth, he was an austere, melancholy man, slow to anger and temperate in the show of it, wanting in severity and firmness. Alexander Llewelyn, the cross-bearer of the martyr, used to say of the three archbishops whom he had known that when they came to town the first place S. Thomas visited was the court ; Richard, the grange ; Baldwin, the church. He was, in fact, a Cistercian of the best sort, a man who lived but little for the world, and that to make it better. A certain infirmity of purpose may be traced in his career, for which the rapid changes which attended his promotion may account, if they cannot excuse it. He adapted himself perhaps too easily to the quickly changing circumstances of his life, and so failed to carry out in his higher position the hopes and promise which had led to his attaining it. According to Giraldus, his friend, as well as to Urban III., his bitter enemy, he was more zealous as a monk than as an abbot, as an abbot than as bishop, as bishop than as archbishop. In the mouth of Urban this was almost praise. We, judging him by a better standard, may admire the honesty and clearsightedness in which, as an abbot, he chose to perform the duty of an abbot rather than to humour the prejudices of his monks ; and, when he became archbishop, tried to do his duty as an archbishop, instead of playing into the hands of the monastic party, a course which would have insured him a much more quiet life, and, considering the circumstances of his death, might have entitled him to canonisation. The

His errors of temper

errors of temper, harshness, arbitrary severity, and want of tact, of which he cannot be acquitted on the evidence of the letters (in vol. R. S.), are not perhaps really inconsistent with the character drawn of him by Giraldus. They seem to be exactly the faults into which

---

[1] Walter Map, De Nugis Curialium, ed. Wright, p. 20. His works are published in the fifth volume of the Bibliotheca Patr. Cistcrciensium, A.D. 1662. There are a penitential and a

volume of sermons by Baldwin in the library at Lambeth.
[2] Gir. Camb., Anglia Sacra, ii. 429, 523. Gervase, 1478.

an unworldly man would be hurried by the influence of unscrupulous and interested advisers.

To Baldwin, as a Cistercian, as a scholar, and as an archbishop, the state of his cathedral monastery was extremely offensive. The luxury and independence of the monks were opposed to all his notions of monastic sanctity : his own claims as abbot, so highly estimated under the Cistercian rule, were practically repudiated. The once famous learning of the school of Canterbury was now represented only by Nigel Wireker the poet and Gervase the chronicler. The archbishop felt himself to be an unwelcome stranger in his own house ; the sense of personal dislike was added to determine his feelings towards the monks ; he knew that he had been forced upon them when they would rather have chosen Theobald of Cluny [1] or Odo of Battle.[2] The state of Christ Church offensive to Baldwin

Still, it may be doubted whether he would have attempted any measure for their humiliation if it had not been for the suggestions of the clerks, scholars, and statesmen who surrounded him in his new position. The former complained that in a monastic cathedral the archbishop had no means of rewarding his faithful servants with places of dignity and profit. All he could do for them was to enrich them with church livings, diverting the means appropriated to the cure of souls, and placing them in positions which they had neither tastes nor time to fill as the laws of the church required. The scholars,[3] such as Peter of Blois and Joseph of Exeter, Baldwin's kinsman,[4] could find ample room for regret that the great revenues should be spent on idle and luxurious monks, which might maintain a university of able and useful students ; with such a plea Baldwin himself had much sympathy, and the poverty of the infant universities presented a disagreeable contrast to the riches of the monasteries. But the statesmen, the court bishops, and clerical lawyers were the bitterest enemies of the monks, whom they regarded as the avowed maintainers of an alien jurisdiction in the country, as the greatest supporters of dangerous and disreputable immunities, and as insurmountable obstacles to an equal and uniform administration of justice. Both king and church were from time to time exasperated by the claim of the monks to elect the primate, a claim which they looked upon as a dangerous innovation, and which, if granted, might lead to a repetition of the miseries of the struggle between Henry and Thomas. Urged by these, the The instigation of his dependents The influence of the scholars and statesmen.

---

[1] Benedict. Peterb. ad 1184.
[2] Gervase, 1466.
[3] Cf. No. clxx. p. 146, vol. R. S. ; and Gervase, 1478.
[4] The author of the lost *Antiocheis* and of the extant *History of the*

Trojan War. Baldwin intended him to be the poet of the third Crusade. Gir. Camb., Ang. Sacra, ii. 492. He is mentioned once in No. ccxlviii. p. 230, as in correspondence with the dean of Rheims.

archbishop began his attack upon the convent, and, advised by these, he conducted his approaches by those crooked ways in which a man cannot walk at once honestly and successfully.[1]

Opposite accounts of Baldwin's design

If we are to accept the account given by Baldwin and his adherents, his intention was only to build a large collegiate church, such as had been projected by S. Anselm and S. Thomas, in honour of S. Stephen and S. Thomas, to be tenanted by men of learning, usefulness, and distinction. For the maintenance of this establishment sufficient could be easily spared from the archiepiscopal property if it were freed from the claims by which the liberality or piety of the series of monks who had filled the see had impoverished it for the enrichment of the convent. The monks, on the other hand, declared that this foundation was intended to supplant their own church, as the mother church of England. It was to be built and endowed out of their estates; its canons were to be the bishops, who already claimed a voice in the election of the primate; that voice would be heard in exclusion of the convent. The archbishop, backed by the king, would have supreme jurisdiction; he would be

Fears of the monks

pope and the suffragans his cardinals; beyond him no appeal would be suffered to go; not only would the monasteries lose their money,

---

[1] It may be as well to give here in a note, before entering upon the chronological sketch of the struggle, a list of the monks who were engaged in the dispute with Baldwin, 1187–1189 (page references are to vol. in R.S.):—

Honorius, prior, 1186–1188.
Geoffrey, subprior, 1186–1191.
Alan, third prior.

Robert, sacrist, ⎫
Hervey, cellarer, ⎬ Obedientiaries in 1187.
Simon, chamberlain, ⎭

Ralph, almoner, d. 1188.

Roger Norreys, ⎫
John of Boching, ⎬ Treasurers, 1187,
Ralph of Orpington. ⎭ p. 60.

Symon, treasurer, 1187, p. 55.
Felix, cellarer, 1189, p. 299 ; deposed, 1191 ; sacrist, before 1197 ; prior of Dover, 1197.
Osbert de Bristo, prior, 1190.
John de Bremble, probably third prior until 1188. See No. ccxxxii. pp. 298, 308.

Edmund, ⎫
Humfrey, ⎬ Died at Rome in 1188
Haymo de Thanet, ⎪
Symon, ⎭

Gervase, sacrist in 1193, p. 315.
Nigel ' Wireker,' pp. 315, 317.
William, precentor in 1198, pp. 258, 311.

Hervey, precentor in 1189.
Alexander of Dover, pp. 94, 308,
Henry, pp. 226, 230, ⎫
Jonas, p. 271, ⎬ Employed abroad.
Elias, p. 278, ⎪
R., p. 226, &c. ⎭

Willelmus Ascelinus, p. 311, ⎫
Robertus Medicus, p. 312, ⎬ Partisans of Roger Norreys.
Walter de Ba, p. 169. ⎭

R., chaplain to S. Thomas.
—, chaplain to S. Thomas.
R. de Tumba, p. 308.
O. de Tumba, p. 314.
R. de Cripta, p. 298.
Helyas Magnus, p. 315.
Aaron, pp. 67, 315, 317.
Isaac, pp. 311, 317.
James, p. 315.
Walter de Stura, p. 311.
R. de Eastry, p. 313.
Zacharias, p. 312.
Benjamin, p. 312.
Lodovicus, p. 312.
Badewinus, p. 311.
Ralph de Harundel, p. 311.
Symon of Dover, p. 67.
John of Dover, p. 430.   Abbot of Battle, 1200–1213.

but their stay and support, their connexion with Rome would be cut off, recourse to the Holy See would be forbidden, and a schism in the Western Church would follow. It is curious to note how nearly their instincts led them to the results which four centuries later did follow the abolition of the monastic order in England.

The first measure taken by the archbishop was to procure a letter from the pope, Lucius III.,[1] empowering him to reclaim the possessions alienated from the see by his predecessor. This licence was necessary, because the alienations in question had been confirmed by Alexander III., and by Lucius himself.[2] It was uncertain how far such a permission would be allowed to be valid in opposition to the papal privileges which might be adduced by the convent; but there could be no doubt that if the archbishop had proceeded without it he would have put himself out of court at once. Of these alienated possessions the principal ones were the oblations of the church, which canonically belonged to the archbishop,[3] and the four churches appropriated to the almonry, Monkton, Eastry, Mepehám, and Eynesford, and these had been confirmed to the convent by the Holy See. The alienations which had not been so confirmed the archbishop could reclaim with no risk of coming in direct conflict with the court of Rome. His measures would probably be appealed against, but when the appeal was once admitted, the price of justice at Rome was notorious, and the longest purse, the weightiest influence, or the most determined pertinacity might reckon on victory.

Baldwin obtains a papal licence to reclaim the alienated property of the see

Armed with this permission, Baldwin, on the 15th of December, 1185, the first anniversary of his enthronement, came to Canterbury and confiscated the xenia.[4] It is probable that the news of the death of the pope, which occurred at Verona on the 24th of November, reached England about this time, and that for that reason the archbishop did not proceed at once to seize the churches of the almonry. His agents at Verona, however, lost no time in obtaining the renewal of the licence from Urban III.[5] This was issued on the 19th of December, and on the 25th of January 1186, the archbishop's clerks, by virtue of his presentations, took possession of the churches of Monkton and Eastry. They borrowed the keys, says Gervase,[6] pretending that they wished to hear the gospel, and fraudulently inducted the new incumbents. At the same time certain of the vills of the convent were seized and committed to lay stewards under the archbishop's authority.

He seizes the xenia,

and the churches of the almonry

The monks, immediately on the receipt of this news, appealed to Rome against the archbishop, who in consequence proceeded to take

---

[1] No. i.
[3] Can. Apost. xl.
[5] No. ii.

[2] Battely's *Canterbury*, p. 97, and vol. R. S. p. 5.
[4] Gervase, 1478.
[6] Gervase, 1478.

possession of all the estates of the church.   As in Theobald's time,
a mediation was proposed and accepted.   The archbishop restored
the estates, and the convent renounced the appeal.   Baldwin
retained, however, both the xenia and the disputed churches, as he
had a right to do, on the renunciation of the appeal, and proceeded
to bestow the latter on some of those influential ecclesiastics whose
interest he was anxious to secure either at home or abroad.[1]
Eynesford he gave to John of Poictiers, now archbishop of Lyons.[1]

The convent were not unanimous in their submission ; one monk,
Haymo of Thanet, refused to join in the compromise, and carried the
appeal (contrary to the good faith of the convent), first by letter and
then in person, to Pope Urban.

The next step the archbishop took was, pursuant to the policy of
Theobald, to get rid of the prior and substitute a creature of his own.
Alan was made abbot of Tewkesbury,[2] and to maintain the balance
of justice Robert of Hastings, Baldwin's chief supporter among the
monks, was rewarded with the abbacy of Chester.   Honorius, the
cellarer of Christ Church, who had been chaplain to the archbishop,
was elected to succeed Alan.[3]   This appointment is said to have been
made at the petition of the convent, who perhaps knew Honorius
better than the archbishop did, the latter accepting him as a man
who would easily be amenable to his influence.   This was done on
the 13th of July.

Matters being now ripe for futher progress, a letter was issued to
the clergy and people of England, instituting a brotherhood for
collecting contributions towards the building of a new collegiate
church, to be dedicated to the martyrs Stephen and Thomas.[4]   In
confirmation of this design letters were produced from the pope,
which had been granted to the earnest petitions of the bishops and
archbishop.[5]   One of these, which was published in November,
confirmed the foundation of the college ; another readjusted the
oblations of Christ Church, giving one quarter to the monks,
another to the poor, another to the fabric of the cathedral, and the
remainder to the archbishop, to be used at his pleasure.

During the last week of November, Baldwin and his clerks came
down to Canterbury, intending to install his new foundation for a
time in the parish church of S. Stephen at Hakington, the northern
suburb of Canterbury, about three furlongs from the cathedral.   If

---

[1] John of Poictiers was a native of
Canterbury.   Walter Map, De Nugis
Curialium, p. 70.
[2] Received benediction June 15.
Gervase, 1480.
[3] Alan of Tewkesbury ; ep. xiv.

Gervase, 1480.
[4] No. viii.   This expedient for
raising funds was not unusual.   See
Ann. Winton. (ed. Luard), p. 78, and
Du Cange, Confratria.
[5] Nos. vi., dlx., dlxi.

we are to credit Gervase [1] the college was already incorporated. It was to consist of sixty or seventy prebendaries : one stall was assigned to the king, and one to each of the confederate bishops, who were each to endow and appoint his prebendary and vicar. Every incumbent of a church in the gift of the archbishop was to be a canon, and this included also all the churches properly in the gift of the convent. By a singular coincidence it happened that on the night of the feast of S. Catherine a young monk, named Andrew John, saw a wonderful vision. The venerated form of S. Thomas appeared to him, bade him rise from his pallet and follow him from the dormitory into the choir, and through the choir into an adjacent tower. There the saint showed him a huge Catherine wheel, shooting out blue flames. Having withdrawn a little way, he saw the archbishop approach. He took three swords, and having leaned upon each to try whether it would bend, chose one of them, and summoned the prior Honorius. ' I wish,' said Baldwin, ' to destroy this new work [the unfinished cathedral], and for this purpose I have made this wheel, but without you I cannot move it.' The prior reluctantly complied, and other monks were called to help. Andrew John was now terribly frightened, and implored the saint to interfere. S. Thomas drew his sword, a blade of inconceivable brightness, inscribed with letters of gold, at the first sight of which the archbishop and his satellites vanished. He then delivered the sword to Andrew, showing him the inscription, ' Gladius beati Petri apostoli,' and bade him give it to the prior, who should smite with it and destroy the Catherine wheel. The monk now awoke, but the dream was thrice repeated before he ventured to tell it to the prior, who immediately saw in the wheel the archbishop's new college, and in the sword of S. Peter the ready weapon of appeal to Rome. About the same time another of the brethren saw in a vision the archbishop trying to cut off S. Thomas's head, and losing his mitre in the attempt.

This strange vision, whether true or fictitious, was believed by the brethren, and had the effect of settling prior Honorius in his fidelity. [2] On the 8th of December the convent united in a second appeal, which was announced to Baldwin on the 14th at Gillingham, by Gervase the historian, who fixed the date of appeal for the following Mid-Lent Sunday. [3] The archbishop received Gervase with calmness and allowed the appeal. On the 16th, however, he came to Canterbury, and on the next day proceeded to Hakington, where he said mass, and instituted his canons in spite of the opposition of the convent. Returning to Christ Church the same day, he suspended the prior

His plan for the college

Vision of Andrew John

Second appeal of the convent

---

[1] Gervase, 1481.
[2] There are numerous references to this vision in the letters (vol. R. S.); especially Nos. lxix., ccxciv.   [3] Gerv. 1484. No. ix.

and the appellant brethren, closed the monastery, and ordered the monks on their obedience to remain within.[1] Then, as a mark of his profound displeasure, he went to keep Christmas at Otford, thereby laying his cathedral open to an unheard-of insult, for on Christmas eve two papal legates, Hugh of Nunant and Cardinal Octavian, neither of them a bishop, were suffered to enter the church with their mitres on and their crosses erect. The prior, regardless of the prohibition, fled from Canterbury immediately after Baldwin's departure, and, crossing the straits, landed on the 22nd in Flanders,[2] whence he pursued his way to Verona.

The prior goes to Italy

The contest was now to begin in earnest, and each party looked round for supporters, both at home and abroad. The state of Europe was such that neither had any difficulty in finding patrons. Baldwin was strong in the assistance of Henry, who was believed to have suggested the tactics of the archbishop, and the convent consequently betook themselves to solicit the friendship of those who openly or secretly wished to embarrass the king. All who had shown sympathy with S. Thomas during his life, or reverence for him after his death, were claimed as friends by the convent. Philip of France and Philip of Flanders were drawn to this side either by dislike to the king or by duty to the martyr. The Emperor Frederick was appealed to by the convent ;[3] Henry the Lion, as the king's son-in-law, was favourable to the archbishop, and his example was followed by the king and queen of Sicily.[4] The whole Cistercian order, at home and abroad, espoused the party of Baldwin from principle and inclination ; and the whole order of Cluny, at home and abroad, undertook the defence of the convent, to which they were attached by their earliest traditions. Thus the monastic party in England was itself divided, and whilst the convents of Faversham, Reading, and Lewes were found among the willing agents of the monks, those of Boxley and Robertsbridge were always ready to defeat any step injurious to the archbishop. Of the greater monasteries, those of Peterborough, Battle, and Tewkesbury were ruled by abbots who had been priors of Canterbury, and Evesham by a Cluniac monk. S. Augustine's, hating impartially both the archbishop and the convent, stood aloof from the strife. In France the abbeys of S. Bertin and Cluny afforded a home to the exiles and provisions to the messengers of the convent. One Cistercian monk, Peter, who had been abbot of Cîteaux, and was now bishop of Arras, offered a lukewarm support to the monks, but actually played into the hands of Baldwin. Ralph de Serra (Sarr in Thanet), dean of Rheims, who had been a friend of S. Thomas, and was personally

The two parties and their allies

The Cistercians support Baldwin, the Cluniacs the convent

---

[1] Gervase 1485.
[2] No. xix.
[3] No. xi.
[4] No. clxxxiii.

attached to the convent, was their most zealous supporter among the secular clergy in France.

In the college of cardinals the same differences prevailed. Of the cardinal bishops, Henry of Albano, who had been abbot of Clairvaux when Baldwin was abbot of Ford, undertook the defence of his friend ; he was supported by Cardinal Albert, the chancellor, who is also claimed by the Cistercians,[1] and who had known the king of England in former years, and by the cardinal deacon Octavian. On the other hand, Theobald, bishop of Ostia and dean of the Sacred College, had been abbot of Cluny, and also a candidate for the see of Canterbury when Baldwin was elected ;[2] both good reasons for supporting the monks. Among the less eminent cardinals who were glad to pursue the ordinary policy of the papacy by weakening the authority of the bishops and supporting the demand of the monks, the latter found great favour. Of these were William of Champagne, archbishop of Rheims, who, though not resident, had influential agents at Verona ; Gratian, the cardinal of SS. Cosmas and Damian, the friend of S. Thomas, who called him the Son of Grace, and the mortal enemy of Henry, who had contemned his mediation in 1169 ; Cardinal Hyacinth, who afterwards became Celestine III. ; the French cardinals, Melior and Ralph Nigel ; Gerard Allucingoli, nephew of Lucius III. ; Peter of Piacenza, Soffred of S. Mary in Via Lata ; and John of Anagni, cardinal priest of S. Mark, to whose family was attached a young ecclesiastic, his kinsman, whose friendship gained at this time was fraught with great issues both to the convent and to their country ; Lothario[3] dei Conti di Segni, afterwards Pope Innocent III. Last, if not least, Urban III., or Pope Turban as the imperialists called him, once archdeacon of Bourges, and an ally of S. Thomas,[4] threw himself with his characteristic violence into the party opposed to Baldwin.

The archbishop took up his position with the best advice. He found himself backed by the majority of the bishops at home. Geoffrey of Ely,[5] the archidiabolus of S. Thomas, was ready to depose that in that loving intercourse which they had enjoyed the departed saint had often spoken of his design of building a church in honour

Parties in the college of cardinals

Position of the bishops at home

---

[1] Ciaconius.
[2] Benedict Peterb. ad ann. 1184.
[3] P. 68, vol. R. S.
[4] Conrad of Ursperg, p. cccxi. (ed. 1540.) Herb. Bosham, vii. 1.
[5] No. xxiii. It is not improbable that there may be some traces of a design of this sort on the part of S. Anselm and S. Thomas in their different lives ; I have not, however,

been able to discover them. There is so great an a priori probability that S. Thomas, who had a great veneration for S. Stephen, had some such plan, that Geoffrey might safely assert it, whether true or not. Peter of Blois tells an even more circumstantial story of S. Anselm's wish to do the same. Ep. 216. (Appendix, vol. R. S. No. dlxxi.)

of S. Stephen.   Hugh of Nunant, the elect of Coventry, nephew of
Arnulf of Lisieux,[1] the inheritor of the diplomatic abilities and
courtly habits of a long race of astute Norman prelates, and the inveterate enemy of monachism, was prepared to go any lengths of violence
in the same direction.   John the Chantor, bishop of Exeter, was
bound, both as an Exeter man and as a newly consecrated bishop, to
take the side of his townsman and primate.   The bishop of Norwich,
John of Oxford, needed no persuasion to take up arms against his old
enemies.   Gilbert of Rochester was the near kinsman of the king's
justiciar, and at constant war with the monks of his own church.
Seffrid of Chichester and Reginald of Bath, with a view probably to

Opinion of
S. Hugh

future elections, took the opposite side.   Hugh of Lincoln stood
aloof, and, according to his biographer, faithfully remonstrated with
Baldwin, explaining the difficulties and dangers of the course he was
beginning, so clearly and sensibly that the result almost entitled him
to the reputation of a prophet.[2]

The kings
ministers

Of the king's ministers, Ranulf Glanvill professed attachment to
the convent, but Hubert Walter, his nephew, was designated for
one of the new prebends, as were also Richard FitzNeal, the king's
treasurer, and several others who rose to eminence in the following
reigns, among whom were William of S. Mere l'Eglise, afterwards
bishop of London ; Henry of Northampton, canon of S. Paul's ; and
Ralph of S. Martin, the persecutor of the convent under John.[3]

The arch-
bishop tries
to usurp the
management
of the
estates of
the convent

Before sending his representatives to Rome to answer the prior,
the archbishop took a step towards recovering the administration of
the conventual estates.   He forbade the tenants to pay rent to the
monks, and, having summoned three of the brethren, presented them
with a commission to manage the affairs of the house during the
absence of the prior.[4]   The convent refused to recognise the authority, and Baldwin, having pleaded the precedent of Theobald, not
feeling very sure of his ground, waived his claim.[5]   The king, who
had spent Christmas at Guildford and was now going abroad, about
this time sent, at the archbishop's request, the bishops of Norwich
and Worcester, with Hugh of Nunant,[6] to propose an arbitration ; but
this was rejected by the subprior Geoffrey, a man of great firmness

Henry II.
visits Can-
terbury

and much practical ability, who two days afterwards had an interview with the king at Chilham, and left him favourably impressed

[1] Hugh was nephew to Arnulf,
bishop of Lisieux, and John FitzHar-
douin, bishop of Séez, and adminis-
trator of Rochester : grand-nephew of
John, bishop of Lisieux. See Epist.
Arnulfi, pp. 97, 121, 137, &c. (ed.
Migne) ; and Ord. Vital. xi. 31, xii. 35.
Hugh was legate of the Apostolic See

for Ireland in 1186.
[2] Magna Vita S. Hugonis (ed.
Dimock, pp. 133-136).
[3] Fœdera, i. 99.   Foss's Judges, i.
418.
[4] Nos. lxxxiv. lxxxv.
[5] Gervase, 1486.
[6] No. xcix.

with his eloquence and moderation. On the 11th of February, 1187, Henry came in person to Christ Church, and prayed the monks to renounce the appeal and accept an arbitration. This failing, he addressed himself to Baldwin, with whom he was acting in concert. 'Let the archbishop remove the suspension of the offending monks ; the king was in despair at losing so many valuable intercessors.' The archbishop insisted on a confession to be made in the presence of witnesses ; the convent pleaded the privilege by which strangers were forbidden to be present on such an occasion. The archbishop, however, granted a general absolution before he left.

He now despatched his agents to Verona : Peter of Blois, archdeacon of Bath, and William of S. Faith (*sans* faith, according to the convent), precentor of Wells. He also changed the site of his new church, from the churchyard of Hakington to the vacant space in front of S. Dunstan's church, now known as S. Thomas's hill.[1] The foundations were begun on the 18th of February, a day marked by the heaviest hailstorm ever known in Kent.

Baldwin sends agents to Verona, and changes the site of his college

The prior and his companions, well furnished with letters of introduction, had now reached Verona, and found the pope already active in their behalf. He had listened favourably to the first appeal, and before the arrival of the prior, on the 19th of January, had issued a mandate for the restoration of Eastry and Monkton, the execution of which was committed to the bishop of Lincoln and the abbots of Boxley and S. Augustine's.[2] As, however, this appeal had been formally renounced, these letters were not brought forward in the controversy. Notwithstanding the absence of Theobald of Ostia,[3] Honorius obtained an audience of the pope, and on the 1st of March, a week before the term of the appeal, was able to send papal letters to England ordering the archbishop to remove his suspension, and the abbots of Battle, Faversham and S. Augustine's to enforce compliance.[4] As the archbishop's agents had not arrived on Mid-Lent Sunday, Urban adjourned the hearing of the cause to the 10th of April, in the meanwhile granting several privileges to the prior, and

Honorius at Verona, obtains a mandate for his restoration

[1] Gervase, 1491 ; Sommer, p. 47; and No. dlv. vol. R. S. Although the new site was in the parish of S. Dunstan, the college continued to be called that of Hakington.
[2] Nos. iii. v. The churches of Eynesford and Mepeham are not mentioned in this letter. Mepeham was in fact held by Master Virgil, to whom Archbishop Richard had given it at the request of Alexander III., and whose rights he had reserved in the act of appropriation. Eynesford had been long in litigation between the convent and the heirs of William FitzRalph, the original donor. This ended in Archbishop Richard's time. He gave it to Gentilis, a nephew of Alexander III., to revert on his death to the almonry. Gentilis died shortly before Richard, who then confirmed the appropriation.—Fragment of a chartulary of the almonry, Lambeth Charters, vol. xiii. p. 1, No. 15, and Bodl. MS. Tanner, xviii.
[3] No. xxxiv.
[4] Nos. xxvi. xxvii.

especially vesting the whole of the oblations of the church in the hands of the convent.

Baldwin's contempt of the papal mandate

Baldwin received the letters ordering the removal of the prior's suspension on the 25th of March, at Otford ; he took no further notice of them, but, by way of showing his contempt for the convent, consecrated, at S. Paul's in London on the following day, the chrism for the diocese of Canterbury.[1] The abbot of Battle executed his commission on the 11th of April,[2] declaring the sentence against the prior and monks to be invalid ; the other points of the mandate, which proceeded to enjoin the restoration of the *status quo ante appellationem*, he was afraid to proceed with, and referred them back to the pope. On the 14th[3] the archbishop's clerks appealed to the pope against the commissioners, and Baldwin replied to the attack by confining to the monastery Ralph of Orpington and John

He builds a wooden chapel

of Boching, the managers of the estates, and by building a chapel of wood, eighty feet in length, on the chosen site.

The pope issues two new mandates

This was duly reported to the pope, who, on the 9th of May, the representatives of Baldwin having not yet appeared, addressed two peremptory letters[4] to the archbishop, in the first of which he forbade him to proceed with his buildings, and in the second ordered him to restore the property of the convent. He also wrote to the prelates of England abolishing the new brotherhood, and to the abbots of Battle, Faversham and S. Augustine's, to compel Baldwin to restitution.[5] Honorius and his party, having succeeded so well, prepared to return home, leaving the cause in the hands of Master Pillius, an eminent advocate, with injunctions to watch the arrival and the machinations of the archbishop's agents. The letters were sent forward by Haymo of Thanet, the original appellant.[6] Brothers Humfrey and Edmund prepared to accompany the prior.[7]

Baldwin again contemns the mandates

The apostolic mandates were served on the archbishop as he was going on a legatine visit to Wales,[8] the first at Bredon, on June 10th, and the second at Shrewsbury, on the 23rd, by brothers Symon and Aaron. To both he returned answer in writing, ' We have seen the pope's mandates, and what we have to do thereupon we will do.' His practical reply was to press on the building ; the papal letter had miraculous power to turn the wooden edifice to stone ;[9] the canons began to build their houses, and took upon themselves the responsibility of proceeding with the church. John of Boching and Ralph of Orpington were now excommunicated, and immediately

---

[1] No. xxxiii.   Gerv. 1493.
[2] No. xxviii.   Gerv. 1494.
[3] Gerv. 1494.
[4] Nos. xl. xlii.
[5] Nos. xli. xliii.
[6] Gerv. 1497.   Nos. lxx. lxxix.

[7] Nos. liii. liv.
[8] Not to be confounded with his expedition to Wales in the following year on the business of the Crusade.
[9] No. lxvi.

carried their complaint to the pope.[1] The royal interference was also invoked. Ranulf Glanvill forbade the execution of the second mandate, and summoned the subprior to Westminster on the 25th of July.[2] Geoffrey declined the obey the summons, but sent two aged brethren in his place ; whom the justiciar charged to recall the prior, and to send the subprior with five or six of the monks to exhibit their privileges and charters before the king in Normandy.[3] Ranulf Glanvill forbids the execution of the mandate

The convent were thrown into the greatest dismay by these proceedings. That the prior should have left Verona under the circumstances seemed little better than treason. Brother Haymo, who had foolishly ventured home without a protection,[4] had been instantly sent back. Other messengers were sent off to the brethren at Verona, and to Cluny, Tours, and Rheims, to meet Honorius.[5] Haymo met him at Vercelli,[6] but, not being in possession of the latest news, could not induce him to return to the court. He proceeded homewards, and reached Soissons, where he took up his residence with the dean of Rheims,[7] until he received peremptory directions to return to Verona.[8] These he obeyed, and arrived there on the 11th of September.[9] In the meantime important events had occurred both there and nearer home. Honorius leaves Verona, and is ordered back

We have seen how the archbishop had been foiled in his attempt to get the management of the conventual estates intrusted to his nominees during the absence of the prior. On his return from Wales he made another effort to secure it, which led to further difficulties. He began by again seizing the whole estates of the convent. Then, on his way to Dover, where he was going to embark for the continent, he sent for the officers of the convent, and made them a new proposition. The property of the convent was apportioned partly to the cellarership for the victualling of the house, partly to the chamberlainship for the furniture of the cells and clothing of the monks, and partly to the sacrist for the use of the church.[10] The manors appropriated to these purposes were not, however, managed by the obedientiaries themselves, but by three stewards, bursars or treasurers, who received the whole revenue, and divided it in proper proportions. The three treasurers were John of Baldwin determines to usurp the management of the estates

---

[1] Nos. lxxiii. lxxxiii. lxxxix. xc. They were absolved on the day of their arrival at Verona, and immediately returned home.
[2] No. lx.
[3] Nos. lvi. lxv. Gervase, 1504.
[4] No. lxxx.
[5] Nos. lxxvii. lxxx.
[6] Gervase, 1497.
[7] Whether the dean of Rheims

Ralph of Sarr, was also archdeacon of Soissons, I cannot make out. It was at his house that Honorius stayed at Soissons, and he seems to be addressed as archdeacon in No. xv. Gerv. 1497. No. lxxix.
[8] No. lxxxii.
[9] No. cxxvii.
[10] No. cxix.

Boching[1] and Ralph of Orpington,[2] whom the archbishop had excommunicated, and Roger Norreys,[3] who, with the aged sacrist Robert, had been sent on private business to the king in France. The remaining two obedientiaries, Hervey the cellarer and Symon the chamberlain, obeyed the archbishop's summons. His proposal to them was that they should consent to hold their offices under him, instead of the convent, and of course should render their accounts to him only.[3] This they refused to do, declaring that they would hold their places on the same terms on which their predecessors had done. The archbishop refused to restore the estates on any other conditions, and forbade the cellarer to meddle any more with the affairs of the house. He then, having appealed to the pope against the abbots of Faversham and Battle, sailed to Normandy, on the 11th of August.[4]

The envoys of the convent at the king's court The king was at Alençon, where a great court was to be held on the 28th. To Alençon accordingly the archbishop betook himself, and to his alarm found that the messengers of the convent had had an interview with the king. These were Alexander of Dover and an old monk named Robert or Richard, who had been chaplain to S. Thomas.[5] Henry had expressed himself in friendly terms, and so far imposed upon the envoys that Alexander returned home. The archbishop proceeded to lay his statement before Henry, insisting on resigning his see if the monks were not compelled to obedience.[6]

Baldwin invests the sacrist and cellarer at Alençon At the court on the 28th the messengers of the convent who were sent in obedience to the command of the justiciar presented themselves, Robert, who had been sacrist for forty years,[7] and Roger Norreys. Robert was very old and stupid, Roger was a traitor. By the king's persuasion these were induced to accept the archbishop's terms : Roger he appointed cellarer, and Robert he re-appointed as sacrist. They allowed themselves to be invested by him, acknowledging him as their feudal lord, and as the source of their jurisdiction over the manors appropriated to their obediences. They returned home with letters to the convent announcing their appointment, and to the bishop of Rochester, requiring him to institute them, and also to re-invest Symon the chamberlain as the archbishop's servant.[8] The king either supposed, or pretended to do so, that these messengers had full powers to treat on behalf of the convent, and that by yielding in this point they had satisfied the archbishop, which was all that was wanted. He wrote, therefore, to

---

[1] No. cxix.
[2] No. cvii.
[3] Gerv. 1504.   No. xcvi.
[4] Gerv. 1505.
[5] No. cxxi.
[6] Gerv. 1505.
[7] Nos. cxxi. cxviii.

[8] Nos. cxi. cxii. The king also commissioned Ranulf Glanvill and the bishop to invest the new obedientiaries, which, of course, increased the fear of the convent of being subjected to secular power.

the pope, and to Prior Honorius, claiming the credit of having restored peace to the church.[1]

Roger and Robert were received at Canterbury with well-deserved indignation. Symon refused to accept institution from the bishop, and the aged sacrist was ordered to repudiate his act at Alençon, as forced on him by the king. Roger Norreys was arrested and confined in the infirmary.[2] The sacrist with three other brethren was sent back to the king, to declare that from him only, and not from the archbishop, would the convent accept restitution, and that such restitution must be made to the prior and convent, not to the obedientiaries.[3] These messengers were not allowed to have access to the king ; the archbishop was still more exasperated, and attempted to close the courts of justice held by the convent in their own name.[4] He also directed his servants to take possession of the estates of the convent, and displace their officials. A fresh complaint was accordingly carried to Rome : not only had the archbishop violated the ancient customs of the convent, but, by investing the obedientiaries in the king's court, he had recognised a secular jurisdiction in matters ecclesiastical. This was the news from home which reached the prior soon after his return to the papal court.

The reception of the sacrist and cellarer at Canterbury

There Baldwin's envoys had been working zealously during Honorius's absence. Peter of Blois and William of S. Faith had arrived at Verona, a week after the prior had left, early in June.[5] They seem to have held back, as if uncertain of their reception. They had delayed their arrival until his departure ; now they refused to open their budget in the presence of Master Pillius. When he had been got out of the way, they produced on behalf of the king and primate their answers to the charges of the monks : on these Pope Urban reserved his decision. They then delivered petitions in favour of the new church, and for the revocation of the privileges which the prior had obtained in March. Master Pillius was recalled to state the arguments of the convent against this. He declared that the royal letters on behalf of the new church were a mere matter of form, and such as would necessarily be granted to any influential person. To the claims of Baldwin he replied by stating the rights of the convent, and denying those of the archbishop, who had moreover put himself in the wrong by proceeding with the prohibited building. The pope then questioned Peter of Blois as to the use and necessity of the new college. ' The church of Canterbury,' said Peter, ' is very high exalted and glorious, and therefore needs much help against princes and powers, especially

Peter of Blois at Verona

The pope hears both sides

---

[1] Nos. cxiv. cxv.
[2] Gerv. 1506. Nos. cxvii. cxviii. cxxi.
[3] Gerv. 1506. No. cxxiii.
[4] Gerv. 1507.
[5] Gerv. 1497-8-9.

such help as would be supplied by wise clerks, who are much more prudent and experienced in affairs than are monks.' 'But are not,' asked the pope, 'the monks the ministers of the cathedral?' Peter admitted it. 'If so, then why does not the archbishop use them as his councillors?' Here Master Pillius broke in : 'My Lord, the archbishop is bishop of the church of Canterbury, and also, as our opponents say, abbot of these same monks. If, then, he is abbot, he ought to change or alienate nothing without consent of his monks, neither in his character of bishop can he build a church on the estates of his chapter without their consent.' The pope next inquired what was the archbishop's purpose in building : 'was the see, or the body of the martyr, to be translated?' Peter answered that no such proceeding was contemplated ; the archbishop was merely carrying out the purpose of S. Anselm and S. Thomas. 'Stop,' said the pope ; 'did S. Thomas wish to build a church in his own name?' Peter, so said the monks, was silenced by this august quibble. The arguments lasted several days, but this is all that is preserved to us of the actual discussion.[1]

The pope silences Peter of Blois

Urban III. leaves Verona

The result of the hearing was to embitter Urban more than before against the archbishop. After Honorius's return the cause was pressed still more urgently on him by both parties. The pope's mind was at this time unsettled and soured by his quarrel with the emperor, whom he threatened to excommunicate. The people of Verona begged him not to issue his sentence whilst he was their guest ; and during the last week of September he left the city, intending, according to some authorities, to go to Venice to equip a fleet of crusaders. He took, however, the way to Ferrara. Peter of Blois rode with him the first day. They had been fellow-students in former days ; now the envoy began to sing the praises of Baldwin. The pope, who was in bad health, and never had much command of temper, was bored by the importunity of the archdeacon. ' May it please God,' he cried out, ' that I may never dismount from this horse, or mount steed again, if I do not shortly dismount him from his archbishopric.' Scarcely were the words spoken, when the cross of gold, carried before him by the subdeacon, fell broken at his feet.[2] That day he reached a place which Peter calls Sutoro or Futuro.

Illness of the pope

There he was seized with dysentery, and was obliged to proceed by water to Ferrara. At Ferrara he issued a mandate to the archbishop on the 3rd of October, directing him to demolish his new buildings and

---

[1] Gerv. 1497-9.

[2] This account is given by Peter of Blois in a fragment of a letter which, so far as I am aware, occurs in only one MS., New College, 127. I have ventured to give it in the Appendix,

vol. R. S. (No. dlxxi.), as it is a necessary adjunct to the series of letters ; but the text is corrupt and shows that the transcriber could not read his copy.

desecrate the site, to dissolve the collegiate foundation, and replace the convent *in statu quo*. Thirty days were allowed for compliance; after that term the bishops of Bath and Chichester were to enforce it. At the same time he wrote to the king, insisting on the execution of the mandate, and to the convent, annulling all sentences of excommunication, suspension, or interdict that Baldwin might launch against them.[1] Urban's last
mandate

On the day these letters were issued Jerusalem was taken by Saladin, and sixteen days after the pope died. The news of both these events reached England nearly at the same time.[2] It is scarcely possible that Urban should have heard of the capture of the Holy City, but he may have known that the sultan had begun the siege, and that defence was hopeless. His death was ascribed to the bitterness of his grief. It is observable, however, that the letters in this volume make no mention of the surrender as a cause of his death. No such blow indeed was necessary to despatch an old man worn out with heavy anxiety and stormy passions; the dysentery caught on his journey doubtless caused his end. In him the convent lost a very zealous, if not a discreet patron, and the archbishop a furious enemy. The event was announced to both parties by their agents, Peter of Blois exhibiting a most unbecoming and heartless joy.[3] Two days after the death of Urban, the new pope was chosen. The bishop of Albano, Baldwin's friend, took a leading part in the election. The cardinals nominated three candidates, the bishops of Albano and Palestrina, and Albert, the chancellor. The bishop of Palestrina was persuaded to retire on the plea of infirmity; Henry of Albano refused to undertake the responsibility; and the chancellor succeeded, as Gregory VIII.[4] His first measure was to confirm all the acts of his predecessor done within three months of his death;[5] his second, to make an exception in favour of the archbishop of Canterbury, thus annulling the mandates which had been gained with so much perseverance and at so great a price. This was done on the 29th of October. Death of
Urban III.

Election of
Gregory
VIII.

He annuls
the mandates
of Urban III.

The mandate arrived in England at the end of the same month, and the privilege exempting the convent from Baldwin's sentence was read in the synod of the diocese at Canterbury on the 1st of November.[6] The archbishop received his letter at Caen, from Brother Haymo,[7] and declared himself willing to do justice. The king also professed to be friendly. Matters seemed a little more favourable,

---

[1] Nos. cxxviii. cxxix. cxxx. cxxxi.
[2] William of Newburgh says that it was the news of the battle of July 6 that killed the pope. Lib. iii. 21. Benedict of Peterborough and Hoveden confirm the statement; as also

Gervase.
[3] Nos. cxxxiv. cxxxv.
[4] No. cxxxv.
[5] Nos. cxxxviii. cxxxix. Diceto, 636. Hoveden, 365.
[6] No. clxxvi.   [7] Gerv. 1511.

The proceedings of Baldwin after the death of Urban

when the news of Urban's death spoiled all. King and primate alike threw off the mask. Henry ordered the justiciar to take the new college under royal protection, which was done on the 18th of November ; [1] and Baldwin issued injunctions for thankgiving at Hakington for the annulling of the papal mandate.[2] On the 17th of December he forbade the holding of the courts of the convent.[3] Ralph of S. Martin, one of their bitterest enemies, visited them with advice to throw themselves on the archbishop's mercy ; and the venerable Herbert of Bosham, with more regret, gave them the same counsel.[4] But the spirited subprior was proof against all such recommendations, and Herbert left him convinced, according to Gervase, of the duty of resistance.

Honorius follows the new pope to Pisa

Prior Honorius was now pleading his cause over again with the cardinals, and trying to get an interview with the new pope. He was assured privately that justice would be done ultimately, but that for the time it was necessary to move cautiously. He followed the court from Ferrara, by Bologna and Modena, to Parma, and thence to Pisa, where he arrived on the 10th of December.[5] The pope professed that he had no time to listen to him ; he was engrossed with receiving embassies and preparing for the crusade ; the bishop of Albano was still hostile. But just as he was congratulating himself on the dismissal of his most dreaded opponent,[6] who was sent to conduct the matter of the crusade in Germany, the pope sickened and

Death of Gregory VIII.

died after a reign of less than two months. No time was wasted in filling up the vacant throne. The Cistercian bishop of Albano was absent, and the succession was offered to the Cluniac Theobald of Ostia, the friend and patron of the monks of Canterbury. Theobald declined the dangerous honour, and Paul Scolari, bishop of Palestrina, who two months before had been shouldered out of it by the bishop of Albano, ascended the papal throne under the name of Clement III., on the 19th of December.[7] The bishop of Ostia

---

[1] No. cxxxiii.

[2] No. cxl.

[3] No. cxxiv. Gerv. 1513.

[4] Gerv. 1513. The appearance of Herbert in this place ought to have refuted at once the notion that appears in some of our early bibliographers, and in the lists of cardinals, that Herbert of Bosham became, after S. Thomas's death, a cardinal and archbishop of Benevento. The story is compounded from the following ingredients:—1. Lombard of Piacenza, a friend of S. Thomas, was cardinal and archbishop of Benevento from 1171–1179. He probably gave Alan of Tewkesbury his prebend at Benevento. 2. Herbert,

archbishop of Compsa 1138–1180. He was a native of Middlesex, and Ralph de Diceto makes him archbishop of Cosenza, and swallowed up by an earthquake in 1185. 3. A different person, named Ruffus, who was archbishop of Cosenza, and perished in that way in 1185. See Ughelli, Italia Sacra, viii. 192, &c. ; Ciaconius, i. 1094.

[5] Nos. cxlviii. cliv.

[6] No. clxi. Henry proceeded into Germany, where he gave the cross to Frederick Barbarossa, and proceeding thence through the Low Countries, died at Arras, July 14, 1188.

[7] No. clxii.

announced the result to the convent, advising them to authorise the continued stay of the prior at the papal court.[1]

In England the death of Urban was regarded as insuring the triumph of the archbishop. Hitherto he had managed to render nugatory the whole procedure of the convent. He now prepared to return, and, in concert with the king, sent the bishop of Rochester with a proposal to the convent on the 9th of January, 1188.[2] The bishop, attended by a few knights and by the canons of Hakington, harangued the monks in the chapter-house, extolling the virtues of Baldwin, and counselling submission. He did not, however, offer any relaxation of the harshness which had been hitherto exercised by the archbishop, and ended by confessing that he was sent to inspect and place under seal the treasure of the church. The subprior took a day for consideration, and on the morrow replied, refusing to let the bishop inspect the treasure, and declining to surrender the seal or to receive restitution of the estates on the archbishop's terms. Having said thus much, he solemnly appealed to the pope, and asked the bishop for licence to proceed to Rome with his appeal. The bishop, unable to answer, retired in dismay, and the knights who accompanied him attempted to seize the court of the monks.[3] The next day, Monday, January 11,[4] Ranulf Glanvill arrived in person, and had a peaceable interview with the subprior. The same day Baldwin landed at Dover. On the Wednesday Geoffrey sent two monks on horseback to Wingham, to offer him the customary procession. He replied by excommunicating the messengers and seizing their horses. They returned in great tribulation on foot, and were followed by William FitzNeal,[5] the faithless steward who had

Marginal notes: Clement III. succeeds

Baldwin sends the bishop of Rochester to Canterbury

Violent proceedings against the convent

---

[1] No. cl.

[2] Gervase, 1514. Nos. cxlvii. clxviii. It is necessary, in order to understand the proceedings, to remember the position of the conventual buildings. The archbishop's palace and court stood to the north-west of the church. East of them stood the cloister, adjoining the nave; east of that was the convent garden, and east of that, round the east end, and down the south side of the church as far as the gate of the close, extended the cemetery, which was divided into an outer and inner portion by the *porta cœmeterii*: this is called the court of the cemetery. Immediately adjoining the cloister on the north and east were the dormitory and refectory; beyond which on the north was the court of the convent, surrounded by the offices, brewhouse, storehouses, &c., which joined nearly the city wall. It will

thus be seen how, the court of the monks being seized by the soldiers, their provisions were cut off, and they were confined to the dormitory, refectory, cloister and church buildings. The seizure of the gates of the close and of the cemetery stopped all access from without to the church, and put the monks to great straits for provisions. There is a good map in Somner's *Canterbury*, and two beautiful plans, one copied from a twelfth-century MS., in a memoir on the conventual buildings read by Mr. Mackenzie Walcott before the Institute of British Architects, Dec. 15, 1862.

[3] Nos. cli. cliii.

[4] Gervase, 1516. Nos. clviii. clix. clxvi.

[5] Gerv. 1516; Foss's Judges, i. 241; Fitz-Stephen, 297, 298; Roger of Pontigny, 160–161.

deserted S. Thomas in the hour of his last peril. William found the
court of the convent closed against him, broke through the wall, and
occupied the gate and the outer offices ; [1] whereupon the subprior
suspended divine service, and stripped the altars as in the time of
interdict.[2] The next day the servants of the convent were compelled
to swear that they would prevent the monks from going outside the
walls ; the inner wall of the court was scaled, and the monks shut
up within the line of the cloister, their provisions now falling into
the enemies' hands. After an ineffectual attempt at reconciliation,
made by the bishop of Rochester and Hugh of Nunant, Baldwin on
the following Sunday excommunicated the subprior and his advisers.[3]
The very next day he received the news of Pope Gregory's death,
and, thinking that he had gone too far for his own safety, left
Wingham, and, having preached an apologetic sermon at Hakington,
hurried to London. He also made another offer of restitution, by
the prior of S. Gregory's and the sheriff of Kent, and entreated the
convent to resume divine service. The subprior answered the
proposal as usual, and refused the request. The messengers, however, opened the little door in the gate of the cemetery for the
admission of pilgrims, and a few days later the gate itself was opened
by the sheriff, but it was still strictly guarded. In this way the
monks were kept in a state of imprisonment for eighty-four weeks,
during which time they were dependent for food on the gifts of the
pilgrims ; even Jews were found among their benefactors. They
were so well supplied, it seems, that two hundred strangers were
daily fed with the superfluous contributions ; nor were these confined
to absolute necessaries, for fish, vegetables, and pepper cake were
among the constant offerings ; even poultry was presented for the
use of the sick.[4] About the end of January Roger Norreys, the
intruder cellarer, escaped from durance by making his way through
the cloaca of the monks,[5] and betook himself to Baldwin at Otford.[6]

The monks confined to the monastery

Escape of Roger Norreys

[1] Nos. clvi. clvii.
[2] Gerv. 1517. No. clxvii.
[3] Gerv. 1518. No. clxvii.
[4] Gerv. 1520, to Aug. 12, 1189.
[5] This building occupies a conspicuous place in the ancient plan of the
convent, extending from the infirmary
across the court of the monks almost
as far as the dormitory. If Roger was
still confined in the infirmary he could
have easily escaped into the cemetery,
or if not, through the cloaca in the court
of the convent, which, as well as the
cemetery, was in the hands of the enemy.
It may be well just to point out here
that Roger Cloacarius, who is men-

tioned once or twice, is, of course,
Roger Norreys. The play on the name
of Norreys occurs several times, as
Rogerus ab Aquilone, and the brother
who has set his throne in the sides of
the north. Similar are the references
to William de Sancta Fide, W. Malæ
Fidei, and W. Sine Fide : to the unhappy pretensions of Brother Felix ;
and to the *unnecessary* service of
Roger Norreys after his escape. Who
the little priest was who ' crebrius
ostrea captat,' No. lxxxi., I do not
know, unless it was the abbot of
Faversham.
[6] Gerv. 1519. No. ccviii.

The king landed at Winchelsea on the 30th of January,[1] and was prevented from visiting Canterbury by the news of the suspension of divine service. He sent on the 4th of February[2] to the subprior orders to resume it, and summoned him with six of the brethren to the council which was to be held at Gaitington on the 11th. Geoffrey refused either to appear or to send representatives. The council assembled, and the archbishop stated his complaint against the convent in very bitter language; he also demanded the arrest of the subprior as excommunicate. The convent were defended by Reginald, bishop of Bath, who prevented the request of Baldwin from being granted. The king proposed an arbitration, and sent two bishops to Canterbury to persuade the convent to send representatives to court. Four monks were accordingly sent on the 24th of February,[3] and presented themselves before Henry at Clarendon on the 1st of March, with copies of the charters and privileges on which the convent relied. To the horror and disgust of the monks, the king declared with a magnificent oath that the royal charters were not genuine, all his councillors, except Roger the almoner and William of S. Mere l'Eglise, confirming the statement. Before he dismissed them he bade them meet the archbishop and himself at Winchester, and they were afterwards summoned on to Cirencester, where they met the archbishop going into Wales to preach the crusade. When they came into his presence, they saluted him. Baldwin returned no answer; his clerks received the attention with mockery and insult. Henry now renewed the proposal of an arbitration, to which Baldwin consented. The envoys replying that they could not get a fair arbitration in England, where the archbishop was supreme, Henry administered a reproof for the uncharitable suspicion, and proposed the recall of the prior. 'If we consent to recall the prior, who,' the brethren asked, 'will engage to provide for the sustenance of the convent until his return?' Henry would not promise; the monks were sent back to consult their brethren, and the three oldest members of the convent were summoned to appear before the king. Geoffrey replied to the summons that it was impossible to send them; one was ruptured, another afflicted with hæmorrhoids, the third was a paralytic: he sent two others, who were immediately sent back by the king as unfit for his purpose. Henry was now called away by serious business, and Baldwin spent the spring in Wales.[4]

The suit was in the meantime being vigorously pressed at Rome. Immediately after the bishop of Rochester's visit on the 9th of

Marginal notes:
Cause of the convent at the council of Gaitington

Interview of the monks with Henry at Clarendon,

and with Baldwin at Cirencester

---

[1] Gerv. 1520.
[2] Gerv. 1520. Nos. clxxxvi. cclxxvi.
[3] Gerv. 1523. Nos. clxxxvi. ccxl.
[4] Gervase, 1528.

John de
Bremble
goes to
Rome

January, four brethren were sent to the pope,[1] one of whom, brother John de Bremble, was from this time the life and soul of the cause. His letters are all worth reading ; perhaps they are the best in the volume.   He crossed the Great S. Bernard in February,[2] and reached Rome on the 27th of the month.[3]   Prior Honorius had not been idle.   As early as the 26th of January he had procured a mandate dated at Siena,[4] reaffirming the last letters of Urban, but not accompanied by a commission to enforce execution.   The news brought by Brother John of the outrages committed in January was delivered to the pope on the 1st of March,[5] and on the 17th Clement commissioned the prior of Faversham and Master Farreman, warden of the hospital of S. James at Canterbury, to excommunicate the persons who had violently entered the monastery.[6]   By the same

New man-
dates issued
and a legate
promised

messenger the prior ordered the subprior to resume divine service.[7] On the 11th of April the pope promised to send a legate with full powers to settle the whole cause, and hopes were held out that the bishop of Ostia would be chosen.[8]

The arch-
bishop con-
temns the
mandates of
Clement

The mandate of January 26th was served on Baldwin on the 22nd of March, in the presence of two bishops, probably at or near Llandaff.   To the bearers he returned no answer, but wrote to Hakington directing his servants to intrench the new buildings, and put them in a state of defence.[9]

On the 15th of April, being Good Friday,[10] the letter of March 17th was received at Canterbury, with the prior's command to resume the service.   The monks reluctantly obeyed this direction, and the prior of Faversham on the 23rd executed the mandate.   This produced

---

[1] No. clxv.
[2] No. cxcvii., a very amusing letter.
[3] No. ccv.
[4] No. cxciii.
[5] No. ccv.
[6] No. ccxiii.
[7] No. ccxvi.
[8] No. ccxxviii.
[9] Gerv. 1529. No. ccxxiii.   The two bishops were Peter of St. David's, who accompanied Baldwin on his tour, and the bishop of Llandaff, in whose diocese he was at the time.   The data for fixing the chronology of Giraldus, who gives the history of the tour in his Itinerarium Cambriæ, are very scanty.   He makes the expedition start from Radnor about Ash Wednesday, March 2 ; Ranulf Glanvill having just returned from thence to England.   But it is clear from No. ccxl. that Ranulf Glanvill was on the 1st of March at Clarendon, whilst

the archbishop did not reach Cirencester, or indeed Winchester, until some days later.   At least a week must have elapsed after the 2nd of March before they left Radnor : in about ten days they reached Llandaff, where they spent two nights, the bishop of Llandaff having met them two days before at Caerleon : about a fortnight later they reached Llanbadarn, and on April 10 were at Nevyn.   The place where the mandate was delivered was thus between Caerleon and Abergavenny, where the bishop of Llandaff left them.   Master Silvester, who treated the pope's mandates so contumeliously in No. cci., was not Giraldus, but the steward of the archbishop's household, who is mentioned in Benedict of Peterborough and elsewhere.
[10] Gerv. 1530.

a riot, in which a nephew of S. Thomas took a conspicuous part, and was committed, with several other partisans of the convent, to prison, greatly to the scandal of the faithful.[1] Master Farreman, who had gone to London to avoid acting in the matter, came in nevertheless for a share of the indignation of the archbishop's party. Robert de Bechetune, one of the canons of Hakington,[2] led a detachment of rioters against the hospital, and the warden was obliged to appeal to the pope on behalf of his leprous old women. The parish priests of Canterbury took part with the canons, and publicly announced that the papal excommunication against the aggressors was invalid.[3]

Through the early part of the summer the convent were cheered with reports from Rome of the speedy mission of the legate ; they were also relieved from the presence of Baldwin, who sailed for France on the 16th of June.[4] War had broken out, and the king's foreign dominions were in imminent danger. Henry followed in person on the 10th of July ; [5] and about the same time the communications from the brethren at Rome stopped suddenly for a very melancholy reason.

As soon as the pope had given his promise to send a legate *a latere*, John de Bremble started for home. Honorius, who seems to have looked on his energetic assistant with a little jealousy, remained behind with five other monks, Haymo of Thanet, Edmund, Humfrey, Symon, and Ralph the almoner. The letters of Edmund and Humfrey are preserved. They are the compositions of puzzle-headed men, whose studies had lain in mystic interpretation of Scripture and in unfulfilled prophecy. Haymo was, as we have seen, a very active and determined man, but imprudent. John, on the other hand, was a shrewd observer, plain-spoken and witty ; a man of business, with a considerable command of money, and a fixed and efficacious conviction that at Rome money was all-powerful. Honorius seems to have felt it hard to keep up with the energy of John, and John evidently kicked against the devout simplicity and leisurely management of the prior. He accordingly went northward, and reached Arras on his way home.[6] The bishop of Arras was the one Cistercian friend of the convent, and Brother John persuaded him to offer his mediation with the archbishop. He therefore visited Canterbury in July or August, with proposals from the archbishop, which received the usual answer.[7] The bishop offered then to

Marginal notes:

Reception of the mandates at Canterbury

Riot at Canterbury

Baldwin and Henry leave England

John de Bremble returns homewards

John de Bremble engages the advocacy of the bishop of Arras

---

[1] Nos. ccxviii. ccxix. ccxxvii. Ralph, probably a brother of the person called in the Great Roll of the Pipe, 1 Ric. I. ' Johannes filius Rohesiæ sororis Sancti Tom.' Cf.

Robertson's *Becket*, p. 353.
[2] Gerv. 1532.   [3] No. ccxxiv.
[4] Gerv. 1535.   [5] Gerv. 1535.
[6] No. ccxliv.   [7] No. ccxlvii.

represent the cause of the convent at the general chapter of the Cistercians in September. The offer was accepted, and a deputation of the brethren attended with him. The matter was brought before the chapter, but the abbot of Cîteaux undertook Baldwin's defence, and nothing further resulted from the proceeding.[1]

Death of the brethren at Rome It was perhaps at Cîteaux that the terrible news was received by the brethren that a plague had broken out in Rome, and that five of the monks left with Honorius were dead. Haymo, the promoter of the first appeal, went first on the 7th of July. Edmund and Humfrey followed on the 11th and 13th, Symon on the 15th, Ralph the almoner on the 18th. The prior wrote the sad story to the convent,[2] but the letter does not seem to have reached them until the middle of September. The subprior did immediately the best possible thing: John de Bremble returns to Rome directed John de Bremble to return to the papal court at once.[3] He took with him Brother Elias and a second Symon. John borrowed a mark at Rheims from a friendly canon, and set out in faith. Before he reached Siena he met a servant of the archbishop of Lyons, who told him that the prior was dead. Between Siena and Rome he heard of the death of the bishop of Ostia. When he reached Rome, but one of the brethren, William, was alive, and he was in great danger. The mortality had extended to the servants; John's first act was to attend the cook's funeral.[4] He lost no time in besieging the pope, and on the 10th of December succeeded in getting a mandate reiterating the injunctions of Pope Urban, and committed for execution to Ralph Nigel, cardinal of S. Praxedes.[5]

He starts with the legate Ralph Nigel With Cardinal Ralph Brother John set off forthwith for England. By way of making a favourable impression on the legate he offered him a magnificent reliquary. Ralph, however, was a conscientious man, and refused the implied bribe, but he borrowed the prior's packhorse, and further commended John to the care of one of his retinue, whose expenses he was expected to pay. When the cavalcade reached Parma, his friend's horse fell lame, and John had to buy him a substitute. The new horse, which had cost a mark, turned out to be useless, and a second was bought, also at John's expense.[6] Having thus propitiated both the legate and his kinsman, he was in hopes that at last the cause was prospering, when, sad to say, the Death of the legate cardinal himself fell ill at Pavia, and having got on with difficulty to Mortara, died there on the 30th of December.[7]

Brothers John, William, and Symon turned back to Rome in

---

[1] No. cclxxiv.   [2] No. cclxxii.
[3] No. cclxxv.
[4] No. ccxcii. Brother John must have fallen behind his companions, as he heard of the death of the bishop between Siena and Rome, whereas

the other brethren arrived at Rome four days before the bishop's death. No. cclxxxviii.
[5] No. ccxci.   [6] No. ccxc.
[7] Nos. ccxcii. ccxciii. ccxciv. Gerv. 1538.

despair. Their second journey was hardly more cheerful than the John's second visit to Rome first. At Bardi, in the country of Parma, the prior's packhorse, from which so much had been hoped, was lost.[1] At Siena they found one of their servants dead. At Rome the king's agents were in full force, Simon of Apulia and four companions urging that Cardinal Octavian might be sent to England as legate, that Baldwin might be permitted to proceed with his church, and that the disposition of the oblations might be restored to him. The pope refused to listen to The pope refuses to hear the king's agents their arguments, and doubted their credentials. They quitted Rome in chagrin, leaving their business in the hands of Robert of Rouen and Richard of Norwich, ' an enemy with a very fat face and a hoarse voice.' In January or February 1189, the monks had their audience ; the pope was very gracious, and asked their advice in the choice of a legate.[2] The brethren proposed their three friends, Gratian, Soffred, and Peter of Piacenza, the last of whom was anxious to undertake the expedition.[3] Clement, however, explained that it would be imprudent to send one whose very name was hateful to the king, as was Gratian's ; the other two were employed elsewhere : he suggested John of Anagni, cardinal of S. Mark. The mandate[4] was renewed John of Anagni appointed legate with the insertion of John's name instead of Ralph's, and John and Elias set out in his company. They reached Paris in April, and went from there to Le Mans,[5] where they had an interview with the king on S. Dunstan's day.[6]

During the winter of 1188 little had happened at home to cheer the imprisoned convent. Gervase notes only a grand aurora borealis on the 20th of December. The letters from Rome were few and sad. The king and his counsellors in Normandy were supposed to be meditating further oppressions ; Baldwin also was abroad ; the correspondence that seems to fall in with this period consists of letters The convent ask aid of other monasteries of condolence from other monasteries, and of complaints and petitions for help from that of Canterbury.

After Christmas they sent two envoys, H. and R., to the king in They send envoys to Henry in France France. They took Rheims on their way, and there fell in with the messenger from Rome,[7] who had been sent on with a copy of the mandate intrusted to Cardinal Ralph. In company with him they went on to Chaumont in the Vexin, where Brother H. left the other two, being afraid to meet the king. From Chaumont they proceeded to Gisors, and thence to the king at Le Mans, where they found the archbishop as well. It happened that the papal letters were delivered to Baldwin the very day that he heard of the death of Cardinal Ralph. The bearer, Brother Jonas, having discharged his commission, quitted the city, and left Brother R. to face the king alone. He had his

---

[1] No. ccxcii.   [2] No. ccxcvi.   [5] No. ccv.   [6] No. cccvii.

[3] No. ccxcv.   [4] No. cccviii.   [7] No. ccxcvii.

audience on the 1st of February, 1189. The king, who was under
the influence of Roger the almoner, a friend of the convent, listened
to the monk with unusual calmness, and ended the conference by
swearing that the convent should have their rights. Roger the
almoner and Hubert Walter were directed to draw up a letter to
them in the king's name. The letter was written and sealed, when
the archbishop, according to Brother R., came down in a passion,
and ordered Hubert and Peter of Blois to break the seal and read the
contents.[1] He then added three clauses. This letter, when it
arrived at Canterbury, contained an assurance of the king's goodwill ; an account of the attempt that he had made to bring about a
reconciliation, to which he found the archbishop not indisposed, and
a proposal to send the bishops of Ely and Rochester, with Ranulf
Glanvill and the deans of York and Lincoln, to negotiate. With
them on their return he charged the convent to send representatives
with full power to treat of peace. The letter concludes with a
strong recommendation to submit, and a threat in case of obstinacy,
which were probably the clauses added by the archbishop.[2]

These commissioners visited Canterbury on the 24th of March.[3]
They put the question, Would the convent send plenipotentiaries to
the king ? The subprior politely refused : ' None of the brethren
dared to undertake such a responsibility, nor would the convent
venture on such a measure whilst the cause was before the pope.'
The justiciar suggested that, if they dared not send an envoy with
full powers, they might at least send a deputation to propitiate
Henry. The subprior hinted that after the events at Alençon in
1187 the king was not to be trusted. Ranulf could hardly gainsay
this, so the bishop of Rochester replied with a prayer that they
would confide in the king, and not refuse his good offices. The subprior would refuse no man's good offices, but ' rumor de veteri faciet
ventura timeri.' At this juncture arrived the courier from Rome
with the news of the appointment of John of Anagni as legate. This
broke up the debate ; the messengers returned to the king pricked at
the heart. Two days after Osbert de Bristo, an unworthy monk,
escaped from the convent into the court of the archbishop's palace,
and took the oath of fidelity to Baldwin.[4] Gervase says that he
expected to be rewarded with a bishopric. The subprior, now
thinking himself safe under the protection of the legate, condescended to send four brethren to the king ; they were stopped,
however, at the gate of the cemetery on the Saturday in Easter
week, and not allowed to proceed.

John of Anagni reached Le Mans in May, and was present when,

[1] Gerv. 1539.   [3] Gerv. 1540.
[2] No. dlxii.   [4] No. cccii. Gerv. 1540.

on the 19th, John de Bremble presented the mandate to the archbishop.[1] Baldwin received it with reverence, but in silence; his clerks heaped abuse on Brother John, who had formerly been a member of the archbishop's household. This he bore patiently; the archbishop took no more notice of him. The next day John called on the legate, who told him that Baldwin denied the charges made against him, and professed himself ready to restore all the property of the convent on the ancient terms. As they were conversing, Baldwin himself arrived and argued his case; John tried to provoke him into a passion, and soon succeeded. The conference broke up in confusion, and more important events interfered to prevent its being resumed. *The legate reaches the court at Le Mans*

A colloquy was held between the kings of England and France at Le Mans on the 9th of June,[2] which resulted in an outbreak of war. Ranulf Glanvill was sent to England to levy forces, and on his way paid his devotions at Canterbury. He had an interview with the subprior, who hinted to him in a gentle way that the king, being in great straits, might, if prudently approached, see at last the use of mercy. Ranulf answered that the monks had yet to learn what what mercy was, if they would, for the love of Rome, do nothing to please the king, the archbishop, or anyone else. On the subprior's repeating that experience had shown that neither Henry nor his advisers were to be trusted, Ranulf quitted him in indignation: 'Rome is all you seek: Rome alone will be your ruin.' Geoffrey did, however, send a small deputation to the king, hoping to find him softened by his misfortunes. These penetrated to the seat of war, and found Henry at Azai, just after he had been compelled to accept terms of peace.[3] They approached with a salutation: 'The convent of Canterbury salute you as their lord.' The king replied, 'I was once their lord, and am still, and will be yet'; adding between his teeth, 'small thanks to you, wicked traitors.' He then listened to their petition, and dismissed them with a promise of letters.[4] They went from Azai to Rouen, where the legate was, the king having forbidden him to go to England. With the advice of the legate, the monks offered to accept restitution from the archbishop. Baldwin tried to temporise, and ended by declaring that he would do nothing without the king. That week the king died at Chinon. *Outbreak of war*
Ranulf Glanvill visits Canterbury
Last interview of the monks with Henry II.
The king's death

Baldwin returned to England, after more than a year's absence, on the 31st of July.[5] He seems to have determined to make some sort of an arrangement with the monks before the coronation, and on the day after his landing summoned the officers of the convent *Baldwin returns home and visits the convent*

---

[1] No. cccvii.   [2] Gerv. 1543.   [4] No. cccxii.   [5] Gerv. 1546.
[3] No. cccxi.   Gerv. 1544.

to Wingham.[1] Alan, the third prior, appeared, with a few of the brethren. The archbishop began by demanding the deposition of the subprior and John de Bremble. Alan answered that he came only as a messenger, and had no power to treat of such matters. The archbishop lifted up his hands to heaven, and cried three times, ' God avenge me on the subprior.' Alan replied, ' If the subprior were now where he will be before a hundred years are over, it would make no difference ; we will never yield.' ' Well,' said Baldwin, ' I tell you judgment is passed on him, and his punishment is at the door.' On the 5th of August, the archbishop came to the cathedral, and gave the benediction after the Gospel. He also invited some of

Baldwin tries to compel the convent to submit

the elder monks to dine with him, which they refused to do under the circumstances. On the morrow he sent to offer them restitution of their possessions, saving their rights and his own and the pope's mandate. This was accepted, and Alan received seisin by the gift of a book. But no sooner was this done than Baldwin broke out against the subprior, declaring he would take him wherever he could catch him ; he also deposed Hervey the cellarer, and nominated a monk named Felix in his place. This immediately caused a tumult ; the monks insisted upon being put in bodily possession of the restored estates, and Baldwin attempted to force upon them the compact of Alençon. The convent replied with a prayer that the archbishop would fulfil the pope's mandate. He offered to do it, on condition that he should appoint the obedientiaries, the convent managing the estates as before. This they were disposed to accept, but Baldwin repented of his offer, and demanded the nomination of the treasurers as well. He did not, however, wait for an answer, but went off to Tenham. The subprior, feeling himself no longer safe, fled from Canterbury on the 9th,. and crossing the straits proceeded first to Arras and then in search of the legate. The queen regent Eleanor and Ranulf Glanvill were

The queen and the justiciar prevail on the convent to accept restitution

not less anxious than the archbishop to settle the quarrel before the arrival of Richard in England, and after the subprior's departure sent the abbot of Hyde and the prior of Bermondsey to Canterbury, who by threats tried to induce the convent to accept the cellarer appointed by Baldwin, and to receive restitution from them in the archbishop's name. After another angry discussion this was done,. on the 12th of August, the rights and privileges on both sides being reserved.[2] The gates, which had been shut since the 13th of January,

The blockade of the convent raised

1188, were opened, and the convent gained possession of their house ; the questions in dispute being, however, as far off as ever from settlement.

It is possible that Baldwin was content to make this concession

---

[1] No. cccxiv.   [2] Gerv. 1549.

in ignorance of what the new sovereign's sentiments might be on the case. But Richard soon showed himself even more determined than his father that his rights and dignity should not be infringed. He ordered the legate into Poictou to collect the Saladin tithe, and bade him leave the monks of Canterbury for himself to deal with.[1] The legate remonstrated with the ministers, Walter of Coutances and Hugh of Nunant, but in vain. Brother John began to mistrust the legate, and wrote in haste to Canterbury for a present to secure his wavering friendship, a handsome grey greatcoat, or a robe of martens' skins. It was indeed neccessary to strike whilst the iron was hot. For at Rome the archbishop's friends were rising ; Octavian was promoted to the see of Ostia ; Albinus, ' a convertible man,' to Albano ; Bobo, an open supporter of Baldwin, to Portus ; the Tuscan party, Gratian and Soffred, the only friends left to the convent, had deserted the court.[2]

Richard's treatment of the legate

The coronation of Richard was celebrated on the 3rd of September. Eight monks represented the convent on the occasion,[3] and the bishops of Durham and Bath were prepared to resist the petition that Baldwin was expected to make for his new church. Baldwin, however, kept a discreet silence. From London the court moved to Gaitington, where a parliament was held on the 17th, at which the king confirmed the charters of the convent. The legate was still forbidden to enter England, and the archbishop was allowed to have his own way. He resolved to proceed to extremities, came down to Canterbury on the 6th of October,[4] and, to the horror of the monks, appointed as the new prior Roger Norreys ; he then seized the cemetery gate, that messengers might not be sent to the legate. Roger immediately took Osbert de Bristo into his counsels, and committed to him the management of the estates.

The coronation and council at Gaitington

Baldwin makes Roger Norreys prior

It is hardly conceivable that Baldwin ever intended to maintain Roger Norreys in the position of prior ; he was certainly and notoriously a most unfit person for any spiritual office, a man with neither character, temper, nor tact.[5] The archbishop probably thought that such an appointment would compel the monks to submit, and that done, the obnoxious prior might bo provided for elsewhere. The measure did in fact reduce the monks to despair. They sent

Despair of the convent

---

[1] No. cccxv.   [2] No. cccxv.
[3] No. cccxxiv.
[4] No. cccxxvi. Gerv. 1551.
[5] Of the bad character of Roger Norreys there can be no doubt. See the account given of him by Giraldus, in his Speculum Ecclesiæ (Ang. Sac. i. 139) ; by the historian of Evesham (ed. Macray, pp. 104–107) ; and by Gervase himself, c. 1506. It may

perhaps be supposed, in Baldwin's favour, that Roger had not yet exhibited his bad propensities ; certainly nothing is said about them in the correspondence ; and Gervase wrote his book ten or eleven years later. His conduct as prior was evidently such that Baldwin would not support him, and he was deposed within two months.

to the king, who had recommended them strongly to compromise, first to treat of terms, next to offer a bribe; that failing, they threw themselves on his mercy. On November 8th their messengers were received at Westminster. Among them were nearly all the brethren who had taken active part in the struggle; the old sacrist Robert, Symon the treasurer, John of Boching, Ralph of Orpington, Gervase the historian, Nigel the poet, Master William, and Roger Norreys.[1] Baldwin attempted to get the first word; Master William had been excommunicated: he must leave the court. The whole convent he accused of embezzling the treasure of the church. The brethren on their part demanded the removal of Roger Norreys, refusing him the title of prior. Reginald of Bath, as usual, supported the convent. Hugh of Durham tried to act as mediator; their other friends advised them to accept the king's arbitration; and on the following day they yielded so far as to produce their powers, and accept the proposal of a compromise. The king nominated the committee, the monks challenging only two Cistercian abbots whom he proposed. At last a jury was empanneled, eight bishops, five abbots, and the prior of Merton. The monks were now asked to declare that they would accept the decision of the committee, when Master William insisted that it could be done only on the understanding that the judgment should be guided by the charters and privileges of the church. A division followed; the monks withdrew their consent to the arbitration; the object of the meeting was defeated, and nothing remained but an appeal to force. Baldwin threatened to seize the monastery and to disperse the brethren; the king insisted on the proposed arbitration; the legate was still forbidden to cross the straits; and the last hope from Rome was extinguished.

Richard and his whole court arrived at Canterbury on the 27th of November. He was received with great pomp by the convent in the presence of all the bishops: in his train were the king of Scotland and Geoffrey Plantagenet, the elect of York. The day after the reception the archbishop of Rouen came from the king, to ask the convent whether they were still in the same mind. They replied that whilst Roger Norreys was called prior, and the church of Hakington still in being, there could be no peace. 'Will you,' he asked, 'consent to an arbitration, if the archbishop will yield on these two points?' They agreed, on condition that their charters should receive a fair consideration. The king, hearing this, sent word that on this understanding he would himself depose the prior and demolish the buildings, if the archbishop could not be prevailed upon to do it. Baldwin justly complained of this; it was not fair

They send to the court at Westminster

Failure of the king's first attempt at a compromise

The king comes in state to Canterbury

He tries to make peace

---

[1] No. cccxxix. Gervase, 1553–1562.

that he should yield two of the chief points of the quarrel, and after all have to submit to arbitration on the rest. Seeing that the king and bishops thought him unreasonable, he called for a copy of the rule of S. Benedict, and insisted on his rightful position as abbot on the first principles of regular order.

Richard now struck out a new plan. It was clear that the archbishop would not yield on these points, and yet submit to an arbitration on the rest. It was not to be expected ; but if the archbishop would yield those two, would the convent consent to throw themselves on his mercy for the rest ? If so an agreement might be secured. Baldwin would surrender the college and the prior ; the monks would allow him to decide the other points by his own sense of justice. The brethren, persuaded by their friends, at last consented on condition that for form's sake a few of their charters should be read. The king whispered to the archbishop some words that were not heard, and then, turning to the monks, bade them not to be afraid if in the terms of the agreement language were introduced to spare the feelings of the archbishop. Both parties were then called to the chapter-house.

Baldwin yields the two chief points, and the convent accept his mercy on the rest.

It was growing dark, being late in the afternoon, and a fog, which Gervase considered supernatural, added to the gloom ; even the king in his glittering robes could scarcely be distinguished. The archbishop of Rouen rose and said, ' Blessed be the God and Father of our Lord Jesus Christ, the Father of mercies and God of all consolation : the Day-spring from on high hath visited us.' The words stuck in his throat ; he stopped for a moment and added, ' A certain discord between the lord archbishop and the monks of this convent has been long protracted ; but by the advice of the king and of the bishops who are present, ourself among them, a way of peace has been found. We have adjudged that the archbishop had power to build himself a church wherever he pleased, and to institute his own prior. Let the convent beg the mercy of the archbishop, and he will remit his anger against them.' The monks were thrown into consternation at this : the two points that the archbishop was to yield were decided in his favour ; they themselves were at his mercy : this had come of the king's whispering. When they were called up before Richard, one of them attempted to speak, but the king beckoned to him to be silent, and ordered them all to kneel. They obeyed, and one of the oldest in the company faltered out, ' If, reverend father, we have in any part of this dispute offended your grace, we beg that you will remit your anger against us and consent to preserve the rights of the church.' Baldwin answered, ' I remit my indignation against you, and all yours, except the subprior, who by his own authority suspended my church from divine service.'

The final compromise effected

The compromise effected by the king's contrivance

The monks remained on their knees entreating pardon for the sub-prior. At last the archbishop said, ' Let him come, then, as you have done and ask pardon, and he may have it with the rest of you ' ; he added, ' As you ask that my anger may be remitted against you and yours, so I ask you to forgive, from your heart, me and mine, what-ever we have offended in word or deed.' The bishop of Rochester then rose and announced that the prior should be deposed and the college demolished ; when thanks had been given and *Te Deum* sung, the archbishop would give his reconciled children the kiss of peace. This was done, and Baldwin on the following day, in the chapter-house, restored the estates of the convent which remained in his hands, and relieved the prior from his office. A deed was drawn up and attested by the king and arbitrating prelates, recording the termination, by compromise, of the whole cause.[1] Richard then left Canterbury, and the legate, who had been waiting at Dover for ten days, was allowed to visit the church. Even this, however, was not suffered without deliberation. Some few of the bishops proposed that he should be honourably received ; others urged that he should be compelled to depart at once. The archbishop voted for admitting him, but sending him back as quickly as could be done. He came, therefore, and lodged in the palace at the archbishop's charges, being closely watched that he might not be tampered with by the convent. The monks succeeded in getting a private interview with him, at which Baldwin, who saw that nothing was to be feared from him, probably connived. He informed the monks that the king had told him of the compromise, by which the collegiate buildings at Hakington were to be demolished, and the chapel to be served by a few priests, who should pray for the soul of king Henry. The monks declared that they had accepted no such condition. The legate could do nothing but groan over the wickedness of the persecutors ; not daring to advise the convent to resist, and anxious to get away without committing himself, he recommended them to temporise. He was conducted with great reverence to Dover by the archbishop's clerks ; but before he went he executed a secret deed, declaring that the compromise had been extorted from the convent by fear, and was null and void of effect prejudicial to their rights. This was kept a profound secret, and reserved for future use.[2]

The king left England for the crusade on the 14th of December.[3] The archbishop remained in the country till March, arranging his affairs before his pilgrimage. Roger Norreys having been made abbot of Evesham, Baldwin instituted Osbert de Bristo as prior ; and on the 19th of February, 1190, at Westminster, appealed to the

The visit and act of the legate

Baldwin goes on the crusade

---

[1] No. cccxxxv.   [2] Gerv. 1563, 1678.   [3] Diceto, 650.

Holy See against all who should attempt to alter the state of his church during his absence.[1] He also directed the destruction of the collegiate buildings at Hakington, and the removal of the materials to Lambeth, where he proposed to build his church according to the compromise. For this purpose he exchanged with the convent of Rochester a piece of land in the Isle of Grain for twenty-four acres at Lambeth for a site. The exchange was confirmed by the king, as was the foundation of the church in honour of S. Thomas and S. Stephen, on the 20th of March at Rouen.[2] The archbishop had left England for ever on the 6th. He wrote but one letter afterwards to the convent, announcing his arrival at Acre on the 12th of October.[3] He died there about the 20th of November, but the news did not reach England before March 1191. The only matter of interest mentioned by Gervase or referred to in these letters, during this interval, was a dispute as to the consecration of William elect of Worcester and Geoffrey of York. The details differ little from those of the hundreds of similar squabbles in which the convent engaged on the question. In the former case they were successful ; in the latter they were defeated.[4]

The men whom Richard placed at the helm of ecclesiastical affairs were, with one exception, those who as lawyers or ministers had been the faithful servants of his father, but whom Henry, recollecting his sad experience with S. Thomas, had refused to reward with the episcopal dignity.[5] It may be said of them all, that however they came by their promotion, their use of it was wise and pure.[6] Hubert Walter, the new bishop of Salisbury, was a man who set himself to do what his hand found to do with all his might. As a bishop, a soldier, a lawyer, or a statesman, he came up fully to the standard of his time. Of the others, Richard of London was a famous organiser in the business of the treasurership ; and he, as well as Godfrey de Lucy of Winchester, was a good average bishop. Of the older prelates, Hugh of Puiset was as ambitious and bustling as he had been forty years before ; Hugh of Lincoln kept as much as possible out of the affairs of state ; Reginald of Bath was quietly laying his plans for the primacy.

That Richard began his reign by imprisoning two of his father's

Richard's new bishops

---

[1] Gerv. 1564. Nos. cccxliii. cccxliv.
[2] No. cccxxxvii. Fœdera, i. 51.
[3] No. cccxlv.
[4] Nos. cccxxxviii.–cccxliv.
[5] In 1186, Godfrey de Lucy, Richard FitzNeal, and Herbert le Poor had been nominated by the canons of Lincoln for the vacant see in 1186, but Henry refused his consent for the

reason given in the text. The same year Hubert Walter had been elected archbishop of York, but was set aside by the king. Godfrey le Lucy had refused Exeter. Benedict. Peterb. ad annum.
[6] For the character of Richard Fitz-Neal, see Ann. Winton., Ang. Sac. i. 304.

ministers, Ranulf Glanvill and Stephen de Marzai,[1] is alleged by one
or two trustworthy historians. We are left in ignorance of the real
cause of this harsh treatment of these men, unless we follow the belief
of the chroniclers that it was for the purpose of extortion. It is
possible that Ranulf Glanvill was suspected of too great attachment
to John, whose guardian he had been, and in whose favour Henry
was said to meditate the disinheriting of his elder son. Whatever
the cause, the imprisonment was short, and both the obnoxious
ministers were promoted to important commands in the crusade.
The king showed no further mistrust of his father's servants.

The one exception to the rule, the one new man who came on
the stage of politics at Richard's accession, was William of Longchamp, bishop of Ely.[2] Of this prelate such contradictory characters have been drawn, that is impossible to say whether he was a
hero or a mere unprincipled adventurer. In the latter light he was
regarded by Hugh of Puiset, by the followers of Geoffrey and John,
and probably by the majority of Norman nobles. By the monks
and their friends he is spoken of as a pious and conscientious
man. Of his public policy it may be fairly said that no legal
charge was ever brought against him; that his enemies were in all
cases the enemies of his master; that his designs were actually
followed up by his rivals when they attained to power. He was
doubtless an upstart; probably a clever and not very scrupulous
politician; possibly a person of haughty, supercilious demeanour.

But the greatness of his position was enough to draw upon him a
great deal of odium. Few men have ever wielded the power that
was placed in his hands by the king and primate when they left

---

[1] Richard of Devizes, pp. 6, 7. If
the statement depended only on the
testimony of this ill-natured historian,
it might be considered doubtful; for he
never misses an opportunity of speaking ill of anyone, and here he has a
hit at all the three parties. Benedict
of Peterborough mentions the deposition of Glanvill from the justiciarship
after the coronation, and the manner
in which Richard made all the officials
in the kingdom repurchase their
places: the fine levied on Stephen was
30,000 pounds Angevin down, and a
promise of 15,000 more. The Angevin
'pound' was a quarter of the English.
Ranulf's fine was 15,000 pounds of
silver (R. Devizes, 7). These were
both very heavy fines if we consider
that the price of the chancellorship
was 3,000 pounds when William of
Longchamp bought it; possibly, however, Richard let him have it cheap, as

we know he refused an offer of 4,000
from Reginaldus Italus. Of the fact
of the exaction I have no doubt, but
of the imprisonment there is less certainty. It can have continued, if real,
only a very short time; and when we
next meet with Ranulf and Stephen, it
is in places of honour. Stephen de
Turnham, who fought in the crusade
with Richard, seems to be the same
person with Stephen de Marzai.
William of Newburgh tells a wonderful fortune-telling story about him.
Lib. v. c. 6.

[2] A good character is given to Long-
champ by the monks of Winchester,
Ang. Sac. i. 302; and by those of
Canterbury, p. 538, vol. R. S.; Nigel
Wireker; Peter of Blois; Ang. Sac. i.
632. A bad one by Giraldus Cam-
brensis, Hugh of Nunant, William of
Newburgh, Richard of Devizes.

England ; the combined burden of the legatine office [1] and the chancellorship proved a few years later too great for Hubert Walter, who was a comparatively popular minister ; and the position of William Longchamp was made still more invidious by the absence of the king. It was by the manœuvres of John [2] and Geoffrey that he was overthrown ; he must be credited at least with the merit of faithful service.

When in March 1191 the rumour of the death of Baldwin reached the convent, they immediately petitioned the king for a free election.[3] If they had any expectation that their prayer would be granted, they were speedily undeceived, for on the 6th of May was delivered the king's letter from Messina ordering them to postulate William, archbishop of Montreal.[4] Their first thought, however, was not whom to elect as archbishop, but how to get rid of Prior Osbert, who, although a man of very different character from Roger Norreys, was hardly less a creature of the late archbishop, and equally obnoxious to the extreme party. The certainty of Baldwin's death inspired the monks with courage ; in a vacancy of the see they possessed the undoubted right of electing their own prior. It is uncertain when or how the subprior Geoffrey had returned from exile. We find him at Canterbury on the 10th of May.[5] On that day, four days after the receipt

Marginal note: Deposition of Prior Osbert

---

[1] He was appointed legate by Clement III., June 5, 1190. On Clement's death his legation seems to have expired, and he applied for renewal to Celestine III., shortly before his downfall ; Ben. Peterb. ii. 693, ed. Hearne. He ceases after the news of the death of Clement, who died March 27, 1191, to call himself legate. It does not appear when Celestine renewed the legation, but it was evidently before Dec. 2, on which day Celestine names him legate in a letter to the prelates. Hoveden, 402. Cf. W. Newburgh, iv. 18. He could hardly have been treated as he was by the archbishop of Rouen if he had been recognised as legate at the time of his deposition. The letter of July 30, given by Giraldus (Ang. Sac. ii. 390), seems to be opposed to this, but it may not be an exact copy ; and in the letter of Aug. 25 the title is omitted. His consecration of the bishop of Worcester on the 5th of May must have been about his last legatine act.   Pope Clement IV. decreed that the legation did not expire at the death of the pope. VI. Decr. i. tit. xv. c. 2.

[2] The immediate cause of William's overthrow was the imprisonment of Archbishop Geoffrey of York at Dover, by his creatures. Gerv. 1576. There can be little doubt that the act was one of indiscreet zeal on their part ; but it is a curious question where the chancellor was at the time. The writ for the apprehension of Geoffrey is dated ' apud Preston, xxx. die Julii.' Gir. Camb., Anglia Sacra, ii. 390. The prohibition to Walter of Rouen to visit Canterbury is dated ' apud Releiam, xxv. die Augusti,' ib. p. 395. The letter of excuse for the arrest (No. ccclxxi.) is dated Sept. 29th, 'apud Bromd.' It was at Norwich that the bishops of London and Norwich upbraided him with his conduct in the matter ; Gir. Camb., A. S. ii. 392. He then went to London (p. 394), and thence to Windsor ; from which place he went to the colloquy at Lodbridge on the 5th of October. ' Bromd,' in No. ccclxxi., must, therefore, be somewhere between Norwich and London. The struggle closed on Oct. 10.

[3] No. cccli. Gervase, 1567.

[4] Nos. cccxlviii. cccliv. Gervase, 1568.

[5] No. cccliv. Gervase, 1570.

of the royal letter, the brethren under Geoffrey's guidance demanded the dismissal of Felix the cellarer, Robert the doctor, and Zacharias, an unfaithful monk. Prior Osbert was unable to make any resistance. Having assented to the act, he imprudently asked, ' Are there more ? ' ' You yourself,' was the ready answer, ' must resign the priorate.' Osbert behaved with some little dignity. He rose and said, ' Hear me, sirs, as you would have God hear you. You know how well and firmly I stood by you in your troubles, for which I was excommunicated by the archbishop and suffered much hardship. When by the counsel of certain great persons and of some of the brethren I quitted you for the archbishop, I always exercised my influence for your good, never for your harm. When I was made prior, at the archbishop's command and with the royal assent, no voice from the convent was raised against me. I thought until to-day that I had your assent as well. God knows that if I had not thought so I would never have taken either the priorate or any other office upon me. As it is I will not hold it against your good pleasure.' The seniors accepted this as a resignation, and the subprior was dragged into the prior's chair. Little notice was taken by the legate chancellor, for the best of reasons. The convent would certainly have a voice in the election of the archbishop, and William Longchamp intended the choice to fall upon himself.[1]

Geoffrey made prior

There can be little doubt, if the few letters that passed between the convent and the legate may be depended upon, that had the election been free the monks would have elected him. There were many points in his favour. He was already at the head of a chapter of monks and on friendly terms with them. His enemies were the old enemies of the convent, the worldly clerks, and unprincipled ministers of Henry. He himself was or seemed to be high in the favour of both king and pope. Nigel the poet was an intimate friend and admirer of William, and he was one of the most able men in the convent.[2]

William Longchamp a candidate for the primacy

[1] See No. ccclxxiv. Jocelin of Brakelond says of Longchamp (p. 38), ' Dicebatur olfacere archiepiscopatum ; ' see also W. Newburgh, iv. 18.

[2] Nigel Wireker, as he is generally called, was one of the best mediæval poets : see Leyser, *Hist. Poematum Medii Ævi*, p. 751 ; Wright, *Biographia Brit. Lit.* pp. 351, &c. In a copy of some of his poems in the Cotton MS. Vesp. D. xix. he is styled, in a hand of the fourteenth century, ' Nigellus de Longo Campo.' It is uncertain whether this is a simple mistake arising from his connexion with

William, to whom he dedicates his *Speculum Ecclesiæ*, or *De Abusu ecclesiastico*, and some of his poems, perhaps also the *Speculum Stultorum* ; more probably they were either relations or fellow-townsmen. There is one letter in this series which may have been written by him, No. cccxxii. The *vir quidam magnus* in this letter may have been the future chancellor : the second of the four lines with which the letter ends, ' Maxima pars nostri, dimidiumque mei, ' bears a strong likeness to the fourth line of the dedication of the *Speculum Stultorum*, ' Maxima pars animæ, dimi-

Other heads, however, were at work to prevent this. Foremost Walter of Coutances brings the king's commands there was the archbishop of Rouen, who had been sent over by the king with the commission of justiciar,[1] with especial directions as to the election of the primate. Walter of Coutances was an ambitious man, and would gladly have accepted the translation for himself. William Longchamp prevented him from visiting Canterbury as long as he remained in power,[2] and until he could do so the king's pleasure could not be known or the election proceeded with. It can never be certainly known why Richard nominated William of Montreal ; the influence of his sister, Queen Joanna, whose husband, William of Sicily, had greatly trusted and promoted him, may have been used in his favour ; possibly Richard thought that by appointing him he might prevent the primacy from becoming a bone of contention among the greedy courtiers at home. Possibly the recommendation was bought and paid for, but never intended to be carried out. No effort was made to effect the promotion of the archbishop of Montreal, who was probably dead before the day of election.

Reginald Fitz Jocelin,[3] bishop of Bath, had stood by the convent The bishop of Bath, Reginald Fitz Jocelin in their troubles more faithfully than any other prelate, although he had never gone so far as to imperil his own position. He had powerful friends and an unwearied agent in his kinsman Savaric, archdeacon of Northampton, who called himself cousin of the Roman emperor.[4]

diumque meæ ' ; it is possible, however, that this may be a quotation in both cases from some other poet. The French words that precede it, ' Cinc cenz deehez ait il, ki pur archeveskc u pur celerier a cose revan [?],' mean ' Five hundred plagues have he, who for archbishop or for cellarer has husked bran ' : but it is not clear in what signification they were spoken.

[1] On this see Sir F. Palgrave, preface to ' Rotuli Curiæ Regis,' vol. i. pp. lx, &c.

[2] No. dlxvi.

[3] Reginald Fitz Jocelin was the son of Jocelin de Bohun, bishop of Salisbury ; he was brought up in Lombardy (Herb. Bosham, vii. 1), and hence bore the name Reginald Lumbardus ; he is probably also the Reginaldus Italus who, according to Richard of Devizes (p. 9), offered Richard 4,000 pounds for the chancellorship.

[4] Savaric is a person whose career, if it could be explored, must have been very interesting. His first appearance is in the 18th of Henry II., when he was fined 26l. 4s. 4d. for trying to take a

bow from the king's servants in a forest in Surrey (Madox, Hist. Exch. p. 390). He was probably made treasurer of Salisbury by his cousin Jocelin de Bohun before 1184, and held also the archdeaconry of Northampton, the revenues of which were sequestered in 1186 for the payment of his debts. On Richard's accession he followed him to Sicily, where he obtained a letter to the justiciars, giving the royal assent for his admission to any bishopric to which he might be elected ; and this he got confirmed by the pope. Having taken a prominent part in securing the election of Reginald Fitz Jocelin, he succeeded him as bishop of Bath and Wells, and was consecrated at Rome in 1192. During Richard's captivity he visited him and got two letters from him, recommending him for the see of Canterbury. In 1196 he was chancellor of Burgundy under Henry VI. (Hoveden, 420). After Henry's death he seems to have returned to England, and spent the rest of his life in his contest with the monks of Glastonbury. He died in 1205, and was described in his

Reginald's testimonials

He forwarded letters to Canterbury from both Philip of France and Henry VI., recommending them to take the advice of Savaric and elect a faithful friend whom he would recommend to them, and whom they could easily recognise by that description. These letters were not without effect.[1]

Proceedings in the election of archbishop

As soon as Walter of Coutances and Earl John had expelled the chancellor from the country, they hurried on the election of archbishop. The monks were summoned to London for the 22nd of October.[2]

epitaph, 'Hospes eras mundo, per mundum semper eundo, Sic suprema dies fit tibi prima quies.' Godwin, *De Præsulibus*, 370. The following account of his lineage may afford some clue to the nature of his relationship to the emperor, the fact of which is certain, although the exact degree is not yet known. On his father's side the pedigree is as follows. In the early part of the eleventh century one Savaric was viscount of Le Mans. He was succeeded by his brother Ralph, lord of Beaumont and S. Suzanne, who was twice married: 1, to Emma, niece of Hubert, bishop of Angers, who bore him Hubert, his successor. Hubert married Ermengard, daughter of William, count of Nevers, by whom he had two sons, Ralph and Hubert, and a daughter, Godechildis; from the eldest son the viscounts of Beaumont were descended. 2. Ralph's second wife was Chana, daughter of Geldewin, lord of Saumur, by his wife Aanordis. Chana had been married before to Frangalus, lord of Fougères, by whom she had children. By Hubert she had Savaric Fitz Chane, who succeeded to the estates in England conferred by the Conqueror, or William Rufus, on his uncle Goffred, lord of Chaumont. Savaric Fitz Chane had three sons, Ralph, Savaric, and Geldewin. Ralph and Savaric died childless. Geldewin married a lady named Estrangia, by whom he had Savaric, bishop of Bath and Wells, and Franco de Bohun, who died in 1192. (Ann. Waverley, p. 164.) Estrangia may have been a German lady; the name of Franco, or Francus, may point to a Franconian origin. The relation between Savaric and Reginald Fitz Jocelin is also obscure. Humfrey I. de Bohun had three sons: Robert, who died s. p.; Humfrey, who was the ancestor of the Bohuns of Hereford; and Richard

de Meri. Richard de Meri made his heir Engelger, a noble of the Cotentin, who was almost certainly his son-in-law. This Engelger had a son, Engelger II. who married Adeliza, daughter of Count Stephen of Aumale, and was living to nearly 1180. He is called by William Fitz Stephen, p. 290, the '*patruus*' of Jocelin, bishop of Salisbury, who and his brother Richard de Bohun, bishop of Coutances, may have been sons of Alexander, son of Engelger I.; but were more probably brothers than nephews of Engelger II. The heir of Engelger II. was Savaric Fitz Savaric, and after him Franco, the son of Geldewin, who thus became Franco de Bohun. Engelger II. must have been too young to be grandfather to Savaric Fitz Savaric, and could not have been father-in-law, or the inheritance would not have descended to Franco. It would seem, therefore, most probable that Savaric Fitz Chane married another daughter of Richard de Meri, and that on the default of issue to the Engelgers, his great-grandchildren came in as heirs to the Bohuns of Midhurst. The estates of the Bohuns were in Sussex, where lay also those of Albini and Percy, who were connected with the dukes of Louvain. It was probably on the side of his Burgundian mother that Henry VI. was connected with his Burgundian chancellor. The authorities for the foregoing statements are Stapleton's preface to the Rolls of the Norman Exchequer, ii. p. 31, &c. and the Chronicles in Mart. et Dur. *Amplissima Collectio*, i. 439; Dachery, *Spicilegium*, iii. 277; and Ordericus Vitalis.

[1] Nos. ccclxxxi. ccclxxxii.

[2] The summons to the monks was issued on the 10th of October, the very day of the chancellor's deposition, No. ccclxxvii.

They attended accordingly.   The prior was asked whether he would accept the nomination of William of Montreal.   Geoffrey declared that it was unworthy of the English Church to go begging for a foreigner when the realm was so full of able clerks, but declined giving a decided answer until he had had time for consideration and prayer.   Having been thanked by the justiciars, who never intended to elect the archbishop of Montreal, he returned home.[1]   A second letter was now issued in the king's name; the justiciars would attend at Canterbury on the 3rd of December to complete the election.   Nearly a week before the day appointed the justiciars and some of the bishops arrived, and by so doing roused the suspicion of the prior, who remembered that the suffragans had succeeded in forcing Archbishop Baldwin upon the convent.   He tried, therefore, to sound the chief justiciar as to who would be accepted by the king.   Walter, as Gervase hints,[2] intended the monks to choose himself ; he must, if so, have failed either to express himself intelligibly or to convince the prior of his merits.   'Would the bishop of Bath be admissible?'   The archbishop did not say Yes, but the monks interpreted his looks as favourable.   'We elect,' cried the prior, 'the bishop of Bath.'   The monks re-echoed the nomination, and, laying violent hands on Reginald, thrust him into the archiepiscopal chair.[3]   The archbishop of Rouen retired in alarm to London, and, having called together the nobles, in their presence demanded of the bishop whether he was prepared to abide by the election.   Reginald declared that he would, and defended the legality of the proceeding.   The prior was also present and refused to retract a step.   Further proceedings were threatened by the ministers, and for the first time the deposition of Prior Osbert was bought forward.   The death of Reginald, within a month of the election, settled speedily the more important question.   Queen Eleanor's protection was invoked by the convent, and the matter of Osbert was soon forgotten in more pressing troubles.   Reginald was seized with paralysis or apoplexy on Christmas Eve at Dogmersfield, and died on S. Stephen's day.[4]   The monastic habit for which he had sent to Canterbury did not arrive until he had breathed his last.   The convent lamented a faithful and powerful friend.   He was buried on the feast of S. Thomas.

The year 1192 is almost a blank in the history of the convent.   The state of the country was not such as to suffer them to attempt an election : the news from the Holy Land was scanty and uncertain.   Richard was taken prisoner at Vienna on the 12th of December.   After three months' captivity he wrote to the convent, directing them to take the

The bishop of Bath elected to the primac

Death of Reginald

A new election during Richard's imprisonment

---

[1] Gervase, 1578.   No. ccclxxxvi.
[2] 'Spe fraudatus.'   Gervase, 1580.
[3] Gervase, 1580.
[4] Gervase, 1580.   Pet. Bles. ep. 216.

E E

advice of William of S. Mere l'Eglise in their choice of a new arch-bishop ; at the same time he wrote to his mother and to the justiciars to secure the election of Hubert Walter.[1] He was sorely pressed at this time ; the indefatigable Savaric, who had become bishop of Bath, was now a candidate on his own account ; the imperial relation-ship was brought to bear upon Richard, who wrote two letters to the convent in his favour.[2] William Longchamp also got a letter from the king, and so, perhaps, did some others.[3] The real choice of the captive prince was undoubtedly Hubert, in whose favour he wrote pressing letters both to the convent and to Queen Eleanor. Hubert was elected without much delay [4] on the 30th of May. Strange to say, two months after the election was over, a letter was brought from the king, dated July 10, forbidding the convent to elect him. It is hard to say what this meant : [5] the letter may have been ex-torted from the king by the influence of those about him, to which, as he complains to his mother, he is compelled to seem to yield. The election was by this time perfected, and Hubert busily engaged in reducing the kingdom to order and in procuring the king's release.

We have now to return to the old question of the college of clerks. Prior Osbert,[6] shortly before his deposition, had sent to Rome for an injunction for the destruction of the remaining buildings at Hakington, for the confirmation of the secret act of John of Anagni, and the renewal of the mandates of popes Urban and Clement. These were readily granted by the pope Celestine III., who had succeeded Clement III. in the spring of 1191. The bishop of Bath and the abbots of Reading and Waltham were the delegates for executing the mandates.[7] The buildings were finally demolished, but the chan-cellor interfered to prevent the ejection of the clerks from the four disputed churches. The chapel of Hakington was destroyed on the 21st of July.[8] Reginald's participation in this act helped to endear

Hubert Walter elected archbishop

Demolition of Baldwin's college

[1] Nos. cccxcix. cccc. cccci.
[2] No. ccccii.
[3] No. cccciii. Gervase, 1583.
[4] The monks anticipated the elec-tion of Hubert by the bishops, by electing him themselves before the day appointed. Gervase, 1584.
[5] Giraldus (Opp. ed. Brewer, iii. 19), who hated Hubert, declared that he obtained the election by unfair means. ' Nisi enim rex Ricardus in Alemannia detentus fuisset, et ibi multipliciter in carcere circumventus, longe aliter proculdubio Anglicanæ ecclesiæ pro-vidisset.' The appointment of Hubert must have been arranged between himself and Richard at Spires : for

the management of it is intrusted to William of S. Mere l'Eglise, who accompanied Hubert on his visit to the captive king. Hoveden, 413.
[6] No. cccl.
[7] Nos. ccclvi. ccclvii. ccclviii. A month later Celestine renewed the privilege granted by Urban III. to the convent, which appears as No. xlvi. in the volume (Rolls Series). As the privilege of Celestine is word for word the same as that of Urban, I have not thought it worth while to put it into the Appendix, R. S. It is dated June 20, 1191, S. Peter's ; and is printed by Wilkins in the Concilia, i. 524.
[8] Gervase, 1572-3.

him to the convent, and added a new claim to the many he already possessed to the primacy.

The fears of the monks were now directed to another quarter. The original privilege by which Urban III. had permitted Baldwin to found his college had specified Lambeth as one of the places where it might be settled. The manor of Lambeth was the property of the convent of Rochester, to which it had come by royal gift soon after the Conquest. The archbishops of Canterbury had been the tenants of the manor-house since the time of Anselm, who had ordained in the chapel and held a council there in 1100. His two successors used the chapel for the consecration of bishops. Archbishop Theobald seems to have made some arrangement with the owners, which ended in the house being recognised as the town residence of the primates,[1] and for this reason doubtless it was named by Pope Urban. The archbishop did not, however, possess any part of the estate until the year 1190, when, as was mentioned above,[2] Baldwin acquired twenty-four acres of the demesne of the manor in exchange for land in the Isle of Grain, with the express intention of founding a church of canons. The parish church of Lambeth and the manor itself were not acquired until some years later. *(margin: The Lambeth estate)*

On this piece of ground the foundations were laid before Archbishop Baldwin sailed,[3] but owing to the want of his presence and support the scheme languished. The buildings had, however, in 1192 attained such dimensions as to offend the convent of Canterbury. In the May of that year a mandate was procured from Rome, directing the bishop of Chichester and the abbots of Waltham and Reading to release the canons of Lambeth from the oath they had taken to the late archbishop, and to close the church.[4] It seems probable that the canons appealed against this sentence, for there is a bull of Pope Celestine III., of January 30, 1193,[5] in which he takes them and their lawful possessions under the care of the Holy See. *(margin: Celestine III. orders the dissolution of the Lambeth college)*

Matters were in this state when Hubert was elected. He received the archiepiscopal cross from Gervase, now become the sacrist,[6] at Lewisham on the 3rd of November, and the pall at Canterbury on the 7th. In the first year of his pontificate the convent held their courts as in former times; although the affair was now becoming urgent, not a word had been spoken about it. Hubert was the *(margin: Hubert's revival of the scheme)*

---

[1] Ann. Roffenses, Ang. Sac. i. 344. This may, however, refer only to Theobald's settlement of a dispute between the bishop of Rochester and the convent on the ownership of the manor. It would seem, from the act of exchange of the manor between Hubert and the convent of Rochester, that the estate was managed as a cell under a 'prior de Lammedhe.' Mon. Angl. i. 177.
[2] P. 411. Fœdera, i. 51.
[3] Gervase, 1564.
[4] No. cccxcvii.
[5] No. cccxcvi.
[6] Gervase, 1585.

intimate friend of Baldwin and the executor of his will; he had been himself one of the canons of Hakington, and may have felt some resentment for the extinction of that design, but this would hardly have led him into a new dispute if he had not been pressed by his old friends the clerks. With a view of compromising matters, he offered to remove the college to Maidstone, and build there on the estate of the convent.[1] But to this plan the monks would not listen; the original intention was therefore reverted to. In 1196 Gervase records that the monks remonstrated with the archbishop. After a long conversation, in which the historian himself probably took a leading part, and in which the history of the former controversy was reviewed, the archbishop honestly declared that, sorry as he might be to act in opposition to the church which had placed him at its head, he could not for his own honour's sake leave imperfect the work that he had begun. The two parties separated with the expressed intention of seeking divine counsel by prayer.[2]

Outbreak of the new quarrel

The new storm broke in 1197. On Christmas Day 1196 the archbishop visited Canterbury, but was prevented by illness from taking part in the service. After his recovery, on the 21st of January, he had a conference with the convent in the chapter-house; his own clerks were excluded, and his cross was carried by John of Dover, one of the monks.[3] The discussion lasted for three days, and the result was kept a profound secret. We may guess almost to a certainty at one subject of consideration. Hubert had already arranged for

Acquisition of the manor of Lambeth

the acquisition to his see of the manor of Lambeth. As early as April 7, 1195,[4] and again June 13, 1196, the king had confirmed an exchange, between Hubert and the church of Rochester, of Darenth for Lambeth.[5] It was most probably on this occasion that the archbishop first tried to secure the assent of the convent to the completion of Baldwin's design. Although we cannot suppose that he succeeded in this, he must either have lulled the suspicious watchfulness of Prior Geoffrey, or have miscalculated the strength of the old feeling in the convent. He proceeded in April, 1197, to perfect the exchange, which was again confirmed by the king,[6] and on the conclusion of the bargain he sent an envoy to Rome to obtain the countenance of Celestine III. The pope, who was far beyond ninety, was growing very infirm, and had, perhaps, forgotten the part that in former days he had taken on the side of the monks. Hubert at any rate procured from him a letter which placed the collegiate church of S. Stephen and S. Thomas at Lambeth in his hands.[7] He was now lord of the manor of Lambeth, and had by

---

[1] Gervase, 1593.
[2] Gervase, 1595.
[3] R. de Diceto, 696.

[4] Foedera, i. 65.   [5] No. dlxvi.
[6] No. dlxvii. Gervase, 1597.
[7] No. ccccxiii.

the common law the right to build a religious house of any order he chose upon his own estate.

He was called away from England on the 17th of June,[1] long before the arrival of Celestine's grant, and remained on the continent until the 3rd of November.[2] On his return he took up the business immediately. After paying a visit in person to the convent, he sent, on the 16th, the abbots of Chertsey, Waltham, and Reading with new proposals.[3] The envoys declared that their purpose was not to ask the consent of the monks to the foundation of the college of Lambeth, that was not required, but to lay before them the scheme which the archbishop had drawn up for the securing of their rights. The principal points of this scheme were these : every newly-appointed canon should swear that he would never attempt to assert for the college any voice in the election of the archbishop ; that he would not connive at the translation of S. Thomas to any other church ; that he would not consent to the consecration of the chrism elsewhere than at Canterbury ; he would never seek or suffer another to seek relief from this oath. Every canon should be installed *in propria persona*, and immediately after his installation should go to Canterbury and take this oath, under pain of privation. The prior of Christ Church should hold a prebendal stall at Lambeth, and be present at all chapters in the habit of a canon. To these conditions the archbishop was prepared to secure the consent of both king and pope.[4]

(margin: Hubert proposes certain cautions for the security of Christ Church)

The answer of the monks to this offer was conveyed by one of their own body, probably Gervase again ; they professed the utmost affection for Hubert, but positively refused to consent to his design ; as for the securities he offered, they would take the advice of their friends.[5]

(margin: The convent reject the proposal)

The archbishop visited Canterbury again early in the next year to receive the deliberate answer of the convent to his proposals. The allegations which the monks brought forward in reply were probably those embodied in the very curious memorial with which our MS. closes, and which is unfortunately imperfect. They amount to a downright refusal. Hubert then proposed that the Holy See should be consulted by both parties, on the strict understanding that neither should apply for any mandate without the knowledge of the other. The monks assented in words ; and the archbishop left them,

(margin: Both parties agree to consult the pope)

---

[1] Gervase, 1597.
[2] Gervase, 1598. R. de Diceto says that he returned on the 8th, having been absent twenty weeks and six days.
[3] Gervase, 1598. Nos. ccccxxvii. ccccxxviii.
[4] No. dlvi. Gervase, 1598. This

was the second time these propositions were made : Hubert sent them first by John of Dover, and afterwards summoned the monks to Coventry for their answer. No. cccclxv.
[5] Gervase, 1599. The answer was given on the 17th.

deceived, according to Gervase, by their mild speeches; for their envoys were already on the way to Rome.

Geoffrey was still prior; but he seems to have lost some of his earlier energy, or else to have considered the propositions of the archbishop not unreasonable. Two of the brethren, who looked upon him as dilatory or lukewarm in the cause, had left the convent secretly early in January, and proceeded to Rome to lay their case before Pope Celestine.

On hearing of the gross deception that had been practised upon him, Hubert was very angry, and came down to Canterbury to make inquiry. The prior answered that the monks had left without his permission, and produced a letter from the delinquents confessing their offence, and appealing to the Holy See against the archbishop. Hubert, having a strong suspicion of collusion, excommunicated the fugitives in spite of their appeal. It is not very easy to say what share the prior had in the transaction. Perhaps if he had been left to himself he might at this time have agreed with the archbishop; but the precedent which he had created against himself by the deposition of Osbert was a dangerous one; it would be fatal to him to be suspected of a deficiency of zeal; his hesitation, if hesitation there was, was but for a moment. It is more charitable to suppose that such was the case than to assume that he actually connived at the deceiving of the archbishop.[1]

The result of the manœuvre was not long delayed. The two brethren found when they reached Rome that Celestine was dead; that his successor, Innocent III., was their old friend, the lord Lothair. Their business was expedited at once. Without waiting to hear the representations of Hubert, Innocent, on the 24th of April, issued a letter to him, insisting on the demolition and abolition of the college within thirty days,[2] on pain of suspension, and accompanied it with an injunction to the suffragan bishops to withdraw their obedience in case of his refusal. This was granted on the hearing of one party only, but in dependence on the mandates of Urban, Clement, and Celestine.

The news of the issue of these letters reached Lambeth, where Hubert was staying, on the 31st of May.[3] After a sleepless night,

---

Marginal notes:

Two monks go secretly to Rome

Hubert excommunicates the fugitives

The Prior Geoffrey

First mandate of Innocent III.

Hubert appeals against the mandate

---

[1] Gervase (1601) defends the deception practised by the monks on the grounds that the archbishop had already sent messengers with a great supply of money to Rome. It is probable that Hubert had agents generally at Rome; but the whole tenor of the succeeding controversy shows that he had acted in good faith on this occasion. In fact, he believed himself to have power to do all that he wanted in the matter; and even if he did send an agent to obstruct any petitions the convent might make, it was no more than he had a right to do on the terms of the agreement.

[2] Nos. ccccxxxiv. ccccxxxv.

[3] No. cccl. Gervase, 1601.

he called together his advisers early the next morning, and in their presence appealed against the mandate as obtained under false pretences; the bishop of Rochester joined in the appeal, and Symon, archdeacon of Wells, also appealed on behalf of the canons. Hubert then proceeded to send the abbots of Chertsey and Waltham to Canterbury with a letter of remonstrance, and a strict command that the monks should write a true statement of the whole case to Innocent. *He remonstrates with the convent*

The convent demanded time for consideration before answering, and in the meanwhile sent four monks to serve the obnoxious letters on the archbishop. They arrived at Lambeth on the 7th of June, but were kept waiting two days before they were suffered to execute their office. The information had now reached the king in Normandy, and provoked him to great indignation. He immediately prohibited the archbishop from obeying the mandate, and wrote to the pope and cardinals, protesting vigorously against so monstrous an invasion of English liberties in Church and State. *The mandate is served on Hubert, and the king forbids him to obey*

Hubert had already summoned the bishops to Canterbury to the consecration of Geoffrey Muschamp, elect of Coventry, which was fixed for the 21st. He himself arrived there on the 19th. On the 20th he visited the convent, and complained bitterly of the ill faith of the prior. On the Monday after the consecration the abbots of Waltham, Chertsey, and Reading again appeared as his messengers; with them came several of the bishops, and Geoffrey Fitz Peter and Hugh Bardolf, on the part of the king. These produced a letter from Richard, in which he forbade the execution of the mandate, and himself appealed against it, at the same time taking the college at Lambeth under royal protection, and summoning the prior to account for the offence against the liberties of the realm. When this had been read, the archbishop appeared in person, and tried by persuasion to prevail on the monks to renounce the papal sentence, and to accept an arbitration. Finding all argument useless, he left Canterbury in disgust on the 23rd, and directly on his departure the royal officers entered on the possessions of the convent. This first occupation lasted only a few days, and was withdrawn at the archbishop's request. *Council of the bishops, and attempts at mediation*

Both parties now sent accredited messengers to Rome. Hubert, in the simplicity of his heart, furnished his with a load of the relics of SS. Albinus and Rufinus;[1] not neglecting, however, to send a great treasure of ready money with them. His envoys were the Cistercian abbots of Boxley and Robertsbridge, who had already *The archbishop sends envoys to Rome*

---

[1] Honorius had before taken a quantity of the relics of these saints to Rome to work upon the feelings of Pope Clement. No. ccxxxiv.

attempted to act as mediators.[1] They were furnished with letters in
defence of the archbishop from all the suffragans of the province,
and from the Cistercian abbots of England.

The king
insists on an
arbitration

Although Hubert deemed it wise to appear at Rome by his
agents, he could foresee the sentence of the pope, and was not inclined
to acquiesce in it. He devoted himself, therefore, to another attempt
to persuade or to compel the convent to a compromise. He again
applied to the king, who issued a letter on the 23rd of July, ordering
the convent to choose five bishops and five abbots as arbiters.[2] The
prior refused on the old grounds, that as all the prelates in England
were committed to the design of Hubert, no fair arbitration could be
obtained.

Hubert in
Wales

The month of August passed away without any alteration in the
position of parties, the archbishop being called away by the war on
the Welsh marches,[3] and no new mandates being received from

Hubert
surrenders
his justiciar-
ship

Rome. Hubert was employed further in surrendering the justiciarship, which, according to Hoveden and Matthew Paris, the pope, at
the suggestion of the monks, had forbidden him to retain. It is
curious that not a word on this subject is found in the present
volume. If it were not for the strong contemporary evidence, the
statement would seem improbable ; as it is, we must suppose that
the allegations were made by word of mouth, or the letters containing
them were destroyed, as dangerous documents, should they fall into
the hands of either Hubert or the king. In the midst of business,
however, the archbishop found time to send for the third time to
Canterbury the schedule of cautions with which he was prepared to
secure the status of the mother church in case the new foundation
should take effect.

Richard
sends to
enrol the
treasure of
the church

Richard was not disposed to let matters rest even for a time.
The treasures of the church had not been exhausted by his ransom ;
sufficient yet remained to swell considerably the hoard he was laying
up in France, and this he would not suffer to flow into the pockets
of the Roman courtiers. He renewed the struggle early in September
by a command addressed to the justiciars to visit Canterbury and
make an inventory of the treasures of the convent.[4] This was to be
followed by a similar visitation of the other cathedral monasteries.[5]
The visit was paid on the 26th of September ;[6] the royal officers

---

[1] Gervase, 1606.
[2] No. cccclxx. Gervase, 1608.
[3] Gervase, 1614. The archbishop
defeated the Welsh in a great battle
at Payn's Castle a few days after the
death of Peter, bishop of S. David's,
which happened on July 16. Giraldus,
Opp. i. pp. 95 96 He then returned

to London, and surrendered the justiciarship, to which Geoffrey Fitz
Peter succeeded in August. The
writ by which the king relieved Hubert from his office is dated July 11.
Fœdera, i. 71.
[4] No. cccclxv.   [5] No. cccclxxiv.
[6] Gervase, 1614, 1680.

presented themselves in company with Henry of Castillon, archdeacon of Canterbury, and the abbot of Faversham, on the part of the archbishop. The prior stoutly refused to suffer the treasure to be seen by profane eyes ; the envoys did not choose to use force, but departed as they came. The refusal was an act of rebellion against the king ; on the 28th,[1] therefore, the conventual estates were the second time occupied by the king's officers. On that day Hubert left the kingdom ; but on hearing of what had been done he wrote an urgent letter to the king, begging him, out of consideration for himself, to recall the order. Such an act of violence would, he saw, effectually destroy any favour he might have found at Rome ; and although he did not expect a favourable sentence, it would be better not, by following the violent policy of his predecessor, to lay the foundation of future difficulties, or arm the monks with their favourite plea of ' *vis et metus.*'[2] The king complied with the petition, and the estates were restored by a letter dated October 29th.[3] Before this, Prior Geoffrey, notwithstanding his age and the melancholy precedent of Honorius, had determined to carry his appeal in person to Rome. Since the 31st of May no news had been received from the brethren there ; the messengers despatched with the report of July 6th had not yet certified their arrival ; the pope was known to be away from the city, and the worst anticipations began to prevail as to the fate of the absent monks.[4] Not content, therefore, with sending a reinforcement of three brethren, Geoffrey himself, about the middle of October, started in company with Brother William, the precentor, and proceeded slowly to Rome. At Lucca he met Brother Salomon, one of the third set of envoys, returning in triumph.

The two brethren who had carried the first appeal were dead ; the arrival of the abbots of Boxley and Robertsbridge was expected early in September, and the pope, anticipating the action of the

(margin notes: Hubert tries to mitigate the king's anger against the monks. The prior goes to Rome. He meets brother Salomon at Lucca.)

---

[1] Gervase, 1615, 1680.
[2] No. cccclxxxiii.
[3] No. cccclxxxiv,
[4] Unfortunately the names of the monks chiefly concerned in the second quarrel are only indicated by initials. The two who left the convent secretly in January were S. and N. Gervase says (c. 1601) that these monks, having received the mandate of April 24, returned home. In this, however, he is clearly wrong, for they write from Rome that they shall wait to hear of the receipt of the mandate, No. ccccxlviii. ; and they had not arrived at home in June. See No. cccccl. Two others followed with the archbishop's licence to consult the

pope, after the visit of Hubert to Canterbury in January ; these must have been Jo. and Hubert, whom the archbishop excommunicated after their departure (see above, p. 422) ; S. and R. (No. ccccxcvi.) apparently followed in July with the letter No. cccccl., and reached the pope in September. The two monks who had died before Sept. 5, No. cccclxxx., were most likely the first party, S. and N. What had become of the others the prior did not know in September, but sent out three more, B., B., and T.,to reinforce them. Nos. cccclxxxvii. and ccccxcvii. He himself with William the precentor followed early in the next month.

convent, wrote urgently on the fifth of that month for new advocates to be sent.[1] This letter was not received at Canterbury until after the prior's departure, but the arrival of the two or three reinforcements sent out from home had rendered it unnecessary to regard it. The brethren John and Hubert must have reached the court, which was now at Perugia, before the 11th of September, on which day the pope wrote to the priors of S. Augustine's and S. Gregory's at Canterbury, to declare invalid a sentence of excommunication which the archbishop had fulminated against them.[2] About the same time, before the arrival of the archbishop's agents, Innocent wrote to the king rebutting his arguments in Hubert's favour, and declaring his intention of walking in the footsteps of his predecessors.[3] A few days after this, before the 17th, the abbots arrived at Perugia.[4] But the cause was not heard before the 21st of October, after the court had returned to Rome. On that day [5] the pope heard the abbots on behalf of Hubert, and listened to a long letter on the same side from the archbishop of Lyons.[6] On the 22nd he heard the answer of the monks, and the following day the abbots were suffered to reply. The monks on this occasion secured the all-powerful advocacy of Ugolino, the pope's chaplain, the very eminent canonist who afterwards filled S. Peter's chair as Gregory IX.[7]

Innocent took a month to draw up his judgment, which was delivered on the 6th and despatched on the 20th of November. It contained a clear and tolerably fair statement of both sides of the question, but concluded with reiterating the former mandate. It must be executed within thirty days, or Hubert would be deprived ; this was notified to the suffragans, and the king himself was threatened with spiritual punishments if he should interfere to prevent the execution.[8] Such was the news that Brother Salomon had for the prior at Lucca.[9] Great, however, as were the advantages thus assured, Geoffrey was aware that all was not yet gained, and he had his own appeal to prosecute. He therefore went on to Pisa, whither he summoned three of the brethren who were at Rome. He also retained Salomon, and sent the mandates home by William the precentor. When he had ascertained the state of affairs, he proceeded to Rome, where he arrived on the 11th of December,[10] and soon after had an interview with the pope. He laid his complaint

---

Arrival of Hubert's envoys

The hearing by Innocent III.

The second mandate of Innocent III.

Geoffrey proceeds to Rome

---

[1] No. cccclxxx.
[2] No. dlxix.
[3] No. dlxx.
[4] The archbishop's agents had reached the papal court before this, for on the 17th Innocent issued to Hubert the letter printed in the Fœdera, i. 71 ; and on the 18th and 19th others commissioning him to reclaim the

alienated property of his see. Epp. Innoc. III., ed. Baluz. lib. i. epp. 370 and 371.
[5] Gervase, 1616.
[6] See No. ccccxcviii.
[7] Nos. div. dix. &c.
[8] Nos. ccccxcviii. ccccxcix. di. dii.
[9] Nos. ccccxcvii.
[10] No. dx.

formally against the archbishop and the justiciars for the visitation
of September 26.   Innocent, without waiting to hear how his second
mandate was received, wrote on the 22nd to the king, urgently
enjoining on him, 'in remissione peccatorum,' to recall the measures
he had taken against the convent ; he also wrote to the archbishop
of Rouen and the bishop of Ely to enforce canonical punishment
against all offenders, including implicitly the king himself.[1]

The archbishop received the second mandate on the 2nd of
January 1199,[2] and prepared immediately to fulfil it.   The offending
chapel was levelled with the ground on the 27th ; the collegiate
buildings, however, were left standing.   The bishops of Ely and
Lincoln and the abbot of S. Edmund's, to whom the execution of
the mandate was committed by the pope, summoned the rectors of
the alienated churches to appear at Westminster on the 10th of May
to give account to the convent.[3]   Whilst the latter were congratulating themselves on the obtaining of an unprecedented success, the
letters which the pope had issued at the prior's request arrived.[4]
The monks, being wise enough to see that it would be ruinous to
them to provoke the king by making use of these, abstained from
presenting them.[5]   It is probable, however, that the royal agents at
Rome had informed their master of the issue, and on the 13th of
March[6] the estates were again seized, on the pretext that the convent
had refused to allow the king's officers to inspect their treasure, the
very point upon which the papal letter had been most urgent. This
time the archbishop refused to intercede with the king.   The
messengers who were sent to Richard himself were informed on their
way into Poictou[7] that he had fallen under that fatal bolt which
ended so many high hopes and opened the way for the bitterest
humiliation of the house of Anjou.   Richard died on the 6th of
April.   The monk who was sent to him returned without redress ;
but Geoffrey Fitz Peter, hearing that his lord was dead, very shortly
after restored the estates of the convent. The monks would not,
however, regard this as an act of reparation, but pretended to look
upon it as a reinvestment or confirmation, such as was usually

Marginal notes: Hubert's action on the second mandate, and proceedings of the delegates

The conventual property seized the third time

Death of Richard

---

[1] Nos. dxix. dxx. Gervase, 1623.
In this letter Innocent expresses the
great regard which he had for Richard
above all the princes of the world.
He had honoured him especially by
sending him a precious ring, the first
gift that was offered him after his
consecration, and which Richard bestowed on Abbot Samson of S.
Edmund's.   Jocelin de Brakelonda,
p. 72.   The letter to 'the king of
England, which occurs in the first
book of the epistles of Innocent III.
(May 29, 1198), explaining the mystical
meaning of four jewelled rings accom-
panying it, belongs, according to M.
Paris, to the year 1207, and to King
John.

[2] No. d. Gervase, 1623.
[3] No. dv.
[4] Nos. dxix. dxx.
[5] Gervase, 1626. No. dxxi.
[6] Gervase, 1626.
[7] Gervase, 1627.

Fresh complaints sent to Rome
obtained on the succession of a new prince.[1] They despatched accordingly a third series of complaints to Rome, the burden of which was the continued detention of the disputed churches in contempt of the papal mandate, and the fact that the condemned buildings of the college were still suffered to stand.[2]

The archbishop changes his tactics
The archbishop had now determined on a new plan. He probably thought that the pope might be satisfied with the obedience exhibited in the demolitiom of the chapel, and that he would be willing to listen to an application on behalf of the college, if it were made to himself first. Immediately after the demolition of the chapel he sent his agents to Rome to announce that so far the mandate had been fulfilled, and that he was ready to grant the convent further redress for any injuries that they could prove to have been inflicted on them in consequence of their opposition to the new college. He prayed further that a papal licence might be granted him to found a college in honour of S. Stephen and S. Thomas at Lambeth, but on a new

Innocent issues a commission to adjudge the case
site. This application the pope could not well refuse to entertain ; he directed, therefore, a commission to the bishops of Lincoln and Ely, and the abbot of S. Edmund's,[3] to examine into the whole case.

Instructions of the commission
They were instructed first of all to use their best endeavour to restore concord between Hubert and his convent ; if that failed, they were first to compel the archbishop to restore all that had been taken from the convent to enrich the new foundation, or in consequence of their opposition to it, and then to adjudicate on the question itself ; or if they could not do that, to hear evidence and refer the decision back to the pope. They were further empowered to visit Canterbury, and to examine into the condition of the monastery, both external and internal.

Hubert's further aggressions
Whilst his envoys were at Rome, Hubert had been provoked to fresh acts of aggression. He had seized the marsh of Appledore, and the oblations of the high altar. After his return to England in Easter week,[4] he had, towards the end of May,[5] closed the conventual courts of justice. These acts were made the burden of fresh complaints : the pope was further informed that the archbishop refused to let the monks approach him, even in the solemn processions of the church, but hedged himself in with clerks before and behind ; the very dress of the clerks was a ground of accusation. Wearied with these petty complaints, Innocent once more wrote, on the 11th of September,[6] to the archbishop, to induce him to more fatherly behaviour : he had also ordered him, on the 21st of August, to restore all the churches on the estates of the convent.

Proceedings of the delegates
The delegates, on receiving their commission, summoned the parties to appear before them at Westminster on the Friday after

---

[1] No. dxxiii.   [2] No. dxxiv.   [4] Giraldus, Opp. iii. 81.
[3] No. dxxv.   [5] No. dxxiv.   [6] No. dxxix.

Michaelmas.[1] The monks did not condescend to obey. Hubert appeared, and laid before the judges his terms of reconciliation. The convent were informed of this, and notice was given that the delegates would hold their visitation at Canterbury on the 18th of November.[2] It does not appear on what day it actually took place : the result was signified to the pope by the convent ;[3] they had offered the archbishop fair terms ; they would remit three years' revenue of their posses- sions, and the mesne profits of the disputed churches and the xenia, in all fifteen thousand pounds sterling; the churches were to be confirmed to their incumbents for life, at a small annual pension, and Hubert was to retain the xenia for his life. The convent undertook the completion of the building of the cathedral ; and further they offered, when the cathedral was finished to consent to Hubert's building in some unsuspected place a college of canons regular. The archbishop refused to listen to this proposition, and insisted that the convent should throw themselves upon his mercy. *Proposals of the convent for peace*

The formal hearing of the case was resumed, as it would seem, on the 26th of January, 1200, at Westminster :[4] for that day the delegates peremptorily summoned the convent, who had failed to attend on the 30th of September and the 27th of November ; if they refused the third summons, judgment would go against them by default. When they had presented themselves, the archbishop made a formal claim to be allowed to build his college.[5] The monks insisted that, before the question could be entertained, their claim of restitution according to the mandate should be satisfied. Everything that had been taken from them, on account of the chapel at Lambeth, must be restored. So the commission ran ; the delegates were warned not to go beyond the letter of their authority. Hubert sheltered himself under a verbal ambiguity ; and this having been reserved by the judges, they proceeded to hear evidence. They decided that the convent had failed to prove that they had lost anything on account of the interdicted chapel : they notified the decision to the pope, with the points reserved ; thus, virtually, giving sentence in favour of Hubert. His clerks began to triumph ; the king forbade the papal judges to enter on the question of the disputed advowsons ;[6] the quarrel broke out again with its old bitterness. Innocent was prevailed upon by the convent to rescind the powers of the delegates, and to recall the cause to Rome, the parties to appear before the pope himself on the feast of S. Martin. This letter was issued on the 21st of May.[7] *Argument before the delegates*

The powers of the dele- gates re- voked

Before, however, the letter was received, a sudden change had taken place in the feelings of the combatants. The delegates had *Sudden change in the position of the parties*

[1] No. dxxxi.   [2] No. dxxxii.   [5] No. dxxx.   Gervase, 1680.
[3] No. dxxxiv. &c.   [4] No. dxxxiii.   [6] No. dxxxiv.   [7] No. dxlv.

appointed the Thursday before the feast of S. Simon and S. Jude [1] for the last day of hearing. What produced the change in the archbishop's tactics it is impossible to say ; according to the monks, he was prevailed upon by the arguments of certain foreign scholars who visited Canterbury ; [2] it is more likely that he had found by experience that he must not reckon on the continued support of the king ; it is probable also that, most of the original promoters of the college being now provided for, less pressure was brought to bear upon him than had been before. Of one thing we may be sure, that he was anxious that the cause should not be referred to Rome, but should be settled in a way that was compatible with the laws of the kingdom.

Hubert proposes to choose the delegates as arbitrators

On whatever motive he acted, he came down to Canterbury before the day of hearing, and proposed that, instead of proceeding on the apostolic letters, himself and the convent should agree to elect the delegates to arbitrate in the case. The bishop of Lincoln was dying ; Roger of Rolveston, the dean, might fill his place. The convent having now, by Innocent's letter [3] revoking the commission, the means of quashing further proceedings if they should be unfavourable, accepted the archbishop's proposal. The bishop of Ely, the dean of Lincoln, and the abbot of S. Edmund's sat at Westminster, not as papal delegates, but as umpires chosen by the parties to the suit.[4]

Final award of the arbitrators

They pronounced their decision on the 6th of November. It was highly favourable to the monks. The archbishop might build at Lambeth, not, however, on the forbidden site, a church of canons, but the church must be a small one, and the canons Premonstratensians. It might be endowed from the archiepiscopal estates or churches, but not from those of the convent or of the almonry, or to an amount of more than a hundred pounds per annum. No consecrations or ordinations were to be celebrated in it; no church of secular canons must be built by the archbishop without the consent of the convent. As for the alienated churches, they were to be held by their present possessors, John, late archbishop of Lyons, Ralph of S. Martin, Symon of Wells, and Master Virgil, at a small rent for life ; when vacant they should be apportioned between the almonry and the archbishop. Hubert was to have the xenia for his life. The question of the marsh of Appledore should be settled by a jury of twelve men.

The several parties signified this arrangement to the pope, who ratified it on the 30th of June, 1201.

Character of the proceedings

In the foregoing sketch of this famous struggle I have not thought it necessary to be constantly recurring to the legal character of the

---

[1] No. dxlvi.   [2] No. dxlvi.   [4] No. dxlviii. &c. R. de Diceto, 708.
[3] No. dxlvii.   Hoveden, 458. Ann. Winton. 305.

proceedings. These were, in fact, a series of repetitions, and may be dismissed in one sentence. The whole case turns on the persistence of the convent in compelling obedience to the papal mandates, and on the persistence of the king and archbishop in defeating them by law, by force, or by fraud. The case was never tried on its merits. Whatever was the opinion entertained upon them both in Rome and in England—and they are found frequently discussed in the unofficial, sometimes in the official, correspondence—the proceedings turned at Rome on the disobedience of the primates, in England on the contumacy of the convent. The same has been the case with the few writers who have ventured to dip into the history. On one side the reasonable rights of the archbishops have been obscured by the arbitrary means they took to secure them ; on the other, all sympathy has been alienated by the dishonesty and litigiousness of the monks. *The case not tried on its merits*

There were, however, from beginning to end, points in dispute that were quite open to free discussion, both at canon and at common law. What right had the former archbishops to sacrifice the interests of their successors ? What authority did the papal confirmation give to acts *ipso facto* uncanonical, such as the alienation of the oblations from the archbishop ? What were the powers of the convent to restrain the acts of the primate as archbishop, or what, as abbot of Christ Church ? These points were never considered *pro tribunali* at Rome. Each party avoided appearing before the pope in the presence of the other. The popes themselves issued their letters on *ex parte* statements. The constant argument of the monastic party was that the right of appeal must be maintained ; they would not have a second pope at Canterbury. It might indeed have been tolerable, had they been his cardinals, but as it was the liberties of the whole Western Church were imperilled. To this representation the successsive mandates were granted ; when they were contemned they were followed up with others, and on the non-fulfilment of these the decision of the whole case, had it been decided at Rome, would have turned. *Points for canonical discussion*

In England, on the other hand, the questions for legal decision were manifold, but the actual proceedings were as simple as at Rome, and probably, with some few exceptions, more directly opposed both to law and equity. What was the real state of the law on the question of appeals ? They were not unlawful, for the Constitution of Clarendon that forbade them had been renounced by the king, and never renewed. Yet every possible means was taken to defeat the prosecution of them. The mandates delivered from Rome were actually illegal, but Henry did not venture to prohibit the publication of them. Richard, on the other hand, did so prohibit them, and in both cases with manifest advantage ; still the transgressors were not *Points for decision at home* punished. Other questions might have been entertained at law without any risk of coming in contact with the papal authority : What was the validity of the charters of the convent which the king denied ? What was their interpretation, if genuine ? What was the nature of the tenure of their property, immediate of the crown, or through the person of the archbishop? What right had they to refuse to answer in the king's court except through the archbishop, and yet to refuse his officers leave to hold the private courts in which, as their abbot, he was the source of justice ? These questions were avoided. The law was not strong enough to assert itself. If the monks were guilty of illegal conduct, it was not by excommunication or by confinement and blockade that they were legally punishable. If they were never tried, they ought not to have been persecuted. The archbishop was at Rome, admitting the legality of an appeal by answering the appellants, whilst at home he was excommunicating them, and throwing every obstacle in the way of a judgment that he seemed to be soliciting.

Inconsistency of the conduct of the archbishop

The power of the Church of Rome was exerted and the spirit of the court of Rome was aroused on the one side, on the other were the national feeling and the majesty of the law of England. Irrespective of law, the pope and cardinals were engaged in sympathy with one side, and the king, clergy, and lawyers on the other. Yet they avoided coming to an actual collision, and in a manner tried to gain a triumph rather by checking their adversaries in alternate moves than by fairly facing the difficulties of the situation. In this game the popes had a decided advantage, for they confined themselves to ground which, on their own hypothesis, was strictly legal, and to a series of measures, each of which sprang naturally and logically from its predecessors. Their adversaries, on the other hand, afraid to bring about a collision, moved in crooked paths and fought with weapons that no law could justify. The policy of Rome was not hampered with either the fear of law or the desire of peace ; the popes played accordingly the more open game ; but they had nothing to lose : whatever loss resulted would fall on insignificant monks ; the law of England had the better cause, but it was enthralled by the fear of spiritual weapons, or a second excitement such as had been so fatal in the earlier years of Henry's reign.

Contrast between the tactics of the courts of Rome and England

The two struggles were conducted by the monks on the same principles. In each case appeal was made against the acts of the archbishop, and in each the appeal was withdrawn, or the archbishop was persuaded that it was so. In each the withdrawn appeal was secretly prosecuted, so that the convent might get the first word at Rome, and yet be able to recognise or disavow, as occasion served, the acts of their messengers. In each the result of the appeal was

The same plan pursued in both the disputes

an unfair judgment.   A mandate was issued on *ex parte* representations.   The archbishops were warranted in the belief that such acts were null or illegal, or tried to anticipate the blow by excommunicating the appellants ; the excommunication was made the *gravamen* of a new appeal ; so mandate followed mandate, and appeal followed appeal.   At last extreme spiritual censures were threatened and defied.   In both the matter was settled by compromise ; in the former the good sense of Richard and his advisers prevented a schism or an interdict ; in the latter Hubert was wise enough to yield ; he saw, in fact, that the time for successful resistance was still far off. *Both decided by compromise*

The characters of the two archbishops gave, however, a distinctive colour to each of the disputes.   Baldwin, with his Cistercian notions, his learning and unworldliness, was a very different man from Hubert the legate, chancellor and justiciar, primate and commander-in-chief, holding more than regal power in England, and possessing supreme influence over the royal mind.   Baldwin might be expected to conduct the struggle as a priest, Hubert as a statesman or a soldier.   Possibly, as has been remarked above, the proceedings of Baldwin may be regarded as characteristic of an unworldly man under the influence of unprincipled advisers : but Hubert certainly acted for himself.   Hubert was careful to observe some regard to the law, and was ready to yield where he saw he could not succeed.   But Baldwin, or those who acted with his authority, uniformly perverted the process of the law, and preferred the weapons of terrorism.   Yet in the final arbitration it was by a side wind that Hubert saved the dignity of the country, losing at the same time all that he had contended for ; whilst, in the first, Baldwin gained all that he wanted except one unimportant point.   The difference of the result probably arose from the different characters of Richard and John, and the decreased interest that Hubert took in the design.   He could not reckon on John's support as he could upon Richard's.   He was content to sacrifice his own interest to save the law.   The papal commission and the long series of mandates were all set aside, and so far the law was upheld ; but the points in dispute wore all given against him ; and the very arbitrators who decided the award were the persons whom the pope had commissioned as delegates.   The law was strong enough to rob the papal proceedings of their logical conclusion, but not strong enough to decide the cause on its merits or by its own virtue. *Contrast between the procedures of Hubert and Baldwin*

The law kept, but not vindicated

And this is not to be wondered at ; for, not to speak of the constant and accumulated aggravations of papal interference, the administration of the law of the land was in the hands of men too rough and self-willed to handle so delicate an instrument.   For the law

F F

itself was not in its infancy, and was fully competent to decide on nearly all the points involved ; but though the weapons were ready and appropriate, they were crushed by the hands that wielded them, and the law was broken in the attempt to enforce it more than in the attempt to evade it.

Illustrations of character

The character of Richard is illustrated in some minor points by his course in these disputes. He stands in pleasant contrast with his father in respect both of his openness and of his firmness. His stout determination not to yield is manifest from the first. He would not suffer the law of the land to be overridden by a rescript from Rome. He condescended to none of what S. Thomas called his father's mousetraps : the tricks by which that astute king managed to put his adversaries in the wrong without committing himself to a decided course. ·He not only threatened, but actually defeated, the legate, John of Anagni, in a way worthy of his father's bolder days. He forbade the execution of the mandate of Innocent, instead of trying to elude it either by chicanery or by bullying. And the success of his resistance fully justified the more manly line he took.

Position of Hubert

Not less conspicuous is the influence exercised over him by Archbishop Hubert. Hubert's character has suffered a good deal from his connexion with Richard. From S. Hugh downwards, judgment has been passed upon him as a man of secular mind, ambitious, unscrupulous, the willing minister of a greedy tyranny. In some respects his position was one of his own seeking. He was the first archbishop of Canterbury who had retained secular power after his accession to the primacy. With the exception of S. Thomas, he was the only primate since the Conquest who had been chosen for any other reason than learning or sanctity ; he was raised to the high position which he filled simply for secular reasons. But it should be taken into account that Hubert never worked for himself alone ; he never enriched or aggrandised himself ; [1] if he grasped a power, there were no other hands capable of grasping it, or even of holding it for a moment. No one exercised over Richard an influence to be compared with that of Hubert. In the recollection of this lies the excuse for much of that arbitrary conduct that has offended his critics. If the yoke when held by Hubert was heavy, what must it have been

---

[1] Giraldus Cambrensis gives Hubert a very bad character for dishonesty, incontinence, ambition, avarice, and tyranny. Besides this, he was both utterly unlearned, and only saved by his ignorance from being heretical. See Giraldus's Invectiones, *passim* ; especially Opp. iii. 28, 38, 39. These calumnies would be utterly unworthy of attention if the inventor had not thought fit to retract them. As it is, we must set against them the character given by Gervase, 1681, 1682. Giraldus accuses Hubert further of aspiring to the cardinalate, and even to the papacy : Opp. iii. 23.

in the hands of William Longchamp, a man who, not inferior in zeal and faithfulness, and perhaps even superior in political acuteness, had not the tact or the moral influence or a particle of the English feeling that characterised the archbishop. That the influence of Hubert over Richard was not a mere accident, but the result of something in the character of the former, can scarcely be questioned ; for he exercised the same among the haughty nobles and among the citizens of London. The extent and character of this influence was especially apparent in the pacification of England during Richard's captivity and in the management of the election of John.[1] On the former of these occasions it is almost amusing to remark the way in which the minor actors, who had acquired some importance in the medley, vanish before his strong and sensible proceedings. William of Longchamp dwindles down into the king's chancellor ; Walter of Coutances disappears almost entirely from the arena of English politics ; Hugh of Puiset and Hugh of Nunant are compelled to keep order ; John and Geoffrey are both put in their proper places ; Richard reigns as powerfully from Spires or Worms as he did from Roche d'Andeli or Azai. Hubert was himself a Norman nobleman, and allied with the greatest names of the period of amalgamation. He had stood face to face with Saladin both in the field of battle and in the council. He who knew how to keep the lion-hearted king in something like order was not likely to cower before a fellow-noble. He was not, perhaps, the best conceivable minister for Richard, but he was probably the best, if not the only one, possible. He was a true patriot, a man of honest purposes and of pure life. That such a man should have the authority he had with Richard is enough to outweigh any charges that can be brought against him as a minister, and the details of the association bring out some of the better features of the king's character at the same time.

If we regard him as a bishop, other considerations come in. The exchequer of a Norman sovereign could hardly be a good school of financial honesty, much less of theological training. Hubert was sadly deficient in both the scholarship and the doctrinal learning that become a bishop. The secular occupations to which he devoted himself could not be satisfactorily pursued without some dereliction of his spiritual work. It can only be said for him that the greatness of his country's need was his best excuse. Yet the results of the system which he represented were very terrible. Under an archbishop whose time was filled with secular work, and whose energies, however commanding, could scarcely have grappled alone with the evils of the

Side notes: Influence of Hubert as a minister

Hubert as a bishop

Unhappy state of religion

---

[1] The influence which he maintained over John is especially noted by Gervase as a proof of his wonderful prudence. Gerv. c. 1681.

disordered church, the state of religion in the country was extremely bad.

Nigel, the monk of Canterbury, and author of the *Speculum Stultorum*, whose name is found two or three times in the following pages (vol. R. S.), has left us in his book *De Abusu Ecclesiastico* a picture of the state of the church as viewed by a sincere and by no means prejudiced monk. The following of secular pursuits by the superior clergy had the double effect of laying open the spiritual offices to unworthy persons, and of perverting religious endowments to mere secular uses. Immorality and simony were crying sins in the portion of the clergy that was supposed to be devoted to spiritual duties, and these were rather encouraged than restrained by their poverty. The superior clergy were generally free from these stains, but ignorance, meanness, avarice, and servility were common among them. Nigel doubtless attributed much of this to the inherent corruptness of secular life ; but a careful study of these letters will show that there was another cause at work, that did not lie, indeed, so deep in human nature, but was almost as difficult to eradicate as if it had done so. This was the paralysis of discipline in the church itself. There can be no reasonable doubt that the hands of the bishops were tied by the sufferance of appeals to Rome, contrary to the ancient custom of the realm : the evil that had called for the Constitutions of Clarendon ; the old evil, foreign to the English Church, which had been

gradually creeping in since the Conquest. It was practically in the power of any contumacious priest to lodge an appeal to Rome, which at once removed him from the authority of his diocesan, and placed him, whatever his merits might be, under the protection of the Holy See. Neither the spiritual nor the lay courts could try him ; no bishop would subject himself to the annoyance and expense of a suit which would almost to a certainty be decided against him. All-powerful money could purchase, or wearisome pertinacity extort, a mandate ; pains and penalties would follow the refusal of the bishop to obey ; from that moment he ceased to be a judge and became a defendant ; and that under a charge on which the Italian lawyers never acquitted a bishop. The great proportion of English cases which are found in the Decretals of Gregory IX., and the space that English letters occupy in the letters of Alexander III. and his successors, which are of course only picked cases and letters of supposed importance, speaks more convincingly than any complaints of the historians of the paralysis of judicial power in the English Church. Although Hubert was neither a learned man nor a great theologian, he did his best, by the means of councils and legatine visitations, to remedy the evils that he saw existing. He failed under circumstances in which S. Hugh of Lincoln and Baldwin of Canterbury failed too.

With the ideas that prevailed during this period on the subject of church preferment, there was doubtless a difficulty in attracting a superior class of minds to mere clerical work. The better endowments were heaped upon men who were ready to serve the king in the business of the State. The monasteries engrossed a vast proportion of tithe and only scantily provided for the duties legally attached to the possession. Piety was driven out of the church and choked in the monastery. The foundation of colleges and enrichment of the cathedrals would have served to provide for the learned and legal clergy, and have left parochial endowments to their natural purpose. But this could only be done at the expense of the monastic order, either by alienating their revenues or by diverting that stream of pious liberality that had flowed so long in their direction. It was partly with this view that Henry II. and his ministers encouraged the design of Baldwin; and this, like every effort after reformation that proceeded from the bishops, was foiled by the appeal to Rome.

The Hakington and Lambeth foundations may be regarded as the last attempt to utilise the property of the monasteries before the Reformation. It failed signally, and the need of the moment was satisfied within a few years by the introduction of the mendicant orders, who undertook the religious revival of the people; these in their turn provoked the parochial clergy to greater activity, and so reform worked itself out; later the lawyers set themselves to oust the clergy from their secular occupations, and thus what was lost to the state was gained for the well-being of the church. The monastic system was left to itself until the sins of the fathers were visited upon the children, and the endowments, which might have nursed learning and amply provided for monastic peace and hospitality, served to enrich the greedy courtiers of Henry VIII. and Edward VI.

From the end of the twelfth century until the Reformation, from the days of Hubert Walter to those of Wolsey, the monasteries remained magnificent hostelries; their churches were splendid chapels for noble patrons; their inhabitants were bachelor country gentlemen, more polished and charitable, but little more learned or more pure in life than their lay neighbours; their estates were well managed, and enjoyed great advantages and exemptions; they were, in fact, an element of peace in a nation that delighted in war. But, with a few noble exceptions, there was nothing in the system that did spiritual service; books were multiplied, but learning declined; prayers were offered unceasingly, but the efficacious energy of real devotion was not found in the homes that it had reared. The monastic body had sacrificed the opportunity of doing good work for the triumph of a moment. The great prize of their ambition,

Preversion of church endowments

Sacrifice demanded of the monastic orders

Importance of the Hakington and Lambeth cases in church history

Decline of monastic power dates from this time

the government of the church, fell from their hands. The position occupied from henceforth by the monks of Canterbury—and their state and weight may be taken as a fair criterion of the whole system —was void of all political importance ; their action in the election of the primate was merely nominal ; in spite of many efforts to elect men of their own order, only once more did a monk fill the throne of Augustine. With the exception of Simon Langham, whose merits were by no means those of a monastic saint, Baldwin was the last monk who governed the Church of England.

THE HISTORICAL COLLECTIONS OF
WALTER OF COVENTRY

[IN the following pages will be found a very remarkable sketch of the character and life of King John. Bishop Stubbs shows how the reforms of Henry II. had greatly strengthened the Crown, and emphasises the fact that no adequate checks upon its still further growth had been provided by the new system. Such power could be safely intrusted to Henry II., who had himself recognised the existence of checks upon the royal despotism. But when a tyrant like John arose, whose power was restricted by no constitutional limits, the clergy, barons, and people were forced into a union the outcome of which was Magna Carta. Bishop Stubbs had nothing but scorn for the saying that John 'was the ablest of the Plantagenets,' and his words on that subject which are here reproduced carry conviction with them.]

  *   *   *   *   *   *

WHAT marks out John personally from the long list of our sovereigns, good and bad, is this—that there is nothing in him which for a single moment calls out our better sentiments ; in his prosperity there is nothing that we can admire, and in his adversity nothing that we can pity. Many, most perhaps, of our other kings have had both sins and sorrows : sins for which they might allege temptations, and sorrows which are not less meet for sympathy because they were well deserved ; but for John no temptations are allowed to be pleaded in extenuation of guilt, and there is not one moment, not one of the many crises of his reign, in which we feel the slightest movement towards sympathy. Edward III. may have been as unprincipled, but he is a more graceful sinner ; William Rufus as savage, but he is a more magnificent and stronger-willed villain ; Ethelred the Unready as weak, false, and worthless, but he sins for, and suffers with, his people. John has neither grace nor splendour, strength nor patriotism. His history stamps him as a worse man than many who have done much more harm, and that—for his reign was not a period of unparalleled or unmitigated misery to his subjects—chiefly on account of his own personal share in the producing of his own deep and desperate humiliation.

(margin note: John the worst of the kings of England)

None of the contemporary historians has left us a portrait of John that can be compared for minuteness and graphic reality with those drawn of Henry II. by Peter of Blois, Ralph Niger, William of Newburgh, and Giraldus Cambrensis. The last-mentioned writer, in his book *De Instructione Principum*, published at the beginning and revised at the end of his own long career, has recorded his early impressions, and his by no means sanguine hopes, together with their bitter disappointment. When he began to write John was young ; his levity might, he thought, pass away and leave the elements of greatness unimpaired.[1] But when he registers his final sentence it is that of all the tyrants of history John was the very worst.[2] Ralph of Coggeshall ventures on no inferences from his acts to his character.[3] Matthew Paris, after averring that it is not safe to write of him even when he is dead, puts his opinion of him into the mouth of another critic, and a most trenchant one it is : he was a tyrant rather than a king, a destroyer rather than a ruler ; an oppressor of his own and a favourer of strangers ; a lion to his subjects, a lamb to his enemies and to foreigners ; he had lost Normandy and his other lands by his sloth, but England he thirsted to overthrow and destroy ; he was of money an insatiable exactor, of his own natural possessions the invader and destroyer ; he was a corrupter of daughters and sisters, and spared not the honour of his peers and kinsmen. As to the Christian faith, he was unstable and unfaithful.[4] Matthew of

[1] See the passage in which he is compared with his brother Geoffrey of Brittany, in the De Instructione, ii. 11 (p. 35, ed. Brewer) ; and in the Topographia Hiberniæ, iii. 52 ; Opp. v. 199. 'Ille in spica, hic messis in herba.' History seems fully to confirm Giraldus's notion of the similarity of the two brothers in character, whilst it entirely belies the good auguries which he imagines in the case of John.

[2] 'Longe atrocius cæteris tyrannis omnibus, tam in sacerdotium quam regnum Anglicanum suis insanire diebus et debacchari.'—'Dictus enim Johannes . . . quoniam fratres egregios atque parentes in bonis æquiparare non potuit, puta sicut annis inferior, sic animis amaris et actibus pravis longe deterior existens, non solum ipsos in malis verum etiam in vitiis enormibus vitiosos vincere cunctos, et maxime tyrannos omnes quos vel præsens ætas vel longævæ memoriæ recolere potuit antiquitas, detestandis pravæ tyrannidis actibus totis tran-

scendere nisibus elaboravit.' De Inst. Pr. iii. 28 ; p. 162.

[3] This writer, although generally prone to run into descriptions of character, draws none of John ; only an occasional adverb, 'dolose,' 'crudeliter,' or 'ignaviter,' shows what he thought.

[4] Ed. Wats, pp. 244, 288. It is difficult to regard the embassy of John to the emperor of Morocco as altogether fabulous, in the teeth of the evidence adduced by Matthew Paris. Thomas of Herdington, Ralph Fitz Nicolas, and Robert of London, whom he names as the envoys, were real persons, and the first of them was employed on an embassy to Rome in the very year, 1213, in which this transaction is placed. Rot. Claus. ed. Hardy, i. 126. It is observable that Innocent III. comments on the absence of three out of the six envoys sent in 1213, and of these three Thomas of Herdington was one. Ep. xv. 234. The words, however, which are put in the mouth of the envoy are probably Matthew Paris's own.

Westminster long afterwards, when it was possible to record the Opinion of historians common belief, specifies his sacrifice of his kingdom by tribute, his extortionate tyranny, his vile impurity, and his cruelty to Arthur, as the chief points of his history.[1]

But although these writers either dared not or could not draw a His great faults frequently remarked on full-length picture of John, they are unsparing of comment on his acts as the occasion for comment arises. His vanity, his atrocious ingratitude to his father and brother, his unprincipled and purposeless avarice, his mercenary meanness,[2] his utter lack of truth and honour; his inertness in the defence and recovery of his dominions;[3] the insincerity with which he treated his barons, and which more than warranted them in their distrust of his most solemn assurances;[4] his reckless neglect of his opportunities; his desperate impotency of rage under defeat that he had not troubled himself to avert; his cruelty, his obstinacy,[5] his idiotic vindictiveness wreaking itself on the innocent to his own harm; his real incapacity for any great design: all these are frequently remarked on by writers who saw Censures of the historians the daily proofs of them. The acts that call forth the censure are not of the class which may allege the misrepresentations of interested writers as a reason for mitigation. They are too manifest to be doubted, and their character too obvious to be excused. Adultery, falsehood, extortion, ill success, are matters on which the public censors cannot have two opinions.[6]

<hr />

[1] Ed. Howard, p. 276. 'Et quia iste Johannes se multis exosum præbuit, cum propter mortem nepotis sui Arturi, tum propter suam incontinentiam qua fœdus lecti matrimonialis dirupit, tum propter suam tyrannidem, tum propter tributum quo sub perpetua servitute regnum Angliæ compedivit, tum propter guerram quam sua merita provocarunt, vix alicujus meruit lamentationibus deplorari. Istæ sunt terræ quas rex Johannes amisit scilicet pro angariis et oppressionibus, multimodis fornicationibus et variis injuriis quæ communiter non cessavit. . .'

[2] As early as 1185, it was remarked that in Ireland he defrauded his mercenaries of their pay: Hoveden, ii. 305. M. Westm. speaks of his 'insatiabilis avaritia,' p. 268.

[3] 'Desidiam regis torpentis incorrigibilem.' M. Westm. 265; M. Paris, 209.

[4] R. Coggeshall, who is not generally severe upon him, repeatedly accuses him of forging letters: 'fraudu-

losam pro more suo stropham commentatus,' p. 253; cf. p. 250. See also M. Paris, p. 255.

[5] 'Proterva obstinacia,' Wykes, 56; Ann. Wav. 282.

[6] No one can have failed to notice that the most damning charges against John are stated most fully by Matthew Paris; that they do not appear in Wendover or in the earlier contemporary annalists. When it is considered that they would touch the honour of many noble houses, we cannot wonder that they are passed over by those who lived in the first generation. Enough, however, remains, without the circumstantial charges of Matthew Paris, to condemn the wretched king; nor is there any reason to suppose that that historian uttered more than the intelligent opinion of his own time justified. John's career must be read as a whole, including the portion of it preceding his accession, to be rightly comprehended. Of course the notion that Matthew wrote in the papal

It is, however, fortunate for us that the history of the time furnishes us with more than these generalities ; that we have not only the comment but the text as well, in abundant records of all John's proceedings, and that from the study of his actions we can evolve a more real, lifelike, and individual presentment.

John was a
mean copy
of his family
type

John, then, as far as I can read his character from his acts, was a mean reproduction of all the vices and of the few pettinesses of his family, of their intellectual as he was of their physical conformation.[1] I say a mean reproduction, because although his crimes were really greater, they are on a smaller scale, from smaller motives, significant of that more unbridled vice that checks at no obstacle and yields to the least temptation. Like his father he is a profligate,[2] but his sins are complicated with outrage and ingratitude ;[3] like Richard he is an extortioner, but unlike him he is meanly mercenary, parsimonious, unsuccessful. Like Geoffrey he is faithless, but unlike Geoffrey he is obstinate rather than impulsive. He never repents, even if it be only to sin again ; he has no remorse, even for his failures. He contemns both the spirit and the form of law ; of religion he has none, scarcely sense enough of it to make him found a monastery ; he neither fears God nor cares for the souls of his people, but he is amenable to superstitions that his father would have spurned. He is passionate, like the rest of the Conqueror's descendants, but it is not the lion-like transport of Henry and Richard ; he is savage, filthy, and blasphemous in his wrath ;[4] but he sulks where he dare not reply, and takes his revenge on the innocent

---

interest is absurd ; he was strongly antipapal, and the papal interest was marshalled on John's side. He often gives point to otherwise vague accusations, but in most particulars he is borne out by other evidence. See further on this point, pp. lxxxii to lxxxiv (vol. R. S.).

[1] Gir. Camb. De Inst. Pr. ii. 11; p. 35. Exp. Hib. p. 199. 'Ambo hi [sc. Geoffrey and John] staturæ modicæ, pauloque mediocri plus pusillæ.' The word 'lubriculus' applied by Wykes to one feature of his character is very significant.

[2] Wykes, p. 53, 'quod nobilium regni sui filias et consanguineas rapuit et concubitu polluit adulterino, erat enim lubriculus, æquiparans vel excedens petulantiam Salomonis.' So also Ann. Wav. p. 282, ' uxores filiasque eorum violabat.' M. Westm. 265, 'effeminatus et fluens in libidinem.' 'Nonnullos uxoribus suis zelotypavit, filias defloravit ; ' ' etiam exosum

habuit uxor propria quam de adulterio adulter defamavit,' ib. 268. See also Wendover, iii. 240 ; M. Paris, 232 ; M. Westminster, 271.

[3] In 1216 his brother William Longespee joined Lewis, ' hac sola speciali causa ductus, quia ei certo innotuit relatore, dictum Johannem regem cum ipsius uxore, rupto fœdere naturali, commisisse incestum, dum ipse esset in Francia incarceratus.' Will. Arm. Bouquet, xvii. 110.

[4] John's oaths, ' per dentes Dei,' M. Paris, 226 ; 'per pedes Domini,' M. Paris, 243 ; compared with the Conqueror's 'By the splendour of God,' are characteristic enough. M. Paris gives an instance of his capacity for profane jesting, p. 245 ; he mentions also John's false opinions on the resurrection of the dead. This may be an invention, but it reminds one of the debate between his kinsman Amalric of Jerusalem and William of Tyre on the same subject. W. Tyr. xix. 3.

and in the dark. His ingratitude is not the common ingratitude of kings, to forget a benefactor when the benefit has grown cold ; he heaps neglect on insult, and scatters scorn on the dead, whose chief fault has been that they have served him too well.[1] Unlike his father and brother, he makes no friends among his ministers ; they are faithful to him, but his only friends are his own creatures, whom he has raised and whom he need not fear to sacrifice.

His conspicuous ingratitude

In the neutral tints of common character his pettiness is not less apparent. The favourite son of Henry II. and the pupil of Glanvill could hardly be without a taste for law ; the instinct that in his father produced great legal reforms, in John works only to the multiplication of little methods of extortion,[2] or the devising of new forms of torture ;[3] like him he sits in the judgment seat,[4] but only for the wages of unrighteousness. Henry's promptness and energy is in John undignified fussiness ; the lofty self-assertion of conscious strength is represented in him by the mere vaunt that can plead no justification ;[5] his recklessness in running into danger is only equalled by the shamelessness with which he retreats before the evils that he has provoked. Of himself he does nothing great, and what is done for him by others he undoes by alienating or insulting them.[6]

Pettiness of John's general character

His recklessness and shamelessness

[1] See his remark on the death of Geoffrey Fitz Peter, M. Paris, 243. His treatment of William de Braiose, who had greatly helped in securing the succession, is remarked on in the Annals of Margam, p. 25.

[2] M. Westm. 265. He took of the Jews, in 1210, 66,000 marks : Madox, *Hist. Exch.* p. 151. Abundant instances of the expansion of the system of fines will be found in the same work.

[3] 'Multa mala et pessimas crudelitates fecerat, quæ non sunt scripta in libro hoc.' Liber de Ant. Legg. p. 202. For example, the ' capa plumbea,' in which Geoffrey the archdeacon of Norwich was starved to death, R. Wendover, iii. 229 ; the punishment of the suspected servant of Queen Isabella, Chron. Lanercost, p. 13 ; the torture of the Jews, M. Paris, 229 ; the 22 noble prisoners starved to death at Corfe, Ann. Margam, 26 ; the fate of Matilda de Braiose and her son, Ann. Theokesb. p. 59. He intended to starve Oliver of Argentan to death also, R. Coggesh. 251.

[4] See Madox, *Hist. Exch.* p. 129, ' præceptum est per regem qui præsens fuit super scaccarium.' Rot. Pip. 6 Joh.

[5] When in 1203 Philip was over-running Normandy, John's remark was, ' Sinite illum facere: ego quicquid modo rapit uno die recuperabo.' Wendover, iii. 171. When Philip took Rouen, ' rex Johannes cachinnando comminabatur, jurans per pedes Dei quod sterlingi Anglorum omnia restaurarent.' M. Westm. 266.

[6] John's greatest exploit was the subjugation of Ireland in 1210, the conquest, with a magnificent army, of a half-armed and divided population, exhausted already by war and plunder. Our author, who (ii. 202, 203) makes the most of his successes at this period, mentions also victories in Wales and Scotland : no great glory could be won from either : he had in 1211 to retreat from the former, and sold a peace to the latter in 1209. He was not, however, devoid of personal valour or of skill in arms ; but his rashness and irresolution constantly brought him into situations in which he must either fight or fly, and he chose the latter. R. Coggeshall describes him on Lewis's landing in 1216, ' perterritus fugit flens et lamentans, et omnis exercitus ejus cum eo,' p. 258. Yet he had been waiting to intercept Lewis, and had a superior force.

His faults increased by his education

He had a bad political education

Although the faults which come out in this form in him are faults so ingrained in the Angevin family that they can scarcely be regarded, except in the particular manifestation, as distinctive of John, somewhat of the result is no doubt to be attributed to his age and training. The youngest of the sons of Henry and Eleanor, he was born[1] long after the arrangement was made by them for the distribution of their states, and consequently lost that education for government which his elder brothers had, and which made a Norman of Henry, a Poictevin of Richard, and a Breton or Angevin of Geoffrey. The title of lord of Ireland did not make John an Irishman; although a stay-at-home, he did not learn the feelings of an Englishman ; he remained, until he became king, without local connexion, a plotter and conspirator against his father and brother, unidentified with any national or provincial interest, representing no party but his own.

He was more or less of an adventurer

And the result of this was that it stamped him more or less with the character of an adventurer. In his earliest childhood his father was busy in seeking to make him a fortune by marriage ; the rebellion of his brother Henry was provoked by an attempt to carve out a portion for John ; for John's sake the attack on Ireland was carried out and the crown of peacock's feathers obtained from Rome ;[2] the final rebellion of Richard was caused by the demand that Poictou should be given up to John ; and during the whole of Richard's reign John was trafficking on the jealous hostility of Philip.

He was born too late to be impressed by the Becket quarrel

Further, he was born too late to be much affected by the Becket quarrel. The archbishop was murdered when John was not four years old, and the matter was condoned before he was six. He thus missed the impression which, partly perhaps unconsciously, but in a measure no doubt through the instructions of Lewis and Eleanor, produced in Richard and in the younger Henry something approaching to a religious feeling, or at least the desire to stand well with the dominant ecclesiastical sentiment of the day. He reproduces in the utmost coarseness the blasphemous profanity of his father's ancestors ; his whole education, such as it was, was carried on during the most

[1] The date of John's birth is fixed by Robert de Monte (ed. Pistorius, i. 903) in 1167; by Ralph de Diceto (c. 540) in 1166. The compiler from whom the late Bishop Stubbs borrowed placed it in 1166, vol. i. p. 186. Robert de Monte is the best authority, especially as he has just mentioned Queen Eleanor's return to England. Diceto, however, who may be regarded as correcting Robert de Monte, is followed by the Annalists generally. The common statement that he was born on the 24th of December, and that two meteors were seen the same evening, is taken from the margin of Robert of Gloucester's Chronicle (ed. Hearne, p. 486); both the facts appear to be taken from Robert de Monte, with the alteration of a year, and placed in the 13th of Henry II., i.e. 1166 instead of 1167. Trivet, p. 60, follows Robert de Monte and gives the right date, Dec. 24, 1167.

[2] Hoveden, ii. 306, 307.

unsettled part of his father's reign ; from the time he was eight years He had no good home influences old to his twenty-third year his mother was practically a prisoner, and if he were allowed to associate with her we may be sure that her lessons were not of the wisest sort. If, as is more probable, she was kept in seclusion, she lost that influence over him during the time when it would have been most beneficial, which it is but justice to her to say was always exercised, where it is at all traceable, in the direction of honesty and manly energy.

His early history is distinctly affected by these facts, especially Appropriateness of his surname *Lackland* the former. The name of *Sansterre* or *Lackland*,[1] whenever and however it was given him, affords one clue at least to the reading of his character and career. Even his infancy is rendered eventful by his father's anxiety to provide for him.

He was born in England in 1167,[2] and seems to have remained His father's anxiety to provide for him under his mother's charge until her imprisonment. Afterwards he is generally found in attendance on his father. In 1170, when Henry believed himself at the point of death,[3] he commended him to his eldest brother, with strict injunctions to make for him such a provision as he would himself have done ; and immediately on his recovery he set to work to obtain a settlement for him, entertaining the idea, possibly as early as this, of fixing him in Ireland and securing him the county of Mortain.[4] In 1173 he arranged a marriage for him with The Maurienne marriage project the heiress of the county of Maurienne and Savoy, by which John was to succeed to the possessions and claims of the marquis of Italy, and consolidate the power of the Angevin house from the Atlantic to the Alps.[5] It was the very natural question of the count, what provision would be made for the little bridegroom to answer to so great a portion,[6] that provoked the revolt of the other sons of Henry, none of whom would consent to part with a single fief for the endowment of their father's darling. John was too young to take part in the war that followed, but he was old enough to understand that it was for his sake that his father had incurred it, a fact which seems to have inspired him rather with a feeling of his own importance than

[1] William of Armorica (lib. vi. p. 303, ed. Pith.) says that the name was given by Henry II. He seems to have shared it before the middle of the thirteenth century with John of Brienne, king of Jerusalem, to whom it is given in the *Chronique de Rains* (ed. Paris), p. 84. Matthew of Westminster (p. 276) explains it with a further reference to his losses in France and his deposition in England, p. 270. Cf. Liber de Antiquis Legibus, pp. 200, 202.

[2] See above, p. 444, note 1. Like Richard he is said to have been born at Oxford : Rob. Gloucester (ed. Hearne), p. 486.

[3] Bened. i. 7.

[4] On the date at which the county of Mortain was given to John, see Hoveden, ii. p. 6, note, and iii. p. xxiv. note.

[5] Bened. i. 36, 37, &c. Gir. Camb. De Inst. Princ. lib. ii. c. 1. Rob. de Monte, ad ann. 1171.

[6] Bened. i. 41.

with any idea of gratitude.   On the peace of 1174,[1] his interests were secured, although not liberally enough to satisfy Henry's wishes ; and in 1175 the revenues of the earldom of Cornwall, which was vacant by the death of Earl Reginald, were detained in his favour.[2] The next year, the Maurienne settlement being endangered by the fourth marriage of the count, and a better opportunity being opened at home by the prospect of the inheritance of Gloucester,[3] John was betrothed to the eldest daughter of Earl William, the Lady Hawis,[4] whom he discarded soon after his accession to the throne, and who afterwards, as wife of Geoffrey de Mandeville, helped to swell the tide of national feeling against him in 1215.[5]   In 1177 he was made lord of Ireland, and received the homage of the native chiefs as their future king,[6] not, however, being intrusted with real authority until many years later.   In 1185 he was knighted and sent to Ireland,[7] where he signally failed.   He lost his forces in petty struggles with the Irish, and devoted himself to the plundering of all who came within his reach.[8]   He was therefore recalled in disgrace, but only to be used as before for his father's political ends.   Two of his elder brothers, Henry and Geoffrey, were now dead ; the king mistrusted Richard and pitted John against him,[9] partly no doubt in the hope of keeping him faithful from a sense of interest, but partly with the view of providing more lavishly for his favourite child.   The result of this policy was most unfortunate in every way ; John threw himself on the side of his father's enemies, and, rendering himself eternally infamous for his ingratitude, broke his father's heart and hastened his death.[10]

Up to this date, then, Henry had made of him, as he had in a less degree of his brothers, a plaything of policy : one of his stakes in the great game he played, but the favourite plaything, the most precious stake. He could scarcely have had a worse political education.   It made him a gambler, through his partner-

Margin notes:

Provision from the earldom of Cornwall

Marriage with the heiress of Gloucester

John lord of Ireland; where he fails completely

Becomes a rival to Richard in his father's hands

Wretched result of his training

---

[1] Bened. i. 78.
[2] Robert de Monte (ed. Pistorius, i. 917), ap. Pertz, viii. 524.
[3] Earl William of Gloucester died in 1183. R. de Monte, ap. Pertz, viii. 534. His son Robert in 1170, ib. 519.
[4] Bened. i. 124.
[5] Walt. Cov. ii. 225.
[6] Bened. i. 161, 165 ; Walt. Cov. i. 308.
[7] Bened. i. 339; Hoveden, ii. 303, 305.
[8] Gir. Camb. Exp. Hib. ii. 36 (Opp. v. 388).
[9] As early as 1183 Henry proposed

that John should have his mother's inheritance, Richard being now his father's heir. Richard refused : Bened. i. 308. The next year he is allowed to invade Richard's states : Bened. i. 311. The jealousy of the brothers goes on increasing, and in 1189 Richard, believing that his father intended to disinherit him, refused to go to Palestine unless John were sent with him : Bened. ii. 66. The same year the king proposed to marry him to Alesia, who had been long betrothed to Richard : Hoveden, ii. 363.
[10] Gir. Camb. De Inst. Princ. iii. 26 Hoveden, ii. 366.

ship and interest in his father's game. Devoid of sound principle and incapable of reading the secrets of Henry's design, he learned to grasp at the advantage of the moment, to trust as no other prince of his age did to the chapter of accidents; having as yet nothing very great to risk, to hazard what he had on the throw of the instant, or, without troubling himself about present losses, to leave all to the chances of the future. Richard and Eleanor saw probably that this was the case, and that, devoid as he was of either force of character or strength of principle, the only chance of keeping him safe and innocuous was to intrust him with a substantial gift of power. He might be steadied by permanent and engrossing interests of his own. His marriage was accordingly pressed on, and that done, Richard, in the lavish improvidence of his heart, touched, perhaps, by remorse for his conduct to his father, and showing it in his bounty to the favourite, heaped on him an enormous appanage,[1] merely guarding himself by the retention of some of the castles of his honours.

John a political gambler

Richard tries to steady him by the gift of power

Notwithstanding the plausibility of the view that prompted this measure, Richard showed his usual shortsightedness by such exaggerated confidence, or else he was over-persuaded by Eleanor's influence in John's favour. Richard had a most contemptuous opinion of his brother's abilities,[2] and perhaps was not quite aware of the extent to which he was himself influenced by the spirit of hazard. John, it might seem, would be faithful if intrusted with the substance of power; if not, he was too weak to be dangerous. But there were other elements of danger besides John, and Richard really risked the welfare of his kingdom on the issue. So long as he was by Eleanor's side, he might be kept in order; but the return of Philip from the crusade, and his obstinate underhand policy, which Richard might have learned, so long and persistently had it been tried upon himself, he, clearly, had not calculated on.[3]

Bad policy of this liberal treatment

But in the true gambling spirit, John, instead of contenting himself with his improved position, used it simply to play a still more dangerous game. The oath which Richard had demanded from him on his departure for the crusade, binding him to absent himself for three years from England, was remitted at his mother's request,[4] and no sooner had the king fairly started than John returned. And here he immmediately found himself in a situation full of temptation and full of opportunity. Rich beyond his earlier dreams, holding the actual administration of a broad belt of

John's rashness and ingratitude during Richard's absence on the crusade

---

[1] Bened. ii. 73, 78, 99.
[2] 'Johannes frater meus non est homo qui sibi vi terram subjiciat, si fuerit qui vim ejus vi saltem tenui re-

pellat.' Hoveden, iii. 198.
[3] Hoveden, iii. pref. pp. lii, sqq. lxxxvii, sqq.
[4] Ric. Devizes, p. 15.

His position somewhat tantalising

territory covering the fairest counties of middle and southern England ; already, as the eldest adult prince of the royal house, attracting to his court all the elements of opposition to the royal officials ; entitled, by his titular sovereignty of Ireland, to all the retinue and pomp, if not to the name of royalty ; he yet saw himself with no recognised position of authority ; the most powerful baron, but not the regent ; the nearest in blood, but not the heir ; close to the throne in both ways, but with no definite claim on the succession or inherent hold on power. Between him and the throne stood young Arthur, the recognised heir, growing more dangerous every year ; and between him and the regency, not only his mother, whom even her love for him could not bend beyond a certain point of compliance, but the rough, unpopular, yet very able justiciar, the king's constitutional lieutenant, a man unscrupulous, insolent, unjust, but indisputably faithful.[1]

His first object is to supplant Arthur as heir

Next to supplant Richard himself

He obtains recognition as heir, and intrigues against Richard

To secure the succession to the exclusion of Arthur was John's first aim ; had not King Henry purposed to exclude Richard to make him king ?[2] Next, to supplant Richard himself by Philip's aid, and trust to the chances of his death or captivity for an escape from his vengeance. A hazardous game, but not the less tempting. The first step was to unseat the justiciar. After two desultory struggles John succeeded in effecting this, and in obtaining from the baronage a more or less occult engagement to accept him as heir to the crown.[3] So great a success was too much for him ; he could not wait ; if he had let England alone, Richard might and probably would never have returned from Palestine. He took the readiest way to bring him home. In vain the warning voice of Eleanor pleaded, commanded, and reproached ;[4] as soon as the king of France returned John entered into his designs at once. The threat of forfeiture brought him to his mother's side, but he was not proof against a bribe. The exiled chancellor purchased his promise to consent to his return ; the barons offered a higher sum ;[5] John withdrew the promise and left his old competitor in the lurch.

His conspiracy with Philip of France

Then came the news of Richard's capture, and again John was in France conspiring with Philip. Now raising money for the ransom and putting it in his own pocket ;[6] now offering the emperor a

[1] Hoveden, iii. pref. xl–xliii.
[2] Hoveden, ii. 363. The words of the historian may be interpreted merely of Henry's intention to exclude Richard from the succession to the continental estates, as in Gir. Camb. De Inst. Princ. p. 91 ; but it is observable that he never allowed homage to be done to Richard as his successor either in England or in Normandy.

[3] Hoveden, iii. pref. lix, lxxix.
[4] Itiner. R. Ricardi, p. 359 ; Ric. Devizes, p. 57 ; Bened. ii. 237.
[5] R. Devizes, p. 59 ; Bened. ii. 239 ; Hoveden, iii. 188 ; Gir. Camb. V. Gaufr. Ang. Sac. ii. 402.
[6] The measures taken in 1193 for ascertaining the amount of his receipts on this head put the fact beyond a doubt. Hoveden, iii. 217.

bribe to prolong the captivity;[1] now brought by his mother to reason, now tempted by Philip to hazard a larger stake; unable to defend his own servants, and unwilling to make the least sacrifice, he fails signally on both sides. The barons, who had clung to him as the leader of the constitutional opposition, will have nothing to say to him as a traitor; even those who were afterwards the most faithful to him took the leading part in his discomfiture: the same week [2] saw him excommunicated and condemned to forfeiture by the man who was afterwards to be his prime minister, and the return of Richard, which he had been unable to prevent, found him an abject suppliant. Humiliated as he was, he was too mean for Richard's vengeance.[3] He pardoned and enriched him, but he trusted him no more. Failure of his attempt against Richard

Up to the time of Richard's death it may be safely affirmed that John had shown none of the qualities that would have fitted him to reign; not even the energy which comes out on one or two occasions in his later career. If it had in any considerable degree depended on himself, he would never have reigned. The uncertainty of the rule of succession, which is so often adduced in illustration of our early history, is scarcely anywhere brought out more clearly than on this occasion. It is probable that Richard had never seriously considered the subject before he received his death-wound. Arthur had been, early in the reign, put forward as the heir, in the idea possibly of repressing the ambition of John, for Richard was not of an age to despair of having children of his own; and later on there were indications that Otho of Saxony, to whom he had given the county of Poictou, and for whom he had tried to secure the succession to the throne of Scotland, might be substituted for the nearer claimant.[4] But in the year before Richard's death Otho had been chosen king of Germany, and Arthur only remained in John's way. Richard on his deathbed set Arthur finally aside,[5] and that we may suppose for good reasons, although John did his best to discredit them. Eleanor's influence was used for John, and the most faithful Uncertainty of John's prospect of succeeding to the crown He is recognised as heir at Richard's deathbed

[1] Hoveden, iii. 229, 232.
[2] Hoveden, iii. 236, 237.
[3] Itin. R. Ricardi, p. 449. 'Excellentia siquidem animi dedignabatur inferiorem punire; reputans sibi sufficere se posse vendicare.'
[4] Richard left Otho his jewels: Hoveden, iv. 83. Otho's presumptive claim is recognised by the pope in 1216, although his elder brother Henry the Count Palatine was alive : R. Wendover, iii. 375. It is observable also that Otho had already, early in

Richard's reign, been promised the counties of York and Poictou, and that, although he was elected king of Germany by his uncle's influence, that influence Richard had intended to be used in favour of his elder brother Henry, thus leaving Otho free for any further provision that might be made for him. Hoveden, iv. 38. Henry, however, was in Palestine when the election took place.
[5] Hoveden, iv. 83.

of Richard's ministers made it their business to carry out his final disposition.

Opposition to his succession, in Anjou and Maine;

But for this John would have had little chance of being king. Both in England and on the continent there were strong parties against him. In France the barons of Maine and Anjou were anxious to have Arthur for their count; they had been in the interest of his father, and had a close connexion with Brittany, which his mother Constantia had striven to maintain. At her instigation they rose on the news of Richard's death, declared for Arthur, and placed him

put down by himself and his mother

in the hands of Philip as his legal guardian.[1] Eleanor thereupon took the command of Richard's mercenaries and reduced Anjou to obedience,[2] whilst John enforced the submission of Maine. In England there was a strong party which was unwilling to accept John at all, or prepared to accept him only under very definite conditions; and there the securing of the crown depended on the services of Richard's ministers.

Opposition among the English barons

It would be very interesting if we could ascertain the exact standing-ground and programme of the opposition, but only the names of the leaders are known, and they seem to have been only

Rigorous administration of Richard's last years

partially actuated by dislike to John. In truth the administration of the last few years of Richard's reign had been somewhat rigorous,[3] and his absence from England a matter of policy. Hubert Walter had carried out Henry's system of abridging the power of the great nobles : not a few of the heirs to earldoms had been for some years uninvested,[4] and therefore deprived of a portion of their revenues ; and the adjustment of their rights, which was to become an important rallying point in the later part of the reign, was loudly

Attempt of the barons to make terms with John

called for.[5] It is not unlikely that, whilst accepting John as an ultimate necessity, they would still try to make good conditions. Besides these there were a few who had always hated him : Richard

His political and personal foes

de Clare, earl of Hertford, the husband of one of the disinherited daughters of Gloucester, and the ally of the justiciar in the struggle of 1191 ;[6] the earl of Chester, who had married Constantia of Brittany, and whose policy halted between the temptation of being stepfather to a king and the hatred of his unfaithful wife ;[7] David of Huntingdon, whose line would be dictated by his brother the king of Scots, and who would attempt by prolonged neutrality to keep open the question of restoring Northumberland and Cumberland to him. The heads of the houses of Mowbray, Ferrers, and Beaumont

[1] Hoveden, iv. 86, 87.
[2] Hoveden, iv. 88.
[3] Hoveden, above, p. 302.
[4] It is observable that even William Marshall and Geoffrey Fitz Peter were not formally invested until

the coronation of John. Hoveden iv. 90.
[5] Hoveden, iv. 88.
[6] Hoveden, iii. 137.
[7] Hoveden, ii. 325 ; iv. 7, 97.

were also suspected, on the general ground, it would seem, of their hereditary opposition and strong feudal antecedents. But the prompt action of the ministers of Richard decided the point. Hubert Walter, Geoffrey Fitz Peter, and William Marshall summoned the barons to Northampton before they had had time to communicate with one another, and there by promises and arguments obtained their adhesion.[1] Not a voice was raised in England for Arthur, and Hubert on the day of coronation was enabled to appeal safely to the assembled baronage on behalf of John as the elective king.[2]

They are brought over by Hubert Walter

John elected

The strength of John at the beginning of his reign consisted chiefly in the support of four persons : his mother Eleanor, who maintained by prestige and intrigue his hold on the continent ; Hubert Walter, Geoffrey Fitz Peter, and William Marshall, who, as the chief officers in church and state, continued the régime of Henry II. in England. Their support was strong enough not merely to obtain his succession, but to keep up his position for many years, notwithstanding his neglect of their advice and the many acts of tyranny and folly which they strove in vain to counteract. And it is important to note that just as the position of the Angevin dynasty in France collapses on the death of Eleanor, so in England the death of Hubert Walter marks the break-up of friendly relations between the king and the church, and the death of Geoffrey Fitz Peter the final rupture with the baronage ; after which the very existence of the royal line depends for years on the adhesion of William Marshall and on the political influence of a new agency, the direct interference of the popes. Under these heads it may be convenient to range the points of remark which present themselves in this general view of the reign.

Important position of Eleanor, Hubert Walter, Geoffrey Fitz Peter, and William Marshall

John's power collapses on the death of his mother and his ministers

Few women have had less justice done them in history than Eleanor. I do not speak of her moral qualities : although probably her faults have been exaggerated, she can hardly be said to shine as a virtuous woman or a good wife ; but of her remarkable political power and her great influence, not only in her husband's states, but in Europe generally ; of her great energy, not less conspicuous than her husband's, both in early youth and extreme old age, there can be

Career of Eleanor

Her energy and long activity

---

[1] Hoveden, iv. 88. Ralph of Coggeshall, however, seems to say that the country was already in the greatest confusion; and that the barons or some of them broke into open ravages on Easter day, having received the news of Richard's death the day before (ed. Dunkin, 170).

[2] Doubt is thrown on Hubert's famous speech on this occasion, in which he distinctly declares the elective character of the English crown, because it is not mentioned by Roger of Wendover, but is inserted by Matthew Paris, and, considering his strong views on constitutional points, might be regarded as a composition of his own. But it is referred to distinctly by Lewis of France in his delaration against John in 1216. Fœd. i. 140. See also Dr. Pauli's note, Gesch. v. Engl. iii. 297.

no question. In an age of short-lived heroes one scarcely realises the length of her adventurous life or the great area of her wanderings. Fifty years before this she had gone on crusade, and by her undisguised flirtations had spread confusion and dismay and discord in the noblest host that ever went to the East.[1] Her divorce had overthrown the balance of power in two kingdoms, producing in one of them a disruption which it required four hundred years of warfare to remedy. Her quarrel with her second husband long retarded the reforming schemes of his great administrative genius, and consigned her to fourteen years of captivity. Yet those fourteen years appear but a short episode in her long life. Henry's death brought her from prison to supreme power.[2] As Richard's representative in England, she repressed the ambition of John and thwarted the designs of Philip; she found time and strength, at seventy, to journey to Messina with a wife for her son,[3] to Rome on an embassy,[4] and to Germany with the ransom that her energy had helped to accumulate.[5] After a few years of rest she is again on foot at Richard's death. To her inspiration John owed his throne; her

Her long journeys in her old age

---

[1] Richard of Devizes, who writes with a barbed pen, says of her, ' Regina Alienor, femina incomparabilis, pulchra et pudica, potens et modesta, humilis et diserta, quod in femina solet inveniri rarissime ; quæ non minus annosa quam quæ duos reges maritos habuerat et duos reges filios, adhuc ad omnes indefessa labores, posse cujus ætas sua mirari potuit . . . Multi noverunt quod utinam nemo nostrum nosset. Hæc ipsa regina tempore prioris mariti fuit Hierosolymis. Nemo plus inde loquatur ; et ego bene novi. Silete' (p. 25). The facts of the case seem to be these : Eleanor and her first husband went together on the second crusade, he as a monk, she in the usual spirit of a gay and courtly pilgrim. Her extravagance was encouraged by her uncle, the prince of Antioch, who hoped through her influence to sway the councils of Lewis ; and in this he failed. Lewis was made doubly miserable by the levity and by the political meddling of his wife. William of Tyre puts the case well (lib. xvii. c. 8) : ' injuriarum memor, quas in via et in toto peregrinationis tractu uxor ei irrogaverat.' The king divorced her on his return home. The divorce took place in 1154, so that he must have nursed his grievances for nearly seven years. From William of New-

burgh, however, it would seem more probable that Eleanor herself desired the divorce, owing to incompatibility of temper, or to a passion she had formed for Henry. From the fact of the divorce orginated the stories of her criminal misbehaviour ; for these William of Tyre is answerable, though not intentionally, his statement being clearly based on his inference from the divorce : ' erat, ut præmisimus, sicut et prius et postmodum manifestis edocuit indiciis, mulier imprudens, et contra dignitatem regiam legem negligens maritalem, thori conjugalis fidem oblita ' (lib. xvi. c. 27). On this basis'the Romancers very early concocted an amour of Eleanor with a Saracen knight, and later identified the knight with Saladin himself : ' la ducoise Elienor qui fu male feme . . . quant la roine Elienor vi la defaute (moleche et nichete) que li rois avoit en lui, et elle oï parler de la bonté et dou sens et de la proueche Salhedin,' she offered to elope with him. Chron. de Rains, pp. 4, 5. The divorce was the origin, not the result of the accusations. The innuendos of Giraldus, De Instr. Pr. iii. 152, are of the same value.

[2] Benedict, ii. 74 ; Hoveden, iii. 4.
[3] Bened. ii. 157 ; Hoveden, iii. 95.
[4] Hoveden, iii. 100.
[5] Hoveden, iii. 226, 233.

influence excluded, no doubt, the unhappy, misguided Arthur; she herself took the command of the forces that reduced his friends in Anjou to submission;[1] she travelled to Spain to fetch the grand-daughter whose marriage was to be a pledge of peace between France and England.[2] She outlived, it would seem, the grandchild who had outraged her. She lived long enough to see Philip's first attacks on Normandy;[3] from her deathbed she was writing to the barons to keep them in their allegiance,[4] and her death at the age of eighty-two was followed by the subversion of all the continental projects of her husband. But her own dominions in great part remained to her son's son, as if her mighty shade were able to defend them at least from the hated offspring of Lewis VII. *Her dominions previously served to John's descendants*

Eleanor no doubt loved John as her youngest son; she seems to have disliked Arthur and his mother, moreover, for their own sakes. Further, little as she had loved Henry II., she was naturally averse to the dismemberment of his empire. Hence, notwithstanding her great age at the time of Richard's death, she set herself heartily to work to remedy the existing dangers, to resume the negotiations for peace which had been begun by Richard just before, and to complete the pacification by detaching Philip from Arthur's side. And this she succeeded in doing, although not without aid from other sources. Philip had for the moment discarded the pretext of helping Arthur, and was warring on his own account;[5] the Angevins were thus induced to throw themselves and their chosen count into the arms of John; the example was followed by a crowd of French nobles who had quarrelled with Philip, and he himself was at the moment threatened with an interdict.[6] Taking advantage of the crisis, Eleanor brought hastily from Spain her grand-daughter Blanche of Castile, and, by the bestowal of a few Norman counties as her marriage portion, John obtained a peace which lasted until Philip's difficulties ended. Then in 1202 war broke out again; Philip declared John to be, as a contumacious vassal,[7] deprived of his fiefs; *Her exertions for the reconciliation of John and Philip*

Conclusion of peace in 1200

---

[1] Hoveden, iv. 88.

[2] Hoveden, iv. 107, 114.

[3] On the 22nd of July, 1202, Eleanor had licence to dispose of her revenue by will: Rot. Pat. i. 14. A few days after, she was besieged in Mirabel and rescued by John, on the 1st of August: R. Coggeshall, ed. Dunkin, p. 210.

[4] There are two letters enrolled on the Charter Rolls of 1201 of great interest; one from the viscount of Thouars and another from Eleanor, both addressed to John, and giving an account of an interview between the

two writers at Fontevraud, where Eleanor had invited the viscount to visit her, and had obtained from him a promise of fidelity to John. Rot. Chart. pp. 102, 103.

[5] Hoveden, iv. 96. Philip's refusal to surrender Ballon to Arthur opened the eyes of the Angevins. The French malcontents were in treaty with John before (ib. p. 95), as they had been with Richard.

[6] Hoveden, iv. 94, 112.

[7] The summons was addressed to John as Philip's liegeman for Anjou and Poictou, and the day fixed for the

Attack and extinction of Arthur

Arthur in the most foolish and wanton way attacked his grand-mother at Mirabel; there he was defeated and taken by John;[1] his imprisonment at Falaise followed, and his final disappearance; which left the disaffected and alienated barons of Normandy no alternative but the choice between Philip and John.[2]

The Norman kings had never ruled without a competitor

And this was a state of things which had not existed since the early days of William Rufus; and even then, in Stephen of Aumale, the Norman barons had found a competitor for their support in rivalry with the son of the Bastard. Henry I. during the whole of his reign knew that there was a strong party in favour of his brother and nephew. Stephen and Matilda had fought out the quarrel. Against Henry II. his own sons had been set up, and John had been utilised to thwart and irritate Richard, as Arthur in his turn had been used to rouse the fears and compel the good

second Sunday after Easter, 1202; Rigord, p. 202 (ed. Bouquet, xvii. 54); R. Coggeshall, p. 208; R. Wendover, iii. 167. The sequence of events is very obscure. According to William of Armorica (Bouquet, xvii. 75), John pledged two castles, Tillières and Botteavant, for his compliance with the summons; on John's non-appearance the castles were seized. So also Alberic of Trois Fontaines, p. 423. Ralph of Coggeshall asserts that the summons was made at the suit of Hugh le Brun and Ralph of Eu, 'de nimia infestatione,' p. 208.

[1] R. Coggeshall, pp. 210, 211 (ed. Dunkin).

[2] Le Baud, in his history of Brittany (Paris, 1638), gives a circumstantial account of the proceedings taken by the Bretons on the news of the death of Arthur: they assembled at Vannes in great force, the historian naming the barons and bishops who were present. They determined to complain to Philip, and sent by Bishop Peter of Rennes a formal charge against John demanding that he should be summoned before a court of the peers of France; 'et, non comparant, fut fait son procez solemnellement, et par celle Cour des Pers fut donnee contre luy sentence diffinitive par arrest, de la quelle il fut dit et declaré que pour sa desloyaute, et pour son crime de parricide et de majesté leze, toutes et chacunes ses seigneuries qu'il tenoit du dit Roy Philippe estoient et seroient confisquees à la coronne de France et y furent unies' (p. 210). See also

Morice, Hist. de Bretagne, i. 132, who says that the charge was made fifteen days after the murder. Le Baud quotes as his authority Robert Blondel, who wrote the 'Reductio Normanniæ' in the fifteenth century. This work is published in the Rolls series: it contains no mention of the matter; and Le Baud's reference is probably to Blondel's 'Oratio Historialis,' which is yet in MS. The value of Le Baud's account consists simply in its circumstantial character. Knighton, c. 2420, gives the same account less circumstantially, but without date. The earliest statement seems to be that contained in Lewis's proclamation, in 1216, Fæd. i. 140; 'satis notum est quomodo de murdro Arturi nepotis sui, in curia karissimi domini regis Franciæ, cujus ambo erant homines ligii, per pares suos citatus et per eosdem pares tandem condempnatus.' See Wendover, iii. 373; M. Paris, p. 283. The second process must have taken place in 1203, where it is placed in the Chronicle of Lanercost, p. 2. 'Rex Johannes citatus ad parliamentum super forisfacturis suis et semper procrastinans, tandem ibi conventus, Normanniam pro nece innocentis amisit.' If Arthur's death was believed to have occurred in Holy Week, 1203 (Apr. 3, Ann. Margam, 27), and Philip's march began a fortnight after Easter (Rigord, 204), the date may be closely approximated to. The account of the trial in the Margam Annals is noteworthy.

behaviour of John. The disappearance or death of Arthur not only shocked the Norman and English nobles, who were now far advanced beyond the barbarism which had tolerated the brutal cruelties of Henry I. ; but it also showed them that they must face for the first time a king who would rule without a competitor. Among the descendants of Henry in the female line there was not as yet anyone recognised as fit to succeed on John's defeasance. The Saxon dukes had claims enough of their own to struggle for. Raymond of Toulouse was out of the question. King Alfonso was too far away, and his rights had devolved (so the French said) on his daughter ; and to accept Lewis was the same thing as to accept Philip. And this the Normans seem to have thought the best course ; a series of defections begins immediately on Arthur's capture. John showed no intention of repelling the attacks of Philip, and his English barons took leave of him in shame and disgust. The second sentence of forfeiture issued by Philip, a thing which in ordinary times would have roused the vassals to an indignant assertion of the rights of their lord, seems to have had now the effect of an ecclesiastical excommunication. It paralysed ·John's few friends, and gave his many enemies the excuse for desertion or open hostility which they were anxiously seeking. In the meantime the southern provinces were bitterly provoked by the circumstances of John's second marriage, and only the life of Eleanor stood between him and entire forfeiture there also.[1]

It is unfortunate that the historians have not preserved the dates of the death of Arthur and the second sentence of forfeiture. It seems, however, certain that Eleanor, who died in the spring of

The barons have no choice but between John and Philip

Second sentence of forfeiture

Alienation of the south

Eleanor dies in 1204

[1] Eleanor made over Poictou to John as her heir in September 1199, Rot. Chart. p. 30 ; but wisely received his homage for it, so that during her life there could be no hazard of forfeiture to the suzerain. She had previously the same year done homage for it to Philip : Rigord, ap. Bouquet, xvii. 50. The possession of the fief of Poictou must always have been complicated by its union with the duchy of Aquitaine. Richard had been made both duke and count in 1176 or 1179, whether or not to the exclusion of his mother's title : but in 1185 he had been compelled to restore Poictou and probably the duchy also to his mother. Her rights, whether lost for the time or not, reverted to her at the end of his reign. During that reign, however, she was still duchess of Aquitaine, Richard was also duke, and under him Otho was count of Poictou. On Richard's death, Otho's tenure being supposed to lapse at his election in Germany, she renewed her own title by doing homage to Philip (for the duchy), and then received that of John as count. Yet John also calls himself duke of Aquitaine. It would be tedious, if not uninteresting, to work out the legal bearing of the several titles, all different, by which the duchy of Normandy, the counties of Anjou and Maine, and the duchy of Aquitaine and county of Poictou, were held ; certainly the legal difficulties were much greater than Philip's hasty sentences of forfeiture could solve ; John did homage to Philip for Brittany as well as for his other lands in 1200, R. Coggeshall, 172.

1204, must have survived both events; but we lose sight of her
personal action after the battle of Mirabel.[1] John's fortunes in
France could not survive his contemptuous negligence; after that
victory his vanity became insufferable, and when he had alienated
the barons by whose sword and counsel it was won it became
contemptible. The whole of his continental dominion slipped out of
his hand.[2] The grand inheritance of the sons of Rollo; the conquests of William in Maine and the Vexin; all the peculations of
the Angevins in Brittany and Touraine; the coveted and but lately
secured superiority of Brittany: all that Henry and Richard had
plotted and fought for, was lost without one strong blow struck to
save it. And it was lost needlessly; notwithstanding the turbulent
insubordination which was inherent in the Norman baronage, so
many of them still had estates in England that, at the very lowest
estimate, revolt must have cost them dear; all the relations of the
clergy were with England rather than with France : the commons
of Normandy had enjoyed under their dukes a semblance of English
liberty. Henry II. had legislated for Normandy as well as for
England, [3] and had never touched the rights that set the free
Norman, on most social and legal points, far above the mere Frenchman. Nor could the hostility of three centuries, during which
Norman and Frenchman had been continuously struggling, have
failed to create an abiding feeling of separate interests and traditions.
But neither self-interest nor sentiment availed to save John. The
great families began to divide their heritages : the French estates,
impoverished by neglect and non-residence, might go to the younger
sons and cousins, if they could avoid forfeiture ; and they might do

Decline of John's fortunes in France

He throws away Normandy

The Normans were more closely connected with England than with France

Absence of any feeling for John in Normandy

---

[1] The date of Eleanor's death is
given by Sandford (p. 60) as June 26,
1202, at Mirabel, the year being certainly two years wrong. The day
seems to depend on an entry in the
Necrology of the monastery of Fontevraud, printed in Bouquet among the
notes to Ralph of Coggeshall, vol.
xviii. p. 98. The Annals of Waverley,
however, say distinctly (p. 256),
' Alienor regina obiit in kalendis
Aprilis.' And this would seem to be
the true date, for John, in an ordinance for the bakers of Winchester
(Rot. Pat. i. 41), issued April 15, 1204,
says, ' facta est autem hæc constitutio
ad Pascha proximum post obitum
Alienoræ Reginæ matris meæ.' Easter
fell on the 25th of April in 1204. On
the 2nd of May John confirms a gift
to Fontevraud ' pro salute animæ
Alienoræ Reginæ,' Rot. Chart. p. 127.

[2] When the castellans of Normandy
applied to him in 1204, ' per nuncios
significavit omnibus, ut nullum ab
ipso exspectarent auxilium, sed
facerent singuli quod sibi melius
videbatur.' Wendover, iii. 181 ; M.
Paris, 212.
[3] See the passage quoted from
Robert de Monte in the preface to
Benedict, vol. ii. p. lix (R.S.), which
shows that Henry was employed in
legal reforms in Normandy as early
as 1160. Geoffrey's ordinance on
primogeniture in Brittany is also
probably his handiwork. The simila-
rities and differences between Norman
and English law at the middle of the
thirteenth century will be seen well
illustrated in the *Codex Legum Nor-
mannicarum*, printed in J. P. de
Ludewig's Reliquiæ Manuscriptorum,
vol vii. pp. 149-418.

homage to King Philip:[1] the English barons were rich enough to spare their Norman farms, and not unwilling to escape the responsibility of defending them. The great earls could make their own bargains;[2] the bishops,[3] the slowest to move because safest and strongest in neutrality, made no sign of adhesion to the fallen house. The two limbs of the great inheritance parted without a struggle. In Anjou and Touraine there was not even a sign of reluctance;[4] no great English estates had been accumulated by the barons of those lands, nor had their separation from the body of France ever been so complete as that of Normandy. Aquitaine, with the exception of Gascony, went for the moment the same way.[5]

Thus the territorial work of the Conquest was undone.[6] With how great advantage to the English it is unnecessary now to work out at length. It is sufficient to observe that the kings could no longer look on Normandy as their natural home, but found themselves obliged to live face to face with their people. The people, gaining strength at the same time from other causes, learned to look with less tolerance on the vices, and to endure with less patience the extortions, of the kings. The long-existing confusion between the duties of the barons as English and as Norman feudatories ceased: John's loss of Normandy undoes the territorial work of William the Conqueror

[1] A list of the barons of Normandy who, like Baldwin Wake, adhered to John; who like the Hommets adhered to Philip; or like the Longchamps divided into branches, would be an invaluable help to the reading of the earlier as well as the later history: and considerable materials for it are already in print in the *Rotuli Normanniæ* of Stapleton, and in the Rolls of the Reign of John, edited by Sir T. D. Hardy, especially the *Rotuli Normanniæ*, i. 122–143. The county of Aumale is the best known and most curious instance of the effects of the change of lords: the conquest of Normandy having turned the English estates of the dignity into an English earldom with a foreign title, the earldom of Albemarle.

[2] The earl of Chester received Richmond and Dovedale in compensation for his Norman estates: Ann. Wigorn.

[3] Among them Walter of Coutances, whose early career was entirely English, who had been vice-chancellor, bishop, and justiciar in England; Henry de Beaumont of Bayeux, who had been on the closest terms with Henry II. and Geoffrey of York, and was a kinsman of the earls of Leicester and Warwick; and Jordan de Humet of Lisieux, a member of the family which gave constables to Normandy under Henry and Richard.

[4] W. Cov. ii. 197. 'Johannes quippe a suis destitutus Normannia recesserat.' It is one story of mutual mistrust; the garrison of Andeli surrendered 'eo quod de subventione regis sui diffidebant.' John could bring them no succour, 'eo quod suorum proditionem semper timeret.' R. Coggeshall, 217, 218. Rouen and Verneuil were lost for the same reason, 'eo quod quorundam suorum proditionem suspectam haberet.' Ib. 219. This seems on some occasions to have amounted to a panic on the king's part; as when he shut himself up for a fortnight in Nottingham castle: Ann. Margam, 32. The story is repeated again in 1214 in Poictou, where Wendover amusingly describes John and Lewis, both at the head of strong armies, running away from each other. Wend. iii. 287; M. Paris, 250.

[5] R. Coggeshall (ed. Dunkin), p. 220; W. Cov. ii.

[6] The prophecy of Merlin was fulfilled. 'Gladius a sceptro separatus est.' R. Cogg. p. 219; Ann. Wigorn. p. 407.

the constant influx of foreigners regarded as half English because
they were Norman was stopped ; and England began to be ruled
more distinctly on national principles, for English purposes and by
Englishmen. The crown became more distinctly dependent on the
goodwill of the nation, and the nation became, more than it had
been since the Conquest, both in church and state, in law and
revenue, in war and peace, distinctly conscious of its unity, and, so
to speak, of its personal identity. The fusion of the races was
accomplished under Henry II. ; but the loss of Normandy had the
effect of separating the consolidated mass from the extraneous
matter which was still mechanically attached to it.

The death of Eleanor, who had impersonated and concentrated
the political influence of the family in France and on the continent
generally, was followed in little more than a year by that of the
archbishop Hubert Walter, who had played the Lanfranc to the
second Rufus. The parallel is by no means merely superficial,
different as were the antecedents and the characters, probably, of the
two prelates. As Lanfranc had placed William Rufus on the
English throne [1] in spite of the deficiency of title and the opposition
of a considerable body of nobles who maintained the rights of
the heir, so Hubert had secured the succession of John. And the
authority which Lanfranc as long as he lived exercised over William,
Hubert exercised as long as he lived over John : by personal influence
with him he repressed his more extreme attempts at tyranny,[2] and
by his influence with the baronage he obtained the most patient
toleration, and put the best colour on the character, of his acts.
Hubert had done this in the affairs of the state as well as in those of
the church. As finance minister to Richard he had learned how the
country could be taxed with the least outcry and with the greatest
profit ; and of the credit which his financial successes procured him
he had availed himself to improve the facilities for the administration
of justice, and to secure the promotion of good men.[3] Richard had
had an unfeigned respect for him, earned no doubt by the common
endurance of great perils and privations in Palestine, and by the
services which had gained the regard of Saladin in the East [4] and
Henry VI. in the West.
Everything that Hubert had done for Richard he had done for
John, having as chancellor even a more intimate intercourse with
him and more constant occasion for remonstrance and reproof.

---

[1] Eadmer (ed. Selden), pp. 13, 14.
[2] As, for example, in his attack on
the Cistercians in 1200 : R. Coggeshall,
p. 181.
[3] Hoveden, above, pp. 186–199.

[4] Itiner. R. Ricardi, p. 437. ' Tam
in militia transmarina quam in regimine sanctæ sedis Cantuariensis
ecclesiæ floruerat.' R. Coggeshall,
p. 234.

John might have been sensible of the merits, ungrateful as he was for the support of Hubert, for notwithstanding the decisive line that he had taken against him when in arms against Richard, he had never maintained, as William Longchamp had done, the claims of Arthur to the English succession : he, as his uncle Ranulf Glanvill had been,[1] seems to have become through old association at Henry's court, and perhaps by the unconscious influence of the king's affection for his youngest son, personally attached to John ; and his brother Theobald, the chief butler of Ireland, was one of John's ministers long before he came to the crown. But John was incapable of gratitude as of every other better sentiment. He had felt the indispensable and irrefutable counsels of the archbishop to be a curb on his instinct for unbridled tyranny.

There are indications that Hubert's influence was on the wane in political affairs before his death. But the immediate result of it— and it is this that gives force to the parallel with Lanfranc—was the rupture of that tacit concordat between the hierarchy and the sovereign which had been instituted by the Conqueror and his great adviser, and which had, with the two great exceptions of S. Anselm and S. Thomas, been maintained by the representative men of the church for a century and a half. *His influence diminished before his death. His death was the signal for the break-up of the concordat between king and clergy*

The principle of this arrangement had been the permission of as much spiritual and ecclesiastical liberty to the clergy as was consistent with the fulfilment of the obligations of citizenship, as understood under a mainly feudal constitution. The Anglo-Saxon system had been too hierarchical. In that respect, as in some others, it was possible only in a state in which the differences of race and religious and political views were few. The Danes had accepted it as a part of English Christianity ; but the Norman Conquest introduced a foreign race, a foreign baronage, and a hierarchy obnoxious to the influences of the Hildebrandine awakening. And it was to meet this that the king and archbishop on the one hand organised the spiritual courts as distinct from the secular, whilst on the other hand they bound the conquered and the conquerors by the feudal tie, covering uniformly the ecclesiastical as well as the merely territorial relations. The bishops became on the one side barons and on the other free and spiritual judges ; as barons they were bound to the feudal obligations, as spiritual judges they claimed for themselves and for their clergy immunity from the secular tribunals. Such a concordat left, however, very many points unsettled, especially that of election to bishoprics, which had been the bone of contention in all the countries of the West, and was ultimately settled, on different *Relation of church and state under the Norman kings* *Church measures of William the Conqueror and Lanfranc*

[1] Gir. Camb. Exp. Hib. p. 380.

principles and in the course of many centuries, according‘ to the
particular circumstances of each national church. It was in England
left to the good understanding between the king and the higher
clergy, being in theory free, but in practice a matter of arrangement
between the king, the chapters, and the consecrating primate : and
of course a pacific carrying out of such an arrangement required
delicate handling on the part of each.

It had been in the main a successful device, although in the
Norman reigns the terrors of the king's court had at least as much
to do with the submission of the chapters as had the manipulation
of the archbishop. The only serious case of disputed election which
had yet occurred was that to York [1] in the reign of Stephen, at a
moment when the king was very weak, when the emancipation of
the disputed see from the obedience of Canterbury had been just
vindicated, and when the hands of both king and archbishop were
tied by the legation of Henry of Winchester. The death of Hubert
Walter not only made the vacancy which proved the object of contention, but removed the influence by which only the contention
could under other circumstances have been allayed.

It is necessary, however, to take a wider view of the circumstances,
and to regard the extent to which the quarrel that followed Hubert's
death was the break-up of the old relations between the church and
the Crown. The particular circumstances are in this aspect less
important; indeed the power of monasticism—and it was monasticism
that provoked the struggle—was so much on the wane that it ceases
henceforth to be one of the motive forces or colouring influences of
English political history.[2]

During the long struggle which the Norman kings and their
successors had waged against aggressive feudalism, the clergy had
stood almost to a man on the royal side. In the best of them, nay
in the great majority, it is probable that this attitude was suggested
by the conviction that the strength of the king was the salvation of
the people. With this mingled, no doubt to a large extent, the
desire of vindicating their class immunities, which could only be done
by making their support valuable to the king; but much more than
this is implied in their constant maintenance of the Crown against
the great feudatories. It was not this that placed S. Wulfstan at
the head of the Worcestershire fyrd to put down the rebellion of the
earls ; [3] or that kept the bishops faithful to William Rufus and
Henry I. ; or that united the whole of the clergy in the support of

Marginal notes:

Election of bishops left to the good understanding between king and primate

Only one serious dispute, before the reign of Henry II.

Hubert's death peculiarly unfortunate in this point

Its effects still more extensive and important

Hitherto the clergy had adhered to the king against the feudatories

[1] See the account in John of
Hexham (ed. Twysden), cc. 269, sqq. ;
Tho. Stubbs, cc. 1721, 1722 ; Will.
Newb. lib. i. cc. 17, 26 ; Raine, Fasti

Ebor. i. 210-233.
[2] See preface to Epistt. Cantuar.
above, pp. 436-38.
[3] Flor. W. ap. W. Covent. i. 91.

Henry II. against his sons. The victory of the barons would, as they saw, have been at that time the destruction of the people. From this resulted the constant employment, by the early kings, of clerical ministers ; and their monopoly of state offices of course increased the attachment of the prelates to the Crown as the fountain of honour, profit, and power. Not only were bishoprics the appropriate reward of official labours, but bishops were felt by the kings to have so many interests in common with themselves that they were the safest men to trust. And even the great quarrels with Anselm and Becket did not interrupt this relation ; for although after Becket's desertion (as Henry deemed it) of the royal cause the king tried to commit himself less and less to the bishops as state servants,[1] and to educate a legal nobility of his own to take their place, the bishops supported the Crown against their primates in the latter case as much as in the former ; and the archbishops found more sympathy among the barons than among their brethren. Nor should it have been otherwise so long as the primates were, with the highest motives it may well have been, risking the destruction of national in defence of ecclesiastical liberties. What is true of the bishops is true for other reasons of the lower clergy, who, mostly of English birth and in thorough sympathy with their flocks, viewed the aggressions of the baronage with terror and hatred, and on every occasion supported the government against them. The monks also had until the middle of the twelfth century maintained a national attitude ;[2] but from the reign of Stephen, partly in consequence of the great increase of foundations by barons, who took this method of compounding for their religious duties, and partly because they felt that their obligations to the papacy were stricter than either to the king or to the nation, they either became neutral or tried to thwart the royal policy with respect to the church. Notwithstanding great local influence they were opposed in view and interest to the seculars, whom on every occasion they misrepresented, and out of whose revenues they were endowed.

But the days were come in which a continuance of this relation was no longer possible. Henry II. had not only humiliated the feudal baronage, but created a new one from the ministerial houses, free from the traditions of French feudalism. The machinery of government had been so arranged as very largely to increase the safety and comfort of society, the speedy attainment of justice, and the education of the people in its administration. But the power of the sovereign had enormously increased at the same time and by the same causes, and no adequate checks upon its still further growth were provided in the new system, which had been devised by a royal

Marginal notes:
Employment of clerical ministers by the Norman kings

The bishops had not sympathised with Anselm or Becket

The lower clergy also faithful to the kings

The monks cease to maintain a national attitude

Rivalry of seculars and regulars

Reforms of Henry II. had greatly strengthened the Crown

[1] Bened. i. 346.   [2] Epp. Cantuar. above, pp. 370-73.

brain and carried out by men who saw in the royal power the only safeguard of the church and people. Such power had been safely intrusted to the great monarch who created it, and who throughout his life felt the restraining influence of the old checks which actually he had destroyed. And even Richard, who had spent so few days during his whole reign in England, and had administered the government by safe men, had possessed this power, masked though it may have been in the using. But John stood face to face with his people, an unmitigated tyrant ; a sovereign whose power no constitutional limits as yet restricted, and whom no scruples, no counsel, held back in the exercise, the abusive exercise, of it. The ecclesiastical struggle of his reign comes in, then, most happily to break the old connexion, to make it impossible for the church to become the tool of a despotic king ; and perhaps no less shock would have sufficed.

From this date the clergy had to choose between the Crown and the nation, and they chose the side of the nation ; in spite of or irrespective of the attitude of the papacy, sometimes in sympathy with it and sometimes in opposition to it, they maintained the cause of liberty hand in hand with the barons against the king, as they had before maintained the cause of liberty hand in hand with the king against the barons. Stephen Langton, S. Edmund, Robert Grosteste, Adam Marsh, the Cantilupes, Robert Winchelsey, John Stratford, and William of Wykeham, although men of very different character, struggling in the most dissimilar circumstances and for the most dissimilar proximate ends, form a string of episcopal statesmen whose claims on national gratitude nothing but professional jealousy can overlook or disparage. After the wars of the Roses the constitutional cycle recurs ; again the baronage is annihilated and the king becomes all-powerful ; but then, most unfortunately, the prelates, unsupported either by a new nobility or by a strong and righteous policy at Rome, placed themselves at the mercy of the Crown ; the balance of the estates was overthrown, never to be restored, and England after the fall of Wolsey saw both her political and her religious constitution made the plaything and victim of a tyrant.

When, however, we say that the church struggle of John's reign was in its result a happy thing for English liberty, it must not be forgotten that the parties who waged the struggle were by no means conscious of the line which events were taking, nor even contemplated the result as a contingency. The baronage in particular, although their turn in the battle was to begin as soon as that of the clergy was over, do not seem in the least to have anticipated it.[1]

---

[1] ' Orta est statim discordia inter papam Innocentium et Johannem tyrannum Angliæ, faventibus ei et consentientibus omnibus laicis et

They had their grievances, but they saw no connexion between them and the clerical grievances : did not even see that the victory which should place the church under the king's feet would make him too strong for them to resist. And it is probable that they were not much to blame in this, for in the first place the adroit management of Hubert Walter had covered many of John's worst faults, and the loss of Normandy, which had occupied the king's time largely up to the year 1205, had only just become a certainty; but, secondly, the circumstances of the ecclesiastical quarrel were not such as to invite the sympathies of men like the barons, who had been brought up in the principles of the Constitutions of Clarendon, and saw in appeals to Rome a breach of national organisation, in the triumph of Innocent III. an unprecedented national humiliation. As the struggle proceeded, it was only those of them who had a real zeal for righteousness that would move to thwart the king, who by his usurpation of ecclesiastical revenue was enabled to dispense with heavy general taxation, or that would incur the risk of the injuries which he never hesitated to inflict. The suspension of general taxation must have been really the secret how the king was able to prolong the struggle. The people were under interdict, but the pecuniary burdens were comparatively light.[1] And the interdict was probably observed but loosely [2] after the flight of the bishops. The great

clericis fere universis, sed et viris cujuslibet professionis multis.' Ann. Margam, p. 28.

[1] Or, to put it in the homely way of the monastic annals, ann. 1209, ' Magna tribulatio fuit hoc anno et præterito super omnes ecclesiasticas personas quia a cura Christianitatis omnes fere laici pedem reflectebant; sed victualium plena fuit abundantia.' Ann. Wigorn. 397.

[2] Roger of Wendover states that it was strictly kept, iii. 222. See also Gesta Innoc. iii. c. 131 : but this must not be strictly interpreted, cf. Ann. Dunst. ed. Luard, p. 30. And even better evidence exists in the letters of Innocent himself. One of these (Martene and Durand, Thesaurus, i. 810) contains the forma interdicti. Prayers are to be said and sermons preached on Sundays in the churchyards ; baptisms are to be performed with full service, but in private houses ; confessions may be said as usual ; burials are forbidden in the churchyards, but may be performed anywhere else ; the priests may not attend the funerals of the laity, but

may say the offices of the dead in private houses. The chief burden was of course the cessation of the Eucharistic service, the closing of the churches and churchyards to the laity, and the prohibition of the ceremonies of marriage and extreme unction. Marriages, however, according to the Annals of Dunstable, did take place in the porches of the churches, and the viaticum was given to the dying. In another letter (Ep. xi. 102), dated June 14, 1208, the pope allows the use of chrism in baptism, the old, if new cannot be got ; in the case of the dying, where the viaticum cannot be obtained, ' in hoc casu credimus obtinere, " Crede et manducasti," ' and greatest of all, ' si tamen viris religiosis ab initio licuisset juxta suorum privilegiorum tenorem, exclusis excommunicatis et interdictis, clausis januis, non pulsatis campanis, suppressa voce divina officia celebrare, nec nobis fuisset molestum, nec absonum exstitisset: possetque per illud tam in hoc quam in aliis congruum remedium adhiberi, præsertim ut per oblationem hostiæ salutaris Divina placaretur in

confiscations affected the prelates far more than the parochial clergy, and the latter would in many cases prefer the spiritual welfare of their flocks to a hazardous compliance with the papal sentence. But even if it were not so, it is not to be supposed that the majority of an uneducated population would balance the loss of religious rites against a comparative freedom from taxation such as seems to have prevailed from 1208 to 1213. To this we may attribute the absence of anything like a popular rebellion, and the postponement of the general rising until the end of the religious struggle ; the influence of the chief ministers, Geoffrey Fitz Peter and William Marshall, both of them men of great experience and great territorial importance, being unquestionably both exercised and felt. But some caution is necessary in speaking of the financial history of these years, because our records and chronicles furnish us with but little trustworthy or exact information upon it.

Conduct of Innocent and John It is not, however, difficult to form an accurate estimate on the two points which have been most frequently controverted in relation to this crisis of our history : the conduct and policy of Innocent III. and the conduct and policy of John. In John's conduct there is no occasion to suspect any special criminality greater than imprudent levity and wilful obstinacy in the treatment of a matter of the highest constitutional importance. It is a signal illustration of the extreme measures into which an unprincipled man may be drawn, without any definitely malicious intention, by his own lack of counsel and unscrupulousness in circumstances which require patient, con-

John was gradually drawn into his extreme position scientious, and yet politic treatment. There is no reason to suppose that John had conceived, or was capable of conceiving, a deliberate plan for suppressing the liberty of the church or throwing off the influence of the pope ; at the worst his design in the first instance was but to place a creature of his own on the archiepiscopal throne, a measure which was only twice attempted during the middle ages by any English sovereign, and in both instances with the greatest danger to the state. And on the other side we should not

Innocent followed the traditional policy of the Curia exaggerate the aggressiveness of Innocent III. The curiously elaborate and persistent policy of the court of Rome has invested that body, in the mind of historians and politicians, with a sort of personal idiosyncrasy, which is very slightly affected by the special characteristics of the individual who happens to be pope ; and so with one school the papacy is a standing conspiracy against the

hac necessitate majestas.' Where privileged orders and monasteries were so many, the hearing of mass must have been within the power of most people, see Ann. Oseney, p. 54 ; Wigorn. 397 ; W. Cov. ii. 201, 205 ; Wil- kins, *Conc.* i. 526 ; but at the worst, the observance of the interdict would not reduce the mean religious services below the model voluntarily adopted by some Protestant communities at the present day.

freedom of mankind, with another a divinely guided organisation for the religious regeneration and moral discipline of the world. And thus sometimes it seems as if there were very little difference between the ecclesiastical acts of a good pope and those of a bad one. But it is quite unnecessary to antedate the existence of the political system of the Jesuits, or to suppose a definitely elaborated plan of aggression even in a far-seeing pontiff like Hildebrand or his most successful follower. Innocent III. in 1205 no more thought of reducing England to the condition of a fief of the Apostolic See than John did of enriching himself with the spoils of the bishops. But the Roman court has a policy in which Innocent himself had been educated, and of which he is, perhaps in all medieval history, the most illustrious exponent : the policy of never overlooking an advantage, or any course of events which might be turned to advantage to the Roman court. In England, where, as we have seen, the secular clergy had until now been consistently ranked on the royal side in questions of church and state alike, the monastic interest was that which it was most important for the papacy to promote ; for the monastic interest was most opposed to the authority of the bishops, most ready to appeal against the Crown, most influential among the people, and both from traditionary religious feeling and from the hope of advantage most kindly disposed to Rome. The monastic interest in England was moreover now in close communication with the monastic interest on the continent, where it was fighting with varied circumstances the same battle.[1]

Neither of them contemplated the actual result

It was most unfortunate for John that he had to deal with such a man as Innocent III. So sound and astute a lawyer, so ingenious and plausible a politician, so high-principled a man, acting in behalf of a cause in which he entirely believed, was unlikely either to leave an opening for his own discomfiture, or to spare the exercise of the power which he thought he was using beneficially, when his own opportunity came. But he neither made nor snatched at the opportunity ; every step of his proceeding was strictly legal, and if in the decisive act of the struggle, the election of Langton, his legality verges on captiousness or chicanery, it must be remembered that his course was provoked by the detected fraud of John. If Innocent had had to deal with Henry II., or even with Hubert Walter, he would have been met with his own weapons : the delays and evasions of the canon law would have been made serviceable on both sides ; the crisis would have been staved off, and the result almost certainly would have been a compromise. John's policy in the matter was

The two principal actors in the struggle were ill-matched

[1] See Epp. Cantuar. above, pp. 386, sq.

H H

simply the blundering, floundering, pettifogging, obstinate, and yet irresolute procedure of a violent man, devoid of real courage or counsel, and ignorant of the strength of his cause. It is unnecessary to enter into the details, but a clear notion of the string of the story is indispensable.

Hubert Walter died July 12, 1205 ; before he was buried,[1] the younger monks of Canterbury, without asking the royal licence, elected their subprior Reginald to succeed him, enthroned him and sent him to Rome for confirmation, with strict injunctions of secrecy as to the purpose of his journey. Reginald as soon as he landed in Flanders, announced himself as the archbishop elect and so exposed the plot. The news reached England in due time ; the king was enraged ; the bishops were provoked at the contempt of their claim to share in the election ; and the monks frightened at their own temerity, and divided into two factions. The bishops appealed to Rome on behalf of their rights, and the monks appealed on behalf of theirs.[2] John announced his intention of nominating John Gray, bishop of Norwich, and both the bishops and the senior party among the monks were ready to elect him. The king, unwilling to wait for news from Rome, obtained in December from the resident monks a renunciation of their appeal and transacted the formal election, placed John Gray in possession of the archiepiscopal revenues,[3] and sent envoys to Rome to demand the papal recognition.[4] Here, then, John took his first false step ; he had not

[1] ' Antequam corpus ejus sepulturæ traderetur.' R. Wendover, iii. 183.

[2] The agents of both the appealing parties appeared before the pope before any mention was made of the election of the bishop of Norwich ; a deputation of five monks from the convent and Master Peter of Inglesham on behalf of the bishops. Peter was robbed of his credentials at Parma, but the pope accepted a caution of 1,000 marks from him, and the security of the bishop of Winchester and Master John, canon of S. Paul's, and admitted him to a hearing. From his statement the pope concluded that the election of the subprior had been made (1) in spite of an appeal ; (2) in contempt of the rights of the bishops ; and (3) in breach of engagement made between the bishops and the monks, to meet for the election on the 30th of November. Accordingly he wrote to the abbots of Reading and S. Alban's, and to the dean of S. Paul's, to examine witnesses, and to send the

necessary persons and depositions to Rome before the 1st of May, 1206. Innoc. III. Epp. lib. viii. ep. 161, dated Dec. 11, 1205. A few days before, Dec. 8, he had written to the bishops, ordering them not to molest the monks. M. Paris, 212, 213.

[3] M. Paris, 213 ; Wendover, iii. 185.

[4] On the very day that Innocent wrote for the witnesses, Dec. 11, John wrote to him, saying that both parties had on Dec. 6 renounced their appeals ; he had himself gone to Canterbury on the following Sunday, and then and there the monks, acting with his consent, had elected John, bishop of Norwich, to be archbishop. Rot. Pat. Joh. i. 56. On the 20th of the same month he sent to Rome Archdeacon Honorius, Master Columb, Geoffrey of Derham, and six monks of Canterbury, on behalf of the bishop of Norwich, and issued a letter to the bishops desiring their seals to a letter to the pope for the same purpose. Rot. Pat. i. 57.

acted with sufficient promptness to stop the election and appeal of the subprior, he had not patience to consider that no pope could allow a suit that was brought before him to be stopped by the renunciation of it in the king's court by men whose interest in it was one of the points to be debated ; and he threw over the rights of the bishops on which his father had always insisted, placing the formal right unreservedly in the hands of the monks.[1] Although, then, three appeals may be said to have been pending, he acted in contempt of them all, and yet forwarded a fourth appeal to the very tribunal whose cherished jurisprudence he was ignoring. Innocent, on the other hand, accepted all the appeals, ignored the renunciations, and set to work to inform himself of the merits of the case, adjourning the hearing of it from time to time,[2] and urging on the several parties concerned to prepare their evidence carefully and to accredit their representatives with full power. John made a show of complying, but he forwarded with the evidence a large sum of money to bribe the papal officials,[3] and whilst he pretended to give the monks whom he sent full powers to complete the election, and a formal assent to any election they might make, he bound them secretly to elect no one but Gray. The imbecile cunning of this policy practised on a man like Innocent is very characteristic of John. In the week before Christmas 1206 the cause was finally heard, before the representatives of all the parties.[4] The election of

Innocent acts on the supposition that the appeals are bona fide

John tries to impose on the pope

[1] Although he desired the bishops to seal the letters on behalf of the bishop of Norwich, he distinctly says that the election was made by the prior and convent (ib. p. 56).

[2] On the 30th of March, 1206, Innocent writes to the convent. After rehearsing his letter of Dec. 11, he announces the arrival of Archdeacon Honorius and his companions with the news of the election of John Gray; the agent of the subprior had insisted that that election should be quashed, alleging that it was made during appeal, that the person chosen was a stranger to the convent, and that it was made under undue influence. On the last ground he declined to confirm the election. Archdeacon Honorius then demanded the rejection of the claim of the subprior; and the latter having replied, the pope summons sixteen monks, ten by name, and six to be named by the convent, with full powers to act for the whole body, to appear at Rome on the 1st of October. The bishop of Rochester and the abbot of S. Augus-

tine's are to see the mandate obeyed (Epp. ix. 34). He also orders the suffragans to send their proctors, and requests the king to do the same (Epp. 35, 36, 37). W. Cov. ii. 198.

[3] On the 8th of May, John writes to the bishops desiring their seals to the letters written by the bishops of London, Rochester, Winchester, Ely, and Norwich : Rot. Pat. i. 64. On the 26th he gave letters of credit to the amount of 3,000 marks to Thomas of Herdington and Anfrid of Dene, who were going to the court of Rome : Rot. Pat. i. 65. The letter which he wrote to the pope bears the same date : ibid. The abbot of Beaulieu followed, with letters of credit for 40 marks only, on the 26th of August : ibid. 67. Of the sum intrusted to them, the envoys spent 2,025 marks before they returned.

[4] The letter condemning the claims of the bishops is in M. Paris, pp. 214, Innoc. Epp. ix. 205, dated Dec. 20. The letter to the king announcing the definite sentence and the election of Langton is in Innoc. Epp. ix. 206 ;

Final deci-
sion of
Innocent

the subprior was annulled as informal ; the election of Bishop Gray was also null because it had been transacted during the appeal ; the claims of the bishops were condemned, as it would seem, on an *ex parte* statement at which the king had connived. The see was therefore vacant ; and the only body that had a right to elect was plenarily represented at Rome, with the royal consent already obtained to ratify their choice. It had been vacant now a year and a half, to the great detriment of the church ; it was desirable that there should be no

Stephen
Langton
elected by
the monks
at Rome

more delay. The pope suggested Cardinal Stephen, an Englishman and a scholar ; not a monk, but also no courtier. And the representatives of the chapter, forgetful with one exception of their secret bond to the king, elected the cardinal. We may strongly suspect that Innocent knew both of the corrupt arrangement by which he was to be hoodwinked, and of the bribes that were lavishly

Strict
legality of
Innocent's
proceedings

spent on his kinsmen :[1] it is probable also that he regarded Bishop Gray as a mere creature of the king, and was anxious for the sake of the church to place in the seat of Augustine the first scholar of the first University of Christendom, a man on whom he could rely in the interests of religion, and whom John himself respected so much that he thrice congratulated him by letter on his elevation to the Cardinalate.[2] But he did nothing in haste, nothing underhand, or in defiance of the common understanding between the Christian princes and their spiritual guide. Where he verges to-

He acts
leisurely,
but finally
takes his
own course

wards over-legality, it is that he may defeat fraud. Nor when Langton was elected did he proceed hastily ; he would not consecrate him before he had attempted to obtain from John a real instead of

and that to the monks, nearly in the same words, is in Innoc. Epp. ix. 207, dated Dec. 21. In these the king's envoys, the abbot of Beaulieu (Hugh, afterwards bishop of Carlisle), Thomas (of Herdington), sheriff of Staffordshire, and Anfrid (Dene), knight, are mentioned. They refused to give the royal assent ; but the deputation of monks had full powers from the convent. The pope writes at the request of the king's envoys for an express assent, although it was not necessary for an election at Rome. The secret history is told by Matthew Paris : 'Rex posuerat verbum suum in ore duodecim monachorum Cantuariensium ut quemcunque eligerent ipse acceptaret. Convenerat autem inter regem et eos, præstito juramento et fidei interpositione, quod nullo modo alium quam Johannem episcopum Norwicensem eligerent. Habebant et similiter regis litteras.' M. Paris, p. 222.

And this statement is, in one part at least, abundantly confirmed by the language of the Barnwell canon (Walt. Cov. ii. 198) : 'a conventu Cantuariensi et episcopis Angliæ, necnon et a rege, sufficienter esset cautum, quod eorum apud sedem apostolicam acta rata haberentur et indiscussa.'

[1] The letters patent of Feb. 20, 1207 (Rot. Pat. i. 69), mention fees of 230 marks to Peter, son of Richard, the pope's brother ; 60 marks to P. Hannibalis ; Stephen Rom. Cassolii, 50 marks ; and 20 marks to the nephew of the bishop of Porto. The pension was still paid to P. Hannibalis in 1214 (Rot. Pat. i. 108) : so also that of Octavian Rom. Cassolii (ibid. p. 117).

[2] So Innocent says in the letter addressed to John, dated May 26, 1207. Wilkins, Conc. i. 517, 518 ; Innoc. Epp. x. 219.

the fraudulent assent to the act.[1] John replied to the announcement with an absolute refusal, supported only by special pleading and unhesitating falsehood. He did not so much as know the obscure person who was forced upon him.[2] Then the successor of S. Peter clad himself in the zeal that so well became him, and consecrated the archbishop.[3]

John had thus contrived, not without cunning but without any true policy, to place hinself in the wrong in every possible way. He had carried an appeal to a tribunal by whose decision he did not intend to be bound ; he had attempted, by an illusory undertaking on his own part and a corrupt bargain with his nominal opponents, to deceive the judge, and such a judge as Innocent. The pope defeated him by treating him as if he were an honest man. Further, he had failed ignominiously, he had lost the cause, he had wasted his bribes, and he had been betrayed by his own tools.[4] But even now there were ways open by which a king like his father or a minister like Hubert would have gained time, or even a reversal of the sentence : even in Scotland William the Lion had managed to keep a similar trial for ten years in suspense ; but John had not self-command enough to temporise. He declared that no earthly consideration should ever make him receive the archbishop, and directed the severest measures to be taken for the punishment of the monks.[5] And it was this that provoked the pope to the use of that

John's want of policy in this matter

---

[1] This he asks for in the letter of Dec. 21, Ep. ix. 206.

[2] John's letter is known chiefly from the pope's answer, Epp. x. 219 : Wendover, 216 ; Wilkins, Conc. i. 517. Wendover gives an abstract of it, pp. 215, 216 ; M. Paris, 224. The messengers would arrive home towards the end of January. They were immediately despatched back again with recommendatory letters dated Feb. 20, and letters of credit of the same date for 2,000 marks, and a strict charge not to spend any of it, 'sicut diligunt corpora sua, ante consummationem negotii pro quo remittuntur ad curiam.' They had also to give account of 1,000 marks which were still in their hands. Rot. Pat. i. 69.

[3] Innocent's letter in answer to John's threat is dated May 26 : Langton being not yet consecrated, Wilkins, Conc. i. 517. John had said that he had never received the papal letters requiring him to send proctors, and had never been asked by the monks for his consent. The pope accounts for this by saying that the

two monks sent for the assent had been stopped at Dover, but that their letters had been forwarded to the king by his own messengers. He should ask for that consent no more, but proceed to do his duty. Langton was consecrated at Viterbo on the 17th of June, and the fact was announced in a letter to the convent dated June 24. Wilkins, i. 517.

[4] 'Dixit enim quod in præjudicium suæ libertatis sine ipsius assensu suppriorem suum elegerant, et postmodum, ut quod male gesserant quasi sibi satisfaciendo palliarent, elegerunt episcopum Norwicensem, et pecuniam de fisco accipientes ad itineris expensas, ut electionem de episcopo memorato factam apud sedem apostolicam impetrarent confirmari, in cumulum iniquitatis suæ elegerunt ibi Stephanum de Langetune.' Wendover, iii. 214 ; M. Paris, 223.

[5] Fulk Cantilupe and Reginald of Cornhill were sent to Canterbury to seize the goods of the monks on the 11th of July : Rot. Pat. i. 74. The bishop of Worcester was also in

The inter-
dict

John hesi-
tates about
receiving
the arch-
bishop

Failure of
negotia-
tions

most fearful and suicidal weapon of the medieval church, the interdict,. which was proclaimed in the spring of 1208.[1]

It is difficult to say with certainty what effect this produced on the king who, although, without religion, was not without superstition ;. whether for the moment he was staggered in his resolution, or merely dissembled in order to test the result of the cessation of religious rites among the people generally : anyhow he offered to allow Langton to receive the royalties of his see,[2] and even gave him permission to visit England provided that he were not expected to receive him as a friend.[3] But the pope suspected deceit in this ; the refusal to receive Langton was too like Henry's refusal of a kiss to Becket.

trouble about the business : Rot. Claus. i. 92. Langton's prebend at York was given away on Nov. 8 : ibid. 96.

[1] On the 27th of August 1207 the pope wrote to the bishops of London, Ely, and Worcester, begging them to use their influence to prevail on John to receive Langton ; and ordering them in case of his refusal to impose an interdict, and threatening still severer measures. Wilkins, Conc. i. 519; Innoc. Epp. x. 113. He had heard, it would seem, already the hardships of the monks. On the 19th of November he wrote to the same prelates to enforce the interdict (Wilkins, Conc. i. 524) ; to the bishops generally, reproving their inertness (ib. p. 523) ; and to the barons, urging them to advise the king to comply (ibid. 524 ; Innoc. Epp. x. 159, 160, 161). On the 21st of January John signified to the three bishops that he was willing to comply : Rot. Pat. i. 78. On March 12 Simon Langton, who had had a safe-conduct on the 19th of February, presented himself to the king at Winchester, and prayed him to receive his brother as archbishop ; and when the king spoke of saving his own rights, Simon insisted that he should place himself altogether at the archbishop's mercy. Such is the king's statement, Rot. Pat. i. 80 (Mar. 4). The interdict was formally proclaimed on the 23rd, M. Paris, 226 ; or on the 24th, R. Coggeshall, 238.

[2] The abbot of Beaulieu was again the envoy, and had orders for his passage from Dover on the 4th of April, ten days after the promulgation of the interdict. The pope's letters in answer are dated May 27. From these we learn the proposals made through the abbot. John was willing to accept Stephen as archbishop and to reinstate the monks : the royalties of the see he placed in the pope's hands. He could not, however, prevail on himself to receive Stephen as a friend, ' nondum animus tuus poterat inclinari ut familiarem eidem archiepiscopo gratiam exhiberes.' The pope in reply urges him to confer the royalties himself and receive the archbishop's fealty ; if he still declines, the bishops of London, Ely, and Worcester are to receive the royalties and confer them in the pope's name : Epp. xi. 89, 90. At the same time he wrote to the three bishops directing them, when the terms of the agreement were fulfilled, to relax the interdict : Epp. xi. 91.

[3] On the 14th of July John granted safe-conduct to Simon Langton and the three bishops to pass to and fro between Dover and the continent in the process of negotiation until Sept. 8, Rot. Pat. i. 85 ; and this is renewed for three weeks from Sept. 8, on the 11th of August, Rot. Pat. i. 82 ; on the 9th of September Stephen himself has a safe-conduct from Sept. 29, for three weeks, Rot. Pat. i. 86. This he did not use, but the three bishops waited in vain for two months for an interview with John : Ann. Wav. 261. Long before this, however, the pope's suspicions as to John's sincerity were aroused ; on the 22nd of August he had written to the three bishops forbidding them to relax the interdict until all promises were fulfilled : Epp. xi. 141. See also R. Coggeshall ad ann. 1208. ' Rex Anglorum misit Romam et se satisfacturum . . . promisit, sed minime tenuit ' (p. 238).

John was not the man to risk a second martyrdom, but there were many ways of silencing an enemy besides murder. Langton came to Dover, but all attempts at a reconciliation failed.[1] John found that the country bore the interdict with equanimity, or at least with submission, and made or allowed no more advances towards reconciliation.[2] Then came the full burst of the storm ; the bishops, relieved from their duties, fled from their flocks, and John seized their revenues ; the inferior clergy were for a moment practically outlawed and the convents reduced to starvation ; and although on second thoughts the king interfered to protect the former, and allowed a fraction of their income for the maintenance of the latter,[3] the

John seizes the estates of the bishops

---

[1] The news of the failure of negotiations having reached Rome, the pope wrote to John on the 12th of January 1209, and, distinctly imputing to him the breaking off of the pacification, insisted on his performing the promises made by the abbot of Beaulieu. If this were not done within three months after the receipt of this letter, he is declared excommunicate, and the three bishops are ordered to publish and execute the sentence : Epp. xi. 211 ; Wilkins, i. 528. At the same time he wrote to the bishop of Winchester enjoining on him to obey the three bishops : Epp. xi. 218. He had not, however, quite given up hopes : for, writing to the archbishop about the same time, he gives him leave to modify the interdict and to absolve the officers who had dispossessed the monks of Canterbury : Epp. xi. 216, 217 ; and on the 23rd of January wrote a letter rather remonstrating with the king than threatening him : Epp. xi. 221. The excommunicatory letter, being enclosed in a letter to the three bishops, was regarded as an ultimatum ; and that of Jan. 23rd would reach the king first. Simon Langton had on the 23rd of March safe-conduct for three weeks after Easter that he might confer with the bishops of Winchester and Bath and the justiciar on the pope's last letter : Rot. Pat. i. 90. There is no evidence of anything being done in this interview. In the meantime the bishops who had fled from England committed the task of publishing the excommunication to their brethren, who of course declined to do so : M. Paris, 228. On the 21st of June the sentence was still unpublished, and

the pope wrote (Epp. xii. 57) to the abbot of S. Vedast at Arras, empowering him to promulgate it in conjunction with any two of the three bishops, whenever the archbishop should demand it. Soon after another interview was proposed, and during the preliminary negotiations matters seem to have advanced so far that a beginning of restitution was made : Ann. Waverley, p. 263. It was otherwise when the archbishop presented himself at Dover, where he landed on the 2nd of October. The king came to Chilham on his way to meet him, and sent the justiciar and the bishop of Winchester to discuss matters with him. These ministers refused to ratify the articles drawn up in the earlier stages of the business, and the archbishop left without seeing the king : Ann. Wav. 264. John made another attempt soon after, summoning the archbishop again to Dover. But to this Stephen replied in a letter still preserved (Wilkins, i. 529), refusing to comply until the terms before arranged were fulfilled, but offering to see the king's agents at Witsand or Gravelines. R. Coggeshall mentions an invitation sent by John to the archbishop in 1210, which failed because he did not give a safe-conduct : p. 239 ; Ann. Winton. 81 ; Ann. Waverl. 266 ; W. Covent. ii. 200. The excommunication, according to the Annals of Dunstable, was published in France but not in England (p. 32).

[2] Especially after the quarrel of the pope with Otho : W. Cov. ii. 202.

[3] M. Paris, 226, 227. On the 6th of April 1208 the king orders a reasonable maintenance to be allowed to the

Intercourse with Rome was not at first stopped by the interdict

Sentence issued against John

result of the infliction was in every way calamitous.   Yet, strange to say, whilst the people were perishing, negotiations on other matters went on between England and Rome, though not without disturbance.[1] The new bishop of Lincoln [2] sought confirmation from the pope and consecration from Langton ; the machinery of the court of final appeal went on ; the nation was under interdict, but the king's excommunication was suffered to be in suspense ; they perished, he grew rich.   At last in 1212 [3] the special excommunication was pronounced, and with it the sentence of deposition.[4]   Even against this

religious, Rot. Claus. i. 109, 110, where several measures of confiscation are ordered of lands seized on account of the interdict. The abbots of Abingdon and Michelney are respited. On the 11th of April the king issues an edict which shows the length to which the outlawry of the religious and the clergy had proceeded : ' Præcipimus tibi quod clamari facias sine dilatione per comitatum tuum, quod nulli, sicut diligunt corpora et catalla sua, malum faciant vel dicant viris religiosis vel clericis contra pacem nostram, et si quem inde attingere possimus ad proximam quercum eum suspendi faciemus.' Rot. Claus. i. 111. See also W. Covent. ii. 200.

[1] Not, of course, on so extensive a scale as usual. But the letters of Innocent III., if not misplaced and misdated, show that long after the interdict was proclaimed and the sentence of excommunication issued the pope was writing to John on the claims of Berengaria : Epp. xi. 223. He wrote also to the chapters of the vacant churches, urging them to elect : Epp. xi. 212; other business is treated of in Epp. xi. 248 ; xii. 100, 166 ; xiii. 52, 74, 208 ; xv. 141.

[2] He went to France, according to Wendover, to be consecrated by the archbishop of Rouen, but went instead to Langton.   Several letters of Innocent concern this election (Epp. xii. 56, 91).

[3] In 1211, ' Reges et alios omnes tam pauperes quam potentes, ad coronam Angliæ spectantes, a regis fidelitate et subjectione absolvit.' M. Paris, 231 ; Wendover, iii. 237.   In 1212 he issued the bull of deposition, the execution being committed to Philip. M. Paris, 232 ; Wendover, iii. 241 ; W. Cov. ii. 209.

[4] According to the Annals of Wa-

verley (ed. Luard, p. 266), in 1211, soon after S. James's day, Pandulf and Durand landed in England, and on the Thursday after the feast of S. Bartholomew held a conference with the king at Northampton. The conference is, however, placed both in the Burton and in the Waverley Annals in the year 1212; so that some mistake is certain, and unfortunately the Rolls of the year are missing. As, however, John was at Northampton on the 29th of August 1211, and not at all during that month in 1212, the conference, if it ever took place, must have been in 1211; and with this conclusion agree the words of the Barnwell book (W. Cov. ii. 204) : ' Duo nuncii a sede apostolica ad Anglicanæ ecclesiæ reconciliationem in Angliam missi sunt, sed pace infecta redeuntes nihil afflictis contulerunt.'   This enables us to understand the letter of Innocent III. dated Feb. 27, 1213, in which he tells John that he has received letters in which the king promises to perform all that the abbot of Beaulieu, A. Marcel, and four other messengers shall undertake on his behalf.   Of these messengers, however, only three have presented themselves : ' ii vero tres nuncii nobis ad ultimum obtulerunt quod secundum illam formam satisfacere promittebas quam per dilectos filios Pandulfum subdiaconum et fratrem Durandum familiares nostros tibi curavimus destinare. Verum cum per te steterit quo minus secundum eandem formam pax fuerit reformata, et postea pejora prioribus attentaveris, nos ad eam . . . minime tenemur.'   Fœdera, i. 108 ; Ann. Burton, 218 ; Innoc. Epp. xv. 234. Of the envoys, the abbot of Beaulieu, Thomas of Herdington, and Philip of Worcester had expenses allowed for their journey, on the 11th

John was obstinate ; the dread of treason, too, failed to subdue him ; but the prophecy of Peter of Wakefield,[1] as the contemporary writers assert, effected what the successor of the apostle had attempted in vain. John's submission was as abject as his conduct hitherto had been wilful ; and he obtained the support of the pope, not merely to disarm Philip Augustus, or to justify him in hanging Peter of Wakefield, but to turn it against his own people. *He gives in at last*

I have stated by anticipation the effect of this struggle on the English church ; its effect on the relations between England and the papacy is read in the history of the country from 1213 to this day. It may be true that John's struggle was in this, as it was in the other contests of his reign, the logical conclusion of a series of events that must have had some conclusion of the kind, that he really bore the brunt of the battle which the policy of the Norman sovereigns had necessitated ; but it is not the less true that he provoked the crisis which they had contrived to avert, at a moment the most unfavourable for himself, and that he fought it with weapons which they would have scorned ; and thus, although the result was to the ultimate benefit of England, it was to the immediate humiliation of the sovereign and to the permanent embittering of every element in the complication. *Important consequences of John's submission* *The result was imminent, but was precipitated by John*

The pacification with the pope was arranged in May 1213, and measures were forthwith taken for the satisfaction of the pecuniary claims of the clergy and the relaxation of the interdict. The negotiations lasted more than a year, and have a constitutional importance of their own on which we cannot enter in detail. The *Measures taken, after the pacification with the pope, to insure good government*

of November 1212. Rot. Claus. i. 126. The others were W. de S. Audocno and Richard de Merton. The pope thus declares that the mission of Pandulf and Durand had failed, and that severer measures had been taken against the king in consequence. These can scarcely have been other than the absolution of his subjects from their allegiance, and the direction to Philip to depose John : W. Cov. ii. 209 ; Wendover, 241. Possibly these commands were given in the letter ' expectantes hactenus exspectavimus,' all copies of which were ordered, after the homage done to Nicolas of Tusculum, to be destroyed (Epp. xvi. 133). Dr. Pauli rejects the earlier mission of Pandulf and Durand, iii. 365, 374. But the authority of our chronicle is very strong ; and it is confirmed by the Annals of Tewkesbury under the year 1211 : ' Nuncii

domini papæ venerunt Angliam propter pacem ecclesiæ, sed infecto negotio redierunt,' p. 60 : and those of Margam mention the discussion at Northampton, p. 31 ; also Ann. Wikes and Oseney, p. 55 ; M. Paris, 230 ; Ann. Winton. p. 81. But I fear the details are too graphic to be true, especially the story of Pandulf going out of the council to look for a candle to excommunicate the king, whereon John forthwith yielded his point. Ann. Burton, 217.

[1] Walt. Cov. ii. 208 ; Ann. Margam, p. 60 ; Wendover gives four reasons for his submission : his long excommunication ; his fear of Philip ; his apprehension of treason ; and ' quartam vero causam aliis plus omnibus timebat,' namely, the approach of the day of the fulfilment of Peter's prophecy. Wendover, iii. 248 ; M. Paris, 235.

king, on the occasion of the absolution in July,[1] renewed his coronation oath with additional promises of good government. In August an assembly was held at S. Alban's under the justiciar Geoffrey Fitz Peter, in which those promises were fully stated, and directions for their fulfilment were laid on the sheriffs ;[2] and the same month Archbishop Langton at S. Paul's laid the charter of Henry I. before the clergy,[3] as affording a programme upon the lines of which the king's reforms should be undertaken. Unfortunately for John, on the 2nd of October the justiciar died, and from that moment he seems to have either lost or deliberately cast away the hold which he had until then retained on the baronage.[4]

We know too little of Geoffrey Fitz Peter to allow us to describe him as a model or as a representative minister. The few notices preserved of his personal character lead us to regard him rather as a vigilant and astute man of business than as a statesman or a patriot. His origin is somewhat uncertain ; he was, however, probably one of those obscure persons whose fortune was made by Henry II. and Richard I. through the marriage of heiresses. He had obtained the hand of one of the co-heiresses of William de Mandeville, and in her right the succession to the earldom of Essex. In the following out of this claim he had shown a grasping and litigious spirit which may or may not have been brought out by a legal education ;[5] and

Production of the charter of Henry I.

John quarrels with the barons

Geoffrey Fitz Peter; one of the legal barons

---

[1] July 20. M. Paris, 239.

[2] August 4, Wendover, iii. 261; M. Paris, 239 : where in an assembly of the magnates, attended by the archbishop and bishops and the reeve and four men out of each of the king's demesne townships, it was ordered 'quatenus leges Henrici avi sui ab omnibus in regno custodirentur.' What those laws were does not seem to have been ascertained until the 25th of the same month, when the archbishop produced the charter of Henry I.

[3] August 25. M. Paris, 240; Wendover, iii. 263.

[4] The words of Matthew Paris are so remarkable that I give the passage entire : ' Anno vero sub eodem Gaufridus filius Petri totius Angliæ justitiarius, vir magnæ potestatis et auctoritatis, in maximum regni detrimentum diem clausit extremum, secunda die Octobris. Erat autem firmissima regni columna, utpote vir generosus, legum peritus, thesauris reditibus et omnibus bonis instauratus, omnibus Angliæ magnatibus sanguine vel amicitia confœderatus. Unde rex

ipsum præ omnibus mortalibus sine dilectione formidabat ; ipse enim lora regni gubernabat. Unde post ejus obitum facta est Anglia quasi in tempestate navis sine gubernaculo. Cujus tempestatis initium fuit mors Huberti Cantuariensis archiepiscopi, viri magnifici et fidelis : nec post mortem istorum duorum potuit Anglia respirare. Cum dicti Petri mors regi Johanni nunciaretur, cachinnando dixit, " Cum venerit in infernum salutet Hubertum Cantuariensem archiepiscopum, quem procul dubio ibi inveniet." Et conversus ad circumsedentes subintulit dicens, " Per pedes Domini, nunc primo sum rex et dominus Angliæ." Habuit igitur ex tunc potestatem liberiorem, juramentis suis et pactis quæ cum ipso Gaufrido dolente fecerat contraire, et initæ pacis vinculis quibus se involverat denodare. Pœnituit igitur ipsum graviter et amarissime quod ad prædictæ pacis consensum inclinaretur.' M. Paris, 243.

[5] See Hoveden, above, p. 222. Mon. Angl. iv. 145.

it is far from improbable that he suggested some of the captious and pettifogging exactions of John. He had been in the Exchequer under Henry II.; [1] in the commission of the justiciarship under Richard I., [2] and was made by him chief justiciar on the archbishop's resignation in July 1198. [3] With the exception of a campaign against the Welsh in the same year, [4] his exploits seem to have been achieved rather in the council than in the field; and his financial policy is marked by the increased stringency of the exactions under the forest law, and the severe measures against the regular clergy which were taken directly after his appointment; [5] the augmentation of the carucage at the beginning of John's reign may also have been suggested by him, for it was a measure unlikely to recommend itself to a newly-crowned king as either popular or necessary. [6] Besides these slight and early indications, there is quite enough in the history of the reign to show that Geoffrey was neither a scrupulous minister nor a man of rigid principles, religious or political. He seems not to have hesitated to carry out the king's orders against the clergy, nor to have interposed to alleviate the severe measures of precaution which John took against the suspected barons. Comparatively free from class influences, and yet closely connected with the nobles, he was able with a very little holding back to make himself necessary to his master. As John Gray and Peter des Roches served his purposes in the church, Geoffrey had with less guilt and less responsibility served him with the baronage; his great fault being that he served him too well. But although Geoffrey, like Hubert Walter, had been willing no doubt to strain the law to its full extent and to take the fullest reasonable responsibility for the measures of the government, he could not forget that he was a baron and a lawyer, and the necessity of being served by him had been irksome to John. Untaught by the lessons of the last eight years to feel either gratitude or respect, John, on hearing of the death of the justiciar, scoffingly observed that when he got to hell he would meet Hubert Walter there and might carry him his greetings. Then, turning to his courtiers, he said, 'By the feet of God, now for the first time am I king and lord of England'; words which, spoken of Henry I. in reference to the banishment of Robert of Belesme, have so different a meaning. [7] With Henry the joy was felt for the riddance of a tyrant who was persecuting alike

Margin notes:
Career of Geoffrey Fitz Peter

He had been a faithful minister, but had acted as a check on his master

John's joy on hearing of his death.

---

[1] He was one of the forest justices in the 31st of Henry II. Madox, *Hist. Exch.* p. 380.

[2] Hoveden, iii. 16, 28, 96.

[3] Hoveden, iv. 48. July 11, Fœdera, i. 71.

[4] Hoveden, iv. 53. The Dunstable Annals mention an expedition into Wales in 1209, but no fighting, p. 32.

[5] Hoveden, above, p. 302.

[6] See Hoveden, ibid.

[7] Ord. Vit. XI. iii. ' Omnis Anglia, exulante crudeli tyranno, exultavit, multorumque congratulatio regi Henrico tunc adulando dixit, " Gaude, rex Henrice, Dominoque Deo gratias age,

the king and the people ; with John it was for the death of a faithful
servant who stood between him and his destined victims. Matthew
Paris records the story, and adds that 'after his death England
became a ship in a storm without a helm. The beginning of the
tempest was the death of Hubert ; after the death of Geoffrey the
country could not even breathe.' [1] It is clear that Geoffrey's
influence had had the effect of keeping the king under some sort of
restraint, although what the extent of the restraint may have been
can be gathered only by a calculation of the difference between the
preceding and following acts of tyranny and extortion. John, however, probably regarded Geoffrey as responsible for the mention
of the laws of Henry I. at S. Alban's, and as having put a most
dangerous weapon in the hands of the barons. Anyhow with
Geoffrey's death the loss of all remaining influence over the barons
does in point of time coincide, and the series of events begins which,
broken in the middle by the extortion of Magna Carta, lasts throughout the remainder of the reign of John and the early years of his
successor. During these years, had it not been for the support of
the papacy, they must have lost England as John had lost his
continental states before.

The grievances of the barons are not now heard of for the first
time ; but it is the first time that they see it necessary to throw
them into the same scale with those of the church and the nation at
large. It is necessary to look back to the beginning of the reign,
and at the risk of a little repetition to trace the growth of them.
The old feudal gravamina had most probably ceased to be felt : he
would have been a bold man who had refused to admit the royal
justices into his franchise, or claimed to exercise the right of coinage
or high judicature among his own vassals. True, the constable
Roger de Lacy had, in 1193, hanged two of his knights as traitors,
but Roger was on the king's side at the time the act was committed,
when the country was in a state of civil war, and the excitement which, notwithstanding the palliating circumstances, followed
the execution was such as shows it to have been in the highest
degree exceptional.[2] But under the system of Henry II. there
were some points which were felt to be abuses, and which the
new nobility as well as the old feudatories, as soon as they had
made good their footing, attempted to reform. Such were the disparagement of heiresses by unequal marriages,[3] common under both

*The death of
the justiciar
followed by
the breach
between
John and
the barons*

*The growth
of the
baronial
grievances*

*Their juris-
dictions
were already
limited*

quia tu libere cœpisti regnare, ex quo
Rodbertum de Belismo vicisti, et de
finibus regni tui expulisti," ' ed. Duchesne, 808.

[1] M. Paris, p. 243, quoted in note to
p. 474.

[2] Benedict, ii. 232, 233 ; Hoveden,
iii. 172.

[3] Ralph Niger, p. 169 : 'Filias
miseræ conditionis corruptas et op-
pressas copulans clarissimis, hæredes
omnes mechanicos creavit. Servis

Richard and his father; the continued retention of the castles of the The disparagement and detention of estates earls who had ceased to be formidable; the postponement of the investiture of heirs by the exaction of enormous reliefs, or the wanton detention of their estates irrespective of the reliefs; the Great exactions, wardship, and marriage whole traffic in wardship and marriage; all these have their exact analogies in ecclesiastical affairs, from which the abuses had been probably borrowed; the constant occupation of the estates of the prelates and monasteries by the king's officers, and the prolonging of vacancies of sees that the revenue might run into the Exchequer.

It seems to have fallen to the lot of the great earls to act as Discontent of the great earls at the beginning of the reign spokesmen of the baronage on these and the like heads. It was by a promise that the king would redress their grievances that Hubert Walter obtained their adhesion to the cause of John and their consent to his succession;[1] and in 1201, when their services were demanded for the war in Normandy, they met at Leicester and refused to follow the king unless their rights were restored to them.[2] They had then been summarily and peremptorily silenced.

But to these grievances John's own reign had added the increase New grievances under the rule of John of taxation to a degree before unimagined, and the exaction by way of fines of sums arbitrarily demanded, assessed, and enforced; and the question of foreign service entered into and complicated most of the other questions of taxation and finance. It is unfortunate that we are only able to account by way of inference for the present state of this question. The obligation of the royal vassals to serve in Obligation to foreign service foreign warfare did not and could not come into dispute so long as those vassals owed allegiance to the sovereign as duke of Normandy and Aquitaine. And in the earlier Norman reigns, under William Rufus at least, there is some evidence to show that the obligation was regarded, or construed, as binding not on the vassals only, but on the national militia, the old fyrd of the Anglo-Saxon times. Al- How the obligation to foreign service had grown up though that force had never been actually taken across the Channel, it had been brought down to Hastings for the purpose, and had there been dismissed, on surrendering its travelling money for the king's necessities.[3] In the war of Toulouse, the first war waged by him as duke of Aquitaine, Henry II. had come upon all the English baronage; and the application of the rule of scutage for the purpose of that war,[4] both to the bishops, who could have no foreign fiefs, and to the entire body of the knights, who in most instances were

generosas copulans pedaneæ conditionis fecit universos. Hæreditates retinuit aut vendidit.' This is of course rhetorical, but the grievance was real. See Benedict, ii. 71, 72.

[1] Hoveden, iv. 88: 'redderet unicuique illorum jus suum.'

[2] Hoveden, iv. 161: 'ex communi consilio mandaverunt regi quod non transfretarent cum illo nisi ille reddiderit eis jura sua.'

[3] Floren. Wig. ad ann. 1094.

[4] Ben. Pet. above, pp. 150–152.

exclusively English, would show that in 1158 no legal difference
was made between service on the continent and service in Britain,
in all parts of which, Scotland, Galloway, Wales, and perhaps in
Ireland also, it was rendered or accounted for without hesitation.

Scutage Still the introduction of the scutage for the first Aquitanian war
may be interpreted as implying a misgiving as to the right of demanding service from the English in a land where they had no fiefs.
In 1177 Henry II. summoned to Portsmouth all the tenants of the
Crown in arms for the invasion of France : [1] the purpose was not
carried out, in consequence of the peace negotiations opened with
Lewis VII., but the summons was obeyed, the earls, barons, and
knights crossed the Channel, and there is no record of any show of
reluctance on the part of the feudatories. The reign of Richard
does not afford any evidence of such occasion having arisen until

Refusal of a grant to Richard 1198. A scutage was raised for war in Normandy in 1195,[2] but
three years after, when the justiciar proposed in the great council
that a grant should be made for the maintenance of 300 knights for
war in France, the bishops of Lincoln and Salisbury declared that
their estates were held on a tenure of military service within the
borders of England, and there only.[3]

Result of the military policy of Henry II. It would appear, then, that the present phase of the question had
been thus produced. In the first place Henry II. had introduced
great reforms into the military and financial administration, re-
creating for internal defence the national militia, which could not be
expected to serve abroad, and using for foreign warfare an army of
stipendiaries whom he did not bring to England, but whom he paid
by funds raised by scutage from the whole landed interest of the
country.[4] The vassals had thus got into the way of leaving the
king to manage his foreign wars in his own fashion : the few who
went with him to France either had French interests to maintain or
received from him pay for their men if not for themselves. In the
second place, the number of vassals who held land on both sides of
the Channel was diminished, many of the Norman families having
already broken up into two branches, a French one and an English
one, while the new nobility of Henry II. either had, as a rule, a very
small stake in Normandy compared with their possessions at home,
or else possessed no Norman estates at all.[5] It cannot be pretended

---

[1] Benedict, i. 160, 167, 168, 190.
[2] See Hoveden, above, p. 297. Red
Book of the Exchequer (ap. Hunter,
Three Catalogues, p. 15); Madox,
Hist. Exch. 444.
[3] Hoveden, iv. 40; Magna Vita S.
Hugonis, p. 248 Hoveden, above, p.
99

[4] Dialogus de Scaccario, i. 9.
[5] The passage of the canon of
Barnwell, preserved by Walter of
Coventry, ii. 217, is of the greatest
importance on this point; the
northern barons insist that they owe
no service abroad, or scutage for
foreign service. John replies that he

that the law spoke very distinctly on the subject of obligatory service, for it is clear that it was unsettled in the reign of Edward I., when the recalcitrant earls Bohun and Bigod raised the same cry as had been so potent under their predecessors in 1214. Indistinctness of the state of the law

Another of the new grievances was the increase in direct taxation which had been demanded immediately upon the king's accession. The rate of carucage was then raised from two to three shillings,[1] and that of scutage from twenty shillings to two marks, and the latter impost was levied for six years in succession. In 1203 a seventh of movables was exacted from the baronage;[2] in 1204 an aid was taken from all the knightly landholders of the country;[3] in 1207 a thirteenth of movables,[4] the amount of which may be estimated by the fact that in 1224, when the country was much more impoverished than it was in 1207, a fifteenth so raised amounted to nearly 60,000*l*.[5] Besides these general taxes enormous sums were exacted from individuals, especially the Jews,[6] and the persons on whom John could bring his legal chicanery to bear, by the system of fines which was elaborated under his directions into that minute and grotesque instrument of torture which all the historians of the reign have dwelt on in great detail. It is further to be observed that much of this money was raised unconstitutionally; the taxation imposed, not with the silent or sulky acquiescence of the council, but in opposition to the protest of the barons. Archbishop Geoffrey of York, an unfortunate person to be chosen as Increase of direct taxation Irregular exactions System of fines Money raised in spite of refusal of the payers

has a right to it, for it was done in the days of his father and brother. John was right as to the fact; the barons as clearly had the reason of the thing on their side. Compare R. Coggeshall, p. 243.

[1] 'Exiit ergo edictum a justitiariis regis per universam Angliam ut quælibet caruca arans tres persolveret solidos : quæ nimirum gravis exactio valde populum terræ extenuavit, cum antea gravis exactio scutagii præcessisset; nam ad scutum duæ marcæ persolvebantur, cum nunquam amplius quam viginti solidi ad scutum exigerentur.' R. Coggeshall, ed. Dunkin, p. 180; Ann. Winton. 73; M. Paris, 200. The scutages of John's reign are thus enumerated in the Red Book of the Exchequer (apud Hunter, p. 15): 'Aº. 1. primum scutagium post coronationem regis ; on each fee two marks; 3º, 4º, 5º, 6º, 7º, 8º; six assessments of two marks each, pro exercitu Normanniæ; 12º, pro passagio regis in Hiberniam, on each fee two marks; 13º, pro exercitu Walliæ,

on each fee two marks; eodem, pro exercitu Scotiæ, on each fee two marks.' Notwithstanding the great authority for this statement, it is impossible not to suspect that some of the scutages were merely arrears of past years. The scutage of Wales in 1211 is mentioned by M. Paris, 230.

[2] Matt. Paris, p. 209.

[3] Two marks and a half. M. Paris, p. 209.

[4] Ann. Waverley, 258; M. Paris, 221; Rot. Pat. i. 72.

[5] Liber Ruber (ap. Hunter, p. 22) : 'Summa xvˡᵐᵃᵉ assisæ per Angliam anno regni regis Henrici filii regis Johannis octavo, 86,758 marc. et 2 d.'

[6] From the Jews in 1209 he raised 66,000 marks; and from the Cistercians the next year 33,333 marks, Liber de Ant. Legg. p. 201. M. Paris states the latter sum as 40,000 pounds, p. 230; and adds to it 100,000 pounds obtained the same year from the regulær clergy. Cf. W. Covent. ii. 200, 201, 202.

a champion of law, provoked an attack on himself as early as 1200 by his opposition to the carucage,[1] and in 1207 the thirteenth was exacted although the clergy had absolutely refused to grant it,[2] and Geoffrey went into exile in consequence.[3] On these occasions, although the clergy are put forward as the objectors, it is not on ecclesiastical grounds that they oppose: the taxes were no more popular with the baronage, but the bishops were personally safe from the ungovernable savagery of the king; being protected from corporal harm and having no children to seize as hostages, they could speak with comparative boldness, where a temporal baron would have had to take his choice between civil war, imprisonment, and forfeiture.

The clergy put forward as objectors

John's meanness and tyranny more intolerable than his exactions

What, however, was far more galling to a proud and not illiberal body of men like the barons, whom Henry had trained to government and Richard to perfect skill in warfare, was the fact that the money extorted and the service demanded from them were extorted and demanded on false pretences; whilst any attempt at remonstrance on their part was met by the exercise of irresponsible tyranny. The taxes were raised for the defence of the country and the recovery of his inheritance,[4] yet John made no real attempt to recover Normandy, and England was not yet assailed. The forces summoned to Portsmouth in 1201 were allowed to return home on a payment of money to the king;[5] in 1202 and 1203, having reached Normandy, they found the king indisposed to fight and left him in disgust, for which on his return he forced them to atone by the infliction of enormous fines.[6] In 1205 he assembled another great army and fleet at Portsmouth, and there made a feigned start for France. He sailed from

His treatment of the barons when prepared for foreign service

[1] Hoveden, iv. 140.

[2] Ann. Waverley, p. 258.

[3] M. Paris, p. 221; Ann. Margam, p. 28; Ann. Wigorn. 395; Ann. Winton. 79; Ann. Waverl. 258, 259; Walt. Cov. ii. 198, 199. The northern primate was engaged in this his last struggle with his brother just at the same time that the negotiations on the interdict were going on; and the quarrel is much less known. On the 18th December 1207, the pope wrote to the bishops of Worcester, Ely, and Hereford to urge John to make amends to the archbishop for his extortions, under pain of interdict (Epp. x. 172); and on the 27th of May, 1208, he wrote to the bishops of London and Rochester and the dean of Lincoln, telling the whole story; John had exacted a thirteenth from the religious and the clergy of the province of York, contrary to the liberty of the church: Geoffrey had left England to appeal to the pope, and John had immediately seized all his temporalities, although the pope had written six months before to the bishops of Ely, Worcester, and Hereford without result: the recipients are to admonish the king, and if that fails, after three months, to put the province under interdict: Epp. xi. 87. In 1210, May 6, the pope was still writing on the thirteenth to Geoffrey: Epp. xiii. 67.

[4] 'Ad recuperandam hæreditatem suam in Normannia et in aliis terris suis,' Ann. Wav. 258. Of the thirteenth, W. Cov. ii. 198.

[5] Hoveden, iv. 163. Two marks on the knight's fee, M. Paris, 206.

[6] M. Paris, p. 209.

Portsmouth and landed at Wareham; as soon as he returned to Portsmouth he dismissed his forces and took a pecuniary grant instead of service.[1] On this occasion the historians tell us that Archbishop Hubert dissuaded the king from the expedition, and that the barons were offended and disgusted at the final resolution taken after the labour and expense had been incurred.[2] But if this were really done, we can only suppose that the archbishop made, as he had often done before, a sacrifice of his own dignity to save the character of the king, or, if his appeal were *bona fide*, that he in common with the baronage [3] mistrusted John's capacity and used his influence to prevent unnecessary sacrifice. The barons, too, may well have been disinclined to follow John, and yet irritated by the facile way in which after all their exertions they were thrown over. But more than irritation at this moment they could not show, for they saw themselves in his power. Any sign of resistance he met by demanding their children as hostages.[4] So fortified against the men who would have been his surest defence, he filled his treasury with the spoils of his subjects, and, letting go all that he had inherited of territory and honour, consoled himself with his money-bags, his vicious indulgences, and his petty acts of spite and vengeance. And the mingled shame and malignity of this policy wrought its effects in the long run, although it was not until the great church struggle was over that the long endurance of evil united all parties against the tyrant.

John's measures for silencing opposition

The beneficial provisions of the great charter were not confined to the clergy and the baronage. There was a third estate with distinct interests, and trained under the system of Henry II. for a distinct future of its own. The hardships of the commons were one set of grievances that called for remedy, and the co-operation of the commons was needed if a remedy were to be possible. The people, alienated by the sufferings which, in common with the clergy, they had endured under the interdict, and, in common with the

Grievances of the commons

---

[1] M. Paris, p. 212; R. Coggeshall (ed. Dunkin), p. 227.

[2] R. Coggeshall, p. 228.

[3] The Earl Marshall is mentioned as joining in the appeal of the archbishop: R. Coggeshall, p. 227; all the *optimates*, by the Annals of Margam, p. 28; Ann. Waverl. 256; M. Paris, p. 212; Wendover, iii. 182.

[4] In 1201 William of Albini saved his castle of Belvoir by giving his son as hostage: Hoveden, iv. 161. In 1208, when John demanded hostages, in fear of the pope's absolving the barons from their oaths of fealty, ' alii filios,

alii vero nepotes et carnaliter propinquos nunciis tradebant,' Wendover, iii. 224, 225 ; M. Paris, 227. ' Erant insuper hac tempestate multi nobiles in regno Angliæ, quorum rex uxores et filias illis murmurantibus oppresserat; alii quos indebitis exactionibus ad extremam inopiam perduxerat; nonnulli quorum parentes et carnales amicos exulaverat, eorum hæreditates in suos usus convertens; unde factum est ut idem rex tot fere habuit hostes quot habuit magnates.' M. Paris, p. 232; Wendover, iii. 240.

I I

baronage, during the abeyance of justice, were willing and able to assert their rights, and for the first time since the Conquest ranged themselves on the side of the barons against the king. The text of Magna Carta shows what their grievances were. As the king had treated the barons of the opposite party, he had allowed the barons of his own party to treat the people : what little support he had he had purchased by allowing his favourites the full sway of feudal tyranny.[1] The royal exactions by which all alike suffered were reproduced in the baronial taxation, by which the commons in particular suffered over and above the rest. Under one or the other of these two principles almost all the gravamina of the commons came, for the incidence of feudal hardships was uniform, and of course the accumulation pressed most heavily on the lowest rank. Hence the force and propriety of the clauses by which the barons insist that the king shall secure for their vassals as regards them the same liberties that they obtained for themselves.[2] It was not enough that the status of the commons should depend on the mere benevolence of the great feudatories, who might at any moment purchase from the Crown the liberty of tyrannising : the barons of Runnymede guard the people against themselves as well as against the common tyrant. The provision which Henry I. forced on the nobles on behalf of the people [3] is now forced by the nobles upon the king, in order to make it impossible for the future that class should be set against class.

But besides these, a great number of the articles of the charter have a meaning only when viewed in relation to the rights of the commons. The provision for the city of London is made applicable to all the towns of the country ;[4] the freeholders' interests are everywhere coupled with those of the knights and the barons ;[5] the ancient courts of the nation in which the barons have little or no direct share are restored to full efficiency ;[6] the stock in trade of the merchant, the land qualification of the freeholder, and the wainage of the villein are preserved from over-amercement, as well as the settled estate of earldom or barony.[7] If the knight is freed from compulsory exaction of service, the freeholder is freed from

[1] It is to this that the 15th article of the charter refers, ' Nos non concedemus de cetero alicui quod capiat auxilium,' &c.

[2] Art. Baronum, 48 ; Magna Carta, art. 60. ' Omnes autem istas consuetudines et libertates quas rex concessit regno tenendas quantum ad se pertinet erga suos, omnes de regno tam clerici quam laici observabunt quantum ad se pertinet erga suos.' Compare M. C. art. 15.

[3] M. Carta Henrici I. art. 2 : ' Similiter et homines baronum meorum justa et legitima relevatione relevabunt terras suas de dominis suis.' Art. 4 : ' Et præcipio quod barones mei similiter se contineant erga filios et filias vel uxores hominum suorum.'

[4] Magna Carta, Art. 13.

[5] Articles 14 and 15.

[6] Articles 17, 18, 19, 24, 25, 38, 45.

[7] Articles 20, 21, 22, 23.

compulsory cartage.[1] If it is to the freeholder of land chiefly that the boon is given, it must be remembered that it was in and through the holding of land that a man became obnoxious to the demands that are now restricted. The non-landholding free man was protected by his own status; he had nothing on which feudal tyranny could prey directly; nor could the feudal interest obtain for itself a remission of taxation which would not be directly applicable to all the population. Hence it is, no doubt, that there is so little notice of villeins in the charter; it was not that they had no spokesman, but that they were free from the more pressing grievances and benefited by every general provision. The provisions for equal justice are applicable to the commons as to the baronage; the relief from forest tyranny is a boon to all classes alike.[2] Clause for clause the rights of the freeholders are stated with the rights of the barons, and analogous remedies are provided wherever one rule seems inapplicable to both.

It may very naturally be asked, how came this accord to be effected; was there a treaty made by the barons with the commons previous to the drawing up of the articles by the barons to be presented to the king, or were the demands of the barons for the people the mere outcome of a political stratagem for isolating the public enemy? Read, I think, by the light of the preceding history, the circumstances scarcely allow of either supposition. No doubt when the assembly of the commons of the royal demesne met the bishops and barons under Geoffrey Fitz Peter at S. Alban's,[3] the three estates learned much of each other's desires; and we cannot question that when Langton at S. Paul's expounded to the clergy the great charter of Henry I.[4] he pointed out the duty there enforced, that they should do to their vassals as they would have the king do to them. But the accord lay deeper than this; in fact they could not have entered at all into each other's views if it had not been for the feeling that the English were now become one people, and that the benefits of institutions rapidly becoming spontaneous, instinctive, and free, were making that unity a fact too certain to be controverted, too prominent to be ignored. If we run through the list of the barons who took the leading part in resisting John and in drawing up the charter, we shall see that although it may contain the names of a few who were moved by personal feelings, or by the old leaven of feudal opposition, the great majority are men of English interests, sprung from the English patriots of 1173, the Northern barons[5] who had saved the country in that year, and

Marginal notes:
Amount of co-operation between the barons and the commons

The Northern or constitutional party

---

[1] Articles 29 and 30.
[2] Articles 44–48.
[3] M. Paris, 239.   [4] M. Paris, 240.

[5] 'Barones Northumbriæ,' R. Cogeshall, p. 246. 'Contradixerunt ex Aquilonaribus nonnulli, illi videlicet

Other ele-
ments of
hostility to
the king
who refused to follow John to Poictou in 1213. True, John had
united every sort of hostility against himself : there is Geoffrey de
Mandeville, the son of Geoffrey Fitz Peter and husband of the king's
divorced wife ; [1] Giles de Braiose, bishop of Hereford, who had the
cruel wrongs of his family to avenge ; there is the earl of Clare, who
from the beginning of the reign had maintained an attitude of
suspicion ; Bigod and Mowbray and Aumale, the hereditary representatives of feudal insubordination ; [2] but they are a small element
by the side of the Northern barons, who had never been ranged
against the king before,[3] the loyal Lacies, the Percies, the Vescies,
the Bohuns, the Stutevilles, the Veres, the Vauxes, and the Multons ;
the men who sprang from the chosen servants of Henry II. and his
most valued ministers, whose descendants were the strength of that
great Lancastrian party which maintained the spirit of freedom
in the darkest days of the fourteenth century ; the barons who invariably led and were followed by the commons.

Importance
of Magna
Carta
Magna Carta is, then, the first corporate act of the nation roused
to the sense of its unity ; the first act of the three estates dis-
covering the true oneness of their interests and sinking their
differences under the pressure of the common enemy. That the

Part taken
by the com-
mons in
securing it ;
the barons
acting as
leaders
historians have recorded less of the action of the third estate is
accounted for by the fact that at this period and from this period to
the Reformation the baronage acts as advocate for it ; and there is
as yet no division between the town and country parties. But the
barons could not have done what they did without the help of the
people, and the king would not have been so helpless as he was if
he could, as William Rufus and Henry I. had done, have made
himself strong in the support of the people against the barons. The
effect of his fifteen years of misrule had been to undo all that had
been done to strengthen the royal power since the reign of Henry I. ;
to undo the work of the twelfth century in England, as he had done
in the continental territories of his house ; and thus to set the

qui anno præterito regem ne in Picta-
viam transiret impedierunt ; dicentes
se propter terras quas in Anglia tenent
non debere regem extra regnum sequi
nec ipsum euntem scutagio juvare ' :
Walt. Cov. ii. 217. The canon of
Barnwell, indeed, generally speaks of
them as the Northern party, ii. 219,
221 ; Transhumbrani, p. 222 ; the
Annals of Dunstable call them
Norenses, pp. 40, 43 ; ' licet fuissent de
diversis partibus Angliæ, tamen omnes
fuerunt vocati Norenses,' Lib. de Ant.
Legg. p. 201.

[1] W. Covent. ii. 225 ; Ann. Dunst.

45. John, it is said, had made him
marry her. She married after his
death Hubert de Burgh.

[2] W. Covent. ii. 225.

[3] 'Aquilonaribus supradictis et
pluribus aliis quos longum esset enu-
merare,' Walt. Cov. ii. 219 ; M. Paris,
p. 254. The Vescies, the Stutevilles, the
Vauxes, the Lacies, the lords of Kyme
and Lanvalei, were of Northern houses
risen by the service of Henry II. : the
Percies and the Bruces were Northern
barons less closely connected with
official life. The list will bear the
severest analysis.

nation at one with itself, in a way in which it had not since the Conquest realised its identity. The sentence of Runnymede reversed the sentence of Hastings.

That John saw what he was doing it would be rash to affirm : it cannot be said that even Innocent III. fully realised the position of affairs ; [1] but both showed an instinctive hostility to the claims of the nation which forms a clue to the later history. John attempted to divide his enemies before as well as after the concession. Now he would grant the liberties of the church if the clergy would detach themselves from the cause of the barons.[2] Now he would treat with the barons in the idea of escaping from their constitutional demands by purchasing their adhesion with the gift of feudal privileges.[3] Now he would disarm all hostility by declaring himself a crusader, and involving all opponents in the excommunication resulting from his sacrosanctity.[4] But he failed in each plan, and the bloodless issue of the contest proves, if there were need of proof, the unity of the nation and the isolation of the king. Nor has he the credit of accepting the terms forced upon him with the intention of observing them. When he seals the charter he is demanding absolution from his undertaking,[5] and as soon as he has concluded the reconciliation he sets to work to destroy those whom for that moment he might have made friends. Nor do they trust him any more than he deserves. Already perhaps they saw that they had obtained in word more than they could secure in reality. The history of the century shows that it was so ; the very men who had won the constitutional articles of the charter were, when the supreme power fell into their own hands, unable or unwilling to ratify them ; and it was only after eighty years of striving that they became permanently a part of the law, in the hand of a king who knew how to keep faith, and who saw in a clearer light and with a juster precision the truth of the national unity. The unity which the barons at Runnymede had realised as against the king, Edward, not without a struggle, but, when the struggle was over, with a firm faith and righteous purpose, crowned by the adhesion of royalty itself.

Marginal notes:

The king and pope instinctively hostile to liberty on this occasion

John tries to temporise and fails

The benefits of the char ter only partially secured at first

Edward the First really secures liberty

---

[1] John's idea of the pope is thus interpreted by Matthew Paris : ' Noverat autem et multiplici didicerat experientia, quod papa super omnes mortales ambitiosus erat et superbus, pecuniæque sititor insatiabilis, et ad omnia scelera pro præmiis datis vel promissis cereus et proclivus ' (p. 245).

[2] On the 21st Nov. 1214, and again on Jan. 25, 1215. See Blackstone's remarks, *Charters*, Introduction, p. x.

[3] See his letter of May 10, 1215,

Fœd. i. 128.

[4] March 4, 1215, Ann. Theokesb. p. 61 ; W. Cov. ii. 219. ' Sinistre hoc interpretabantur alii, dicentes eum non intuitu pietatis aut amore Christi hoc fecisse, sed ut eos a proposito fraudaret.'

[5] 'Dum hæc agerentur,' Ann. Dunstapl. p. 43 ; and see at greater length the statement of the canon of Barnwell ; W. Cov. ii. 222.

The popes now had the choice between the people and the king, and threw in their lot with the latter in a way that affects the history of England to the present moment. Had they chosen to support the barons against the Crown, the complications of the reign of Henry III. would have been avoided, but then Henry III. would never have reigned, and England might, after all her early glories and later discipline, have shared the fate of France. Thus much the papal alliance did for John : it saved the throne for his son, and saved the son's throne in the evil days in which the constitutional struggle was renewed. But when Edward I. found himself in the position in which he chose to conquer by yielding, he cast to the winds the compact in which his father and grandfather had sought their strength. The papal alliance had maintained the Plantagenet hold on England, but it had almost destroyed its hold on the English. Edward, too, had to choose between the continuance of his vassalage and his glorious status as a national king. Unlike

John, he chose the latter, to the enormous increase of his own power in church and state, and to that adjustment of the relations between the papacy and England which continued to the Reformation, and which, read politically, without reference to the spiritual questions, continue in the direction of their course to the present day. The statutes of Præmunire and Provisors, the principle of which was, politically speaking, the germ of the Reformation, followed naturally from the determination of 1297. The Bull *Clericis laicos* stands to the Confirmation of Charters in the same relation as the submission of Dover stands to the Great Charter itself. The first dissolved the concordat which was established by Pandulf, the second crowned the work that was made feasible at Runnymede.

Innocent III. had no successor even second to himself. He would not, like Honorius III., have attempted the ignoble policy of supporting the foreign malcontents against the patriotic ministers of Henry III. He would not have descended to the sordid contrivances, or allowed himself to be forced into the self-defeating arbitrary impotence, of Gregory IX. He would not have broken the heart and spirit of S. Edmund, or connived at the faithless tyranny of Henry III., or the cruelties of Charles of Anjou. Nor would he, like Boniface VIII., have precipitated a crisis that threw the papacy into exile, and opened the way to the general disruption of the

Western Church at the Reformation. But he would not have been able in all probability to alter the result, or to thwart the policy of tradition. The high Hildebrandine policy would have sought realisation by nobler but not more effective devices ; and with regard to England, only a king like Edward I. was required to undo what John had done, as well as to complete what he and Innocent together had failed to prevent.

For John even in the abject humiliation of his end we have no word of pity as we have had none of sympathy. He has deserved none. He has no policy of either aggression or defence. We do not credit him with a deliberate design on the rights of his people, simply because he never showed the consciousness of any rights they had, but took his own evil way in contempt of law, and in a wilful ignoring of dangers he dared not face. He made no plans and grasped at no opportunities. He was persistent only in petty spite and greedy of easy vengeance. He staked everything on the object of the moment and made no effort to avert his ruin until it was consummated. He looked neither before him nor behind him, drew as little from experience as he sacrificed to expediency, or as he utilised the present for the ends of the future. He had not sufficient regard for virtue to make him play the hypocrite, and lost even the little defence that such a cloak gives to kings. He had neither energy, capacity, nor honesty; he availed himself neither of the help of those who had common interests, nor of the errors of those whom he regarded as his enemies. He met honest service with contempt, and the best advice with the treatment due to dangerous conspiracy. He is an exception to the class of men who are well hated only in this, that none even pretended to love him. And as he is without wisdom for himself, he has no care for his people ; on them, the weaker and more innocent the better, he wreaks the vengeance, the savage vengeance, that the stronger and less innocent have provoked,[1] as if burning villages and slaying peasants was an enjoyment to be set against defeat in council and disgrace in the field. And now the heart that was obdurate against the sufferings of the people, that had been unmoved by the cries of the tortured as it was inexorable to the prayers of friendship, virtue, and sorrow, is broken by the loss of his treasure.[2] And he who had defied God by word and deed all his life, sought shelter from the terrors with which superstition, not conscience, had inspired him, by being buried in the habit of a monk : a posthumous tribute to religion, which he had believed only to outrage.[3]

John deserves no commiseration

Selfishness and isolation of John

* * * * * *

[1] This is a marked feature in John's proceedings both in his French wars and in the cruel measures he adopted in the last year of his reign : for example he burnt Tours most wantonly in 1202 (R. Coggeshall, p. 211); and Le Mans the same year : compare his treatment of Rochester in 1215 (R. Coggeshall, p. 252); and the work of his mercenaries in the fens (p. 254) : his ravaging of Axholme in 1216 (Walt. Cov. ii. 231), and of Lincolnshire generally : after setting up the dragon standard at Winchester, he fled before Lewis, and set the city on fire in four places : R. Coggesh. p. 258. Instead of relieving Rochester, ' perambulabat terram et incendiis ac rapinis quæcunque potuit consumpsit ' : ib. p. 259.

[2] ' Quia res ei minime cesserant ad votum,' Ann. Wav. 286; cf. M. Paris, p. 287.

[3] It was Merlin's prophecy : ' inter sanctos collocabitur,' Wikes, 59

CHRONICLES OF THE REIGNS OF EDWARD I.
AND EDWARD II. VOL. I.

[THE following Preface to the *Annales Londonienses* and the *Annales Paulini*, two valuable authorities for the reigns of Edward I. and Edward II., contains much that is of interest. Attention is called to the mixture of ecclesiastical and civil matters which characterises the *Annales Londonienses*, and to the impressions of London life to be derived from the *Annales Paulini*. The author of the latter was present at Edward II.'s coronation, which he describes with minuteness. He also gives evidence to prove how divided political feeling was in London in the year 1321. Bishop Stubbs, after devoting 99 pages of his Preface to an examination of these two Annals, concludes with a sketch of (1) a portion of the reign of Edward I. and (2) the reign of Edward II.]

*   *   *   *   *   *

Important illustrations of contemporary history

RESERVING [for the later portion of this collection] our review of the more important crises of the reign of Edward II., I will devote the remaining pages of this introduction to the elucidation, rendered more easy by the documents accumulated of late years, of two of the subordinate incidents of a period fraught with great issues to English liberty. Of these the first will be the final struggle of Edward I. with Archbishop Winchelsey ; the second, the abortive attempt of the Lancaster party to wrest the supreme power from Isabella and Mortimer at the opening of the reign of Edward III.

The difficulties of government under Edward I.

To the student of the reign of Edward I. every difficulty and embarrassment under which the king laboured serves to enhance the greatness of the man who with such drawbacks on his activity could do so much. There are, of course, emergencies and contingencies which help to draw out the strong points of the character of a ruler ; such are the exigencies of national defence, the necessities of political reconciliation, the reconstruction of shattered institutions. But Edward's difficulties were of a much more trying, penetrating, and homely character. He was throughout his reign deeply in debt, and, in every section of his government, hampered by opposition from the leading prelates of his time. Personally he was very economical and truly devout. He inherited from his father a poverty which his own

The king's poverty and

obligations, incurred during the Crusade, increased into a lifelong burden; and he inherited from his father certain ecclesiastical traditions which he found it indeed more easy to break through than it was to pay his debts, but which in their results and in combination with his debts have a perceptible influence on the colour of his reign, his popularity whilst he lived, and the reputation which he left behind him. Setting aside his treatment of the Scots, which may, of course, be read in two ways, all the events of the reign which fall short of the ideal events of such a king's reign are attributable to these two causes, separately or conjointly. From the very day of his accession Edward was financially in the hands of the Lombard bankers; hence arose, no doubt, the difficulty which he had in managing the city of London; hence came also the financial mischief which followed the banishment of the Jews; and hence an accumulation of popular discontent, which showed itself, in the king's lifetime, by opposition to his mercantile policy, and, after his death, supplied one of the most efficient means for the overthow of his son. But more than this : Edward's pecuniary exigencies forced him to the invention or development of a great system of customs duties, in the collection of which he had to employ foreign agents, and to an amount of pecuniary dealings with the see of Rome which imperilled his independence as a king, and brought him into collision with the independent ecclesiastical instincts of his people. *Results of Edward's pecuniary exigencies*

It had rarely happened in English history that a strong king and a strong primate had ruled together or in anything but rivalry. The archbishops of Canterbury, inheriting a very special preponderance in England from the days of the Heptarchy, had been rather joint rulers than subjects until the Conquest, and since the Conquest the relations of the heads in church and state had always been somewhat strained. William I. and Lanfranc, both foreigners, and men of high intellect and policy, had worked together ; but since that time, except where a weak king had strong archbishops or weak archbishops had a strong king, there had been scant peace between church and state. Anselm had had to fight against William Rufus and Henry I., Becket against Henry II., Langton against John. All these were strong men in their way, but the weak Theobald had had his struggle with the weak Stephen, and the weak Edmund with the weaker Henry III. In general it had happened that the ecclesiastical interest had coincided with the interest of popular liberty, but sometimes that coincidence had been the result of a common determination to resist those measures of strong government which were necessary for national consolidation. So it had been in the great Becket quarrel, and so it was in a less degree and with less calamitous results in the reign of Edward I. Archbishop Winchelsey *Coincidences of strong kings and strong primates*

Edward I. and his archbishops

was probably the ablest man who had sat at Canterbury since Langton, and his predecessor Peckham, of whom the same might be said, had borne part of the burden of the struggle before him.

Peckham's conduct in opposition

Peckham, however, although a papal nominee in opposition to the king's choice, and a bold and independent politician, had never come into personal antagonism with Edward. He had been obliged to submit his conciliar proceedings to the king's fiat; he had been obliged to withdraw from his aggressive attitude in the publication of the charters, to acquiesce in an unprecedented amount of ecclesiastical taxation, and to agree to the limitation of ecclesiastical acquisitiveness in the statute *De religiosis*, and of ecclesiastical jurisdiction in the legislation of the *Circumspecte agatis*. But with the single exception of the episode of the charters he had not set

Winchelsey in opposition

himself up as a secular champion. Winchelsey, on the other hand, either placed himself at the head of the baronial opposition, or by playing into the hands of the discontented earls had practically connived at the great humiliations of Edward's career. Although he was an English priest and an Oxford scholar, and although he attained the primacy by a free election and with the full agreement of all the competing parties, who so very seldom could agree on such a point, he was from the moment of his promotion in opposition.

Personal and political motives

Personally he disliked the king's ministerial bishops, one of whom, Walter de Langton, was his political rival and enemy as long as he lived; and, although Edward and he must have entertained some respect for one another, it was never such as reached the measure of personal friendship. Consecrated in 1294, Winchelsey crossed the Rubicon in 1296, when, relying on the papal Bull *Clericis laicos*, he

His successive offences against Edward

refused to help the king with money; in 1297 he leagued with the earls in forcing the king to confirm the charters, and in 1301 he finally cut off all chances of future co-operation by his conduct in the parliament of Lincoln. In each of these cases his conduct was capable of an easy defence, and the king's policy was tenable only on

Edward's resentment

the ground of bitter necessity, but it is clear that Edward saw in the archbishop's behaviour more than mere official or political opposition; he felt the treatment, which he had not deserved, as personal insult; and the great king was unquestionably a good hater. For the political manœuvre by which, in the Lincoln parliament, he had been obliged to submit to have his minister impeached and his own honour doubted, he never forgave the archbishop. But for a time both parties had to deal with a pope who was difficult to manage.

Winchelsey moves the pope against the king's minister

Boniface VIII., with all his faults, was incapable of becoming a political tool, and he was quite capable on occasion of acting up to his great idea of his office; both sides in the personal struggle waited on his decision. Immediately after the parliament of

Lincoln we find Winchelsey's agents at the Roman court urging bitter accusations of personal depravity against Langton, and at the same time the archbishop himself was subjected, as we have seen, to a piece of petty persecution at which the king must have connived, in the matter of Theobald of Bar;[1] but in the end the pope acquitted Langton and absolved Winchelsey. This part of the quarrel ended in 1302, and the same year, by usurping the appointments to the sees of Worcester and Norwich, the pope showed both the great litigants that it was unwise to recognise in him too unreservedly the supreme authority that he claimed. Boniface VIII. met his calamitous doom in 1303, and in that and the following year Edward was fully employed in Scotland. Benedict XI. was not strong enough, and did not reign long enough, to interfere much in England ; only on one or two occasions do we come upon traces of his action. I have already called attention to the attempt which he made through Gerard de Petoraria to collect a tenth which Boniface had made over to the king.[2] That attempt was peremptorily foiled by Edward, but not finally dealt with until the pope was dead; Benedict died on the 6th of July; the order for the arrest of Gerard is dated on the 5th of July, but he was not sent about his business until the 10th of December, 1304. In the preceding April the pope had written to the bishop of Durham, directing him to appoint the bishop of Byblus to the priory of Coldingham, a proposition which was rejected by the king in the next parliament,[3] as prejudicial to himself and his royal crown. Other cases of interference with patronage might be found. Edward himself never hesitated to use the papal influence for his own purposes ; in the interregnum that followed the death of Benedict, he is found writing to Rome advocating the archbishop of York's claim to carry his cross erect in the province of Canterbury,[4] a small matter in itself, but one in which Winchelsey was specially susceptible ; and there are letters of the same date, in which he undertakes not to write to the Curia in opposition to appeals which had been carried there against the decisions of the ecclesiastical courts at home ;[5] but, although, perhaps as a political necessity, he had to counteract the aggressive pretensions of his own bishops more frequently than those of the popes, he took advantage of the vacancy in the popedom to press through his parliament of April 1305 an act which forbade the export of money from the alien monasteries.[6] This act, which was no doubt aimed partly at the papal collectors, did not apparently

Marginal notes:
Boniface VIII. difficult to use

Benedict XI. and Gerard de Petoraria

Dismissal of Gerard de Petoraria

Benedict's attempts in England, and the king's connivance

Legislation against export of money by alien monasteries

---

[1] See vol. in R. S. p. xxxv.
[2] Ibid. p. xxxvii.
[3] Fœdera, i. 969, 970; Prynne, Records, iii. 1059.
[4] Fœdera, i. 969.
[5] Prynne, Records, iii. 1041.
[6] Statutes of the Realm, i. 150.

receive the assent of the clergy, and did not become law until it was confirmed by the statute of Carlisle two years after. It is possible that for the moment it was retarded by the influence of Winchelsey, whose day of account was now at hand.

Edward was too wise to begin an open struggle with the archbishop whilst the Scots were on his hands. In the spring of 1305 Scotland seemed to be completely subdued; Wallace was taken and executed; Bruce was still at the English court. In the summer the papacy was filled by the election of Bertrand de Goth, a Gascon nobleman, archbishop of Bourdeaux, born and promoted within Edward's French dominions. Bertrand received the triple crown as Clement V. on the 14th of November, 1305; but before this, as soon as the news of the election reached England, Edward had concerted his attack on Winchelsey. Clement was anxious that the ceremony of his coronation should be graced by the presence of the king or his eldest son, and immediately on his election sent to England, with the invitation, Raymond, bishop of Lescar, and William de Testa, archdeacon of Aran, in the Pyrenees,[1] a person who soon after becomes a leading figure in the negotiations. The king declined the offer on behalf of himself and his son, but he sent an embassy to Lyons, including among its members Bishop Langton, the treasurer, Hugh le Despenser, and his two most trusted friends, Henry de Lacy, earl of Lincoln, and Otho of Grandison. Besides mere formal credentials in which these envoys were authorised to treat on the matters of the Crusade, the canonisation of Thomas Cantilupe, and other points of smaller interest, they had letters of recommendation by which the pope was requested to listen to them on certain businesses which were deep in the heart of the king, 'quæ valde insident cordi nostro.'[2] One of these businesses was the obligations to which in 1289 and 1301 the king had been forced to submit, in reference to the forest charters. To the request for absolution from the oath which the king had taken, Clement V. listened readily; the Bulls were expedited before the end of the year. On the 29th of December the king was released from his oath,[3] and, on the first of January, 1306, a formal prohibition was issued, by which it was decreed that no sentence of excommunication, suspension, or interdict should be issued against him without special leave from the pope.[4] This prohibition left Winchelsey both personally and politically defenceless, and his agents at Lyons were able to warn him that worse was coming.

Clement V. becomes pope

He invites the king to his coronation

Envoys sent with special instructions

Edward's Bulls of absolution

[1] Fœdera, i. 973; Prynne, Records, iii. 1068.
[2] Fœdera, i. 973, 974, 975.
[3] Fœdera, i. 978. The Ordinance of the Forest, issued in consequence of the absolution, is printed among the statutes of the realm, dated at Westminster, May 27. Statutes, i. 147–149; Prynne, Records, iii. 1140.
[4] Fœdera, i. 978, 979.

Bishop Langton was not likely to let the matter rest. He was not, perhaps, a good bishop, but there is no reason to believe that he fell below the ordinary moral level of episcopal politicians ; yet, with Winchelsey's connivance, he had been charged with adultery, concubinage, simony, and intercourse with the devil. Boniface VIII. had on these representations suspended him in 1301, but Edward had explained to the pope that the charges really proceeded from Winchelsey's malice, and Langton was acquitted and reinstated in 1303.[1] *Langton urges the pope against Winchelsey*

Now his turn was come, and he had the pope's ear. On the 12th of February Clement suspended the archbishop and summoned him to the Curia. The news reached him on the 25th of March through Master Thorp,[2] the dean of the Arches, whom, in anticipation perhaps of some hostile move, he had sent to Lyons in the preceding January. The Bull had not yet arrived, so Winchelsey betook himself to the king to ask for his gracious intercession. *He is suspended and summoned to the papal court*

Edward answered him by recounting the disgrace, contempt, and injuries which he had heaped upon him : told him how he had nearly driven the kingdom into rebellion, and that it was no fault of the archbishop's that he was not dethroned ; kindness and patience had been tried in vain, one of the two must quit the kingdom.[3] Winchelsey could scarcely have replied effectively, for the charges, although somewhat exaggerated, represented a feeling in the king's mind which the archbishop's perversity had justified. Instead of interceding, Edward wrote to the pope declaring that the archbishop's continued presence was a standing danger to peace. The letter was written on the 6th of April.[4] Winchelsey had to wait in patience ; on the 18th of May the letters of suspension reached him,[5] and on the morrow before sunrise he set out for Lyons and crossed the sea. He left no substitute, and from the 18th of May to the 6th of June the spiritual and temporal administration of the see was in abeyance. Nothing seems to have happened in consequence. Winchelsey, however, did not return to England until after the coronation of Edward II. *Winchelsey's remonstrance and Edward's persistence*

Winchelsey goes abroad

Edward I. had not to wait long before he found out with what dangerous tools he had been playing. Even the accommodating Clement was not going to lose his vantage-ground ; he was already prepared to undertake the spiritual and temporal administration of the archbishopric. William de Testa had spied out the country when he came to invite the king to the pope's coronation. On the

---

[1] Fœdera, i. 939, 943, 956, 957.
[2] Somner's Battely's Canterbury, part ii. App. p. 31. See vol. in R. S. p. 145.
[3] Birchington, Ang. Sacr. i. 16.

[4] Fœdera, i, 983 ; Prynne, Records, iii. 1092.
[5] See vol. in R. S. p. 144 ; Somner, p. 31.

6th of June, at Bow church, he and his colleague, William Geraldi de Sora, published letters dated on the 20th of April, by which the spiritual administration was committed to them ; in the king's presence they delivered a similar letter to Bishop Langton, by which the temporal administration was committed to him. We are curious to know how this had been contrived, whether the pope was anxious to make his claim on the temporal administration effectual by appointing the king's confidential minister, or whether Langton had miscalculated his master's patience by asking for the office for himself. However it was, the king was very angry, and immediately replied that he would never permit the bishop, or anyone else, clerk or lay, native or alien, deputed or to be deputed by the pope, to interfere with any temporal matters in his kingdom, any more than the pope permits him to do in spiritual matters. And having said this he committed the temporalities of Canterbury to Humfrey of Walden, knight.[1]

Before the king set out for Scotland in the summer, on the 2nd of July he wrote again [2] to the pope begging that Winchelsey might not be restored, and at the same time negotiated for the transfer to himself of a biennial tenth which had been imposed for the purposes of the Crusade. This was one of the curiously discreditable shifts to which Edward's poverty drove him, and which the pope's pliability rendered easy. But the spiritual administration of William de Testa was not successful ; it consisted principally in the direction of the court of Arches and the collection of firstfruits. The archbishop's dean of Arches was superseded on the 6th of June, and Philip Turbeville appointed commissary-general.[3] That much was easy. The collection of the firstfruits of vacant benefices, which was committed to the papal agents by another Bull, immediately produced difficulties. The canons of Merton, in Surrey, refused to pay the impost and prevented the collectors from proceeding with their task. On the 27th of August the pope wrote to the king to complain of this.[4] Edward had already found that with the Scottish war on his hands he could not maintain the position which his brave words had claimed. If the pope was to keep Winchelsey innocuous, it must be made worth his while. The 11th of September the king wrote from Bradley, on the Scottish march, to Clement,[5] giving up to him all the profits of the temporal administration to be applied to his own uses, but adding a petition that Nicolas of Tingewick, his physician, might be allowed to retain the church of Reculver, to which he had presented him whilst the temporalities

---

[1] Somner, pp. 31, 32. See also Prynne, Records, iii. 1095, 1098, 1099.
[2] Fœdera, i. 989 ; Prynne, Records, iii. 1095.
[3] See vol. in R. S. p. 147.   [4] Fœdera, i. 997.
[5] Fœdera, i. 999.

were in his hands.[1] The pope graciously accepted the surrender and confirmed the physician in his living. He also determined to send Cardinal Peter of Spain to attempt the negotiation of a general peace. Matters were in this state when the famous parliament of Carlisle was called. The writs were issued on the 3rd of November,[2] and the assembly, which was to be a complete representation of the estates, was to meet on the 20th of January, 1307, the cause of the meeting being the settlement of Scotland. The parliament was a very full one ; the names of the representatives of both clergy and laity are preserved.[3] On the 19th of January the king empowered Bishop Langton and the earl of Lincoln to open the session, he himself being at Lanercost. The meeting took place on the 20th, and the estates sat on the 21st and 29th. Some of the legal transactions of the session are dated in full parliament on the 9th of February, others as late as the 18th and 23rd of March. How long the formal session continued is uncertain. The cardinal who was expected to meet it did not reach Carlisle until March. He arrived on or about the 12th.[4] The chief thing that he did was to excommunicate Robert Bruce, and to make some engagements for Philip IV., which that king did not confirm. The parliament of Carlisle had thus time to act whilst waiting for the cardinal. The statute of 1305 forbidding the alien monasteries to export money was confirmed, and on the 20th of March notified to the sheriffs for execution.[5] A more important feature of the time was the address to the pope, drawn up on behalf of the clergy and people of England, recounting the abuses, oppressions, and exactions which they had suffered from the maladministration of the papal power.[6] Another petition to the king to the same effect was presented by the nobles and commons, stating the national grievances in language which subsequently became classical and was adopted in the great statute of Provisors.[7] In this document William de Testa and his commissaries are singled out for special animadversion ; and in consequence a series of articles was exhibited against him.[8] He was interrogated in full parliament, and, being unable to allege in excuse anything beyond his general authority from the pope, was regarded as convicted, and forbidden by a resolution of the whole parliament to proceed with his exactions; his money was to be seized, a report was to be sent to the pope of

Margin notes:
Parliament of Carlisle, Jan. 20, 1307

Duration of the session

The Act of 1305 confirmed

Petitions against papal aggressions

William de Testa questioned in parliament

---

[1] Fœdera, i. 1000, 1006.
[2] Fœdera, i. 1008.
[3] Rot. Parl. i. 188, 189, 204.
[4] The day fixed for the cardinal's visit was March 12, and on the 16th letters of safe-conduct were issued for his departure (Fœdera, i. 1009) ; but it is not improbable that he arrived earlier, and he certainly stayed longer.

[5] Rot. Parl. i. 217; Statutes of the Realm, i. 150–152.
[6] Rot. Parl. i. 207, 208; Prynne, Records, iii. 1174.
[7] Rot. Parl. i. 219; Prynne, Records, iii. 1168–1170.
[8] Rot. Parl. i. 220: Prynne, Records, iii. 1171.

his misdoings, and the sheriffs were directed to arrest his agents and bring them before the king in the ensuing Trinity term. The

writs for this purpose were issued on the 22nd of March.[1] It is therefore probable that the whole of these proceedings had been prepared before the arrival of the cardinal. He is not mentioned as present during the discussion, but unfortunately stayed with the king after the estates had separated. Notwithstanding the writs of the 22nd of March which had been issued with parliamentary

authority, the cardinal persuaded the king on the 26th to restore the temporal administration of Canterbury to William de Testa,[2] and on the 4th of April to take the culprits into his protection, and to sanction the collection of the firstfruits.[3] By other writs he empowered William de Testa to execute his office as envoy of the pope and administrator of Canterbury. The day fixed for the trial of the agents came, but, at the beginning of Trinity term, instead of appearing as culprits they presented to the council a series of complaints that they were hindered from the performance of their

duty. They presented the letters of April 4, and the council examined them.[4] They found, in close agreement with the policy of their master, that the latter writs only empowered the papal agents to collect the firstfruits, so far as it was in the king's power to authorise it ; and forbade them to persist in the oppressions which were injurious to the king and his faithful subjects. These saving words explained away all that the writs seemed to have granted, and a peremptory prohibition against their further proceedings was issued on the 27th of June.[5] This was delivered to them by the mayor and aldermen of London. Before they could

determine on the next step to be taken Edward I. died. Nothing more was done in the matter. The whole of the situation changed. Within a few days Bishop Langton was removed from office, to be arrested, kept in prison and disgrace for years. Winchelsey was to return in triumph. From this time, although the flame broke out again and again, as in the parliament of Stamford, when a bill of gravamina, corresponding with that of Carlisle, was drawn up and sent to the pope, the new quarrels of the new reign were for the

most part on other points. For a short time Winchelsey was on the side of Edward II., but he very soon found himself hand and glove with Lancaster. When his opposition became overt, after the publication of the ordinances, Edward made his peace with Langton and restored him to liberty and office. But Winchelsey died before

[1] Rot. Parl. i. 221, 222.
[2] Fœdera, i. 1012 ; Prynne, Records, iii. 1179.
[3] Fœdera, i. 1014 ; Rot. Parl. i. 222 Prynne, iii. 1178, 1179.

[4] Rot. Parl. i. 222, 223 ; Prynne, Records, iii. 1181.
[5] Rot. Parl. i. 223 ; Prynne, Records, iii. 1182.

the king's difficulties became insurmountable, and after his death his rival became insignificant ; he too died before the final crisis of the reign, during the period which intervened between the banishment and the recall of the Despensers.

It is interesting to know that William de Testa, after Winchelsey's restoration, faithfully accounted to him for the receipts of his administration, making him much richer than he had ever been before.[1] William himself was made a cardinal in 1312, and long survived all the other actors in the struggle. *Fortunes of William de Testa*

The story I have told shows us a curious close of a great and in some respects glorious reign ; we see the old king fighting with those favourite weapons from which he had never gained anything but discredit ; holding by the letter of an engagement, taking his stand on the wording of a writ ; balancing between the pope and the national clergy ; buying the leave of the one to tax the other, and availing himself of the independent spirit of the one to avoid paying the price of the services of the other. His poverty and his ecclesiastical troubles, throughout his reign, are connected together, and serve to bring out the weak points of his character as a king and as a man. We have to remember, however, in an equitable view of the matter, the greatness of his exigencies, and the overwhelming power and prestige of the papacy. It was comparatively easy for Edward I. to overawe the national clergy, to cripple its acquisitiveness, to limit its judicial ambitions, and to put the whole of its members into outlawry. But with the pope he must temporise. A later king whose exigencies were less pressing, of much stronger will and much less scrupulous integrity, in a still more critical juncture, had to play with a weaker pope a game of diplomacy still more complicated and still more full of snares for honest dealing. Henry VIII. in his dealing with the annates and Peterpence had not less than Edward I. to play fast and loose with his people ; to make the execution of his statutes contingent on the next move of the Curia. *Curious light thrown on the character of Edward I.* *His excuses in the great difficulties of his position*

Another somewhat obscure episode of our history, on which the annals now edited and the companion records throw a fresh light, is the period of the dominion of Mortimer and Isabella, who for nearly four years exercised supreme power in England, which they lost by a revolution more abrupt and scarcely less just than that by which they had gained it. The fall of Edward II. was the result, no doubt to a great extent, of his own incapacity for government or for attracting the affections of his people, and to a great extent, also, of a general rising against the tyranny of the Despensers. But if we look more narrowly at the influences which guided the rising and *Another historical crisis*

[1] A. Murim. p. 12; cf. Angl. Sac. i. 51.

K K

took the benefit of the revolution we shall see that it was not mere incapacity or mere tyranny provoking a general outburst. In truth Edward's victory over the discontented barons in 1322 had been too great a victory : it had destroyed the forces between which it would have been safer to hold the balance. Throughout the reign there had been three parties in the country : a royal party, comprising a few powerful bishops and barons, strong, however, rather in hereditary or official than in personal greatness ; a party, under the headship of the earl of Lancaster, which was hereditarily opposed to royal aggression, which to some extent represented the baronage of 1265, and which, although unfortunate in its leader, who was an ill-tempered and violent man, still to a certain extent possessed claims on popular affection as the ' good lords ' or party of freedom. There was a third, a mediating party, a party of *politiques*, without any affection for the king or any aspirations for freedom, which was simply anxious to gain and hold power. This party was led at one period by Badlesmere, D'Amory, and Pembroke, the last of whom was personally faithful to the king. In the early struggle of the reign, when Piers Gaveston was the object of detestation to both court and people, these two parties had acted together. After the fall of the favourite they had broken up into two sets, and had been rival aspirants to supreme power over the king. At one time he was held in the fierce grip of Lancaster, at another in the more friendly but scarcely less irksome hold of Pembroke. The two Despensers under whose influence he ultimately won his victory, and who shared his doom, had not been consistent in adhesion either to him or to either of the rival parties in the baronage, and it is a curious fact that the very assertion of principle which was set by the earlier barons at the head of their attack on Gaveston, the doctrine that the allegiance of the subject is due to the office rather than to the person of the king was, in so many words, made the ground of a charge against the younger Hugh in 1321.[1] Another charge made against him, of forming a political league with Sir John Giffard and Sir Richard Grey[2] for exercising undue influence over Edward, bears exactly the same relation to the covenant between Pembroke, Badlesmere, and D'Amory for the creation of the third party.[3] In 1311 the elder Hugh le Despenser had been supposed to be on the side of Gaveston, whilst in 1316 the younger Hugh had filled the high office of chamberlain under the Lancaster administration. We may conclude that the father and son, when they finally threw in their lot with the king, would be regarded as deserters of the parties

The three great parties

Creation of party leagues

---

[1] See vol. in R. S. p. 153.   [2] Statutes of the Realm, i. 182.
[3] Parliamentary Writs, II. ii. 120.

to which they had belonged before, and the son was the most formidable claimant of the Gloucester honours in rivalry with Audley, who belonged to the Lancaster, and D'Aamory, who belonged to the Badlesmere alliance. Hostility to the Despensers again united these parties in 1321, and the Despensers were exiled. The following year the king had his revenge; Lancaster's hatred for Badlesmere enabled the king to crush them both, and he had no mercy. He was after the battle of Boroughbridge master of the situation. But if he had destroyed his enemies, he had not learned to make or to manage his friends; he could not govern and they misgoverned. The desertion and treason of his wife, brothers, and son left him at the disposal of the Despensers; the earl of Pembroke was dead; the personal friends of the king were powerless where they were not dangerous. Thus the wretched man perished. Again all parties rallied against his favourites; the Lancastrians under Earl Henry and Bishop Stratford, the Badlesmere party under bishops Orlton and Burghersh; the hold on the queen and her son possessed by Mortimer obtained for him the aid of the latter party, and they accomplished the revolution. The prizes of dominion were divided among the victors : Lancaster was to guide the council, the queen's bishops were to administer affairs ; Mortimer's personal influence with Isabella and Edward lodged the real power, unfettered by council or ministry, in his unscrupulous hands. Mortimer himself had not been a politician; as Despenser hereditarily represented the popular party of 1265, Mortimer hereditarily represented the royal party, but in both personal ambitions outweighed constitutional propensions.

I do not propose to follow into detail the events of 1327 and 1328 ; it is enough to say that, whereas the new government by its unpopular foreign policy lost the national regard which it had won by domestic legislation, it contained in itself an element of division which was incurable. The old Lancaster party had revenged its wrongs and now fell back on its old political principles ; the dominant court party knew that they had no political strength and held to office as the end and guarantee of their existence. Moreover the Lancastrian party had never been actuated by the personal hatred of the late king which was a leading feeling in Mortimer and Isabella. After the death of Edward II. the rift widened ; Lancaster found his position a sinecure and a pretence, with no real power and no real responsibility ; his friends were left out of office, and his very safety was problematical. The queen and the young king, and not less the great ministries of state, were under Mortimer's hand ; and Edward was beginning his reign with proceedings of wanton terrorism and extortion. Parliaments were multiplied, but no

Marginal notes: Combinations of the parties, for the overthrow of the Despensers. The king's revenge and fall. Revival of the old parties. Unpopularity of Mortimer's government. The Lancaster pary strengthened.

remedial legislation resulted; taxes were granted, but every proper function of government was in abeyance.

Parliament of Salisbury, Oct. 1328

Matters were in this stage when the parliament of Salisbury was called to meet on the 16th of October 1328; it was the fourth parliament of the year; two sessions had been held at York and one at Northampton. The archbishopric of Canterbury was just filled up by the appointment of Mepeham. The country had been kept alive with tournaments, which were probably the pretexts for dangerous meetings of the discontented lords. And many lords were discontented. The two younger sons of Edward I., Kent and Norfolk, were drawing nearer to Lancaster. Bishop Stratford of Winchester was the political guide of that party. Orlton and Burghersh were with Mortimer. Other prelates halted between the two, for they knew that the whole order was unpopular. The misgovernment of the last reign was generally attributed to the prelates, some of whom were distinctly evil men, and the great majority weak ones.

Tumultuous proceedings

It was not without apprehensions that the estates met; and the leaders came at the head of armed retinues. This was contrary to rule, and contrary even to an order which the government had just issued. The rival factions had fights on Salisbury Plain. The earl of Lancaster refused to come into the city, and remained with his friends and retainers at Winchester, whither the king, at Mortimer's suggestion, marched in hostile guise against him. The earl fled before the king, but the intention of resistance was regarded as a crime for which pardon had afterwards to be obtained.[1] The prelates ran still greater risks; Bishop Stratford, who was lodged at the nunnery of Wilton, narrowly escaped assassination by Mortimer's emissaries.[2]

The king marches against the Lancaster party at Winchester

Parliament opened

The parliament was opened by the bishop of Lincoln, the chancellor, and Walter Hervey, archdeacon of Salisbury, as the king's commissioners.[3] It continued in session until the 31st of October. It is probable that the assembly met, as in 1384, in the great hall of the bishop's palace, and that the estates when they separated sat in the houses of the canons or in the chapter-house. The prelates certainly met in a separate house. Of the debates nothing is known. The deliberations of the bishops were broken in upon by Mortimer and his armed force;[4] Bishop Stratford fled in alarm first to his manor at Downton[5] and thence to Winchester, notwithstanding the king's express order that none should leave the city during the

Flight of Stratford

---

[1] Rot. Parl. ii. 52, 255, 443.
[2] Birchington, Anglia Sacra, i. 19.
[3] Fœdera, ii. 752, 753; Report on

the Dignity of a Peer, i. 492; Rot. Parl. ii. 443.
[4] Rot. Parl. ii. 52.
[5] Birchington, Ang. Sac. i. 19.

session. No statutes were passed, no taxes granted; a few entries on the Close Rolls represent all the business that was transacted; and the creation of three new earls, one of whom was Mortimer himself, was the whole ostensible result. But the break-up of the parliament was the first great overt sign of the general discontent. *Creation of earls*

At the close Edward and the court removed to Wallingford, whence on the 11th of November were issued letters ordering the sheriff of Hampshire to bring Bishop Stratford before the king in the ensuing Hilary term to answer for his contempt of the royal order.[1] The bishop did not comply, but fled from Winchester to Waltham, hiding occasionally in the neighbouring woods. The court from Wallingford went to London, spent a week at Westminster early in December, and then proceeded northwards. *Attempts to arrest Stratford*

As soon as the court had left the opposition set to work. Archbishop Mepeham saw before him a chance of following in the steps of Stephen Langton; he came to S. Paul's on the 18th of December and met a company of earls and bishops.[2] The first thing to be done was to collect a body of magnates who could be depended upon. That day were issued letters of summons, in the names of the earls of Kent and Norfolk, for a meeting at London to treat of the dangers imminent; the king was riding about the country with an armed multitude, and, contrary to the Great Charter and his coronation oath, was plundering, seizing, and destroying his faithful peers.[3] Among the lords who took upon them this dangerous responsibility were, besides the two royal earls and the bishops of London and Winchester, the lord Wake, son-in-law of the earl of Lancaster, and brother-in-law of the earl of Kent, and Hugh of Audley, the competitor with Hugh le Despenser for the Gloucester earldom.[4] The news of the negotiation soon reached the court, and Mortimer prepared to set up the royal standard. The lords, who were not quite ready for open war, sent the archdeacon of Essex, John of Elham, to persuade the king to desist, but the appeal was in vain. The earl of Lancaster kept Christmas at Waltham, the earl of Norfolk at Blackfriars, and the archbishops and bishops at S. Paul's. The earls of Norfolk and Lancaster had been at feud in consequence of the execution of Robert, lord Holland, who had been beheaded as a traitor to the late earl Thomas, whilst in some way or other he was under the protection of the earl of Norfolk. The prelates spent an anxious week, for the king sent no answer, and the earl of Lancaster gave no sign. The bishop of Rochester excused himself on account of his health, and on receiving an express command from the archbishop, who was his liege lord in temporals as well as spirituals, returned the same answer. Mepeham was very *Meeting of prelates and barons at S. Paul's, Dec. 18* *Summons issued to faithful lords* *Composition of the party* *Message to the king* *Uneasy Christmas* *The abstention of the bishop of Rochester*

---

[1] Fœdera, ii. 753.
[2] See vol. in R. S. p. 343.
[3] W. Dene, Ang. Sacra, i. 368.
[4] See vol. in R. S. p. 344.

angry, and remarked with a scoff, ' The bishop of Rochester delights himself in quietness ' ; whereto one of his people pleasantly said, ' He wants to be " A per se," alone by himself.' This being told to the bishop he said, ' I would rather be " A per se " than with the other letters,' meaning the other bishops assembled at London. He was astonished that the primate in the depth of winter should go to London to treat behind the king's back on false pretext and real motives which were not revealed to the archbishop himself.[1] It is probable that the royal earls were mistrusted by the baronage at large, and the assemblage that accepted their invitation was not a large one.

Meeting of
the lords,
Jan. 1, 1329However, on New Year's Day, the earl of Lancaster came up from Waltham with a large retinue, paid his respects to the bishops at S. Paul's, and went on to Blackfriars, where he was formally reconciled with the earl of Norfolk.[2] The next day a solemn assembly was held in the cathedral, and articles were drawn up containing the points of grievance against the king, with which the archbishop, the bishop of London, and the king's two uncles were Demands of
the lordssent to the court. They demanded that Mortimer and the queen should live on their own property and allow the king the proper use of his own ; that inquiry should be made as to the causes of the success of the Scots ; that account should be given of the transfer of authority from the royal council appointed at the coronation, of the expenditure of the late king's treasure, the surrender [3] of the king's rights over Scotland, and the disparagement of his sister by Mortimer
ravages the
Leicester
earldomher Scottish marriage. Mortimer was on the alert. He had already begun to ravage the earl of Lancaster's estates, and was leading a large force against the town of Leicester,[4] the capital of the earl's possessions in middle England. On the 4th of January the royal army occupied Leicester, and he ravaged the country for eight days. The embassy had no influence with the king, but the earls of Kent and Norfolk were persuaded to detach themselves from the enter- Lancaster
marches
against himprise which they themselves had started. Lancaster accordingly, with the bishops of London and Winchester, and the lords Wake and Audley, marched towards Leicester. They were joined by several other barons who had taken a prominent part in the politics of the late reign ; the old adventurer, Henry de Beaumont, who had been involved in Gaveston's disgrace, and had deserted Edward II. in his later troubles ; Sir William Trussell, the proctor of the parliament who had in the name of the nation renounced allegiance to Edward of Carnarvon ; Thomas de Wyther, who had beheaded Robert of Holland, and Sir Thomas de Roscelin.[5] The Londoners

[1] W. Dene, Ang. Sac. i. 369. [3] Barnes, Edward III. pp. 31, 32.
[2] See vol. in R. S. p. 343. [4] Knighton, c. 2554. [5] Ibid.

helped the Lancastrian cause with a contingent of 600 men, an offence for which they were afterwards called to account. With such an army as these influential lords could collect, Lancaster marched to Bedford, where he encamped, intending to await the approach of Mortimer ; and at Bedford he received the information that the two earls, the king's uncles, had gone over to Mortimer. He had difficulty in keeping order in his own camp, and as soon as the royal forces appeared he had no better policy than submission. The king's grace was vouchsafed to him at the petition of the archbishop and in consideration of a fine of 11,000*l.* A promise was made that the complaints alleged should receive redress in the next parliament, a promise made compulsory by the alarm of a general rising. Lancaster was able to obtain immunity for his own immediate friends, but Henry de Beaumont, Trussell, Wyther, and Roscelin had to leave the kingdom, and the citizens of London, among whom Hamo of Chigwell was the representative man, were left at the king's mercy.[1] This pacification must have taken place about the 12th or 13th of January.

The London contingent

Lancaster reaches Bedford, where he has to give way

Punishment of his adherents

As soon as the tumult was over Mepeham went to Canterbury to celebrate the festival of his enthronement, and before the end of January was again in London holding an ecclesiastical council. On the 22nd Edward, as the *Annales Londonienses* record, was setting the legal machinery to work, to punish Hamo of Chigwell and his companions ; and on the 9th of February parliament was to meet, by adjournment from the abortive session at Salisbury. This assembly was in session from the 9th to the 22nd of February, but it has left no act on the statute roll and no record of proceedings.[2] The citizens of London who had taken part in the rising were indicted on divers pretexts during the sitting of the parliament, and several of them were hanged. We have seen how narrowly Hamo of Chigwell escaped.

Church council

Proceedings against Hamo of Chigwell

Parliament of February 1329

It is needless to observe that the promises of redress which Mortimer had made at Bedford were never fulfilled ; nor were the recalcitrant earls, even after penitence, really forgiven. In the summer of 1329 the young king and queen went to France ; a grand ceremonial of pacification took place in September after their return ; and early in 1330 Queen Philippa was crowned. Thus time was given for the concocting of the cruel plot by which Mortimer wreaked his first vengeance on the earl of Kent, whom he found means of persuading that his hapless brother Edward of Carnarvon was still alive. The curious evidence which from time to time has been fabricated to show that Edward escaped from Berkeley Castle

Further proceedings

Mortimer's revenge

[1] Knighton, cc. 2554, 2555.
[2] Fœdera, ii. 756 ; Report on the Dignity of a Peer, i. 492.

and lived and died in exile must be reserved for separate treatment hereafter. Such as it was, it tempted earl Edmund to his doom ; the terror of his fate roused up in the royal house and in the young sovereign himself the determination to get rid of Mortimer. By one

Curious
sequence of
events

of the strangest pieces of medieval placability, within little more than half a century we find the heir of Mortimer heir of the crown of England ; the daughter of the earl of Kent married to the son of Sir Robert Holland, and the house of Holland joined in unhappy marriages with the families of the White and Red Rose, until the middle ages close in the deluge of civil war.

Permanence
of heredi-
tary politics

The struggle between the rival administrations which had risen by the support of the Mortimer and Lancaster parties continued as a struggle between two court factions long after the death of Mortimer, and the animosity which long survived the chief actors broke out in 1841 in the quarrel between Edward III. and Archbishop Stratford : Burghersh was dead, but Orlton was as malicious as ever. But this portion of history lies for the present too far ahead, and is itself perhaps only a link in the later complications of a long and tedious reign.

*   *   *   *   *   *

CHRONICLES OF THE REIGNS OF EDWARD I. AND EDWARD II. Vol. II.

[The following is a portion of the Preface to a volume containing four works dealing with the reign of Edward II. In one of these works, the *Commendatio Lamentabilis*, is to be found a comparison of Edward I.'s personal appearance, with that of Henry II. 'Henry was of middle height, Edward was very tall, a head taller than the generality of his subjects; Henry had a small nose, Edward a long one; Henry was ruddy, red-haired, and blue-eyed; Edward had black and curly hair, and his eyes were probably dark also.' Such is Bishop Stubbs's summary of a portion of the chronicler's description of the two kings. Both men were fond of hunting, both able and original legislators, both eloquent, cautious, and patient. Edward II. was very different from both Edward I. and Henry II.; Bishop Stubbs's sketch of his reign brings out many interesting points.]

*　　*　　*　　*　　*　　*

THE reign of Edward II. possesses, in its more prominent events, an extraordinary amount of tragic interest; but outside of the dramatic crises it may be described as exceedingly dreary. There is a miserable level of political selfishness which marks without exception every public man; there is an absence of sincere feeling except in the shape of hatred and revenge; there is a profession of economic and reforming zeal which never comes into practice, and there is no great triumph of good or evil to add a moral or inspire a sympathy. This absence of inspiring topics renders certain parts of the reign simply unreadable; yet there are great quantities of records which are, as a series, instructive enough, and capable of a good deal of antiquarian illustration. This is true of the whole of the reign, but especially true of the years that intervene between the death of Gaveston and the attack on the Despensers. During this period the national history may be summed up as a series of attempts made by the party of the earl of Lancaster to reduce the king to impotence, on the pretext of compelling him to observe the Ordinances; interrupted from time to time by renewals of the Scottish war, which constrained the conflicting parties to a show of reconciliation and

Character of the reign of Edward II.

The middle of the reign especially dreary

Party warfare

joint action; and by a series of intrigues and counter-intrigues to obtain, for a party independent of the earl of Lancaster, a hold on the royal administration. The king all the time, whether working underhand against Lancaster, or acting overtly against him under the influence of a body of allies in whom he had no confidence, is gradually being thrown more and more completely and helplessly on the support of the Despensers, who finally get him entirely under their hands.

Reconcilia-
tion after
Gaveston's
death

Gaveston perished in June 1312; the second half of that year and the whole of the next were occupied with negotiations for reconciliation; the parties reconciled joined in the war with Robert Bruce; the battle of Bannockburn furnished Lancaster with a convincing argument of the king's incapacity and of the importance of the Ordinances. Gradually almost all power slipped out of the

Lancaster
supreme in
1316

king's hands, and in the parliament of Lincoln, held in January 1316, the earl was made chief counsellor, and restraints were placed on the action of the king, who was to undertake nothing important or arduous without the consent of the earls and barons. Edward had nothing better to do than to confirm the Ordinances, and try, by satisfying the demands of the clergy, to secure some measure of peace and some supplies of money.

Intrigues of
the year 1317

This state of things did not continue long. The king tried to make a party of his own, and different clusters of courtiers organised themselves in parties too, to take advantage of the first opportunity that might arrive of gaining power on the pretext of freeing him.

New ordi-
nances pro-
posed

The year 1317 was a period of intrigue and private war. Lancaster, as we learn from a valuable letter preserved by the Bridlington historian,[1] had attempted, in his office of chief counsellor, to impose some new ordinances. A committee had been appointed in the Lincoln parliament to reform the administration, and of this committee, which included bishops and earls, the leading men were Lancaster himself, Archbishop Reynolds who was supposed to be committed heart and soul to the king's side, and Bartholomew, lord Badlesmere, who was an enemy of Lancaster and only cared for the king as the fulcrum to be used for the promotion of his own ambition of governing. Ordinances were framed and were sent in writing to the king by the hands of Badlesmere and Inge the chief justice. Of course nothing was done, and the precise purport of the ordinances

Lancaster
offended

themselves is not now to be recovered. The earl was violently offended, and his sulky attitude strengthened the hands of the intriguing parties at the court. But matters went further. Early in 1317 the king called councils which Lancaster refused to attend.[2]

[1] See vol. in R. S. pp. 50, 51.
[2] Mon. Malmesb. vol. in R. S. pp. 226–228, and notes.

He sent to the pope to ask for absolution from his oath to the Edward applies to the pope Ordinances and for a sentence against the Scots. The pope declined both requests ; the Ordinances were drawn up by men who could be trusted with the interests of both church and crown ; the Scots were not to be condemned until the cause had been tried on its merits ; if the king would devote his energies to the crusade the clergy might grant him money, not otherwise. The pope's advice was thrown away. The courtiers advised defiance of Lancaster and Intrigues against Lancaster the prosecution of the Scottish war, to which the great earl was known to be opposed. The earl of Warenne was now the king's confidant. By his agency the countess of Lancaster [1] was enabled to elope from her husband ; and it was believed that the scheme for her abduction was contrived in royal council at Clarendon. The earl immediately began to prepare his revenge by enlisting strong Threatenings of civil war forces of retainers and by collecting the barons of his party and the numerous and powerful vassals of his own five earldoms. To counteract these machinations, and to draw his own force to the north, the king issued orders for the assembly of the council at Nottingham on the twenty-first of July, followed by a summons to muster at Newcastle on the morrow of S. Lawrence, August 11. Lancaster refused to attend the council. His letter in answer to Lancaster's refusal to attend a council the king's remonstrance is preserved by the Bridlington annalist,[2] and the Malmesbury historian furnishes the argument which his agents offered in the court. He would not attend the council because the business to be treated of was such as, according to the Ordinances, could only be treated in parliament. He would, however, obey the summons to Newcastle. In the meantime he collected his forces at Pomfret.[3] Edward, after holding the council at Nottingham, took up his quarters at York on the 8th of September. For a fortnight The king and earl watch one another in arms the two rival powers watched one another ; the earl refused the king's followers leave to cross the Aire at Castleford ; the king did not feel strong enough to dislodge him ; the bishops and barons interposed their good offices and a meeting was agreed on. The earl was told that if he attended the conference it was at the peril of life or liberty, and the meeting did not take place.[4] But the autumn was wasted ; on the 24th of September[5] it was determined that a parliament should be held in the following January at Lincoln where all complaints were to be satisfied, and the king marched The king goes to the south southward, passing by Pomfret, notwithstanding the remonstrances of the earl of Pembroke, in full battle array.[6]

[1] The most circumstantial account of this business is, I think, given by Hall's Continuator of Trivet, pp. 20, 21, 22.

[2] See vol. in R. S. pp. 50, 51.

[3] Mon. Malmesb. vol. in R. S. p. 230.

[4] Mon. Malmesb. ibid.

[5] Parl. Writ. II. i. 171.

[6] See vol. in R. S. p. 231; Cont. Trivet, pp. 23, 24.

Neither party had taken much by the move; the private war between Lancaster and Warenne had really broken out in Yorkshire, where Lancaster had taken the castles of his rival, and some of his riotous followers had seized Knaresborough.[1] On the 3rd of November the king issued stringent orders for peace. The parliament summoned for January was not held, being postponed by successive writs to March, and afterwards to June. The capture of Berwick by the Scots in April 1318 served for a warning of the necessity of reconciliation.

Order for peace

Capture of Berwick

It is at this juncture that we come upon a very extraordinary document thoroughly illustrative of the state of political morality. On the 24th of November, that is just at the moment when both Edward and the earl had put themselves decidedly in the wrong, and each had shown that he was too weak to coerce the other, a new party is formed to grasp at the reins of power. The leaders of this confederation were Badlesmere and Pembroke. Badlesmere was the open enemy of the earl of Lancaster; Pembroke, who perhaps was the king's wisest and truest friend, had never forgiven the stain thrown on his honour by the seizure of Gaveston; but he probably saw through the designs of Lancaster, and had determined to head the opposition. In the curious indenture referred to, we find Roger D'Amory, the husband of one of the Gloucester heiresses, binding himself in a sum of 10,000l. sterling to give his whole diligence and legal influence with the king to induce him to let himself be guided and governed by the counsels of Pembroke and Badlesmere and to trust their counsels beyond all other people on earth, so far as they shall advise him to the honour and profit of himself, his crown, and his kingdom; he will himself act according to their counsels, and will not trespass against them in any point; nor will he agree to the king making grants beyond twenty pounds in land, or doing any other business of importance without their acquiescence.[2] It is possible that this agreement is one of a set by which others of the king's council formed themselves into an inner council to hold power and restrain the king's extravagance. But it is clear that the purpose of the league was hostile to Lancaster; and, although we do not know that it included the earl Warenne and the other Gloucester claimants, we are told by the Malmesbury writer that Audley and Despenser as well as D'Amory were among the great earl's enemies.

Confederation between Pembroke and Badlesmere

League made by indenture

The parliament called for January 27, 1318, was on the 4th of

<hr>

[1] It will be remembered that this important Honour, which was afterwards and is still a considerable member of the Duchy of Lancaster, was now in the king's hands, having fallen, with the rest of the possessions of the earldom of Cornwall, as an escheat on the death of Gaveston.

[2] Parl. Writs, II. ii. 120.

[3] See vol. in R. S. p. 235.

that month postponed to the 12th of March by the advice of the Postpone- lords who were desirous of making terms with Lancaster. It was parliament to have met at Lincoln, but the difficulties which led to the first postponement led to a second, and on the 3rd of March it was countermanded, to meet on the 19th of June at the same place. In the interval a council was held at Leicester,[1] to which the Bridlington writer gives the name of parliament, but which was really a conference of representative members of both parties attended by the chancellor.

Berwick was taken by the Scots on the 2nd of April, and the Great Council at council at Leicester, which sat on the 12th, was awed into harmony. Leicester, April 1318 The archbishop and five bishops, three earls, twenty-eight barons, and two judges swore to maintain the Ordinances; a new scheme for general reconciliation was set on foot, and one of the terms of pacification was that the two Despensers were to be retained by the earl of Lancaster with a service of two hundred horse; prisoners were to be released and charters of pardon issued.[2] The earl of Warenne, however, was not to be pardoned for assisting in the countess of Lancaster's elopement. It was time that something should be done. The Scots had burned Northallerton and carried their devastations as far as Bolton. The king ordered the gentlemen Military preparations of Yorkshire to collect the forces of the county, and prepared to go northwards himself. But the earl would not obey the summons to parliament, and on the 4th of June the king gave up the idea of holding one, recalled the summons to Lincoln, and issued writs for a military levy to meet at York on the 26th of July.[3] On the 8th of June at S. Paul's he declared himself ready to confirm the Ordinances.[4] Early in July he came to Northampton, the earl being at Tutbury.[5] The court was at Northampton from July 4th to the 4th of August, during which time the chancellor travelled backwards and forwards to negotiate a treaty of peace between the two.[6] On the 31st of July a general pardon was issued to the Lancaster General pacification partisans,[7] and on the 14th of August the cousins met at Hathern,[8] in August 1318 near Loughborough, and gave each other the kiss of peace. The

---

[1] Mon. Malmesb. p. 233; Bridlington, p. 54; Parl. Writs, II. ii. 122.

[2] Bridlington, vol. in R. S. p. 55.

[3] Parl. Writs, II. i. 501.

[4] Annales Paulini, i. 282; Parl. Writs, II. i. 181.

[5] The conversations between the earl and the chancellor are recorded by Knighton, c. 2535, who says that they took place at Tutbury, the head of the Derby earldom. The bishops of Norwich and Ely were the messengers, the latter being chancellor.

[6] Parl. Writs, II. ii. 123, 124.

[7] Ibid. 125.

[8] Ann. Paul. i. 283; Cont. Trivet, p. 27. Knighton, c. 2534, makes the place of meeting Syroches brigge, 'quæ modo vocatur Sotesbryge'; and the Bridlington writer, vol. in R. S. p. 55, calls it 'Sortebrigge juxta Lughteburghe.' Possibly it is the place called Zouch-bridge in the Ordnance map, where the Soar is crossed near Hathern.

terms had been sealed on the 9th at Leek in Staffordshire, and were to be submitted to a parliament which was to meet on the 20th of October at York. Any plan of a campaign against the Scots was now impracticable. The parliament met at York and confirmed the terms of what was really a surrender on the part of the king.

Terms of agreement

Edward had been represented in the negotiations by Pembroke and Badlesmere, who may thus be understood to have made good their position to the council, with the earl of Arundel, four bishops and four barons, one of whom was Roger Mortimer.[1] These agreed that the king should confirm the Ordinances and issue the requisite pardons ; and that a standing committee of council should be appointed to reside constantly with the king. Two bishops, one earl, one baron, and one banneret nominated by Lancaster were to attend for three months at a time ; what could be done without parliament they were to do, and their administration was to be reviewed by parliament. The estates at York ratified the scheme, and continued the earl's nominees in their places. The younger Despenser was also appointed or confirmed as chamberlain.[2]

Operations of 1319 and 1320

I must pass over the two following years, during the greater part of which the king was employed in the north, the court being at York from October 1318 to January 1320, and the siege of Berwick being pressed with more ardour than vigilance. The rapid incursion of the Scots in September 1319, during which the archbishop with the men of Yorkshire was defeated at Myton, and which carried devastation over Airedale and Wharfedale and to the gates of Pomfret, had the effect of raising the siege of Berwick, and rousing in their bitterest form the king's suspicions of Earl Thomas. The earl did indeed offer to purge himself of the charges against him,[3] but he would not attend a council which was held without a parliament. His declaration that that parliament should not be held *in cameris*[4] is perhaps the most distinct enunciation that we have of his constitutional policy. After the king's visit to France in the summer, and an uneasy parliament held in October at Westminster, the alarms of civil war began to be heard again.

Battle of Myton

Edward's visit to France

Gathering of the storm against the Despensers

As I am attempting in this sketch mainly to direct attention to the material additions to our knowledge contributed by the authorities before us, I will not repeat the story of the quarrel about Gower, which seems to have thrown the younger Despenser into permanent hostility to the party supported by Lancaster. The earl himself was not directly concerned in the Glamorganshire quarrel, but, as usual, was willing to contribute to any movement of disturbance. By this time also the influence of Badlesmere had waned, and the king had

Parl. Writs, II. i. 184, 185.   [3] Mon. Malmesb. vol. in R. S. p. 249.
[2] Statutes of the Realm, i. 181.   [4] Ibid. p. 250.

yielded himself entirely to the guidance of the Despensers. It may, however, be useful here again to mark the dates of the more important incidents.

As soon as Edward returned from France, in July 1320, he summoned on the 5th of August a meeting of the lords and commons in parliament, for the 6th of October. It was well attended, but Lancaster, as usual, absented himself, and sent Nicolas Segrave as his proxy.[1] The session was not a quiet one. Although we do not know that the question about Gower was mooted in it, the estates refused to confirm grants which the king had made to the pope's relations, and petitioned for a severe inquiry by the justices into the unlawful confederations for breach of the peace which were doing mischief in every county.[2] The session ended on the 25th of October, and on the 18th of December commissions of oyer and terminer were issued in compliance with the parliamentary petition. On the 14th of January, 1321 the justices itinerant at the Tower were directed to examine into unlawful 'colligations, confederations, and conventions by oaths' which were known to have been formed in the city.[3] The disturbed state of Glamorganshire was now known: on the 20th the king directed a special commission for the apprehension of malefactors in Gower,[4] and on the 30th wrote to the earls of Hereford, Arundel, and Warenne, forbidding them to attend an illegal gathering which had been summoned to treat of matters touching the Crown.[5] The same day the sheriffs of the northern counties were ordered to warn all men against attending unlawful meetings. It is clear, therefore, that the king knew what the matter in contention was, who were the chief combatants, and from what quarter they looked for assistance. As the season advanced, and matters grew more threatening, Edward prepared to go westward. He reached Gloucester late in March, and on the 28th wrote to the lord Hastings, the earl of Hereford, the two Rogers of Mortimer, the younger Despenser, John Giffard of Brimsfield, and Thomas and Maurice of Berkeley; all of them men whose names have an unhappy prominence in the later records of the reign. He has heard, he tells them, that there is war on the March; they must come to a council at Gloucester on the 5th of April.[6] Two days later the king seems to have fixed on Hugh of Audley as the chief delinquent; he was specially bound to the king by covenant; he had again and again refused to obey the royal summons. He was now peremptorily ordered to appear,

Marginal notes:
Parliament in October 1320

Disturbed state of Gower

The king in the west, March 1321

Proceedings against Hugh of Audley and Roger D'Amory

---

[1] Ann. Paul. i. 290.   [2] Fœdera, ii. 438; Rot Parl. i. 371.
[3] Fœdera, ii. 441; Ann. Paul. i. 290, 291; Parl. Writs, II. ii. 154, 155.
[4] Parl. Writs, II. ii. 155.   [5] Ibid.
[6] Ibid. II. i. 231.

and the Earl Marshall and Justice Spigurnel were to try him.[1]   The other confederates, who had ventured to write to urge the king to dismiss Despenser, or place him in the hands of Lancaster, were Roger D'Amory, John Mowbray, Roger Clifford, and the earl of Hereford. On the 9th of April the sentence of forfeiture was issued against Audley,[2] and about the same date the king seized the castle of S. Briavel, which belonged to Roger D'Amory, whom he had warned

Edward fails to make peace and returns to London

by a letter of the 27th March.[3]   On the 21st of April he was at Bristol, whence he again wrote to warn the Berkeleys and sixty-two other great lords ;[4] two days after this he set out on his return to London. He had failed to quiet the disturbance, and probably was unable to muster a force that could overawe the discontented.   Before leaving Bristol, however, he wrote to the earl of Hereford, who was his brother-in-law, remonstrating with him for his disobedience in not attending the council, arguing that, as Hugh le Despenser was appointed chamberlain by the parliament, he could not properly dismiss him, and to commit him to custody would be contrary to the Great Charter, the common law of the kingdom, the Ordinances, and the coronation oath.   The letter, which is sufficiently dignified, ended with a summons to council at Oxford on the 10th of May.[5] When the king reached Wallingford he issued other letters ; the council was postponed to the 17th, and Hereford and Despenser were both forbidden to continue their private war.[6]   As soon, in

The lands of the Despensers ravaged

fact, as Edward had turned eastward the confederates had overrun all Despenser's estates in Wales.[7]   Hugh himself was believed to be in attendance on the king.   On the 15th of May the summons was issued for the meeting of parliament on the 15th of July.[8]

Lancaster assembles his allies at Pomfret, May 24

The hand of Lancaster, the Malmesbury writer tells us,[9] was in all this ; but he had not stirred overtly.   His enemy was the elder Hugh, not the younger.   It is to the Bridlington annalist that we owe our most exact information about the part which the great earl was now about to take.[10]   On the 24th of May, as soon, that is, as the parliamentary summons was received, he called together at his castle of Pomfret the great lords of the north country, Multon of Gilsland, Furnivall of Sheffield, the baron of Greystoke, the Deyncourts, Fitzhugh of Middleham, Percy of Topcliffe, Marmion of Tanfield, Philip Darcy, William Fitz-William, Fauconberg, Meynell,

---

[1] Parl. Writs, II. ii. 158.
[2] Ibid.
[3] Mon. Malmesb. p. 246 ; Fœdera, ii. 445.   [4] Parl. Writs, II. ii. 160.
[5] Ibid. II. i. 231.
[6] Ibid. II. ii. 161.
[7] They began to ravage the estates of the son on the 6th of May ; the attack on the father began in

Wiltshire on June 11th, *i.e.* after Lancaster had declared himself. These dates are given in the petition for the restoration of the Despensers in 1398, from the petition of 1322; Rot. Parl. III. 361, 362.
[8] Parl. Writs, II. i. 234.
[9] See vol. in R. S. p. 257.
[10] See vol. in R. S. p. 61.

Thwing, and Constable ; all these, for themselves and their retainers, agreed on a league of defence ; if anyone attacked the earl or any of the league, all would join to punish the aggressor and to secure the peace. The covenant, which was written in French, was sealed by each of the lords.

A confederation drawn up and sealed

So far, perhaps, the earl had gone no further than the usage of the time, however illegal and unconstitutional, warranted ; he had as much right to make an alliance, offensive and defensive, as Badlesmere and D'Amory had had in 1317. The covenant which the king himself had made with Hugh of Audley was distinctly a party or personal covenant superadded on the feudal relation, or on the right of the king to the allegiance of his subject. Hugh le Despenser, as we learn from Dugdale,[1] had a similar covenant with the earl of Louth, and it was by an attempt to draw in John Giffard to such a confederation that he laid himself open to the charge on which the first article of his condemnation was framed.[2] But the earl's next proceeding was very strange. He summoned the archbishop of York, the bishops of Durham and Carlisle, and the other prelates of the province to meet at Sherburn in Elmet, on the 28th of June ;[3] and at the same time invited the chief of the malcontent lords, who had been harrying the estates of the Despensers, to meet them. In a word, he tried to bring together a parliament of his own, prelates, barons, bannerets, and knights.

Legality of this

Other examples

Lancaster assembles the clergy at Sherburn in Elmet, June 28

At Sherburn, then, which is a village about halfway between Pomfret and Tadcaster, dignified as being a very ancient residence of the archbishops, a very extraordinary assembly met. There was Archbishop Melton, who throughout his life was a faithful friend of the king, Bishop Lewis of Durham, brother of Edward's favourite Henry Beaumont, and the old Bishop Halton of Carlisle, who had lived in alarms from the Scots for thirty years. What could have induced Melton to attend, unless it was the hope of being able to mediate, it is impossible to say ; perhaps he felt that he could not trust the king, and that it was not wise to disappoint the earl ; he certainly came and brought a considerable quota of his clergy with him. With Lancaster appeared the earls of Hereford and Angus, and a goodly number of lay lords of north and south, who were prepared to cast in their lot with them. They met in the parish church, and the proceedings opened as in parliament by the reading of articles at the earl's command. The articles were in French and included the agreement concluded at Pomfret in the preceding month, with a statement of grievances to be discussed and if possible provided with remedies. The grievances were the bad ministers

Lancaster's parliament at Sherburn

Statement of grievances

[1] Baronage, p. 391.   [2] Statutes of the Realm, i. 182.
[3] Bridlington, vol. in R. S. p. 62

who were appointed contrary to the Ordinances ; the banishments and forfeitures which had been decreed without assent of peers; the visitation of the special commissions for putting down conspiracies ; the action of the justices itinerant at London on the writ *Quo warranto* ; the abuses of the staple, and the imprudent treaties made with foreign nations. It was also declared that the king had too many lawyers about him, so many in fact that the persons whom the court wanted to implead had the greatest difficulty in finding advocates to undertake their causes.[1] This bill of articles having been read by Sir John de Bek, acting as chancellor to the almost sovereign earl, the earl himself requested the prelates to retire and

Separate de-
liberation

consider their answers. They left the church and held their quasi-convocation at the house of the rector. Lancaster and the lords deliberated apart. The result of the consultation was, in the chamber of the lords, a determination to adhere to Lancaster and to maintain the quarrel of the earl of Hereford and his confederates

Indenture of
confedera-
tion

against the Despensers. This was drawn in an indenture in which were inserted the names of the earls of Lancaster and Angus and thirty-three men of rank, including some of the confederates of Pomfret, and among them Sir Robert of Holland, the trusted friend of Lancaster, who afterwards betrayed the good cause, and Sir William Trussell, who took the leading part four years afterwards in

The elder
Despenser
attacked

the deposition of the king.[2] It was by the influence of Lancaster that the elder Hugh le Despenser was included in the accusations prosecuted against his son ; and in all probability the act of condemnation, which was passed a month after in the real parliament, may have been drawn up on this occasion.

Answer of
the clergy
after de-
liberation

After the lords had deliberated the clergy sent in their reply, addressed to the earl as 'domine reverende.'[3] They expressed their sincere gratitude to the earl for the heartfelt anxiety he showed for the kingdom and country, and declared themselves willing to the utmost of their ability to join in the defence against the Scots. But further than that they were not disposed to go : as to the 'motions of late set on foot' (that is, the political quarrel), 'they humbly and devoutly supplicate your reverend lordship and the others in company with you, that for reverence and honour of God and holy church, the salvation of the realm and the quiet of the people, there be a tolerance or forbearance of the said motions' (that is a suspension of hostilities), 'and that in the next parliament concord and unity may be ordained between our lord the king and his lieges by peaceful considerations in Christ as to what is most expedient. And if this be done they trust that upon all the articles here exhibited, by the favour of God,

---

[1] Bridlington, vol. in R. S. pp. 62–64.   Tyrrell, iii. 280.
[2] See the Indenture printed in   [3] Bridlington, vol. in R. S. pp. 64, 65.

an opportune remedy will be ordained in the said parliament.' The answer was a good one, creditable to the religious spirit of the clergy, and a clever one, foiling the earl for a moment with his own weapon, and recommending confidence in parliament. Nor is the freedom with which it is given less creditable to the earl, who evidently might have extorted stronger expressions and promises of support. 'This answer in writing having been read before the earl, he in right royal fashion returned special thanks to the prelates and clergy, and so having received licence to depart all retired.' Policy of the answer

It is to the Bridlington annalist that we owe the most striking of these details, but it is most probable that either in the public records, or in some of the episcopal registries, even a fuller account may be preserved. Tyrrell, in his History of England, has preserved a copy of the indenture, from the register of Christ Church, Canterbury, and some of the particulars are referred to in the proceedings for setting aside the exile of the Despensers. But Tyrrell placed Sherburn[1] in Dorsetshire, a mistake corrected by Carte, who, however, extracted his list of the confederates from Tyrrell's work.[2] It is curious that Walsingham, who knew of the Sherburn gathering, but did not know where Elmet was, wrote the name so that of his editors one read Clivedon, and the other Elmedon.[3] In the popular histories of the epoch scarcely a word is found that shows any knowledge of this most curious and important episode of the struggle. Tyrrell's account of these proceedings

Our authorities do not, I think, furnish us with any new details of the parliamentary proceedings against the Despensers, or of the war which followed, over and above the anecdote of the younger Hugh which is preserved by the canon of Bridlington.[4] Nor do the few particulars recorded of the king's flight from Byland to Bridlington in 1322,[5] although interesting in themselves, add anything important to our knowledge of the period. The dreary years of the Despenser government from 1322 to 1326 are unbroken by any ray of political light or poetical incident. And even when we reach the great crisis at the end of the latter year, we have to contend with a dearth of such minute detail as would give life or reality to any picture we might attempt to draw. As, however, in the preface to the first volume,[6] I undertook to devote a few pages to an attempt to arrange the chronology and determine some of the local features of the revolution, at least in London, I will endeavour, with the aid of the Pauline Annals and such other materials as are within reach, to fulfil the promise. No material addition to our information between 132? and 1326

Edward, it may be remembered, had been very much isolated

---

[1] Hist. of England, iii. 279.
[2] Carte, Hist. Engl. ii.
[3] Walsingham, ed. Riley, i. 159.

[4] Vol. in R. S. p. xxx.
[5] Ibid. pp. 79 sq.
[6] Vol. i. p. lxxxv, R. S.

since his tragic victory over Earl Thomas. He had lost his faithful
friend and cousin, Earl Aymer of Pembroke in 1324 ; he had sent
the queen, his brother the earl of Kent, and his son Edward to
France in 1325 ; the Earl Warenne, who had been for two years in
command in Gascony, had only just returned, and at no time had
he shown himself a wise counsellor. Henry of Lancaster, now
known as earl of Leicester, was a man of noble character, but Edward
might well distrust him, as having his brother's wrongs to avenge,
and a claim, as yet unsatisfied, on his brother's inheritance. The
earls of Hereford and Warwick were minors, and so in a position in
which the king could not obtain help from them as friends, nor
strengthen himself by destroying them. The earl of Arundel was
faithful, but carried little weight ; all the will and executive force of
the government depended on the Despensers. The chancellor
Baldock shared the unpopularity of the court, and Archbishop
Melton, the treasurer, who was faithful and not unpopular, had his
means of usefulness curtailed by the watchful enmity of the weak
and ungenerous primate at Canterbury.[1] The leading men of the
episcopal body were men who had forced themselves upon the king
by means of papal intrigue or usurpation, and who attributed their
loss of influence at court to the hostility of Baldock, whom they
had supplanted in the way of preferment, or to the Despensers, who
had kept them out of their temporalities on legal pretexts. With his
kinsmen alienated, his great nobles in minority or retirement, his
bishops untrustworthy, and his ministers unpopular, a really able
king could scarcely have failed to strengthen himself by alliance
with such strong political elements as were to be found in the cities
and in the country party which in the next reign showed itself so
strong. There is indeed some evidence that Edward had tried to
propitiate the Londoners,[2] and we can scarcely think that the Despensers had so entirely lost their heads as not to have attempted to
create a party of personal adherents. But the result shows that if
they had done so the attempt had failed. The earl of Leicester was
son-in-law of the Lady Despenser, and may have hoped by using the
family connexion wisely to obtain recognition as his brother's
successor ; but in all these family ties at this period of history we find
causes and occasions of enmity quite as often as of friendship; nor
could Leicester be expected to forget that the father and son were
really responsible for the death of his brother. He had a party in
the great and mighty host of vassals which since the battle of Evesham had rallied round the banners of Leicester, Lancaster, Derby,
and Lincoln. The new-made earls of Winchester and Gloucester

---

[1] Mon. Malmesb. vol. in R. S. p. 283.   [2] Walsingham, i. 180.

had none.   Their sole source of strength seems to have been their Helpless-ness of the Despensers
hold on the person and will of their master, and their ability to use
the little influence that still remained to him after he had lost his
wife and son, sacrificed his relations to his revenge, and signally
failed at Bannockburn, at Byland, and at Berwick to prove that he
inherited his father's prowess.   It was this helplessness and isolation that ruined him ; for, though the queen's invasion was cleverly
managed, and the boldness and promptitude with which her
advisers acted might, so far as adroitness deserves success, have been
fairly entitled to some great advantage, she had no great force nor
any sound political cry.   No one believed in her alleged wrongs, but
she gained a following as the avenger of the earl who was more
honoured in his death than in his life.   She won a great victory, Easy victory of the queen
but it was over a foe that put in no appearance, without a battle,
but not without wanton and cruel bloodshed, prolific of quarrels,
vengeances, and further bloodshed for long years to come.

All through the summer there had been rumours of an invasion ; Alarm of invasion
the king had not been put off his guard by his knowledge of the very
small resources that were at his wife's disposal.   He had been
nervously alive to the danger, all the more as it was for long altogether uncertain on what side it was likely to come.   After spending Movements of the king
the spring at Kenilworth, and June and July in London, he had
gone in August to Clarendon,[1] where he had in former years spent
so much time in laying out his park and improving his forest
domain, and had in September been at Porchester issuing writs of
array and taking other precautions.   In this month he was informed
where the queen was likely to land, and on the 2nd [2] directed the
march of forces to Orwell, where in fact she did land three weeks
later.   On the 23rd of September he was in London, and there the
news that she had landed on the 24th reached him on the 27th.[3] The queen lands
She had landed at noon near Harwich, at Colvasse, and lodged the
first night at Walton.[4]   She had ten ships, and the disembarkation was
so rapidly effected that nine of them were cleared before sunset, the
tenth was brought by the king's sailors to London, and, with the news
of his wife's arrival, presented to him at the Tower.[5]   He remained Flight of Edward
in London for a few days longer, was at Westminster on the 2nd of
October, and on that day set out for the west,[6] leaving in the Tower
his son John of Eltham, a mere child, as nominal governor, with
Sir John Weston the constable.[7]   Isabella marched towards London,

---

[1] Parl.   Writs, II.   Chronological
Abstract, pp. 439–448.
[2] Parl. Writs, II. i. 758.
[3] Ibid. II. ii. 292.
[4] Ann. Paul. i. 313, 314.

[5] Ibid. p. 314.
[6] Parl. Writs, II. ii. 294. Edward was at the Tower on the 28th
of September.
[7] Walsingham, i. 183.

Progress of
Isabella
expecting to find her husband still there, and being joined by all classes as she proceeded. At Bury St. Edmund's she borrowed 800 marks of the king's money deposited in the abbey ;[1] she went on to Cambridge and stayed a day or two at Barnwell,[2] then to Baldock in Hertfordshire,[3] where she enjoyed the pleasure of plundering the chancellor's property, and then to Dunstable.[4] At Dunstable the earl of Leicester joined her.[5] On the way she must have heard that Edward had left London. She then turned westward and passed on to Oxford, where she laid her cause before the University in a sermon preached by Bishop Orlton, on the text 'Caput meum doleo.'[6] From Oxford she went to Wallingford,[7] where she was on the 15th of October; thence to Gloucester, where she was joined by Percy, Wake, and other northern lords ;[8] thence to Berkeley, where she secured the allegiance of the heir of the castle by restoring to him the estate which Hugh le Despenser had seized on the ground probably of his

She reaches
Bristol
father's treason.[9] From Berkeley she went on with a constantly increasing host of retainers to Bristol, where on the 26th of October the carnage of the revolution began.

Retreat of
the king
Helpless and unready the unhappy king, with his chancellor Baldock, the younger Despenser, and a few other followers, started from London on the 2nd of October. On the 10th he was at Gloucester,[10] still issuing letters of summons for the men of the districts nearest, especially those of South Wales. He had, if we may trust Sir Thomas de la Moore,[11] sent a quantity of supplies to Lundy Island, which he regarded as a last refuge. But, although he may before the last extremity arrived have thought of Lundy as a place of security, we can hardly think that either despairing foresight or simple cowardice was so strong in him as to suffer him to provide himself with such a resource long before.

The king's
movements
in his flight
Anyhow he made for the Severn ; on the 12th of October he was at Westbury,[12] on the 14th at Tintern ;[13] and from the 16th to the 21st at Stroguil or Chepstow,[14] whence he sent the elder Despenser to take the command at Bristol. There the old counsellor of Edward I., the son of Simon de Montfort's justiciar, fell into the hands of his enemies and gave his life in expiation of the wrongs of Lancaster.[15]

---

[1] Ann. Paul. i. 314.
[2] Ibid.   [3] Ibid.
[4] Ann. Paul. i. 315.
[5] Knighton, c. 2546.
[6] T. de la Moore ; see vol. in R. S. p. 310.
[7] Fœdera, ii. 645, 646 ; Twysden, Scriptores, c. 2764.
[8] Walsingham, i. 183.
[9] Ibid.

[10] Parl. Writs, II. ii. 294, 295.
[11] See vol. in R. S. p. 309 ; Walsingham, i. 183.
[12] Parl. Writs, II. i. 760.
[13] Ibid. II. ii. 295.
[14] Ibid. II. i. 761 ; Walsingham, i. 181.
[15] Compare Ann. Paul. i. 317, 318 ; Wals. i. 183 ; Knighton, c. 2544 ; Bridlington, vol. in R. S. p. 87.

We lose sight of the king between October 21st, when he was at Chepstow,[1] and October 27th, when we find him at Cardiff ; [2] and it is to the intervening days that we must assign the unsuccessful attempt to reach Lundy Island. Unable to effect a landing, he is said to have disembarked in Glamorganshire.[3] From Cardiff on the 27th and 28th he sent out letters, for he still had the chancellor and the great seal with him, to bring in the men of the neighbouring lordships. At Caerphilly, where the third and youngest Despenser was in command, on the 29th and 30th he issued commissions of array for the same districts.[4] Again we lose sight of him for nearly a week. He is found at Neath on the 5th of November, still entreating aid from the men of Gower.[5] The end was now very near. The queen knew where to find her husband, for, as he had made no secret of his residence at Neath, it is needless to suppose that treachery was at work. Which of the parties opened the negotiations that ended in surrender it is impossible to say. On the 10th of November, however, the abbot of Neath, Rhys ap Griffith, and Edward Bohun, had letters of safe-conduct from the king as his messengers to his wife and son.[6] On the 16th he was taken at Llantrissaint,[7] having apparently made no attempt to save his friends, a fact which may seem to prove that the whole party were taken by surprise. Henry of Lancaster and Rhys ap Howel made the capture, and the prisoners, with the great seal, were delivered to the queen at Hereford on the 20th. The earl of Arundel, who was taken at Shrewsbury by John Charlton, was beheaded on the 17th,[8] and Hugh le Despenser on the 24th.

We must, however, now turn back to London, which the king had quitted at the beginning of October, leaving his son John of Eltham and his niece the countess of Gloucester in the Tower. The city was, as usual, divided in opinion. Hamo of Chigwell had been maintained by royal influence in the mayoralty for three years in succession,[9] but Nicolas of Farringdon, the head of the rival party, was nearly as strong, and much stronger when it was known that the tide had turned. Before Edward left London Hamo had failed to get from the citizens a promise to shut out the queen, although they would undertake to shut out the foreigners ; [10] as soon as it was known that the queen's cause was prevailing he lost his power

Marginal notes:
Attempt to reach Lundy

The king at Cardiff, Caerphilly, and Neath

Negotiation for the king's surrender

Capture of Edward and execution of his friends

State of London

Hamo of Chigwell the mayor

[1] Parl. Writs, II. ii. 296.
[2] Ibid. II. i. 761.
[3] T. de la Moore ; see vol. in R. S. p. 309 Walsingham, i. 183.
[4] Fœdera, ii. 646, 647 ; Parl. Writs, II. i. 760–762 ; Walsingham, i. 183, 184.
[5] Parl. Writs, II. i. 763.

[6] Fœdera, ii. 647.
[7] Lantrosin, Ann. Paul. i. 319 ; Laturssan, Wals. i. 184.
[8] Bridlington, vol. in R. S. p. 87.
[9] See vol. i. pp. lxxxii. sq. R. S. French Chronicle of London, pp. 42, 48, 49, 51.
[10] Walsingham, i. 180.

Communications from the queen

altogether. The queen had lost no time before asking the aid of the citizens. Her letters had been sent out on the 29th of September,[1] but so long as the king was in the neighbourhood the receipt of them was kept secret.[2] On the 9th of October another letter was found at the dawn of day posted on the cross in Cheap,[3] praying the faithful Londoners to join in destroying the enemies of the land, especially Hugh le Despenser. The city was troubled, but remained quiet for nearly a week. There was a strong force of bishops in the neighbourhood, and with their counsel the mayor was able to keep peace.

Conduct of Archbishop Reynolds

On the 13th, the Monday after the letter was published,[4] the poor foolish archbishop, who on the 30th of September had tried to delude the people by publishing at S. Paul's an old Bull against the Scots as if it had been directed against the queen,[5] got together at

Assembly of bishops at Lambeth

Lambeth the bishop of London, Stephen of Gravesend, Hamo of Hythe, bishop of Rochester, and Bishop Cobham of Worcester, who were all three pious learned men, but not statesmen ; Bishop Stapleton of Exeter, who had been treasurer when the queen's estates were seized, and who was only less unpopular than the chancellor ; and Bishop Stratford of Winchester, who was probably committed already to the queen, and who later on was the head of the

Proposed meeting at S. Paul's

Lancaster party in the new government.[6] The archbishop proposed to hold a meeting at S. Paul's, preparatory to sending a mission of mediation ; but the bishop of Rochester strongly advised him not to cross the river or attempt to enter the city. The more cautious counsels prevailed, and the debate was postponed to the Tuesday.

Proposed mission of mediation

Then again the prelates met at Lambeth. A mission should be sent, but who would go ? Bishop Stratford was willing to go—he knew that he was safe—but only if he had a companion ; all declined for themselves and pressed the bishop of Rochester to go. He resolutely excused himself. In fact it was now too late. He returned to Rochester Place, near the archbishop's palace ; Stratford to his house in Southwark, and the bishops of London and Exeter to their respective lodgings ; Bishop Gravesend probably to his house by S. Paul's, and Bishop Stapleton either to the mansion which he was building on the site of the Outer Temple or to the house in Old Dean's Lane close to where Stationers' Hall and Amen Court now stand, and not far from Chancellor Baldock's house of canonical

Proposed session at Blackfriars

residence in Ivy Lane. The bishops of London and Exeter were to meet the next morning at Blackfriars with the judges, possibly to contrive means for securing the city.[7]

---

[1] French Chronicle, p. 51.
[2] Ibid.   [3] Ibid.
[4] W. Dene, Ang. Sac. i. 366.
[5] Ann. Paul. i. 315. Knighton, c. 2544, writes as if the Bull so used

had been duly applied for and was intended by the pope for this purpose.
[6] W. Dene, Ang. Sac. i. 366.
[7] Ibid. ; cf. Leland, Collectanea, i. 467.

On the 15th of October the city broke into rebellion.[1] The Rising in the city mayor and aldermen had gone out early to Blackfriars to meet the bishops; they were recalled by a rising of the citizens, who forced them to the Guildhall, the mayor Hamo imploring mercy with clasped hands, and only able to save himself by granting to the 'commune' all that they asked, and especially undertaking to drive out of the city all enemies of the queen.[2] One unfortunate man, Murder of John le Marchal John le Marchal, a citizen who was regarded as a spy of the Despensers, was caught in his inn in Walbrook, dragged into Cheap, stripped and beheaded.[3] Just at this time the unfortunate Bishop Perilous entry of Bishop Stapleton Stapleton, who had been visiting his new house outside Temple Bar, came riding into the city with two of his squires, William Wall, who was his nephew,[4] and John of Padington, the latter being steward of the new mansion. The mob, which seems to have been disappointed not to find him at Blackfriars, was on the watch for him; and it was believed also that he intended to claim the charge of the city at the Guildhall. He entered the city by Newgate, and, on his way to the Tower, was to stay in Old Dean's Lane to take his noonday meal.[5] He had reached the church of S. Michael le Quern, which stood at the west end of Cheapside, near the cross. Hearing the cries of 'Traitor! traitor!' he turned his horse and attempted to reach S. Paul's; but at the north door he was seized, dismounted, and dragged into the Cheap, through the middle of S. Paul's churchyard,[6] and there stripped and beheaded with a He is murdered in S. Paul's churchyard panade[7] or butcher's knife which one of the bystanders offered, by a certain R. de Hatfield.[8] The bishop's two squires perished with him. His body was left on the spot until evening; his head was set on the pillory[9] and afterwards sent to the queen at Bristol.[10] His house had been already plundered, and seems to have given the rioters Plunder and devastation in London their first taste of spoil as well as of violence; for before order was restored the chancellor's houses in Ivy Lane and Finsbury were destroyed;[11] the treasure of the unfortunate earl of Arundel, deposited at Trinity, Aldgate, was seized;[12] the chancellor's treasure at S. Paul's shared the same fate; and the banking-house of the

---

[1] Ann. Paul. i. 315.

[2] French Chronicle, p. 52.

[3] Ann. Paul. i. 315, 316; French Chronicle, p. 52.

[4] Leland, Coll. i. 463.

[5] Ann. Paul. i. 316; W. Dene, Ang. Sac. i. 366; French Chronicle, p. 52.

[6] Ann. Paul. i. 316.

[7] Ibid. i. 350.

[8] Ibid. i. 345.

[9] W. Dene, Ang. Sac. i. 366.

[10] It is said that the queen received the head from the mayor, Hamo of Chigwell, and thanked him for it, adding that it was an excellent piece of justice. It is very improbable that Hamo did this, as he was very shortly removed from office. See Aungier's note, French Chronicle, p. 53.

[11] French Chronicle, pp. 53, 54.

[12] Ann. Paul. i. 321.

Bardi, where the Despensers' treasures were, was despoiled in the night. Other houses of rich citizens were likewise robbed.

In the evening, after vespers, the minor canons and vicars choral of S. Paul's took courage and came with cross before them and took up the bishop's body. It remained in the church all night, and in the morning was carried to S. Clement Danes, a church standing near the bishop's new mansion, the advowson of which he had lately procured from the brethren of the Holy Sepulchre at Warwick by an exchange for Snitterfield, in Warwickshire.[1] The tumult had not yet subsided ; the bishop's treasurer was killed the same morning at Holywell, close to the church,[2] and the cowardly rector, John Mugg, refused to admit the mutilated corpse of his patron. The bearers were told that the bishop had died under sentence of excommunication,[3] and they fled. There stood then near S. Clement's an old deserted and half-ruined church of the Holy Innocents, with a cemetery that had once belonged to the Pied Friars, a small order of mendicants which had been suppressed in 1273. Stapleton, it was said, had applied some of the materials of this church to the building of his new house ;[4] if it were so, the treatment of his lifeless body was a fearful example of the punish-

ment of sacrilege. Covered with a ragged cloth, it was deposited, without service of priest or clerk, without the trouble of digging a grave, in a hole among the ruins ;[5] there it remained until on the 17th of February, when the court was becoming ashamed of the outrages of the revolution, it was disinterred and taken to Exeter.[6]

The primate and his brethren may well be excused for taking timely measures to secure themselves. The noise in London on the morning of the 15th was so loud as to reach the bishop of Rochester as he sat at dinner in his house at Lambeth, and he immediately sent to his great neighbour to learn what had happened. Archbishop Reynolds had not only decamped, but had borrowed the bishop's horses and gone off to Kent without giving him warning.

Poor Bishop Hamo started off on foot to Lesnes, where he stayed all night ; the next day he got some food at Stone, and went on to Halling. There he was told that the road to Rochester was unsafe, at all events for a bishop who was reckoned rich ; he therefore took

---

[1] Ann. Paul. i. 316 ; French Chron. p. 52 ; Leland, Collectanea, i. 468.

[2] French Chronicle, p. 53, note.

[3] French Chronicle, p. 52 ; cf. Walsingham, i. 182.

[4] Leland, Collectanea, i. 468.

[5] Ann. Paul. i. 316 ; French Chron. p. 52.

[6] The Annales Paulini (p. 317) give the date of the transfer ; Dr. Oliver

(Exeter Cathedral, pp. 63, 68) doubts whether it was really made, as the executors' accounts do not mention it. But if it was done in consequence of a royal command, the king may have paid for it. See Boase's Register of Exeter College, pref. pp. ii. 3, where March 28 is mentioned as the date of burial at Exeter.

boat as far as Boxley. Next morning, having breakfasted at the
abbot's grange, he got a horse and rode into Rochester, where he
stayed a week, and on All Saints' day entertained the bettermost folk
of the neighbourhood at his table. After dinner he went to Halling,
but the populace who had not been invited to the feast assembled at
the church and were with difficulty prevented from plundering.[1]
The trouble had by this time extended far beyond London, and the
example set there of opening the prisons and releasing criminals
had filled the country towns with malefactors.[2]

Release of criminals

It is not certain that until the king was captured the weaker party
among the bishops sent in their submission to the queen. Some
of them had sent her money, and some, like Bishop Hamo, had
sent excuses for non-appearance when she was at Gloucester.[3] But
it was not until the 7th of December that the archbishop at
Maidstone made up his mind to desert his old pupil and indulgent
lord. The bishop of Rochester tried to dissuade him and refused to
go with him, but he feared the queen more than the King of Heaven,
and went to join her at Wallingford, where Bishop Stratford was
already framing the articles which would justify the deposition of
the king.[4] The rest of the revolutionary programme was carried
through in the parliament of January 1827. The archbishop of
York, with the bishops of Rochester, Carlisle, and London, attempted
a slight obstruction, but it was of course in vain. The archbishop
of Canterbury, although now numbered in the victorious party,
narrowly escaped ill-treatment at the Guildhall, the Londoners who
flocked together ' to see the bishops sacrifice to Mahomet ' [5] apparently thinking that cowardice and ingratitude constituted no
particular title to respect, although they accepted fifty casks of wine
in token of reconciliation.[6]

The arch- bishop joins the queen

Progress of the revolu- tion

The details of the insults and tortures inflicted on the miserable
king, from the day of his capture in November 1826 to his death in
1827, are known to us chiefly through the narrative of Sir Thomas
de la Moore, and, being recorded full twenty years after the event,
are susceptible of some criticism, if any conflicting statements can
be brought against them. A conspiracy for a restoration was
detected in June,[7] which probably alarmed the queen and her advisers into more cruel proceedings. On these the other contemporary
writers throw little light ; they must indeed have been secrets at the
time and as long as Mortimer lived. We learn from Bishop Orlton's

Narrative of Sir Thomas de la Moore

---

[1] W. Dene, Ang. Sac. i. 366, 367.
[2] Walsingham, i. 183.
[3] W. Dene, Ang. Sac. i. 367.
[4] W. Dene, Ang. Sac. i. 367 ;
Knighton, c. 2764, 2765.

[5] W. Dene, Ang. Sac. i. 367.
[6] French Chron. p. 58 ; W. Dene,
Ang. Sac. i. 367 ; Ann. Paul. i.
323.
[7] Ann. Paul. i. 337.

defence that when in the spring of 1327 he went to Avignon [1]
Edward was still at Kenilworth in the charge of the earl of Lancaster.
The date of his removal to Berkeley is given as the 3rd of April.[2]

Questions
as to Ed-
ward's im-
prisonment
Sir Thomas mentions a period of imprisonment at Corfe Castle and
at Bristol between his leaving Kenilworth and arriving at Berkeley,
and tells of the miserable incident of the king being shaven with
ditch water as having happened in the marshes of the Severn between
Bristol and Berkeley.[3] Such at least was the story that William
Bishop, who had been one of the escort, told him after the great
plague of 1349, twenty-three years after it had happened.[4] According
to the Peterhouse Chronicle, as abridged by Leland, it was at Corfe
that Gourney and Maltravers received the order to put the king to
death. The exact mode of the murder is mentioned by the same
writer, and appears in the Polychronicon, which must have been
finished long before De la Moore wrote.[5]

Secrecy of
the king's
murder
It is not to be wondered that, as the whole treatment of the
king was secret, there should be a great mystery about his end. He
was indeed buried at Gloucester with sufficient pomp, but there
were suspicious, ' marvellous ' circumstances about the whole matter.[6]
In 1328 Edmund of Kent, his penitent half-brother, was prevailed
on to believe that he was living on the continent. Mortimer, it
was inferred, had contrived the letters that induced him to take
Letter of
Fieschi on
the king's
escape
measures which were construed as treason. A few years ago there
was discovered among the archives of the department of Hérault a
letter from Manuel Fieschi to Edward III. purporting to contain
the confession of Edward II. after his escape from Berkeley, and
certain mysterious adventures which had ended in his finding a
resting-place in Italy. The letter is curiously accurate in the
character of its details, and contains no anachronism or inconsistent
statements by which its falsehood could be distinctly proved. I am
indebted for my acquaintance with it to two articles published by
Mr. Bent in ' Macmillan's Magazine ' and in ' Notes and Queries ' for
the year 1880. It is printed from the original in No. 37 of the
Publications de la Société Archéologique de Montpellier (December
1877), with a translation and notes by M. A. Germain.

' In nomine Domini Amen. Ea quæ audivi ex confessione
patris vestri, manu propria scripsi, et propterea ad vestri domina-
tionem intimari curavi. Primo dicit quod sentiens Angliam in

---

[1] Twysden, Scriptores, c. 2766.
Orlton had letters of credence to the
pope on the 24th of March; Fœdera,
ii. 698, 699.

[2] Walsingham, i. 188; Knighton,
c. 2551; Mon. Malmesb. from the
Polychronicon; vol. in R. S. p. 290.

[3] See vol. in R. S. p. 316.

[4] Ibid. p. 317.

[5] See Polychr. (ed. Lumby), viii.
324; Knighton, c. 2552; Walsingham, i. 189.

[6] Leland, Coll. i. 469.

subversione contra ipsum, propterea monitu matris vestræ recessit a familia sua in castro comitis Marescali supra mare quod vocatur Gesosta.   Postea timore ductus ascendit barcham unam com dominis Ugone Dispensario et comiti Arundele et aliquibus aliis et aplicuit in Glamorgan supra mare, et ibi fuit captus, una com domino dicto Ugone et magistro Roberto de Baldoli ; et fuerunt capti per dominum Henricum de Longo Castello ; et duxerunt ipsum in castro Chilongurda, et alii fuerunt alibi ad loca diversa ; et ibi perdidit coronam ad requisitionem multorum.   Postea subsequenter fuistis coronatus in proximiori festo Sanctæ Mariæ de la Candelor.   Ultimum miserunt eum ad castrum de Berchele.   Postea famulus qui custodiebat ipsum post aliqua tempora dixit patri vestro : Domine, dominus Thomas de Gornay et dominus Symon d'Esberfort milites venerunt causa interficiendi vos ; si placet, dabo vobis raubas meas ut melius evadere possitis.   Tunc condictis raubis hora quasi noctis exivit carcerem, et dum pervenisset usque ad ultimum ostium sine resistentia, quia non cognoscebatur, invenit ostiarium dormientem, quem subito interfecit ; et receptis clavibus ostii, aperuit ostium, et exivit, et custos suus qui eum custodiebat.   Videntes dicti milites qui venerant ad interficiendum ipsum quod sic recesserat, dubitantes indignationem reginæ, ymo periculum personarum, deliberarunt istum prædictum porterium, extracto sibi corde, ponere in una cassia, et cor et corpus prædicti porterii, ut corpus patris vestri, maliciosæ reginæ præsentarunt, et ut corpus regis dictus porterius in Glocestari fuit sepultus.   Et postquam exivit carceres castri antedicti fuit receptatus in castro de Corf con socio suo, qui custodiebat ipsum in carceribus, per dominum Thomam castellanum dicti castri ignorante domino, domino Johanne Maltraverse, domino dicti Thome, in quo castro secrete fuit per annum cum dimidio.   Postea audito quod comes Cancii, quia dixerat eum vivere, fuerat decapitatus, ascendit unam navim cum dicto custode suo, et de voluntate et consilio dicti Thomæ qui ipsum receptaverat, et transivit in Yrlandum ubi fuit per viii. menses.   Postea dubitans ne ibi cognosceretur, recepto habitu unius heremite, rodivit in Angliam, et aplicuit ad portum de Sandvic, et in eodem habitu transivit mare apud Sclusam.   Postea direxit gressus suos in Normandiam, et de Normandia ut in pluribus transeundo per Linguam Occitanam, venit Avinionem, ubi dato uno floreno uni servienti pape, misit per dictum servientem unam cedulam pape Johanni ; qui papa eum ad se vocari fecit, et ipsum secrete tenuit honorifice ultra xv. dies.   Finaliter, post tractatus diversos, consideratis omnibus, recepta licentia, ivit Parisius, et de Parisius in Braybantiam, de Braybantia in Coloniam ut videret iii. reges causa devotionis, et recedendo de Colonia per Alimaniam transivit, sive perexit Mediolanum in Lombardiam, et de Mediolano intravit

The retreat to Chepstow:

landing in Glamorgan :

surrender and captivity

Arrival of Gourney and Berford to murder the king

The king's escape from Berkeley, and concealment at Corfe

The earl of Kent beheaded

The king goes to Ireland, returns to England, and then goes to Sluys

He goes by Avignon to Paris, Cologne, and Lombardy.

He lives as
a hermit in
Lombardy

quoddam heremitorium castri Milasci, in quo heremitorio stetit per
duos annos cum dimidio ; et quia dicto castro guerra supervenit,
mutavit se in castro Cecinie, in alio heremitorio diocesis Papiensis
in Lombardiam ; et fuit in isto ultimo heremitorio per duos annos
vel circa, semper inclusus, agendo penitentiam et Deum pro nobis et
aliis peccatoribus orando. In quorum testimonium sigillum con-
templatione vestre dominationis duxi apponendum. Vester Manuel
de Flisco, domini pape notarius, devotus servitor vester.' Cartul. de
Mag. Reg. A. fol. 86 vo.

This letter was discovered by M. A. Germain on a leaf of the
Cartulary of the ancient bishopric of Maguelonne, among the
departmental archives of the Hérault.[1] The Cartulary in which it
was found is one drawn up in 1368 by order of Gaucelin de Deaux,
bishop of Maguelonne and treasurer to Pope Urban V.

Examina-
tion of the
letter

The letter is extremely curious, and, whenever and however
written, must have been the work of some one sufficiently well
acquainted with the circumstances of the king's imprisonment to
draw up the details without giving an opening for ready refutation.
It is certain, as we have seen, that the king was at Chepstow, and
' Gesosta ' is not an improbable form for the name to take in Italian
ears. The earl of Arundel is not indeed mentioned as a partner in
the flight to Lundy, but it is not impossible that he was one of the
unlucky company, and that he may have left them after they landed ;
Henry of Lancaster was the person who captured Edward and his
companions ; the king was imprisoned at Kenilworth and there
deprived of his royal character ; he was, after the coronation of his
son on the day before Candlemas, removed to Berkeley. Thomas

Accuracy of
the facts
detailed up
to a certain
point

de Gournai was believed to have murdered him, and in 1330 was
condemned as a traitor, while in the same parliament Simon of
Berford was executed as an acccomplice of Mortimer in his designs
against the king. The two may have been sent to Berkeley to

Possibility
of the latter
part of the
story

expedite the murder. Here the exact correspondence of the letter
with recognised fact ceases, but the later details include no im-
possibilities. Edward is said to have changed dresses with his
servant, to have killed the porter, and to have escaped to Corfe
Castle, which was then under the command of John of Maltravers.
John of Maltravers was warden of Corfe Castle on the 24th of September 1329, and for a year after. If the king lived there a year
and a half, from September 1327, part of this time may have been
spent under Maltravers' tenure of the office.[2] It was to Corfe Castle
that the earl of Kent was induced to go in search of his brother, and
there he was assured by Sir John Deverel that he was alive, part of

[1] Publications de la Société Archéologique de Montpellier, No. 37 (December 1877), pp. 118–120.
[2] Hutchings' Dorset, i. 504.

Mortimer's scheme of alluring him to his death.[1] Thus far, then, the letter may be made to agree with the invented story. Supposing the king to have escaped from Corfe in the spring of 1329, and spent eight months in Ireland, to have returned to England and passed through Normandy by Languedoc to Avignon, he would find John XXII. still on the papal throne; the rest of the story is of course incapable of being subjected to a crucial test. The supposed writer, Manuel Fieschi, was a canon of York and had been archdeacon of Nottingham; [2] he may be supposed to have been personally acquainted with Edward II. There is thus in the letter itself little that could justify a charge of forgery. Yet the improba- Improba-
bility of bilities that forbid us to receive it as genuine are insuperable. It is some of the impossible that John Deverel should have acknowledged that details Edward II. was alive if he had really been at Corfe in 1329. It is impossible to suppose that by accident he told the real truth to the earl of Kent, himself being ignorant of it. Such a coincidence is incredible. It is impossible that John XXII., who, whatever else he Probability may have been, was a fearless and restless pope, would have kept that the
story is a silence as to the true character of his royal visitor. It is to the last fabrication degree improbable that Edward, especially after the report that he was alive had been in circulation, should have moved about England, France, and Italy undetected. It is by no means improbable that, like many other kings who have died mysteriously, he should become the hero of a tale of wonder; but this does not explain the existence of the letter. I can only suggest three theories to account for it: Can it be either it was part of a political trick devised in the French court at accounted
for? the beginning of the great war to throw discredit on Edward III. and possibly to create disaffection in England; or it was the pretended confession of some person well acquainted with the circumstances of Edward's death and probably implicated in it, who wished to secure his own safety and subsistence by counterfeiting the character; or it was the real confession of a madman. There is great difficulty in the last supposition, for there is too much true and consistent detail to have been arranged by a thoroughly disordered brain; if the first be accepted, the plan of which the letter was a part must have been so completely abortive as to be otherwise unknown, and the second supposition seems almost as improbable as the authenticity of the letter. There the fact remains, at present inexplicable.

*   *   *   *   *   *

[1] This part of the story is best given in Barnes's Life of Edward III., pp. 39–41.   [2] Hardy's Le Neve, iii. 150, 168.

INDEX

M M